About Pearson

Pearson is the world's learning company, with presence across 70 countries worldwide. Our unique insights and world-class expertise comes from a long history of working closely with renowned teachers, authors and thought leaders, as a result of which, we have emerged as the preferred choice for millions of teachers and learners across the world.

We believe learning opens up opportunities, creates fulfilling careers and hence better lives. We hence collaborate with the best of minds to deliver you class-leading products, spread across the Higher Education and K12 spectrum.

Superior learning experience and improved outcomes are at the heart of everything we do. This product is the result of one such effort.

Your feedback plays a critical role in the evolution of our products and you can contact us - reachus@pearson.com. *We look forward to it.*

NTA

UGC NET/SET/JRF

Paper 1
Teaching and Research Aptitude

Second Edition

KVS Madaan

Faculty cum Founder-director
netmentor.net, Chandigarh

Former Associate Director
Arni School of Business Management
Arni University
Himachal Pradesh

Pearson

To

my revered gurus, my parents Smt. Devika Rani and

Late Shri. Prem Singh Madaan

Senior Editor—Acquisitions: Pradeep Sharma
Editor—Production: M. Balakrishnan

ISBN 978-93-325-5173-2

First impression, 2016
Thirteenth impression, 2019
Fourteenth impression,

Published by Pearson India Education Services Pvt. Ltd, CIN: U72200TN2005PTC057128.

Head Office: 15th Floor, Tower-B, World Trade Tower, Plot No. 1, Block-C, Sector 16, Noida 201 301, Uttar Pradesh, India.
Registered Office: 4th Floor, Software Block, TS-140, Block 2 & 9, Rajiv Gandhi Salai, Taramani, Chennai 600 113, Tamil Nadu, India.
Fax: 080-30461003, Phone: 080-30461060
Website: in.pearson.com, Email: companysecretary.india@pearson.com

Compositor: Cameo Corporate Services (P) Ltd., Coimbatore.
Printed in India by Gopsons Papers Ltd.

Contents

Preface

With new frontiers of knowledge being explored every moment, the role of a teacher in the society can only get bigger. It is only a teacher who imparts knowledge, inculcates values, and teaches norms of the society to the youngsters. There has always been an insatiable demand for people who adopt teaching as a long-term career option.

NTA-UGC NET/SET/JRF Paper I—Teaching and Research Aptitude has been written for students who aspire to eke out a career in academics and research. This book not only focuses on preparing the candidates for qualifying the NET Examination but also focuses on developing teaching and research aptitude in real terms. It is primarily designed to help students assess their **reasoning ability, comprehension, divergent thinking, and general awareness.**

The book has been divided into 10 units as per the prescribed syllabus. The discussion throughout the book has been supported by updated facts, figures, and diagrams as per the previous years' examination pattern. A NET aspirant's Teaching and Research aptitude is tested through Papers I of NTA-UGC Net Exam and subject knowledge is assessed on the basis of performance in Paper II. Exam pattern was made totally objective in June 2012. Now the marks obtained in Paper 1 are counted for the preparation of final list of qualifying candidates. Thus performance in this paper has become very crucial.

A genuine attempt has been made to incorporate concepts on which questions can be asked in the forthcoming examinations. The language is simple, short, and crisp. Each unit is followed by extensive practice questions, so as to instill candidates with the confidence. The solutions offered at the end of the papers actually come in handy. The variety and scope of probable questions is expanding with each examination, but, importantly, the level of difficulty has remained almost the same.

For suggestions and feedback you may write to: kvsm2003@yahoo.co.in or contact at 09417315300.

Acknowledgments

I am indebted to Prof. Surindra Lal (formerly Principal of Multani Mal Modi College, Patiala, and a renowned authority on Physics) who has always been a mentor and continuous source of inspiration to me at a personal level. I am thankful to my friends and faculty colleagues—Dr Sukhwinder Kaur (Director Career Spot, Chandigarh), Dr Kiran Thakur (NIT, Hamirpur), Prof. (Dr) Pankaj Thakur, School of Chemistry, Shoolini University, Solan (HP), and Mr Parveen Bansal (MD, Abhimanu IAS Visions, Chandigarh) who have always been forthcoming to offer their help and support.

I would like to extend my gratitude to the Team Pearson, Ms Sharel Simon, Mr M. Balakrishnan, and Mr H. R. Nagaraja who have always been prompt in offering help during different stages of publishing. My special gratitude is due for Mr Vikas Sharma, who is actually the motivation behind the whole project, and like an elder brother to me, provided inputs that enabled me to come out with the improvised second edition as per requirements of the NET career aspirants. It is not possible for me to put his contribution into words. My younger brother Parminder Madaan also provided me motivational support.

Last, but not the least, I am indebted to my better half Anshu Bala for keeping me motivated during all stages of project. I always feel a divine power supporting my efforts when kids Jiya, Srijan, and Jappan are around. They actually made me work harder on the project.

KVS Madaan

About NTA

The National Testing Agency (NTA) has been established as a premier, specialist, autonomous and self-sustained testing organization to conduct entrance examinations for admission or fellowship in higher educational institutions. It has been set up with the following specific objectives.

1. To conduct tests in an efficient, transparent and international standard in order to assess the competency of candidates for admission and recruitment purposes.
2. To undertake research on educational, professional and testing systems in order to identify gaps in the knowledge systems and take steps for bridging them.
3. To identify experts and institutions in formulating examination questions.
4. To produce and disseminate information and research on education and professional development standards.

The NET exam is conducted on behalf of UGC for determining the eligibility of candidates opting for the post of Assistant Professor only or Junior Research Fellowship (JRF) and Assistant Professor both in Indian universities and colleges. The JRFs being selected will acquire essential stipend while pursuing PhD/Fellowship.

Until recently, the CBSE conducted NET exam in 84 subjects at 91 selected cities spread across the country. From December 2018, the UGC-NET (Eligibility for Assistant Professor only or Junior Research Fellowship and Eligibility for both Assistant Professor) is to be conducted by NTA.

The NTA intends to create a question bank for all subjects using modern techniques. The administration of NTA has been entrusted to the governing body with Shri R. Subrahmanyam, Secretary, Department of Higher Education, MHRD, being its first chairman.

Eligibility

Candidates who have secured at least 55% marks in Master's degree or equivalent examination from recognized universities in Humanities (including languages) and Social Science, Computer Science and Applications, Electronic Science, etc., are eligible to appear for this test. A relaxation of 5% for other reserved categories has also been entitled to candidates.

Candidates who are pursuing their Master's degree or equivalent course should comply to all the eligibility criteria. It is essential for the candidates to complete their Master's degree or equivalent examination within two years from the date of NET result with required percentage of marks, failing to which they will be treated as disqualified.

The Ph.D. degree holders whose Master's level examination had been completed by 19th September 1991 (irrespective of the date of result declaration) shall be eligible for a relaxation of 5% in aggregate marks, i.e., from 55% to 50% for appearing in NET.

Candidates are advised to appear in the subject of their post-graduation only. The candidates, whose post-graduation subject is not covered in the list of subjects, may appear in a related subject.

About the Author

KVS Madaan is Faculty cum Founder-director of netmentor.net – a Mock Test platform for various prestigious competitive exams. A post graduate in Business Administration from Haryana School of Business, GJUST, Hisar, he qualified for UGC-NET in the subject area of Management and is currently pursuing his Ph.D. With more than eighteen years of rich teaching and research experience, he has helped thousands of career aspirants to realise their goals.

He has worked as Associate Director, School of Business Management, Arni University, Kathgarh (Himachal Pradesh); Director, Punjab Business School, Mohali and Head of Department – Management, MM University, Solan, Himachal Pradesh; and also as Faculty for Management with Chandigarh University, SAS Nagar, Mohali.

A trainer cum keynote speaker at many UGC and AICTE sponsored Faculty Development Programmes; he has conducted training sessions with many renowned institutes across the country.

Syllabus

UNIVERSITY GRANTS COMMISSION
NET BUREAU

PAPER-I
Subject: General Paper on Teaching and Research Aptitude

The main objective is to assess the teaching and research capabilities of the candidates. Therefore, the test is aimed at assessing the teaching and general research aptitude as well as their awareness. They are expected to possess and exhibit cognitive abilities. Cognitive abilities include comprehension, analysis, evaluation, understanding the structure of arguments and deductive and inductive reasoning. The candidates are also expected to have a general awareness and knowledge of sources of information. They should be aware of interaction between people, environment and natural resources and their impact on quality of life.

NOTE: (i) Each section gets equal weightage: five questions and 10 marks from each section.
(ii) Whenever pictorial questions are set for the sighted candidates a passage followed by equal number of questions should be set for the visually handicapped candidates.

I. Teaching Aptitude

- Teaching: Nature, objectives, characteristics and basic requirements;
- Learner's characteristics;
- Factors affecting teaching;
- Methods of teaching;
- Teaching aids;
- Evaluation systems.

II. Research Aptitude

- Research: Meaning, characteristics and types;
- Steps of research;
- Methods of research;
- Research Ethics;
- Paper, article, workshop, seminar, conference and symposium;
- Thesis writing: its characteristics and format.

III. Reading Comprehension

- A passage to be set with questions to be answered.

IV. Communication

- Communication: Nature, characteristics, types, barriers and effective classroom communication.

V. Reasoning (Including Mathematical)

- Number series; letter series; codes;
- Relationships; classification.

VI. Logical Reasoning

- Understanding the structure of arguments;
- Evaluating and distinguishing deductive and inductive reasoning;
- Verbal analogies: Word analogy- Applied analogy;
- Verbal classification;
- Reasoning Logical Diagrams: Simple diagrammatic relationship, multi-diagrammatic relationhip;
- Venn diagram; Analytical Reasoning.

VII. Data Interpretation

- Sources, acquisition and interpretation of data;
- Quantitative and qualitative data;
- Graphical representation and mapping of data.

VIII. Information and Communication Technology (ICT)

- ICT: meaning, advantages, disadvantages and uses;
- General abbreviations and terminology;
- Basics of internet and e-mailing.

IX. People and Environment

- People and environment interaction;
- Sources of pollution;
- Pollutants and their impact on human life, exploitation of natural and energy resources;
- Natural hazards and mitigation

X. Higher Education System: Governance, Polity and Administration

- Structure of the institutions for higher learning and research in India; formal and distance education; professional/technical and general education; value education: governance, polity and administration; concept, institutions and their interactions.

SAMPLE QUESTIONS

I. Teaching Aptitude

1. Which one of the following is the main objective of teaching?
   (a) To give information related to the syllabus.
   (b) To develop thinking power of students.
   (c) To dictate notes to students.
   (d) To prepare students to pass the examination.

Key: (b)

2. Which one of the following is a good method of teaching?
   (a) Lecture and Dictation
   (b) Seminar and Project
   (c) Seminar and Dictation
   (d) Dictation and Assignment

Key: (b)

3. Teacher uses teaching aids for
   (a) Making teaching interesting
   (b) Making teaching within understanding level of students
   (c) Making students attentive
   (d) The sake of its use **Key: (b)**

4. Effectiveness of teaching depends on
   (a) Qualification of teacher (b) Personality of teacher
   (c) Handwriting of teacher (d) Subject understanding of teacher **Key: (d)**

5. Which of the following is not characteristic of a good question paper?
   (a) Objectivity (b) Subjectivity
   (c) No use of vague words (d) Reliable. **Key: (b)**

II. Research Aptitude

1. A researcher is generally expected to:
   (a) Study the existing literature in a field (b) Generate new principles and theories
   (c) Synthesize the ideas given by others (d) Evaluate the findings of a study.
   Key: (b)

2. One of the essential characteristics of research is:
   (a) Reliability (b) Generalizability (c) Usability (d) Objectivity
   Key: (d)

3. The Government of India conducts Census after every 10 years. The method of research used in this process is:
   (a) Case study (b) Developmental (c) Survey (d) Experimental
   Key: (c)

4. An academic association assembled at one place to discuss the progress of its work and future plans. Such an assembly is known as a
   (a) Conference (b) Seminar (c) Workshop (d) Symposium
   Key: (a)

5. An investigator studied the census data for a given area and prepared a write-up based on them. Such a write-up is called:
   (a) Research paper (b) Article (c) Thesis (d) Research report
   Key: (b)

III. Reading Comprehension

Read the following passage and answer the question nos. 1 to 5:

The Constitution guarantees every citizen the fundamental right to equality. Yet after 50 years of independence, just one perusal of the female infant mortality figures, the literacy rates and the employment opportunities for women is sufficient evidence that discrimination exists. Almost predictably, this gender bias is evident in our political system as well. In the 13th Lok Sabha, there were only 43 women MPs out of a total of 543; it is not a surprising figure, for never has women's representation in Parliament been more than 10 per cent.

Historically, the manifestos of major political parties have always encouraged women's participation. It has been merely a charade. So, women's organizations, denied a place on merit, opted for the last resort: a reservation of seats for women in parliament and State Assemblies. Parties, which look at everything with a vote bank in mind, seemed to endorse this. Alas, this too was a mirage.

But there is another aspect also. At a time when caste is the trump card, some politicians want the bill to include further quotas for women from among minorities and backward castes. There is more to it. A survey shows that there is a general antipathy towards the bill. It is actually a classic case of doublespeak: in public, politicians were endorsing women's reservation but in the backrooms of Parliament, they were busy sabotaging it. The reasons are clear: Men just don't want to vacate their seats of power.

1. The problem raised in the passage reflects badly on our
   (a) Political system (b) Social behaviour
   (c) Individual behaviour (d) Behaviour of a group of people

Key: (b)

2. According to the passage, political parties have mostly in mind
   (a) Economic prosperity (b) Vote bank
   (c) People' welfare (d) Patriotism

Key: (b)

3. "Trump Card" means
   (a) Trying to move a dead horse (b) Playing the card cautiously
   (c) Sabotaging all the moves by others (d) Making the final jolt for success

Key: (d)

4. The sentence "Men just don't want to vacate their seats of power" implies
   (a) Lust for power
   (b) Desire to serve the nation
   (c) Conviction in one's own political abilities
   (d) Political corruption

Key: (a)

5. What is the percentage of women in the Lok Sabha?
   (a) 10 (b) 7.91 (c) 43 (d) 9.1

Key: (b)

IV. Communication

1. Informal communication network within the organization is known as
   (a) Interpersonal Communication (b) Intrapersonal Communication
   (c) Mass Communication (d) Grapevine Communication

Key: (d)

2. TV Channel launched for covering only Engineering and Technology subjects is known as
   (a) Gyan Darshan (b) Vyas (c) Eklavya (d) Kisan

Key: (c)

3. In which state the maximum number of periodicals are brought out for public information:
   (a) Uttar Pradesh (b) Tamil Nadu (c) Kerala (d) Punjab

Key: (c)

4. The main objective of public broadcasting system i.e. Prasar Bharti is
   (a) Inform, Entertainment and Education (b) Entertain, Information and Interaction
   (c) Educate, Interact and entertain (d) Entertainment only

Key: (a)

5. The competerrcy of an effective communicator can be judged on the basis of:
   (a) Personality of communicator (b) Experience in the field
   (c) Interactivity with target audience (d) Meeting the needs of target audience.

Key: (d)

V. Reasoning (Including Mathematical)

1. Which one of the following belongs to the category of homogeneous data:
   (a) Multi-storeyed houses in a colony. (b) Trees in a garden
   (c) Vehicular traffic on a highway (d) Student population in a class.

Key: (a)

2. In which of the following ways a theory is not different from a belief?
   (a) Antecedent – consequent (b) Acceptability
   (c) Verifiability (d) Demonstrability

Key: (b)

3. The state – "Honesty is the best policy" is
   (a) A fact (b) An value
   (c) An opinion (d) A value judgement

Key: (d)

4. Which one is like pillar, pole and standard?
   (a) Beam (b) Plank (c) Shaft (d) Timber

Key: (a)

5. Following incomplete series is presented. Find out the number which should come at the place of question mark which will complete the series:
   4, 16, 36, 64,?
   (a) 300 (b) 200 (c) 100 (d) 150

Key: (a)

VI. Logical Reasoning

1. The following question is based on the diagram given below. If the two big circles represent animals living on soil and those living in water, and the small circle stands for the animals who both live on soil and in water, which figure represents the relationships among them?

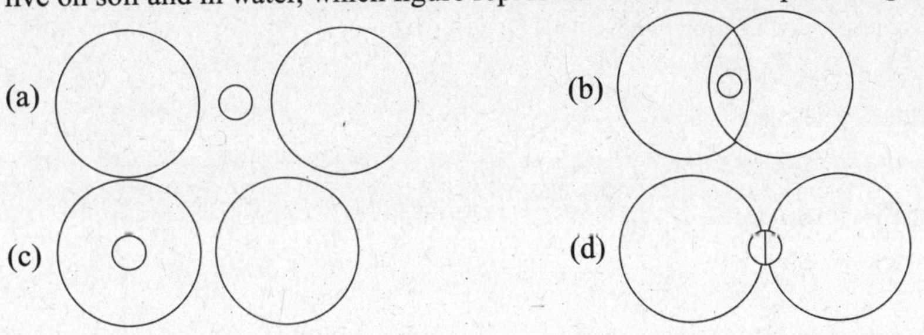

Key: (d)

2. Of the following statements, there are two statements both of which cannot be true but both can be false. Which are these two statements?
   (i) All machines make noise
   (ii) Some machines are noisy
   (iii) No machine makes noise
   (iv) Some machines are not noisy
   (a) (i) and (ii) (b) (iii) and (iv) (c) (i) and (iii) (d) (ii) and (iv)

Key: (c)

3. In the following question, a statement is followed by two assumptions (i) and (ii). An assumption is something supposed or taken for granted. Consider the statement and the following assumptions and decide which of the following assumptions is implicit in the statement.

Statement: We need not worry about errors but must try to learn from our errors.

Assumptions:

(i) Errors may take place when we are carrying out certain work.

(ii) We are capable of benefiting from the past and improve our chances of error-free work.

(a) Only assumption (i) is implicit
(b) Only assumption (ii) is implicit
(c) Either assumption (i) or (ii) is implicit
(d) Both the assumptions are implicit

Key: (d)

4. The question below is followed by two arguments numbered (i) and (ii). Decide which of the arguments is 'strong' and which is 'weak'. Choose the correct answer from the given options below:
   (a) (b) (c) (d)
   Should the press exercise some self-restraint?
   (i) Yes, they should not publish news items which may incite the readers to indulge in wrong practices.
   (ii) No, it is the responsibility of the press to present the truth irrespective of the consequences.
   (a) Only the argument (i) is strong
   (b) Only the argument (ii) is strong
   (c) Neither argument (i) nor argument (ii) is strong
   (d) Both the arguments (i) and (ii) are strong

Key: (a)

5. Study the argument and the inference drawn from that argument, given below carefully.
   Argument: Anything that goes up definitely falls down. Helicopter goes up.
   Inference: So the helicopter will definitely fall down.
   What in your opinion is the inference drawn from the argument?
   (a) Valid
   (b) Invalid
   (c) Doubtful
   (d) Long drawn one

Key: (d)

VII. Data Interpretation

Four students W, X, Y, Z appeared in four papers, I, II, III and IV in a test. Their scores out of 100 are given below:

Students	Papers			
	I	II	III	IV
W	60	81	45	55
X	59	43	51	A
Y	74	A	71	65
Z	72	76	A	68

Where 'A' stands for absent.

Read the above table and answer below mentioned questions 1 to 5

1. Which candidate has secured between 60–65% marks in aggregate?
   (a) W
   (b) X
   (c) Y
   (d) Z

Key: (a)

2. Who has obtained the lowest average in aggregate?
   (a) W
   (b) X
   (c) Y
   (d) Z

Key: (b)

3. Who has obtained the highest average?
   (a) W
   (b) X
   (c) Y
   (d) Z

Key: (a)

4. In which paper the lowest marks were obtained by the candidates?
(a) I (b) II (c) III (d) IV

Key: (b)

5. Which candidate has secured the highest percentage in the papers appeared?
(a) W (b) X (c) Y (d) Z

Key: (d)

VIII. Information and Communication Technology (ICT)

1. ICT stands for
(a) Information common technology
(b) Information and communication technology
(c) Information and computer technology
(d) Inter connected technology

Key: (b)

2. Computer can
(a) Process both quantitative and qualitative information
(b) Store huge information
(c) Process information and fast accurately
(d) All the above

Key: (d)

3. Satellite Communication works through
(a) Radar (b) Transponder (c) Receptor (d) Transmitter

Key: (b)

4. A computer is that machine which works more like a human brain. This definition of computer is
(a) Correct
(b) Incorrect
(c) Partially correct
(d) None of the above

Key: (a)

5. Information and communication technology includes
(a) E-mail
(b) Internet
(c) Educational television
(d) All the above

Key: (d)

IX. People and Environment

1. It is believed that our globe is warming progressively. This global warming will eventually result in
(a) Increase in availability of usable land.
(b) Uniformity of climate at equator and poles.
(c) Fall in the sea level
(d) Melting of polar ice.

Key: (d)

2. In which parts of India ground water is affected with arsenic contamination?
(a) Haryana (b) Andhra Pradesh (c) Sikkim (d) West Bengal

Key: (d)

3. Sunderban in Hooghly delta is known for
(a) Grasslands (b) Conifers (c) Mangroves (d) Arid forests

Key: (c)

4. Sardar Sarover dam is located on the river
(a) Ganga (b) Godavari (c) Mahanadi (d) Narmada

Key: (d)

5. Which one of the following trees has medicinal value?
(a) Pine (b) Teak (c) Neem (d) Oak

Key: (c)

X. Higher Education System: Governance, Polity and Administration

1. Which one of the following is not considered a part of technical education in India:
   (a) Medical (b) Management (c) Pharmaceutical (d) Aeronautical

   Key: (a)

2. Which of the following is a Central University?
   (a) Mumbai University (b) Calcutta University
   (c) Delhi University (d) Madras University

   Key: (c)

3. Identify the main Principle on which the Parliamentary System operates.
   (a) Responsibility of Executive to Legislature
   (b) Supremacy of Parliament
   (c) Supremacy of Judiciary
   (d) Theory of Separation of Power

   Key: (a)

4. The reservation of seats for women in the Panchayat Raj Institutions is:
   (a) 30% of the total seats
   (b) 33% of the total seats
   (c) 33% of the total population
   (d) In proportion to their population

   Key: (b)

5. Match list I with list II and select the correct answer from the code given below:

List I (Institutions)	List II (Locations)
(1) Indian Veterinary Research Institute	(i) Pune
(2) Institute of Armament Technology	(ii) Izat Nagar
(3) Indian Institute of Science	(iii) Delhi
(4) National Institute for Educational Pannesi and Administrators	(iv) Bangalore

   (a) 1 (ii), 2 (i), 3 (iv), 4 (iii) (b) 1 (ii), 2 (iv), 3 (ii), 4 (iii)
   (c) 1 (ii), 2 (iii), 3 (i), 4 (iv) (d) 1 (iv), 2 (iii), 3 (ii), 4 (i)

   Key: (a)

Strategy about NTA-UGC NET Exam

The National Eligibility Test is a national level exam conducted in India by NTA on the behalf of University Grants Commission (UGC). This test enables Post Graduate students to qualify for university level teaching jobs in India and also to seek admissions in Ph.D. level programmes. The test ensures that a candidate qualifies for the minimum standards in the teaching profession and research. The test is conducted in Humanities (including languages), Social Sciences, Environmental Sciences, Geography, Commerce, Management to name a few.

Career Options after Qualifying in UGC NET Exam

Once you clear UGC NET, you are eligible to become an Assistant Professor or pursue Junior Research Fellowship in distinguished universities. The vacancies are announced from time-to-time and you have to apply for the same.

Assistant Professor

Once you clear NET, you can apply for the post of Assistant Professor as and when the vacancies are announced by the colleges and universities. While clearing NET is a mandatory criterion in many colleges and universities, the final appointment will depend on how well you fare in the interview conducted by the concerned university.

Junior Research Fellowship

Junior Research Fellowship is for those who have their heart set on research. You become eligible for the Junior Research Fellowship if you have applied for it in your application form and you have subsequently cleared NET. Once you get selected, then you can pursue research in any prestigious university and get the tuition fees reimbursed. In some universities, the students even get direct admission into M.Phil. programmes in case they qualify NET Exam.

Tips and Techniques to Prepare for UGC NET

- **Preparing well in time:** The preparation for UGC NET Exam starts while undergoing Post Graduate course. Once Post Graduation is complete, a focused preparation of three to six months is mandatory. Preparation should be planned and implemented in such a manner that it leaves scope for revision also.
- **Refer to past questions:** The previous years' questions help the career aspirant to get familiarity with pattern of the exam. Go through them, and try to solve at least few of them. This will give you an idea of what to expect in the exam, and it also builds the confidence in you. Take help of the teachers or seniors if required. Better, if can, make a list of important topics, though it is an objective pattern now.

- **Gaining familiarity with the syllabus:** Run through the syllabus thoroughly. It is important that you understand the syllabus completely and prepare for each topic accordingly. As all papers are objective now, do not leave out any topic.
- **Prioritising the subjects:** Out of the three papers, Paper II and Paper III will be based on the subject of your choice, whereas Paper I will be based on General Awareness and Aptitude. It is very important that you have a complete hold over your subject, as you can score well there. While focusing your attention on the subject papers, start preparing for the General Awareness test by solving sample papers.

  UGC NET Paper I, which is not merely qualifying now, marks are calculated towards the final score also. Therefore, students are taking this paper seriously now. Earlier, Paper I was only qualifying in nature, and one had to score only 40% in this paper, only then Paper II and Paper III would be evaluated.
- **Making personal notes:** This is applicable for all the subjects and Paper I also. These notes work as a kind of 'ready reckoner' once the exam is nearing fast. In general, go for big page note books or registers, divide the page into three columns—on the left-hand side, write main topics, titles, serial number, etc., the middle column is for main discussion of the topic, and right-hand side for any addition, updations, references, etc., that may be required to be done at some later date. The notes help in revision. The same may be done in case of Paper I also.
- **Build upon speed and quality of preparation:** While your aim should be on completing all the topics mentioned in the syllabus, quality must also be kept in mind. While preparing, concentrate on improving the quality of your preparation, which means you can concentrate more on zeroing down on what exactly has to be studied and how much has to be studied.
- **Time management:** Time management depends upon the nature of subject. Some subjects are purely theoretical, some are technical, and some are both. Utilise time in an efficient manner. Have a strategy in place as to how to complete all the questions within the given time. It is best if you time yourself while preparing the subjects.
- **Be confident:** There is no substitute of confidence. Confidence is the outcome of your degree of preparation. Once you decide that you have to eke out a distinguished career in teaching, then UGC NET Exam is the stepping stone.

"All The Best and Do Your Best"

1

TEACHING APTITUDE

Educationists should build the capacities of the spirit of inquiry, creativity, entrepreneurial and moral leadership among students and become their role model

—Dr. APJ Abdul Kalam

These words reflect the whole idea of what it means to be a teacher.

INTRODUCTION

The progress and prosperity of a nation depends upon the development of its human resources. For this purpose, we need highly competent teachers.

Teaching aptitude is all about evaluating candidates who want to enter teaching profession on the basis of their knowledge and skills. It refers to basic qualities required to become a successful teacher. This includes qualification, intelligence, attitude, and many other qualities expected from a person who wants to become a successful teacher.

Apart from teaching concepts, teaching objectives, teaching methods, and teaching aids that are specifically mentioned in the syllabus, many questions have been asked on classroom situations in NET examination. The ensuing discussion will help candidates to correctly comprehend these types of questions.

CONCEPT OF TEACHING

Teaching can be both formal and informal. Informal teaching is carried out within the family or in community, during initial years of life. It is also called home schooling. On the other hand, formal teaching is carried out by paid professionals called editors, teachers or faculty.

Teaching can be defined in the following ways:

1. Teaching is the purposeful direction and management of the learning process.
2. Teaching is a process of providing opportunities for students to produce relatively permanent change through engagement in experiences provided by the teachers.
3. Teaching is skillful application of knowledge, experience, and scientific principles with an objective to set up an environment to facilitate learning.
4. Teaching is a planned activity, and effective teaching depends on the following:
   (a) How clearly the students understand what they are expected to learn
   (b) How accurately their learning can be measured.
5. Teaching is a process in which the learner, teacher, and other variables are organized in a systematic way to attain some predetermined goals.
6. Teaching is an activity that causes the child to learn and acquire the desired knowledge and skills and also the desired ways of living in the society.

Basic Teaching Models

There is no basic model of teaching that augurs well for all the situations. Two contrasting models are discussed here; these models separately or in combination could be used for different courses.

Instructor-centred Teaching

Instructor-centred teaching is a conventional approach. In this method, the instructor, more or less, controls the material to be learned and the pace of learning while presenting the course content to the students. The purpose of this method of learning is to acquire and memorize new knowledge or learn new skills.

Instructor-centred teaching can also be described as 'pedagogical approach'. Pedagogy is the art and science of teaching. It determines 'how the teaching occurs, the approach to teaching and learning, the way the content is delivered, and what the students learn as a result of the process'.

In pedagogical approach, the learner is dependent upon the instructor for all learning, and the teacher assumes full responsibility for what is taught and how it is learned. The teacher or instructor evaluates the learning processes of the students.

Learner-centred Teaching

In this model, the learner is mostly self-directed, and is responsible for his/her own learning. The students learn best not only by receiving knowledge but also by interpreting it, that is, learning through discovery and, at the same time, setting the pace of their own learning. In this method, the instructors facilitate the learning of participants and help them by offering opportunities to learn themselves and acquire new knowledge and develop new skills. This type of teaching is also referred to as andragogical approach.

Self-evaluation is also the characteristic of this approach.

Nature or Characteristic Features of Teaching

The characteristic features of teaching include the following:

1. It has different levels of teaching.
2. It takes place in a dynamic environment.
3. It is closely related to education, learning, instruction, and training.
4. It is essentially an intellectual activity.
5. It is an art as well as science.
6. It tends towards self-organization.
7. It is a social service.
8. It includes lengthy period of study and training.
9. It has high degree of autonomy.
10. It is a continuous process.
11. Teaching is a profession.

Different Levels of Teaching

Teaching takes place at three levels progressively—memory level of teaching, understanding level of teaching, and reflective level of teaching.

Memory Level of Teaching (MLT)

1. Herbart is the main proponent of memory level of teaching.
2. It is the initial stage of teaching.
3. It induces the habit of rote memorization of facts and bites of information.
4. The teaching–learning process is basically 'Stimulus–Response' (S–R) here.
5. It enables the learner to retain and also to reproduce the learnt material whenever required.
6. The evaluation system mainly includes oral, written, and essay-type examination.
7. Good memory includes rapidity in learning, stability of retention, rapidity in recalling, and ability to bring only desirable contents to the conscious level.

UNDERSTANDING LEVEL OF TEACHING (ULT)

1. Morrison is the main proponent of understanding level of teaching.
2. It is 'memory plus insight' as it goes beyond just memorizing of facts. It focuses on mastery of the subject.
3. It makes pupils understand the generalizations, principles, and facts.
4. It provides more and more opportunities for the students to develop the 'intellectual behaviour'.
5. It provides active role for both the pupil and the teacher for the assimilation of facts.
6. The evaluation system mainly includes both essay and objective-type questions.

REFLECTIVE LEVEL OF TEACHING (RLT)

1. Hunt is the main proponent of reflective level of teaching.
2. It is the highest level of teaching and includes both ULT and MLT.
3. It is problem-centric approach of teaching.
4. The students are assumed to adopt some sort of research approach to solve the problem.
5. Classroom environment is to be sufficiently 'open and independent'. The learners are motivated and active.
6. The aim is to develop the reflective power of learners so that they can solve problems of their lives by reasoning, logic, and imagination, and lead successful and happy lives.
7. The pupil occupies the primary place and teacher assumes the secondary place.
8. Essay-type test is used for evaluation. Attitude, belief, and involvement are also evaluated.

Dynamic Environment

Teaching is dominated by communication that itself is very dynamic in nature. Teaching changes according to time and place. Its environment consists of interaction among three variables, namely, independent, dependent, and intervening variables.

As students depend upon teachers for learning, students are assumed to be dependent variables. Teachers are in a position to manipulate the behaviours of students, and hence, teachers are considered as independent variables. Teaching methods, teaching aids, and motivational techniques which also facilitate the teaching–learning process are termed as intervening variables.

Closely Related to Education, Learning, Instruction, and Training

Teaching is basically causing to learn. Nothing is assumed to be taught unless it is learnt by the students. Thus, learning and teaching go hand in hand. Teaching is the main tool to educate a person.

IMPORTANT CONCEPTS RELATED TO TEACHING

Education: In its general sense, is a form of learning in which knowledge, skills, and habits of a group of people are transferred from one generation to the next through teaching, training, research, or simply through 'autodidacticism' (self-learning).

Learning: Learning means activities and experiences. Learning can be defined as the relatively permanent change in an individual's behaviour (current and potential) as a result of experience or practice. This can be compared to other primary processes producing relatively permanent change, 'maturation', that comes with biological age.

Some methods of active learning are discussion, practice sessions, structured exercises, team projects, and research projects. Different aspects of learning have been explored later in this chapter.

Instruction: It is delivery of contents by the teacher. It does not involve an interaction between the teacher and the learner; but still it facilitates achievement of teaching objectives. Teaching is a wider concept and instruction is a part of teaching.

Training: The main purpose of imparting training is to equip candidates with specific or job-related or technical skills. Again teaching is a wider concept than training.

Indoctrination: Indoctrination can be termed as the highest order of teaching. In indoctrination, the beliefs and ideas are impressed upon others and can be included in teaching. Teaching can be done without indoctrination but no indoctrination is possible without teaching.

Syllabus: Syllabus is an outline and summary of topics to be covered in an education or training course. It is descriptive in nature. A syllabus is either set out by an exam board or prepared by the professor who supervises or controls the course quality.

Curriculum: A curriculum usually refers to a defined and prescribed course of study, which the students must fulfill in order to pass a certain level of education. Curriculum can also be defined as the sum total of all the experiences that a student undergoes in the school including academic, cocurricular activities and other types of exposure.

Intellectual Activity

Teaching is essentially an intellectual activity. It is not merely talking or expressing one's ideas; it requires conscious and continuous organization of learning activities. It entails creation of a conductive and supportive learning environment. A teacher has to evolve a suitable plan of action to achieve desired changes in the behaviour of a group of learners. In teaching–learning process, learners constitute the raw material. Learners are prepared to teach in continuous involvements in the society with varied expectations.

Teaching Is a Science as well as an Art

The teaching profession is based upon a systematic body of knowledge, which has been derived from social, psychological, historical, political, and economical spheres of life. It is also influenced by the religious, spiritual, and ethical beliefs of the society. Teaching techniques are systematic, have definite steps to be followed, and are easily communicable. On the basis of assumptions of science, a teacher can be trained. There are definite steps that are followed in training a teacher.

Teaching is an art as well. It takes places in a dynamic environment. The teacher has to deal with individual differences in a class in a tactful manner, it needs a lot of individualized approach and discretion.

Self Organization

The people in teaching profession are sensitive towards growth and development because it is self-organized. They evolve a definite mechanism to sustain and promote the standards of teaching profession. The growth in teaching profession is organic in nature, that is, the growth happens in a spontaneous manner.

Social Service

It has been accepted that education is a potent tool to bring about changes in any nation. It is useful to develop the society.

High Degree of Autonomy

There is a high degree of autonomy in teaching profession right from curriculum development, planning activities of a year, identifying instructional objectives, deciding upon the method of teaching, media, evaluation criteria, and techniques to divide the admission and promotion rules, and autonomy in planning and execution of co-curricular activities.

Teaching as a Profession

Teaching is the profession that makes other professions possible. There are many courses such as B.Ed, M.Ed, etc. Which impart knowledge and skills that establish the foundation for a successful pathway to a teaching career. It entails a number of years of study and intermittent training periods. A teacher has to improve his/her qualification for advancements in the teaching career.

Effective Teaching Practices

Maxims of Teaching

A maxim is a ground rule or fundamental principle that has evolved over a period of time. It is a guide for future action or behaviour. Teaching has also its own set of maxims, which have been discussed below.

1. *From simple to complex:* The teacher should start with simple things and ideas, and these can be done with day-to-day examples, if possible. Then gradually, a teacher can move towards concepts and technical terms. This creates interest among learners to acquire new knowledge. This is helpful in better retention.
2. *From known to unknown:* This is related to first maxim. Retention is always better if new knowledge can be linked with the known one.
3. *From seen to unseen:* The students should be imparted knowledge about the present; then they can understand the past and the future better.
4. *From concrete to abstract:* The mental development of students happens better with the concrete objects, they become familiar with and define micro-words for them at a later stage.
5. *From particular to general:* The students should be presented with examples first and then general laws and their derivations can be explained to them. The experiments and demonstrations serve this purpose.
6. *From whole to part:* Gestalt psychologists have proved that we first see the whole object and then its parts. For example, we first perceive the tree and then its trunk, branches, leaves, etc. Thus, the introduction or overview of the topics is important.
7. *From indefinite to definite:* The teacher should help to transform indefinite knowledge into definite one and aim to clarify the doubts of students.
8. *From psychological to logical:* During initial stages, psychological order is more important, whereas for grown-up learners, logical order is emphasized more.
9. *From analysis to synthesis:* Initially, the students have little or vague knowledge about the topics. Analysis means dividing problems into its constituent parts, and then, these are studied.

   Synthesis means to understand by connecting the knowledge acquired through analysing the parts. A teacher should use analytic–synthetic method.
10. *Follow nature:* It means to regulate the education of a pupil according to his nature.
11. *Training of senses:* Senses such as sight, hearing, taste, smell, and touch are gateways to knowledge. It is better if all or maximum of these senses can be applied in teaching. Montessori and Froebel are the main proponents of this maxim.
12. *Encouragement to self-study:* Dalton's system is based on self-study.

Principles of Teaching

They are closely related to maxims. Teaching methods are based on two types of principles: general principles and psychological principles.

General Principles

1. *Principle of motivation:* It creates curiosity among students to learn new things.
2. *Principle of activity (learning by doing):* Froebel's Kindergarten (KG) system is based on this principle. It includes both physical and mental activities. For example, students are asked to make charts and models.
3. *Principle of interest:* By generating genuine interest among the learner's community, the effectiveness of the teaching-learning process can be increased.
4. *Principle of linking with life:* Life is a continuous experience, and learning linked with life can be more enduring.
5. *Principle of definite aim:* This is important for optimum utilization of teaching resources and making learning more focused.

6. *Principle of recognizing individual differences:* Every student is unique in terms of intelligence, attitude, abilities and potentialities, and socio-economic background. The teaching method should be devised in such a manner to make all the students to avail equal opportunities in life.
7. *Principle of selection:* The horizon of knowledge is expanding each day. The teacher should be able to pick contents that can be more relevant and updated to the learners' objectives.
8. *Principle of planning:* Every teacher has certain time-bound objectives, and hence, teaching should be systematic to make optimum use of resources within the time limit.
9. *Principle of division:* To make learning easier, the subject matter should be divided into units, and there should be links between the units.
10. *Principle of revision:* To make learning enduring, the acquired knowledge should be revised immediately and repeatedly.
11. *Principle of creation and recreation:* This principle is a must to make the classroom environment humorous and creative.
12. *Principle of democratic dealing:* It entails students in planning and executing different activities; it helps in developing self-confidence and self-respect among the learners.

Psychological Principles

1. *Principle of motivation and interest:* A teacher needs to understand that every student is a unique psychological entity, and a student can be motivated after identifying his/her motives and needs.
2. *Principle of recreation:* Recreation is necessary to tackle fatigue after attending lengthy classes. This breaks monotony and prepares students for learning again.
3. *Principle of repetition and exercise:* This is specifically true in case of small children.
4. *Principle of encouraging creativity and self-expression:* This is specifically applicable in subjects such as mathematics and in learning languages.
5. *Principle of sympathy and cooperation:* This principle is required for the motivation of students.
6. *Principle of reinforcement:* Students should be suitably rewarded for their desired behaviour.
7. *Principle of imparting training to senses:* The use of multimedia makes many senses get involved simultaneously, which is crucial for enduring learning.
8. *Principle of remedial teaching:* This principle is necessary for the teacher to identify mistakes and suggest better answers to the problems.

Microteaching

Microteaching is a teacher training technique for learning teaching skills. It employs real teaching situation for developing teaching skills and helps to get deeper knowledge regarding the art of teaching. This Stanford technique involves the steps of 'plan, teach, observe, re-plan, re-teach, and re-observe'. Most of the pre-service teacher education programs widely use microteaching, and it is a proven method to attain gross improvement in the instructional experiences. Effective student teaching should be the prime quality of a teacher. As an innovative method of equipping teachers to be effective, skills and practices of microteaching have been implemented.

Objectives of Teaching

In a knowledge-driven society where information has increasingly short shelf life, it is important for the teachers to focus on long-term goals of preparing our students for life activities, thereby equipping them with more than a finite and rapidly obsolescent body of knowledge, and developing them to understand, apply, and create knowledge, as well as to constantly refresh and upgrade their knowledge.

An objective describes an intended result of instruction rather than the process of instruction itself. Thus, instructional objectives communicate the intended learning outcomes at the end of instruction and state the changes that an instruction should make in the student's behaviour. A good objective should be specific, outcome based (i.e., it should emphasize on the output rather than the process of instruction), and measurable.

The first and the foremost point to be considered in teaching–learning process is what a student will be able to do at the end of an instruction. The objectives of teaching and learning must integrate at the end of the instruction.

Classification of Teaching and Instructional Objectives

There are two main ways of classifying instructional objectives. One classification is given by Bloom, whereas another classification is given by Gagne and Briggs.

Bloom's Classification of Teaching and Instructional Objectives

According to this classification, instructional objectives fall under one of the following three categories:

1. *Cognitive domain:* It is related to development of intellectual capability (i.e., thinking or knowledge); it is the core learning domain. The other domains (i.e., affective, and psychomotor) require at least some cognitive components. It functions at six levels, which are as follows:
   (a) *Knowledge:* It is basically about recalling information or contents.
   (b) *Comprehension:* It is the ability to grasp the meaning of a material.
   (c) *Application:* It converts abstract knowledge into practice.
   (d) *Analysis:* It involves breaking down a communication into its constituent parts in such a manner that relationship of ideas is understood better.
   (e) *Synthesis:* It is basically about combining the constituent parts to make it a whole. It is antonym of analysis.
   (f) *Evaluation:* It involves judgement made about the value of methods and materials for particular purposes.
2. *Affective domain:* It deals with attitude, motivation, willingness to participate, valuing what is being learned, and ultimately incorporating the values of discipline into a way of life. It asks for better student participation. It includes the following levels:
   (a) *Receiving:* willingness to listen
   (b) *Responding:* willingness to participate
   (c) *Valuing:* willingness to be involved
   (d) *Organizing:* willingness to be an advocate of an idea
   (e) *Characterization:* willingness to change one's behaviour or way of life
3. *Psychomotor domain:* It is mainly concerned with the acquisition of technical skills. Following are the five different levels of instructional objectives in psychomotor domain:
   (a) *Imitation:* It includes demonstration of a skill by a skilled person and learner tries to follow the same.
   (b) *Manipulation:* A learner tries to experiment with various aspects like manipulating machinery, equipment, etc.
   (c) *Precision:* Accuracy in performing various acts increases with practice.
   (d) *Articulation:* Achieving a desired level of efficiency and effectiveness through practice.
   (e) *Naturalization:* Skill is internalized and an individual is able to adapt, modify, or design new techniques, methods, or procedures according to the requirements of a situation.

Gagne and Briggs Classification of Teaching and Instructional Objectives

According to this classification, the learning outcomes fall under one of the following categories:

1. *Intellectual skills:* These skills are crucial for dealing with the environment. They include concept learning, rule learning, and problem solving.
2. *Cognitive strategies:* These include methods and techniques for one's own learning, remembering, and thinking skills.
3. *Verbal information:* It refers to organized bodies of knowledge that an individual acquires.
4. *Motor skills:* They are basically about motions carried out when the brain, nervous system, and muscles work together.
5. *Attitudes:* They refer to an internal state of an individual.

Methods of Teaching

If a child can't learn the way we teach, we should teach the way they learn

—Ignacio Estrada

Once the instructional objectives are specified, the next step is to select an appropriate instructional method to achieve them. The teacher has a number of methods at his disposal to select from. These methods are as follows:

1. Large group teaching methods
2. Small group teaching methods
3. Individualized teaching methods

In order to make efficient and effective use of these said methods to attain the desired learning outcomes, the user must have thorough understanding of the characteristics and appropriate uses of various instructional methods. Some of the important methods of instruction are given in Table 1.1.

Table 1.1 Important Methods of Instruction

Teacher-centred strategy	Mixed strategy	Student-centred strategy
Large group methods	**Small group methods**	**Individualized methods**
1. Lectures	1. Group discussion	1. Tutorials
2. Team teaching	2. Seminar	2. Assignments
3. TV or video presentation	3. Panel discussion	3. Project work
	4. Brainstorming	4. Case study
	5. Project method or work	5. Programmed instruction
	6. Tutorials	6. Computer-assisted learning
	7. Case study	7. Interactive video
	8. Role play	8. Open learning
	9. Simulation	9. Personalized system of instruction (PSI)
	10. Demonstration	10. Heuristic method

Large Group Teaching Methods

Lecture Method

Formal lecture helps in building up basic theoretical knowledge that must be gained before practice or before participative sessions. In certain situations, such as large audience, scarce teaching resources, or shortage of time resource, lecturing may be the only alternative.

Lectures can be either one-way or two-way depending upon the presence or absence of the facility to seek further information, clarification, and explanation. To make lecture method more effective, the three factors, namely preparation, presentation, and evaluation, must be given due consideration.

Advantages

1. Economical as it can cover large audience in less time.
2. Stimulates further learning.
3. Flexibility of adapting the lecture according to time and equipment available.

Limitations

1. Student may be a passive listener so teacher has to make conscious efforts to make it two-way communication.
2. Not very suitable for developing mental skills.
3. Stressful for the audience who does not have efficient skills on taking notes.

Team Teaching Method

Team teaching is an innovative approach in teaching large groups in which two or more teachers are involved in planning, executing, and evaluating the learning experiences of a group of students.

Advantages

1. Sharing the best faculty by more students.
2. Optimum use of multiple teaching techniques and devices.
3. Improvement of teaching quality.

Limitations

1. Finding teachers with special competencies is a difficult task.
2. More teachers are required for this method.
3. Not useful for teaching all subjects.
4. Requires much time for planning and scheduling.

TV or Video Presentation

Television or video presentation is an improved presentation of radio or audio presentation, and it can virtually bring the whole world inside the classroom. Screening of video presentation is followed by a discussion or task.

Advantages

1. Many important personalities and experts are brought to the classroom through video presentation.
2. Specifically useful for adult learners.
3. Illustrated lectures and demonstrations can be supplemented by other teaching aids such as slides, models, specimens, etc.
4. Easily accessible for learners in remote areas.
5. Specifically useful for subjects such as geography, astronomy, etc.

Limitations

1. Less possibility for two-way communication.
2. There can be difficulty in adjusting to complicated schedules to telecast period.

Small Group Teaching Methods

Most of the methods of instructional delivery for the learning of smaller groups numbering between 3 and 12 trainees lean towards trainee-centred approach. Some of these methods are group discussion, seminar, project work, tutorials, role playing, etc. These are briefly discussed below.

Group Discussion (GD)

Group discussion is one of the basic methods of teaching smaller groups. It can be described as communication and interaction within a group around a topic, skill, issue, or problem presented to the group by the trainer or moderator for discussion.

Group discussion can be any one of the following:

1. *Planned:* There is certainty about the conclusions and objectives. The discussion is guided by the trainer in an appropriate sequence.

2. *Partly Planned:* Here, the concluding and opening statements are known, but the discussions in-between is not directed or very loosely guided.
3. *Unplanned:* The topic presented for discussion is without any opening statement and the discussion that follows is entirely spontaneous without any guidance from the trainer.

Advantages

1. Participation of all the group members.
2. Critical thinking can be developed as trainees are free to express their ideas and opinions.
3. Good for the development of oral, nonverbal, and written communication skills.

Limitations

1. Time consuming when it is not very systematic.
2. Possibility of domination by a few participants on the basis of their better communication skills.
3. Leading a discussion requires a change of roles which may not be realized by the trainer.
4. Assessment of trainees is difficult and can be biased also.

Seminar

It is a type of group discussion where one trainee, or several, prepare a paper on a given topic, issue, or problem, which is then presented to the whole group for discussion and analysis. A series of seminars can be presented by the trainees around a major topic, so that they form a linked series of discussions. The main stages in seminar are preparation of paper, presentation of paper, and discussion on it.

Advantages

1. This method gives more independence, which leads to development of presentation skills of the participants.
2. It provides opportunity for the trainees to prepare and contribute to a particular topic thoroughly.
3. It provides opportunity to the trainees towards practical group leadership and allows them to use analytical skills, research on conclusions, solve a problem, etc.

Limitations

1. It is time consuming and may cause stress to participants.
2. It needs a group of trainees with fairly highlevel of attainment.

Panel Discussion

A panel consists of a small group of six to eight persons. They carry on a guided and informal discussion before an audience. For example, a panel discussion takes place on the issue of climate change. The leader must, in addition, take special care to select the panel members who can think and speak effectively. He must also be sure that they prepare themselves to discuss the subject.

Advantages

1. Panel discussions, if well conducted, are usually more interesting to the audience than the single-speaker forum.
2. Usually on socially relevant issues.

Limitations

1. Bringing experts to a single forum can be difficult.
2. The audience is not actively involved.

Brainstorming

Brainstorming is a creative group work in which group members produce a large number of ideas quickly on a given topic or problem for subsequent evaluation. In this method, anyone can exchange remarks with anyone except that the participants are not allowed to criticize the ideas at the time when views are being invited. Sometimes quantity of ideas is more important than quality. Spontaneity is the hallmark of brainstorming sessions.

Several rounds of brainstorming are conducted till all the ideas are exhausted. Participants are then asked to evaluate all ideas and list the best one.

Advantages

1. It encourages creativity that helps trainers to produce, think, and explore ideas.
2. Scope for larger participation.
3. It is economical as it does not require much preparation.

Limitations

1. It is not a very systematic way of studying a subject.
2. There is possibility of some trainees being reluctant to participate.

Project Method

This can be described as both a small group and an individualized instruction. In this method, students are allowed to explore and experience their environment through their senses and direct their own learning by their individual interests. Very little is taught from the textbooks, and the emphasis is on experiential learning rather than rote learning and memorization. A project method classroom focuses on democracy and collaboration to solve purposeful problems.

Advantages

1. Students are likely to develop the habit of critical thinking.
2. They develop the habit of working in teams.

Limitations

1. Continuous monitoring may be required.
2. Additional resources may be required.

Role Playing

Role playing has been used effectively by many teachers to help solve classroom interpersonal problems and to teach human-relations skills in the classroom. Role playing has also been used to facilitate subject-matter learning through the dramatization of literary and historical works and historical or current events. In all these uses, role playing provides the student with a dramatic confrontation and clarification of (1) his relations with others, (2) his information about and expectations of the society, (3) his evaluation of himself and his life style, and (4) the ways in which academic material may be relevant to his daily tasks.

Advantages

1. It is the semblance to real-life situations.
2. Interactive and interesting, it entails participation of every member of the group.
3. It gives immediate feedback.
4. It develops social, decision-making, problem-solving, negotiating, and manipulating skills.
5. It is effective to change the attitude of the participants.

Limitations

1. It has unpredictable outcomes.
2. Real-life situations are usually more complex.
3. It requires a considerable amount of resources.

Simulation

Simulation means creating conditions that are quite similar to actual conditions. Then the training is provided under those conditions. For example, the training of pilots and astronauts takes place in conditions that are quite similar to actual flight conditions. Simulation is specifically used for training purpose.

Advantages

1. They are economical in the long run.
2. Safety aspects are taken care of.

Limitation

1. It entails high initial investment in machinery equipment, etc.

Tutorials

Tutorial method is a method employed for teaching small groups for developing skills for solving numerical problems, providing individual guidance, and sorting personal problems. It is appropriate for taking care of individual differences and guiding the students as per their needs, mastery, learning, comprehending concepts, principles and their applications, and for remedial exercises.

Advantages

1. Focused attention
2. Generates more ideas
3. Better control over pace of teaching–learning process

Limitations

1. It is difficult to find a suitable pace if the trainees vary greatly in ability.
2. It can be time consuming.

Demonstration Method

This method is based on the principle of learning by doing and learning from concrete to abstract. The term demonstration means to show. It is adopted in the classroom for the achievement of cognitive, affective, and psychomotor objectives.

Demonstration can be defined as a combination of verbal explanation coupled with a live display of using apparatus for presenting important facts, ideas, or processes. It may entail audio–visual explanation.

Advantages

1. It is effective in explaining materials, objects, and ideas.
2. It is effective in explaining abstract concepts.
3. It is useful for achieving objectives in cognitive, psychomotor, and affective domains as there is mental and physical participation of students.

Limitation

1. Only few get opportunities to participate in the experimental process.

Individualized Teaching Methods

The individualized methods of instruction can be defined as instructions designed to meet the needs of an individual learner and to accommodate the differences displayed between the learners. The main teaching methods include assignments, case-study approach, computer-based learning, open learning, personalized system of instruction, and programmed instructions, which are discussed below.

Assignments

Assignments are given to students for a number of purposes, such as for acquiring additional information, surveying, application of knowledge, and solving numerical problems. Although the main role is of the learner, the teacher too has a crucial role. The teacher has to plan the assignments and guide the student regarding references for collecting relevant information.

Assignments can be prepared on any type of topic, but the nature of assignment should be such that the students may not merely copy from the books. The assignments should be open-ended and should promote creativity among the students.

Advantages

1. It helps students work independently.
2. It helps in sharpening the student's comprehension, analytical, and problem-solving abilities.
3. It helps in inculcation of creativity among the students.

Limitation

1. Students may copy each others material unless the assignments are carefully planned.

Case Study

Unlike traditional lecture-based teaching where student participation in the classroom is minimal, the case method is an active learning method that requires participation and involvement from the student in the classroom.

For students who have been exposed only to the traditional teaching methods, this calls for a major change in their approach to learning.

A case is usually a "description of an actual situation, commonly involving a decision, a challenge, an opportunity, a problem, or an issue faced by a person or persons in a social set up such as an organization". In learning with case studies, the student must deal with the situation described in the case, that is, in the role of a decision maker facing the situation. This method has applications across disciplines such as psychology, management, biology, law, sociology, history, etc., to name a few.

By allowing the students to gain hands-on experience of the real world and shifting the work focus from professor to the student, the case-study method becomes an efficient tool for the creation of a learner-centred education rather than a teacher-centred education. The student becomes actively involved in the course and is no longer an observer in class developments.

Cases can be short from brief classroom discussions to long and elaborate semester-long projects. It is important for bringing real-world problems into a classroom or a workshop. They ensure active participation and may lead to innovative solutions to the problems.

Advantages

1. It provides opportunity to the participants to analyse, critically examine, evaluate, and express reasoned opinions.
2. It enhances decision-making and problem-solving skills.
3. It ensures active participation, which may lead to innovative solutions.

Limitations

1. It requires training for the teachers to use this method.
2. It is not useful for all subjects and situations.

Programmed Instruction

Programmed Instruction (PI) is a general term for a highly structured system of learning, which is based on logical sequence of self-paced, learning steps with feedback between each step. The learner gets immediate feedback after each step.

Advantages

1. There is regular feedback.
2. This ensures active participation of the learner, and it can be used for any subject.

Limitation

1. Learner motivation may get diminished after sometime.

Personalized System of Instruction

Personalized System of Instruction (PSI) can be used for all subject matters except where the students are to select the contents. Learners must achieve mastery of a series of written mastery units, assisted by teachers, proctors, and enriching lectures before proceeding to the final test. PSI consists of five basic elements comprising (i) mastery learning, (ii) self-pacing, (iii) stress on written material, (iv) proctors, and (v) lectures.

It is best suited for contents that are usually conveyed through written material.

Advantages

1. It is based on mastery learning.
2. It facilitates self-paced learning.

Limitations

1. It is not suitable for rapidly changing course contents.
2. It is not suitable for psychomotor and affective domains.

Computer-assisted Learning

Computer-assisted Learning (CAL) is concerned with the use of a computer to mediate the flow of information in a learning process. A computer has the ability to process information very quickly, accurately and to adapt and respond to the learner's need, difficulties, and progress, which is much greater than that of a book or video tape.

Advantages

1. It has more flexibility and better control in comparison to other methods.
2. It can be effectively used for drilling and practicing, simulation, and modelling.

Limitation

1. It is impersonal and costly.

Open Learning

It is a flexible method of delivering the instruction, where the learner has open access to learning resources of people, material, equipment, and accommodation, although regular class attendances are not necessary. There are no or minimal restrictions on admissions.

The face-to-face interaction between teachers and students through tutorials should form a part of open learning. For open learning, learning packages are to be developed, making use of multimedia. Open learning instruction is, however, not suitable for the rapidly changing nature of content as this involves time, expertise, and resources.

Advantage

1. It offers flexibility to learner.

Limitations

1. It is not suitable for achieving psychomotor and affective learning objectives.
2. It requires time, expertise, and resources, and hence, not suitable for subjects of rapidly changing nature.

Interactive Video

The interactive video approach to teaching can be employed to achieve cognitive, psychomotor, and affective objectives. It allows the learner to randomly access any piece of information and provide immediate feedback regarding the consequences of their action. The essence of the interactive video experience is video simulation with more number of video presentations of real images as possible.

Advantage

1. Interactive video approach enhances the decision-making power of the individual.

Limitation

1. This method is time consuming and requires resources and expertise.

Heuristic Method

This method was advocated by Professor Armstrong. In this method, the student has to find out the answer to his/her own problem by unaided efforts. Thus, the child becomes a discoverer of knowledge by developing a spirit of inquiry. The main aim of teaching by this method is not to provide much facts about science, mathematics, grammar, etc. but to teach how knowledge of these can be obtained.

Advantage

1. Self-learning approach

Limitation

1. Not much focus on factual knowledge

Differentiated Instruction (DI)

Differentiated instruction is a dynamic, proactive method of teaching. It means that the teacher plans and uses a variety of ways to teach learning. It is a combination of whole group, small group, and individual instruction methods.

In this method, qualitative aspects are given more weightage than quantitative aspects. It uses multiple approaches to accommodate multiple intelligences. It is student-centred, meaning that lessons are engaging, relevant, interesting, and active. It is an organized and planned method of teaching.

Blended Learning: The term originated in USA. There is no clear single definition available for it. Blended learning combines online learning with face-to-face learning. It is also defined as the combination of multiple approaches to pedagogy or teaching, for example, self-paced, collaborative or inquiry-based study. The goal of blended learning is to provide the most efficient and effective instruction experience by combining delivery modalities.

Learning and Learner's Characteristics

Learning Defined

It appears quite simple to define the term 'learning'—after all we have spent our entire lives learning new things. Learning is basically psychological in nature; a few definitions offered by psychologists are given below:

1. Learning is the process whereby the behaviour of an organism undergoes changes as a result of experience.
2. Learning is relatively a permanent change in capacity for performance, which is acquired through experience.
3. Learning is the way through which human beings acquire new skills, knowledge, attitudes, and values. The outcomes of learning are the new capabilities possessed by the learner.

Learners' Characteristics Are Mainly about Individual Differences

Learners have many common characteristics at various ages and stages, but they also differ significantly in many ways. Teachers need to understand both the commonalities and the differences in order to meet the students' needs as no two individuals are alike. There are variations among learners in respect to their age, cultural environment, past experiences, physical, mental and emotional make up, goals, needs, etc.

Furthermore, different learners have different learning styles, and as heterogeneity is increasing day by day, they may perceive, interpret, and evaluate the same learning event in different ways.

Learners' characteristics, therefore, merit consideration in selection of media. Learners benefit from those media that match their individual learning styles. Therefore, it is understandable why a variety of methods, resources, and paths should be provided for different students to achieve a particular objective. Thus, while designing an instructional plan, the important task for the designer is to identify the most critical characteristics for the attainment of instructional objectives.

Elements of Learning Event

The main components of learning event are as follows:

1. *Learner:* The learner must interpret the stimulus, differentiate, and combine them, and give them some meaning.
2. *Stimulus:* Any stimulus or set of stimuli to which learner is sensitive can become a part of his learning situation.
3. *The internal conditions of the learner:* These are perception, cognitive structure, self-concept, attitudes, needs, motives, intelligence, previous learning. etc.
4. *Response:* Any action or reaction to a learning situation.

Main Steps in Learning Process

In NET Exam, there may be direct or indirect questions on learning process.

Reception: Gaining attention by making some abrupt changes in stimulus or stimuli.

Expectancy: Informing learners of the objective and what they will be able to do after learning.

Retrieval to working memory: Stimulating recall of prior knowledge.

Selective perception: Displaying contents with distinct features.

Semantic encoding: Learning guidance.

Responding: Asking learner to perform.

Reinforcement: Providing feedback to the learner.

Retrieval and reinforcement: Additional performance by learner; it entails feedback also.

Generalization: More practice of varied problems so as to increase retention.

Types of Learners

In the past, many direct and indirect questions have been asked in the NET exam. There are main three categories of learner characteristics: general characteristics, specific entry competencies, and learning styles.

Learner Characteristics

1. *On the basis of personal and social attributes:* They help in planning instructional objectives as it may reveal physical characteristics that are relevant to training or instructional decisions. The social factors mainly include the following:
   (a) Age and maturity level
   (b) Motivation and attitude towards the subject
   (c) Expectations and vocational aspirations
   (d) Special talents
   (e) Mechanical dexterity
   (f) Ability to work under various environmental conditions.

   Table 1.2 enlists some of the differences in learner characteristics between the youths and the adults.

Table 1.2 Differences between Adult and Youth Learners

S.No.	Adult learners	Youth learners
1.	Problem centred	Subject oriented; focus on course completion
2.	Result oriented	Future oriented
3.	Self-directed	Dependent upon adults for direction
4.	Sceptical about new information	More likely to accept new information
5.	Accept responsibility for their own learning	Dependence upon others

2. *Learner characteristics on the basis of learning styles:* Learning styles are traits that refer to how learners receive and process information. Felder and Silverman developed one set of category for analysing an individual's learning styles.

   Table 1.3 shows the differences between the types of learners and their learning styles.

Table 1.3 Learner Type and Learning Style

Learner type	Effective learning style
Visual	Pictures, diagrams, and demonstrations
Auditory	Words and sounds
Intuitive	Insights and hunches
Inductive	From facts to generalization
Deductive	From theory to individual facts
Actively	Physical engagement or discussion
Reflectively	Introspection
Sequentially	Series of related steps
Globally	Large jump or holistic approach

3. *Learner characteristics on the basis of listening skills:* Listening in an important skill, and there are four types of listening styles, which are as follows:
   (a) *Active listening:* It is listening with a purpose.
   (b) *Empathic listening:* It is a form of active listening in which you attempt to understand the other person.
   (c) *Evaluative listening or critical listening:* In this type, the listener evaluates the accuracy, meaningfulness, and utility of speaker's message.

(d) *Appreciative listening:* Listening for enjoyment involves seeking situations involving relaxing, fun, or emotionally stimulating information.

4. *Learner characteristics on the basis of thinking styles:* There are different thinking styles of learners, which are mentioned below:
   (a) Reflective thinkers
      (i) View new information with respect to the subject
      (ii) Relate new information to past experiences
      (iii) Always ask 'why?'
      (iv) Examine their feelings about what they are learning
   (b) Creative thinkers
      (i) Like to play with new information
      (ii) Always ask 'why?'
      (iii) Create their own solutions and shortcuts
   (c) Practical thinkers
      (i) Always look for factual information
      (ii) Seek the simplest and the most efficient way to do their work
      (iii) Not satisfied until they know how to apply their new skills to their job or other interest
   (d) Conceptual thinkers
      (i) Accept new information only after seeing the big picture
      (ii) Want to know how things work, not just the final outcome
      (iii) Learn the concepts that are presented but also want to know the related concepts that may not have been included

Factors Affecting Teaching

Teaching is an art and a skill; its acquisition depends upon so many factors, which are briefed below:

1. *Educational qualification of a teacher:* It is generally assumed that highly qualified teachers should teach higher classes and less qualified teachers should teach lower classes.
2. *Skills:* Adequate skill set helps a teacher to do his or her job in more effective manner. Some teaching skills may come with birth, but for many others, a prospective teacher has to make conscious efforts.

National Council of Educational Research and Training (NCERT) in its publication ***Core Teaching Skills*** (1982) has laid stress on the following teaching skills:

1. Writing instructional objectives
2. Organizing the content
3. Creating set for introducing the lesson
4. Introducing a lesson
5. Structuring classroom questions
6. Question delivery and its distribution
7. Response management
8. Explaining
9. Illustrating with examples
10. Using teaching aids
11. Stimulus variation
12. Pacing of the lesson
13. Promoting pupil participation
14. Use of blackboard
15. Achieving closure of the lesson
16. Giving assignments
17. Evaluating the pupil's progress
18. Diagnosing pupil learning difficulties and taking remedial measures
19. Management of the class

3. *Experience of teacher:* Teacher himself is a learner all the time. A good teacher would always like to share his enhanced knowledge with the students, and the experience also helps in better handling of student queries and classroom management.
4. *Classroom environment:* A teacher has to take initiative in creating a classroom

environment that supports teaching–learning process.

5. *Economic factor:* Teaching professionals always seek independence of thought. If that is constrained by financial problems, the quality of teaching is affected. The same applies to learner's situation as well.
6. *Administrative policies of school, college or university:* As discussed, a teacher always seeks independence in handling classroom situations; however, administration intends to bring standardization in teaching practices.
7. *Subject matter:* Sometimes, when a teacher teaches a subject in which he is not specialized, he cannot create any effect through his teaching, but the same teacher can teach his specialized subject in a better way.
8. *Parental expectations:* Parental expectations may work as an intervening variable. They may put stress on the learner and ultimately teaching may also get affected.

Different Approaches in Education

Three Basis of Education: The educational process is decided on the basis of three questions: 'Why', 'How', and 'What'. Here, the question of 'Why' is most important. This is answered by philosophy. The 'How' is decided by the psychology and 'What' is decided by the social needs. Hence, education is based on the basis of philosophical, psychological, and sociological basis.

The important approaches in education are discussed below:

1. *Behaviourism:* This assumes that learner is a passive organism who may be conditioned to learn new behaviours. Therefore, learning could be explained by change in observable behaviour. E.L. Thorndike postulated the law of exercise and the law of effect.
   (a) *Law of exercise:* Repeating a conditioned response would strengthen the bond between the stimulus and the response. In other words, practice makes a man perfect.
   (b) *Law of effect:* Law of effect is the principle of reinforcement and punishment. Any behaviour followed by pleasure would strengthen the behaviour and any behaviour followed by pain would decrease the behaviour.
2. *Gestalt psychology:* It believes that the whole is greater than the sum of its parts. For example, in the human body, there are cells, tissues, bones, etc., yet the sum of all these components (human body) is greater than the sum of its parts. This is because the parts are interrelated to each other. Gestalt psychology demonstrated the significance of perception. It also showed that complex learning need not occur gradually through lengthy practice but may develop through insight.
3. *Constructivism:* The learner actively constructs knowledge. Jean Piaget and J. S. Bruner believed that learning involves an active processing of information and that each individual activity organizes and constructs knowledge for itself. Educational psychology believes that there are developmental stages for knowledge organization. According to Jean Piaget, 'accommodation' and 'assimilation' are basic to learning. A learner developes new 'schema' through accommodation. New experiences are assimilated into already existing schemas or they may be accommodated by creating new schemas.
4. *Idealism:* The mind is central in understanding the world. The idealists emphasize the spiritual aspects of learning. God is the source of all creation and knowledge; spirit and mind constitute reality. Values are absolute, eternal, and unchanging. Man has a superior nature, and it is expressed in the form of intellectual

culture, morality, and religion. The main thinkers are Froebel, Kant, Plato, Swami Dayanand, Vivekananda, and Sri Aurobindo.

5. *Naturalism:* It considers nature as the whole of reality. Our senses are the gateway to knowledge, and nature is the source of all knowledge. Mind is subordinate to nature. The educative process must be pleasurable and set in natural surroundings. The main protagonists are Tagore, Rousseau, and Herbert Spencer.
6. *Pragmatism:* It focuses on activity or doing. According to pragmatists, there are no absolute values of life. Truth is created during the course of experience. Humans are active being and have the ability to solve their problems through the logic of experiments and scientific methods. The main thinkers are C. S. Pierce and John Dewey.
7. *Humanism:* It is a reasonable balance in life and regards humans as the centre and measure of all activities. Humanism believes in the interests and welfare of all human beings. Thus, the life of a human being should be transformed so that the welfare of all becomes the goal. The form of learning is on self-actualization. It advocates cooperation, mutual tolerance, and social understanding.
8. *Rationalism:* Rationalists claim that there are significant ways in which our concepts and knowledge are gained independently of sense experience. Empiricists claim that sense experience is the ultimate source of all our concepts and knowledge.
9. *Existentialism:* It is a philosophy that emphasizes individual existence, freedom, and choice. This emphasizes the uniqueness and isolation of the individual experience in a hostile or in different universe, regards human existence as unexplainable, and stresses freedom of choice and responsibility for the consequences of one's acts.

Table 1.4 Important Concepts in Education and Its Proponents

Concepts	Main proponents
Basic education (Wardha Education System)	Mahatma Gandhi
Learning to take place in nature and from nature	Rabindranath Tagore
Integral education	Sri Aurobindo
Focus on spiritual aspects of Indian philosophy	Dr. Sarvepalli Radhakrishnan
Education to transform human mind	J. Krishnamurti
Experiential learning	John Dewey
Self-education through development of individuality	Maria Montessori
Kindergarten—focus on self-activity, creativeness, and social cooperation	Froebel
No formal learning—nature is the only teacher	Rousseau

Evaluation Systems

Interdependence of Teaching, Learning, and Evaluation

Teaching has been defined as the process of facilitating learning, and learning is broadly defined as the process of acquiring knowledge, attitude, skills, habits, and abilities. To determine whether teaching has facilitated learning, evaluation is carried out. In other words, teaching, learning, and evaluation are the three interdependent aspects of the educative process. This interdependence is clearly seen when main purpose of instruction is conceived in terms of helping students achieve a set of learning outcomes that include changes in the cognitive, psychomotor, and affective domains. The instructional objectives or the desired changes in students (learning) are brought about by planned learning activities (teaching), and the students' progress is determined by tests and other devices (evaluation).

There is a direct relationship among the four important factors of the educational system such as objective, curriculum, method, and evaluation. As Indian Education Commission (1944–1966) has remarked, 'It is now agreed that evaluation is a continuous process, forms an integral part of the total system of education, and is intimately related to educational objectives; it exercises a great influence on pupil's study habits and the teacher's method of instruction, and this helps not only to measure educational achievement but also to improve it'.

Desirable Characteristics of Evaluation

1. *Comprehensiveness:* It must try to assess all aspects of a child's development. Thus, different techniques might be used by the teachers to evaluate the performance of the child.
2. *Continuous:* Evaluation is a continuous process as education. It is not just an examination but a part of the evaluation process. There is no fixed time limit for the completion of evaluation work, but it is a continuous process.

   CBSE's Continuous and Comprehensive Evaluation (CCE) is based on the above two parameters. CCE helps in improving student's performance by identifying his/her learning difficulties at regular time intervals right from the beginning of the academic session and employing suitable remedial measures for enhancing their learning performance.

Functions of Evaluation

Evaluation does not end with the summarization of results. It has direct bearing on the improvement of the system as a whole. The functions of evaluation are as follows:

1. *Feedback:* To assess strengths and weaknesses.
2. *Motivation:* The mere realization that you would be evaluated propels a student to work hard.
3. *Better guidance:* Crucial for the growth of pupils.
4. *Remediation:* It helps in locating the areas that require remedial measures.
5. *Facilitates planning:* It helps the teacher in planning, organizing, and implementing learning activities.
6. Revision of curriculum.
7. Inter-institutional comparison
8. *Educational decision-making:* It relates to selection, classification, placement, promotion, etc.
9. Submission of progress report to parents.

Classification of Evaluation Techniques

A good evaluation device is one which secures valid evidence regarding the desired change of behaviour. A teacher needs to know the various devices that are helpful in gathering evidence on the changes taking place in a pupil.

They can be categorized into quantitative and qualitative techniques:

Quantitative Techniques

1. *Written examination:* It is also known as paper pencil test. In this technique, the answers are to be written as per the instruction of questions.
2. *Oral examination:* They supplement the written examination. Examples are test of reading ability, and pronunciation; viva voce is also an example.
3. *Practical examination:* These tests are necessary to test experimental and manipulative skills of a learner, particularly in subjects such as science, technology, agriculture, craft, and music.

Qualitative Techniques

1. *Observation and interviews:* Observation is used to evaluate the behaviour of the pupil

in controlled and uncontrolled situations. It is purposive and systematic, and carefully viewing or observing the behaviour and recording it. Interview is sometimes superior to other devices. It is because of the fact that pupils are usually more willing to talk than write.

2. *Checklist:* A checklist is an instrument that is used for collecting and recording evidence regarding significant behavioural tendencies of the pupils or specific problems they present in the classroom.
3. *Rating scale:* Rating is a term applied to the expression of opinion or judgement regarding some situation, object, or character. Rating scale is a device by which judgements can be quantified.
4. *Cumulative records:* Anecdotal records, cumulative record cards, and diaries of pupils are some other devices used in evaluation process to know the details about a child's behaviour.

Type of Evaluation on the Basis of Phase of Instruction

In the various phases of instruction, evaluation is integrated. The four types of evaluation are placement, formative, diagnostic, and summative.

1. *Placement evaluation:* It determines the knowledge and skills the students possess, which are necessary at the beginning of instruction in a given subject area. The purpose of placement evaluation is to check the aptitude of a candidate for the course or subject, whether the candidate has calibre or not. Various entrance exams can also be conducted for the same purpose. This is also done to see the knowledge base of students, and a teacher can start discussion keeping that in view.
2. *Formative evaluation:* A formative evaluation (also referred to as internal evaluation) is a method for judging the worth of a programme while the programme activities are in progress. It focuses on the process. This evaluation provides the student with feedback regarding his or her success or failure in attaining the instructional objectives. It also identifies the specific learning error that needs to be corrected.

   For instance, a student learns and scores high on the objective part of the test but fails in the essay part; he is reinforced to exert more effort in answering essay questions in the succeeding tests. For a teacher, formative evaluation provides information for making instructions and remedies more effective. Quizzes, unit tests, and chapter tests are examples of evaluative instruments used in this type of evaluation.
3. *Diagnostic evaluation:* The formative evaluation determines the extent to which students accomplish the learning targets; therefore, it focuses on the measurement of the intended outcomes. The diagnostic evaluation goes a step further and tries to provide an explanation for the possible causes for problems in learning. Diagnostic tests are, thus, more comprehensive and detailed.
4. *Summative evaluation (external evaluation):* Summative evaluation is a method of judging the worth of a programme at the end of the programme activities (summation). The focus is on the outcome. It determines the extent to which objectives of instruction have been achieved and is used for assigning course grades. Summative evaluation generally includes oral reports, projects, term papers, and teacher-made achievement tests, and it shows how good or how satisfactory the student is in accomplishing the objectives of instruction.

Teaching Aids

I hear and I forget, I see and I believe, I do and I understand

—Confucius

These are also termed as instructional aids that assist an instructor in the teaching–learning process. They supplement teaching methods and are themselves not as self-supporting as teaching methods.

The teaching aids include audio–visual aids. They follow the assumption that learning originates from senses' experience. They help in better learning, retention and recall, thinking and reasoning, activity, interest, imagination, better assimilation, and personal growth and development.

Table 1.5 depicts some of the benefits of using teaching aids.

Table 1.5 Benefits of Teaching Aids

Important benefits			
1.	Motivational Effect	10.	Facilitates healthy classroom environment
2.	Supplement verbal instructions	11.	Promotion of scientific temper
3.	Complement verbal instructions	12.	Development of higher faculties
4.	Clear images	13.	Flexibility in learning
5.	Vicarious experience	14.	Opportunities to handle and manipulate
6.	Variety	15.	Better retention
7.	Based on teaching maxims	16.	Reinforcement
8.	Vividness	17.	Positive transfer of learning and training
9.	Catering to individual differences	18.	Positive creativity

Educational Technology

Educational technology can be divided into two categories: hardware approach and software approach.

1. *Hardware approach:* It mechanizes the process of teaching so that teachers are able to deal with more students with less expenditure in educating them. Hardware includes computer, epidiascope, overhead projector, radio, slide and film projector, teaching machines, television, etc.
2. *Software approach:* This makes use of the principle of psychology for building in the learner a complex repertoire of knowledge, modifying a learner's behaviour. It evolved through the pioneering work of Skinner and other behaviourists. Software approach is characterized by task analysis, writing precise objectives, selection of appropriate learning strategies, immediate reinforcement of responses, and constant evaluation. Newspapers, books, magazines, educational games, flash cards, etc. also form a part of software approach.

According to the senses involved, the educational technology can be divided into audio aids, video aids, and audio–video aids:

1. *Audio aids:* They are instructional devices through which message can only be heard. We spend more than 50% of our time in hearing. This reflects the importance of audio media in our life. Examples of audio aids include Language labs, radio sets, sound distribution sets, etc.
2. *Visual aids:* Instructional devices through which the message can only be seen are known as visual aids. Examples include posters, flashcards, charts, bulletin boards, maps, models, photographs, etc.
3. *Audio–visual aids:* Audio–visual aids are those aids that help in completing the triangular process of learning, that is, motivation, classification, and stimulation. They are instructional devices in which the message can be heard and seen simultaneously. Out of five senses, seeing at 87% and hearing at 7% are the major ones to attract attention and increase learning. Examples of audio–visual aids include television, video films, documentary films, etc.

Functions of Audio–visual Aids

When properly used, audio–visual aids contribute to one or more of the following functions.

1. More clarity and understanding
2. Better attention, interest, and retention

3. It helps in faster and comprehensive learning
4. Better access
5. Save the instructor's time
6. Supplement the spoken words—by compining audio and visual stimuli

Limitations of Audio–visual Aids

1. Learners may form distorted impressions unless audio–visual aids are supplemented with required explanations.
2. Teaching may be narrowed down to only a few big ideas, not giving the complete picture of a subject.
3. There is the possible risk of spectatorism instead of the attitude of thoughtful enquiry. Some extension workers acquire the mistaken idea that they have little to do when audio–visuals are used.
4. *Multimedia:* It is a combination of more than one media, but it could include several forms of media and audios, texts, still images, animations, graphics, videos, and films.

Types of Teaching Aids According to Projection or Show

Teaching aids according to projection or show are divided into projected and non-projected aids.

1. *Projected aids:* Visual instructional devices that are shown with a projector are called projected aids. Examples include slides, filmstrip, silent films, cartoons, etc. These are projected through an opaque projector (epidiascope) or an overhead projector.
2. *Non-projected aids:* Visual instructional devices that are simply presented without any projection equipment are non-projected aids. Examples include blackboard, chart, etc.

Apart from these aids, there are two additional categories of the teaching aids: display aids, and presentation aids.

1. *Display aids:* Visual aids that are spread before the audience for viewing information and instruction. Examples are poster, bulletin board, models, exhibits, etc.
2. *Presentation aids:* Visuals aids that are presented or projected before the audience for viewing, explaining or presenting the message of the visuals, so that the audience gets meaningful understanding of the subject. Examples are flashcards, slides, filmstrips, etc.

Table 1.6 shows the different types of teaching aids according to projection or show.

Table 1.6 Projected and Non-projected Aids

Projected aids	Non-projected aids				
	Graphic aids	**Display boards**	**3-D**	**Audio aids**	**Activity aids**
Films	Charts	Blackboard	Models	Radio	Field trips
Slides	Flash cards	Whiteboard	Mock ups	Recordings	Experimentation
Overhead projector	Posters	Bulletin board	Objects and specimens	Digital Audio Player	Dramatics
Epidiascope	Pictures and photographs	Flannel board	Puppets	Television	Teaching machines
Video projectors	Graphs	Magnetic board		Telephone and mobile	Programmed instructions
Film strips	Maps Diagrams	Peg board			

Mind Mapping

Mind Mapping as a method of teaching was developed by Tony Buzan in 1960. A 'mind map' is a diagram for representing tasks, words, concepts, or items linked to and arranged around a central concept or subject. It uses a non-linear graphical layout that allows the user to build an intuitive framework around a central concept, and it can turn a long list of monotonous information into a colourful, memorable, and highly organized diagram that works in-line with a learner's brain's natural way of doing things.

Mind Map

Using mind maps as an innovative thinking tool in education helps students to visualise and externalise concepts and understand the connections between different ideas. It is commonly used in presentations, critical thinking, brainstorming, decision making, and project management.

Projected Visual Aids

Any visual aid that is used for magnification of image on a screen in dark or semi-dark conditions can be called a projected visual aid. There are three important methods of projection:

1. *Direct projection:* Slide and film projectors
2. *Indirect projection:* Overhead projector
3. *Reflected projection:* Opaque projector and epidiascope

Slides

A slide is a transparent-mounted picture that is projected by focusing light through it. The projection may be made on a screen or on a white wall. Slides of 35-mm films mounted on individual cardboard or plastic frames are common and are extensively used in extension work during training programmes, seminars, workshops, group meetings, campaigns, exhibitions, etc.

Overhead Projector (OHP)

The overhead projector projects the picture over the head of the speaker on the screen. Drawings, diagrams, letterings, etc. are made on transparent sheets and are put on the glass platform of the overhead projector, through which a strong light is passed. The rays of light are made to converge with a lens and are reflected by a mirror held at an angle on the screen at the back.

Transparencies can also be made through photographic, xerox, or electronic processes as well. Overhead projection is used in training programmes, group meeting, seminar, symposium, workshop, etc.

Advantages include synchronization of projections with talk, facing audience, and observing their reaction, sustaining audience interest, clear presentation of complex ideas, time saving, and easy availability of materials for making transparencies.

Handheld Projector

It is also known as a pocket projector, a mobile projector or a pico-projector. It is an emerging technology that applies the use of a projector in a handheld device. It is a response to the emergence of compact portable devices, such as mobile phones, personal digital assistants, and digital cameras, which have sufficient storage capacity to handle presentation materials with an attached display screen.

Video Projector

A video projector is also known as a digital projector, which is now popular for many applications for extension and development. All video projectors use a very bright light to project the image.

Opaque Projector (Epidiascope or Episcope)

It is a device that displays opaque materials by shining a bright lamp onto the object from above. The material can be book pages, drawings, mineral specimens, leaves, etc.

Film Strips

The filmstrip was a common form of still image instructional multimedia. It was once commonly used by educators in primary and secondary schools, now overtaken by newer and increasingly low-cost, full-motion videocassettes and DVDs, since 1940s till 1980s.

Microsoft PowerPoint Presentations

PowerPoint is an application program of presentation that is found in Microsoft Office. Nowadays, many of the audio–visual teaching aids have been replaced with PowerPoint presentations. Here, the slides give us the flexibility in terms of fonts, visuals, sizes, ability to change, etc. It allows the teachers to reflect on a lesson and correct any changes, and they can create perfect lessons and can print them out. Using PowerPoint improves the students' learning motivation, increases authentic materials for study, and encourages interaction between the teacher and the students.

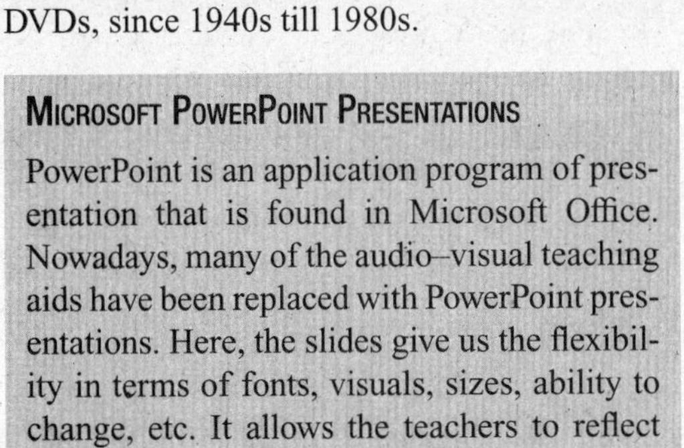

Non-Projected Visual Aids

Non-projected visual aids are those aids that are used without projection or help of any projector. Advantages include easy availability, no specific power supply requirement, economical, and ease in handling. They can be useful in small group situations. Many of them can be converted into projected aids. For example, charts, flannel graphs, and flash cards can be photographed or scanned and converted into slides. Some of them can be projected through an opaque projector.

Charts

A chart is a symbolized visual aid with pictures of relationships and changes, which are used to tabulate a large mass of information or show a progression. Charts can help communicate difficult and dull subject matter in an interesting and effective way. They make facts and figures clear and interesting, show or compare changes, and show the size and placement of parts. They are also helpful in summarizing information and presenting abstract ideas in visual form.

Types of Charts

There are many varieties of charts. Some common types of charts are briefly discussed below for your understanding:

1. *Bar chart:* Bar charts are made of a series of bars along a measured scale. They are used to compare quantities at different times or under different circumstances.
2. *Pie chart:* Pie charts are in the shape of circles and are used to show proportions and percentages.
3. *Tabular chart:* Tabular charts are used to bring together mass-related data in compact form (e.g., timetable).
4. *Tree chart:* Tree charts are used for showing development or growth of a programme or project. The origin is shown in a single line or as a tree trunk, and various developments are shown as branches.
5. *Flow chart:* Flow charts show organizational structure of departments, institutions, and resources with lines and arrows.

6. *Pictorial chart:* A pictorial chart gives the viewer a vivid picture and creates a rapid association with the use of graphic messages, such as cartoons and illustrations. This type of chart is more useful for illiterate audience.
7. *Overlay chart:* An overlay chart consists of a number of sheets that can be placed one over the other conveniently. On each individual sheet, a part of the whole concept is drawn. This enables the viewer to see not only the different parts but also how they appear when one is placed over the other. After the final overlay is placed, it shows full view of the whole picture. This type of chart presentation is dramatic and effective.
8. *Pull chart:* It consists of written messages on a large sheet. Messages are hidden by strips of thick paper held in position by the slits provided on either side. The messages can be shown to the viewer one after another by pulling out the concealing strips.
9. *Striptease chart:* It is similar to the pull chart; however, messages are concealed by strips of thin paper instead of thick paper. The ends of thin paper strips are pinned or pasted at both ends of the message. Whenever the message is to be exposed, one end of paper strip is stripped off. This has the advantage of surprise and anticipation.
10. *Flip chart:* A flip chart is a series of visuals drawn onto large sheets of paper or cardboard, which are fastened together at the top. These are turned over or flipped one at a time. This kind of chart exposes the audience to segments of the subject in sequence and holds their attention remarkably well.

Flash Cards

Flash cards are brief visual messages on poster board. The cards are flashed (turned over at short intervals) before the audience to emphasize the important points in a presentation. Flash cards are held like a pack of cards and are flashed to the audience one at a time in a sequence along with the talk.

Poster

A poster is displayed in a public place with the purpose of creating awareness among the people. A poster is generally seen from a distance and the person glancing at it seldom has the time or inclination to stop and read. The job of the poster is to stop the persons hurrying past and thrust the message upon them.

1. Posters give only an initial idea and cannot furnish detailed information. They need to be reported for further information by another aid or method (e.g., leaflets and demonstration).
2. The production of good posters is a technical job and requires skill and time.
3. It cannot be repeated; for each occasion, a new poster has to be made.

Pictures and Photographs

A picture is a representation made by drawing, painting, or photography, which gives an accurate idea of an object. A good picture may tell a story without using a single word. Pictures may be in black and white or in colour. Nowadays, digital cameras are popular.

Graphs

A graph is an image that represents data symbolically. A graph is used to present complex information and numerical data in a simple, compact format. Bar graphs, line graphs, scatter graphs, and pictographs are some types of graphs. In a two-dimensional graph, the information is represented along two co-ordinates: X coordinate and Y coordinate. An independent variable is shown along X axis and dependent along Y axis. More about graphs is discussed in Chapter 7 on Data Interpretation.

Maps

A map is a visual representation of an area—a symbolic depiction highlighting relationships between elements of that space such as objects, regions, and themes. Cartography or map-making is the study and practice of crafting representations of the Earth upon a flat surface.

Diagrams

A plan, sketch, drawing, or outline designed to demonstrate or explain how something works or to clarify the relationship between the parts of a whole is called a diagram.

Display Boards

Blackboard or Chalkboard

It is one of the oldest teaching aids; the chalkboard is probably the simplest, cheapest, most convenient, and widely used non-projected visual aid in extension teaching. It is a vehicle for a variety of visual materials.

The chalkboard is suitable for use in lectures, training programmes, group meetings, etc.

It facilitates step-by-step presentation of the topic, creates a dramatic impact, and sustains audience interest. Presentations may be adjusted according to the receptivity of the audience. It helps the audience to take notes. It helps in comprehension and retention of knowledge.

White Board

Modern classrooms are equipped with boards also called marker boards or multipurpose boards. They require special erasable markers. A felt eraser is required to erase the surface soon after use. Markers are available in different colours. It may be used as surface for projecting films, slides, and overhead transparencies. A white board with a steel backing can be used as magnetic board for display.

An interactive white board is a large interactive display that connects to a computer and projector. A projector projects the computer's desktop onto the board's surface, where users control the computer using a pen, finger, or other device. The board is typically mounted to a wall or to a floor stand.

Bulletin Board

A bulletin board displays messages. It is a surface on which bulletins, news, information, and announcements of specific or general interest can be displayed. Bulletin boards are of different sizes with provisions to hold pins, book exhibits, and other materials.

Flannel Board and Flannel Graph

A flannel board is a visual aid in which messages are written or drawn on thick paper and presented step-by-step to the audience to synchronize with the talk. The board is a flannel-covered flat surface. Flannel is stretched and then glued to a piece of plywood or heavy cardboard.

Magnetic Board

It can be a sheet of tinplate; it is simply a type of chalkboard, and the surface of which is treated or coated with a porcelain-like substance. The base of the board is steel, and pictures and objects can be pasted or mounted with small magnets and can easily be moved about.

Peg Board

Perforated hardboard is tempered hardboard, which is pre-drilled with evenly spaced holes. The holes are used to accept pegs or hooks to support various items, such as tools in a workshop.

Three-dimensional Models

Real things may not be available all the times, and in the desired form. Hence, models help to tide over this problem. A model is a recognizable representation of real things in three-dimensional view—height, width, and depth. This makes the understanding better and easy.

Models can be of three types: (i) solids, (ii) cut away or cross sections, and (iii) working models. They have advantages of reality depiction, illustration, and are complex and intricate. They are long lasting and cheaper.

Objects, Specimens, and Globe

Objects are collections of real things for instructional use. Specimen is any typical object representing a class or group of things.

A globe is the spherical model of earth.

Audio Aids

Radio

The popularity, availability, and low cost of radio made it a convenient and practical medium for use in programmes for distance learning. It is mostly used in combination with other media, such as with print medium followed by face-to-face teaching, etc.

Gyan Vani (Educational FM Radio Channel of India) was launched in 2001. The publicity material has been developed by IGNOU. The target group is students of open or conventional universities. It is a unique decentralized concept of extending mass media for education and empowerment, which is suited to the educational needs of the local communities.

Recordings

A tape recorder or any other kind of audio recording is suitable for extension work in meetings, training programmes, campaigns, recording radio programmes, etc. It facilitates on-the-spot recording of sound. It is easy to operate and preserve. It has low operational cost as the same tape may be used again.

Digital Audio Player

A digital audio player is sometimes referred to as an MP3 player and has the primary function of storing, organizing, and playing audio files. Some digital audio players are also referred to as portable media players as they have image viewing and video-playing support. The example is iPod (fourth generation audio aid).

Telephone and Mobile

Usually, two persons can communicate at a time through a telephone; the system serves many people in a given area if a speaker is attached to it like Cell Phone-Operated Mobile Audio Communication and Conference System (COMBACCS). This technology is seeing a phenomenal growth in many developing countries. Short message service (SMS) and wireless application protocol (WAP)-enabled cell phones with cameras can be effective in offering always available extension between experts and people. COMBACCS can help community members at different locations build relationships and understanding.

Television

Television is an effective tool in expressing abstract concepts or ideas. Abstract concepts are usually produced and conveyed with words. Besides this, in making an abstract concept concrete, the role of animation and visual experimentation is very important.

Activity Aids

1. *Field trip:* A field trip is a structured activity that occurs outside the classroom. It can be a brief observational activity or a longer, more sustained investigation or project. Field trips offer an opportunity to students to get exposure to real people, events, and opportunity to make connections with others. Students on field trips visit people and places that they are not normally exposed to during the schooldays.
2. *Experimentation:* The experiments are specifically useful in science subjects so as to relate theory with practice.
3. *Dramatics:* They can convey some message to society or public at large. These are usually theme-based and students are assigned different roles.
4. *Teaching machines:* There are many types of teaching machines. In general, they all work on the same method, which is to present a question, have the user indicate the answer, and then provide the user with the correct answer. They are usually programmed. They are particularly useful in subjects that require drill, such as arithmetic or a foreign language. Users can proceed at their own pace and also have an opportunity to review their work. If the machines are used in a classroom, they relieve teachers of some of the time-consuming aspects of drilling students and allowing them to give more attention to

individuals with specific problems or to concentrate on some particularly difficult area of instruction.

5. *Programmed instructions:* It is mentioned on page 1.13 under Individualised Teaching Methods.

Other Activity Aids

The computer-aided learning, demonstration, and programmed instructions have been discussed under teaching methods. Whether these are full-fledged teaching methods or just teaching aids, depends upon the degree of their use.

Factors Influencing the Selection of Teaching Aids

No single rule-of-thumb can be given for the selection and use of various audio-visual aids to ensure effectiveness in all situations. In order to get the most effective results, the following aspects are important:

1. Selection of appropriate aids
2. Suitable combination of the selected aids
3. Their use in proper sequence.

Audio–visual aids are used singly or in combination, thereby taking into consideration the following factors:

1. *Nature of audience:* Printed media are meant for literate people, whereas exhibits, pictures, and symbols are for less literate people.

2. *Size of audience:* A video show or whiteboard cannot be used effectively when the number of participants exceeds 30; internet can be used for large audiences.

3. *Teaching objective or expected nature of change:* Select the audio–visual aids based on the objective of extension teaching, that is, to bring about a change in (i) thinking or knowledge, (ii) attitude or feeling, and (iii) actions or skills.

   If you merely want to inform or to influence a large number of people slightly, use mass media such as radio or television.

4. *Nature of subject matter:* In case new practice is simple and familiar, a news article, a radio message, or a circular letter will be effective, whereas complex or unfamiliar practices will require audio–visual aids.

5. *Availability of aids:* Despite the availability of the Internet two decades back, it was not being used on a large scale. With availability of speed, due to better technology, and cost effectiveness, more people are now using Internet-based technologies as teaching aids.

6. *Relative cost:* Effective aids need not be necessarily costly. The amount expended on audio–visual aids, in relation to the extent of effectiveness, is also an important consideration in their selection and use.

Dale's Cone of Experience

Dale's Cone of Experience is a model that incorporates several theories related to instructional design and learning processes. During 1960s, Edgar Dale theorized that learners retain more information by what they 'do' as opposed to what is 'heard', 'read', or 'observed'. His research led to the development of the 'Cone of Experience'. Today, this 'learning by doing' has become known as 'experiential learning' or 'action learning'.

How can instructors use the cone of experience? According to Dale's research, the least effective method at the top involves learning from information presented through verbal symbols, that is, listening to spoken words. The most effective methods at the bottom involve direct, purposeful learning experiences, such as hands-on or field experience. Direct purposeful experiences represent reality or the closet things to real, everyday life. The cone charts the average retention rate for various methods of teaching. The further you progress down the cone, the greater the learning and the more information are likely to be retained. It also suggests that when choosing an instructional method, it is important to remember that involving students in the process strengthens knowledge retention. It reveals that 'action–learning' techniques result

Cone of Experience

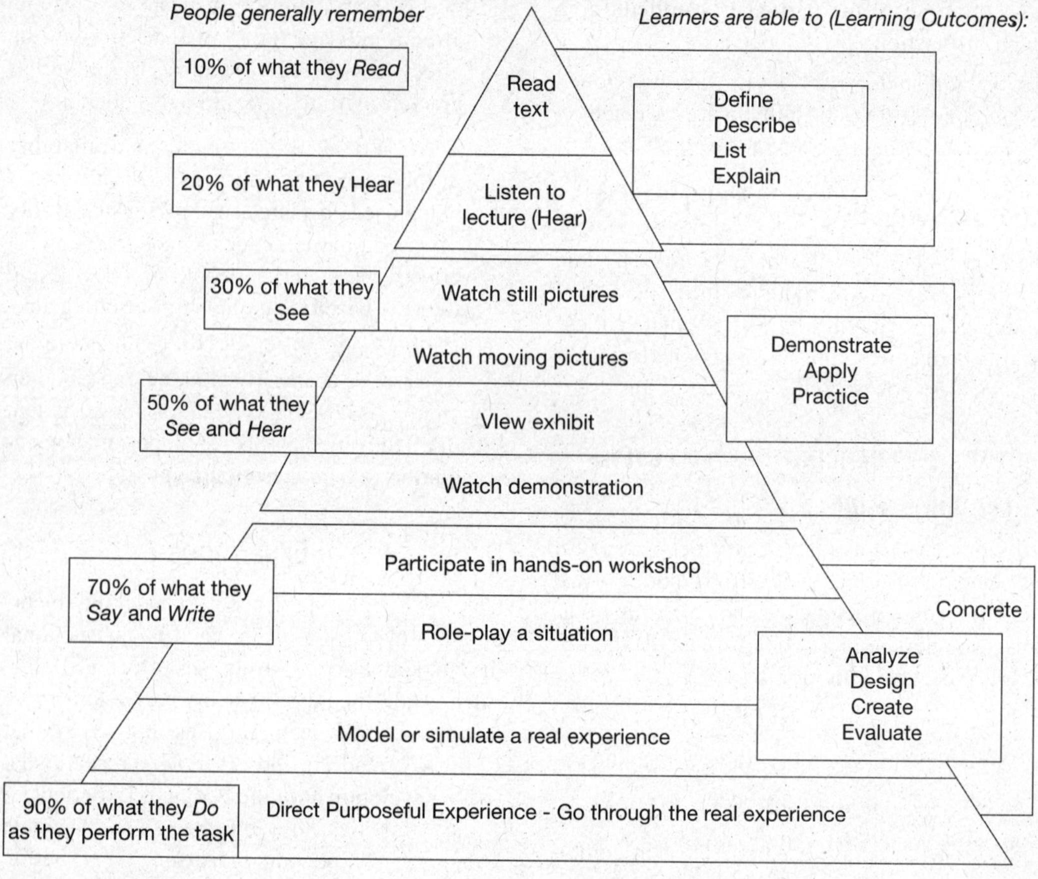

in up to 90% retention. People learn best when they use perceptual learning styles, and these learning styles are sensory based.

The more sensory channels possible in interacting with a resource, the better chance that many students can learn from it. According to Dale, instructors should design instructional activities that build upon more real-life experiences. Dales' cone of experience is a tool to help instructors make decisions about resources and activities.

Important Tips for Better Classroom Management

In NET examination, there are questions about class indiscipline and how to deal with the situation. There are number of things a teacher must keep in mind when dealing with students who do not behave in a disciplined manner in the class. There is a basic rule that the teacher must consider that he or she does not hurt them physically or emotionally. This would prove psychologically harmful to the student, and our purpose is surely not to harm them but to modify their behaviour as individuals.

Punishments, if any, should be seen as reasonable and fair, and never vicious. The ability to control a group of students depends on the personality of the teacher and also the rapport that he or she develops with them. There are some tips to be kept in mind.

1. *Immediate action:* If the students indulge in deviant behaviour, the teacher must take

instant action and not allow it to persist for a long time. If a student is coming late to school repeatedly, the teacher should speak to the student immediately after the class.

2. *Stop teaching in case of misbehaviour:* Stop teaching whenever the students disrupt the class; the teacher must stop teaching and should tell the students to stop doing so immediately. The moment the teacher stops teaching, it is clear that the teacher means business and will not tolerate misbehaviour in the class.

Teaching with Sense of Humour

- Laughter is a natural, universal phenomenon, with beneficial effects - both physical and psychological.
- Everyone loves a teacher with an infectious sense of humour
- It builds cordial relationship.
- It has the ability to relax people and reduce tension.
- It is an effective advertising strategy.
- Teaching with the help of cartoon is a very effective way.
- When there is a willingness to change, there is hope for progress in any field.
- Students enjoy humour in forms of funny anecdotes.

3. *Change seats:* If few students disrupt the class, change their seats. Separating the troublemakers is quite effective in controlling indiscipline.
4. *Adapt and be sensitive:* In case the entire class is gradually getting out of control, then it's a signal that the activity is boring; the best way of controlling them is by changing the activity, for example, if they are reading, immediately switch over to a writing task, which would keep them all quiet and involved. The teacher must learn to adapt and be sensitive to the mood of the class.
5. *Counsel after class:* One of the most effective ways of tackling a student is by giving counselling after class. A heart-to-heart talk explaining the anti-social behaviour to the student and giving them an opportunity to explain why they misbehaved would prove beneficial in sorting out many issues. The teacher should also clearly explain the consequences of not improving.
6. *Talk to the parents:* In several cases, a talk with the parents will improve the behaviour of the student. It would also give a better insight into the reasons for indiscipline by individual students.

Education and Teaching-Related Important Days

Table 1.7 Important Dates Related to Education

Dates	Important days
January 04	World Braille Day—A form of written language for blind people, in which characters are represented by patterns of raised dots that are felt with the fingertips
January 24	National Girl Child Day also called as Balika Divas
February 21	International Mother Language Day
February 28	National Science Day—To commemorate invention of the Raman Effect in India by the Indian physicist, Sir Chandrasekhara Venkata Raman on the same day in 1928
June 21	International Day of Yoga—United Nations proclaimed 21 June as International Yoga Day
September 5	Teachers' Day is celebrated on 5th September every year, which is also the birthday of Dr Sarvepalli Radhakrishnan, the first Vice-President of independent India and the second President of the country.

(Continued)

Table 1.7 *(Continued)*

Dates	Important days
September 8	International Literacy Day—To highlight the importance of literacy in life and remind ourselves of the status of literacy and adult learning worldwide
September 14	Hindi Day
October 5	World Teachers' Day—UN World Teachers' Day commemorates the work of teachers and their contributions to society
October 11	International Day of Girl Child
October 20	World Statistics Day
November 1	National Education Day—It is also the birthday of Maulana Abul Kalam Azad, eminent educationist and the first Education Minister of independent India
November 14	Children's Day—It is also the birthday of independent India's first Prime Minister Pt. Jawaharlal Nehru
November 20	Universal Children's Day

Concepts, Nature, and Characteristics

1. Which of the following is/are the basic paradigms in classroom teaching?
   (a) Learning paradigm
   (b) Instructional paradigm
   (c) Both (a) and (b)
   (d) None of the above
2. The prime requirement to become a good teacher is to have
   (a) Genuine interest in teaching
   (b) Knowledge about controlling students
   (c) Subject knowledge
   (d) Good expression
3. Which of the following statement/s is/are NOT true? *(June 1997)*
   (a) Teaching is just an art
   (b) Teachers can be trained only
   (c) Teachers are born
   (d) All of the above
4. The most desirable skill of teacher is to
   (a) Make the students understand what the teacher says
   (b) Cover the prescribed course
   (c) Keep students relaxed while teaching
   (d) Keep higher authorities informed about the class activities
5. Match List I with List II

List I (Level of teaching)		List II (Main proponent)	
A	Memory Level	I	Herbart
B	Understanding Level	II	Morrison
C	Reflective Level	III	Hunt

Codes:
(a) A-I, B-II, C-III (b) A-I, B-III, C-II
(c) A-II, B-III, C-I (d) A-II, B-I, C-III

6. Which of the following is the sequence of different levels of teaching?
   (a) Memory level–understanding level–reflective level
   (b) Understanding level–memory level–reflective level
   (c) Reflective level–understanding level–memory Level
   (d) Memory level–reflective level–understanding level
7. Which of the following is an independent variable in teaching–learning process?
   (a) Teacher (b) Student
   (c) Institution (d) Parents

8. Which of the following method should be used by each teacher?
(a) Analytical–synthetic
(b) Synthetic–analytical
(c) Only analytical
(d) Only synthetic

9. Match List I with List II

List I (Teaching maxims)		List II (Main proponents)	
A	From whole to part	I	Gestalt psychologists
B	Self-study	II	Dalton
C	Training of senses	III	Montessori and Froebel

Codes:
(a) A-I, B-II, C-III (b) A-I, B-III, C-II
(c) A-II, B-III, C-I (d) A-II, B-I, C-III

10. Which of the following reflects the nature of teaching?
(a) It is an art.
(b) It is a science.
(c) It is an art as well as science.
(d) It is neither art nor science.

11. Which of the following orders are the three levels of teaching?
(i) Memory level of teaching
(ii) Understanding level of teaching
(iii) Reflective level of teaching
(iv) Pedagogical level of teaching
(a) (i), (ii), and (iii) (b) (ii), (iii), and (iv)
(c) (i), (iii), and (iv) (d) (i), (ii), and (iv)

12. Nowadays, teaching is becoming more and more
(a) Learner-centred
(b) Instructor-centred
(c) Group-centred
(d) None of the above

13. When the learner is self-directed, it is termed as
(a) Pedagogical learning
(b) Andragogical learning
(c) Distance education learning
(d) None of the above

14. Instructional objectives are written for the student and they state what the student is expected to do. These objectives should be
(a) Specific (b) Observable
(c) Measurable (d) All of the above

15. In context of dynamic teaching environment, which of the following statement is true?
(a) Teacher is a dependent variable and student is an independent variable.
(b) Teacher is an independent variable and student is a dependent variable.
(c) Both teacher and student are intervening variables.
(d) None of the above

16. At which of the following teaching levels, classroom environment is required to be sufficiently 'open and independent'?
(a) Memory level
(b) Understanding level
(c) Reflective level
(d) All of the above

17. What is meant by the term 'curriculum'?
(a) The subject of study offered by an educational institution.
(b) Organized whole of learning and other experiences provided by educational institutions to realize set goals.
(c) The prescribed syllabi in the various subjects, plus practical courses and project/dissertation.
(d) Theory and practical courses to be completed to qualify for a level of education.

18. The classification of cognitive domain was presented by
(a) Benjamin S. Bloom
(b) Skinner
(c) Krathwohl
(d) Simpson

19. To make use of previously learned material in new situation is
(a) Comprehension (b) Application
(c) Knowledge (d) Analysis

20. The highest level of cognitive domain is
(a) Synthesis (b) Analysis
(c) Comprehension (d) Evaluation

21. At authoritarian level, teaching is
    (a) Teacher-centred
    (b) Child-centred
    (c) Headmaster-centred
    (d) Experience-based
22. Match List I with List II

List I (Characteristic)		List II (Philosophy)	
A	Learning by doing	I	Naturalism
B	Education through environment	II	Idealism
C	Realization of truth, beauty, and goodness	III	Pragmatism
D	'World as it is here and now'	IV	Realism

Codes:
    (a) A-I, B-IV, C-II, D-III
    (b) A-III, B-I, C-II, D-IV
    (c) A-I, B-III, C-II, D-IV
    (d) A-III, B-II, C-IV, D-I
23. The intellectual skills are reflected by
    (a) Cognitive domain
    (b) Affective domain
    (c) Psychomotor domain
    (d) None of the above
24. Attitudes, values, and interests are reflected by
    (a) Cognitive domain
    (b) Affective domain
    (c) Psychomotor domain
    (d) None of the above
25. Which domain is concerned with physical and motor skills?
    (a) Cognitive domain
    (b) Affective domain
    (c) Psychomotor domain
    (d) None of the above
26. Which of the following can be cited as an example of cognitive domain?
    (a) Describe a specific topic
    (b) Develop a photographic film
    (c) Typing an essay
    (d) Take responsibility for maintenance
27. Which of the following can be taken as an example of psychomotor domain in the context of teaching?
    (a) demonstrates awareness to environmental pollution
    (b) performing an experiment
    (c) computing results of two experiments
    (d) narrating a story
28. Which of the following statements is false?
    (a) Teaching and instruction are the same concepts.
    (b) There is difference between teaching and learning.
    (c) Education is a wider term than teaching, training, research, etc.
    (d) All of the above are true.
29. Teaching is based upon the mastery of
    (a) Knowledge of concepts
    (b) Teaching skills
    (c) Decision-making skills
    (d) All of the above
30. Who has the least chance of becoming an effective teacher? (*December 2002*)
    (a) One who is a strict disciplinarian
    (b) One who knows his subject well
    (c) One who has no interest in teaching
    (d) One who teaches moral values
31. Which of the following is/are the teaching maxims?
    (i) From psychological to logical
    (ii) From analysis to synthesis
    (iii) From concrete to abstract
    (iv) Follow nature
    (a) (i), (ii), and (iii) (b) (i), (ii), and (iv)
    (c) (i), (iii), and (iv) (d) All of the above
32. Analysis means
    (a) Ability to break a problem into its constituent parts
    (b) To combine the constituent parts
    (c) Both (a) and (b)
    (d) None of the above
33. The rules of presenting the contents to make them easy are called

(a) Methods of teaching
(b) Maxims of teaching
(c) Techniques of teaching
(d) Teaching strategies

34. With smaller classes, teachers are much more able to
(a) Identify learning problems
(b) Provide individual attention
(c) Adapt instruction to individual differences among students
(d) All of the above

35. The single most important factor in the beginning of the teaching career is
(a) Meritorious academic record
(b) Communication skills
(c) One's personality and ability to relate to class and students
(d) Organizing ability

36. Effective teaching, by and large, is a function of
(a) Maintaining discipline in the class
(b) Teachers' honesty
(c) Teachers making students learn and understand
(d) Teachers' liking for the job of teaching

37. In List I, the names of the philosophers are given, and in List II, statements regarding the philosophy are given. Match List I with List II in correct order:

List I (Characteristic)		List II (Philosophy)	
A	Tagore	I	Harmonious development of personality
B	Vivekananda	II	The doctrine of karma
C	Mahatma Gandhi	III	Child is more, important than all kinds of books
D	Buddhism	IV	Yoga as a method of education
		V	The doctrine of dharma

Codes:
(a) A-V, B-I C-II D-IV
(b) A-III, B-IV, C-II D-V
(c) A-III, B-IV, C-I D-II
(d) A-IV, B-II, C-I D-III

38. Who said this 'Education is man-making. It is that by which character is formed, strength of mind is increased, intellect is expanded and by which man can stand on his own feet'?
(a) Swami Vivekananda
(b) Guru Rabindranath Tagore
(c) Swami Dayanand Saraswati
(d) None of these

39. Prior to teaching, the teacher does
(a) Identification of objectives
(b) Preparation of teaching lesson plan
(c) Know the interest of students
(d) All of the above

40. Effective teaching includes
(a) Teacher is active but students may or may not be active
(b) Teacher may be active or inactive but students are active
(c) Teacher is active and students are active
(d) All of the above

41. The most expected immediate outcome of teaching is
(a) Changes in the behaviour of students in desirable direction
(b) Development of total personality of students
(c) Building characters of the students
(d) Getting selected for a suitable job

42. Basic requirement of teaching efficiency is
(a) Mastery on teaching skills
(b) Mastery over use of different techniques of teaching
(c) Mastery over appropriate use of media and technology in teaching
(d) All of the above

43. Which of the following statements is NOT correct? *(June 1997)*
(a) A good communicator cannot be a good teacher
(b) A good communicator has good sense of humour

(c) A good communicator has wide reading knowledge
(d) A good communicator has command over language

44. A teacher is successful only if he
(a) Knows his subject thoroughly well
(b) Produces cent per cent result
(c) Is approachable
(d) Publishes papers in journals of repute.

45. If a teacher wants to enhance his income, he should
(a) Teach in coaching institutes during extra time
(b) Take more remunerative works in the school/college
(c) Join contractual assignments other than teaching
(d) Write books

46. As a principal, you will encourage your teacher colleagues to
(a) Participate in seminars and conferences in India and abroad
(b) Participate in refresher courses for enhancement of subject knowledge
(c) Doing community services for the upliftment of down trodden
(d) All of the above

47. Which of the following activities can help a teacher inculcate social and moral values among the students?
(a) Delivering lectures on values
(b) Showing TV programmes
(c) Involving students actively in co-curricular activities
(d) Observing religious festivals

48. A teacher will become an effective communicator if (*December 1997*)
(a) He uses instructional aids
(b) He helps students get meaning out of what he teaches
(c) He asks question in between teaching
(d) He helps students get correct answer to the questions on the topic

49. Teaching in higher education implies (*December 1997*)
(a) Presenting the information given in the textbook
(b) Asking question in the class and conducting examinations
(c) Helping students prepare for and pass the examination
(d) Helping students to learn

50. Teaching will be effective if the teacher (*June 1998*)
(a) Is the master of the subject
(b) Has much experience in teaching the subject
(c) Starts from what students know already
(d) Uses many instructional aids

51. A college teacher will really help the students when she (*June 1998*)
(a) Dictates notes in the class
(b) Is objective in her evaluation
(c) Encourages students to ask questions
(d) Covers the syllabus completely in class

52. Which is the most desirable outcome of teaching in higher education? (*June 1998*)
(a) Increase in student achievement
(b) Increase in the level of independent thinking of students
(c) Higher percentage of result
(d) Increase in the number of students who opt for the subject

53. Books can be a powerful source of communication, provided (*December 1998*)
(a) The content is abstract
(b) The content is illustrative
(c) The medium is hindi
(d) The content is presented through good print

54. Good teaching is best reflected by (*December 1998*)
(a) Attendance of students
(b) Number of distinctions
(c) Meaningful questions asked by students
(d) Pin-drop silence in the class

55. The main aim of classroom teaching is (*December 1998*)
(a) To give information
(b) To develop inquiring mind

(c) To develop personality of students
(d) To help students pass examinations

56. Students prefer those teachers who (*December 2000*)
(a) dictate notes in the class
(b) give important questions before examination
(c) can clear their difficulties regarding subject matter
(d) are themselves disciplined

57. Which of the following is the main objective of teaching?
(a) To give information related to the syllabus
(b) Prepare the students for examination
(c) Help the students in getting jobs
(d) To develop thinking capability of students

58. The teacher's role in higher education is to
(i) Provide information to the students
(ii) Only prepare students for examination
(iii) Motivate students for self-learning
(iv) Encourage competition among students
(a) (i) and (ii) (b) (ii), (iii), and (iv)
(c) (i), (iii), and (iv) (d) All of the above

59. An effective teacher will ensure (*December 2002*)
(a) Cooperation among his students
(b) Laissez-faire role
(c) Competition among students
(d) Competition or cooperation as the situation demands

60. A new teacher to start with will have to (*December 2002*)
(a) Enforce discipline in class
(b) Establish rapport with the students
(c) Cut jokes with the students
(d) Tell the students about his qualifications

61. A teacher can establish rapport with students by
(a) Playing the role of a guide who desires to help them
(b) Becoming a figure of authority
(c) Impressing the students with knowledge
(d) Implementing strict rules

62. The quality of teaching can be assessed
(a) By the result in annual exam
(b) By the attendance of students
(c) By the quality of interaction of students in the class
(d) By the silence in the class

63. Which of the following is the least important aspect of the teacher's role in the guidance of learning?
(a) The development of insight to overcome the pitfalls and obstacles.
(b) The development of insight into what constitutes an adequate performance.
(c) The provision of encouragement and moral support.
(d) The provision of continuous diagnostic and remedial help.

64. Which of the following should not be the main role of the teacher at the higher educational level?
(a) Provide information to students
(b) Promote self-learning in the students
(c) Encourage healthy competition among students
(d) Help the students to solve their personal problems

65. Arrange the following activities of interaction in logical order.
(i) Analysis of the work done
(ii) Planning and preparation
(iii) Presentation of material
(iv) Modification and improvement
(a) (i), (ii), (iii), and (iv)
(b) (ii), (iii), (i), and (iv)
(c) (iv), (i), (ii), and (iii)
(d) (i), (iii), (iv), and (ii)

66. Effective teaching means all of the following except
(a) A teacher teaches with enthusiasm.
(b) A teacher finds fault in his students.
(c) A teacher puts emphasis more on teaching than on class control.
(d) A teacher is interested in making the subject matter understood rather than on completing the course.

67. If some students fail in the examination, it is the fault of
(a) The teacher
(b) The principal

(c) Students themselves
(d) It cannot be generalized

68. A teacher who is not able to draw the attention of his students should
(a) Evaluate his teaching method and improve it
(b) Resign from the post
(c) Find fault in his pupils
(d) Start dictating

69. The primary task of a teacher is
(a) To teach the prescribed curriculum
(b) To stimulate and guide student's learning
(c) To provide diagnostic and remedial aid wherever desired
(d) To promote habits of conformity to adult demands and expectations

70. Which of the following teacher's behaviour suggests a dimension of 'unsuccessful' teacher behaviour? A teacher who is:
(a) Always motivating students
(b) Business-like and friendly approach
(c) Aloof and focused on routine tasks
(d) Understanding and sympathetic

71. A teacher
(a) Should provide overview of the topic to be taught in the class
(b) Should have good communication skills
(c) Should command over his subject
(d) all of the above

72. Which of the following is desirable from a new teacher as his/her professional responsibility is
(a) Changing the course curriculum
(b) Cooperate with the fellow teacher despite the differences
(c) Follow the procedures of the institute
(d) None of the above

73. The greatest important cause of failure in beginning for a teacher lies in the area of
(a) Interpersonal relationship
(b) Verbal ability
(c) Knowledge of the teacher
(d) Tight handling of the students

74. 'Mirambaka'—The school based on ideas of free progress education was advocated by
(a) M.K. Gandhi (b) Vivekanand
(c) John Dewey (d) Aurobindo

75. The most important single factor of success for a teacher in the beginning of teaching career is
(a) Verbal fluency and organizational ability
(b) Positive attitude and outlook towards life
(c) Personality and ability to adjust to classroom
(d) Competence and professional ethics

76. For a teacher in higher educational institution, which of the following is the best option to do in leisure time?
(a) Taking rest in teacher's room
(b) Reading magazines in library
(c) Talking to administrative staff
(d) Doing research

77. What are the components of Tyler's model of curriculum?
(a) Aims, subject content, teaching, evaluation
(b) Purpose, educational experiences, effective organisation of experiences, verification of goal
(c) Aims of education, organisation of content, testing, feedback
(d) Subject content, teaching, learning, testing

78. The experienced teachers do not require the detailed lesson plan of a topic because
(a) They can teach more effectively without its help.
(b) There are just few curious students in the class.
(c) The teacher is not likely to face any challenges from students even if they are wrong.
(d) They can equip themselves with brief outline as they gain specialization in it through experience.

79. The ideal teacher
(a) Covers the whole syllabus in class
(b) Helps his students in learning
(c) Is a friend, philosopher, and guide
(d) Is a strict disciplinarian

80. The field of education is permeated by conflicts and misconceptions because
(a) Subjectivity of interpretation
(b) Problems are not amenable to rigorous scientific investigation
(c) Lack of good teaching methods
(d) All of the above

81. In the introduction part of a lesson plan, a teacher aims to get student's
(a) Assignments
(b) Aptitude
(c) Attention
(d) Abilities

82. With the development of technology, the role of a teacher in future will be
(a) To provide information
(b) To develop new textbooks
(c) To guide students
(d) To use the Internet in teaching

83. Which of the following is not a level of teaching learning?
(a) Differentiation level
(b) Memory level
(c) Reflective level
(d) Understanding level

84. What does the cognitive domain of Bloom's Taxonomy of Educational Objectives affect in learners?
(a) Thoughts (b) Emotions
(c) Skills (d) All of the above

85. Integral education concept is propounded by
(a) Sri Aurobindo
(b) Mahatma Gandhi
(c) Swami Dayanand
(d) Swami Vivekananda

86. The standard of education can be raised by
(a) Appointing good teachers
(b) Providing physical facilities in schools
(c) Reforming examination system
(d) Providing computer in schools

87. Which of the following skills are needed for the present-day teacher to adjust effectively with classroom teaching?
I. Knowledge of technology
II. Use of technology in teaching learning
III. Knowledge of students' needs
IV. Content mastery

Codes:
(a) I and III (b) II and III
(c) II, III, and IV (d) II and IV

88. The primary duty of a teacher is to
(a) Raise the intellectual standards of students
(b) Improve the physical standards of students
(c) Help in all-round development of students
(d) Imbibe value system in students

89. Which one of the following is the most important quality of a good teacher?
(a) Punctuality and sincerity
(b) Content mastery
(c) Content mastery and reactive
(d) Content mastery and sociable

90. The primary responsibility for the teacher's adjustment lies with
(a) The children
(b) The principal
(c) The teacher himself
(d) The community

91. Which one of the following statements is correct?
(a) Syllabus is an annexure to the curriculum.
(b) Curriculum is the same in all educational institutions.
(c) Curriculum includes both formal and informal education.
(d) Curriculum does not include methods of evaluation.

92. A successful teacher is one who is
(a) Compassionate and disciplinarian
(b) Quite and reactive
(c) Tolerant and dominating
(d) Passive and active

93. The most important quality of a good teacher is
(a) Sound knowledge of subject matter
(b) Good communication skills
(c) Concern for students' welfare
(d) Effective leadership qualities

94. Most important challenge in teaching a resource teacher is
   (a) Identification and assessment of the disabled children
   (b) Sensitization of public, parents, and peer groups
   (c) Establishing resource room and supplying assistive devices
   (d) Teaching plus curricular activities

Teaching Methods and Teaching Aids

95. Micro teaching is more effective (*December 2009*)
   (a) during preparation for teaching practice
   (b) during teaching practice
   (c) after the teaching practice
   (d) always

96. Micro-teaching is useful to students of
   (a) Primary classes only
   (b) Junior classes only
   (c) 10 + 2 classes only
   (d) Both for primary and higher classes

97. Which of the following university was the pioneer in micro-teaching concept started in 1961?
   (a) Stanford University
   (b) Oxford University
   (c) Delhi University
   (d) J L N University, New Delhi

98. In which of the following is instructional procedure the main component?
   (a) Synectics teaching model
   (b) Basic teaching model
   (c) Inductive model
   (d) Social stimulation

99. In education, John Dewey stressed on
   (a) Learning by doing
   (b) Authoritarian teaching methods
   (c) Rote learning
   (d) None of the above

100. Symposium is a type of
   (a) Discovery method
   (b) Discussion method
   (c) Lecture method
   (d) Demonstration method

101. Questioning skill in teaching is most useful in
   (a) Ensuring students' active participation in learning
   (b) Memorizing the facts by students
   (c) Making students disciplined
   (d) Preparing students for examination

102. Which of the following statement is incorrect about microteaching?
   (a) It is a method of teaching.
   (b) It consists of core teaching skills.
   (c) Each skill is practised separately.
   (d) Questioning is one component of microteaching.

103. Armstrong was the main exponent of
   (a) Problem-solving method
   (b) Project method
   (c) Discussion method
   (d) Heuristic method

104. Discussion method is useful if
   (a) The topic is very easy
   (b) The topic is difficult
   (c) The topic is very difficult
   (d) In all situations

105. Educational technology is useful because
   (a) It is the need of the hour
   (b) It is adopted by famous institutions
   (c) It makes teaching effective and efficient
   (d) It attracts students towards teaching and learning activities

106. Which component(s) might be included in a lesson plan?
   (a) Development or outline of a lesson
   (b) Varied materials and media to supplement and clarify content

(c) Specific objectives of the lesson
(d) All of the above

107. One of the most popular forms of drill and practice is
(a) Questioning
(b) Direct instruction
(c) Experiential instruction
(d) None of the above

108. Practice is made in
(a) Inductive method
(b) Deductive method
(c) Drill method
(d) Discussion method

109. In which of the following subjects, role playing can be mainly useful for teaching?
(a) History
(b) Science subjects
(c) Mathematics
(d) Language

110. Which is not the advantage of team teaching?
(a) Better utilization of resources
(b) Better planning
(c) Better use of teaching techniques
(d) Better financial benefits of teachers

111. A teacher performs practically and explains in
(a) Lecture method
(b) Discovery method
(c) Demonstration method
(d) Problem-solving method

112. The main assumption underlying team teaching is
(a) Teachers feel bored while working alone
(b) Teachers are not competent
(c) The best teachers can be shared by more students
(d) The single teacher cannot control the class

113. CAI stands for
(a) Computer-analysed instruction
(b) Computer-assisted instruction
(c) Computer-assisted intelligence
(d) None of the above

114. Which is not the mode of CAI?
(a) Tutorial mode
(b) Drill mode
(c) Simulation mode
(d) Question mode

115. When presenting materials, teachers should consider which of the following?
(a) Structuring (b) Balancing
(c) Motivating (d) All of the above

116. The technology in education is making teaching
(a) Learner oriented
(b) Teacher oriented
(c) Both (a) and (b)
(d) None of the above

117. Which of the following is/are true of whole-group instruction?
(a) Permits students to progress at their own pace
(b) Convenient for teaching the same skills or content to the entire class
(c) Gives the teacher a chance to introduce new skills at a level suited to particular students
(d) All of the above

118. Which of the following methods of communication is the most effective
(a) Verbal communication
(b) Oral Communication
(c) Multimedia method
(d) Difficult to generalize and depends upon the situation

119. Maximum participation of students is possible in teaching through
(a) Lecture method
(b) Discussions
(c) Textbook method
(d) Audio–visual aids

120. Which type of teaching paradigm would focus on a technical or 'one right way to teach' approach to presenting content?
(a) Learning paradigm
(b) Instructional paradigm
(c) Value-added paradigm
(d) None of the above

121. Which of the following cannot be a good way of communication in promoting literacy among villagers?
   (a) Demonstration
   (b) Reading and writing
   (c) Providing material on TV and film projector
   (d) Large group discussion

122. The main advantage of giving home assignments to students is
   (a) Keeping them busy in studies all the time
   (b) To stop them from watching TV
   (c) To develop the habit of self-study
   (d) None of the above

123. Instruction-medium affects the absence and escape from class teaching.
   (a) Agreed
   (b) Indefinite
   (c) Disagreed
   (d) None of the above

124. The main task of educational computer is
   (a) Scoring the answers
   (b) Preserves the information
   (c) Analysis of data
   (d) All of the above

125. The computer-based teaching model has been developed by
   (a) Gilbert
   (b) Stolurow and Davis
   (c) Robert Gagne
   (d) Mecner

126. Which of the following expectation students have from group learning?
   (a) To get appreciation from the group
   (b) To distribute the work equally
   (c) To ignore individual view point
   (d) To motivate isolated students to become members of the group

127. Which of the following combines scopes of large group, small group and individualized teaching methods:
   (a) Group discussion
   (b) Differentiated instruction
   (c) Brainstorming
   (d) None of the above

128. Which combination of teaching methods listed below would encourage the learner-centred paradigm?
   (a) Individualized instruction and lecture method
   (b) Simulation and demonstration
   (c) Lecture method and experimentation
   (d) Projects and direct experiences

129. What is the limitation of the project method of teaching?
   (a) It is learner-centred
   (b) Learners get practical experience
   (c) The learners are usually not properly supervised
   (d) None of the above

130. The heuristic approach is based on
   (a) Rote memorization
   (b) Home work
   (c) Spirit of inquiry
   (d) None of the above

131. A teacher uses the learning aids to make learning
   (a) Simple
   (b) More knowledgeable
   (c) Quicker
   (d) Interesting

132. Which of the following is a teaching aid?
   (a) LCD projector (b) Green board
   (c) Tape recorder (d) All of the above

133. Teacher uses visual aids to make learning
   (a) Interesting (b) Passive
   (c) Quicker (d) Complex

134. Which of the following is not true about projects as a learning activity?
   (a) It is a purposeful activity
   (b) It is proceeds in social environment
   (c) It is accomplished in real-life situations
   (d) It is teacher-centred activity

135. Use of telecast materials facilitates
   (a) Better concentration and learning
   (b) To reach large number of people
   (c) Better retention of topics taught
   (d) All of the above

136. Which of the following is a benefit associated with the overhead projector?
   (a) They are relatively inexpensive
   (b) Overhead transparencies can be made relatively quickly
   (c) They offer teachers the option of writing on transparencies during the class activity
   (d) All of the above

137. What is most important while writing on blackboard?
   (a) Good handwriting
   (b) Clarity in writing
   (c) Writing in big letters
   (d) Writing in small letters

138. Blackboard can be included in which group/category of teaching aids?
   (a) Audio aids
   (b) Visual aids
   (c) Audio–visual aids
   (d) None of the above

139. Which of the following is related with teaching skill?
   (a) Blackboard writing
   (b) Solving questions
   (c) Asking questions
   (d) All of the above

140. Why do teachers use teaching aid?
   (a) To make teaching fun filled
   (b) To teach within the understanding level of students
   (c) For students' attention
   (d) To make students attentive

141. Which among the following gives more freedom to the learner to interact?
   (a) Use of film
   (b) Small group discussion
   (c) Lectures by experts
   (d) Viewing country wide classroom programme on TV

142. Which of the following is more interactive and student centric?
   (a) Seminar (b) Workshop
   (c) Lecture (d) Group discussion

143. An effective teaching aid is one which
   (a) Is colourful and good looking
   (b) Activates all faculties
   (c) Is visible to all students
   (d) Easy to prepare and use

144. Which of the following belongs to a projected aid?
   (a) Blackboard (b) Diorama
   (c) Epidiascope (d) Globe

Learner Characteristics

145. Understanding theories and principles of children's learning is of fundamental importance
   (a) For effective teaching
   (b) For effective curriculum planning
   (c) For motivation of the learner
   (d) All of the above

146. The most appropriate meaning of learning is
   (a) Inculcation of knowledge
   (b) Modification of behaviour
   (c) Personal adjustment
   (d) Acquisition of skills

147. Teachers knowledge on student's needs and interests are covered by the subject
   (a) Philosophy of education
   (b) Psychology of education
   (c) Sociology of education
   (d) Politics of education

148. The most important challenge before a teacher is *(June 1997)*
   (a) To maintain discipline in the class
   (b) To make students do their homework
   (c) To prepare question paper
   (d) To make teaching–learning process enjoyable

149. The psychological aspects of the classroom are best managed by *(December 1998)*
   (a) The class teacher
   (b) The subject teacher
   (c) The principal
   (d) The student themselves

150. Students can be classified into four types on the basis of their learning. Which one of the following seeks meaning and reasoning to the learning? (*December 2000*)
(a) Innovative learner
(b) Analytic learner
(c) Common sense learner
(d) Dynamic learner

151. Instruction that takes into account various types of learners and learning styles and is adapted accordingly is said to be
(a) Teacher-centred
(b) Differentiated
(c) Direct instruction
(d) None of the above

152. A heavy emphasis on measurable outcomes leads to
(a) Rote learning
(b) Memorization
(c) Both (a) and (b)
(d) None of the above

153. Teachers who are enthusiastic in the classroom teaching
(a) Lack proficiency in the subjects, which stays hidden under their enthusiasm
(b) Simply dramatize to hold the student's attention
(c) Involve their students in the teaching–learning process
(d) All of the above

154. Diversity in student demographics requires common academic standards to
(a) Provide a common benchmark for assessment
(b) Promote genuine learning for high-performing students
(c) Ensure that all states have the same requirements as required by the central government
(d) None of the above

155. Intuitive thinking
(a) Is part of the process of discovery.
(b) Has been encouraged by traditional teaching
(c) Is not a cognitive process
(d) None of the above

156. While presenting your ideas in a classroom it is better to (*December 2000*)
(i) Recognize that there can be other views
(ii) Recognize that students are not a homogenous mass
(iii) Take dissenting views also in consideration
(a) Both (i) and (iii)
(b) Only (iii)
(c) Only (ii) and (iii)
(d) (i), (ii), and (iii)

157. 'Individual differences' in learning process are given the least importance in
(a) Naturalism (b) Realism
(c) Idealism (d) Pragmatism

158. Arrange the following experimental learning activities adopted by a teacher in cyclic order.
(i) Accommodation
(ii) Converging
(iii) Assimilation
(iv) Diverging

Codes:
(a) (i), (ii), (iii), and (iv)
(b) (iv), (iii), (ii), and (i)
(c) (ii), (iii), (iv), and (i)
(d) (iii), (i), (ii), and (iv)

159. We usually say that no two students are alike. They may differ from each other in terms of
(a) Upbringing and social status
(b) Aptitude
(c) Attitude
(d) All of the above

160. Reinforcement is provided by any factor that increases the probability that a response will be repeated. Which of the following can be factor(s) of reinforcement?
(a) Praise
(b) Token reward
(c) Simply succeeding in a task
(d) All of the above

161. When you complete your math's exercise, you can play the computer game. Using such kind of reinforcement wherein student's favourite activity can be used to reinforce a student's engagement in a less popular activity is termed as
(a) Premack Principle
(b) Thorndike Law
(c) Pavlov Experiment
(d) None of the above

162. Morphographs is the term associated with
(a) Corrective spelling
(b) Corrective reading
(c) Corrective learning
(d) Corrective behaviour

163. Which of the following description(s) apply in context of constructivist approach and Cognitive Theory of learning?
(a) Learners as active participants in learning process
(b) Seeking to interpret
(c) Using multiple sources of information
(d) All of the above

164. Organized bodies of knowledge that we build up about particular objects, situations, or phenomena are termed as
(a) Schemas or mental schemata
(b) Memory
(c) Cognition
(d) None of the above

165. The taking in of new information is termed as
(a) Assimilation (b) Accommodation
(c) Cognition (d) Reception

166. The term used to refer to the variety of ways in which teachers and others help or support learners to move beyond their current level of understanding by giving them cues, suggestions, or even direct guidance at appropriate moments in their investigations or activities is known as
(a) Scaffolding
(b) Cognition
(c) Reinforcement
(d) None of the above

167. The changes in behaviour (learning) are the net result of environmental influences, interacting with innate predispositions and processes within the learner
(a) Neo-behavioural Theory
(b) Cognitive Theory
(c) Behavioural Theory
(d) None of the above

168. The students or individuals may develop beliefs (positive or negative) about their own ability to cope effectively in a variety of situations. This can be termed as
(a) Self-efficacy
(b) Self-regulation
(c) Ego
(d) Confidence

169. The ability of an individual to think about one's own thought processes, self-monitor, and modify one's learning strategies as necessary is termed as
(a) Metacognition
(b) Self-regulation
(c) Simple cognition
(d) None of the above

170. Teachers blame a student's learning problems on
(a) Lack of motivation
(b) Lack of intelligence
(c) Casual parental attitude
(d) None of the above

171. The memory that refers to our memory of meaningful facts, rules, definitions, concepts, and principles is termed as
(a) Semantic memory
(b) Episodic memory
(c) Procedural memory
(d) None of the above

172. An individual's awareness of his or her own memory processes and the ways in which storage and retrieval of information can be enhanced is termed as
(a) Semantic memory
(b) Episodic memory
(c) Procedural memory
(d) Meta memory

173. Which of the following can impact process listening in an adverse manner?
(a) Excess of listened material – message overload
(b) Very high speed of speaking
(c) A good amount of hearing loss
(d) All of the above

174. The most important aspect of communication – listening can be improved by
(a) Linking listening to monetary reward system
(b) Making the contents interesting and need based
(c) Enhancing voice effectiveness and impressiveness
(d) All of the above

175. Listening to a lecture is basically
(a) Informational listening
(b) Evaluative listening
(c) Emphatic listening
(d) Dynamic Listening

176. The evaluative listening is basically about
(a) To accept or reject an idea given to the listener
(b) To evaluate the speaker's credibility and personality
(c) Both (a) and (b)
(d) None of the above

177. According to Francis Gallon, heredity does not go to immediate parents but to remote ancestors. Only 50% of the heredity is due to
(a) Parents
(b) Great-grandparents
(c) Grand parents
(d) None of the above

178. Arrange the following teaching processes in order
(i) Relating the present knowledge with the previous knowledge
(ii) Evaluation
(iii) Re-teaching
(iv) Formulation of teaching objectives
(v) Presentation of materials

Codes:
(a) (i), (ii), (iii), (iv), (v)
(b) (ii), (i), (iii), (iv), (v)
(c) (v), (iv), (iii), (i), (ii)
(d) (iv), (i), (v), (ii), (iii)

179. A student helps a teacher to solve the problem during the course of lecture in classroom. He is
(a) An emphatic listener
(b) An evaluative listener
(c) A realistic listener
(d) None of the above

180. The process of communication enhances through
(a) The feeling of belongings and commonness
(b) Security and freedom to make choices
(c) Informal environment
(d) All of the above

181. Which one of the following is a product of learning?
(a) Intelligence (b) Maturation
(c) Skills (d) Memory

182. Which of the following explains the mental growth most suitably?
(a) A growth pattern runs parallel to the physical growth.
(b) It is an erratic pattern
(c) It is not an erratic pattern
(d) Uniform rise to the middle teens and gradual levelling off during middle twenties

183. While comparing hearing and listening, we can say that
(a) Hearing is a physical process; listening is a psychological process.
(b) Hearing is a psychological process; listening is a physical process.
(c) Both are mainly physical processes.
(d) Both are biological processes.

184. Which of the following statements is true?
(a) The human relationships are not affected by listening.
(b) When communicating, college students spend over half of their lives listening.

(c) Listening constitutes just a small fraction of our overall communication.
(d) None of the above

185. When a person listens and attempts to understand the other person's viewpoint, it can be termed as
(a) Active listening
(b) Empathetic listening
(c) Critical listening
(d) None of the above

186. Which gender tends to listen in order to solve problems, is less attentive to nonverbal cues, and interrupts to switch topics?
(a) Men (b) Women
(c) Both genders (d) Neither gender

187. Critical thinking
(a) Focuses solely on the details instead of the main point
(b) Ignores the context in which communication is occurring
(c) Is important when making judgments about the message being presented
(d) Is only associated with listening

188. Asking questions to clarify information, paraphrasing messages, and identifying confusing areas are basically
(a) Barriers to listening
(b) Listening for fun
(c) Techniques for checking your understanding of a message
(d) None of above

189. Suggestions for lecture listening include
(a) Focusing on the delivery part and avoiding summarizing and reviewing the information
(b) Poor attention in order to think creatively, listening for details, and ignoring lecture cues
(c) Not to make notes so as to focus better on lecture and message delivery
(d) Finding areas of interest to you, avoiding distractions, and listening for main ideas

190. The ability to locate, evaluate, and effectively use information is an important trait known as
(a) Critical thinking
(b) Information literacy
(c) Hearing
(d) Selective attention

191. At primary level, it is better to teach in mother language because
(a) It develops self-confidence in children
(b) It makes learning easy
(c) It is helpful in intellectual development
(d) It helps children to learn in natural atmosphere

192. The best approach to motivate students is by
(a) Giving them suitable prizes
(b) Providing them proper guidance
(c) Giving examples all the time
(d) Delivering speech in class

193. The best way a teacher can try to inculcate good values among students is
(a) Storytelling
(b) By developing sense of discipline
(c) Ideal behaviour of teacher themselves
(d) To take their parents into confidence

194. How the students should be motivated to get success in life?
(a) Selected study
(b) Incidental study
(c) Intensive study
(d) Rote learning

195. The problem of absenteeism can be tackled in a better way through
(a) Reduction of the weight of curriculum
(b) Sympathy of teachers
(c) Attractive environment of the school
(d) Motivation of the students

196. The best remedy of a student's problems related with learning is
(a) Suggestion for hard work
(b) Supervised study in library
(c) Suggestion for private tuition
(d) Diagnostic teaching

197. Emotional adjustment of students is effective in

(a) Personality formation
(b) Class teaching
(c) Discipline
(d) All of the above

198. Who among the following is described as 'Father of Psychoanalysis'?
(a) Erik H. Erikson
(b) Jean Piaget
(c) Jerome S. Bruner
(d) Sigmund Freud

199. The main proponent of the Cognitive Theory of teaching is
(a) N. L. Gage
(b) Shiv Kumar Mitra
(c) B. F. Skiner
(d) McDonald

200. Practical knowledge of language is learnt at
(a) School
(b) Language laboratory
(c) Language teaching
(d) Language instruction

201. In which domain does the following objective fall? At the end of the lesson, the learner should be able to hit the football using the head.
(a) Affective domain
(b) Cognitive domain
(c) Psychomotor domain
(d) Both (a) and (c)

202. Planning or arranging the student's environment in order to predict the consequences of a student's behaviour is referred to as:
(a) Prompting (b) Reinforcement
(c) Shaping (d) Stimulus control

203. Which theory of learning has found that knowledge of internal processes is crucial to the understanding of learning?
(a) Cognitive Theory
(b) Stimulus–response theory
(c) Operant conditioning theory
(d) Classical conditioning theory

204. Which aspect of evaluation is used when a teacher ensures that students complete an exercise in mathematics and also makes sure that instructions are clear and specific?
(a) Validity
(b) Practicality
(c) Reliability
(d) Consistency

205. Which of the following is not a characteristic of a slow learner?
(a) Limited vocabulary
(b) Short span of attention
(c) Abstract thinking
(d) Limited range of interests

206. A teacher used the following statement to change the behaviour of a student who was a smoker. 'Smoking is healthy for the nation'. This is an example of:
(a) Cognitive dissonance
(b) Conceptual conflict
(c) Meaningful learning
(d) Challenge

207. The best way to memorize is
(a) Study for long time
(b) To understand the concept
(c) To read loudly
(d) To write the concept

208. Attitudes, concepts, skills, and knowledge are products of
(a) Learning (b) Research
(c) Heredity (d) Explanation

209. Which of the following is not a product of learning?
(a) Attitudes (b) Concepts
(c) Knowledge (d) Maturation

210. Some students in a class exhibit great curiosity for learning. It may be because such children
(a) are gifted
(b) come from rich families
(c) show artificial behaviour
(d) create indiscipline in the class

Classroom Situation Management

211. The best way to react to a wrong answer given by a student is (*December 1997*)
   (a) To scold him for not having learnt the lesson
   (b) To explain why the answer is wrong
   (c) To ask another student to give the correct answer
   (d) To ignore the wrong answer and pass on the next question

212. When a student asks a question to which the teacher has no direct, correct answer, he should (*December 1997*)
   (a) Give some vague answer and satisfy the student
   (b) Tell the student not to ask much irrelevant questions
   (c) Tell the student that he would give the correct answer later
   (d) Ask the student to find out the answer himself from the books in the library

213. Failure of teacher to communicate his ideals well to the students may result in (*December 2002*)
   (a) Classroom indiscipline
   (b) Loss of students' interest in topic being taught
   (c) Increased number of absentees in the class
   (d) All of the above

214. If the students do not understand what is taught in the class, the teacher should (*December 1997*)
   (a) Repeat the lesson once again
   (b) Teach the lesson again citing suitable examples
   (c) Check the previous knowledge of the students in the topic
   (d) Proceed to the next topic

215. An ideal situation in a classroom would be where (*December 2000*)
   (a) A teacher comes fully prepared to deliver his lecture
   (b) Students come fully prepared and discuss the subject with each other in teacher's presence
   (c) Teachers and students discuss the subject
   (d) The teacher uses audio–visual aids while learning
   (a) Both (a) and (c)
   (b) Both (c) and (d)
   (c) Only (b)
   (d) Only (d)

216. Which of the following categories of teachers tend to favour the traditional, formal seating pattern of rows of students directly facing the teacher at the front of the classroom?
   (a) Direct instruction
   (b) Indirect instruction
   (c) Student centred
   (d) None of the above

217. Which of the following teacher can be identified with authoritarian teaching style?
   (a) Democratic teacher
   (b) Indirect teacher
   (c) Laissez-faire teacher
   (d) Direct instruction teacher

218. What is more desirable in a classroom? (*December 2000*)
   (a) A teacher delivering a lecture on the basis of the text and his own research
   (b) A teacher delivering a lecture on the basis of course content and standard books
   (c) A teacher answering questions raised by students
   (d) A teacher maintaining strict discipline and taking attendance regularly

219. Which process of communication is the best for controlling noise in a classroom?
   (a) Saying 'do not talk'
   (b) Raising one's voice above students' voice
   (c) Remaining calm and just looking at the students
   (d) Continue teaching without caring for noisy class

220. As a teacher, what will you do if students do not attend your class?
(a) Blame students for their absence from the class
(b) Ponder over the present attitude of students in a calm manner
(c) Think about using some interesting techniques of teaching
(d) Try to understand the reasons and try to eliminate them

221. A teacher is strict in maintaining discipline in the class both in curricular and extracurricular activities. However, there is always room for discussion regarding clarification of doubts in teaching–learning and conducting other activities. What is the approach of teacher towards students?
(a) Authoritative (b) Democratic
(c) Flexible (d) Rigid

222. Better classroom management means
(a) Effective group work and interaction among the students
(b) Proper planning and preparation in developing suitable teaching aid
(c) Punctuality of the teachers and ability to complete course in time
(d) All of the above

223. Which of the following can be described as the most probable characteristic of an ineffective teacher?
(a) Always focus on achievement of instructional objectives
(b) Always focus on observance of teaching standards
(c) Always focus upon control of immediate situation
(d) None of the above

224. If majority of students in your class are weak, as a teacher you should
(a) Not care about the intelligent students
(b) Keep your speed of teaching fast so that students' comprehension level may increase
(c) Keep your teaching slow
(d) Keep your teaching slow along with some extra guidance to bright pupils

225. If some of the students misbehave with the teacher in the college campus, which kind of solution can help in the long run
(a) Report to their parents
(b) Teacher should improve their behaviour by their own character and scholarship
(c) Report the matter to the principal
(d) Mobilize other teachers against these guys

226. A teacher in the class should keep the pitch of his voice
(a) High enough
(b) Low
(c) Moderate
(d) Sometime low and sometime high

227. Which of the following should a teacher adopt in a lecture? (*December 2002*)
(a) Precise and low tone
(b) Elongated tone
(c) Precise and high tone
(d) Moderate tone

228. If students do not understand what is taught in the classroom, the teacher should feel (*June 2002*)
(a) Terribly bored
(b) To explain it in a different way
(c) That he is wasting time
(d) Pity for the students

229. With specific reference to classroom environment, all except one of the major components of listening is
(a) Hearing
(b) Being attentive
(c) Answering
(d) Understanding and remembering

230. Which of the following will not hamper effective communication in the classroom? (*June 2002*)
(a) A lengthy statement
(b) An ambiguous statement
(c) A precise statement
(d) A statement which allows the listener to his own conclusions

231. If backbenchers are always talking in the classroom, a teacher should
(a) Let them do what they are doing
(b) Punish them
(c) Ask them to sit on the front benches
(d) None of the above

232. If a teacher is not able to answer the question raised by a student in the classroom, he should
(a) Say that he will answer after consultation
(b) Rebuke the student
(c) Try to manipulate the students
(d) Feel shy of his ignorance

233. If students are not able to follow, you should
(a) Give them prompt explanation
(b) Make the matter easy
(c) Illustrate with examples
(d) All of the above

234. If students pass remarks on you while you are working as a teacher, you will
(a) Punish them
(b) Expel them from the college
(c) Take revenge while evaluating internal test copies
(d) Be impartial at the time of evaluation

235. Discussion in class will be more effective if the topic of discussion is

(*December 2002*)

(a) Not introduced
(b) Stated before the start of the discussion
(c) Written on the board without introducing it
(d) Informed to the students in advance

236. Which of the following is the most important single factor in underlying the success of beginning as a teacher?
(a) Scholarship
(b) Communicative ability
(c) Personality and its ability to relate to the class and to the pupils
(d) Organizational ability

237. All of the following are the characteristic features of an effective teacher except
(a) Emphasis upon maintaining standards of education
(b) Emphasizing group discussion for the purpose of clarifying the objectives
(c) Emphasis upon providing solution of immediate problems
(d) Differential treatment meted out to students of his class

238. Some students send a greeting card to you on teacher's day. As a teacher, you will
(a) Not respond at all
(b) Say thanks to them
(c) Ask them to not to waste money
(d) Reciprocate wishes to them

239. A student comes late in your class. As a teacher you will
(a) Inform to principal and parents
(b) Punish him to set an example
(c) Try to know the reason
(d) It is not worth paying attention

240. When a number of students regularly fail in the exams, it can be understood that
(a) The system has failed
(b) The teacher's failure
(c) The textbooks failure
(d) The individual student's failure

241. If a student asks questions on some unrelated topic in the class, as a teacher you will
(a) Allow him to ask unrelated questions
(b) Not allow him to ask unrelated questions
(c) Answer the question after the class
(d) Consider it as an act of indiscipline

242. A guardian never comes to see you in school. As a teacher, you will
(a) Ignore the child
(b) Write a letter to the guardian
(c) Go to meet him yourself if possible
(d) Start punishing the child

243. To maintain interest among students in class, a teacher should
(a) Make maximum use of teaching aids
(b) Discuss
(c) Ask questions intermittently
(d) All of the above

244. A teacher asks the questions in the class to
   (a) Keep students busy
   (b) Maintain discipline
   (c) Attract student's attention
   (d) Teach

245. To keep a check on the habit of absenteeism among students
   (a) The principal and parents should get worried.
   (b) The officials should put notice against absentee students on the notice board.
   (c) The teachers should take it as a serious problem.
   (d) They should be given less priority in the classroom in relation to regular students.

246. When the students try to solve the questions in some different way not taught by the teacher from prescribed books, then these students should be
   (a) Always discouraged to consult some other books on the subject
   (b) Always encouraged to consult other books on the subject
   (c) Suggested to seek permission of their respective class teachers before referring to other books
   (d) No action required

247. Students who ask questions in the class should be
   (a) Advised to meet the teacher after the class
   (b) Encouraged to participate in the discussion in the class
   (c) Encouraged to continue asking questions
   (d) Encouraged to search answers independently

248. In order to modify the undesirable behaviour of a student, the most effective method is
   (a) To punish the student
   (b) To bring it to the notice of parents
   (c) To find out the reasons for the undesirable behaviour and provide remedies
   (d) All of the above

249. A majority of classroom tasks initiated by teachers in traditional classrooms are usually
   (a) Low-level cognitive processes
   (b) High-order cognitive processes
   (c) Affective processes
   (d) Both (a) and (b)

250. In totality, the teacher helps student the most in the following way:
   (a) Integrated development of the child
   (b) Physical growth of the child
   (c) For Socio cultural
   (d) Development of the child

251. If students are not able to follow, the teacher in the class should
   (a) Give them prompt reply
   (b) Illustrate with suitable examples
   (c) Make the contents easier
   (d) All of the above

252. If students are not taking interest in your teaching, then you will
   (a) Ignore them
   (b) Leave the class
   (c) Ask them to pay attention
   (d) Review the teaching method

253. What quality the students like the most in a teacher?
   (a) Idealist philosophy
   (b) Compassion
   (c) Discipline
   (d) Entertaining

254. Research has shown that the most frequent symptom of nervous instability among teachers is
   (a) Digestive upsets
   (b) Explosive behaviour
   (c) Fatigue
   (d) Worry

255. Which one of the following is appropriate with respect to teacher–student relationship?
   (a) Very informal and intimate
   (b) Limited to classroom only
   (c) Cordial and respectful
   (d) Indifferent

256. In a lively classroom situation, there is likely to be
(a) Occasional roars of laughter
(b) Complete silence
(c) Frequent teacher–student dialogue
(d) Loud discussion among students

257. For maintaining an effective discipline in the class, the teacher should
(a) Allow students to do what they like.
(b) Deal with the students strictly.
(c) Give the students some problems to solve.
(d) Deal with them politely and firmly.

258. Those teachers are popular among students who
(a) Develop intimacy with them
(b) Help them solve their problems
(c) Award good grades
(d) Take classes for extra tuition fee

259. The essence of an effective classroom environment is
(a) A variety of teaching aids
(b) Lively student–teacher interaction
(c) Pin-drop silence
(d) Strict discipline

260. On the first day of his class, if a teacher is asked by the students to introduce himself, he should
(a) Ask them to meet after the class
(b) Tell them about him in brief
(c) Ignore the demand and start teaching
(d) Scold the student for this unwanted demand

261. Moral values can be effectively inculcated among the students when the teacher
(a) Frequently talks about values
(b) Himself practices them
(c) Tells stories of great persons
(d) Talks of gods and goddesses

262. Suppose a student wants to share his problems with his teacher and he visits the teacher's house for the purpose. The teacher should
(a) Contact the student's parents and solve his problem
(b) Suggest him that he should never visit his house
(c) Suggest him to meet the principal and solve the problem
(d) Extend reasonable help and boost his morale

263. When some students are deliberately attempting to disturb the discipline of the class by making mischief, what will be your role as a teacher?
(a) Expelling those students
(b) Isolate those students
(c) Reform the group with your authority
(d) Giving them an opportunity for introspection and improve their behaviour

264. A teacher is said to be fluent in asking questions, if he can ask
(a) Meaningful questions
(b) As many questions as possible
(c) Maximum number of questions in a fixed time
(d) Many meaningful questions in a fixed time

Learner's Evaluation

265. The most significant approach of evaluation is
(a) Continuous and comprehensive evaluation
(b) Conducting objective term end examination
(c) Maintaining cumulative records of students
(d) Semester system evaluation

266. What type of test is most effective when trying to test memorization?
(a) True/false
(b) Multiple choices
(c) Fill in blanks
(d) Both (b) and (c)

267. Essay-type tests are not reliable because
(a) Their answers are different
(b) Their results are different

(c) Their checking is affected by examiner's mood
(d) Their responding styles are different

268. To raise the standard of education, it is necessary
(a) To evaluate students continuously
(b) To give high salary to teachers
(c) To revise curriculum
(d) To make good school building

269. The best method of checking a student's homework is
(a) To assign it to intelligent students of the class
(b) To check the answers in the class in group manner
(c) To check them with the help of specimen answer
(d) To check by the teacher himself in a regular way

270. A time-bound testing programme for students should be implemented in schools so that
(a) The progress of the students should be informed to their parents
(b) A regular practice can be carried out
(c) The students can be trained for final examinations
(d) The remedial programme can be adopted on the basis of the feedback from the results

271. The most important indicator of quality of education in an educational institute is
(a) Infrastructural facilities of a school
(b) Classroom system
(c) Textbooks and teaching–learning material
(d) Student achievement level

272. Teachers use placement evaluation in order to
(a) Find out what knowledge and skills students have mastered
(b) Discover the causes of students' learning or behavioural problems
(c) Both (a) and (b)
(d) None of the above

273. Summative evaluation is used for which of the following purposes?
(a) To monitor student's progress during the learning process
(b) Primarily to certify or grade students
(c) To find out what a student's interests and work habits are
(d) To assign students to specific learning groups

274. For homework to be effective in accomplishing its purposes, which of the following suggestions for teachers is correct?
(a) Do give homework as punishment
(b) Make up spur-of-the-moment homework assignments for student practice
(c) Do not expect students to always have their homework assignments completed
(d) Do not listen to what students say about their experiences in completing homework assignments

275. When a student takes the same test twice it is referred to as?
(a) Post-test (b) Pre-test
(c) Test-retest (d) After-test

276. Which type of evaluation is carried out at the end of a course of study?
(a) Summative
(b) Assessment
(c) Formative
(d) Both (a) and (b)

277. Which test is carried out to determine the ability of a learner?
(a) Aptitude
(b) Attitude
(c) Achievement
(d) Scholastic

278. The verbs write, list, label, and name when used in an examination, test the
(a) Comprehension level
(b) Application level
(c) Knowledge level
(d) Synthesis level

279. Good evaluation of written material should not be based on
(a) Linguistic expression
(b) Logical presentation
(c) Ability to reproduce whatever is read
(d) Comprehension of subject

280. By which of the following methods, the true evaluation of the students is possible?
(a) Evaluation at the end of the course
(b) Evaluation twice in a year
(c) Continuous evaluation
(d) Formative evaluation

Miscellaneous Topics

281. CHEER stands for
(a) Children Enrichment Education through Radio
(b) Child Health Education Electronic Recording
(c) Children for Engineers and Energy Requirement
(d) None of the above

282. Educational TV was first introduced in India in
(a) 1961 (b) 1959
(c) 1968 (d) 1961

283. SITE stands for
(a) System for International Technology and Engineering
(b) Satellite Instructional Television Experiment
(c) South Indian Trade Estate
(d) None of the above

284. When an action or response produces a pleasant or rewarding outcome that behaviour is likely to be repeated and responses that bring displeasure or pain are likely to weaken and fade, it is called
(a) Thorndike's Law of Effect
(b) Thorndike's Law of Exercise
(c) Both (a) and (b)
(d) None of the above

285. National Literacy Mission was established in
(a) 1996 (b) 1988
(c) 1999 (d) 2000

286. The main aim of National Council for Teacher Education is
(a) To open colleges of education
(b) To promote research in education
(c) To maintain standards in colleges of education
(d) To provide grant to colleges of education

287. Kindergarten system of education was constituted by
(a) T. P. Nunn (b) Spencer
(c) Froebel (d) Montessori

288. 'National Council of Educational Research and Training' was established in
(a) 1961 (b) 1962
(c) 1963 (d) 1964

289. The main purpose of new education policy is
(a) To provide equal opportunity of education to all
(b) To improve the whole education system
(c) To link education with employment
(d) None of the above

290. It is desirable that students play games in the campus as
(a) It makes them physically fit
(b) It lessens the burden on the teacher
(c) It develops co-operation and physical balance
(d) None of the above

291. Family is the main agency of
(a) Informal education
(b) Formal education
(c) Non-formal education
(d) None of the above

292. To whom the responsibility of organization of curricular activities should be stored with?
(a) The principal
(b) The teacher who is appointed for this work

(c) The teachers who take interest in it
(d) All the teachers

293. The aim of education should be
(a) To develop vocational skills in the students
(b) To develop social awareness in the students
(c) To prepare the students for examination
(d) To prepare the students for practical life

294. The contribution of taxpayers in primary education is in the form of
(a) Income tax
(b) Tuition fee
(c) Paying money for individual tuition
(d) Educational cess

295. The priority to girls education should be given because
(a) The girls are more intelligent in comparison than the boys
(b) The girls are lesser in number than boys
(c) The girls were badly discriminated in favour of boys in the past
(d) Only girls are capable of leading for social change

296. The success of integrated education depends on
(a) The support of community
(b) The excellence of textbooks
(c) The highest quality of teaching–learning material
(d) The attitudinal changes in teachers

297. The quality of schools education exclusively depends upon
(a) Infrastructural facilities
(b) Financial provisions
(c) International support
(d) The quality of teacher's education

298. The idea of Basic Education was propounded by
(a) Dr. Zakir Hussain
(b) Dr. Rajendra Prasad
(c) Mahatma Gandhi
(d) Rabindranath Tagore

299. The in-service teacher training can be made more effective by
(a) Using training package which is well prepared in advance
(b) Making it a residential programme
(c) Using cooperative approach
(d) Practicing training follow-up procedures

300. Who developed the interaction analysis category system in education for increasing the teacher's effectiveness?
(a) Flander
(b) Rayon
(c) Amidon and Simon
(d) Richard Over

301. One of the important theories of moral development was proposed by
(a) Laurence Kohlberg
(b) Erik Fromm
(c) Daniel Coleman
(d) Benjamin Bloom

302. Character is developed by
(a) Will power
(b) Conduct and behaviour
(c) Morality
(d) All of the above

303. Spare the rod and spoil the child. This assumption is related to the type of discipline which has been advocated
(a) By naturalist philosophy
(b) By pragmatist philosophy
(c) In Victorian Era
(d) In Democratic Era

304. The determinant of teaching skill training is
(a) Components (b) Pupil–teacher
(c) Supervisor (d) Headmaster

305. Which of the following is an approach to educational planning?
(a) Manpower approach
(b) Social demand approach
(c) Both (a) and (b)
(d) None of the above

306. 'Man is born free but everywhere he is in chains'. This statement was given by
 (a) Abraham Maslow
 (b) Jean Jacques Rousseau
 (c) John Dewey
 (d) W.H. Kilpatrick

307. The purpose of National Education Policy is
 (a) Universalization of primary education
 (b) Vocationalization of education
 (c) To review the education
 (d) To give equal opportunity of education to all

308. The academic performance of students can be improved if parents are encouraged to
 (a) Supervise the work of their wards
 (b) Arrange for extra tuition
 (c) Remain unconcerned about it
 (d) Interact with teachers frequently

309. If a parent approaches the teacher to do some favour to his or her ward in the examination, the teacher should
 (a) Try to help him
 (b) Ask him not to talk in those terms
 (c) Refuse politely and firmly
 (d) Ask him rudely to go away

310. When the children become mischievous and disobedient in the classroom, the teacher should examine
 (a) Home background of the students
 (b) Influence of outside elements in class
 (c) Teaching methods and subject knowledge
 (d) Co-curricular and other attractions in the school

Answer Keys

Concepts, Nature, and Characteristics

1. (c) 2. (c) 3. (d) 4. (a) 5. (a)
6. (a) 7. (a) 8. (a) 9. (a) 10. (c)
11. (a) 12. (a) 13. (b) 14. (d) 15. (b)
16. (c) 17. (b) 18. (a) 19. (b) 20. (d)
21. (a) 22. (b) 23. (a) 24. (b) 25. (c)
26. (a) 27. (b) 28. (a) 29. (d) 30. (c)
31. (d) 32. (a) 33. (b) 34. (d) 35. (c)
36. (c) 37. (c) 38. (a) 39. (d) 40. (c)
41. (a) 42. (d) 43. (a) 44. (a) 45. (d)
46. (d) 47. (c) 48. (b) 49. (d) 50. (c)
51. (b) 52. (b) 53. (b) 54. (c) 55. (b)
56. (c) 57. (d) 58. (c) 59. (d) 60. (b)
61. (a) 62. (c) 63. (a) 64. (d) 65. (b)
66. (b) 67. (d) 68. (a) 69. (b) 70. (c)
71. (d) 72. (b) 73. (c) 74. (d) 75. (c)
76. (d) 77. (b) 78. (d) 79. (c) 80. (b)
81. (c) 82. (c) 83. (a) 84. (a) 85. (a)
86. (a) 87. (c) 88. (c) 89. (d) 90. (c)
91. (a) 92. (a) 93. (a) 94. (d)

Teaching Methods and Teaching Aids

95. (a) 96. (d) 97. (a) 98. (b) 99. (a)
100. (b) 101. (a) 102. (a) 103. (d) 104. (d)
105. (c) 106. (d) 107. (b) 108. (c) 109. (a)
110. (d) 111. (c) 112. (c) 113. (b) 114. (d)
115. (d) 116. (a) 117. (b) 118. (d) 119. (b)
120. (b) 121. (d) 122. (c) 123. (a) 124. (d)
125. (b) 126. (d) 127. (b) 128. (d) 129. (c)
130. (c) 131. (a) 132. (d) 133. (a) 134. (d)
135. (d) 136. (d) 137. (a) 138. (b) 139. (d)
140. (b) 141. (b) 142. (d) 143. (b) 144. (c)

Learner Characteristics

145. (d) 146. (b) 147. (b) 148. (d) 149. (a)
150. (b) 151. (b) 152. (c) 153. (c) 154. (a)
155. (a) 156. (d) 157. (c) 158. (d) 159. (d)
160. (d) 161. (a) 162. (a) 163. (d) 164. (a)
165. (a) 166. (a) 167. (a) 168. (a) 169. (a)
170. (a) 171. (a) 172. (d) 173. (d) 174. (c)
175. (b) 176. (a) 177. (a) 178. (d) 179. (b)
180. (d) 181. (c) 182. (d) 183. (a) 184. (b)
185. (b) 186. (a) 187. (c) 188. (c) 189. (d)
190. (d) 191. (d) 192. (b) 193. (c) 194. (c)
195. (d) 196. (d) 197. (d) 198. (d) 199. (a)
200. (b) 201. (c) 202. (d) 203. (a) 204. (a)
205. (c) 206. (a) 207. (b) 208 (a) 209. (d)
210. (a)

Classroom Situation Management

211. (b) 212. (c) 213. (d) 214. (b) 215. (a)
216. (a) 217. (d) 218. (a) 219. (c) 220. (d)
221. (c) 222. (d) 223. (c) 224. (d) 225. (b)
226. (a) 227. (c) 228. (b) 229. (c) 230. (c)
231. (c) 232. (a) 233. (d) 234. (d) 235. (d)
236. (c) 237. (d) 238. (b) 239. (c) 240. (a)
241. (c) 242. (c) 243. (d) 244. (c) 245. (c)
246. (b) 247. (c) 248. (c) 249. (d) 250. (a)
251. (b) 252. (d) 253. (b) 254. (b) 255. (c)
256. (c) 257. (d) 258. (b) 259. (b) 260. (b)
261. (b) 262. (d) 263. (d) 264. (d)

Learner's Evaluation

265. (a) 266. (d) 267. (c) 268. (a) 269. (d)
270. (d) 271. (d) 272. (a) 273. (b) 274. (c)
275. (c) 276. (a) 277. (a) 278. (c) 279. (c)
280. (c)

Miscellaneous Topics

281. (a) 282. (c) 283. (b) 284. (a) 285. (b)
286. (c) 287. (c) 288. (a) 289. (b) 290. (c)
291. (a) 292. (a) 293. (d) 294. (d) 295. (d)
296. (d) 297. (d) 298. (c) 299. (d) 300. (a)
301. (a) 302. (d) 303. (c) 304. (a) 305. (c)
306. (b) 307. (c) 308. (d) 309. (c) 310. (c)

2

RESEARCH APTITUDE

CONCEPT AND DEFINITION OF RESEARCH

Earlier it might have taken thousands of years to double up the amount of knowledge, but now, this may happen every few years. Progress in any domain of knowledge be it natural science, applied science, or social science won't happen without research.

Research is the lifeblood of any institute of higher learning worth its name. Research is more than a set of specific skills; it is a way of thinking; it examines critically the various aspects of any professional work. It is a structured enquiry that utilizes the acceptable scientific methodology to solve problems and create new knowledge that is generally applicable. The enquiry is aimed at understanding a thing or phenomenon or solving a problem.

The term research comprises of two words, namely 're' and 'search'. Generally, 're' means again and 'search' means to find out. According to Advanced Learner's Dictionary, 'research is a careful investigation or inquiry specially to search for new facts in any branch of knowledge'. According to Creswell, 'research is a process of steps used to collect and analyse information to increase our understanding of a topic or issue'.

From many definitions, there is a general agreement that research (1) is a process of enquiry and investigation, (2) is systematic and methodical, and (3) increases the knowledge.

Scientific method consists of systematic observation, classification, and interpretation of data. Research is basically scientific in nature to provide an objective, which is an unbiased evaluation of data. There is nothing like unscientific research approach even in case of social sciences.

Research is like undertaking a journey, and one must know about its destination and which route to take. The sequence of steps during the journey is not absolute. At every step, there is multiplicity of methods, approaches, and procedures. Here, experience of guide comes handy to guide our actions to achieve our objectives.

As a teacher, the following questions may arise:

1. What are the common conditions prevalent among rural students?
2. What are the possible causes of such conditions?
3. What is the degree of satisfaction of parents with the teaching of school?
4. The change in level of understanding of students with the change in method of teaching.

The list of questions may be endless. Researches have to be undertaken to find answers to these questions.

RESEARCH OBJECTIVES

Research adds to the existing stock of knowledge. The main purpose of research is to discover answers to questions through the application of scientific procedures.

The typical objectives of research can be summarized as follows:

1. Gain familiarity with a new phenomenon or develop new insight into a phenomenon.

2. Review and synthesize the existing knowledge.
3. Investigate some existing situation or problem.
4. Offer solutions to a problem.
5. Explore and analyse more general issues.
6. Construct or create a new procedure or system.
7. Generate new knowledge.

The actual research may encompass one or combination of any of the above objectives.

Important Terms Linked with Research

The research is basically about gaining knowledge for different purposes. To gain knowledge is a human quest. Different approaches were developed over the period to acquire the knowledge through research. In the NET Exams, questions are asked on basic concepts. These concepts will help the candidates in better understanding of various aspects of research as well.

Metaphysics is branch of philosophy that deals with abstract concepts such as being, knowing, identity, time, and space. It is intimately connected with epistemology.

Epistemology is the study of knowledge. It deals with origin, nature, scope, and methods to acquire knowledge. The term was first used by Frederick Ferrier. There are basically two ways to acquire knowledge—rationalism and empiricism.

Rationalism tends to believe that logic and reason as the means of acquiring knowledge. Mind is given the authority over senses. This is basically a priori use of logic and reason come first to conclude something before experience. Rationalism is associated with deduction.

Empiricists claim that sense experience is the ultimate starting point for all our knowledge. The senses give us all our raw data about the world, and without this raw material, there would be no knowledge at all. This is termed as a posteriori. It is related to induction.

Research Paradigms: There is difference between natural sciences and social sciences, and so is the difference between research approaches relating to them. Hence, there are two competing paradigms to acquire knowledge. The paradigms are grouped as positivist paradigm and interpretive paradigms.

Positivist paradigm: It is associated with quantitative research strategies. There is one particular view of how research should be conducted, which suggests that we should carry out research in social sciences in ways that are similar to the methods within the natural sciences (physics, chemistry, and biology). This is called the positivist or scientific approach.

According to the positivist approach, the research design should be highly structured, the methods should be reliable, and the research design should aim to generate large-scale, statistically based studies.

Interpretive paradigm: It is usually associated with qualitative research strategies. It is specifically applicable in social sciences such as sociology, political science, etc.

According to interpretive approach, the research design should be flexible and unstructured, the methods should be valid, and the research design should generate small-scale and intensive data, using insider accounts and based on descriptions of what is seen and what is heard.

Verstehen: The term is closely associated with the work of the German sociologist, Max Weber. In social sciences, such as anthropology and sociology, Verstehen means a systematic interpretive process in which an outside observer of a culture attempts to relate to it and understand others. Verstehen roughly translates to 'meaningful understanding' or 'putting yourself in the shoes of others to see things from their perspective'.

The method of the natural sciences (physics, chemistry, biology, etc.) is explanation (*erklären*), whereas that of history is understanding (*verstehen*).

The understanding about positivist and interpretive paradigms is crucial to differentiate between quantitative, qualitative, and other types of approaches or methods that are basic types of research. These terms have been discussed later in this chapter.

Theory: A theory is a set of systematically related statements, including some law-like generalizations that can be tested empirically. These generalizations provide hypothesis, and these hypothesis determine what must be measured.

Motivation in Conducting Research

Although there is some overlapping between the research objectives and motivation for undertaking research, they are different. Some factors, single or combined, for undertaking any research are as follows:

1. Acquire a research degree along with its consequential benefits
2. Face the challenge in solving the unsolved problems
3. Intellectual satisfaction of doing some innovative work
4. Service to the society
5. Desire to enhance the social status
6. Input for policy decision-making

However, the list for motivating people to undertake research studies is not exhaustive.

Research Characteristics

There are certain common desirable characteristics in the research process. There is word of caution, there is overlapping in the meaning and scope of these characteristics. They ensure that research is free of biases, prejudices, and subjective errors.

1. *Objectivity:* It means research is without any bias. All other characteristics are built around it. Researchers usually take utmost precautions that results are not affected by their own presence, behaviour, and attitude. They critically examine the research methods to avoid any bias.
2. *Reliability:* Reliability in the context of research is consistency. It refers to the extent to which an investigation produces consistent results. It can also be termed as verifiability.

   If any research yields similar results each time, it is undertaken with similar population in the given context and with similar procedures, it is said to be a reliable research.

   Suppose a research is conducted on the effects of watching television on the class performance of the children, and if the results conclude that watching TV causes low grades in class, and if another sample taken from the population shows the same results with the same research procedure, then we can say that the research procedure and the outcome are reliable. The more the similarity in the results, the more is the reliability of research. Coefficient of determination is also termed as reliability coefficient.
3. *Validity:* Here, validity in research mainly stands for accuracy of procedures, research instruments, tests, etc.

   The concept of validity can also be understood by posing a question, 'Are we measuring or able to measure what we originally intended to measure?'.

   Validity means that research must be unbiased and free from any systematic error as these may impact the applicability of research. Without validity, research goes in the wrong direction.

   Generally, validity is termed to be much more important than reliability. To keep the research on the right track, it is must that the concepts are defined in the best possible manner so that no error occurs during measurement. Different types of validity are given below:

   (a) *Internal validity:* With higher internal validity, a researcher is able to establish better causal relationship between two or more variables. This is specifically true in case of laboratory experiments where cause-and-effect relationship is supposed to be more clearly established.

(b) *External validity:* It means that external factors that can affect the study must be controlled. For example, the response of a respondent in social sciences surveys may be affected by mere the presence of a non-participant observer. It also refers to the extent to which research outcome can be generalized and applied to other cases that are not under study.

Sometimes, internal validity is also termed as credibility and external validity is termed as generalizability or transferability. Both credibility and generalizability have been discussed as separate features also in the ensuing discussion.

(c) *Face validity:* By valid, we mean that survey and questionnaire accurately measure what they are supposed to measure. For example, all participants who filled a questionnaire meant for measuring certain personality traits agree that this exercise appears to measure those traits, and not something very different.

(d) *Content validity:* The indicator measures all aspects of the construct (or concept as discussed earlier) and not just a part of it.

(e) *Criterion validity:* The indicator corresponds with and is predictive of measurements using related indicators.

(f) *Construct validity:* The indicator measures the construct in a manner that is convergent with other measures in terms of direction (*e.g.*, the level of education and income level converge). The indicator also allows discrimination of opposing constructs.

4. *Accuracy:* It is closely related to validity. It is also the degree to which research processes, instruments, and tools are related to each other. Accuracy also measures whether the research tools have been selected in the best possible manner and research procedures suit the research problem or not.

   Rigorous scientific methods and procedures have been adopted in research, and each step in the research is tested for accuracy. Thus, choosing the best data collection tool improves the accuracy of research.

5. *Credibility:* It is the use of best source of information and the best procedures in the research. The use of secondary data saves time and reduces cost. However, the excessive reliance on secondary data when the option of primary data is available entails the risk of reducing the credibility of the research. Hence, it has to be trade-off between primary data and secondary data.

   The accurate references in research enhance the credibility of research but fake references also decrease the credibility of research.

6. *Generalizability:* It is closely related to validity. It refers to the degree to which research findings can be applied to a larger population. The sample considered is the representative of the whole population so the findings should also be applicable to the population.

7. *Empirical research:* It is based on real-life experiences, direct experiences, or observation by the researcher. It implies that research is related basically to one or more aspects of a real situation and deals with concrete data that provides a basis for external validity to the results of the research.

8. *Systematic:* For a research to be effective, it has to be systematic. It is the only approach to undertake any research work, and each step must follow the other. There are a set of procedures that have been tested over a period of time and are, thus, suitable to use in research. Each research, therefore, should follow a definite procedure.

9. *Controlled factors:* In real-life experience, there is always more than one factor that

affects an outcome of an event. Similarly, in research, various factors may affect the outcome; some are taken as controlled factors, whereas the others are tested for possible outcome. The concept of control implies that, in exploring causality in relation with two variables (factors), we set up a study in a way that minimizes the effects of other factors affecting the relationship. The controlled factors or variables have to be controlled rigorously.

In physical sciences, it is easier to control such factors as the experiments are conducted in laboratories. In social sciences, it is extremely difficult as research is carried out on the issues related to human beings living in society, where exerting such controls are not possible. Moreover, within social sciences, the level of control may vary significantly from one discipline to another.

10. *Cyclical:* Research is a cyclical process because it starts with a problem and ends with a problem.
11. *Logical:* The statement, a good research is logical, implies that research is guided by the rules of logical reasoning. Induction and deduction are of great value in research, which have been discussed under types of research.
12. *Replicable:* This characteristic allows the results of the research to be verified by replicating the study and thereby building a sound basis for decisions.

Types of Research

Table 2.1 gives an idea about the main basis adopted for the classification of research. Here, it is important to mention that these approaches are not exclusive. The research is usually interdisciplinary. Depending upon the subject area, it is better that the researcher specializes in any one form of research because all research methods have their own advantages and disadvantages.

Table 2.1 below enlists the basis for classification and the types of research that form a part of it. It is important to note that there is overlapping among different types of research.

Table 2.1 Classification of Research

S.No.	Basis of classification	Types
1.	Objectives	1. Descriptive 2. Correlational 3. Explanatory 4. Exploratory 5. Experimental
2.	Outcome	1. Fundamental 2. Applied
3.	Logic	1. Deductive 2. Inductive
4.	Process	1. Quantitative 2. Qualitative
5.	Inquiry mode	1. Structured 2. Unstructured
6.	Idea or concept	1. Conceptual 2. Empirical

Classification of Research on the Basis of Objectives

From the purpose and objectives point of view, a research can be classified as follows:

1. Descriptive research
2. Correlational research
3. Explanatory research
4. Experimental research

Descriptive Research

1. Descriptive research can answer questions such as 'what is' or 'what was'.

   Here, the information is collected without changing the environment (i.e., nothing is manipulated). Sometimes these are referred to as 'correlational' or 'observational' studies. It is 'any study that is not truly experimental'.

2. It includes surveys and fact-finding enquiries with adequate interpretation.

   For example, in human research, a descriptive research can provide information about the naturally occurring health status, behaviour, attitudes, or other characteristics of a particular group.

   Descriptive research can involve a one-time interaction with groups of people (cross-sectional study) or a study might follow individuals over time (longitudinal study).

Two specific examples are being given here, (1) Ministry of Agriculture would like to know about the crop patterns across different states in India and (2) School principal may be interested to know about the result of his own school in comparison to other schools in the district.

Descriptive research is closely linked with *ex post facto*, historical, exploratory, and analytical research, and sometimes, these terms can be used interchangeably.

Ex Post Facto Research

1. It is used in social sciences and business organizations.
2. It is conducted in context of a phenomenon after it has occurred or at the time of its occurrence.
3. It basically deals with non-manipulated variables of a phenomenon.

Historical Research

1. It is another dimension of descriptive research and somewhat similar to *ex post facto research*.
2. It usually focuses on the historical aspect of an issue of interest or problem.
3. Examples are growth of trade unions in India, evolution of modern education system in India, etc.

Analytical Research

1. In this method, the researcher uses facts or information already available.
2. It attempts to make critical evaluation of the material.

Correlational Studies

1. It is undertaken to discover or establish relationship or interdependence between two aspects of a situation. Two or more variables may occur together but that does not mean that one has caused the other to occur.
2. It may identify factors leading to a certain situation. For example, ascertaining the degree of relationship between stress among students to perform in the exam and rote learning. What is the impact of promotional campaign on the sales of a product?

Explanatory Research

Explanatory research attempts to answer how and why between two aspects of a situation or a phenomenon. For example, why examination-related stress leads to rote learning? Why and how stress leads to a heart disease?

Exploratory Research

1. It is generally done in the beginning of a research. It is undertaken to explore an area where little is known or to investigate the possibilities of undertaking a particular research study and is akin to feasibility study or pilot study. A 'small-scale study' is undertaken to decide whether it is worth carrying out a detailed investigation.
2. It attempts to clarify why and how there is a relationship between two or more aspects of a situation or phenomenon.
3. The purpose of exploratory research is to gain background information, to define terms, to clarify the problems, to develop hypothesis, to establish research priorities and objectives, and to develop questions to be answered.
4. It makes use of secondary data (mainly literature review), experience surveys, case studies, interviews (mainly focus groups' interviews), projective techniques, and Delphi techniques.

Experimental Research or Causal Studies

1. It is cause-and-effect finding research; it seeks to uncover cause-and-effect relationships.

2. An action or occurrence can cause other action, for example, smoking causes lung cancer. It brings up a definite cause-and-effect relationship. It identifies the variable that changes the dependent variable. For example, smoking causes weak lungs and not vice versa.
3. If we are able to identify the cause of a problem, then we may be on the way to find a solution to the problem, as is the case in medical science.

Reflexivity refers to circular relationships between cause and effect. A reflexive relationship is bidirectional with both the cause and the effect affecting one another in a relationship in which neither can be assigned as causes or effects. For example, poverty is the main cause of unemployment; and unemployment is the main cause of poverty.

Classification of Research on the Basis of Application

On the basis of application, research is of two types, namely pure (or basic research) and applied research. Table 2.2 gives the classification of research based on application.

Fundamental (Basic or Pure) Research

1. The main purpose of basic research is to add to the existing stock of knowledge and, thus, can be intellectually challenging.
2. The knowledge produced through pure research is sought in order to add to the existing body of research methods.
3. It is not likely to have any practical application at the present time or even in the future.

Applied Research

1. Applied research is done to solve specific, practical questions facing the society.
2. It can be used for policy formulation, administration, and understanding of a phenomenon.
3. It is always done on the basis of basic research and can be carried out by academic or industrial institutions. For example, an academic institution, such as a university, will have a specific applied research program funded by an industrial partner interested in that program.

Action Research

The term 'action research' was coined during 1940s by Kurt Lewin, a German-American social psychologist who is widely considered to be the founder of this field.

Action research refers to a wide variety of evaluative, investigative, and analytical research methods designed to diagnose problems or weaknesses—whether organizational, academic, or instructional—and help researchers to develop practical solutions to address them quickly and efficiently. It may also be applied to programs or educational techniques that are not necessarily experiencing any problems, but that researchers simply want to learn more about the techniques and improve their knowledge. The general goal is to create a simple, practical, repeatable process of iterative learning, evaluation, and improvement that leads to increasingly better results. Action research may also be called a 'cycle of action' or 'cycle of inquiry' because it typically follows a predefined process that is repeated over time.

Table 2.2 Classification of Research on the Basis of Application

Fundamental research	Applied research
Addition to knowledge	Solution to existing problems
Discovery or invention	Innovation or application
Mostly academic	Practical use in solving a problem
Extensive in nature	Intensive in nature

Classification of Research on the Basis of Logic

In research, conclusions are based on two approaches known as the deduction and the induction.

Deductive Approach

It is also termed as top-down or general-to-specific approach.

In deduction, we start from a theory and try to prove it right with the help of available information. The deductive method involves the following three steps:

1. State the hypothesis (based on theory or research literature).
2. Collect data to test the hypothesis.
3. Make decision to accept or reject the hypothesis.

Example

1. All men are mortal (general fact, applies to all men).
2. Socrates is a man.
3. (Therefore,) Socrates is mortal (specific).

Inductive Approach

It is also termed as bottom-up approach.

In inductive research, we move from specific to general. This approach also involves three steps:

1. Observe the different phenomena in the world.
2. Make a search for a pattern in what is observed.
3. Make a generalization about what is occurring.

Example

1. Socrates is mortal (specific).
2. Alexander is mortal (specific), Pluto is mortal, and so on (specific).
3. All men are mortal (general).

Take another example: 3 + 5 = 8 and eight is an even number. 7 + 59 = 66 and the result is again an even number. Therefore, the conclusion is when an odd number is added to another odd number, the result will be an even number.

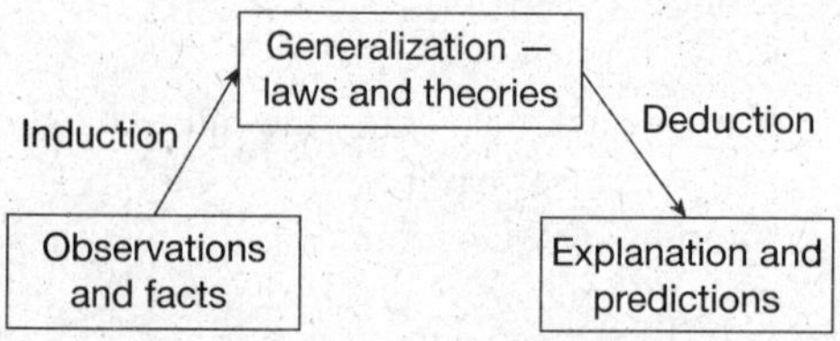

Figure 2.1 Induction and Deduction

Figure 2.1 above shows the main components that form a part of inductive and deductive approach.

Classification of Research on the Basis of Inquiry Mode

Basically, the process adopted to find answers to research questions involves two approaches-structured and unstructured.

Structured Approach

1. The structured approach to inquiry is usually classified as quantitative research.
2. Everything that forms the research process, such as objectives, design, sample, and the questions that a researcher plans to ask of respondents, is predetermined.
3. It is more appropriate to determine the extent of a problem, issue, or phenomenon by quantifying the variation. For example, how many people have a particular problem? How many people hold a particular attitude?

Unstructured Approach

1. The unstructured approach to inquiry is usually classified as qualitative research.
2. It allows flexibility in all aspects of the research process.
3. It is more appropriate to explore the nature of a problem, issue, or phenomenon without quantifying it.

Classification of Research on the Basis of Process

Quantitative Research

It is similar to deductive research. It is also termed as linear research as it typically follows a linear path:

1. Stating with testable hypothesis
2. Collection of data
3. Analysing the data
4. Accepting or rejecting the hypothesis.

Quantitative research is generally associated with the positivist or post-positivist paradigm. It usually involves collecting and converting data into numerical form so that statistical calculations can be made and conclusions can be drawn.

Qualitative Research

1. This is basically an approach and not just a method to conduct research.
2. Qualitative research is basically inductive or spiral in nature and has a very different structure. The researcher starts with a tentative idea or question; these questions become more specific with progress in research. Then, a pattern may emerge in research. Thus, in qualitative research, one starts with observation and ends with a theoretical position or stance. Thus, it is inductive in nature, that is, the research moves from specific to theory.

Qualitative research is appropriate when:

1. The intended research area is not well studied or understood;
2. A subject needs to be studied in depth;
3. A holistic perspective is needed;
4. Behavioural aspects of people need to be studied;
5. Measurement techniques like questionnaires are not considered suitable;
6. A researcher is more interested in the process (how it works) and not the product (the outcome).

The important methods and approaches used in qualitative research have been discussed below.

1. *Focus groups:* In this method, a researcher brings together a small number of subjects to discuss the topic of interest. The group size is kept deliberately small so that the members express themselves more openly and also get more time as well.
2. *Direct observation:* The data are collected by an external observer.
3. *In-depth interviews:* It is unstructured and has face-to-face interviews.
4. *Narrative research:* It is an approach to review the literature. Sometimes, it is contrasted with a systematic review. It tends to be less focused than a systematic review and seeks to arrive at a critical interpretation of the literature that it covers.
5. *Phenomenology:* It is a form of qualitative research in which the researcher attempts to understand how one or more individuals experience a phenomenon. For example, interviewing the wives of 10 prisoners of war and asking them to describe their experiences.
6. *Ethnography:* It is the process of studying and describing a culture (a culture is the shared attitudes, values, norms, practises, language, and material things of a group of people). It intends to provide an insider's picture of a community under study. A researcher may go and live in that specific community and study the culture and their educational practises.
7. *Case study research:* It is focused on providing a detailed account of one or more cases. For example, case study of a class that was given a new curriculum of IT.
8. *Grounded theory:* It is a qualitative approach to generate and develop a theory from data that the researcher collects.

   Role play, simulation, and diary methods are also used in qualitative research.

In qualitative field study, the depth of study is greater and the sample size is usually small, whereas in field survey, there is greater coverage of population but the depth of study may not be great.

Mixed Research

Both quantitative and qualitative researches are not exclusive. Qualitative research may end in a hypothesis that can be quantitatively tested later. Quantitative research may involve qualitative research elements.

Quantitative research may answer questions such as extent and pattern of poverty in India, but it may not be efficient in answering questions such as what is the experience of facing poverty, hardships, consequences, and circumstances that lead to poverty. This may be answered by qualitative research. As quantitative research is generally well known, it may be useful to outline when qualitative research is needed.

Triangulation: There are multiple realities in social research. It is akin to solving a research problem in multiple ways so as to increase the validity of answer. The triangulation is mostly used in the qualitative research. It entails the use of multiple data sources, multiple investigators, and multiple methods. It also overcomes the problem of subjectivity. It involves the use of multiple data sources, multiple investigators, and most importantly, multiple methods (such as participant observation, focus groups, case studies, and so on) to get complete understanding of the social phenomena. This provides validity to research process and also overcomes the problem of subjectivity and biasedness to an extent. It is multiple validations of results.

The use of results from one set of data to corroborate those from another type of data is also known as triangulation.

Classification of Research on the Basis of Concept

Conceptual Research

Conceptual research is generally used by philosophers and thinkers to develop new concepts or to reinterpret the existing concepts. It is related to some abstract idea or theory.

Empirical Research

Empirical research relies on experience or observation alone, which is without due regards for system and theory. It is a data-based research coming up with conclusions that are capable of being verified by observation or experiment.

In this research, the researcher must formulate a working hypothesis. He collects data to prove or disprove his hypothesis. The researcher is in control over the facts. Empirical research is appropriate when proof is sought that certain variables affect other variables in one way or the another.

Research Process

Research process usually adopts the following three criteria:

1. It is conducted within a framework of a set of approaches. It may be qualitative or quantitative and depends upon academic discipline.
2. The logical sequencing of steps undertaken in order to find the answers to the research questions are termed as research methodology. It adopts procedures, methods, and techniques that are tested for their validity and reliability.
3. It is unbiased and objective.

According to the definition given by Cresswell, research consists of three basic steps:

1. Formulating a research question or posing a problem, to which the researcher wants to find answers to.
2. Collecting data to answer the questions.
3. Present an answer to the question.

Table 2.3 Research Process—a Snapshot

Step 1: Formulation of Research Problem	**Step 2: Preparing Research Design**	**Step 3 : Developing Data Collection Instrument (Research Instrument)**	**Step 4: Selecting Samples**
• Literature review • Formulation of objectives • Identifying research variables and measuring scales • Formulating hypothesis	• Problem structure • Study design – Experimental study – Non-experimental study	• Types of data • Methods of data collection • Designing research tool	• Types of samples – Probability – Non-probability • Determining sample design
Step 5: Writing a Research Proposal	**Step 6: Collecting Data**	**Step 7: Processing and Analyzing Data**	**Step 8: Writing a Research Report**
• Main elements – Need – Benefits – Types of data – Justification for funds and other resources	• Observations • Interviews • Questionnaire • Schedules	• Editing and Coding • Classification of data • Tabulation • Analysis • Hypothesis testing • Generalizations	• Title page • Table of contents • Chapters • Bibliography • Appendices

These basic steps have been elaborated further in Table 2.3 and discussed in detail in ensuing paragraphs.

Step 1

Formulation of the Research Problem

The manner in which a problem is formulated determines almost every step that follows.

Steps in Formulation of a Research problem

A reasonable level of knowledge in the broad subject area is required to work through these steps. Usually, the following steps are undertaken to formulate a research problem:

Step 1: Identifying a broad area of interest: What really interests me as a professional? As a teacher, I might be interested in the area of teaching methodology or increasing acts of violence among students, psychology, or existence of common conditions of the students in an area.

Step 2: Dividing broad areas into subareas: Suppose I want to study acts of violence among students. It can have various subareas (1) profile of families these students come from, (2) profile of perpetrators, (3) causes for violence (4) role of politicization of education, (5) impact on society, and so on.

Step 3: Focusing on and selecting an area of interest: The researcher may choose one or two areas for current research because it is not possible to pick many areas simultaneously. Delete the subareas in which you as a researcher do not have any interest and subsequently focus on the area you are passionate about.

Step 4: Identifying the gaps and raising research questions: Within an area, list all the questions the researcher wants to find answers to.

Step 5: Formulation of broad objectives: Objectives grow out of the questions.

Step 6: Assessing and reviewing objectives: As a researcher narrows the research problem, the specific identification of study population is crucial in order to select the appropriate respondents.

Main Considerations in Selecting a Research Problem

These help ensure that your study remains manageable and that you remain motivated.

1. *Interest:* Research is usually time-consuming and entails the use of resources. Many unforeseen problems may crop up. So the topic should be of interest to the researcher to sustain the desired motivation level.
2. *Manageable magnitude:* The topic should be manageable within the available time and resources. The broader topic should be broken down to something that is more relevant for the purpose and manageable. It should be specific and clear to the extent possible.
3. *Concept measurement:* The clarity about indicators and measurement of concepts is required. The idea of construct is important here.
4. *Level of expertise:* The adequate level of skills for the task is required.
5. *Relevance:* Though relevance is again a subjective term, the research should add to the existing stock of knowledge and bridge the current knowledge gaps.
6. *Availability of data:* The availability of data of sources is to be ensured before finalizing the topic.
7. *Ethical issues:* The ethical issues and their remedies must be anticipated before formulating the problem.

Extensive Literature Review

Literature review is an integral part of entire research process. It makes significant contribution to each and every operational step at a later stage. After passing through this stage, a researcher is able to acquaint oneself with the available body of knowledge in the area of interest. The main objectives of literature review are as follows:

1. It broadens the knowledge of researcher about the research problem.
2. It brings better clarity and focus to the research problem; it also helps to improve the authenticity of research.
3. It helps to improve the research methodology.
4. It helps to contextualize the findings. It means how value addition has been done by the researcher to the existing stock of knowledge.

The procedure for reviewing literature covers searching the existing literature, reviewing it, and developing a theoretical and conceptual framework.

The main sources of literature review are books and journals. In both cases, specifically in journals, there can be a gap of two to three years between the completion of a research project and the publication in a journal.

As with books, the researcher needs to prepare a list of journals for identifying the literatures relevant to his research. Nowadays, researchers make extensive use of the Internet sources for literature survey and review, and at the same time, the researcher should be careful about the authenticity of the contents.

Bibliography given at the end of a project gives a clear and complete description of the sources that were used while preparing the report.

Formulation of Objectives

Objectives are the goals you set out to attain in your study. They inform the reader what the researcher wants to accomplish through the research work. The wording of the objective should be very precise and specific.

Objectives can be written under two headings:

1. Main objectives or aims
2. Sub-objectives

The main objective is an overall statement of the thrust of study. It is also a statement of the main associations and relationships that you seek to discover or establish.

The sub-objectives are the specific aspects of the topic that you want to investigate within the main framework of your study.

1. They should be listed numerically.
2. The wording should be clear, complete, and specific.
3. Each objective should contain only one aspect of the study.
4. Use action-oriented words or verbs when writing objectives.

The objectives should start with words such as 'to determine', 'to find out', 'to ascertain', 'to measure', 'to explore', etc. The wording of objectives determines the type of research (descriptive, correlational, and experimental) and the type of research design you need to adopt to achieve them. For example, in case of descriptive studies, the objective can be stated as, 'To describe the types of incentives provided by the organizations in Chandigarh to their employees in IT industry'.

In correlational studies, it may state, 'To ascertain the impact of coaching classes on students' performance'.

Example of Main Objective and Sub-objectives

Main Objective

The main objective is to explore the relationship between the use of modern teaching techniques and student performance.

Sub-objectives

The sub-objectives are as follows:

1. To find out the extent of relationship between the use of modern teaching techniques and student performance.
2. To compare the use of modern teaching techniques in government and private schools.
3. To study the impact of modern teaching and level of motivation of students to learn.

Concepts and Variables

The meanings of terms such as teaching effectiveness, class performance, job satisfaction may vary from one person to another, from one place to another. Concepts (also called as constructs) are mental images, thus are not directly measurable. For research, we have to define concepts so that they are understood in the same sense by respondents in case we collect data.

Again for research purpose, concepts have to be made measurable, otherwise how the data can be collected. It means that concepts should be capable of assuming different values. Here the term indicators and variables come into picture. Anything capable of assuming different values is called as variable.

Let's take another example, if richness is a concept or construct, then assets and income are its indicators; asset values and annual incomes are variables.

Types of Variables

The variables are classified into categorical and quantitative variables. Quantitative variables vary in degree or amount such as annual income, and categorical variables vary in type or kind such as gender.

On the basis of causation, the variables are basically of two types, namely independent and dependent variables.

1. *Independent variables* (symbolized by IV) are presumed to be the cause of another variable.
2. *Dependent variables* (symbolized by DV) are the presumed effect or outcome. Dependent variables are influenced by one or more independent variables. In research, for example, in the study about impact of coaching on student performance, coaching is IV and student performance is DV.

In addition, there can be intervening variables and extraneous variables.

1. *Intervening variables:* These are also termed as mediator variables. They establish link between IV and DV. These are variables through which one variable affects another variable. These are helpful to understand the process.

For example, tissue damage is an intervening variable in smoking and lung cancer relationship. We can use arrows (which mean causes or affects) and draw the relationship that includes an intervening variable like the one given below.

Smoking ⟹ Tissue damage ⟹ Lung cancer

2. *Extraneous variable*: In real-life situations, there can be many factors or variables that may affect the outcome. These variables are termed as extraneous variables. They actually compete with the independent variable in explaining the outcome. If an extraneous variable is the real reason for an outcome rather than IV, it is also called as confounding variable because it has confused or confounded the relationship we are interested in.

The independent variable (also known as the manipulated, experimental, or treatment variable) is the variable manipulated by the researcher in an experiment. The dependent variable (also known as the outcome or response variable) is the variable that changes as a result of changes made with the independent variable. Extraneous variables also affect the dependent variable, although these are not manipulated by the researcher.

On the basis of study design, the variables can be active variables and attribute variables. Active variables can be manipulated or controlled during the study, whereas attribute variables such as gender, age, etc. cannot be changed, controlled, or manipulated.

On the basis of unit of measurement, the variables can be categorical or continuous. Categorical are measured on nominal or ordinal scale, and they can be further classified as follows:

1. *Constant variable:* Only one value such as flower, tree, etc.
2. *Dichotomous variable:* Two categories such as male and female, rich and poor, etc.
3. *Polytomous variable:* More than two categories such as below average, average, above average, etc.

Measuring Variables

Measurement of variables is central to research studies. According to Stevens, measurement scales can be of four types:

1. *Nominal scale:* It is also termed as classificatory scale. A variable being measured on a nominal scale may have one, two, or more subcategories depending upon the extent of variation. For example, gender can be classified into two subcategories—male and female.
2. *Ordinal or ranking scale:* It usually ranks the subgroups in a certain sequence or order. For example, examination marks can be measured either quantitatively, that is, in absolute terms or in percentage terms or qualitatively using subcategories like above average, average, and below average. The distance between these subcategories may or may not be equal.

   The socio-economic status can be categorized as lower class, middle class, and higher class. The middle class can further be divided into lower middle, middle middle, and higher middle. The attitudinal or Likert scale also falls in the same category.
3. *Interval scale:* An interval scale has all the characteristics of an ordinal scale. In addition, it uses a unit of measurement with an arbitrary starting and terminating points. For example, Celsius scale is from 0°C to 100°C.
4. *Ratio scale:* They are used to gather quantitative information. It combines the properties of nominal, ordinal, and interval scales. In addition, it has its own property. It has a fixed starting point. Ratio scale consists of equidistant points and has a meaningful zero point. If we ask respondents about their ages, the difference between any two years would always be the same, and zero signifies the absence of age or birth. A 20-year-old person is twice the age of 10-year-old ones. In order to respect the notion of equal distance between adjacent points on the scale, you

must make each category of the same size. Therefore, if the first category is ₹0 to ₹9,999, then the second category is to be ₹10,000 to ₹19,999, and so on. There should be no overlapping of categories, and they should follow a logical order, in increasing order.

ATTITUDINAL SCALE

If you want to ascertain the attitude of students towards a teacher, the questionnaire framed may be open-ended or close-ended. If the questionnaire is open-ended, it may invite respondents from sample to describe the attitude they hold towards teaching quality. If the researcher has framed close-ended questions, the respondent is given options such as strongly agree (SA), agree (A), undecided (U), disagree (D), strongly disagree (SD).

TYPES OF ATTITUDINAL SCALE

As the attitudinal scales are very important in qualitative research, the different types of attitudinal scales are as follows:

1. *Likert scale:* It is also termed as summated rating scale. It is the easiest one to construct. It is based upon the assumption that each statement or item on the scale has equal attitudinal value, importance, or weight. The quality of a teacher may have many dimensions like use of knowledge base, communication skills, presentation of contents, organization of material, promptness to solve student problems, etc. Respondents may have different attitudes towards different aspects.

Statements about Teacher	SA	A	U	D	SD
1. Knows the subject well (+)					
2. Willing to solve students' problems (+)					
3. Have poor communication skills (–)					
4. Is hard to approach (–)					
5. Good teaching skills (+)					
6. Liking/disliking (+/–)					

Some statements may be positive, some negative, and some neutral. Then, the scores may be assigned to different responses, and the score of each respondent is calculated. Some respondents may have more positive attitude than others. There can be numerical scale as well. Instead of SA, A, U, D, and SD, it will have values 5, 4, 3, 2, and 1.

2. *Thurstone scale:* It may assign weightages to the different statements, such as willing to solve student problem may have a weight of 1, the statement about subject knowledge has weight of 1.5, and statement in context of teaching skill can have weight of 2, and the scores are calculated accordingly.
3. *Guttman scale:* It is mainly based on ratio scale. It is quite difficult to develop.

FACTOR ANALYSIS

Factor analysis allows researchers to describe many variables using few factors, thus reducing the number of variables to a manageable level in terms of factors that can be analysed further.

Formulating Hypothesis (plural - Hypotheses)

Researchers will have one or more hypothesis. These are the questions that they want to address, which include predictions about possible relationships between the things they want to investigate (variables).

As a researcher, we do not know the exact truth but have a hunch about the outcome and, thus, we make some prediction about the outcome. This hunch or prediction about the outcome is called hypothesis. It can also be termed as an educated guess or assumption about some phenomenon. This assumption is tested by collecting information that will enable us to conclude if our hunch was right. Thus, defining hypothesis has the following features:

1. It is a tentative proposition.
2. The validity of a hypothesis is unknown.
3. In most cases, formulating a hypothesis specifies the logical relationship between two variables.
4. It must be generalizable.
5. It should be simple.

Main Functions of a Hypothesis

Formulating a hypothesis, though important, is not absolutely necessary for a research. A perfectly valid research can be conducted even without formulating any hypothesis. In general, formulation performs the following functions:

1. They bring focus, clarity, and specificity in the research study.
2. It helps in making sample design.
3. They make the study more objective.
4. They facilitate the formulation of a theory.

Hypothesis can be of the following types:

1. *Descriptive hypothesis:* It is formulated to describe characteristics. For example, the present rate of unemployment in urban areas of India is 10%.
2. *Relational hypothesis:* They indicate the relationship between two variables. For example, parents residing in urban areas spend more money on the education of their children.
3. *Explanatory hypothesis:* They guide about the cause-and-effect relationship between two variables. For example, when salaries increase, the spending on food items also increase. However, reverse may not be true.

In statistical hypothesis testing, you have a null hypothesis against which you are testing an alternative. The hypothesis concerns one or more characteristics of the distribution.

Concept of Null and Alternative Hypotheses

Prof. R. A. Fisher was the first to use such an experiment for testing hypothesis by scientific investigation. He talked about the principle of replication, randomization, and local control in research.

Observations that run contrary to those predicted are taken as evidence against the hypothesis; observations that are in agreement with those predicted are taken as corroborating the hypothesis. It is the same as we solve everyday problems, but there is only a small twist that is termed as null and alternate hypothesis.

As discussed, a hypothesis is a statement that relates two or more constructs. For example, the greater the stress experienced in a job, the lower the job satisfaction of employees.

Here, you need a clear operational definition of stress and job satisfaction. A good hypothesis is tested by the research that you propose to do.

In classical hypothesis testing, a statement about the population parameter and then a random sample from the population are taken, and the hypothesis are tested with the appropriate sample statistics.

Suppose, as a teacher you are under the impression that a high dropout rate exists among students from rural background or semi-urban areas. Then, we collect data from all the students or some of them to check the validity of the assumption or prediction.

Null hypothesis (H_o) will state that place of residence (rural, urban, semi urban) does not have any impact on dropout ratio. The alternative hypothesis (H_A) will state that dropout rate is higher among students from rural areas. Then, data are collected to challenge the null hypothesis. If null hypothesis is rejected based on the data analysis, the alternative hypothesis will be automatically accepted. Hypothesis can also become the basis of further enquiry. Its formulation is based upon your own or someone else's observation.

Directional and Non-directional Hypothesis

In a studies relating to the academic performance of boys and girls, the null hypothesis would state that boys and girls have equal performance level. The directional hypothesis may state that boys or girls are more able. It tends to be more specific about the outcome. The non-directional alternative would simply state that there is a gender difference. We have no idea whether boys are more able or girls are more able—only say that they are not the same.

Step 2

Preparing Research Design and Study Design

Now, when the setting up of hypothesis is done, the next step is research design. It is a roadmap to carry out the research. It is a step-by-step approach addressing basic questions like, what is the scope of research study?, what type of data is to be collected?, or something like, what methods should be used to collect the data and to analyze them? The justification is required at every step as the resources are at stake. In fact, many of the research methods are basically research designs or closely linked with them.

Research design is an activity and time-based plan keeping in view of the research objectives. It guides about the types of information to be collected and their sources. It is a framework for specifying the relationship among the variables under study. It outlines the procedures. It also answers questions such as, is an intensive study of a small sample more effective than a less intensive study of a large sample? and, should the analysis be primarily qualitative or quantitative?

Research design is also defined as plan, structure, and strategy of investigation conceived so as to obtain answers to research questions and to control variance. It is a master plan specifying the methods and procedures for collecting and analyzing the needed information.

Ghauri (1995) tried to establish a link between research design and problem structure as shown in Figure 2.2.

Research design		Problem structure
Exploratory	→	Unstructured
Descriptive	→	Structured
Causal	→	Structured

Figure 2.2 Research Design

Therefore, research design involves consideration of the following:

1. Objectives of research study
2. Selection of method of data collection
3. Source of information—sample design
4. Tools for data collection
5. Data analysis—qualitative and quantitative

Research design achieves the following purposes:

1. It makes research efficient
2. Optimum utilization of resources—maximum information with minimal expenditure, time, and money
3. Flexibility
4. Minimization of bias
5. Reliability and objectivity

Study Design on the Basis of Number of Contacts

On the basis of contacts, research can be cross sectional or longitudinal. In cross-sectional studies, data is collected only once during the research process. The data are not necessarily gathered simultaneously, and data collection may spread over a period of time such as one week, one month, or so. It may also take a longer period. For example, data may be collected about holiday preference of software professionals in India.

In longitudinal studies, data would be collected at several points of time. For example, a drug has been administered to a group of patients to check the efficacy of drug, and the data may have to be collected many times to check their health conditions. HR department of an organization may collect data about employee satisfaction level before and after raise of pay or promotion. The marketer may be interested in getting information about the impact of advertisement on sales.

Study Design on the Basis of Reference Period

1. *Retrospective study design:* It is meant for a phenomenon or a situation that has occurred in the past.
2. *Prospective study design:* It pertains to likely prevalence of a phenomenon in the future.

Study design based on reference period can be a combination of both retrospective and prospective studies.

Study Design on the Basis of Nature of Investigation

For example, a pharmaceutical company wants to test the impact of a drug in treating people. There is cause-and-effect relationship between the two variables. The research can be broadly classified into two for the purpose of study design, namely experimental study and non-experimental study.

Experimental Study

If a study is done in a manner that we start from cause to establish the effects, the independent variable can be manipulated by the researcher so as to see the effect of change in independent variable (cause) on dependent variable (effect).

The treatment groups (not in terms of medical science) are of two types: experimental group and control group.

1. *Experimental group:* Group receiving treatment is the experimental group (e.g., students of a class being taught with new teaching method, a group of patients being administered a new medicine, etc.).
2. *Control group:* Group not receiving treatment is the control group (e.g., students being taught with same conventional method, a group of patients with no medicine or no new medicine, etc.).

Control in an experiment means that the researcher wants to investigate the effect of various factors one at a time in that experiment.

Randomization

It covers the following aspects:

1. The selection of a group as experimental or control group is random.
2. All participants have equal chance of being chosen for experimental group or control group.
3. The larger the number of participants, the greater the chance that groups will represent the population.

Non-Experimental Study

It is a retrospective type of study. Thus, we start from the effects to trace the cause. Here, the assumed cause has already occurred. Variables are still referred to as IV and DV (e.g., comparing opinions from natural groups).

There can be other types of study designs as well. A few important study designs are as follows:

1. *Action research:* It is a research initiated to solve an immediate problem. It was coined by Kurt Lewin. The aim of fundamental research is the development of theory and that of applied research is on its general application, whereas the action research is focused on immediate application of theory.

   For example, the objective of action research by the teacher will be to identify the problems and then to improve classroom practises himself.
2. *Cohort studies:* It is based on the existence of some common characteristics such as year of birth, graduation, or marriage. For example, the researcher wants to study the pattern of employment of MBAs passed in

1991, when India was facing economic crisis, or study of people born between 1995 and 2000.

3. *Placebo design:* A patient, for example, may have an impression that he is undergoing treatment, but in reality, he is being given only sugar pills. It can play an important role in his recovery. There can be two groups: one receiving the actual treatment and the second receiving placebo treatment. The control group can also be used in this design. The first group receives the actual treatment, the second placebo treatment, and the third group (control group) receives nothing.

Step 3

Developing Data Collection Instrument (Research Instrument)

Data are defined as the information recorded to represent facts. Few points about data are worth mentioning here.

1. Data represent facts about hypothesized variables.
2. Data are analysed to determine consistency with prediction. Prediction is in the form of setting up of hypothesis.
3. If data and prediction are consistent, then null hypothesis is supported.
4. If data and prediction are inconsistent, hypothesis is not supported and is rejected.

The quality and validity of the output are solely dependent on the tools used for data collection. The data can be classified as primary and secondary, objective and subjective, and qualitative and quantitative.

Primary Data and Secondary Data

Primary data are collected for the purpose of current research project, whereas secondary data are collected for some other research purpose. It is collected fresh by the researcher and is based on surveys, observations, and experimentation. It is expensive and difficult to acquire. It is reliable as it has been obtained directly with a specific problem in view. Figure 2.3 shows the various ways be which primary data can be collected.

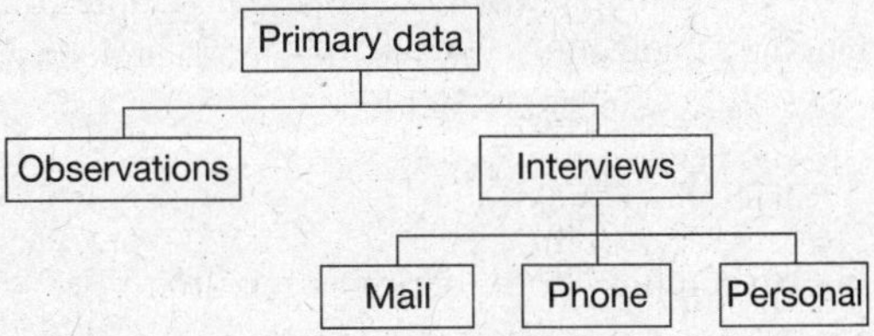

Figure 2.3 Sources for collection of Primary Data

Secondary data are collected from external sources such as TV, radio, the Internet, magazines, books, and newspapers. These data might have been collected for different purposes. It is an inexpensive and a quick method of obtaining information. Sometimes, it is the only way when the original source is inaccessible. It should be ascertained (i) whether the data is relevant to your study? and (ii) is it credible?

Objective Data and Subjective Data

Objective data are independent of any single person's opinion, whereas subjective data can be an individual's opinion or it can be dependent upon the researcher.

Qualitative Data and Quantitative Data

Qualitative data are the description of things made without assigning numeric values. For example, facts generated from unstructured interview. It needs researcher's interpretation.

Quantitative data entail measurements in which numbers are used directly to represent properties of things. It is ready for statistical analysis. The larger sample is required in quantitative data, and with proper sampling design, the ability to generalize is also high.

Observation Method

This is used in behavioural sciences. It is about collecting primary data by investigator's own direct observation of relevant people, actions, and situations without asking from the respondent. For example, a retail chain sends observers posing as customers into competitors' stores to check on cleanliness and customer service.

Observation can yield information which people are normally not willing or able to provide. For example, by observing many copies of classwork, the untidy copies indicate that quality of teaching is not satisfactory.

Types of Observations

1. Structured—for descriptive research
2. Unstructured—for exploratory research
3. Participant observation
4. Non-participant observation
5. Disguised observation

Limitations

Firstly, there are many behavioural aspects that may not be observable directly. For example, marketer as a researcher cannot measure the feelings, beliefs, and attitudes that motivate buying behaviour and infrequent behaviour cannot be observed.

Secondly, the observation method is quite expensive.

Survey Method

Sometimes, observation method is supplemented with survey method. This approach is most suited for gathering descriptive information, and this research may be direct or indirect. It is of two types: structured and unstructured surveys.

1. *Structured surveys:* They use formal lists of questions to be asked from all respondents in the same manner.
2. *Unstructured surveys:* They give the interviewer the flexibility to probe respondents and direct the interview according to their answers.

Advantages

1. Quick and low cost in comparison to observation method.
2. Survey method can be administered to collect many different types of information.

Limitations

1. Privacy issues
2. Reluctance on the part of respondents
3. Biases.

Contact Methods

Information may be collected by mails, telephone, personal interview, etc.

Mail Questionnaires

Advantages

1. It includes collecting large amounts of information at a low cost per respondent.
2. Respondents may give more honest answers to personal questions on a mail questionnaire.
3. It is unbiased as no interviewer is involved.
4. Convenient for respondents who can answer when they have time.
5. Good way to reach people who travel.

Limitations

1. It is not flexible.
2. It takes a longer time to complete than telephonic or personal interviews.
3. It has low response rate.
4. Little control of researcher over the process.

Telephonic Interviewing

Advantages

1. It is a quick method.
2. It gives greater flexibility to interviewer as he can explain questions not understood properly by the respondent.
3. It has greater sample control.
4. It has higher response rate.

Limitations

1. High cost per respondent as interviewer should be more skilled.
2. Privacy issues.

3. Complete standardization is not possible.
4. Wrong entry is possible due to lack of time.

Personal Interviewing

It is very flexible and can be used to collect large amounts of information. Trained interviewers can hold the respondent's attention and are available to clarify difficult questions.

They can guide interviews, explore issues, and probe as the situation requires. Personal interviews can be used in any type of questionnaire and can be conducted fairly quickly. Interviewers can also show actual products, advertisements, or packages, and observe and record their reactions and behaviour. This takes two forms, namely intercept interviewing (for individuals) and focus group interviewing (for groups).

Intercept Interviewing

Advantages

1. It is widely used in marketing research such as tourism.
2. It allows the researcher to reach known people in a short period of time.
3. It is the only method of reaching people whose names and addresses are unknown.
4. It involves talking to people at homes, offices, on the street, or in shopping malls.
5. The interviewer must gain the interviewee's cooperation.
6. It is time-consuming and may range from a few minutes to several hours (for longer surveys, compensation may be offered).
7. It involves the use of judgemental sampling, that is, the interviewer has guidelines as to whom to intercept, such as 25% under 20 years of age and 75% over 60 years of age.

Limitations

1. There is greater room for error and bias on the part of the interviewer who may not be able to correctly judge age, race, etc.
2. Interviewer may not be comfortable talking to certain ethnic or age groups.

Focus Group Interviewing

Advantages

1. It is usually conducted by inviting 6–10 people to gather for a few hours with a trained moderator to talk about a product, service, or organization. The meeting is held in a pleasant place, and refreshments are served to create a relaxed environment.
2. The moderator needs objectivity, knowledge of the subject and industry, and some understanding of group and individual behaviour.
3. The moderator starts with a broad question before moving to more specific issues, encouraging open and easy discussion to bring out the true feelings and thoughts. At the same time, the interviewer focuses on the discussion, hence the name focus group interviewing.
4. It is often held to help determine the subject areas on which questions should be asked in a later, large-scale, structured, direct interview.
5. Comments are recorded through note taking or videotaped and studied later (content analysis).

Limitations

1. It is more expensive than telephonic survey.
2. Group interview studies keep the sample size small enough to keep time and cost down; therefore, it may be difficult to generalize from the results.
3. There is some possibility of interviewer bias.

Construction of a Research Tool (Questionnaire)

Questionnaire depends upon research objectives. For each objective or research questions, list all the associated questions that a researcher wants to answer through study. Then, the information required to answer them is listed, and finally, the questions are listed.

Questionnaire - Concept and Types

A questionnaire consists of a set of questions presented to a respondent for answers. The questionnaire is used during structured surveys or interviews. The respondents read the questions, interpret what is expected, and then write down the answers themselves. It is also called an interview schedule when the researcher asks the questions and records the respondent's reply on the interview schedule. Here, the researcher may have to explain questions to the respondents.

There are many options before the researchers adopt this method, but questionnaires should be developed and tested carefully before being administered on a large scale. There are three basic types of questionnaires: closed-ended, open-ended, and a combination of both.

1. *Closed-ended questionnaire:* Closed-ended questionnaires generally include multiple choice questions or scale questions. This type of questionnaire can be administered to a large number of respondents or sample size. As there is a set format, the data generated from questionnaire can be easily fed into a computer system for the purpose of analysis.
2. *Open-ended questionnaire:* Open-ended questionnaires offer the flexibility to respondents to answer in their own words. It may leave a blank section to write an answer.

   Closed-ended questionnaires might be used to find out how many people use metro rail service in New Delhi, but open-ended questionnaires might be used to find out what people think about the quality of service.
3. *Combined questionnaire:* In this method, it is possible to find out how many people use a service and what they think of the service in the same form. The combined questionnaire may begin with a series of closed-ended questions, with boxes to tick or scales to rank, and then finish with a section of open-ended questions or a more detailed response.

Step 4

Selecting Samples

Researchers usually draw conclusions about large groups by taking a sample. A sample is a subset of the population selected to represent the population as a whole. The main benefits of sampling are as follows:

1. Reduction in overall cost of research
2. Less time-consuming, and in certain cases, this is desirable as well.
3. In case, the population is consistent, this becomes even more desirable.

Ideally, a representative sample should be an unbiased indication of what the population is like. Some of the factors that researchers consider when selecting a representative sample include sex, age, educational level, socioeconomic status, and marital status.

For example, if roughly half of the total population of interest is female, then a sample should be made up of approximately 50 per cent women in order to be representative.

In research, the population does not mean only human population all the times; it can be factories, schools, etc. Population is denoted by N and sample as n.

The factors affecting inferences drawn from a sample are dependent upon the following:

1. *Sample size:* The larger the sample, the more is the accuracy.
2. *Variation in population:* The greater the variation in population, the greater will be the uncertainty of outcome. The higher the consistency in population, the more confident we are about the quality of outcome. The higher the variations in population, the larger should be the sample size.

Types of Sampling Techniques

1. *Probability or Random Samples:* Each person in the population has equal, independent, and known chances of being selected. In case, there are 100 elements in a

population, every element has 1/100 chance of being selected in a sampling exercise. Here, independence means that selection of one element is neither being affected by the selection of other elements nor it will affect the other elements.

(a) *Simple random sample:* Every element or member of the population has a known and equal chance of being selected.

(b) *Stratified random sample:* In case, the population is heterogeneous, the population can be divided into different strata. The population within a stratum is homogeneous with respect to the characteristic under study. Population is divided into mutually exclusive groups such as age groups, and random samples are drawn from each group. The population in a particular stratum may be in proportion to its population. Suppose there are 1,000 students in a college, 600 study humanities and 400 study commerce. In a sample of 100, 60 students will be from humanities and 40 from commerce, that is, in the same ratio as in the overall population.

(c) *Cluster sample:* The simple and stratified sampling is adopted in situations when population size is small and units are identifiable. But if the population is larger, the researcher can go for cluster sampling. The population is divided into mutually exclusive groups, and the researcher draws a sample of the group to interview. For example, in a national level survey, at the first few levels, a few states may be selected. Within the states, a few districts may be selected; then, within each district, blocks may be selected and then villages. It is termed as 'multistage cluster sampling'.

2. *Non-probability Sampling:* It is a sampling technique where the samples are gathered in a process that does not give all the individuals in the population equal chances of being selected. Here, only some elements of the population have a greater chances or unknown chances of being selected.

(a) *Convenience sampling:* The researcher selects the easiest population members from which to obtain information.

(b) *Judgement or purposive sampling:* The researcher uses his/her judgement to select population members who are likely to provide accurate information. This can be used for historical research or descriptive research.

(c) *Quota sampling:* The researcher finds and interviews a prescribed number of people in each of several categories. Here, the main criterion used by the researcher is the ease to access sample population. The sample is selected from a location convenient to him or her; here, there are some possibilities to include people with some visible characteristics. However, the results may not be generalized to larger populations.

(d) *Accidental sampling:* It is akin to quota sampling, but used in market research (in market places) where a researcher can come across any person and they may not have any information.

(e) *Snowball sampling:* In this kind of sampling, the information may be selected from few individuals, and they may identify other people for the purpose of gathering information. They may also become a part of the sample. It creates a network of sample elements.

Determining Sample Design

Designing the sample calls for three decisions:

1. *Sample itself* – Who will be surveyed? It further depends upon what type of information is required.
2. *Sample size* – How many people should ideally be surveyed? Large samples are likely to give more reliable results than small samples. However, it has to be a trade-off between cost and accuracy.

3. *Sampling* – How should the sample be chosen? Sampling can be done by adopting either probability or non-probability method.

The sample size for any research study depends upon four Ps:

1. *Purpose:* The required precision of study
2. *Population:* The size and nature of population under study
3. *Procedure:* The time, budget, and resources available
4. *Publishing:* The importance of the studies

Note: The more heterogeneous or diverse the population is, the bigger should be the sample size.

STEP 5

WRITING A RESEARCH PROPOSAL

A research proposal is a document of usually three to seven pages that informs others of a proposed piece of research. This proposed research is usually a Masters or Doctorate by thesis, but it can also be a work for a corporate purpose.

A research proposal is a document written by a researcher that provides a detailed description of the proposed program. It is like an outline of the entire research process that gives the reader a summary of information discussed in the project. Research proposals are written for various reasons like budget request for the research certification requirements for research, etc.

Main Elements of Research Proposal

1. Need of a specific research project
2. Benefits and beneficiaries
3. The type of data to be collected and the means to collect the data
4. Types of analysis
5. Help required from other organization, if any
6. Duration, facilities, and requirement of funds
7. Profile and credentials of the proposers

STEP 6

COLLECTING DATA

There are many alternatives available to collect relevant data. The researcher should select one of these methods of collecting data taking into account the nature of investigation, scope and objective of inquiry, financial cost, availability of time, and the desired accuracy.

Primary data can be collected either through experiment or through survey. If the researcher conducts an experiment, he will take some quantitative measurements (data). The data are analysed further to test the hypothesis.

In case of a survey, data can be collected by any one or more of the following ways:

1. *By observation:* This entails the collection of information by the way of investigator's own observation without interviewing the respondents. The information obtained relates to the current happenings. This method is very expensive and the information gathered in such a manner is limited. This method is not suitable for research where large samples are required as is the case with quantitative research.
2. *Personal interviews:* The investigator follows structured approach, and the questions are pre-conceived. Here, the output also depends upon the ability of the interviewer to a large extent.
3. *Telephonic interviews:* This method of collecting information involves contacting the respondents on telephone itself. It is used when the survey has to be accomplished in a very limited time.
4. *Mailed questionnaires:* Questionnaires are mailed to the respondents with a request to return after completing the same. It is the most commonly used method in economic and business surveys. A pilot study may be conducted for testing the questionnaire to check its appropriateness for the purpose.
5. *Schedules:* In this method, the enumerators are specially appointed and trained for

gathering information. Schedules consist of relevant questions. The enumerators visit respondents with these schedules. Schedules are filled up by the enumerators on the basis of replies given by the respondents.

Some random checking by the supervisors may be required to ensure the validity of the research process. Although he should pay attention to all these factors, but much depends upon the ability and experience of the researcher.

Step 7

Processing and Analysing Data

After the data have been collected, the next step is to analyse it. It requires a number of closely related operations such as establishment of categories and the application of these categories to raw data through coding, tabulation, and then drawing statistical inferences.

The large data should be condensed into a few manageable groups and tables for further analysis. This is done with the help of classification of data into more relevant, purposeful, and usable categories.

1. *Editing:* The process of cleaning the data is called editing. The purpose of editing is to identify and minimize errors, miscalculations, misclassification, or any gap in information provided by the respondent. Editing improves the quality of the data for coding.
2. *Coding:* It depends upon how a variable has been measured in your research instrument. For coding, the first step is to ensure the nature of data, that is, whether it is quantitative or qualitative. The qualitative data may be descriptive, (case history) categorical or discrete (Gender: male or female; Income: below average or above average; Attitude: strongly favourable, favourable or unfavourable.

Quantitative and categorical information is processed to be converted into numerical values called codes. It is usually done at this stage through which the categories of data are transformed into symbols that may be tabulated and counted. After coding is completed, the data are tabulated.

The descriptive information goes through a process called content analysis with a motive to get an idea about the 'themes' of the descriptive information such as an interview. In descriptive or qualitative data, the researcher may go through the transcription of all interviews in which people may use different words to express the same phenomenon.

Classification of Data

Classification of data is a process of arranging data in groups or classes on the basis of common characteristics. It can be done in following ways:

Classification According to Attributes

The data can be descriptive (e.g., literacy, sex, religion, etc.) or numerical (e.g., weight, height, income, etc.). Further classification can be either simple classification or manifold classification.

1. *Simple classification:* In this classification, we consider only one attribute and divide the universe into two classes—one class consisting of items possessing the given attribute and the other class consisting of items which does not possess the given attribute.

   Example

   Candidates with MBA degree

	Yes	No	Total
MBA degree	21	09	30

2. *Manifold classification:* In this classification, we consider two or more attributes simultaneously and divide the data into a number of classes.

   Example

   Educational qualification of faculty

	Yes		No		Total	
Gender	M	F	M	F	M	F
PG degree						
Ph.D.						

CLASSIFICATION ACCORDING TO CLASS INTERVALS

Classification is done with data relating to income, age, weight, tariff, production, occupancy, etc. Such quantitative data are known as the statistics of variables and are classified on the basis of class intervals. For example, persons whose income is within ₹2,001 and ₹4,000 can form one group or class, those with income within ₹4,001 and ₹6,000 can form another group or class, and so on. The number of items which fall in a given class is known as the frequency of the given class.

Tabulation

Tabulation is a part of the technical procedure wherein the classified data are put in the form of tables. It is the process of summarizing raw data and displaying the same in compact form for further analysis. The mechanical devices can also be used for this purpose. When data are really large, computers can be used for tabulation. It also makes it possible to study large number of variables affecting a problem simultaneously. It is an orderly arrangement of data in columns and rows. It is essential because of the following reasons:

1. It conserves space and reduces explanatory and descriptive statement to a minimum.
2. It facilitates the process of comparison.
3. It facilitates the summation of items and the detection of errors and omissions.
4. It provides the basis for various statistical computations.

Tabulation may also be classified as simple and complex tabulations. Simple tabulation generally results in a one-way table that supplies answers to questions about one characteristic of data only. Complex tabulation usually results in two-way tables, which give information about two interrelated characteristics of data; three-way tables or still higher order tables are also known as manifold tables.

Analysis of Data

After tabulation, analysis is done with the help of different mathematical and statistical techniques such as percentages, averages, coefficients of correlation, regression, and so on. It largely depends upon whether data is qualitative or quantitative.

QUALITATIVE DATA ANALYSIS

The analytical approach may be personalized, and there may be few rigid rules and procedures. Generally, the researcher needs to go through a process called content analysis. Content analysis means analysis of the contents of an interview in order to identify the main themes that emerge from responses given by the respondents. This process involves the following steps:

1. *Identify the main themes:* The researcher needs to carefully go through the descriptive responses given by respondents to each question so as to understand the meaning they communicate. These help in developing broad themes that reflect these meanings. For example, people use different words and languages to express themselves.
2. *Assign codes to the main themes:* Assigning codes is required when the researcher wants to count the number of times a theme has occurred in an interview.
3. *Classify responses under the main themes:* Having identified the themes, the next step is to go through the transcripts of all the interviews and classify the responses under different themes.
4. *Integrate themes and responses into the text of your report:* Having identified the responses that fall under different themes, the next step is to integrate the themes and responses into the text of your report. It entirely depends upon the way the researcher wants to communicate the findings to the readers.

QUANTITATIVE DATA ANALYSIS

This method is most suitable for large, well-designed and well-administered surveys using properly constructed and worded questionnaire. Data can be analysed either manually or with the help of a computer.

1. *Manual data analysis:* This can be done if the number of respondents is reasonably small and if there are not many variables to analyze. However, this is useful only for calculating frequencies and for simple cross-tabulations. Manual data analysis is time consuming. The easiest way to do this is to code it directly onto a large graph paper in columns.
2. *Data analysis using a computer:* If you want to analyse the data using computer, you should be familiar with the appropriate program. In this area, knowledge of computer and statistics plays an important role.

   The most common software is SPSS for windows. However, data input can be long and laborious process, and if data are entered incorrectly, it will influence the final results.

In the process of analysis, relationships or differences, supporting or conflicting with original or new hypothesis should be subjected to tests of significance to determine with what validity the data can be said to indicate any conclusions.

Hypothesis Testing

After analysing the data as stated above, the researcher is in a position to test the hypothesis. As discussed earlier, the qualitative studies may not have any formal hypothesis.

In quantitative studies, we have to see whether the facts support the hypothesis or they happen to be contrary. This is the usual question that should be answered while testing hypothesis. Various tests, such as Chi-square test, t-test, and F-test, have been developed by statisticians for this purpose.

The hypothesis may be tested through use of one or more such tests, depending upon the nature and object of research inquiry. Hypothesis testing will result in either accepting the hypothesis or rejecting it. If the researcher had no hypothesis to start with, generalizations established on the basis of data may be stated as hypothesis to be tested by subsequent researches in times to come.

Generalizations and Interpretation

If a hypothesis is tested and upheld several times, it may be possible for the researcher to arrive at generalization, that is, to build a theory. As a matter of fact, the real value of research lies in its ability to arrive at certain generalizations. If the researcher had no hypothesis to start with, he might seek to explain his findings on the basis of some theory. It is known as interpretation. The process of interpretation may trigger off new questions which in turn may lead to further researches.

STEP 8

WRITING A RESEARCH REPORT

Writing a report is the last, and for many, the most difficult step of the research process. The report informs the world what you have done, what you have discovered, and what conclusions you have drawn from your findings. The report should be written in an academic style. Language should be formal and not journalistic.

Research Report Format

Traditional written reports tend to be produced in the following format.

Title Page

1. Title of the research project
2. Name of the researcher
3. Purpose of the research project, for example 'A research project submitted on partial fulfilment of the requirements of XYZ University, New Delhi, for the degree of ____________'.
4. Date of Publication

Table of Contents

In this section, the contents of the report, either in chapters or in subheadings are listed.

Example

Contents **Page No.**

Introduction

Chapter I Theoretical Framework and Review of Related Literature

List of Tables

This section includes the title and page numbers of all tables.

Example

Table No.	Title	Page No.
1.	Income levels of respondents	
2.	Age distribution of respondents	

List of Figures

This section contains the title and page numbers of all graphs, pie charts, etc.

Example

Figure No.	Title	Page No.
1.	Pie chart showing the age distribution of respondents	
2.	Bar graph showing the popularity of menu items	

Acknowledgements

In this section, the researcher may acknowledge the institute, principal, faculty guides (both research guide and technical guide), research participants, friends, etc.

Introduction

This section introduces the research, setting out the main aims and objectives. It is actually a rationale for the research.

Theoretical Framework and Review of Literature

This section includes all the background research information that has been obtained from the literature review. You must indicate from where all the information was obtained. Thus, it is mandatory to keep a complete record of everything the researcher has read. Otherwise, there are chances that the researcher could be accused of plagiarism, which is akin to intellectual theft.

Research Design

This section includes all practical details followed for the research. After reading this, any interested party should be able to replicate the research study. It includes the methods used for data collection, sampling procedures, tools used for data collection, and analysis of data.

Data Analysis and Interpretation

If you have conducted a large quantitative survey, this section may contain tables, graphs, pie charts, and associated statistics. If you have conducted a qualitative piece of research, this section may be a descriptive prose.

Summary and Conclusion

In this section, you sum up your findings and draw conclusions from them, perhaps in relation to other research or literature.

Recommendations

If the research has been conducted for any client organization, this section could be treated as the most important part of the report. Sometimes, this section is included at the beginning of the report.

Suggestions for Further Research

Research is a continuous process. This section shows how research could be continued. This could happen as some results are inconclusive or the research itself has thrown up many more research questions that need to be addressed. It also shows the honesty and integrity of the researcher that he has a wider perspective and has actually not tried to cover up the shortcomings.

List of References/Bibliography

The list of references contains only the details of those works cited in the text. It includes sources not cited in the main text matter but are relevant to the subject of study, specifically in case of larger dissertations or thesis. Small research projects may need just a reference section to include all the literature that has been referred to in the report.

For Books

1. Authors' surname (alphabetically), followed by their initials
2. Date of publication
3. Title of the book in italics
4. Place of publication, publisher

For Journal Articles

The title of the article appears in inverted commas and name of the journal comes in italics, followed by the volume number and pages of the article.

Example

Madaan KVS; 'Influence of British Rule on Indian Culture'; Journal of Tourism; 10–18.

Appendices

This is specifically required in case of questionnaires or interview schedules constructed for conducting the research; it may be useful to include them in the report as an appendix.

Appendices do not count towards your total number of pages or words. It is a useful way of including relevant material so that the examiner can gain a deeper understanding of your work by reading it.

Certificate

Certified that this research project titled

____

is the bonafide record of work carried out by __________ for final year __________.

Technical guide   Research coordinator   Principal

Place __________

Date __________

Dissertation and Thesis

A dissertation culminates in a postgraduate degree such as MS/M.Tech./M.Sc./MPhil, whereas a thesis leads to a doctoral degree (Europe and India). In American universities, a dissertation leads to a PhD degree and a thesis leads to a Master's degree. We will adhere to the former one.

In a dissertation, it is adequate if one has a decent knowledge of the new discoveries in order to arrive at the conclusion effectively. In a thesis, one has to substantiate the hypothesis with original research work. The hypothesis or the 'synopsis' should contain the gist of the new findings one has made on the subject of research. The written thesis should contain all details of original research work that one has made on the subject. (A thesis may be subjected to scrutiny for any plagiarism to determine the originality of the effort.) Another finite difference between the two is that in a thesis, analysis of any existing literature is added, whereas a dissertation by itself is an analysis of any existing literature. The differences between a dissertation and a thesis are given below:

1. A researcher has to utilize the already collected information in order to prepare a dissertation, whereas thesis is based on the research conducted all by himself.
2. Thesis is lengthier, thus, takes more time to be completed, whereas dissertation is short; therefore, it does not consume too much time to be completed.
3. In thesis, researcher have to include a hypothesis based on your research work. In contrast to thesis, in dissertation, researcher should have a decent knowledge of the new discoveries in order to infer conclusion effectively.
4. In thesis, researcher has to focus on your primary argument in order to prove your standpoint to the readers. In contrast to thesis, dissertation focuses on background work.
5. In Master's dissertation, researcher has to utilize the research work in order to prove his

point; in case of PhD thesis, researcher has to add novel findings to the existing literature.

6. Thesis is written as an academic research paper, whereas dissertation is more like an academic book.
7. Data collected in dissertation is based upon the hypothetical analysis of contents, whereas thesis is comprised of theory and argumentation based on original research.

The structure of a dissertation and thesis writing is normally described in university students' handbook.

Shodhganga and Shodhgangotri: Shodhganga is the name coined to denote digital repository of Indian electronics thesis and dissertations set up by Information and Library Network (INFLIBNET) Centre, an autonomous Inter-University Centre (IUC) of the University Grant Commission. Now, the candidates will have to store the thesis in a compact disc (CD) and upload each chapter in a separate pdf file using naming convention as prescribed by Shodhganga. The CD must be authenticated by Supervisor/Head of Department.

INFLIBNET introduced Shodhgangotri, which has been built to maintain a database of synopsis of on-going M.Phil./Ph.D. in Indian universities and institutions.

Basic Bibliographic Information – APA Format

The American Psychological Association (APA) guidelines specify using sentence-style capitalization for the titles of books or articles, so we should capitalize only the first word of a title and subtitle. The exceptions to this rule would be periodical titles and proper names in a title that should be capitalized. The periodical title is run in title case and is followed by the volume number, which is italicized along with the title.

If there is more than one author, use an ampersand (&) before the name of the last author. If there are more than six authors, list only the first one and use et al. for the rest.

Format Examples

1. *Books Format:* Author's last name, first initial. (Publication date). Book title. Additional information. City of publication: Publishing company.

   Examples

   Madaan, K. V. S. (2009). Fundamentals of retailing. New Delhi: Tata McGraw-Hill.

2. *Encyclopedia and Dictionary Format:* Author's last name, first initial. (Date). Title of Article. Title of Encyclopedia (Volume, pages). City of publication: Publishing company.

   Examples

   Bergmann, P. G. (1993). Relativity. In The new Encyclopedia Britannica (Vol. 26, pp. 501–508). Chicago: Encyclopedia Britannica.

3. *Magazine and Newspaper Articles Format:* Author's last name, first initial. (Publication date). Article title. Periodical title, volume number (issue number if available), inclusive pages.

   Examples

   Harlow, H. F. (1983). Fundamentals for preparing psychology journal articles. Journal of Comparative and Physiological Psychology, 55, 893–896.

4. *Website or Webpage Format for online periodical:* Author's name. (Date of publication). Title of article. Title of Periodical, volume number, Retrieved month day, year, from full URL.

   Format for online document: Author's name. (Date of publication). Title of work. Retrieved month day, year, from full URL.

   Examples

   Devitt, T. (2001, August 2). Lightning injures four at music festival. The Why? Files. Retrieved January 23, 2002, from http://whyfiles.org/137lightning/index.html

   Dove, R. (1998). Lady freedom among us. The Electronic Text Center. Retrieved June 19,

1998, from Alderman Library, University of Virginia website: http://etext.lib.virginia.edu/subjects/afam.html

Main Terms Used in Context of Footnotes and Reference Writing

Ibid is the abbreviation for the Latin *Ibidem*, meaning, the same. It refers to the same author and source (e.g., book and journal) in the immediately preceding reference.

op. cit. is the abbreviation for the Latin *opus citatum*, meaning the work cited. It refers to the reference listed earlier by the same author.
Loc. cit. is of Latin origin and abbreviation for *loco citato*, meaning in the place cited. It is a footnote or endnote term used to repeat the title and page number for a given work.

et al. refers to, and others; it is used when referring to a number of people.

The Indian National Bibliography has been conceived as an authoritative bibliographical record of current Indian publications in Assamese, Bengali, English, Gujarati, Hindi, Kannada, Malayalam, Marathi, Oriya, Punjabi, Sanskrit, Tamil, Telugu, and Urdu languages, received in the National Library, Kolkata, under the Delivery of Books and Newspapers (Public Libraries) Act, 1954.

The main entries are in Roman Script, and the collations and annotations, if any, are in English. The classified portion follows the Dewey Decimal Scheme of Classification, but the numbers from the Colon Classification scheme are assigned to each entry at the bottom right hand to facilitate the use of the bibliography and libraries arranged according to the Colon Schemes of classification. Indian National Bibliography and Central Reference Library fall under the supervision of Ministry of Culture, Government of India.

Research Ethics

Ethics are the principles and guidelines that help us to uphold the things we value. Ethics and law are different aspects, although laws of the land are intended to be based on certain ethics. Almost all societies have legal rules to govern certain behaviour in a country or society, but ethical norms tend to be broader and more informal than laws. An action may be legal but unethical or illegal but ethical. Ethics aim to achieve two fundamental objectives, that is, to tell us how we ought to act in a given situation, and to provide us with strong reasons for doing so.

Ethics always emerge from conflict between values, and research ethics are not an exception. In research, these conflicts may take different forms such as participant's concern for privacy versus some justification for manipulation, openness and replication versus confidentiality, present loss versus future benefits, and so on. Each decision made in research involves a potential compromise of one value for another. However, still researchers must try to minimize the risk to participants, colleagues, and society while trying to optimize the quality of outcome. Research ethics help us to reconcile value conflicts.

The benefits of observing ethics in research studies are as follows:

1. It helps in promoting the aims of research such as bringing out truth and avoidance of errors.
2. It promotes the values that are essential to collaborative work, such as trust, accountability, mutual respect, and fairness.
3. It holds the researcher accountable to the public and society.
4. It helps in building public support for research, which in return can help in getting participants who take part in the research willingly.

Main Approaches to Research Ethics

The following are the three major approaches to ethics:

1. *Deontological approach:* We should identify and use a universal code in making ethical decisions. This is a absolutist approach.

2. *Ethical scepticism approach:* It states that ethical standards are not universal but are relative to one's own particular culture and time. This is based on relativism.
3. *Utilitarianism approach:* Decisions regarding ethics in research should be based on an examination and comparison of the costs and benefits that may arise from a study. If the expected benefits exceed the expected risks, the study is presumed to be ethical. The risk–benefit precaution is a modern version of the end justifying the means. It has its most direct application when those exposed to the risks also receive the benefits. The ratio is more difficult to justify when the participants are subjected to potential harm and when the benefits are directed to other individuals or to the society to be absolute in their requirements.

Some Desirable Elements to Ensure Ethics in Research

The following is a general summary of some research ethical guidelines and principals that various codes address:

1. Honesty in reporting data, results, methods and procedures, and publication status.
2. Objectivity to avoid bias in experimental design, data analysis, interpretation, and peer review.
3. Integrity, acting with sincerity, striving for consistency of thought and action.
4. Carefulness to avoid careless errors and negligence; proper documentation of all aspects.
5. Openness in sharing data, results, ideas, tools, resources and openness to criticisms and new ideas.
6. Respect for intellectual property rights such as patents, copyrights, and other forms of intellectual property.
7. Confidentiality in context of communications, personal records, and privacy issues.
8. Responsible publication with an aim to serve the society. Avoiding wasteful and duplicative publication.
9. Responsible mentoring in terms of guiding research students.
10. Respect for colleagues translates to extending fair treatment to the colleagues.
11. Social responsibility means to serve the society and different stakeholders.
12. Non-discrimination against colleagues or students on the basis of sex, race, or factors that are not related to their scientific competence and integrity.
13. Enhancing competence for own professional advancement or lifelong learning; taking steps to promote competence in science as a whole.
14. Ensuring legality of the whole process by obeying relevant laws, that is, institutional and governmental policies.
15. Animal care through proper experimental designs.

Stakeholders in Research

There are three stakeholders in the research process, namely participants or subjects, researcher, and the funding organization.

Ethical Issues Relating to Participants

There are many ethical issues in relation to participants of a research activity. One of the most commonly cited ethical principles is that we should not cause harm to our research participants. The issue of ethics in research mainly caught the attention of policy makers as a result of many gruesome instances, few of which have been mentioned below.

1. Medical experiments conducted by Nazi doctors in German concentration camps in 1930s. Nazi doctors in German concentration camps killed twin gypsy teenagers in order to determine why some of them had differently coloured eyes while conducting experiments.

2. A South African oncologist experimented with women suffering from cancer to excessive dosages of chemotherapeutics without informing the patients and taking their due consents.
3. Ethical issues during organ transplant, sterilization, and so on.
4. Experiments on animals.

In research, specifically in medical sciences, the observance of ethics is very crucial. Even now, when pharmaceutical companies want to conduct clinical trials in underdeveloped or developing countries, this issue crops up again and again. It is a general understanding that ethical research issues are more moral than legal.

Apart from physical injury, the psychological distress or emotional harm, loss of self-esteem, being persuaded to conduct morally reprehensible acts, and hampering one's physical, intellectual, or emotional development are other important concerns.

We must also be careful about the security of our research records, so that respondents may not be identified or otherwise harmed through loss of confidentiality.

During the initial phase of medical research history, people participating in trials were referred to as research subjects. Now, they are called as trial participants. Now, their role has transformed from a passive subject to that of an active participant. Thus, we can see that research ethics are basically about means of ensuring that vulnerable people are protected from exploitation and other forms of harm. The ethical issues are to be observed at every stage of a research process.

1. *Collecting information:* Before a researcher actually collects information, his request for information may put pressure or create anxiety on a respondent; it may not be ethical, but without research, there will be no intellectual progress or development in the society. A researcher is required to improve the conditions by considering various points in the ensuing discussion.
2. *Seeking consent of participants:* Informed consent refers to an individual's willingness to participate in a study. Individuals who provide informed consent have been made aware of the design and procedures with enough detail to exercise a rational decision to participate.
3. *Providing incentives:* Most people do not participate in a study because of incentives, but they are motivated because of the importance of the study. Giving a gift before data collection is not ethical on the part of a researcher.
4. *Seeking sensitive information:* Some pieces of information can be regarded as sensitive or confidential by some people. This may be akin to invading their privacy. Seeking such kind of information may make them upset. Questions on income, age, marital status, etc. may be considered as intrusive.

   It, however, may not be unethical to enquire if the participants be explained before the research and give them sufficient time to decide if they want to participate without any major inducement.
5. *Possibility of causing harm to the participants:* When you collect data from respondents or involve subjects in an experiment, you need to examine carefully whether their involvement is likely to harm them in any way. Harm may include use of chemicals, drugs, discomfort, anxiety, harassment, invasion of privacy, or demeaning or dehumanizing procedures. Even after the consent, the researcher must make sure that the risk is minimal.
6. *Maintaining confidentiality:* In case, the researcher has to identify the respondent as information needs to be sought more than once, sharing information about a respondent with others for purposes other than research is not ethical and at least the information provided by the respondent should be kept anonymous.

Ethical Issues Relating to the Researcher

1. *Avoiding bias:* Objectivity in research means to avoid bias in the research process as it is considered unethical. Bias means deliberate attempt to either hide facts or to under represent or over represent them. It may undermine the truth.
2. *Provision or deprivation of a treatment:* This is specifically true in case of medical research. Is it ethical to provide to a study population with an intervention or treatment that has not yet been conclusively proven effective? However, without administering it to patients, its real effects may never be known, and patients may be deprived of its potential benefits. Thus, it imposes an ethical dilemma before researchers. Informed consent, minimum risk, and frank discussion can help to resolve the ethical issues.
3. *Using inappropriate research methodology*: The deliberate use of a highly biased sample, method, or procedure is unethical.
4. *Incorrect reporting:* This can be done to advance the interests of the researcher.
5. *Inappropriate use of the information:* Sometimes, it is possible to harm individuals in the process of achieving benefits for the organization. An example would be a study to help in formulation of a policy by the organization. New policy may not serve the interests of certain individuals but may be good for the organization as such. Should you ask respondents for information that is likely to be used against them?

Some of the key terms used in the context of ethical issues concerning researchers are as follows:

1. Fabricating behaviour: Creation of spurious data by researcher, their recording, and drawing inferences.
2. Falsification manipulates the research material, equipment, and processes, or changes or omits data or results such that the research is not accurately represented in the research records.
3. Plagiarism is the act of appropriating somebody else's ideas, thoughts, pictures, theories, words, or stories as your own. If a researcher plagiarizes the work of others, the integrity, ethics, and trustworthiness of the sum total of his or her research becomes questionable. Plagiarism is both an illegal and punishable act and is considered to be on the same level as stealing from the author who originally created it. It can take the following forms:
   (a) *Intra-corpal:* A case of plagiarism where one student has copied from another in the same submission is known as intra-corpal plagiarism.
   (b) *Extra-corpal:* It is an instance of plagiarism where a student has copied the material from an external source (e.g., book, journal article, world wide web, etc.).
   (c) *Autoplagiarism:* It is citing one's own work without acknowledgement.
4. *Multiple authorship:* There can be many improprieties in authorship. Improper assignment of credit, such as excluding other authors, inclusion of others as authors who have not made a definite contribution towards the work published, or submission of multi-authored publication without the knowledge of all the authors.
5. *Peer review:* It is the process in which an author submits a written manuscript or an article to a journal for publication. The journal editor distributes the article to experts or reviewers. The peer review process seldom proceeds in a straight line. The entire process may involve several rounds of communication between the editor, the reviewers, and the original author before an article is ready for publication.

The two most important ethics in the process are maintaining confidentiality and protection of intellectual property. Reviewers and author should not know the names of each other. Only then, the peer review process can be genuinely open and beneficial. None in the process can publicly disclose the information in the article or use the information in a submitted article for personal gain.

6. *Duplicate and partial publication:* It is publishing the same data and same results in more than one publication or journal. This is unethical but may be acceptable in certain cases such as publishing results in a journal to provide research participants with a summary of the results. Partial publication involves publishing parts of your results in different journals. It is specifically unethical for a small, focused study. However, in case of large studies with many variables, this may be acceptable as different publications involve different research questions and different data, and it actually advances the interest of the study.

Important Measures to Make Research More Ethical

1. *Informed consent:* The provision of informed consent also includes the knowledge that the informed participation is voluntary and that participants can withdraw from the study at any time.
2. *Protective research design:* This involves estimating the probability of happening of harmful effects, their severity, and the likely duration of these effects.
3. *Screening:* It is an attempt to select only those individuals for study who show a high tolerance for potential risks.
4. *Pilot studies:* When the potential harms are uncertain, a useful precaution involves a pilot study with follow-up diagnostic interviews to assess the effects and request advice from the participants.
5. *Outside proposal review:* Requesting others to review research proposals is a helpful precaution in minimizing risks.
6. *Professional codes:* Two features of professional codes are important for discussion. First, professional codes have been developed inductively from the wide research experiences of professionals. Second, professional codes place strong emphasis on researchers' responsibility for their research.
7. *Government regulations:* Government regulations such as state and central laws are designed to protect or advance the interests of society and its individuals. Thus, researchers are required to take certain precautions.

Papers, Articles, Workshop, Seminar, Conference, and Symposium

Paper

A paper is defined as an essay or dissertation read at a seminar or published in a journal. It is either a result of research effort or an intellectual exercise. A research paper may entail all the steps of research such as literature survey, data collection and so on. It usually follows the journal's editorial policy. Conceptual papers are not based on data. It presents facts of research in a logical and lucid style. They can be analytical or argumentative. The paper usually requires that the sources are cited in a bibliography given at the end.

Article

The articles are usually informative in nature, which typically address the topic in a general scope as a means of introduction. They may appear in newspaper, magazine, consumer or industry publication.

A research article is written by and for researchers for the purpose of making specific findings known to the scientific community at large. It includes a problem or question, method of research, data, and conclusions. Research article is found exclusively in a peer-reviewed scientific or medical journal, such as Journal of Medical Research.

A research article illustrates the outcome of scientific research with supporting clinical data. A research article could be used as a reference when writing a research paper.

Meeting

A meeting is an assembly or coming together of people whether it is a symposium, workshop, conference, or so. In a very remote sort of a way, all of them convey the same meaning—that is, people coming together for a purpose.

Symposium

It is usually a formal meeting at which specialists deliver short addresses on a topic or on related topics and then answer the questions relating to these topics. It is especially one in which the participants form an audience and make presentations.

Symposium is also defined as a collection of writings on a particular topic, as in a magazine.

Colloquium

It is usually an academic meeting at which specialists deliver addresses on a topic or on related topics and then answer the questions relating to these topics. A colloquium is targeted to a well-educated but not specialized audience.

Conference

A conference is a meeting of people who confer about a topic. It is a meeting where people come for discussion.

It features keynotes and presentations delivered to all attendees, as well as multiple break-out sessions. Attendees expect to receive information about industry trends and developments.

It can be an academic conference (a formal event where researchers present results), a business conference (organized to discuss business-related matters), or a parent–teacher conference (meeting with a child's teacher to discuss grades and school performance), a peace conference (a diplomatic meeting to end conflict), and so on.

Webinars or Web Conferences

Webinars or web conferences are presentations that involve an audio and video component. The audio portion of the event is delivered via phone or over the Internet, so that participants can listen via their computer speakers. The video portion of the event is delivered via the Internet, giving participants a presentation to watch while listening to the instructor.

Seminar

The word seminar is derived from the Latin word *seminarium*, meaning seed plot. It is a formal presentation by one or more experts to a small group of audience. It can be conducted on recurring or regular basis, monthly or even weekly; there is an invited speaker, and audience is much more technically versed or specific in nature.

The motive behind the seminar system is to familiarize the students extensively with vital aspects of their study and also to allow them to interact with examples of practical problems that always occur during study or research work. A seminar is, thus, a form of academic instruction either at an academic institution or offered by a commercial or professional organization.

Seminars focus on some particular subject in which everyone present is requested to actively participate.

Colloquia and seminars both happen in an academic setting. Phenomena such as global warming and climate change, and nuclear power accidents are discussed but from the perspective of a scientist; however, well-educated audience is able to understand it.

Teleseminars are seminars are delivered via a conference call over the telephone and/or over the Internet.

Workshops

Workshops tend to be smaller and more intense than seminars. This format involves students practising their new skills during the event under the watchful eye of an instructor.

Hands-on workshops typically involve participants doing work on a particular issue during the program. The promise is that when they leave, they'll have at least a rough plan or tools in place to address the challenge.

Impact Factor

The **impact factor** of an academic journal is a measure reflecting the average number of citations to recent articles published in the journal. It reflects the relative importance of a journal within its field. The journals with higher impact factors are deemed to be more important than those with lower ones.

The *h*-index is an index that attempts to measure both the productivity and the impact of the published work of a scientist or a scholar.

The *g*-index is like *h*-index; it has an averaged citations count.

The *i*10-index indicates the number of academic publications an author has written that have at least ten citations from others. It was introduced in July 2011 by Google as part of their work on Google Scholar, a search engine dedicated to academic and related papers.

Research – Basic Concepts

1. Research is
   (a) A purposeful, systematic activity
   (b) Conducted for purely academic purposes.
   (c) Conducted to answer questions about practical issues.
   (d) A random, unplanned process of discovery
2. The research is always (*December 2008*)
   (a) Verifying the old knowledge
   (b) Exploring new knowledge
   (c) Filling the gaps between the knowledge
   (d) All of the above
3. All good research aims at
   (a) Betterment of the society
   (b) Developing generalizations, theories, and principles
   (c) Solving routine problems
   (d) None of the above
4. A grand theory
   (a) Explains interrelationships among concepts
   (b) Is highly abstract
   (c) Broad explanation of phenomenon in a discipline
   (d) All of the above
5. The idea that knowledge comes from experience is
   (a) Rationalism
   (b) Deductive reasoning
   (c) Logic
   (d) Empiricism
6. A theory is defined as
   (a) Set of systematically related statements
   (b) Law like generalizations
   (c) Both (a) and (b)
   (d) None of the above
7. Epistemology refers to
   (a) A term specifically used in the social sciences
   (b) A term used to study the types of diseases
   (c) Acceptable level of knowledge in a field of study
   (d) A type of interviewing technique
8. Which of the following is a function of theory?
   (a) Integrating and summarizing current knowledge
   (b) Making predictions
   (c) Explaining phenomena
   (d) All of the above
9. Which of the following term explains the idea that knowledge comes from experience?
   (a) Rationalism (b) Empiricism
   (c) Logic (d) Deduction
10. In every field, research pursuits promote systematic and gradual advancement of knowledge but discoveries are rare because (*December 1997*)
   (a) Result is a continuous critical investigation.

(b) It is not common to be able to think beyond a grooved channel.
(c) Sustained experimental work needed for discovery is not easily forthcoming.
(d) Most people lack the depth of knowledge needed for it.

11. One of the following is not a quality of a researcher? (*December 2005*)
(a) Unison with that of which he is in search
(b) He must be of alert mind
(c) Keenness in enquiry
(d) His assertion to outstrip the evidence

12. 'Metaphysics' means
(a) A branch of Physics
(b) Exploring the nature of ultimate reality
(c) Physics of metals
(d) Physics of weather

13. The quality of research is judged by the (*December 1998*)
(a) Relevance of research
(b) Methodology adopted in conducting the research
(c) Depth of research
(d) Experience of researcher

14. Which of the following is defined as a systematic method of evaluating statistical data based on the results of several independent studies of the same problem?
(a) Factor analysis
(b) Meta-analysis
(c) Systematic analysis
(d) None of the above

15. The quality of a research study is mainly evaluated on the basis of
(a) The place of publication
(b) The manner in which the recommendations are implemented
(c) The rigour with which it was conducted
(d) None of the above

16. Which statement is NOT correct? (*June 1997*)
(a) A researcher is expected to be a well-read person.
(b) One research gives birth to another research.
(c) All researchers contribute to existing knowledge.
(d) A good researcher is a nice person.

17. Which of the following periodical is specifically meant for publishing research work?
(a) Magazine (b) Monographs
(c) Journals (d) Books

18. Which of the following options are the main tasks of research in modern society? (*June 2006*)
(I) To keep pace with the advancement in the knowledge
(II) To discover new things
(III) To write a critique on the earlier writings
(IV) To systematically examine and critically analyze the investigations/sources with objectivity
(a) IV, II, and I (b) I, II, and III
(c) I and III (d) II, III, and IV

19. Which of following description is true in context of defining 'theory'?
(a) An organized body of concepts and principles intended to explain a particular phenomenon
(b) Tentative explanations that new data either support or do not support
(c) Apt to drive further research
(d) None of the above

20. Research can be conducted by a person who (*December 2006*)
(a) Has studied research methodology
(b) Holds a postgraduate degree
(c) Possesses thinking and reasoning ability
(d) Is a hard worker

21. The best quality of a researcher is
(a) Curiosity
(b) Active imagination
(c) Ability
(d) All of the above

22. The result of building up information from pieces of information is known as
(a) An analysis
(b) A synthesis

(c) A synopsis
(d) None of the above

23. The result of setting out a reasoned argument in steps is known as
(a) A comparison (b) A debate
(c) An evaluation (d) An analysis

24. A researcher is generally expected to
(a) Study the existing literature in a field
(b) Generate new principles and theories
(c) Synthezise different ideas
(d) None of the above

25. What do you consider as the main aim of interdisciplinary research? (*June 2006*)
(a) To bring out holistic approach to research
(b) To reduce the emphasis of single subject in research domain
(c) To oversimplify the problem of research
(d) To create a new trend in research methodology

26. One of the essential characteristics of research is
(a) Replicability
(b) Generalizability
(c) Usability
(d) None of the above

27. The depth of any research can be judged by (*June 2006*)
(a) Title of the research
(b) Objectives of the research
(c) Total expenditure on the research
(d) Duration of the research

28. Which of the following statements is true about the theory?
(a) It explains phenomenon in simple manner.
(b) It explains the 'how' and 'why' questions.
(c) It can be a well-developed explanatory system
(d) All of the above

29. Which of the following is a function of theory?
(a) Summarizing the current knowledge
(b) Making predictions
(c) Explaining phenomena
(d) All of the above

30. The feasibility of a research study generally depends upon
(a) Cost factor
(b) Time required to conduct research
(c) Skills set of the researcher
(d) All of the above

31. An empiricist believes that
(a) Natural science methods should not be applied to social science research.
(b) Social science methods cannot be applied in natural sciences.
(c) Knowledge is acquired through our sensory perceptions.
(d) None of the above

32. The experimental study is based on
(a) Law of single variable
(b) Manipulation
(c) Both (a) and (b)
(d) None of the above

33. What is the position held by a positivist as far as acquiring knowledge is concerned?
(a) A general positive attitude towards research.
(b) Scientific research should be based on value-free, empirical observations.
(c) Exact knowledge can be acquired from the society.
(d) None of the above

34. The approach which is based on the assumption that social phenomena can be explained by observing cause and effect is
(a) Positivism
(b) Interpretivism
(c) Qualitative
(d) None of the above

35. An ontological question is usually about
(a) Diagnose of a medical problem
(b) Study of things outside ourselves, an external reality
(c) Use of questionnaires or interviews in project
(d) Acceptable level of knowledge

36. Which of the following is not a characteristic of a researcher?
    (a) Industrious and persistent
    (b) Specialist rather than a generalist
    (c) Objective
    (d) Not versatile in his interest and even in his native abiiities

37. An important practical issue to consider while designing a research project is
    (a) An interesting theoretical perspective
    (b) Add to knowledge of researcher only
    (c) Availability of time and other resources
    (d) None of the above

Types of Research

38. Research can be classified as *(December 2006)*
    (a) Basic, applied, and action research
    (b) Quantitative and qualitative research
    (c) Philosophical, historical, survey, and experimental research
    (d) All of the above

39. The two main approaches of a research are
    (a) Data collection and data analysis
    (b) Surveys and questionnaires
    (c) Sampling and data collection
    (d) Qualitative and quantitative

40. A researcher designs an experiment to test how variables interact to influence how well children learn spelling words. In this case, the main purpose of the study is
    (a) Explanation (b) Description
    (c) Influence (d) Prediction

41. Qualitative research is
    (a) Without any specific purpose
    (b) Primarily concerned with in-depth exploration of phenomena
    (c) Deals with the collection and analysis of numerical data
    (d) None of the above

42. Match List A with List B and choose the correct answer from the code given below. *(December 2004)*

	List I		List II
A	Historical method	I	Past events
B	Survey method	II	Vision
C	Philosophical method	III	Present events
D	Experimental method	IV	Future action

Codes:
(a) A-I, B-III, C-II, D-IV
(b) A-I, B-II, C-III, D-IV
(c) A-I, B-II, C-III, D-IV
(d) A-II, B-III, C-I, D-IV

43. Which of the following research specifically requires objectivity to discover facts and causes from the data gathered for the purpose?
    (a) Quantitative research
    (b) Fundamental research
    (c) Qualitative research
    (d) Action research

44. Which of the following is classified in the category of developmental research? *(June 2009)*
    (a) Philosophical research
    (b) Action research
    (c) Descriptive research
    (d) All of the Above

45. In psychology and education, experimental research is also termed as
    (a) S–R (stimulus–response) research
    (b) Analytical research
    (c) Historical research
    (d) Post Facto research

46. Which of the following is NOT the method of research? *(December 2006)*
    (a) Observation (b) Historical
    (c) Survey (d) Philosophical

47. Fundamental research is usually carried out in
    (a) Classroom
    (b) Field setting
    (c) Laboratory conditions
    (d) Social setting

48. The research that applies the laws at the time of field study to draw more and more clear ideas about the problem is (*December 2008*)
   (a) Applied research
   (b) Action research
   (c) Experimental research
   (d) None of the above

49. The research which is exploring new facts through the study of the past is called
   (a) Philosophical research
   (b) Historical research
   (c) Mythological research
   (d) Content analysis

50. The scientific method can be used
   (a) Only in physical sciences such as physics and chemistry
   (b) Only in social sciences
   (c) Both in physical and social sciences
   (d) None of the above

51. Action research is (*December 2009*)
   (a) An applied research
   (b) A research carried out to solve immediate problems
   (c) A longitudinal research
   (d) Simulative research

52. In the method of naturalistic observation, there will be
   (a) Haphazard behaviour as it naturally occurs
   (b) Setting up of controlled experiments by which they uncover causal elements in behaviour
   (c) Set out to actively observe subjects in their natural environments
   (d) Interview subjects at different stages of life

53. Which of the following is a form of explanatory research in which the researcher develops a theoretical model and empirically tests the model to determine how well the model fits the data?
   (a) Causal modelling
   (b) Predictive research
   (c) Descriptive research
   (d) Exploratory research

54. Match the following two lists

List I		List II	
A	Experimental	I	Criticism
B	Historical	II	Control
C	Case study	III	Interpretative
D	Ethnography	IV	Intensive
		V	Intuitive

Codes:
   (a) A-II, B-III, C-IV, D-V
   (b) A-I, B-II, C-V, D-III
   (c) A-III, B-I, C-IV, D-V
   (d) A-II, B-I, C-IV, D-III

55. One of the aims of scientific method in research is to (*June 2006*)
   (a) Improve data interpretation
   (b) Eliminate spurious relations
   (c) Confirm triangulation
   (d) Introduce new variables

56. The term 'phenomenology' is associated with the process of (*December 2010*)
   (a) Qualitative research
   (b) Analysis of variance
   (c) Correlational study
   (d) Probability sampling

57. Which research approach is the most appropriate to establish a relationship that is causal in nature?
   (a) Causal-comparative
   (b) Experimental
   (c) Correlational
   (d) Descriptive

58. The important pre-requisites of a research in sciences, social sciences, and humanities are (*December 2005*)
   (a) Laboratory skills, records, supervisor, and topic
   (b) Supervisor, topic, critical analysis, and patience
   (c) Archives, supervisor, topic, and flexibility in thinking
   (d) Topic, supervisor, good temperament, and preconceived notions

59. Books and records are the primary sources of data in
(a) Historical research
(b) Participatory research
(c) Clinical research
(d) Laboratory research

60. The type of research that tests hypothesis and theories in order to explain how and why a phenomenon operates as it does is
(a) Descriptive research
(b) Predictive research
(c) Explanatory research
(d) None of the above

61. Fundamental research reflects the ability to (*June 2007*)
(a) Synthesize new ideas
(b) Expound new principles
(c) Evaluate the existing material concerning research
(d) Study the existing literature regarding various topics

62. The classification of studies into exploratory, descriptive, analytical, or predictive research is based on:
(a) Logic (b) Outcome
(c) Process (d) Purpose

63. The strongest evidence for causality comes from which of the following research methods?
(a) Experimental
(b) Causal–comparative
(c) Correlational
(d) None of the above

64. One of the limitations of the case study is that
(a) There are few subjects for which it is applicable.
(b) There are no control groups
(c) It requires a large and expensive sample size
(d) None of the above

65. Which of the following is research method is termed as controlled observation?
(a) Historical research
(b) Philosophical research
(c) Field experimentation
(d) All of the above

66. Fieldwork-based research is classified as (*June 2008*)
(a) Empirical (b) Historical
(c) Experimental (d) Biographical

67. Which of the following is not a longitudinal design?
(a) Panel
(b) Cross-sectional
(c) Trend
(d) Both (a) and (c) are longitudinal designs

68. When a researcher starts with the dependent variable and moves backwards, it is called
(a) Predictive research
(b) Retrospective research
(c) Exploratory research
(d) Descriptive research

69. The study in which investigators attempt to trace an effect is known as (*June 2007*)
(a) Survey research
(b) 'Ex post facto' research
(c) Historical research
(d) Summative research

70. The essence of the experimental method is
(a) Correct calculation of Karl Pearson's Coefficient of correlation
(b) Obtaining direct reports from subjects about their subjective experience
(c) Careful measurement and record keeping
(d) Using control to identify cause-and-effect connections

71. Which research paradigm is based on the pragmatic view of reality?
(a) Quantitative research
(b) Qualitative research
(c) Mixed research
(d) None of the above

72. Which research paradigm is not much concerned about generalizing its findings?
(a) Quantitative research
(b) Qualitative research

(c) Mixed research
(d) None of the above

73. Which of the following best describes quantitative research?
(a) The collection of non-numerical data
(b) An attempt to confirm the researcher's hypothesis
(c) Research that is exploratory
(d) Research that attempts to generate a new theory

74. All of the following are common characteristics of experimental research
(a) It relies primarily on the collection of numerical data.
(b) It can produce important knowledge about cause and effect.
(c) It uses the deductive scientific method.
(d) All of the above

75. Which type of research is likely to provide the strongest evidence about the existence of cause-and-effect relationships?
(a) Non-experimental research
(b) Experimental research
(c) Historical research
(d) None of the above

76. Research in which the researcher uses the qualitative paradigm for one phase and the quantitative paradigm for another phase is known as
(a) Action research
(b) Basic research
(c) Quantitative research
(d) Mixed method research

77. Research that is done to understand an event from the past is known as
(a) Experimental research
(b) Historical research
(c) Replication
(d) Archival research

78. The type of research typically conducted by teachers, counsellors, and other professionals to answer questions they have and to specifically help them solve local problems?
(a) Action research
(b) Basic research
(c) Predictive research
(d) Longitudinal research

79. Which form of reasoning is the process of drawing a specific conclusion from a set of premises?
(a) Rationalism
(b) Deductive reasoning
(c) Inductive reasoning
(d) Probabilistic

80. Research that is done to examine the findings of someone else using the 'same variables but different people' is which of the following?
(a) Exploration (b) Hypothesis
(c) Replication (d) Empiricism

81. Which scientific method is a top-down or confirmatory approach?
(a) Deductive method
(b) Inductive method
(c) Hypothesis method
(d) Pattern method

82. Which scientific method is a bottom-up or generative approach to research?
(a) Deductive method
(b) Inductive method
(c) Hypothesis method
(d) Pattern method

83. The method of drawing conclusions based on the observation of each and every instance of a population is called
(a) Scientific Method
(b) Deductive Method
(c) Inductive Method
(d) Dialectic Method

84. Which of the following is NOT a characteristic of a good theory or explanation?
(a) It is parsimonious.
(b) It is testable.
(c) It is general enough to apply to different situations.
(d) All of the above

85. Which scientific method follows these steps: (i) observation/data, (ii) patterns, and (iii) theory?
(a) Inductive
(b) Deductive
(c) Top-down
(d) None of the above

86. Which scientific method is a top-down or confirmatory approach?
(a) Deductive method
(b) Inductive method
(c) Hypothesis method
(d) Pattern method

87. Which of the following terms can be associated with research in social sciences?
(a) Causal research
(b) Empirical research
(c) Correlational research
(d) All of the above

88. Which scientific method focuses on testing hypothesis developed from theories?
(a) Deductive method
(b) Inductive method
(c) Hypothesis method
(d) Pattern method

89. Which scientific method focuses on generating new hypothesis and theories?
(a) Deductive method
(b) Inductive method
(c) Both (a) and (b)
(d) None of the above

90. Which research method is most appropriate if a researcher is looking for a causal relationship?
(a) Experimental method
(b) Case study
(c) Correlational study
(d) Naturalistic observation

91. A field experiment is one that takes place in
(a) Real world
(b) Laboratory
(c) Both in real world and laboratory
(d) Naturalistic environment

92. Characteristics of the scientific method necessarily include
(a) Lab experiments only
(b) Controlled observation
(c) Analysis formulation
(d) All of the above

93. A correlational study determines
(a) The relationship between independent and dependent variable.
(b) Impact of the observer on the participant
(c) Cause-and-effect relationship
(d) The relationship between two events

94. The qualitative research is usually
(a) Deductive in nature
(b) Inductive in nature
(c) Deductive or inductive in nature
(d) None of the above

95. Which of the following types of research is associated with theory generating?
(a) Inductive research
(b) Deductive research
(c) Both inductive and deductive
(d) None of the above

96. Which of the following types of research is associated with theory testing?
(a) Inductive research
(b) Deductive research
(c) Both inductive and deductive
(d) None of the above

97. A non-government organization conducted a study in a Gram Panchayat to see the impacts of campaign approach on enrolment and retention of rural elementary school children. This is an example of
(a) Descriptive Study
(b) Field Experiment
(c) Ex-post facto research
(d) Historical Research

98. The classification of studies into exploratory, descriptive, analytical, or predictive research is based on
(a) Logic of the research
(b) Outcome of the research
(c) Process of the research
(d) Purpose of the research

99. Research study that take place over a long period of time is termed as
(a) Cross-sectional research
(b) Longitudinal research
(c) Research methodology
(d) None of the above

100. The main difference between longitudinal and cross-sectional researches is in terms of
(a) Frequency of data collection
(b) Primary versus Secondary
(c) The qualification of researcher
(d) None of the above

101. Defining hypothesis is a useful way of approaching research because
(a) It will impress the reader.
(b) It allows the development of testable propositions.
(c) It allows for the development of indisputable proof to be established in research findings.
(d) It looks suitably scientific.

102. The government of India conducts census after every 10 years. The method of research used in this process is
(a) Case study (b) Developmental
(c) Survey (d) Experimental

103. A nine-year-old is taller than seven-year-old ones. It is an example of
(a) Vertical studies
(b) Cross-sectional studies
(c) Experimental studies
(d) Case studies

104. The main difference between basic research and applied research lies in
(a) basic process
(b) sample size
(c) utility
(d) All of the above

105. Which type of method can be used in order to create a real-world laboratory?
(a) Correlational coefficients
(b) Field experiment
(c) Case study
(d) Random assignment

106. In a research study to learn the impact of the Internet surfing on exam performance, it was found that as the number of hours spent on the Internet surfing increases, the exam performance deteriorates. This study is an example of
(a) Experimental method
(b) Correlational research
(c) Case study
(d) None of the above

107. The term associated with the theory and the method of interpretation of human action in social sciences is *(December 2006)*
(a) Theology (b) Hermeneutics
(c) Ontology (d) None of the above

108. A researcher spent several years observing social behaviour of people in their native habitat. The research method used here is
(a) Case study
(b) Experimental method
(c) Correlational study
(d) Naturalistic observation

109. In a study of two variables, when one variable goes up as another goes down in value is known as a
(a) Positive correlation
(b) No correlation
(c) Negative correlation
(d) Fluctuating correlation

Research Process

110. In the context of survey research, the following steps are taken in a certain order
(I) Sampling
(II) Inference
(III) Data analysis
(IV) Data collection
(a) (II), (III), (I), (IV)
(b) (I), (IV), (III), (II)
(c) (III), (II), (IV), (I)
(d) (IV), (I), (II), (III)

111. A research problem is feasible only when *(June 2007)*

(a) It has utility and relevance.
(b) It is researchable.
(c) It is new and adds something to the knowledge.
(d) All of the above

112. The first step of research is (*December 2006*)
(a) Selecting a problem
(b) Searching a problem
(c) Finding a problem
(d) Identifying a problem

113. Which of the following statements is true? (*December 2004*)
(a) In research, objectives can be worded in question form.
(b) In research, objectives can be worded in statement form.
(c) Objectives are to be stated in Chapter I of the thesis.
(d) All of the above

114. A good hypothesis should be
(a) Precise, specific, and consistent with most known facts
(b) Formulated in such a way that it can be tested by the data
(c) Of limited scope and should not have global significance
(d) All of the above

115. Hypothesis cannot be stated in
(a) Null and question form terms
(b) Declarative terms
(c) General terms
(d) None of the above

116. Which of the following statements is correct? (*December 2006*)
(a) Objectives of research are stated in first chapter of the thesis.
(b) Researcher must possess analytical ability.
(c) Variability is the source of problem.
(d) All of the above

117. *sine qua non* (essential elements) of good research is (*June 2000*)
(a) A well-formulated hypothesis
(b) A good research supervisor
(c) Adequate library
(d) A well-formulated problem

118. The accuracy of the research process depends upon the
(a) Unbiased attitude of researchers
(b) The sample size
(c) The research method adopted
(d) All of the above

119. Who is regarded as the father of scientific social surveys?
(a) Best
(b) Booth
(c) Darwin
(d) None of the above

120. A research plan
(a) Should be detailed
(b) Should be given to others for review and comments
(c) Sets out the rationale for a research study
(d) All of the above

121. Sources of researchable problems can include
(a) Researchers' own experiences as educators
(b) Practical issues that require solutions
(c) Theory and past research
(d) All of the above

122. The introduction section of the research plan
(a) Gives an overview of prior relevant studies
(b) Contains a statement of the purpose of the study
(c) Concludes with a statement of the research questions
(d) All of the above

123. Which of the following is not the requirement of a hypothesis? (*June 1998*)
(a) Be based on facts
(b) Be conceivable
(c) Contradict the knowledge of nature
(d) Allow consequences to be deduced from it

124. The objective of a research can be written (*December 1998*)

(a) Only in question form
(b) Only in statement form
(c) Both question and statement forms
(d) In hypothetical form

125. For a proposition to be true, it should have the following characteristics EXCEPT *(June 1998)*
(a) It must be objective.
(b) It must be in tune with accepted beliefs.
(c) It must be consistent.
(d) It must be testable.

126. A statement that predicts the cause-and-effect relationship between variables is known as the
(a) Null hypothesis
(b) Experimental hypothesis
(c) Independent variable
(d) Dependent variable

127. To be confident that a cause-and-effect relationship exists, it is necessary to
(a) Engage in naturalistic observation
(b) Develop a positive correlation
(c) Perform a controlled experiment
(d) Test for a negative correlation

128. Which of the following statement is correct? *(December 2005)*
(a) Objectives should be pin-pointed
(b) Objectives can be written in statement or question forms
(c) Another word for problem is variable
(d) All of the above

129. The first question that a researcher interested in the application of statistical techniques to his problem has to ask is
(a) Whether the data could be quantified
(b) Whether appropriate statistical techniques are available
(c) Whether analysis of data would be possible
(d) Whether worthwhile inferences could be drawn

130. Which one of the following is a data collection method?
(a) The opinion (b) Positivism
(c) The case study (d) The interview

131. In which of the following techniques of data collection, several participants, including facilitator, emphazise on questioning on a specific and defined topic, and interaction within the group and the joint construction of meaning?
(a) Case study
(b) Focus group
(c) Ethnography
(d) None of the above

132. The process not needed in experimental research is
(a) Observation
(b) Manipulation and replication
(c) Controlling
(d) Reference collection

133. The process not needed in experimental researches is *(December 2009)*
(a) Observation (b) Manipulation
(c) Controlling (d) Content analysis

134. Which type of study will be preferred by a researcher to estimate the degree of relationship between the level of education and achievement motivation?
(a) Naturalistic (b) Inventory
(c) Correlational (d) Experimental

135. Which scale is the simplest form of measurement?
(a) Nominal (b) Ordinal
(c) Interval (d) Ratio

136. A satisfactory statistical quantitative method should not possess one of the following qualities: *(December 2005)*
(a) Appropriateness (b) Measurability
(c) Comparability (d) Flexibility

137. Which of the following is the correct order of Steven's four levels of measurement?
(a) Ordinal, nominal, ratio, and interval
(b) Nominal, ordinal, interval, and ratio
(c) Interval, nominal, ordinal, and ratio
(d) Ratio, interval, nominal, and ordinal

138. We use factor analysis (*June 2009*)
(a) To know the relationship between two variables
(b) To test the hypothesis
(c) To know the difference between two variables
(d) To know the difference among many variables

139. Match List I (interviews) with List II (meaning) and select the correct answer from the code given below: (*June 2006*)

List I (Interviews)		List II (Meanings)	
A	Structured interviews	I	Greater flexibility approach
B	Unstructured interviews	II	Attention on questions to be answered
C	Focused interviews	III	Individual life experience
D	Clinical interviews	IV	Pre-determined question
		V	Non-directive

Codes:
(a) A-IV, B-I, C-II, D-III
(b) A-II, B-IV, C-I, D-III
(c) A-V, B-II, C-IV, D-I
(d) A-I, B-III, C-V, D-IV

140. Which of the following correlational values is the strongest?
(a) +0.10 (b) –0.95
(c) +0.90 (d) –1.00

141. The correlation between intelligence test scores and grades is
(a) Positive (b) Negative
(c) Perfect (d) No correlation

142. Which of the following figures reflect the highest value of Karl Pearson's coefficient of correlation?
(a) +0.22 (b) +0.91
(c) –0.49 (d) –0.92

143. A widely used format developed by Resins Likert is used for asking questions about
(a) Attitude
(b) Personality
(c) Morale
(d) None of the above

Research Characteristics

144. Objectivity in research implies (*June 2000*)
(a) Exact judgement of truth
(b) Findings consistent with realty
(c) Inter-researcher agreement
(d) Methodological sophistication

145. How can the objectivity of research be enhanced? (*June 2009*)
(a) Through its impartiality
(b) Through its reliability
(c) Through its validity
(d) All of the above

146. The extent to which an instrument measures a characteristic that cannot be directly observed but is assumed to exist
(a) Face validity
(b) Construct validity
(c) Criterion validity
(d) Content validity

147. Field study is related to
(a) Real-life situations
(b) Experimental situations
(c) Laboratory situations
(d) None of the above

148. The verification that the method of measurement actually measures what it is expected to measure is called as
(a) Content validity
(b) Face validity

(c) Construct validity
(d) Criterion validity

149. The extent to which the results of a research study apply to situations beyond the study itself; the extent to which conclusions can be generalized is
(a) External validity
(b) Internal validity
(c) Situation validity
(d) None of the above

150. The extent to which the design and data of a research study allows the researcher to draw accurate conclusions about cause-and-effect and other relationships within the data is
(a) External validity
(b) Internal validity
(c) Situation validity
(d) None of the above

151. The validity and reliability of a research will be at stake when
(a) The incident was reported after a long period of time from that of its occurrence
(b) The author who is a source of information is biased and incompetent
(c) The researcher is not competent enough to draw logical conclusions
(d) All of the above

152. The term used to describe when a research measures the variable or dimension it is supposed to measure is
(a) Validity
(b) Reliability
(c) Dependability
(d) Suitability

153. Which of the following is not a characteristic of research? (*December 2004*)
(a) Research is systematic
(b) Research is not a process
(c) Research is problem oriented
(d) Research is not passive

154. Which of the following terms is closely related to generalization of outcome of research?
(a) External validity
(b) Inference
(c) Both (a) and (b)
(d) None of the above

155. A research instrument giving inconsistent results has
(a) Low validity (b) High validity
(c) Low reliability (d) High reliability

156. Authenticity of research finding is its
(a) Originality (b) Validity
(c) Objectivity (d) All of the above

157. Manipulation is always a part of (*December 2009*)
(a) Historical research
(b) Fundamental research
(c) Descriptive research
(d) Experimental research

Formulation of Hypothesis

158. An educated guess about what is controlling some behaviour is called
(a) Experimental control
(b) A hypothesis
(c) An experimental variable
(d) A theory

159. It is best to use the method of working multiple hypothesis
(a) During the final stages of research
(b) While planning your research study
(c) At the time of publishing the results
(d) None of the above

160. The basis on which the assumptions are formulated is (*June 2009*)
(a) Cultural background of the country
(b) Universities
(c) Specific characteristics of the castes
(d) All of the above

161. Hypothesis cannot be stated in
(a) Declarative terms
(b) Null hypothesis and question form terms
(c) General terms
(d) Directional terms

162. What type of research would be least likely to include a research hypothesis?
    (a) Intervention research
    (b) Associational research
    (c) Descriptive research
    (d) None of the above

163. A null hypothesis is (*December 2009*)
    (a) When there is no difference between the variables
    (b) The same as research hypothesis
    (c) Subjective in nature
    (d) When there is difference between the variables

164. Research hypothesis are
    (a) A review of current research
    (b) Statements of predicted relationships between variables
    (c) Stated such that they can be confirmed or refuted
    (d) Both (b) and (c)

165. Which of the following best describes the development process for a research question?
    (a) A broad question is made more specific as terms are more clearly defined.
    (b) A broad question is made more specific in order to be more significant.
    (c) A specific question is broadened as terms are more clearly defined.
    (d) A specific question is broadened in order to be more significant.

166. Good research questions are
    (a) Clear, significant, and ethical
    (b) Feasible, clear, significant, and ethical.
    (c) Feasible, clear, significant, and include a hypothesis.
    (d) Feasible, clear, and ethical.

167. The essential characteristic of a researchable question is
    (a) Question seems interesting to answer
    (b) Possibility of data collection that can be collected in an attempt to answer a question
    (c) Possibility of commercialization
    (d) A significant positive change in society

168. A good hypothesis should be
    (a) Formulated in such a way that it can be tested by the data
    (b) Precise, specific, and consistent with most known facts
    (c) Of limited scope and should not have global significance
    (d) All of the above

169. A hypothesis can be described as
    (a) Just as a hunch
    (b) A wild guess
    (c) A type of statement made by researchers when they are attempting to get funding for their research.
    (d) A prediction of some sort regarding the possible outcomes of a study.

170. Formulation of hypothesis may not be required in
    (a) Survey method
    (b) Historical studies
    (c) Experimental studies
    (d) Normative studies

171. An operational definition is
    (a) No relation to the underlying concept
    (b) An abstract, theoretical definition of a concept
    (c) In terms of specific, empirical measures
    (d) None of the above

172. What is the purpose of the conclusion in a research report?
    (a) It explains how concepts were operationally defined and measured.
    (b) It summarizes the key findings in relation to the research questions.
    (c) It contains a useful review of the relevant literature.
    (d) It outlines the methodological procedures that were employed.

173. Which of the following is an advantage of stating hypothesis?
    (a) It forces the researcher to think more deeply and specifically about the possible outcomes of a study.
    (b) It simplifies the study.

(c) It clarifies definitions.
(d) It reduces researcher bias.

174. Which of the following is an example of a directional hypothesis?
(a) There will be a difference between the students' reading levels.
(b) There will be a difference between lecture and group instruction.
(c) Group instruction is more effective than lecture in the elementary classroom.
(d) There will be an increase in learning.

175. Formulation of hypothesis may not be necessary in
(a) Survey studies
(b) Fact finding historical research
(c) Experimental studies
(d) None of the above

176. Which of the following is true in context of a hypothesis?
(a) It is a tentative proposition
(b) The validity of hypothesis is unknown
(c) It must be generalizable
(d) All of the above

177. In mixed methods research, quantitative and qualitative findings should be
(a) Listed in the order of importance
(b) Contained in separate sections
(c) Integrated
(d) Shown fully in appendices

178. To test null hypothesis, a researcher uses *(June 2007)*
(a) *t*-test
(b) ANOVA
(c) χ^2 (Chi-square test)
(d) Factorial analysis

Research Variables

179. Attributes of objects, events, or things which can be measured are called
(a) Qualitative measure
(b) Data
(c) Variables
(d) None of the above

180. A statistical technique used for large number of variables to establish whether there is a tendency of groups to be interrelated is *(December 2006)*
(a) Simple correlation
(b) Multiple correlation
(c) Factor analysis
(d) None of the above

181. When studying an active independent variable, an intervention/treatment given to group of participants is called
(a) Experimental group
(b) Control group
(c) Both (a) and (b)
(d) Neither (a) or (b)

182. Which of the following can best be described as a categorical variable?
(a) Age
(b) Annual income
(c) Grade point average
(d) Religion

183. The experimental studies are based on *(December 2007)*
(a) The manipulation of the variables
(b) Conceptual parameters
(c) Replication of research
(d) Survey of literature

184. A manipulated independent variable is called?
(a) Extraneous variable
(b) Intervening variable
(c) Subject variable
(d) Active variable

185. Control groups and experimental groups are exactly the same except for
(a) Dependent variable
(b) Independent variable
(c) Extraneous variables
(d) Replication variables

186. The behaviour that is measured during an experiment is known as the
(a) Confounding variable
(b) Independent variable

(c) Dependent variable
(d) Control variable

187. This type of longitudinal research studies the same individuals over an extended period of time.
(a) Trend study (b) Panel study
(c) Both (a) and (b) (d) Neither (a) nor (b)

188. An example of a categorical variable is
(a) Teacher's hair colour
(b) Average time it takes a teacher to grade an essay
(c) Distance a teacher has to travel from the office to her class.
(d) None of the above

189. Which variables are those that a researcher chooses to study in order to assess their possible effects on one or more other variables?
(a) Dependent
(b) Independent
(c) Extraneous
(d) None of the above

190. A condition or characteristic that can take on different values or categories is called
(a) A constant
(b) A variable
(c) A cause-and-effect relationship
(d) A descriptive relationship

191. Which of the following includes examples of quantitative variables?
(a) Age, temperature, income, and height
(b) Grade point average, anxiety level, and reading performance
(c) Gender, religion, and ethnic group
(d) Both (a) and (b)

192. In research, something that does not 'vary' is called a
(a) Variable
(b) Method
(c) Constant
(d) None of the above

193. We use factorial analysis (*June 2009*)
(a) To know the relationship between two variables
(b) To test the hypothesis
(c) To know the difference between two variables
(d) To know the difference among many variables

194. A variable that is presumed to cause a change in another variable is called
(a) A categorical variable
(b) A dependent variable
(c) An independent variable
(d) An intervening variable

195. Which of the following independent variables cannot be manipulated in a research study?
(a) Gender
(b) Ethnicity
(c) Intelligence and other traits
(d) None of the above can be manipulated in a research study

196. In an experimental design, the dependent variable is the one
(a) In which any changes are observed
(b) Which is not manipulated
(c) Both (a) and (b)
(d) None of the above

197. This variable depends upon what is done to it by the independent variable.
(a) Extraneous (b) Dependent
(c) Manipulated (d) All of the above

198. Extraneous variables are essentially
(a) Independent variables
(b) Dependent variables
(c) Independent or dependent
(d) Neither independent nor dependent

199. These variables are those that are created by the researcher and are typically found in experimental studies.
(a) Extraneous
(b) Manipulated
(c) Dependent
(d) None of the above

200. An experiment is performed to test the effects of sleep deprivation on rote memory. In this experiment, the dependent variable is

(a) Number of hours subjects go without sleep.
(b) Rote memory scores
(c) Number of subjects deprived of sleep in the experimental group.
(d) Correlation between hours of sleep and fatigue.

201. The variable manipulated by the researcher in an experiment is called the
(a) Response variable
(b) Independent variable
(c) Dependent variable
(d) Extraneous variable.

202. Which of the following would not be an appropriate synonym for the dependent variable?
(a) Outcome variable
(b) Response variable
(c) Effected variable
(d) Experimental variable

203. An example of quantitative variable is the
(a) Date of birth
(b) Highest educational qualification
(c) Time taken to complete a task
(d) Postal code

Sampling

204. Which of the following variables cannot be expressed in quantitative terms? *(December 2010)*
(a) Socio-economic status
(b) Marital status
(c) Numerical aptitude
(d) Professional attitude

205. The process of selecting a subset of a population for a survey is known as
(a) Survey research
(b) Representation
(c) Triangulation
(d) Sampling

206. Researchers ultimately want the answer to a research question to pertain to the
(a) Sample
(b) Accessible population
(c) Target population
(d) World

207. Generalized conclusion on the basis of a sample is technically known as *(December 2007)*
(a) Data analysis and interpretation
(b) Parameter inference
(c) Statistical inference
(d) All of the above

208. An investigator wants to study the vocational aspirations of visually challenged children in a wide geographical area. He should select his sample by using
(a) Simple random sampling
(b) Stratified sampling
(c) Purposive sampling
(d) Convenient sampling

209. The type of sampling where each person in population has equal chance of being selected is
(a) Probability sampling
(b) Non-probability sampling
(c) Judgement sampling
(d) None of the above

210. Here, some people have greater chance of being elected than other members of the population. It is
(a) Probability sampling
(b) Non-probability sampling
(c) Quota sampling
(d) None of the above

211. When a research problem is related to heterogeneous population, the most suitable method is *(December 2008)*
(a) Cluster sampling
(b) Stratified sampling
(c) Convenient sampling
(d) Lottery method

212. A representative sample is essential in
(a) Survey method
(b) Experimental method
(c) Case study
(d) Clinical method

213. Which one is called as non-probability sampling?
(a) Cluster sampling
(b) Quota sampling
(c) Systematic sampling
(d) Stratified random sampling

214. While the statistical measure based upon entire population is called parameter, the measure based upon a sample is known as
(a) Sample parameter
(b) Inference
(c) Statistic
(d) None of the above

215. A researcher selects a probability sample of 100 out of the total population. It is called
(a) A quota sample
(b) A simple random sample
(c) A stratified random sample
(d) A systematic sample

216. A researcher divides the school students on the basis of gender and then by using the random digit table, he selects some of them from each group. This is
(a) Stratified sampling
(b) Stratified random sampling
(c) Representative sampling
(d) None of the above

217. To ensure accuracy of a research, the sample should be
(a) Taken randomly
(b) Fixed by quota
(c) Representative of the population
(d) Purposive

218. A researcher can keep the sample size low if population is
(a) Heterogeneous (b) Inaccessible
(c) Homogeneous (d) All of the above

219. Which technique is generally followed when the population is finite?
(a) Area sampling technique
(b) Purposive sampling technique
(c) Systematic sampling technique
(d) None of the above

220. Cluster sampling is used when
(a) Population is scattered and sample size is to be kept large
(b) Population is heterogeneous
(c) Long survey is needed
(d) Both (a) and (c)

221. A researcher divides his population into certain groups and fixes the size of the sample from each group. It is called
(a) Stratified sample
(b) Quota sample
(c) Cluster sample
(d) All of the above

222. Which of the following is a non-probability sample?
(a) Quota sample
(b) Simple random sample
(c) Purposive sample
(d) Both (a) and (c)

223. If a researcher selected five schools at random and then interviewed each of the teachers in those five schools, the researcher used
(a) Simple random sampling
(b) Stratified random sampling
(c) Cluster random sampling
(d) None of the above

224. Which of the following terms best describes data that were originally collected at an earlier time by a different person for a different purpose?
(a) Primary data
(b) Secondary data
(c) Experimental data
(d) None of the above

225. Which of these is not a method of data collection?
(a) Questionnaires (b) Interviews
(c) Observations (d) Experiments

226. Which of the following is an example of a random sampling method?
(a) Systematic sampling
(b) Convenience sampling
(c) Purposive sampling
(d) None of the above

227. Which of the following is not an example of a random sampling method?
(a) Systematic sampling
(b) Stratified random sampling
(c) Simple random sampling
(d) All of the above

228. Which of the following is an example of a random sampling method?
(a) Two-stage random sampling
(b) Systematic sampling
(c) Convenience sampling
(d) Purposive sampling

229. Which of the following is an example of a non-random sampling method?
(a) Convenience sampling
(b) Stratified random sampling
(c) Simple random
(d) Cluster random

230. The purpose of stratified random sampling is to make certain that
(a) Every member of the population has an equal chance of being selected
(b) For proportionate representation from different categories
(c) Prompt response from respondents
(d) None of the above

231. A correlation coefficient is best characterized as
(a) A measure of the extent of the relationship between two variables.
(a) An index of the causal direction between an independent and dependent variable.
(c) An indication of the likelihood that an experimental finding will be replicated by others.
(d) A measure of the likelihood that observed differences may be attributed to chance.

232. Responding to a substance like a sugar pill as if it were a drug is called
(a) The placebo effect.
(b) An extraneous factor
(c) Variability
(d) None of the above

233. What is a cross-sectional design?
(a) A study of one specific segment of customers
(b) The research design that is free from any personal bias
(c) The collection of data from more than respondent in the same time period
(d) A comparison of two or more variables over a long period of time

Research Ethics/Misc

234. Research is not considered ethical if it *(December 2011)*
(a) Tries to prove a particular point
(b) Does not ensure privacy and anonymity of the respondent
(c) Does not investigate the data scientifically
(d) Is not of a very high standard

235. Ethical transgression is
(a) Following ethical principles
(b) Defying ethical principles
(c) Defining ethics
(d) None of the above

236. Which of the following ideas is not associated with the stance of situation ethics?
(a) Anything goes
(b) The end justifies the means
(c) No choice
(d) All of the above

237. Which of the following is a form of harm that might be suffered by research participants?

(a) Physical injury
(b) Stress and anxiety
(c) Impaired development
(d) All of the above

238. The main purpose of personal data being kept confidential in research studies is
(a) To hide from participants what has been written about them
(b) Apprehension of harm identification or disclosure of personal information
(c) For access by government authorities
(d) To know more about private lives of participants

239. Which method is most directly associated with lack of informed consent?
(a) In-depth interviewing
(b) Content analysis
(c) Covert observation
(d) Case study

240. Which of the following is a form of harm that might be suffered by research participants?
(a) Psychological distress
(b) Physical injury
(c) Loss of self-esteem
(d) All of the above

241. The act of publishing the same data and results in more than one journal or publication refers to which of the following professional issues
(a) Partial publication
(b) Duplicate publication
(c) Full publication
(d) None of the above

242. Why is it important that personal data about research participants be kept within secure, confidential records?
(a) To observe principle of research ethics
(b) To sell the data at a later stage to recover the cost of research
(c) To keep secrecy from other researchers
(d) None of the above

243. The importance of measurement in quantitative research is that
(a) It allows us to delineate fine differences between people or cases
(b) It provides a consistent device or yardstick
(c) It allows for precise estimates of the degree of relationship between concepts
(d) All of the above

244. One of the preoccupations of quantitative researchers is with generalization, which is a sign of
(a) External validity
(b) Internal reliability
(c) External reliability
(d) Internal validity

245. Population generalizability refers to
(a) Conclusions researchers make about a random sample
(b) Conclusions researchers make about information uncovered in research study
(c) The degree to which a sample represents the population of interest
(d) The degree to which results of a study can be extended to other settings or conditions

246. The degree to which results of a study can be extended to other settings or conditions describes
(a) Population generalizability
(b) Conclusions researchers make about a random sample
(c) Conclusions researchers make about information uncovered in research study
(d) Ecological generalizability

247. The research design is
(a) A common method adopted by all researchers to carry out research
(b) The final choice between using qualitative or quantitative methods
(c) Presentation of research findings
(d) A framework for every stage of the data collection and its analysis

248. Recognizing our own values in pursuit of research is essential because
(a) It allows us to eliminate them.
(b) It allows us to be honest with ourselves about what may influence our research.
(c) At least we know what we can ignore
(d) It enables us to persuade others of our values.

249. As the value of one variable is increasing, the value of second variable is also increasing, then the correlation coefficient will be
(a) Positive
(b) Negative
(c) Zero
(d) None of the above

250. Which form of reasoning is the process of drawing a specific conclusion from a set of premises?
(a) Rationalism
(b) Deductive reasoning
(c) Inductive reasoning
(d) Probabilistic

251. It is important that academics produce research that can be widely used and valued by academic community around the world. This is termed as
(a) Research impact
(b) Citation impact
(c) Ethics impact
(d) None of the above

252. The problem of researcher seeing only what they expect to see is called
(a) Researcher bias
(b) Experimenter effect
(c) Leniency effect
(d) Halo effect

253. Which of the following is most appropriate to impart training for SPSS, a software package used for statistical analysis?
(a) Seminar (b) Conference
(c) Workshop (d) Paper

254. Which of the following is essentially an academic meeting?
(a) Colloquium
(b) Conference
(c) Symposium
(d) None of the above

255. In which of the following, it is required to cite sources in a bibliography at the end?
(a) Conference (b) Colloquium
(c) Seminar (d) Paper

256. Which of the following is most likely to make use of the Internet?
(a) Web Conference
(b) Seminar
(c) Symposium
(d) None of the above

257. Which of the following is published in a journal?
(a) Article
(b) Paper
(c) Both (a) and (b)
(d) None of the above

258. A researcher conducted three experiments with 100 subjects each following uniform design instead of one experiment with 300 subjects. This is known as
(a) Replication (b) Manipulation
(c) Observation (d) Validation

Answer Keys

Basic Concepts

1. (a) 2. (d) 3. (b) 4. (c) 5. (d)
6. (c) 7. (c) 8. (b) 9. (b) 10. (d)
11. (a) 12. (b) 13. (b) 14. (b) 15. (c)
16. (d) 17. (c) 18. (a) 19. (a) 20. (c)
21. (d) 22. (b) 23. (c) 24. (b) 25. (a)
26. (b) 27. (b) 28. (d) 29. (d) 30. (d)
31. (c) 32. (c) 33. (b) 34. (a) 35. (b)
36. (d) 37. (c)

Types of Research

38. (d) 39. (d) 40. (a) 41. (b) 42. (a)
43. (a) 44. (d) 45. (a) 46. (a) 47. (c)
48. (a) 49. (b) 50. (c) 51. (b) 52. (c)

53. (a) 54. (d) 55. (b) 56. (a) 57. (b)
58. (b) 59. (a) 60. (c) 61. (b) 62. (d)
63. (a) 64. (b) 65. (c) 66. (a) 67. (b)
68. (b) 69. (b) 70. (d) 71. (c) 72. (b)
73. (d) 74. (d) 75. (b) 76. (d) 77. (b)
78. (a) 79. (b) 80. (c) 81. (a) 82. (b)
83. (b) 84. (d) 85. (a) 86. (a) 87. (b)
88. (a) 89. (b) 90. (a) 91. (a) 92. (b)
93. (d) 94. (b) 95. (a) 96. (b) 97. (b)
98. (d) 99. (b) 100. (a) 101. (b) 102. (c)
103. (b) 104. (c) 105. (b) 106. (b) 107. (b)
108. (d) 109. (c)

Research Process

110. (b) 111. (d) 112. (c) 113. (b) 114. (d)
115. (c) 116. (d) 117. (a) 118. (d) 119. (b)
120. (d) 121. (d) 122. (d) 123. (c) 124. (b)
125. (b) 126. (b) 127. (c) 128. (a) 129. (a)
130. (d) 131. (b) 132. (d) 133. (d) 134. (c)
135. (a) 136. (d) 137. (b) 138. (d) 139. (a)
140. (d) 141. (a) 142. (d) 143. (a)

Research Characteristics

144. (b) 145. (d) 146. (b) 147. (a) 148. (a)
149. (a) 150. (b) 151. (d) 152. (a) 153. (b)
154. (c) 155. (c) 156. (d) 157. (d)

Formulation of Hypothesis

158. (b) 159. (b) 160. (d) 161. (c) 162. (c)
163. (a) 164. (d) 165. (a) 166. (b) 167. (b)
168. (a) 169. (d) 170. (b) 171. (c) 172. (b)
173. (a) 174. (c) 175. (b) 176. (d) 177. (c)
178. (c)

Research Variables

179. (c) 180. (c) 181. (a) 182. (d) 183. (a)
184. (d) 185. (b) 186. (c) 187. (c) 188. (a)
189. (b) 190. (b) 191. (d) 192. (c) 193. (d)
194. (c) 195. (d) 196. (c) 197. (b) 198. (a)
199. (b) 200. (b) 201. (b) 202. (d) 203. (c)

Sampling

204. (d) 205. (d) 206. (c) 207. (c) 208. (b)
209. (a) 210. (b) 211. (b) 212. (a) 213. (b)
214. (c) 215. (b) 216. (b) 217. (c) 218. (c)
219. (c) 220. (d) 221. (b) 222. (d) 223. (c)
224. (b) 225. (d) 226. (a) 227. (a) 228. (a)
229. (a) 230. (b) 231. (a) 232. (a) 233. (c)

Research Ethics/Misc

234. (b) 235. (b) 236. (d) 237. (d) 238. (b)
239. (c) 240. (d) 241. (b) 242. (a) 243. (d)
244. (a) 245. (c) 246. (d) 247. (d) 248. (b)
249. (a) 250. (c) 251. (b) 252. (a) 253. (c)
254. (a) 255. (d) 256. (a) 257. (c) 258. (d)

3

Reading Comprehension

Comprehension Passage

According to Wren and Martin, comprehension exercise can be defined as a passage, upon which questions are set to test the students' ability to understand the content of the given text and to infer information and meanings from it. To put it in simple terms, reading comprehension is the act of understanding what you are reading.

It mainly requires two inputs from the reader, that is, vocabulary knowledge and text comprehension. In order to understand a text, the reader must be able to comprehend the vocabulary used in a piece of writing. A comprehension test requires specific reading skills, ability to grasp the main ideas from the passage, linking them, inferring and drawing conclusions based on the proper understanding of a passage. Further, on the basis of understanding developed, a candidate is supposed to answer the questions given at the end of the passage.

For candidates, even though they have ample choice among questions, reading comprehension (RC) is a must attempt as it does not require any specific study; some practice can help in attempting questions with confidence. Usually, each RC is followed by five to six questions in UGC Paper I Exam.

Solution Guidelines

Here are some techniques that can be used to make comprehension easier:

1. *Identification of key ideas:* There are always certain key sentences that determine the flow of the ideas in a passage. To make comprehension simpler, these sentences are supposed to be identified during the first reading of the passage. The paragraph/s should be read quickly to get a general idea. It should be read again, a little slowly, so as to know the details. The key ideas can also be underlined.
2. *Summarize the paragraph:* While reading the passage, develop a habit of mentally summarizing each paragraph and keep linking them as you proceed. This helps in understanding the overall idea of the passage, and as a result, the candidate may find it easier to answer the questions. Some readers may prefer to study the questions again and turn to the relevant portions of the passage later.
3. *Determine sentence links:* Usually, the sentences within a passage are directly or subtly linked. Here, practice helps a lot in identifying such links, failing which the major ideas could be missed out.

4. *Ask questions:* Whenever in doubt, the reader should always pose questions to oneself. For example, the following questions are asked: Why has the author mentioned this example? What is the purpose of the second paragraph? This kind of reflection helps in developing a deeper perspective about the main ideas.

Main Question Categories

Comprehension passage questions can be classified into the following categories:

Main Theme or Central Idea

These type of questions are based on the passage as a whole; they are typical in nature as they reflect upon the author's motive to write the passage.

These questions test up to what extent the reader is able to understand the paragraph.

Solution Approach

Usually, the answers to such type of questions lie in the introductory or the concluding paragraphs. A quick reading of the first or last or both the paragraphs is helpful.

Examples

1. Which of the following alternatives best narrate the passage?
2. Which of the following sentences reflect upon the main idea of the passage?

Paying attention to single words and phrases helps to understand the relationship between the ideas within a paragraph.

1. *Cause and effect words*—as a result, therefore
2. *Time words*—meanwhile, before
3. *Contrast words*—in contrast, conversely
4. *Addition words*—also, in addition
5. *Emphasis words*—more important, remember

Author's Opinion and Attitude

Such questions are based on the author's view point and the answers are not explicitly mentioned. They have to be derived from the key sentences used by the author to express his thoughts and opinions. The questions are so framed as to test one's ability to judge the author's attitude or his knowledge on the subject by analysing the content, style, and phraseology used in the passage. The candidate needs to be empathetic with the author while attempting such questions. Such a set of questions examine the candidate on many fronts.

Solution Approach

One can look for the writing style and the sentences that determine the tone used by the author, which serve as a clue to the answers. If a particular part of the passage is in question form, then try to understand the reasoning used by the author to explain that part.

Alternatively, the reader could focus on the adverbs and adjectives used by the author to describe something. These words are indicative of the mood and intensity of his thoughts.

Examples

1. What is the author's tone in the second paragraph?
2. According to the author, what can be a logical solution to the issue at hand?
3. Which of the following ideas is most likely to agree with?

Explicit or Direct Information

These are direct questions based on the names, dates, figures, data, facts, or opinions mentioned in the passage and are easily noticed during the first read itself. The answer options may also be direct sentences picked up from the passage. Scan the passage to spot the keywords for specific details.

Some specific detail questions are negative and are singled by the words such as not, except, most, and least. If you cannot find the correct answer for negative-specific details, eliminate the choices given and choose the one that remains as the correct response. It also makes a lot of sense to read the questions first as it gives an idea of what to look for while reading the passage. Questions based on explicit information should be verified by reading specific parts of the passage that contain the answer.

Examples

1. Which one of the following options is true according to the passage?
2. Which one of the following options is no longer a motivation for youth today?

Implicit Information

The answers to these types of questions are not explicitly stated but are implied/inferred/deducted from the passage.

These questions test both our comprehension skills and our ability to relate to author's opinion.

Solution Approach

Understanding the overall idea of the passage helps to answer these questions. While reading the passage, the candidate should try to understand the arguments presented by the author.

Examples

1. According to the passage, which of the following options can be inferred?
2. With which of the following arguments is the author most likely to agree?

Language Expression Questions

These questions are based on specific words or phrases mentioned in the passage; sometimes, there may be synonym- or antonym-based questions, which test our understanding of a word in the context of the passage. The aim of the reader should be to understand the contextual meanings of the words with respect to the passage rather than sticking to their dictionary meanings.

These questions test our ability to move simple, known words and their literal meanings to understand the language usage and the subject matter of the passage. They test our reasoning skills and the ability to relate to the author's ideas while reading the passage.

Solution Approach

A thorough second reading of that part of the passage from where the phrase has been picked up help us in correctly understanding the context of the passage.

Examples

1. In the context of paragraph, what does, as good as it gets, mean?
2. From the options, find the word closest in meaning to the given word as it has been used in the passage.

Organization of the Passage

These questions are based on the structure of the passage and the literary techniques used by the author in expressing his arguments. Questions dealing with strengthening and weakening arguments fall in this category.

These questions test our ability to analyse the structure of the passage and identify sentences and paragraphs as assumptions, arguments, solutions, conclusions, etc.

Solution Approach

A lot of reading can help a reader to acquire literary skills.

Examples

1. Which of these options best represent the structure of the passage?
2. What is the fundamental premise on which the author has based his analysis?
3. What is the assumption made by the author when he says democracy will never fall?

Analogous Argument

A candidate is required to choose the option that is similar or conforms to reasoning along the same lines as the arguments mentioned in the passage.

This question tests our comprehension and ability to illustrate the analysis formed in our mind based on our reading of the passage. It also tests our capacity to associate two separate illustrations that follow a single line of reasoning.

Solution Approach

The key to answering such questions is understanding the base arguments before having a look at the options and then eliminating the options by comparing them with compactness of the line of reasoning provided in the question stem.

Examples

1. Which of the following illustrations best represent the arguments mentioned in the second paragraph?
2. The phrase, to err is human, is applicable in which one of the situations listed below?

Specimen Passage I

The sugar maple is a hard maple tree. It can grow as tall as 100 feet and as wide as 4 feet. The sugar maple is commercially valued for its sap, which is used in making maple syrup. Two northeastern states, Vermont and New York, rank as major producers of maple syrup. In Canada, Quebec's annual syrup production surpasses 2.5 million gallons. To make pure maple syrup, holes are made in the trunk of the tree at the end of winter or in early spring. The water-like sap seeps through the holes and runs through a plastic spout that is put into the hole. Afterwards, the collected sap is transferred into tubes that are hooked up to a tank kept in the sugar house. Then, the sap goes through the boiling process. Boiling enhances flavour and adds colour to the sap. Once the sugar content of the sap is about 65%–66%, the sap is ready to be strained and marketed. Maple syrup found in supermarkets, however, is usually not pure and has other additives. The colour of pure maple may range from golden honey to light brown. Between 35 to 50 gallons of sap is needed to produce 1 gallon of maple syrup. Also, popular for the strength and finish of its wood, the sugar maple tree has been put to use in furniture, interior woodwork, flooring, and crates.

Questions

1. What is the main purpose of the passage?
   (a) To examine the economic viability of making maple syrup
   (b) To list a number of major producers of maple syrup
   (c) To provide information on preparation of maple syrup
   (d) To discuss the use of maple wood in furniture and other products

   This is a general inference question. Most of the passage explains the technique used for making maple syrup. Hence, the correct answer is (c).

2. For which of the following words does the author provide a definition?
   (a) The sugar maple
   (b) A tank
   (c) Additives
   (d) Furniture

   This specific detailed question tests our understanding of a definition. Only sugar maple is defined in the first line of the passage. Other words have just been mentioned in the passage. Hence, the correct answer is (a).

3. According to the passage, which of the following periods is ideal for sapping?
   (a) End of winter or in early spring
   (b) Beginning of winter or in early spring
   (c) End of winter or late spring
   (d) Throughout the year

   This is again a specific question. Based on the information in the passage, sapping takes place at the end of winter and in early spring. Hence, the correct answer is (a).

4. All of the following is true about boiling except
   (a) It enhances the colour
   (b) It improves the flavour
   (c) It increases the sugar content
   (d) It reduces the shelf-life of the syrup

   This specific detail question is negative; we can eliminate choices that are not applicable. Hence, the correct answer is (d).

5. What can be inferred about the production of maple syrup?
   (a) It is simple, but time-consuming
   (b) It is labour-intensive

(c) Its processing demands complex equipments
(d) The higher the volume, the less predictable is the quality

This question tests our inference ability. The answer to the question is not directly stated in the passage.

Hence, the correct option is (a). The production technique is quite straightforward, but it takes time. The producers have to depend on the natural flow of sap.

6. The phrase, to be strained, could best be replaced by
(a) To be tried
(b) To be purified
(c) To be filtered
(d) To be solidified

This is a language/expression question. Hence, the correct option is (c).

Specimen Passage II

Now, India's children have to receive at least eight years of education. The gnawing question is whether it will remain on paper or it will become a reality. One hardly needs a reminder that this right is different from others enshrined in the constitution, that the beneficiary—a six-year-old child—cannot demand it, nor can he or she fight a legal battle when the right is denied or violated. In all cases, it is the adult society that must act on behalf of the child. In another peculiarity, where a child's right to education (RTE) is denied, no compensation offered later can be adequate or relevant. This is so because childhood does not last long. If a legal battle fought on behalf of a child is eventually won, it may be of little use to a boy or girl because the opportunity missed at school during childhood cannot serve the same purpose later in life. This may be painfully true for girls because our society permits them only a short childhood, if at all. The RTE has become a crucial point of law in India's history when the ghastly practice of female infanticide has resurfaced in the form of foeticide. This is 'symptomatic of deeper turmoil' in society, which is compounding the traditional obstacles to girls' education. Tenacious prejudice against intellectual potential of girls runs across our cultural diversity and the system of education has not been able to address it.

Questions

1. With reference to the passage, consider the following statements:
(A) When children are denied education, adult society does not act on behalf of them.
(B) Right to education as a law cannot be enforced in the country.

Which of the statements given above is/are incorrect?
(a) (A) only
(b) Both (A) and (B)
(c) (B) only
(d) Either (A) or (B)

Explanation

(A) is incorrect. The enactment of RTE itself shows that adult society may act on behalf of children to ensure their education.

(B) is incorrect as the passage does not indicate that the right cannot be enforced in the country but rather mentions the shortfalls and difficulties which may occur in the act of enforcing the law.

Both A and B are incorrect statements. Hence, (b) is the right answer.

2. According to the passage, what could be traditional obstacles to the education of girls?
(A) Inability of parents to fight a legal battle when the right to education is denied to their children
(B) The traditional way of thinking about girls' role in society
(C) The prejudice against the intellectual potential of girls
(D) Improper system of education

Select the correct answer from the codes given below:
(a) (A) and (B) only
(b) (A), (C), and (D) only
(c) (B), (C), and (D) only
(d) (A), (B), (C), and (D)

Explanation

(A) is not mentioned in the passage anywhere. (B), (C), and (D) are mentioned as traditional obstacles at the end of paragraph. Hence, (c) is the correct answer.

3. Where a child's right to education is denied, no compensation offered later can be adequate or relevant is reflected through the fact that
(a) Childhood is short
(b) Opportunity to learn missed during specific childhood period may not be compensated later in life
(c) Both (a) and (b)
(d) None of the above

Explanation

Explicitly mentioned in the passage. Both (a) and (b) apply. Hence, the correct option is (c).

4. The expression, symptomatic of deeper turmoil, reflects
(a) Lack of proper girl's education in society
(b) Enactment of right to education
(c) Prevailing political environment in the country
(d) None of the above

Explanation

There is mention of girl's education in the second part of the sentence. Hence, the correct option is (a).

5. Which one of the following statement conveys the key message of the passage?
(a) India has declared that education is compulsory for its children
(b) Adult society is not keen on implementing the right to education
(c) The right to education, particularly for a girl child, needs to be safeguarded
(d) None of the above

Explanation

(a) is incorrect as there is no mention of education being made compulsory. (b) is incorrect, as there is no mention of adults not being keen in implementing the right to education; it simply mentions that it is the adult society which must act on behalf of the child. The author is specifically concerned about girl child's education. Hence, the correct option is (c).

6. Which one of the following statements convey the inference of the passage?
(a) The society has a tenacious prejudice against the intellectual potential of girls
(b) Adults cannot be relied upon to fight on behalf of children for their right to education
(c) The legal fight to get education for children is protracted and prohibitive
(d) There is no sufficient substitute for education received in childhood

Explanation

The option (a) is directly mentioned in the passage and hence is not an inference. (c) has the word 'prohibitive' that cannot be inferred from the passage. (d) is supported by 'if a legal battle ... if at all' which points out the opportunity cost of a missed childhood, particularly for girls. Hence, the correct option is (d).

Specimen Passage III

The concept of creative society refers to the phase of development of a society in which a large number of potential contradictions become articulate and active. This is most evident when oppressed social groups get politically mobilized and demand their rights. The upsurge of peasants and tribes, the movements for regional autonomy and self-determination, the environmental movements, and the women's movements in the developing countries are signs of emergence of creative society in contemporary times.

The forms of social movements and their intensity may vary from country to country and place to place within a country, but the very presence of movements for social transformations in various spheres of a society indicates the emergence of a creative society in a country.

Questions

1. What does the author imply by creative society?
   (A) A society where diverse art forms and literary writings seek incentive
   (B) A society where social inequalities are accepted as a norm
   (C) A society where a large number of contradictions are articulate.
   (D) A society where the exploited and the oppressed groups grow conscious of their human rights and upliftment.

   Select the correct answer using the codes given below:

   (a) (A), (B), and (C) (b) (D) only
   (c) (C) and (D) (d) (B) and (D)

   Explanation

   (A) takes the literal meaning of creative society, which is not appropriate in the given context of the paragraph. (B) contradicts the passage as there is talk of oppressed social groups get politically mobilized and … rights. (C) is mentioned in the first sentence where potential contradictions become 'articulate'. (D) is mentioned in 'this is most evident … creative society in temporary times'. Hence, the correct option is (c).

2. According to the passage, what are the manifestations of social movements?
   (A) Being aggressive
   (B) Involvement of the whole society
   (C) Quest for social equality and individual freedom
   (D) None of the above

   Select the correct answer using the codes given below.

   (a) (A) and (B) only
   (b) (C) only
   (c) (B) and (C)
   (d) (A), (B), and (C)

   Explanation

   Social movements do not need to be aggressive. Hence, (A) is in incorrect. (B) contradicts the passage since social groups get politically mobilized and demand their rights internally and not externally. The entire passage supports (C). Hence, the correct option is (b).

3. With reference to the passage, consider the following statements:
   (A) To be a creative society, it is essential to have a variety of social movements
   (B) To be a creative society, it is imperative to have potential contradictions and conflicts

   Which of the statements given above is/are correct?

   (a) (A) only
   (b) (B) only
   (c) Both (A) and (B)
   (d) Neither (A) nor (B)

   Explanation

   (A) and (B) invert the argument in the passage. Paragraph does not mention having a variety of social movements as a necessary condition to be creative in the entire paragraph, so (A) is incorrect. For (B), just the presence of potential contradictions and conflicts is itself not a necessary condition for social movement, but their 'articulation and (being) active' is also required. So (B) is also incorrect. So answer should be neither (A) nor (B). Hence, the correct option is (d).

4. Which of the following are examples of different social movements?
   (A) Upsurge of peasants and tribes
   (B) The movements for regional autonomy and self-determination
   (C) The environmental movements
   (D) The women's movements

   Codes:

   (a) (A), (B), and (C)
   (b) (B), (C), and (D)
   (c) (A), (B), and (D)
   (d) All of the above

Explanation

Explicitly mentioned in the third line of the passage. Hence, the correct option is (d).

5. Which of following can be described as the most appropriate aim/s for various social movements?
   (A) To achieve the status of a creative society
   (B) To achieve rights
   (C) Social transformation

   Codes:
   (a) (A) and (B)
   (b) (B) and (C)
   (c) (A) and (C)
   (d) Only (C)

   Explanation

   (A) is not the explicit aim of any movement. (B) is mentioned in the second line of the paragraph. Social transformation has been mentioned in the last line of the paragraph. Hence, the correct option is (b).

6. Which of following can be considered as the most suitable title for the passage?
   (a) Creative society and social movements
   (b) Social movement as the prerequisite of a creative society
   (c) Social movements
   (d) None of the above

   Explanation

   Option (a) seems to be the most appropriate option. Option (b) is not the answer; it is nowhere mentioned in the paragraph that social movement is prerequisite of a creative society. Yes, social movements indicate the emergence of creative society. Option (c) is also not the answer as the paragraph is mainly about creative society.

Specimen Passage IV

A country under foreign domination seeks escape from the present in dreams of a vanished age and finds consolation in visions about the greatness of past generations. That is a foolish and dangerous pastime in which many of us indulge.

An equally questionable practice for us in India is to imagine that we are still spiritually great though we have come down in the world in other respects. Spiritual or any other such greatness cannot be founded on lack of freedom and opportunity or on starvation and misery. Many western writers have encouraged the notion that Indians are other–worldly. I suppose that the poor and unfortunate in every country become other-worldly to some extent, unless they become revolutionaries, for this world is evidently not meant for them. So also the subject people.

As a man grows to maturity, he is not entirely engrossed in or satisfied with the external objective world. He also seeks some inner meaning and some psychological and physical satisfaction. Therefore, along with people and civilizations, they mature and grow as adult. Every civilization and every person exhibits these parallel streams of external and internal lives. Where they meet or keep close to each other, there is an equilibrium and stability; when they diverge, conflicts and crises arise that torture the mind and the spirit.

Questions

1. The passage mentions that 'this world is evidently not meant for them'. It refers to people who
   (a) Seek freedom from foreign domination
   (b) Live in starvation and misery
   (c) Become revolutionaries
   (d) All of the above

   Explanation

   The pronoun, them, refers to the poor and unfortunate in every country. Hence, the correct option is (b).

2. Which of the following can be taken as the most valid assumption of the paragraph?
   (a) A country under foreign domination cannot indulge in spiritual pursuit
   (b) Poverty is an impediment in suitable pursuit
   (c) Both (a) and (b)
   (d) None of the above

Explanation

(a) is contradictory to the passage. (b) is an assumption implied from 'Spiritual or any other … starvation and misery'. Hence the correct option is (b).

3. Which of the following can be considered as the main theme of the paragraph?
   (a) The state of mind of oppressed people
   (b) Starvation and misery
   (c) The growth of civilization
   (d) Body, mind, and spirit of people in general

Explanation

(b), (c), and (d) are just references in the passage. Hence, the correct option is (a).

4. According to the passage, the torture of the mind and spirit is caused
   (a) By the ruthlessness of foreign domination
   (b) By the desire to escape from foreign domination and find consolation in visions of past greatness
   (c) By the desire to become either other-worldly or revolutionary
   (d) Due to lack of equilibrium between an external life and an internal life

Explanation

(d) is the correct option. It is mentioned in the last line of the third paragraph—'this has been rephrased in the specimen passage Needs to be rephrased here also. Where they meet or keep … and crises arise that torture the mind and spirit'.

5. As a person grows in maturity, she/he seeks satisfaction in
   (a) Psychological satisfaction only
   (b) Physical satisfaction only
   (c) Both psychological and physical satisfaction
   (d) Neither (a) or (b)

Explanation

It is mentioned explicitly in the last paragraph.

6. Many western writers have encouraged the notion that Indians are other-worldly. What can be the possible meaning of 'other-worldly' in the context of entire passage?
   (a) They are still basking in past greatness and are not in touch with the realities of the present-day world
   (b) Poor, unfortunate, and subject people
   (c) Both (a) and (b)
   (d) Neither (a) nor (b)

Explanation

The term 'other-worldly' has been explicitly used in second paragraph for poor people. In common parlance, it means that poor people are cut off from main stream society. Hence, the correct option is (b).

SPECIMEN PASSAGE V

Ecosystems provide people with a variety of goods and services, food, clean water, clean air, flood control, soil stabilization, pollination, climate regulation, spiritual fulfilment, and aesthetic enjoyment, to name just a few. Most of these benefits are either irreplaceable or the technology necessary to replace them is prohibitively expensive. For example, potable freshwater can be provided by desalinating sea water, but only at great cost.

The rapidly expanding human population has greatly modified the earth's ecosystem to meet their increased requirements of some of the goods and services, particularly food, freshwater, timber, fibre, and fuel. These modifications have contributed substantially to human well-being and economic development. The benefits have not been equally distributed. Some people have actually been harmed by these changes. Moreover, short-term increases in some ecosystems' goods and services have come at the cost of long-term degradation of others. For example, efforts to increase the production of food and fibre have decreased the ability of some ecosystems to provide clean water, regulate flooding, and support biodiversity.

Questions

1. Expanding human population has an adverse effect on
   (A) Spiritual fulfilment
   (B) Availability of potable freshwater
   (C) Employment
   (D) Biodiversity

   Which of the statements given above are correct?
   (a) (A), (B), and (C)
   (b) (B), (C), and (D)
   (c) (B) and (D)
   (d) All of the above

   Explanation

   The last sentence indicates an adverse effect on availability of clean water and biodiversity. Hence, the correct option is (c).

2. The passage mentions that 'some people have actually been harmed by these changes'. It indicates towards
   (a) Inequitable distribution of benefits
   (b) Decrease in the ability of some ecosystems to provide clean water, regulate flooding, and support biodiversity
   (c) Both (a) and (b)
   (d) Neither (a) nor (b)

   Explanation

   Both (a) and (b) indicate inequitable distribution of benefits and resources. Hence, the correct option is (c).

3. Which of the following is correct in the context of the passage?
   (a) The rapid expansion of population has adversely affected some people
   (b) Sufficient efforts have not been made to increase the production of food and fibre
   (c) In short term, some people may be harmed, but in long term, everyone will benefit from modifications in earth's ecosystem
   (d) None of the above

   Explanation

   Only (a) is implied, (b) is irrelevant, and discussion in the passage does not support (c). Hence, the correct option is (a).

4. With reference to the passage, consider the following statements:
   (A) It is imperative to modify the earth's ecosystem for the well-being of mankind
   (B) Technology can never replace all the goods and services provided by ecosystems

   Which of the following statements given above is/are correct?
   (a) Only (A)
   (b) Only (B)
   (c) Both (A) and (B)
   (d) Neither (A) nor (B)

   Explanation

   (A) is incorrect since the passage is almost about positive and negative aspects of the modification of our ecosystem. (B) is mentioned clearly in the passage. Hence, the correct option is (b).

5. According to the passage, which of the following can be taken as the main reason for modification of earth's ecosystem?
   (a) Technology
   (b) Increasing population
   (c) Lack of an integrated approach
   (d) All of the above

   Explanation

   Though both technology and lack of integrated approach may be applicable, both are long drawn inferences. Among the available choices, increasing population is clearly mentioned. Hence, the correct option is (b).

6. Which of the following can be considered as the most suitable title for the passage?
   (a) Modification of our ecosystem
   (b) Our natural resources
   (c) Harmful effect of increase in human population
   (d) Human interference in our ecosystem

   Explanation

   Clearly, (b), (c), and (d) may be relevant to the discussion in the passage, but it is mainly about causes for and effect of changes in our ecosystem. Hence, the correct option is (a).

Practice Passages

Practice Passage I (*June 2001*)

Read the following passage and answer question numbers 1–6.

The great Acharyas have said that everything discovered has a great goal; surrender yourself to that goal and act towards it by drawing your inspiration from that goal whereby you will get a new column of energy. Do not allow this energy to be dissipated in the futile memory of past regrets or failures, or excitement of the present, and bring that entire energy focused into activity, that is, the highest creative action in the world outside, whereby the individual who is till now considered the most inefficient finds his way to the highest achievement and success.

This can be said very easily in a second. In order to train our mind to this attitude, considerable training is needed because we have already trained our mind wrongly to such an extent that we have become perfect in imperfections. Not knowing the art of action, we have mastered artists in doing wrong things; the totality of activity will bring the country to a wrong end indeed.

If each one is given a car to achieve an ideal socialistic pattern and nobody knows driving, but starts driving, what would be the condition on road? Everybody has equal rights on the public road. Then, each car will necessarily dash against the other and there is bound to be a jumble.

There seems to be a very apt pattern of life that we are heading to. Every one of us is a vehicle. We know how to go forward. The point intellect is very powerful and everybody is driving but nobody knows how to control the mental energy and direct it properly or guide it to the proper destination.

Questions

1. What is the effect of wrong training of our mind?
   (a) Becoming perfect in all aspects of life
   (b) Becoming master artists
   (c) Taking the country to wrong destination
   (d) Carrying on activities without knowing how to control mental energies
2. The source of energy according to the author is
   (a) Highest creative action
   (b) Proper training of mind
   (c) Inspiration from past events
   (d) Stimulation obtained from a set goal
3. The author's main focus in the passage is
   (a) Finding out a worthy goal in life
   (b) Regulation of energy in proper channels
   (c) Struggle for equal rights
   (d) Car accidents due to lack of driving skills
4. The country may perish because of
   (a) Failures in past acts
   (b) Wrong deeds performed without proper knowledge
   (c) Complete surrender to anyone goal
   (d) Directing mental energy to the right destination
5. The author considers everyone to be a vehicle that knows how to go forward
   (a) Without driving energy
   (b) With least consideration for others
   (c) With no sense of direction
   (d) With no control on speed
6. Which of the following can be considered as the most suitable title for the passage?
   (a) Human mind versus car
   (b) Channelization of mental energy
   (c) Mental energy
   (d) Life without a goal

Practice Passage II

Read the following passage and answer question numbers 7–12.

Each day at Shantiniketan, the school starts with Saraswati Vandana. When painting competitions are held in the school, images of Hindu gods and goddesses are the most common. Sanskrit is the favourite subject of many students. Nothing is new about it except that the 1,200 odd students studying in the Hindu-run school are Muslims. In 1983, when Ranchodbhai Kiri started Shantiniketan in the all-Muslim Juhapura area of Ahmedabad in Gujarat, only 20% of the students were Muslims, but when riots involving the Muslims of Juhapura and the Hindus of nearby Jivraj Park, Vejalpur, affected the locality, Hindus started migrating. Today, all the students are Muslims and the school is an unparalleled example of harmony. In 2002, when a section of inflamed Muslims wanted the school closed, the parents of the students stood like a wall behind it. Shantiniketan's principal said, 'We never thought of moving the school out of the area because of the love and affection of the local Muslims. Indeed, they value the high standard of education which we have set'. Such is the reputation of the school that some of the local Muslim strongmen accused of involvement in communal riots are willing to protect the school during riots. The parents of Shantiniketan's students believe that it is the best school when it comes to quality of teaching. A large number of students have gone for both graduation and post-graduation studies. Significantly, the only Muslim teacher in the 40-member teaching staff, Husena Mansuri, teaches Sanskrit. In fact, she is so happy with the school that she recently declined the Principalship of another Muslim-run school. Some of the students' entries in a recent inter-school painting competition were truly moving. One drew a picture of Bharat Mata with a mosque and temple, while another portrayed a boy tying rakhi to his sister. Truly, Shantiniketan is a beacon of hope that despite the provocations from both communities, Hindus and Muslims, can live side by side with mutual respect.

Questions

7. How does Shantiniketan school start the day?
   (a) Prayer
   (b) National anthem
   (c) Saraswati vandana
   (d) Puja
8. Write the subject which is most preferred by the students.
   (a) English (b) Hindi
   (c) Sanskrit (d) Gujarati
9. Who protects the school during the riot times?
   (a) Hindus (b) Local Muslims
   (c) Politicians (d) Christians
10. Who is the teacher of Sanskrit?
   (a) Manisha Vakil
   (b) Ranchodbhai Kiri
   (c) Husena Mansuri
   (d) Husena Khatoon
11. What is the hope despite the communal riots?
   (a) Hindus and Muslims can live side by side
   (b) Only Hindus can live
   (c) Hindus and Muslims cannot live side by side
   (d) Only Muslims can live
12. Which of the following can be considered as the most suitable title of the passage?
   (a) Communal harmony—a live example
   (b) Rioting and communal harmony
   (c) Role of Sanskrit in maintaining communal harmony
   (d) Odds in communal harmony

Practice Passage III

Read the following passage and answer question numbers 13–18.

Some religious leaders have taught that man is made up of a body and a soul, but they have been silent about intellect. Their followers try to feed the body to earth and save the soul from perdition after death—but they neglected the claims of the mind. Bread for the body and virtue for the soul; these are regarded as indispensable requisites of human welfare. Nothing is said about knowledge and education. Thus, Jesus Christ spoke of feeding the hungry, healing the sick, and converting the sinners, but he never taught the duty of teaching an ignorant and increasing scientific knowledge. He himself was not a well-educated man, and intellectual pursuits were beyond his horizon. Gautama Buddha also laid stress on morality, meditation, and asceticism, but he did not attach great importance to history, science, art, or literature. St. Ambrose deprecated scientific studies and wrote, 'To discuss the nature and position of the earth does not help us in our hope for life to come'. St. Basil said very frankly and foolishly, 'It is not a matter of interest to us whether the earth is a sphere, a cylinder or a disc'. Thomas Carlyle also followed the Christian tradition and declared that he honoured only two kinds of men and no third, that is, the manual labourer and the religious teacher. He forgot the scientist, the scholar, and the artist. The cynics of Greece despised education at last.

Questions

13. What have the religious teachers taught in the past?
    (a) That man is made up of body only
    (b) That man is made up of soul only
    (c) That man is made up of bubbles
    (d) That man is made up of body and soul together
14. According to the passage, what is food for the soul?
    (a) Bread (b) Virtue
    (c) Vice (d) Education
15. The following philosophers are mentioned in the paragraph:
    (A) Jesus
    (B) Gautama Buddha
    (C) St Ambrose
    (D) Thomas Carlyle
    (E) St Basil

    Which of the following depicts the correct order as they appear in the paragraph.

    (a) (A), (B), (C), (D), and (E)
    (b) (A), (C), (D), (E), and (B)
    (c) (A), (B), (C), (E), and (D)
    (d) (B), (A), (C), (D), and (E)
16. Intellectual pursuits have been neglected because
    (A) They are unnecessary and superfluous
    (B) They make people dwarf
    (C) They lead people to hell

    (a) Only (A) is correct
    (b) Only (B) is correct
    (c) Only (C) is correct
    (d) Only (A) and (B) are correct
17. The style of the passage is
    (a) Narrative (b) Expository
    (c) Critical (d) Analytical
18. Which of the following can be considered as the most suitable title for the passage?
    (a) Neglect of human intellect
    (b) Ignorance of spiritual leaders
    (c) Claims of human mind
    (d) Body and soul

Practice Passage IV

(December 2000)

Read the following passage and answer question numbers 19–24.

The previous decade has reversed the presumptions about development, and more than anything else, it has made it difficult to decide what is in store during the next decade. However, there are some things about which one can make claims with some confidence.

Firstly, education, health, and productive employment are the decisive factors for development and impartiality. We believe that all these are the results of rapid economic development, and to achieve these ends, development only can generate resources. In the present form, it will be best to view it as a better reason than as a result of development. In fact, in every case of successful development, the evaluation of previous reforms in education, technical skills, health, existence, and productive tasks are included.

Secondly, technical ability is a vital resource and explains the high ratio of development in production and trade as compared to ratios of development in more traditional factors such as natural resources or capital formation. There is no requisite capability in research. In fact, industrial momentum in a factory or farm is more important than the presence of a research organization.

Thirdly, essentially required environment also can not be ignored for a long time period, which is next only to the issue of disarmament in the list of international issues. At the national level, there has been a definite rise in ignorance towards the environment due to development.

In the context of India, at least two immediate factors increase the ratio mentioned above. The first one of these is the rise in population level. By giving momentum to expansion of population and the workforce, human resource development has achieved synergistic importance. An increase in population is also a factor but is not the most important one, which delineated environmental decay in rural and urban areas. Second, as a large country, we cannot make an independent place for ourselves in the global system without developing appropriate ability for the development of our self-respect. In order to achieve this objective, the achievement of technical skills is a decisive step.

So far, we have taken human resource development, technical, and environmental issues as supporting factors of the main part of the plan. Along with the expansion of quality of basic infrastructure and targets of production (tonnes of steel and kilowatt hours of electricity), other targets of capacity (kilometres), and other targets (number of schools and students, number of electrified villages), known techniques, full use of natural resources, and maximum possible use of available financial resources have been emphasized upon.

Questions

19. According to this passage, what has been considered to be the most important by us out of the following?
    (a) Basic facilities and increase in the number of achieved targets
    (b) Ideal use of available natural resources
    (c) Maximum use of available financial resources
    (d) All of the above
20. According to the author of the passage, whose effect, out of the following, is felt at the national level?
    (a) Expansion of workforce of high quality
    (b) Lack of care and activism for the protection of environmental resources
    (c) Continuous decay of technical potentialities in urbanized countries
    (d) Emphasis on a slower pace of disarmament as compared to disarmament in other nations
21. According to the author of the passage, which of the following factors is of synergistic importance?
    (a) Population growth
    (b) Workforce
    (c) Human resource development
    (d) None of the above
22. Which of the following areas has not been included among various 'targets' mentioned in the passage?
    (a) Maximum use of financial resources
    (b) Electricity production
    (c) Population growth
    (d) Number of schools and children
23. Which of the following can be the most suitable title of the passage?
    (a) Potential obstacles in economic development
    (b) Main factors of development
    (c) Targets in development process
    (d) Role of population growth in development
24. Which of the following can be considered as reasons rather than as results of development in the context of this passage?
    (a) Education
    (b) Health
    (c) Productive employment
    (d) All of the above

Practice Passage V

Read the following passage carefully and answer the questions from 25 to 30.

The phrase 'What is it like?' stands for a fundamental thought process. How does one go about observing and reporting on things and events that occupy the segments of earth space? Of all the infinite varieties of phenomena on the face of the earth, how does one decide what phenomena to observe? There is no such thing as a complete description of the earth or any part of it, for every microscopic point on the earth's surface differs from every other such point. Experience shows that the things observed are already familiar because they are like phenomena that occur at home or because they resemble the abstract images and models developed in the human mind.

How are abstract images formed? Humans alone, among all other animals on the earth, possess language; their words symbolize not only specific things but also mental images of classes of things. People can remember what they have seen or experienced because they attach a word symbol to them.

During the long record of our efforts to gain more and more knowledge about the face of the earth as the human habitat, there has been a continuing interplay between things and events. The direct observation through the senses is described as a percept; the mental image is described as a concept. Percepts are what some people describe as reality, in contrast to mental images, which are theoretical, implying that they are not real.

The relation of percept to concept is not as simple as the definition implies. It is now quite clear that people of different cultures or even individuals in the same culture develop different mental images of reality and what they perceive is a reflection of these preconceptions. The direct observation of things and events on the face of the earth is so clearly a function of the mental images of the mind of the observer that the whole idea of reality must be reconsidered.

Concepts determine what the observer perceives, yet concepts are derived from the generalizations of previous percepts. What happens is that the educated observer is taught to accept a set of concepts and then sharpens or changes these concepts during a professional career. In any one field of scholarship, professional opinion at one time determines what concepts and procedures are acceptable, and these form a kind of model of scholarly behaviour.

25. The problem raised in the passage reflects on
    (a) Thought process
    (b) Human behaviour
    (c) Cultural perceptions
    (d) Professional opinion

26. According to the passage, human beings have mostly in mind
    (a) Observation of things
    (b) Preparation of mental images
    (c) Expression through language
    (d) To gain knowledge

27. Concept means
    (a) A mental image
    (b) A reality
    (c) An idea expressed in language form
    (d) All of the above

28. The relation of percept to concept is
    (a) Positive (b) Negative
    (c) Reflective (d) Absolute

29. In the passage, the earth is taken as
    (a) The globe
    (b) The human habitat
    (c) A celestial body
    (d) A planet

30. Percept means
    (a) Direct observation through the senses
    (b) A conceived idea
    (c) Ends of a spectrum
    (d) An abstract image

Practice Passage VI

Read the following passage carefully and answer questions 31 to 36.

It should be remembered that the Nationalist Movement in India, like all nationalist movements, was essentially a bourgeois movement. It represented the natural historical stage of development and to consider it, or to criticise it, as a Working Class Movement is wrong. Gandhi represented that movement and the Indian masses in relation to that movement to a supreme degree, and he became the voice of Indian people to that extent. The main contribution of Gandhi to India and the Indian masses has been through the powerful movements that he launched through the National Congress. Through nation-wide action, he sought to mould the millions and largely succeeded in doing so. He changed them from a demoralized, timid, and hopeless mass, bullied and crushed by every dominant interest and incapable of resistance, into a people with self-respect and self-reliance, resisting tyranny, and capable of united action and sacrifice for a larger cause. Gandhi made people think of political and economic issues, and every village and every bazaar hummed with argument and debate on the new ideas and hopes that filled the people.

That was an amazing psychological change. The time was ripe for it, of course, and circumstances and world conditions worked for this change. However, a great leader was necessary to take the advantage of those circumstances and conditions. Gandhi was that leader, and he released many bonds that imprisoned and disabled our minds, and none of us who experienced it can ever forget that great feeling of release and exhilaration that came over the Indian people.

Gandhi has played a revolutionary role of greatest importance in India because he knew how to make the most of the objective conditions and could reach the heart of the masses, whereas groups with a more advanced ideology functioned largely in air because they did not fit in with those conditions and could, therefore, not evoke any substantial response from the masses.

It is perfectly true that Gandhi, functioning in nationalist plane, did not think in terms of the conflict of classes, trying to compose their differences. However, the actions he indulged in and taught the people have inevitably raised mass consciousness tremendously and made social issues vital. Gandhi and the Congress must be judged by the policies they pursued and the action they indulged in. But behind this, personality counts and colours those policies and activities. In case of very exceptional persons like Gandhi, the question of personality becomes especially important in order to understand and appraise him. To us, he represented the spirit and honour of India, the yearning of her sorrowing millions to be rid of their innumerable burdens, and an insult to him by the British Government or others was an insult to India and her people.

31. Which one of the following is true of the given passage?
    (a) The passage is a critique of Gandhi's role in Indian movement for independence.
    (b) The passage hails the role of Gandhi in India's freedom movement.
    (c) The author is neutral on Gandhi's role in India's freedom movement.
    (d) It is an account of Indian National Congress's support to the Working Class Movement.

32. The change that the Gandhian movement brought among the Indian masses was
    (a) Physical (b) Cultural
    (c) Technological (d) Psychological

33. To consider the Nationalist Movement or to criticize it as a Working Class Movement was wrong because it was a
    (a) Historical movement
    (b) Voice of the Indian people
    (c) Bourgeois movement
    (d) Movement represented by Gandhi

34. Gandhi played a revolutionary role in India because he could
    (a) Preach morality
    (b) Reach the hearts of Indians
    (c) See the conflict of classes
    (d) Lead the Indian National Congress

35. Groups with advanced ideology functioned in air as they did not fit in with
    (a) Objective conditions of masses
    (b) The Gandhian ideology
    (c) The class consciousness of the people
    (d) The differences among masses

36. The author concludes the passage by
    (a) Criticizing the Indian masses
    (b) The Gandhian movement
    (c) Pointing out the importance of the personality of Gandhi
    (d) Identifying the sorrows of millions of Indians

Practice Passage VII

Read the following passage and answer question numbers 37–42.

Modern biotechnology, especially the creation of genetically modified (GM) crops, is often presented as a magical solution or universal panacea for the problems of poverty, inadequate nutrition, and even environmental degradation across the world. Conversely, there are people who present the picture of tech-generated monsters and major human health hazards being created by science. Many of the technological changes currently being utilized in agriculture can have unforeseen consequences, and their safety and future viability are far from secure.

The reality, as always, is far more complex than either of these two extremes. Even today, the total food production in the world is adequate to feed the hungry of the world; the problem is rather one of unequal distribution, a large part of the population of developing countries engaged in agriculture, face many problems such as lack of infrastructure, poor or unstable market access, volatile input and output prices, etc. These issues can not be addressed by biotechnology as their solution is a far cry.

It is true that transgenic plants can offer a range of benefits (more effective pest resistance of seeds and crops through genetically controlled methods and leads to improved yield), which are above and beyond those that emerged from more traditional innovations. A basic question, of course, is whether the new GM technology is safe, and whether this is absolutely crucial since the effects may only be known much later. The jury is still very much out on this matter, and the controversy does not appear to resolve quickly.

The trouble is that most governments in developing countries have relatively low food and beverage regulatory standards, and public systems for monitoring and surveillance of such standards are either poor or non-existent. This leaves them open for entry and even dumping of a range of agricultural products of new technology, which may not pass the regulatory standards in more developed countries.

Questions

37. Which of the following is true in context of the passage?
    (a) Genetically modified crops have been universally recognized as a solution to poverty and environmental degradation
    (b) The only way to improve the deficit in food requirement and food production in the world is by adapting genetically modified crops
    (c) Genetically modified crops produce more yield as compared to yield from traditional methods
    (d) Taking advantage of the absence of regulatory standards, scientists have been dumping new products in the market without appropriate approval

38. Choose the word/group of words which is most similar in meaning to OPEN in the context of the passage.
    (a) Vulnerable (b) Capable
    (c) Threatened (d) Uncertain

39. Choose the word/group of words which is most opposite in meaning to VOLATILE as used in the passage
    (a) Never-ending (b) Valuable
    (c) Irreversible (d) Stable

40. The author of the given passage seems to be definitely
    (a) Suggesting the use of traditional methods of agriculture as against biotechnology by developing countries owing to their poor regulatory standards
    (b) In favour of utilizing biotechnology as a tool for the alleviation of poverty in the world
    (c) Urging the policy makers to improve infrastructural facilities so that farmers can maximize the benefits of genetically modified crops
    (d) Unconvinced of the long-term effects and rationale for immediate requirement of genetically modified products

41. Why, according to the author, is genetic modification of crops not an answer to the problem of hunger in the world?
    (A) People being highly doubtful of the long-term effects of genetically modified crops do not buy the products grown by such methods
    (B) The problem of hunger in the world is not due to inadequate production of food but due to unequal distribution of it
    (C) Many developing countries have banned genetically modified products as developed countries have been using such countries as dumping groups for new genetically modified products
    (a) Only (A)
    (b) Only (B)
    (c) Both (B) and (C)
    (d) Both (A) and (C)
42. Which of the following can be described as the most suitable title for the passage?
    (a) GM crops—major issues
    (b) Concept of GM crops
    (c) Harmful effects of GM crops
    (d) None of the above

Practice Passage VIII

Read the following passage and answer question numbers 43–48.

Though top leaders of the nationalist movement were the policy makers, the immediate day-to-day leadership was provided by the middle-class intellectuals. The rural origin of the industrial labour force together with rampant illiteracy and their simplistic docility attracted social workers, mainly drawn from the middle-class intellectuals. They had an obvious advantage. Not being employees, the leaders were free from fear of victimization and immune towards the risks of leadership. Being generally well educated, they had a better perspective and sense of organization. They could see the issue in a broader context. They belonged to a higher social plane than the workers and with good education intellectual development comparable to the best among the employers they could meet the employers on their own plane and carry on negotiations on an equal footing. According to Royal Commission on Labour in India, 'the effect of this surge was enhanced by the political turmoil which added to the prevailing feelings of unrest and assured to provide willing leaders of a trade union movement'. But outside leadership had led to the politicization of the movement.

Politicization of the labour movement in India contributed both to its strength and weakness. While economic hardship was present all along as a latent force, the major impetus for growth of unionism was primarily provided by major political currents, particularly movement for national independence. For the zeal and the organizing ability, which the leaders of the nationalist movement brought to bear upon the Indian Trade Union Movement, it would not have gained the dimensions and the position it had by 1909 within a decade of its formal start.

Questions

43. Leadership to Trade Union was provided by the middle-class intellectuals in India because
    (a) They were the active participants in the nationalist movement
    (b) They were literates among the workers
    (c) They were able to negotiate with employers on equal terms
    (d) The workers did not want any one among them to be their leader
44. During the early years, Trade Union Movement gained greater dimensions because
    (a) The workers accepted outside leaders
    (b) It started along with the independence movement
    (c) The leaders were well educated with broad perspectives
    (d) The leaders were devoted to the welfare of workers
45. Early history of trade union movement in India
    (a) Trade Union Movement in India
    (b) Royal Commission on Trade Union Movement

(c) Outside leadership to trade union
(d) Negotiation with employers

46. What would be the reason for workers not coming forward to take up the leadership in Trade Union Movement in the early years?
(a) Lack of time
(b) Illiteracy
(c) Fear of victimization
(d) Risk in leadership

47. According to the passage, which of the following leadership primarily led to the politicization of the movement?
(a) Inside leadership
(b) Outside leadership
(c) Both (a) and (b)
(d) Illiterate leadership

48. Which of the following category of people provided routine leadership in the nationalist movement?
(a) Top leadership
(b) Middle-class intellectuals
(c) Industrial workers
(d) All of the above

Answer Keys

Practice Passage I

1. (d) 2. (d) 3. (b) 4. (b) 5. (c) 6. (b)

Practice Passage II

7. (c) 8. (c) 9. (b) 10. (c) 11. (a) 12. (a)

Practice Passage III

13. (d) 14. (b) 15. (c) 16. (a) 17. (a) 18. (a)

Practice Passage IV

19. (d) 20. (b) 21. (c) 22. (c) 23. (b) 24. (d)

Practice Passage V

25. (a) 26. (b) 27. (a) 28. (c) 29. (b) 30. (a)

Practice Passage VI

31. (b) 32. (d) 33. (b) 34. (b) 35. (a) 36. (c)

Practice Passage VII

37. (c) 38. (a) 39. (d) 40. (d) 41. (b) 42. (a)

Practice Passage VIII

43. (c) 44. (c) 45. (a) 46. (b) 47. (b) 48. (b)

4

COMMUNICATION

CONCEPT AND DEFINITION

Communication is the most integral part of human nature. Human beings have a compulsive urge to communicate with each other, as more than 70% of their time is spent in communicating with others. No meaningful understanding is possible without communication. Of all the creatures, man has the ability and power to express in words. The evolution of mankind is basically the story of his/her progress in communication methods.

There are many definitions of communication. According to Oxford Dictionary, 'Communication is transferring or conveying of meaning'.

According to Little, 'Human communication is the process by which information is passed between people by means of previously agreed symbols, in order to produce a desired response'.

Berlo tried to explain communication as **S-R Model or sender-receiver model**, where **S**ender stands for stimulus and **R**eceiver stands for response.

This was later extended to **S-M-C-R Model** that stands for Sender-Message-Channel-Receiver. It is the basic communication process.

In communication process, the sender (encoder) encodes the message and then using a medium/channel, sends it to the receiver (decoder) who decodes the message, and after processing the information, the receiver sends back appropriate feedback/reply using a medium/channel.

It is important to mention that effective communication always includes feedback.

FUNCTIONS AND OBJECTIVES OF COMMUNICATION

During recent times, communication by mass media and through social media is the underlying force for changes taking place in society. People communicate to learn what they need and want to know to cope with their physical and social reality. Successful people are usually effective communicators.

The different objectives of communication are discussed as following:

1. *Information to keep oneself updated and for decision-making:* Through communication, people want to reduce uncertainty. Information is actually facts provided about something that is the main input for any decision-making.

   Information is regarded as power; the more informed a person is, the more powerful s/he would be.

2. *Education and instruction:* The key functions of communication include imparting

instructions to younger members of the society educating them, and their socialization as well. The process starts during early stages in life, first in family and then in school, and continues forever. Communication provides us knowledge, expertise, and skills that enable people to participate actively in social life.

3. *Smooth functioning of groups:* Effective systems of communication encourage better coordination. Coordination is viewed as a necessity among groups.
4. *Motivation and morale:* Communication motivates people in an organization by clarifying the people what is to be done, how well they are doing and what can be done to improve performance. The formation of specific goals, feedback on progress towards the goals and reinforcement of desired behaviour, all stimulate motivation and require communication.

   Morale is usually a group phenomenon and has a psychological aspect. High morale is generally associated with successful teams, which is further dependent upon effective communication.
5. *Control:* Communication acts to control a member's behaviour both through formal as well as informal communication channels.
6. *Cultural promotion:* Communication provides an opportunity for cultural values to be maintained and promoted. It stimulates individuals to pursue and fulfil their creative urges.
7. *Integration:* Communication is a great integrating tool. By communicating, the individuals, groups, or cultures understand and appreciate each other's ways of life. They develop tolerance towards each other.

Nature and Characteristics of Communication

The nature of communication can be explained using the following characteristics:

1. *Communication is continuous:* Communication is not a static act, but it is a dynamic process of action and interaction towards a desired goal. Sharing or exchanging information is a continuous process.
2. *Communication is all-pervasive:* Lower levels provide information to the middle level. It is further processed to the top level in the desired format that helps in decision making. Top level issues instructions to the middle and lower levels. This happens in an educational organisation as well.
3. *Effective communication is a two-way process:* Communication is deemed to be effective when there is some kind of feedback mechanism. This basic aspect has been taken into account in Cole and Chan Model as well as given in Figure 4.1.
4. *Communication is always with a context and a relationship aspect:* Both in terms of (i) what you say and (ii) how you say the matter. Same message can be communicated authoritatively or politely. For example, while asking for a glass of water, one can say,

   (a) Please bring me a glass of water

   (b) Give me a glass of water

   (c) Can I have a glass of water?

   (d) Could you please give me a glass of water?

   Each message will have a different effect on the person you are talking to.
5. *Communication exchanges are based on symmetry and complementary:* Symmetry refers to similarity and complimentary refers to the differences in characteristics. For example, two students who are very good in Mathematics will have a good communication relationship. This will be termed as *symmetry*. On the other hand, suppose there are two students, one is good in Mathematics but poor in English and the other is good in English but poor in Mathematics. They may have good complementary communication relationship with each other because they can compensate each other's weakness.

6. *Common language:* This helps developing better understanding between the sender and the receiver of a message, thus making communication more effective.
7. *Meeting of minds is necessary:* The receiver must comprehend the intended meaning of the message that the sender wants him/her to understand.
8. *The message must have substance:* The gist of the message holds importance only until the receiver shows interest in the subject matter. For example, any discussion about cricket will be well received by a cricket fanatic.
9. *Communication can also be conducted through gestures:* Communication should not necessarily be verbal or written. Nodding of heads, rolling of eyes, movement of lips, etc., are some of the gestures used to convey certain basic ideas.
10. *Communication is of different types:* It can be formal or informal, verbal or non-verbal. The different types have been discussed in detail in the ensuing discussion.
11. *Communication always has a context:* Communication always takes place within a context. According to Bateson, 'Without context, words and actions don't carry any meaning at all'. At times, this context may not be obvious, and at times, it may stand out boldly. The context of communication has four dimensions:
    (a) *Physical context:* It refers to the place where communication is taking place—in public, conference room, classroom, etc. It refers to the ambience of the place as well.
    (b) *Social context:* Social context is mainly about (i) role and status relationship between the sender and the receiver of messages and (ii) norms and culture of the society. For example, the social context of friends attending a party will be different from the people attending a meeting in an organization or a doctor attending a patient.
    (c) *Psychological context:* It refers to the environment characterized by formality or informality, friendliness or unfriendliness.
    (d) *Temporal context:* It refers to the time factor in communication such as at what time of the day communication is taking place. In morning, we usually talk about religious and spiritual aspects of life; during day time, it is usually about professional aspects, and so on.

Communication Skills

Communication skills include the following:

1. Listening skill
2. Speaking skill
3. Writing skill
4. Reading skill

Classroom Communication Process – Cole and Chan Model

Classroom teaching still dominates the scene of formal education system wherein face-to-face instructions are given to students. The primary objective of classroom teaching is to achieve instructional objectives in the cognitive domain, namely, those concerned with developing knowledge, comprehension, application, analysis, synthesis, and evaluation abilities.

Communication is an integral part of any teaching–learning process, and its effectiveness is one of the factors that determine the degree to which the intended learning outcomes are achieved. The process of classroom communication is affected by multiple factors pertaining to teachers, students, message, instructional methods and media, and learning environment. However, very few of us understand the nature of communication and make deliberate attempts to improve its effectiveness. Communication skills are acquired through training and can be improved with practice and requires conscious knowledge and strategic judgement. Evidences indicate that by improving communication skills, individuals can have more effective and satisfying communication experiences.

All communication is based upon symbols. It is a process that involves organizing, selecting, and transmitting symbols in an appropriate manner to ensure that the receiver perceives in his/her thought process, the intended meaning of the communicator.

According to Cole and Chan, a typical process of classroom communication (and communication in general as well) includes the following five distinct stages:

1. Formulation of message
2. Message encoding
3. Message transmission
4. Message decoding and interpretation
5. Feedback and evaluation

The process of an effective two-way communication is shown in Figure 4.1.

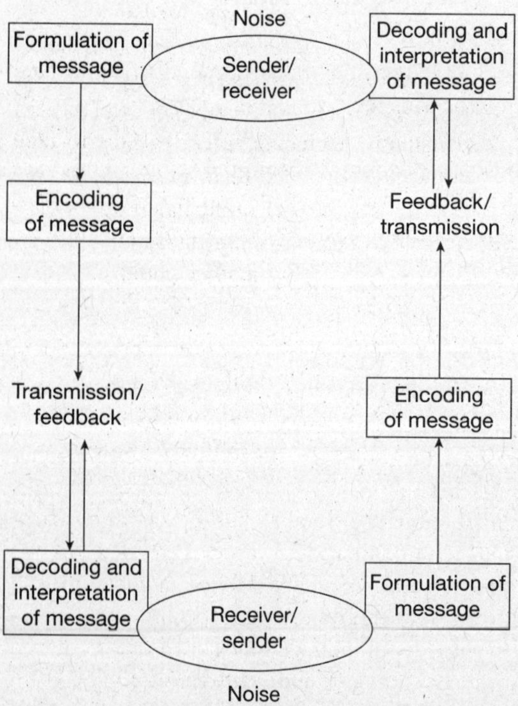

Figure 4.1 Process of Effective Communication

Formulation of Message

The success of communication, therefore, depends on what we say and how we say it.

1. All communication starts with an idea or a message that is to be transmitted to the target audience (individual) with a motive to get a positive response. Communicator (sender or encoder) is the one who initiates the communication process.
2. A message is a set of verbal or non-verbal cues sent by a source. Messages can be spoken or written words, gestures, movements, etc. They cannot have a meaning apart from the person involved in the sending and receiving process.
3. An effective communication depends on the communication skill, knowledge level, and attitude of the communicator and how he/she desires to affect his/her receiver. Ability to think, organize thoughts quickly, and express himself/herself effectively are some of the attributes of a good communicator.
4. Teachers concerned, they conceptualize ideas to be conveyed to students by arranging them in coherent and meaningful sequence. In most of the instances, they will draw on content from curricula. Teachers interpret those ideas and determine the appropriate organization of the content.

Message Encoding

1. The internal shaping, sorting, and sifting of ideas for clarification and organization is called message formulation. Its purpose is to create a clear and meaningful message.
2. Encoding involves converting an idea into a form that can be transmitted to receivers.
3. The communicator not only translates his/her purpose (ideas, thoughts, or information) into a message but also decides on the medium to communicate his/her planned message.
4. The communicator must choose the media (speech, writing, signalling, or gestures)

that the receiver can comprehend well. For instance, an illiterate receiver may fail to understand a written message but can understand it well if told orally.

5. Teachers encode their ideas in different ways according to the demands of various curricula. It is the teacher's responsibility to use appropriate symbolic forms for each subject and to teach students to use these forms.

Message Transmission

1. It is a critical stage in the communication process, and it answers how a message is delivered. The sender selects an appropriate channel or mode of presentation.
2. A 'channel' is the vehicle or means through which a message or stimulus is carried from the communicator to the receiver. There are various options available as channels like written, spoken, verbal, non-verbal, mass media, etc.

   For example, a teacher may use a film or physical demonstration to convey the same idea. Teachers are usually able to use more than one channel in ways that allow for an integrated presentation.

Message Decoding and Interpretation

1. Decoding is interpretation of the message by the receiver. Actually, the receiver looks for meaning in the message that is common to both the receiver and the communicator.
2. If the receiver possesses the background information and is familiar with the form of language used, it becomes easier for him/her to decode and comprehend the message.
3. If the receiver does not have the ability to listen, read, and think, s/he will not be able to receive and decode the messages in the manner the communicator wants him/her to.
4. For effective communication, the receiver is the most important link in the communication process.

Feedback and Evaluation

1. Feedback is the response or acknowledgement of the receiver to the communicator's message. The exchange is possible only if the receiver responds.
2. It involves the receiver reacting to the transmitted messages and conveying the response to the sender.
3. Most effective communicators encourage feedback and adjust the content and presentation of their messages as per the feedback received.
4. Teachers need to be aware of the subtle and direct ways of students for conveying reactions to the messages received. Skilled teachers can also control feedback so as to avoid unnecessary interference in the ongoing communication process.
5. Even by fluttering eyelids, raising an eyebrow, making facial expressions, organizing a point, and asking for explanation, the message is shaped and reshaped by the communicator and the receiver until the meaning becomes clear. In this way, both the participants in communication interact and constantly exchange roles. In face-to-face communication, the receiver responds naturally, directly, and immediately. This provides the communicator an opportunity to improve and make his/her communication effective.
6. Feedback, thus, provides an opportunity to evaluate what is right or wrong about a particular communication. It helps to regulate the conversation among two or more individuals and also stimulates and reinforces an idea that is desired to be communicated.
7. An interactive model of communication (Cole and Chan) has a specific application for classroom teaching and learning. In most classroom interactions, there are constant role changes and many times the communication process is reversed.

Noise

Noise is an interruption that can creep in at any point of time in the communication process and make it ineffective. Environment is one major cause that interferes with message reception like noises from the roadside, constant chattering of individuals, blaring loudspeaker, faulty transmission, etc. Noise can also occur in other forms like poor handwriting, heavy accent or soft speech, communication in a poorly lit room, etc. In fact, these are barriers to effective communication. For smooth and effective communication, it is necessary to eliminate or reduce noise as far as possible.

Noise can mainly be divided into four categories:

1. *Physiological noise:* It is distraction caused by hunger, fatigue, headache, medication, etc.
2. *Physical noise:* It is the most direct form of interference in our physical environment, for example, traffic horns and poor lighting.
3. *Psychological noise:* It refers to the qualities in us that affect how we communicate and interpret others. For instance, if a manager is preoccupied with a very intense problem, then he/she may be inattentive in the meeting. Similarly, prejudice and defensive feelings can also interfere with communication.
4. *Semantic noise:* It occurs when words themselves are not mutually understood. Authors sometimes create semantic noise by using jargon or avoidable technical language.

Types of Communication

People communicate with each other in numerous ways that depends upon the message and its context in which it is being sent. Choice and style of communication channel also affect communication.

Classification on the Basis of Relationship Element

Intrapersonal Communication

1. It is communication within an individual almost all the times, including talking to oneself, listening to oneself, and relating one to oneself.
2. It includes individual reflection, meditation, contemplation, and even praying to God.
3. We conceptualize and formulate our thoughts or ideas before we actually indulge in overt communication.

Muttering 'Oh My God', 'Oh No' (when in trouble), 'Wow', and 'Thank God' are few common examples of intrapersonal communication.

Interpersonal Communication

1. It is also termed as dyadic communication.
2. It is universal form of face-to-face routine communication between two persons, both sending and receiving messages.
3. It may be formal or informal, verbal or non-verbal.
4. It takes place anywhere by means of words, sounds, facial expression, gestures, and postures.
5. It is an effective communication situation because you can get immediate feedback.
6. Due to proximity between the sender and the receiver, interpersonal communication has emotional appeal too; it can motivate, encourage, and coordinate work more effectively than any other form of communication.
7. The efficacy of interpersonal communication depends very much on the mutual relationship between two partners in communication, their status, roles, and skills.
8. It has greater scope for grapevine.

Interpersonal communication can be further subdivided into formal (meeting and conference) or informal (private discussion with family members or friends).

Group Communication

Let us think of a group of people meeting for a particular reason. It may be a group of residents on a street or *mohalla*, students meeting a teacher or a student leader.

1. It is an extension of interpersonal communication where more than two individuals are involved in exchange of ideas, skills, and interests.
2. It provides an opportunity for people to come together to discuss and exchange views of common interest.
3. There could be different groups for different reasons.
4. It includes collective decision-making, self-expression, increasing one's effect, and elevating one's status.
5. It is considered effective as it provides an opportunity for direct interaction among the members of the group, and it helps in bringing about changes in attitudes and beliefs.

Mass Communication

1. It is also termed as 'mediated communication'.
2. It is a special kind of communication with mass audiences and hence the name mass communication.
3. Channels for mass communication are termed as mass media.
4. It uses mechanical devices that multiply messages and take it to a large number of people simultaneously.
5. Examples of mass media include radio, TV, newspapers, magazines, and films (both electronic and print media).

> Communication can also be categorised on the basis of involvement of parties - intrapersonal (reading a newspaper, meditation, introspection), interpersonal (conversation with a colleague), and apersonal (use of mass media, publicity, advertisement).

Communication Types on the Basis of Channels

On the basis of channels, communication is of two types:

1. Verbal communication
2. Non-verbal communication

Verbal Communication

Verbal means the use of words in communication process and in design and formulation of messages. In verbal communication, message is transmitted verbally, that is, by making use of words—oral and written.

In verbal communication, remember the acronym KISS (keep it short and simple).

In order to deliver the right message, the communicator must be empathetic. Verbal communication is further divided into:

(a) Oral communication

(b) Written communication

Oral Communication

In oral communication, spoken words are used. It includes face-to-face conversations, speech, telephonic conversation, video, radio, television, and voice over the Internet. In oral communication, communication is influenced by the following:

1. *Pitch and volume:* Pitch is the degree of highness or lowness of a tone, and it depends upon the frequency of sound waves. It is the key element in teaching–learning process. Teacher's voice and knowing the correct language is the main input in speech. One should be loud enough to be heard. When speaking, one should remember to change the pitch in your voice as a monotone voice may become boring. Excitement is indicated by a high pitch and anger by a low pitch.

   Volume depends upon the proximity and number of people and is measured in decibels.
2. *Rate:* It is the speed at which words are delivered. One should maintain regularity when speaking because a regular or rhythmic voice makes you sound more confident. Irregular speech may show a sign of uncertainty. If a teacher talks at a slow pace, then the students may become frustrated because the information is not being given quickly enough.
3. *Clarity in speaking and articulation:* Proper pronunciation and delivery of words contribute towards the effectiveness of the message. It also depends upon clarity of thought of the

communicator. Pitch, volume, rate, and clarity are termed as components of paralanguage.

The advantages of oral communication are as follows:

1. It is spontaneous and natural.
2. It is, therefore, easy for others to understand.
3. Choice of words generally suits the listeners.
4. It is supported by non-verbal communication.
5. The communicator or the person who communicates is always physically available.
6. It can develop a close relationship between the speaker and the listener.

Limitations of oral communication are as follows:

1. Words spoken disappear into thin air. The words are temporary.
2. Words are not permanent unlike written communication.
3. What is heard is often forgotten.
4. Non-verbal communication that supports oral communication may not be understood by people from other cultures.

Written Communication

In written communication, written signs and symbols, both in printed or handwritten form, can be used. Pictures, graphs, etc., are used to compliment the written text. The communicator's writing skills, style, and knowledge of grammar affect the quality of message. In written communication, message can be transmitted via email, letter, report, memo, etc.

This is the most commonly used communication in a business organization.

The organization needs to communicate with different stakeholders, both in internal and external environments to meet its objectives. Thus, written communication can further have two dimensions—internal and external.

The internal written communication is in the form of memos, reports, bulletins, job descriptions, employee manuals, and emails specifically for internal communication, that is, within the organization.

Emails, Internet, websites (URLs), letters, proposals, telegrams, faxes, postcards, contracts, advertisements, brochures, and news releases are used for external communication.

Even the oral communication is used for both internal as well external communication.

Advantages of written communication are as follows:

1. Messages can be edited and revised many times before being sent, so it minimizes the chances of error.
2. Written communication provides an automatic record for every message sent and can be saved for later study or references.
3. A written message enables the receiver to fully understand it and send appropriate feedback. It brings in the element of impersonality and more objectivity.

Limitations of written communication are as follows:

1. Written communication may not provide prompt and spontaneous feedback.
2. Written communication may take more time.
3. Usually communication is mix of both oral and written.

Mnemonics

This is somewhat in different context, mainly about learning and recalling of words, numbers, facts, etc.

Mnemonics are memory devices that help learners recall larger pieces of information, especially in the form of lists like characteristics, steps, stages, parts, phases, etc. A study conducted by Gerald R. Miller in 1967 found that mnemonics increased recall. Mnemonics can even be used to recall words or remember numbers. For example - BRASS is an acronym for how to shoot a rifle—Breath, Relax, Aim, Sight, Squeeze. They help in taking notes also.

Non-verbal Communication

It is the process of communication through sending and receiving wordless messages. There is a famous quote, 'actions speak louder than words'. Here, action stands for our body movements. Non-verbal communication is all about the body language of the speaker and does not make use of words. Communication, other than oral and written, such as body gesture, eye contact, body language, posture, tone of voice or facial expressions is called non-verbal communication. Non-verbal communication helps receiver in better interpretation of the message.

Non-verbal communication has the following three elements:

1. *Appearance:* It includes both the speaker and the surrounding. Clothing, hairstyle, neatness of the speaker, etc., are taken into account. Surrounding is ambience of the place where communication takes place. It includes a room, lighting, decorations, furnishings, etc.
2. *Body language:* It includes facial expressions, gestures, and postures.
3. *Sounds:* It includes voice tone, volume, and speech rate.

Concept of Kinesics

Kinesics is a major form of non-verbal communication. It is defined as 'the study of non-linguistic body movements such as facial expressions and gestures'. Kinesics is the interpretation of body language such as facial expressions and gestures or, more formally, non-verbal behaviour related to body movement, either any part of the body or the body as a whole.

According to Mehrabian, '**Words** account for 7%, **Tone of voice** accounts for 38%, and our **Body Language** accounts for 55% of communication'. This has become the **7/38/55** Rule. They are abbreviated as the 3 V's, that is, Verbal, Vocal, and Visual.

Thus, in practice, it is always a mix of verbal as well as non-verbal communication.

Classification Based on Purpose and Style

Based on style and purpose, there are two main categories of communication, and they both have their own characteristics.

Formal Communication

In formal communication, certain rules, regulations, conventions, and protocols are followed while formulating and communicating message. It follows an organizational structure. It can be upwards or downwards across hierarchy or authority lines.

In formal communication, use of right language and correct pronunciation is required.

For example, in case an Assistant Professor has to communicate with College Principal, it is usually through Head of Department (HoD).

Informal Communication

Informal communication channels exist along with formal communication channels in any organization. It mainly addresses the social needs of the employees. It is interpersonal and mainly face-to-face and with use of body gestures. It happens among friends and family. In informal communication, there are no formal rules and regulations for communication.

A lot of distortion or filtering may take place in informal communication, and it is termed as grapevine.

Classification on the Basis of Direction

Vertical Communication

1. This is basically formal communication.
2. This can be upwards (bottom up) and downwards (top bottom).

Lateral or Horizontal Communication

1. Communication with people at same level in hierarchy that are peers and colleagues is termed as lateral communication.
2. This may combine both formal and informal communications.

This is the most effective communication, as it is generally not stalled by a chain of command methods. This can help in building teams in an organization.

3. The amount of horizontal communication depends upon the interdependence of different departments.

Diagonal Communication

1. Diagonal communication is effective as hierarchical bindings are removed, and there is a free flow of information, cutting across positions or status.
2. It facilitates in building relationships and bonding between the superior and the subordinate.

Communication Networks

Communication network shows all communication patterns or relationships that may exist in the organization. The various types of communication networks are represented diagrammatically in Figure 4.2.

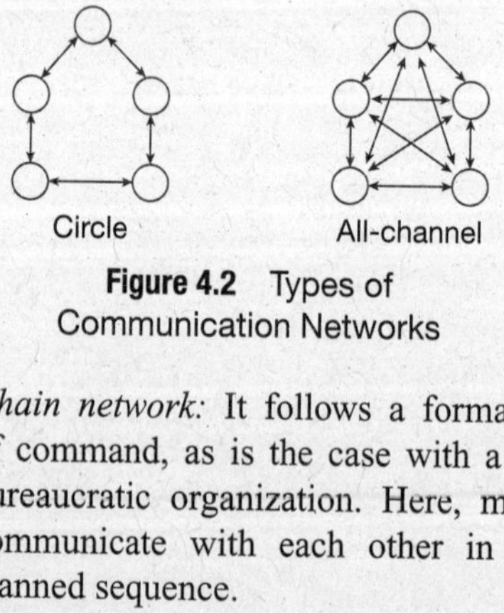

Figure 4.2 Types of Communication Networks

1. *Chain network:* It follows a formal chain of command, as is the case with a typical bureaucratic organization. Here, members communicate with each other in a pre-planned sequence.
2. *Wheel network:* It is also known as 'STAR' network. Here, information flows from one central member of the group to the rest of the members. Other group members may not have to communicate with each other to perform well; all communication is channelized through the supervisor. For examples, one-to-one interactions of Heads of Departments (HoDs) with the college Principal, but little or no interaction of HoDs among themselves. It is not very effective in teams.
3. *Circle network:* Here, members communicate informally with adjoining members generally on the basis of shared experiences, beliefs, areas of expertise, background, or office location. It may have a formal leader as well, but interaction is still lateral. It works in an autonomous team.
4. *All-channel network:* An all-channel network is found in teams. Both the intensity and frequency of interaction is high among members. Information flows in all directions. There is no formal leader and communication may be started by any member.

Communication Barriers

Effective communication can face multiple barriers.

Organizational Barriers

These barriers develop when an organization evolves. They can be attributed to the following conditions:

1. Size of organization
2. Physical distance between employees
3. Specialization of jobs and activities
4. Organizational culture—it impacts freedom and trust
5. Organizational rules and regulations
6. Power structure in the organization
7. Complexity in organizational structure
8. Inadequate facilities and opportunities
9. Lack of cooperation between senior and subordinate

Physical barriers

There are four kinds of physical barriers.

1. *Competing stimulus:* There can be some other conversation going on in the surrounding area, traffic noise in the background, and so on.
2. *Environmental stress:* High temperature, poor ventilation, and so on.
3. *Subjective stress:* Sleeplessness, ill health, effects of drugs, mood variations, and so on.
4. *Receiver's unfamiliarity with medium:* The use of medium with which the recipient is unfamiliar is also a communication barrier.

Psychological Barriers

1. *Frame of reference:* Each person has a frame of reference, a kind of a window to view the world, people, events, and situations. A frame of reference is shaped by our cultural environment (norms, values, and beliefs), childhood experiences, and heredity. All these factors are usually implicit. No two people will have same frame of reference. Our frames of reference modify with passage of time as our needs and experience also change. Here, it is important to mention the concept of reference groups whom we espouse as our own and try to follow in our routine behaviour.
2. *Self-image:* Self-image or self-concept is closely related to frame of reference. People establish their point of view and interpret messages in accordance with their self-concepts. They respond favourably those messages that reinforce their self concept, and reject those messages that are perceived to be threatening self image.
3. *Field of experience:* This barrier occurs when the field of experience is not common to both the sender and the receiver. If a teacher is teaching Einstein's equation to commerce students, he/she will not get any response but if it is taught to science students, his/her communication is likely to be more effective.
4. *Cognitive dissonance:* Cognitive means thinking and dissonance means conflict; thus, it means conflict in thinking. Although a smoker accepts the truthfulness of drug de-addiction in advertisement messages by the Department of Social Welfare, he is not able to react favourably.
5. *Defensiveness and fear:* This is closely related to the desire to maintain status quo and a person always justifies his/her viewpoint or idea.

   Along with the feelings of nervousness, anxiety, and tension, fear is the most restricting of all effects, resulting in narrow thinking, which selects and distorts communication. However, a little fear and anxiety can be turned into a source of energy and enhance confidence as it motivates to perform better.
6. *Selective perception:* It is also characterized as 'I-know-it syndrome'. If somebody says, 'It is a waste of time', is also exhibiting selective perception when one does not apply full mind on communication situation.
7. *Filtering:* A sender's manipulation of information can be seen as more favourable by the receiver.

Linguistic and Cultural Barriers

Language, both verbal or non-verbal, makes use of words. Words are mere symbols. Symbols can be comprehended differently by participants in communication. The communication message might not use vocabulary that is understood by the receiver. For example, excessive use of technical, financial, medical, or psychological terms and jargon.

Most of the native languages are culture specific. When languages are distinct, communication is carried out through translation, which increases the probability of misunderstandings.

Although languages are meant to improve understanding, different cultural contexts and languages can also prove to be a barrier to communication across different cultures.

1. *Semantic barriers:* Semantic barriers occur when there is disagreement about the words

being used, which is based on individuals being from different cultures, thus disallowing the parties involved to determine a common meaning of the words used. This frequently occurs when the parties involved speak different languages.

2. *High-context and low-context cultures:* High-context culture is the culture that relies heavily on non-verbal and subtle situational cues to communicate. A lot of things are left unsaid, but it is already understood by the members that constitute the group. Asiatic societies such as India, Saudi Arabia and Japan are prominent examples of high-context culture.

   Low-context culture relies heavily on words to convey meanings in a communication. A few words can communicate a complex message very effectively to an in-group (in-group is one's own culture) but less effectively outside that group. In a lower context culture, the communicator needs to be much more explicit. Western societies are usually low-context societies.

3. *Cross-cultural communication:* Cross-cultural communication is a field of study that scrutinizes how people from varying cultural backgrounds communicate in similar and different ways among themselves and how they endeavour to communicate across cultures.

Mechanical Barriers

Mechanical barriers can exist in both interpersonal or mass communication. There can be difficulty in reception or some elements of the message may not reach the destination or both. It can be in the form of absence of communication facilities.

Channel noise is a technical term used for such mechanical barriers that includes any disturbance in physical transmission of a message. Some examples of mechanical barriers are disturbances in radio transmissions, blurredness on TV screens, spreading of ink on a newspaper, inaudibility in telephone devices, a barely readable point size, or any kind of improper functioning of a device. They can also be associated with cultural or social issues, language, customs, beliefs, motives, or simply illiteracy.

The various communication barriers at workplaces are as follows:

1. *Language:* The same message can be interpreted differently by different people. Several factors affect how an individual attributes meaning to particular words.
2. *Perpetual biases:* It prevents us to look at reality in a truthful manner. The most common perceptual biases are stereotyping, projection, and self-fulfilling prophecies.

   Stereotyping comes into play when we assume that a person belonging to a certain group will display specific characteristics. However, the person may not actually exhibit those characteristics. This is specifically true in case of traditional societies.
3. *Impersonal relationships:* Our perception is also based on the past experiences with the communicator. The same communication from the highest authority may be perceived differently than that from a subordinate or a colleague.
4. *Cultural differences:* Effective communication requires deciphering the basic motives, values, assumptions, and aspirations that operate across different cultures.

Principles of Effective Classroom Communication

Effectiveness of classroom communication depends on five major factors, namely, teacher, student, message, instructional methods and media, and learning environment. The principles of effective classroom communication have been discussed under the following four headings:

1. Principles for teacher
2. Principles for message design
3. Principles for selection of instructional methods and media
4. Principles for creating conducive learning environment

Principles for Teachers

A teacher should have the following qualities:

1. *Develop a realistic self-concept and a perception about surrounding:* This requires analysis of one's strengths and weaknesses, acceptance of the reality, and efforts to realize one's potential.
2. *Develop proficiency in the subject matter:* Desire to acquire knowledge is a must for the teacher. In the words of Mahatma Gandhi,

    'Live as if you were to die tomorrow
    Learn as if you were to live forever'.

    A teacher should make every effort to remain updated in his/her subject area by independent reading, participation in short-term courses, attending classes of proficient teachers/experts, discussing subject-related issues and problems with other colleagues or seniors, etc. This helps in boosting the confidence of the teacher.
3. *Understand the learners:* A teacher should try to collect as much information about the learners' characteristics as he/she can. Information needs to be collected about the previous knowledge, learning styles, cognitive styles, motivation, and interests. A teacher should accept the fact that no two individuals are alike and thus cannot be treated in the same manner.
4. *Develop effective communication skills (both verbal and non-verbal):* Communication skills can be acquired through training and practice. A teacher can record his/her own audio and analyse the same for identifying the strengths and weaknesses in the spoken language. S/he should remain open to feedback from colleagues, superiors, and students.
5. *Knowledge about pedagogy and andragogy:* This enables the teacher to plan, organize, deliver, and evaluate instructions based upon the sound principles of teaching, learning, and thereby promote learning among students.
6. *Adopt flexible approach:* This helps in modifying instructions as per the needs of the students.
7. *Being objective and unbiased:* A teacher should treat students as equal and not give any preferences to students on the basis of sex, caste, or creed.

Principles for Message Design

The message should have the following characteristics:

1. *Clear and specified objectives:* Objectives should satisfy the criterion of being SMART:
    (a) Specific
    (b) Measurable
    (c) Achievable
    (d) Realistic
    (e) Time framed
2. *Relevant to the objectives:* Contents should be relevant to cover all the objectives.
3. *Properly sequenced:* This is covered in Unit I under the maxims and principles of teaching. It should be seen that the content is organized from
    (a) Simple to complex
    (b) Easy to difficult
    (c) Concrete to abstract
    (d) Known to unknown
    (e) Observation to reasoning
4. *Use language comprehendible to the learners:* The language of the message should be simple and comprehendible to the learners. Technical jargon should be avoided.
5. *Use appropriate symbols:* Symbols used in the message should be technically correct and standardized.
6. *Include relevant exercises:* The exercises selected should be of varying difficulty level and should involve the learners meaningfully.
7. *Make generous use of examples and non-examples:* Examples from daily life and world of work should be used to facilitate understanding of the applicability of content in different settings and thus ensure greater transferability of the learnt materials.

Principles for Selection of Instructional Methods and Media

1. *Select relevant and appropriate methods and media:* The methods and media should be relevant to the objectives, content, and context, and should be appropriate to the level of learners. Instructional methods and teaching methods have been discussed in Unit I.
2. *Use variety of methods and media:* In order to cater to the individual differences among learners and to avoid monotony, a variety of methods and media should be used by the teacher.
3. *Use good quality media:* The quality of media in terms of its visibility, legibility, finish, colours, and printing should be judged before its use.
4. *Integrate media in teaching–learning:* Media should not be used in isolation. For example, if a video film is being used at the end of a lesson to reinforce what has been taught in the class, it should either be followed by a discussion or some quick assessment of students' understanding.

Principles for Creating Conducive Learning Environment

1. *Classes should not be overcrowded:* It really becomes difficult for the teacher to manage a big class and pay attention to each learner, which is the main reason that student–teacher ratio is prescribed by various regulatory bodies.
2. *Ensure proper seating arrangement in the class:* Minimum essential distance should be maintained between the teacher and the students, and among students. Each student should be able to interact with the teacher and other students. Furniture should be comfortable and in proper condition. In addition, there should be proper lighting and ventilation arrangement in the class.
3. *Build rapport with the students:* A teacher should know each and every student in the class by name and be friendly with the students. S/he should try to give due respect to the individuality of students. S/he should have a positive attitude towards the students.
4. *Encourage co-operation and healthy competition among students:* This can be achieved by assigning group activities and pairing bright students with average or poor students.
5. *Feedback mechanism:* It should work both ways.
6. *Encourage experimentation:* A teacher should encourage experimentation with new ideas and techniques by the students. Creativity should be encouraged rather than curbed. Problems having more than one solution need to be posed in the class.
7. *Provide reinforcement:* A teacher should reinforce the desired communication behaviour of learners through praise, appreciation, rewards, social recognition, etc.
8. *Provide non-threatening environment:* There should not be fear of punishment. Prior information regarding schedule of activities, tests, assignments, etc., should be provided to learners in order to avoid any unnecessary anxiety on the part of the learners.

Paraphrasing

Paraphrasing is a skill that is absolutely necessary for good listening. It means stating in your own words, your understanding of what has just been said. It gives the speaker the opportunity to find out what message he/she is getting across to you. S/he can then make any corrections needed. To begin paraphrasing, you might start by saying, 'What I hear you saying is ....' or 'It sounds like ....' or 'Let me see if I'm understanding you ....'

Advantages of Paraphrasing

1. It helps the students know that they are understood by the instructor.
2. It prevents misunderstandings from occurring.

3. It helps to avoid impulsive or angry reactions.
4. It will prevent you from getting distracted easily.
5. It helps to remember what was said frequently.

Some Important Terms

1. *Synchronous media:* Media that takes place in real time such as live television or radio and that requires the audience to be present when the media is being broadcasted or performed is called synchronous media.
2. *Asynchronous media:* Media that does not require the audience to assemble at a given time in order to use it is called asynchronous media. Examples of asynchronous media are printed materials or recorded audio or video.
3. *Time shift:* The recording of an audio or video event, usually by the audience, to be watched later at a time other than when it was originally broadcasted is called time shift. Setting a VCR to record a favourite program is an example of time-shifting.
4. *Surveillance:* Primarily the function of mass communication is to provide information about the processes, issues, events, and other developments in the society.
5. *Convergence:* It is the combining together of computing, telecommunications, and media in a digital environment. Convergence and the changes that it is bringing are fundamentally changing many aspects of mass media and communication.

The 7 Cs provide a checklist for making sure that communication in the form of teaching, instructions, meetings, emails, conference calls, reports, and presentations is well constructed and clear so that the audience gets the message.

According to the 7 Cs, communication needs to be:

1. Clear
2. Concise
3. Concrete
4. Correct
5. Coherent
6. Complete
7. Courteous

Communication: Concept, Nature, and Process

1. When we say that communication is intentional, it means that
   (a) Sender consciously intends to affect the behaviour of receiver of the message
   (b) Effective communication is a process of acting on information
   (c) Through speech communication, people make sense of the world
   (d) None of the above
2. Communication is the transfer and understanding of
   (a) Ideas (b) Concepts
   (c) Meaning (d) Words
3. Which of the following can be termed as the 'context' of communication?
   (a) An interference with message reception
   (b) Effective communication
   (c) Verbal and non verbal responses to messages
   (d) A physical and psychological environment for conversation
4. Which of the following is Berlo's Linear Model of communication?
   (a) S-M-R-C (b) S-M-C-R
   (c) S-R-M-C (d) S-R-C-M

5. Who among the following has stated that people know each other and themselves only through communication?
   (a) George Herbert Mead
   (b) Mahatma Gandhi
   (c) Martin Luther King
   (d) None of above
6. The ability to communicate effectively
   (a) Depends on the education level
   (b) Is a natural talent that cannot be learned
   (c) Always depends upon the use of technology
   (d) Can be learned
7. If it is assumed that communication has no beginning or end, it is termed as
   (a) Mediation (b) Process
   (c) Interaction (d) Transaction
8. The essential components of communication are
   (a) Source, message, interference, channel, receiver, feedback, and context
   (b) Sign, source, destination, interaction, and correlation
   (c) Signs, symbols, understanding, communication, and communicant
   (d) Symbols, understanding, purpose, ideas, opinions, non-verbal, and reaction
9. Which of the following feature is applicable in context of interpersonal communication?
   (a) Forgivable (b) Forgettable
   (c) Reversible (d) Irreversible
10. Two-way communication becomes effective *(December 2003)*
    (a) Never (b) Always
    (c) Rarely (d) None of the above
11. A message can only be deemed effective when
    (a) Good communication skills are used
    (b) Repeated back as proof of understanding
    (c) Understood by receiver and produces the desired response
    (d) Delivered in interpersonal communication
12. Learning to communicate with others is key to
    (a) Eliminating listeners' all physiological noises
    (b) Never being misunderstood
    (c) Establishing rewarding relationships
    (d) All of the above
13. During the communication process, the message is converted to a symbolic form, called
    (a) Decoding (b) Encoding
    (c) Deciphering (d) Expanding
14. One's own description as a person is
    (a) Self-concept
    (b) Self-perception
    (c) Self-awareness
    (d) Self-respect
15. Which of the following term describes the communication between two people that involves sending and receiving of messages?
    (a) Decoding (b) Encoding
    (c) Transaction (d) Dyadic
16. Which of the following is the essence of effective communication?
    (a) Message (b) Feedback
    (c) Encoding (d) Decoding
17. People who engage in frank and open expression of their feelings are considered
    (a) Aggressive (b) Rude
    (c) Assertive (d) Inconsiderate
18. A low context culture is one where
    (a) Most of the information is unspoken
    (b) Most of the information is explicitly stated in a verbal message
    (c) Most of the information is apparent
    (d) Most of the information is non-existent
19. A high-context culture is one where
    (a) Much of the information is about the context or about the person
    (b) Much of the information is spoken
    (c) Most people use sign language
    (d) Much of the information is unspoken
20. A good communicator is one who offers his/her audience *(December 2005)*
    (a) Plentiful of information
    (b) A good amount of statistics

(c) Concise proof
(d) Repetition of facts

21. Which of the following steps would you consider first for an effective communication? (*December 1999*)
(a) Select the channel of communication
(b) Plan the evaluation procedure
(c) Specify the objectives of communication
(d) Identify various media for communication

22. The primary channels used by individuals to communicate with others are
(a) Radio and television
(b) E-mail
(c) Tone of voice
(d) Sight and sound

23. Encoding is important to
(a) Encourage feedback
(b) Eliminate noise
(c) Produce messages
(d) Ensure decoding of message

24. Communication will be effective (*June 1998*)
(a) If it is delivered slowly and clearly
(b) If it is delivered in a calm situation
(c) If it reaches the receiver completely
(d) If it reaches the receiver as intended by the sender

25. Which of the three components are parts of the human communication process?
(a) Message, recording, and feedback
(b) Noise, feedback, and jargon
(c) Message, noise, and feedback
(d) Feedback, message, and critiquing

26. Words are
(a) Connotative (b) Denotative
(c) Symbols (d) Unnecessary

27. Emoticons are
(a) Emotional conference
(b) Specifically expressive bodily gestures
(c) Emotional queries
(d) Typed symbols that communicate facial expressions

28. In the communication process, 'to encode' means to
(a) translate ideas into a code
(b) interpret a code
(c) block a pathway between the sender and receiver of a message
(d) speak to large groups of people

29. A person is more likely to use eye contact while
(a) listening
(b) uninterested in communication
(c) speaking
(d) interpreting

30. Feedback is
(a) a situation in which the sender and the receiver exchange information
(b) confined to the verbal form of communication.
(c) confined to the written form of communication
(d) None of the above

31. Listening is said to be adversely affected by
(a) speaker's fast speed of delivery of words
(b) message loaded with too much of information
(c) improper selection and use of media
(d) All of the above

32. Which of the following terms is closely related to feedback?
(a) Brainstorming (b) Heuristics
(c) Cybernetics (d) None of the above

33. Feedback is a listener's
(a) Verbal critique of your message
(b) Acceptance of a message
(c) Verbal or non-verbal responses to a message
(d) Aversion to a message

34. When we try to organize details in our minds, we are seeking to
(a) Produce new ideas in our mind
(b) Process complex information and then categorize it
(c) Categorize difficult and easy pieces of information
(d) Process simple information and categorize

35. Which is 'feedback' in newspaper's communication? (*December 1999*)
    (a) Articles
    (b) Editorials
    (c) Letters to the Editor
    (d) News
36. To decode a message is to
    (a) Evaluate a message
    (b) Translate ideas into code
    (c) Reject a message.
    (d) Interpret a message
37. A message is a signal that serves as
    (a) Stimuli for a sender
    (b) Stimuli for a receiver
    (c) Stimuli for a mass audience
    (d) Noise reduction
38. The objective definition of a word is its
    (a) Indirect meaning
    (b) Connotative meaning
    (c) Denotative meaning
    (d) Direct meaning
39. The subjective meaning of a word is its
    (a) Denotative meaning
    (b) Indirect meaning
    (c) Antonym
    (d) Connotative meaning
40. Which of the following explains feedback?
    (a) Non-verbal communication only
    (b) Environmental noise
    (c) Verbal and non-verbal receiver responses
    (d) Verbal communication only
41. An effective communication does not require (*June 1997, June 2001*)
    (a) Change in speech pattern
    (b) Appropriate gestures
    (c) Mastery of content
    (d) Handsome personality
42. For which of the following word/s, the term 'chronemics' is used for interpretation of messages
    (a) Smell (b) Taste
    (c) Time (d) All of the above
43. In the communication process, a receiver
    (a) Is a channel
    (b) Decodes a message
    (c) Is the person who encodes an idea
    (d) Responsible for message interference
44. An example of a communication channel is
    (a) Noise
    (b) Context
    (c) Face-to-face conversation
    (d) Feedback
45. The way one interprets information around oneself is
    (a) Always negative
    (b) Always positive
    (c) Related to one's values, beliefs, and past experiences
    (d) None of the above
46. Listening
    (a) May be a complex process involving many steps
    (b) Is always reflexive
    (c) A natural habit
    (d) A physiological process occurring in a spontaneous manner
47. The responding step of listening
    (a) Is non-verbal
    (b) Depends upon human memory
    (c) Can be verbal or non-verbal
    (d) Is always verbal
48. One of the most important communication skills is
    (a) Active listening
    (b) Objective listening
    (c) Passive listening
    (d) Inactive listening
49. A technique that might be used by an active listener is to
    (a) Paraphrase the speaker's meaning
    (b) Express concern
    (c) Explain the speaker's meaning
    (d) Offer a view point when in conversation
50. Effective listening includes
    (a) Filtering out points of disagreement
    (b) Detailed analysis
    (c) Attaching subjective meaning to a message
    (d) Confirming one's understanding of a message

51. A classification of body movements is called
(a) Emblems (b) Non-verbal
(c) Displays (d) Kinesics

52. Movements of the face that convey emotional meanings are called
(a) Displays
(b) Emblems
(c) Eye contact
(d) None of the above

53. Touch is an important element in
(a) Business communication
(b) Interpersonal communication
(c) Intrapersonal communication
(d) None of the above

54. Which of the following is less important in the context of effective communication? (*June 2004*)
(a) Total control over language
(b) Good vocabulary
(c) Attractive personality of the speaker
(d) Total control on the content to be transacted

55. Which of the following statements is correct? (*December 2005*)
(a) Communicator should have fine senses
(b) Communicator should have tolerance power
(c) Communicator should be soft spoken
(d) Communicator should have good personality

56. Which of the following are parts of active listening?
(a) Eye contact
(b) Nodding
(c) Seeking clarification
(d) All of the above

57. Evaluative listening is successful when we
(a) Accurately distinguish stimuli in a message
(b) Infer the meaning of a message
(c) Critically assess the accuracy of facts stated in a message
(d) None of the above

58. One will be an effective communicator if one (*December 1997*)
(a) Is a humorous speaker
(b) Has histrionic talents
(c) Is very clear about what one communicates
(d) Communicates in one's mother tongue

59. Effective communication will make the receivers (*December 1997*)
(a) Enjoy it
(b) Accept it
(c) Pass it on to others
(d) Think about it

60. Effective communication takes place when
(a) Source is attractive and authoritarian
(b) Message design incorporates audience
(c) Modern communication technologies are used
(d) Receivers are passive components

61. Which of the following is not a successful communication? (*June 2002*)
(a) One who presents material in a precise and clear way
(b) One who is able to adopt himself/herself according to the language of the communicatee
(c) One who knows a lot but is somewhat reserve in his/her attitude
(d) One who sometimes becomes informal before the receiver and develops rapport

62. The most important aspect of communication, that is, listening can be improved by (*June 2003*)
(a) Making the attention fully paid
(b) Making the communicated material novel-interesting and need based
(c) Making voice effective and impressive
(d) All of the above

63. The process of communication is enhanced through (*June 2003*)
(a) Belongingness
(b) Security and freedom to make choices
(c) Information of meeting and avoidance of pressure
(d) All of the above

64. Which of the following can help the most in enhancing the effectiveness of active listening?
(a) Developing apathy with the sender
(b) Developing a system to minimize the noise in the area
(c) Paying attention to the body language of the sender
(d) Developing empathy with the sender

65. Which of the following statements is not connected with communication?
(a) Medium is the message
(b) The world is an electronic cocoon
(c) Information is power
(d) Telepathy is technological

66. Postmodernism is associated with
(a) Newspapers (b) Magazines
(c) Radio (d) Television

67. In communication, the language is
(a) The non-verbal code
(b) The verbal code
(c) The symbolic code
(d) The iconic code

68. Media that exist in an interconnected series of communication points are referred to as
(a) Networked media
(b) Connective media
(c) Nodal media
(d) Multimedia

Types of Communication

69. Writing in a personal diary or otherwise recording one's thoughts and feelings are examples of
(a) Mediated intrapersonal communication
(b) Mediated interpersonal communication
(c) Mediated mass communication
(d) None of the above

70. In communication, chatting in internet is (*June 2009*)
(a) Verbal communication
(b) Non-verbal communication
(c) Parallel communication
(d) Grapevine communication

71. Interpersonal communication occurs only when
(a) A person exchanges idea with another one as a unique individual
(b) A large number of people are communicating with each other at the same time
(c) Only friends are talking
(d) None of the above

72. Non-verbal messages are
(a) Overestimated in importance
(b) Attempts at manipulation and should be ignored
(c) Generally irrelevant to overall message meaning
(d) Important for a listener to understand

73. Intrapersonal communication helps one
(a) Learn about oneself
(b) To know what others are thinking
(c) Communicate with the general public
(d) To become a talented public speaker

74. Communication between two or more people is called
(a) Organizational communication
(b) Interpersonal communication
(c) Extrapersonal communication
(d) Intrapersonal communication

75. In interpersonal communication, ethics are
(a) Important
(b) Communication barriers
(c) Ineffective
(d) None of the above

76. Which of the following is also termed as mediated communication?
(a) Intrapersonal communication
(b) Interpersonal communication
(c) Group communication
(d) Mass communication

77. Public communication tends to occur within a more (*June 2011*)
(a) Complex structure
(b) Political structure
(c) Convenient structure
(d) Formal structure

78. Non-verbal communication includes
(a) Delivering a speech
(b) Telephonic conversation
(c) Singing a song
(d) Shaking hands

79. Leadership roles first emerge in which of the following kinds of communication?
(a) Intrapersonal communication
(b) Small group communication
(c) Face-to-face public communication
(d) Media-like cell phones and instant messenger

80. A negative reaction to a mediated communication is described as (*December 2005*)
(a) Flak
(b) Fragmented feedback
(c) Passive response
(d) Non-conformity

81. Another term used for interpersonal communication is
(a) Group communication
(b) Face-to-face public communication
(c) Dyadic communication
(d) Traditional communication

82. Non-verbal message interpretation largely
(a) Depends upon cultural context
(b) Depends upon physical context
(c) Depends upon noise level
(d) Varies from person to person

83. Audio-conferencing may be classified among the following types of communication (*June 2004*)
(a) One-sided verbal
(b) Two-sided verbal
(c) One-sided non-verbal
(d) Two-sided non-verbal

84. Recording a television programme on a VCR is an example of (*December 2005*)
(a) Time-shifting
(b) Content reference
(c) Mechanical clarity
(d) Media synchronization

85. Four conditions influence the effectiveness of an encoded message: the skills, attitudes, knowledge of the sender, and __________.
(a) Social cultural system
(b) Knowledge of the receiver
(c) Age of the sender
(d) Environmental issues

86. Communication becomes circular when
(a) The decoder becomes an encoder
(b) The feedback is absent
(c) The source is credible
(d) The channel is clear

87. The information function of mass communication is described as
(a) Diffusion
(b) Publicity
(c) Surveillance
(d) Diversion

Communication Barriers

88. Disturbances that interfere with the transmission, receipt, or feedback of a message are called
(a) Feedback (b) Feed forward
(c) The channel (d) Noise

89. A disruption in the communication process is called (*June 2004*)
(a) Transgression (b) Feedback
(c) Noise (d) Interaction

90. The most powerful barrier of communication in the class is (*June 1997 and June 2001*)
(a) Noise in the classroom
(b) Confusion on the part of teacher
(c) More outside disturbance in the classroom
(d) Lack of teaching aids

91. Which of the following is not true about the grapevine?

(a) It is faster than formal communication network
(b) It is less accurate than formal network
(c) It is found in almost all organizations
(d) It is preferred over formal communication

92. Level C of the effectiveness of communication is defined as *(December 2005)*
(a) Channel noise
(b) Semantic noise
(c) Psychological noise
(d) Source noise

93. All of the following are barriers to effective communication except
(a) Absence of noise
(b) Distortion of information
(c) Information overloads
(d) None of the above

94. Informal transmission of information or filtered information is called
(a) Gossip
(b) Grapevine
(c) Vertical communication
(d) Horizontal communication

95. An example of physiological noise is
(a) Feeling hungry
(b) A humming air conditioner unit
(c) A lawn mower
(d) A speaker using complex terms

96. A speaker using complex terms is an example of
(a) Physiological noise
(b) Psychological noise
(c) Semantic noise
(d) Physical noise

97. A noise in the communication process
(a) Causes listeners to listen to messages more carefully
(b) Interferes with a message
(c) Focuses wandering thoughts
(d) Enhances a message

98. A fixed and categorized impression of a group of people based on a predetermined set of qualities is called
(a) Generalizing
(b) Consistency
(c) Stereotyping
(d) Oversimplification

99. The goal of perception checking is
(a) Confirmation
(b) Cultural sensitivity
(c) To further explore the thoughts and feelings of others
(d) Control

100. Which is a characteristic of prejudice?
(a) Generalized evaluation, specifically of out-group members
(b) Negativity
(c) Biased perceptions
(d) All of the above

101. The main assumption of 'primacy effect' is
(a) The most information is always that comes first
(b) The most important piece of information comes in the last
(c) The degree of importance depends upon the situation
(d) All pieces of information carry the same weight

102. In communication, a major barrier to reception of messages is
(a) Audience attitude
(b) Audience knowledge
(c) Audience education
(d) Audience income

Classroom Communication

103. If a student raises a hand to speak in class, the person is using
(a) Modifier (b) Emblem
(c) Regulator (d) Display

104. The psychological aspects of the classroom are best managed by *(December 1998)*
(a) The class teacher
(b) The subject teacher

(c) The principal
(d) The student themselves

105. Books can be powerful source of communication, provided
(a) Content is abstract
(b) Content is illustrative
(c) Medium is Hindi
(d) Content is presented through good print

106. Which of the following statements is not correct?
(a) A good communicator cannot be a good teacher
(b) A good communicator has good sense of humour
(c) A good communicator has wide reading
(d) A good communicator has command over language

107. Which of the following cannot be a good way in promoting literacy among villagers? (*June 2003*)
(a) Demonstration
(b) Reading and writing
(c) Providing material on TV and film projector
(d) Large group discussion

108. Which of the following are the main constituents of paralanguage?
I. Tone
II. Pitch
III. Quality of voice
IV. Rate of speaking
(a) I, II, and III
(b) II, III, and IV
(c) I, II, and IV
(d) All of the above

109. A teacher will become an effective communicator if (*December 1997*)
(a) He/she uses instructional aids
(b) He/she helps students get meaning out of what he/she teaches
(c) He/she asks question in between teaching
(d) He/she helps students get correct answer to the questions on the topic

110. Communication in the class fails because (*June 1998*)
(a) The students are inattentive
(b) The teacher is monotonous in delivering the message
(c) The students have no interest in the lesson being taught
(d) There is very much noise in and around the classroom

111. Which of the following will make communication more effective? (*June 1998*)
(a) Cracking jokes in between
(b) Using multi-sensory appeal
(c) Speaking with high authority
(d) Telling what is useful to the listeners

112. The facial expression of students relate to which element of the communication process? (*December 1998*)
(a) Message (b) Receiver
(c) Channel (d) Sender

113. Which of the following will not hamper effective communication in the classroom? (*June 2002*)
(a) A lengthy statement
(b) An ambiguous statement
(c) A precise statement
(d) A statement that allows the listener to draw his/her own conclusions

114. Which group of communication aspects does not disrupt the communication process in the class? (*December 2001*)
(a) Reversing–evaluating–focussing
(b) Evaluating–focussing–illustrating
(c) Evaluating–focussing–exaggerating
(d) Focussing–illustrating–exaggerating

Miscellaneous

115. Journal-like entries written by individuals and posted on the Internet that sometimes can generate many online discussions.
(a) Weblogs (b) Simple posting
(c) E-journals (d) None of the above

116. According to Mehrabian, the respective contributions of (i) words, (ii) tone of voice, and (iii) body language in overall communication are
(a) 38%, 7%, and 55%
(b) 7%, 38%, and 55%
(c) 55%, 38%, and 7 %
(d) None of the above

117. Paraphrasing is a skill that is absolutely necessary to effective
(a) Listening (b) Hearing
(c) Speaking (d) None of the above

118. The transmission of culture from one generation to another is called
(a) Acculturation (b) Enculturation
(c) Interculturation (d) None of the above

119. Leakage cues refer to
(a) facial expressions that people have misread
(b) one of the characteristic styles of facial expressions
(c) unintended signs of how a person really feels
(d) a technique employed by professional actors

120. A person has a very advanced sense of what is socially appropriate and always knows what to say in every social context. The person has which kind of linguistic competence?
(a) Phonemic (b) Cognitive
(c) Syntactic (d) Pragmatic

121. A sender in communication process has very good grammar. This competence is basically
(a) Phonemic (b) Semantic
(c) Syntactic (d) Pragmatic

122. A location where the Internet users can gain wireless access to the Internet
(a) Extranet
(b) Intranet
(c) Web conference
(d) Wi-Fi hot spot

123. Which of the following statement(s) is/are true in context of paraphrasing?
(A) It is basically about stating in your own words, your understanding of what has just been said.
(B) It gives speaker opportunity to find out what message s/he is getting across to you.
(a) Only A (b) Only B
(c) Both A and B (d) Neither A nor B

124. An example of asynchronous medium is
(a) Radio (b) Television
(c) Film (d) Newspaper

125. In communication, connotative words are
(a) Explicit (b) Abstract
(c) Simple (d) Cultural

126. A message beneath a message is labelled as
(a) Embedded text
(b) Internal text
(c) Intertext
(d) Subtext

127. In analogue mass communication, stories are
(a) Static (b) Dynamic
(c) Interactive (d) Exploratory

128. The ability to understand, communicate with, motivate, and support other people, both individually and in groups, defines which of the following organizational skills?
(a) Hard skills
(b) Soft skills
(c) Conceptual skills
(d) Political skills

Answer Keys

Communication: Concept, Nature, and Process

1. (a) 2. (c) 3. (d) 4. (b) 5. (a)
6. (d) 7. (b) 8. (a) 9. (d) 10. (b)
11. (c) 12. (c) 13. (b) 14. (a) 15. (d)
16. (b) 17. (c) 18. (b) 19. (d) 20. (a)
21. (c) 22. (d) 23. (c) 24. (d) 25. (c)
26. (c) 27. (d) 28. (a) 29. (a) 30. (a)
31. (d) 32. (c) 33. (c) 34. (b) 35. (c)
36. (d) 37. (b) 38. (c) 39. (d) 40. (c)
41. (d) 42. (c) 43. (b) 44. (c) 45. (c)
46. (a) 47. (c) 48. (a) 49. (a) 50. (d)
51. (d) 52. (a) 53. (b) 54. (c) 55. (a)
56. (d) 57. (d) 58. (c) 59. (d) 60. (b)
61. (c) 62. (d) 63. (d) 64. (d) 65. (d)
66. (d) 67. (b) 68. (a)

Types of Communication

69. (a) 70. (a) 71. (a) 72. (d) 73. (a)
74. (b) 75. (a) 76. (d) 77. (d) 78. (d)
79. (b) 80. (a) 81. (c) 82. (a) 83. (b)
84. (a) 85. (a) 86. (a) 87. (c)

Communication Barriers

88. (d) 89. (c) 90. (b) 91. (d) 92. (a)
93. (a) 94. (b) 95. (a) 96. (c) 97. (b)
98. (c) 99. (c) 100. (d) 101. (a) 102. (a)

Classroom Communication

103. (b) 104. (a) 105. (b) 106. (a) 107. (d)
108. (d) 109. (b) 110. (b) 111. (b) 112. (a)
113. (c) 114. (d)

Miscellaneous

115. (a) 116. (b) 117. (a) 118. (b) 119. (c)
120. (d) 121. (c) 122. (d) 123. (c) 124 (d)
125. (d) 126. (d) 127. (a) 128. (b)

5

Reasoning (Including Mathematical)

Introduction

In common language, to reason is to think, understand, and form judgements logically or to find a solution to a problem by considering the possible options. Hence, reasoning, as a part and parcel of logic, means the act of drawing conclusions from facts. Aptitude is a natural ability or propensity to learn. In this unit, apart from reasoning, we will discuss mathematical aptitude also that has become very important in NET examinations.

Reasoning is classified into two types, namely verbal and non-verbal. Verbal reasoning is basically about words rather than things. Verbal reasoning tests use words, letters, and numbers and require logical reasoning and a reasonable knowledge of English. It is also necessary to be familiar with simple, basic mathematical operations such as addition, subtraction, division, and multiplication. Non-verbal is basically about figures.

As far as NET examination pattern is concerned, mathematical reasoning covers mainly verbal and basic mathematical skills such as series completion, coding and decoding, classification (odd man out, and so on), and analogical relationship. Questions on direction sense and seating arrangement also appear regularly in the exam.

Topics such as Direction Sense and Venn Diagrams require both verbal and non-verbal reasoning skills.

Series Completion

A series may be a number series or letter series. There are several kinds of series such as finding the missing numbers, replacing the wrong numbers, finding the missing letters, finding the wrong group of numbers or letters, etc.

Number Series

Prime Number Series

Example 1

2, 3, 5, 7, 11, 13, 17, …

(a) 15 (b) 17 (c) 18 (d) 19

Solution

The given series is a prime number series. The next prime number is 19.

Answer: (d)

Example 2

2, 5, 11, 17, 23, 31, …

(a) 33 (b) 37 (c) 41 (d) 43

Solution

The prime numbers in this range are 2, 3, 5, 7, 11, 13, 17, 19, 23, 29, 31, 37, 41, 43, …

Prime numbers have been written alternatively. Thus, after 31, the prime numbers are 37, 41, … Ignoring 37, the answer is 41.

Answer: (c)

DIFFERENCE SERIES

Example 3

2, 5, 8, 11, 14, 17, …, 23, 26,

(a) 19 (b) 21 (c) 20 (d) 18

Solution

The difference between the numbers is 3. (17 + 3 = 20)

Answer: (c)

Example 4

45, 38, …, 24, 17, 10, 3

(a) 31 (b) 34 (c) 38 (d) 29

Solution

The difference between the consecutive numbers is 7. (38 – 7 = 31)

Answer: (a)

MULTIPLICATION SERIES

Example 5

2, 6, 18, 54, …, 486, 1,458

(a) 152 (b) 182 (c) 162 (d) 108

Solution

The numbers are multiplied by 3 to get the next number. (54 × 3 = 162)

Answer: (c)

Example 6

3, 12, 48, …, 768, 3,072

(a) 192 (b) 216 (c) 512 (d) 72

Solution

The numbers are multiplied by 4 to get the next number. (48 × 4 = 192)

Answer: (a)

DIVISION SERIES

Example 7

720, 120, 24, 6, …, 1

(a) 1 (b) 2 (c) 3 (d) 4

Solution

720 divided by 6 = 120
120 divided by 5 = 24
24 divided by 4 = 6
6 divided by 3 = 2
2 divided by 2 = 1

Answer: (b)

Example 8

32, 48, 72, …, 162, 243

(a) 84 (b) 96 (c) 108 (d) 132

Solution

Each number is being multiplied by 3/2 to get the next number.

Answer: (c)

N^2 SERIES

Example 9

1, 4, 9, 16, 25, 36, …, 64

(a) 42 (b) 44 (c) 45 (d) 49

Solution

The series is squares of 1, 2, 3, 4, and so on.

Answer: (d)

Example 10

0, 4, 16, 36, 64, …, 144

(a) 100 (b) 84 (c) 96 (d) 120

Solution

The series is squares of even numbers such as 2, 4, 6, 8, 10, and 12. Hence, the answer is $10^2 = 100$.

Answer: (a)

$N^2 - 1$ SERIES

Example 11

0, 3, 8, 15, 24, 35, 48, 63, …

(a) 80 (b) 82

(c) 83 (d) None of the above

Solution

The series is $1^2 - 1, 2^2 - 1, 3^2 - 1$, and so on. The next number is $9^2 - 1 = 80$.

Answer: (a)

Alternative solution: The differences between the numbers across the series are 3, 5, 7, 9, 11, 13, 15, and 17. The next number is 63 + 17 = 80.

$N^2 + 1$ SERIES

Example 12

2, 5, 10, 17, 26, 37,…, 65

(a) 50 (b) 48 (c) 49 (d) 51

Solution

The series is $1^2 + 1, 2^2 + 1, 3^2 + 1$, and so on. The next number is $7^2 + 1 = 50$.

Answer: (a)

$N^2 + N$ Series and $N^2 - N$ Series

Example 13

0, 2, 6, 12, 20, 30, …, 56

(a) 36 (b) 40
(c) 42 (d) None of the above

Solution

The series is $0^2 + 0$, $1^2 + 1$, $2^2 + 2$, $3^2 + 3$, and so on. The missing number is $6^2 + 6 = 42$. The next number $= 6^2 + 6 = 42$.

Answer: (c)

First alternative solution: The series is $0 \times 1, 1 \times 2$, ... 1×2, 2×3, 3×4, 4×5, and $5 \times 6 = 30$. The next number is $6 \times 7 = 42$.

Second alternative solution: The series is $1^2 - 1$, $2^2 - 2$, $3^2 - 3$, $4^2 - 4$, $5^2 - 5$, $6^2 - 6$, $7^2 - 7$, $8^2 - 8$, and so on.

N^3 Series

Example 14

1, 8, 27, 64, 125, 216, …

(a) 256 (b) 343 (c) 365 (d) 400

Solution

The series is 1^3, 2^3, 3^3, etc. The missing number is $7^3 = 343$.

Answer: (b)

$N^3 + 1$ Series

Example 15

2, 9, 28, 65, 126, 217, 344, …

(a) 513 (b) 362 (c) 369 (d) 361

Solution

The series is $1^3 + 1$, $2^3 + 1$, $3^3 + 1$, and so on. Thus, the missing number is $8^3 + 1 = 513$.

Answer: (a)

Letter Series

In this type of problem, a series of letters of English alphabet will be given, which follow a pattern or a sequence. The letter series mainly consists of skipping the letters.

To solve these types of problems, assign numbers 1 to 26 to the letters of English alphabet as shown below. In some cases, it is useful to assign the numbers in a reverse order.

Table 5.1 English Alphabet–Position Left to Right

A	B	C	D	E	F	G	H	I	J	K	L	M
1	2	3	4	5	6	7	8	9	10	11	12	13
N	O	P	Q	R	S	T	U	V	W	X	Y	Z
14	15	16	17	18	19	20	21	22	23	24	25	26

Concept of 'EJOTY'

Letters	E	J	O	T	Y
Position	5	10	15	20	25

The candidates can determine the relative positions of various alphabets by just remembering the word '**EJOTY**'. Various types of letter series are given below.

First alphabetical half: A to M → 1 to 13 and second alphabetical half: N to Z → 14 to 26

Table 5.2 English Alphabet–Position Right to Left

Z	Y	X	W	V	U	T	S	R	Q	P	O	N
1	2	3	4	5	6	7	8	9	10	11	12	13
M	L	K	J	I	H	G	F	E	D	C	B	A
14	15	16	17	18	19	20	21	22	23	24	25	26

Tables 5.1 and 5.2 above show both the forward as well as the backward place value of English alphabet. A very important fact about the position of any letter is that the sum of forward position and reverse position for any letter is always constant and equal to 27. For example, sum of both positions of H is $(8 + 19 = 27)$, for W is $(23 + 4 = 27)$.

Table 5.3 Series of Opposite English Alphabet

A	B	C	D	E	F	G	H	I	J	K	L	M
Z	Y	X	W	V	U	T	S	R	Q	P	O	N

One Letter Series

Example 16

A, C, E, G, …, K

(a) I (b) H (c) J (d) M

Solution
The series is A + 2 = C, C + 2 = E, E + 2 = G; G + 2 = I, I + 2 = K. The missing letter is I.

Answer: (a)

Example 17
A, B, D, G, …, P
(a) K (b) L (c) M (d) N

Solution
The series is +1, +2, +3, +4, +5, and so on. A + 1 = B; B +2 = D; D + 3 = G; G + 4 = K; K + 5 = P. The missing letter is K.

Answer: (a)

Example 18
B, E, H, K, N, …
(a) P (b) O (c) Q (d) R

Solution
The series is +3. The missing letter is N + 3 = Q.

Answer: (c)

Alternative solution: Skip two letters to get the next letter, that is, skip O and P after N to get Q. The missing letter is Q.

Example 19
B, D, G, I, L, N, …
(a) N (b) O (c) P (d) Q

Solution
This series is formed by moving +2 and +3 for each pair of letters starting from left. Thus the missing letter is N + 3 = Q.

Answer: (d)

Alternative solution: Skip one and two letters alternately to get the next letter, that is, skip two letters O and P after N to get Q.

Example 20
B, C, E, G, K, …
(a) M (b) N (c) O (d) P

Solution
B = 2, … K = 11 according to alphabet series (Table 5.1). Thus, alphabet series have been constructed according to the prime numbers. The next prime number is 13, and the corresponding letter is M.

Answer: (a)

Example 21
A, E, I, O, …
(a) Q (b) R (c) U (d) S

Solution
These are all vowels.

Answer: (c)

Example 22
A, D, I, P, …
(a) U (b) V (c) X (d) Y

Solution
According to alphabet series, the positions are 1, 4, 9, 16, and so on, which are $(1)^2$, $(2)^2$, $(3)^3$, $(4)^2$, and so on. The next number is $5^2 = 25$ and the corresponding letter is Y.

Answer: (d)

Example 23
D, F, H, I, J, L, …
(a) K (b) O (c) M (d) P

Solution
If numbers are assigned, the series becomes 4, 6, 8, 9, 10, 12, and so on, that is, composite number series. The next composite number is 14, and the corresponding letter is N.

Answer: (c)

Example 24
A, Z, B, Y, C, X, D, …
(a) U (b) V (c) W (d) X

Solution
The sequence consists of two series: one is ascending (A, B, C, D, etc.) and other is the descending series (Z, Y, X, W, etc.).

Answer: (c)

Combined Two Letter Series

The first letters of the series follow one logic and the second letters follow another logic, and then they pair with each other.

Example 25
AM, BN, CO, DP, …, FR
(a) EQ (b) FT (c) GR (d) ER

Solution
The first letters are A, B, C, D, E, and F, and the second letters are M, N, O, P, Q, and R.

Answer: (a)

Example 26
AB, DE, GH, …, MN
(a) HI (b) JK
(c) KL (d) None of the above

Solution
After every pair, one letter is skipped.

Answer: (b)

Example 27
AA, CE, EI, GO, …
(a) IU (b) IQ (c) IR (d) IT

Solution
The first letters of all pairs given in the question follow a sequence of A + 2 = C, C + 2 = E, and so on. The second letters are vowels.

Answer: (a)

Three Letter Series

This sequence consists of three letters in each term. The first letters follow one logic; the second letters follow another logic, and the third letters follow some other logic (or the same logic in all the three cases).

Example 28
ABD, CDF, …, GHJ, IJL
(a) EFH (b) IJL (c) HIJ (d) HIK

Solution
The first letter of each triplet follows a sequence of A, C, E, G, I, and so on. The second letter of each triplet follows a sequence of B, D, F, H, J, and so on, and the third letter forms a sequence of D, F, H, J, L, and so on.

Answer: (a)

Example 29
CKZ, DLY, … , FNW, GOV
(a) EMX (b) ENY
(c) ENX (d) None of the above

Solution
The first letters form a series of C, D, E, F, G, and so on. The second letters form a series of K, L, M, N, O, and so on. The third letters form a series of Z, Y, X, W, V, and so on.

Answer: (a)

Example 30
NAB, OEC, PIE, QOG, …
(a) QPH (b) QUH (c) QUI (d) RUK

Solution
The first letters form a series of N, O, P, Q, R, and so on. The second letters form a vowel series; the third letters form prime number series according to their number position.

Answer: (d)

Example 31
ABC, CBA, DEF, … , GHI, IHG
(a) JKL (b) FED (c) DFE (d) IJK

Solution
The second term is the reverse order of the first term. In addition to the above types, a number of other types can also be identified.

Answer: (b)

Coding and Decoding

The codes are based on various principles or patterns such that the message can be easily deciphered at the other end. They have become almost a regular feature of NET Paper I Exam to judge the candidates' intelligence and mental abilities. They are required to encode and decode words and sentences after observing the pattern and principles involved. These questions can be broadly classified as alphabetical coding, numerical coding, and mixed coding.

Alphabetical Coding

Remembering the positions of different letters is necessary to solve any question on alphabetical series. The English language contains 26 alphabets, and their varied positions are discussed in Tables 5.1–5.3.

In these types of questions, the letters of the alphabet are exclusively used. These letters do not stand for themselves but are allotted some artificial values based on some logical patterns or analogies. By applying those principles or observing the pattern involved, the candidates are required to decode a coded word or encode a word. These can be further classified into the following categories.

Simple Analogical Letter Coding

These are also called arbitrary codes. There are two definite principles or patterns involved. Codes are based on the analogy of one example from which different codes are to be formed.

Example 32

If 'BELONGINGS' is coded as 'TABLESTESF', then how will you code 'LINEN'?

(a) BTEAE (b) BTAEA
(c) BATEA (d) None of the above

Solution

The coding is done as follows:

Letters	B	E	L	O	N	G	I	N	G	S
↓	↓	↓	↓	↓	↓	↓	↓	↓	↓	↓
Codes	T	A	B	L	E	S	T	E	S	F

Accordingly, the code for LINEN is BTEAE.

Letter Coding on Specific Pattern

First, the candidates are required to observe the specific pattern involved and then proceed with encoding or decoding as the case may be.

Example 33

If 'POSTED' is coded as 'DETSOP', then how will you code 'SPEED'?

(a) DEEPS (b) DEESP
(c) DESEP (d) SPEDE

Solution

By careful observation, we can say that the letters have been written in the reverse order. Hence, SPEED will be written DEEPS, therefore (a) is the answer.

Example 34

If 'GREET' is coded as 'FQDDS', then 'CDDO' stands for

(a) EDDP (b) DEEP (c) PEED (d) EPED

Solution

Here, it is −1 for each letter of the word 'GREET'.

Word	G	R	E	E	T
	−1	−1	−1	−1	−1
Code	F	Q	D	D	S

CDDO itself is a code. To find out what it stands for, we have to add +1 to the alphabets to get back the original word.

Code	C	D	D	O
	+1	+1	+1	+1
Word	D	E	E	P

Example 35

If 'PAT' is coded as 'QRBCUV', then how will you code 'GRACE'?

(a) HISTBCDEFG (b) HISTBCDEGF
(c) HISBTCDEFG (d) HISTBCEDFG

Solution

The pattern of coding is such that each letter has been allotted the value of 2 letters following the sequence, that is, A = BC, B = CD, C = DE, etc. Hence, the word GRACE will be coded as 'HISTBCDEFG'. Therefore, option (a) is the answer.

Example 36

If 'EGHJKMKM' is the code for 'FILL', how will you decode 'EGDFDFKM'?

(a) LEEF (b) FEEL (c) DEAL (d) REEL

Solution

Refer to alphabet series in Table 5.1 starting from the LHS pair, E is the antecedent of F and G is the precedent of F. We get EG as code for F; HJ as code for I; and so on.

Similarly, EGDFDFKM is the code for FEEL. F is coded as EG with its precedent and antecedent letters; similarly, 'I' is coded as HJ and L as KM. Hence, EGDFDFKM stands for FEEL. Therefore, option (b) is the correct answer.

Coding with Numerical Digits

Here, the numerical values (not necessarily according to rank of letters in the alphabet series) can be assigned to letters. The values are allotted based on some specific pattern that has to be discerned by the candidate in order to solve the problem.

Example 37

If 'TRAIN' is coded as 23456, how will you code 'RAIN'?

(a) 3456 (b) 3546 (c) 2345 (d) 2456

Solution

Word	T	R	A	I	N
Code	2	3	4	5	6

These values have been assigned arbitrarily. The question can be solved on the basis of the relationship established. For RAIN, the code is 3456, so (a) is the answer.

Analogical Coding with Numerical Digits

Here, the letters are assigned numerical values on the basis of analogy of the example given in the question. There is no set of principles or patterns involved. The candidates are required to study the given examples before getting started with the exercise.

Example 38

If 'SELDOM' is coded as '1 2 4 3 6 5', how will you code 'MODE'?

(a) 3 6 2 1 (b) 6 2 3 1
(c) 5 6 3 2 (d) 6 2 1 3

Solution

Word	S	E	L	D	O	M
	↓	↓	↓	↓	↓	↓
Code	1	2	4	3	6	5

On the basis of the analogical relationship established between the letters and the numbers, we can code 'MODE' as 5632.

Answer: (c)

Coding with Specific Pattern

This is the pattern of coding that exhibits the natural correlation of Arabic numbers with alphabetical letters. For instance, alphabets A to Z are assigned the numeric codes from 1 to 26, where each letter gets the assignment in the pattern as follows A = 1, B = 2, C = 3, etc.

The sequence is classified as follows:

1. *Forward sequence:* For example, A = 1, B = 2, ... Y = 25, Z = 26

   Example 39

   If 'PACE' is code as 16-1-3-5, how will you code 'RACE'?

   (a) 18-1-3-5 (b) 16-1-3-5
   (c) 16-3-5-1 (d) None of the above

   Answer: **(a)**

2. *Backward sequence:* For example, Z = 1, Y = 2, ... B = 25, A = 26

   Example 40

   If 'GREAT' is coded as 20-9-22-26–7, how will you code 'GATE'?

   (a) 20-26-7-22 (b) 20-26-6-22
   (c) 26-20-7-22 (d) 26-20-22-7

   Answer: **(a)**

3. *Random sequence:* The pattern can be established in alternative ways, but in every case, a set pattern is involved, which has to be discovered by careful examination of the example given in the question.

   Example: If A = 3, B = 4, Z = 28; If A = 5, B = 7, C = 9, and so on.

   Example 41

   If 'FRANCE' is coded as 10-22-5-18-7-9, how will you code 'INDIA'?

   Based on the above pattern, the answers will be as follows:

   (a) 13-18-8-13-5 (b) 13-17-6-12-4
   (c) 12-17-7-12-5 (d) None of the above

   Solution

   The pattern of assignment is read as given in the following table.

A	B	C	D	E	F	G	H	I	J
5	6	7	8	9	10	11	12	13	14
K	L	M	N	O	P	Q	R	S	T
15	16	17	18	19	20	21	22	23	24
U	V	W	X	Y	Z				
25	26	27	28	29	30				

Answer: (a)

Mixed Coding (Letters + Digits)

Mixed coding takes the pattern of coding with both the letters of the alphabet and numerical assignment. The candidates are required to study the analogy given in the question.

Example 42

If 'A3T15R' stands for 'ACTOR' and 'D1T5' stands for 'DATE', how will you code 'ROTATE'?

(a) R15T1T5 (b) R16T1T5
(c) R15T1T6 (d) L15C1T7

Explanation

While coding for ACTOR, first, third and fifth letters have been put without any change. C and O are placed at 3rd and 15th position in alphabetical series (Table 5.1). Hence, code for ACTOR is A3T15R. Similar exercise for DATE. Thus, code for ROTATE is R15T1T5. Thus, (a) is the answer.

Example 43

If 'M I S S I O N' is coded '□! ? ? ! φ $' and 'LENS' is coded '@#$?', how will you code 'LION'?

(a) @ ! φ $ (b) @ ! $ #
(c) ? ? # # (d) None of the above

Explanation

LION = L + ION

Pick L from LENS and ION from MISSION. By careful observation, we can identify that code for L is @ and code for ION is !φ $. Hence, (a) is the answer.

Coded Statements

1. In a certain code language, 'do re me' means 'he is late'; 'fa me la' means 'she is early', and 'so ti do' means 'he leaves soon'. Which word in that language means 'late'?
(a) la (b) do (c) me (d) re

Explanation

do re me - he is late (i)

fa me la - she is early (ii)

so ti do - he leaves soon (iii)

Comparing (i) and (ii) we can say that 'me' stands for 'is'.

Comparing (i) and (iii) we can say that 'do' stands for 'he'.

Substituting them in sentence (i) we can say that 're' stands for 'late".

The following arrangement also helps in the solution.

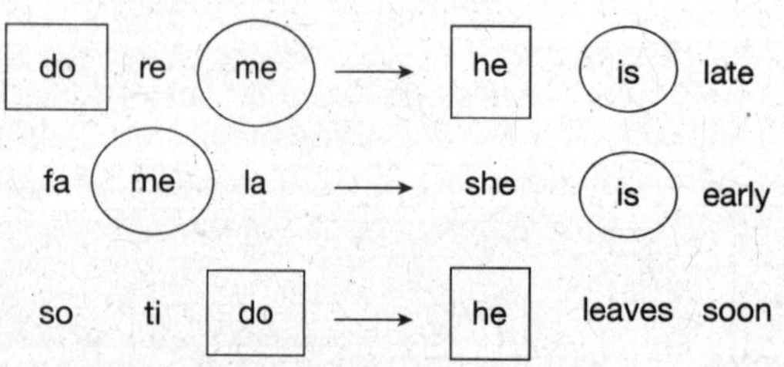

Hence, the code for 'late' is 're'.

2. In a certain code, 'jo ka ra' means 'go for walk'; 'ma fo ka' means 'do not walk', and 'sa ta jo' means 'good for you'. What is the code for 'go'?
(a) ra (b) ka (c) ta (d) jo

Explanation

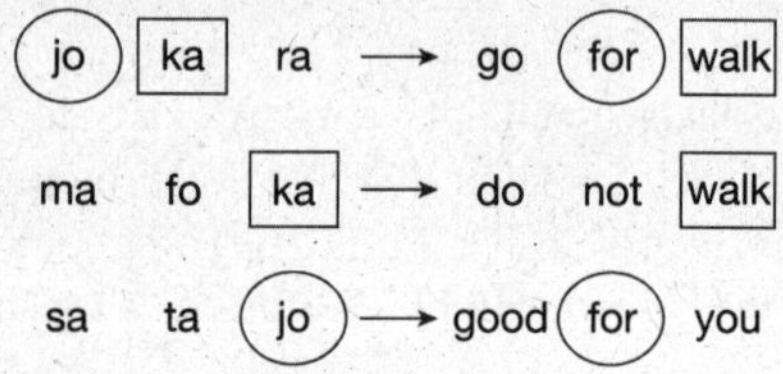

Hence, the code for 'go' is 'ra'.

3. If rain is water, water is road, road is cloud, cloud is sky, sky is sea, and sea is path, where do aeroplanes fly?
(a) Road (b) Sea
(c) Cloud (d) Water

Explanation

The aeroplanes fly in the 'sky' and the 'sky' is called 'sea'. Hence, the aeroplanes fly in the 'sea'.

Answer: (b)

4. In a certain code, '247' means 'spread red carpet'; '256' means 'dust one carpet', and '236' means 'one red carpet'. Which digit in that code means 'dust'?
(a) 2 (b) 3 (c) 5 (d) 6

Answer: (c)

Explanation

In the first and second statements, the common code digit is '2', and the common word is 'carpet'. Thus, '2' means 'carpet'. In the second and third statements, the common code digit is '6', and the common word is 'one'. Thus, '6' means 'one'. Therefore, in the second statement, '5' means 'dust'.

5. In a certain code language, 'Siberia is a cold place' is written as 'a cold is place Siberia'. In the same code, 'Water freezes to ice here' is written as 'freezes here ice to water'. How 'covers ten per cent of earth' will be written?
(a) Covers earth ten per cent of
(b) Covers earth of per cent ten
(c) Earth covers ten per cent of
(d) None of the above

Answer: (b)

Explanation

The first alphabet of the words is to be picked and then written as they appear in alphabetic series.

Classification

The questions based on classification are based on similarity or dissimilarity between a number of items or objects. Some objects are grouped together on the basis of some common characteristics. The candidate has to identify that characteristic and separate out the object that does not belong to the group. This test is also known as 'Odd Man Out'.

Choosing the Odd Word

In these types of problems, some words belong to the real word. They have certain common features except the odd one.

Example 44
Choose the word that is least like the other words in a group?
(a) Calendar (b) Date
(c) Day (d) Month

Answer: (a)

Explanation
All other words are parts of a calendar.

Example 45
Choose the word that is least like the other words in a group?
(a) Peacock (b) Vulture
(c) Sparrow (d) Swan

Answer: (c)

Explanation
Swan is the only water bird in the group.

Choosing the Odd Pair of Words

In each of the following questions, five pairs of words are given, out of which the words in five pairs bear a certáin common relationship. Choose the pair in which the words are differently related.

Example 46
Choose the pair in which the words are differently related?
(a) Man : Crowd (b) Cow : Herd
(c) Sheep : Flock (d) Fish : Shoal

Answer: (a)

Explanation
In all other pairs, the second word is a collective group of the first.

Example 47
Choose the pair in which the words are differently related?
(a) Joule : Energy (b) Ampere : Current
(c) Angle : Degree (d) Pascal : Pressure

Answer: (c)

Explanation
In all other pairs, first is a unit to measure the second.

Choosing the Odd Numeral

In each of the following questions, four numbers are given. Out of these, three are alike in a certain way except one.

Example 48
Choose the number that is different from others in the group?
(a) 139 (b) 177 (c) 144 (d) 183

Answer: (c)

Explanation
Number 144 is the only perfect square number in the group.

Example 49
Choose the number that is different from others in the group?
(a) 127 (b) 345 (c) 361 (d) 514

Answer: (b)

Explanation
All other numbers except 361 are two more than the cube of a certain number.

Choosing the Odd Numeral Pair or Group

Choose the odd numeral pair or group in each of the following questions.

Example 50
Choose the number pair or group that is different from others?
(a) 15 : 46 (b) 12 : 37
(c) 9 : 28 (d) 8 : 33

Answer: (d)

Explanation

In all other pairs, second number = (first number × 3) + 1.

Example 51

Choose the number pair or group that is different from others?

(a) 3, 5 (b) 7, 2 (c) 6, 2 (d) 1, 7

Answer: (b)

Explanation

In all other pairs, the sum of two numbers is 8.

Choosing the Odd Letter Group

In each of the following questions, some groups of letters are given; all of which, except one, share a common similarity.

Example 52

Choose or find the odd letter group

(a) BCD (b) NPR (c) KLM (d) RQP

Answer: (b)

Explanation

All other groups contain three consecutive letters of the alphabet series.

Example 53

Choose the group of letters that is different from others?

(a) KLM (b) IJK (c) PQR (d) RST

Answer: (b)

Explanation

No other group contains a vowel.

ANALOGY

Analogy means correspondence. In questions based on analogy, a particular relationship is given and another similar relationship has to be identified from the alternatives provided. Analogy tests are, therefore, meant to test a candidate for overall knowledge, power of reasoning, and ability to think concisely and accurately. Questions on analogy test the ability of a candidate to understand the relationship between two given objects and apply the same relationship to find what was asked in the question. Some common relationships are given below, which will help you detect most analogies better.

Different types of analogy are given below.

Direct/Simple Analogy

In these types of questions, the first two words have a definite relationship. According to the relationship, we have to choose one word out of the given four alternatives that have the same relationship with the third word as between the first two.

Example 54

Apparel is related to cloth in the same way as footwear is related to

(a) Laces (b) Cobbler
(c) Leather (d) Shoes

Answer: (c)

Explanation

The first is made by the other.

Example 55

As delicious is related to taste, melodious is related to

(a) Voice (b) Speak
(c) Music (d) Highness

Answer: (a)

Explanation

Delicious represents good taste. Similarly, melody describes pleasant voice.

Completion of Analogous Pair

Example 56

Giant : Dwarf : : Genius : ?

(a) Wicked (b) Gentle
(c) Idiot (d) Cunning

Answer: (c)

Explanation

As dwarf is the antonym of giant, idiot is the antonym of genius.

Example 57

Fruit : Banana : : Mammal : ?

(a) Cow (b) Snake
(c) Fish (d) Sparrow

Answer: (a)

Explanation

As banana is a type of fruit, cow is a type of mammal.

Selecting the Right Analogous Pair

In these types of questions, a pair of word is given that is followed by four pairs of words as alternatives. The candidate is required to choose the pair in which the words bear the same relationship to each other as in the case of the words of the given pair.

Example 58
Lamp : Darkness
(a) Fatigue : Exercise
(b) Water : Thirst
(c) Medicine : Illness
(d) Study : Classroom

Answer: (b)

Explanation
Just as a lamp eliminates darkness, water quenches thirst.

Example 59
Weight : Kilograms
(a) Axe : Grind
(b) Ammeter : Current
(c) Power : Ampere
(d) Energy : Joule

Answer: (d)

Explanation
As weight can be measured in kilogram, joule is the unit of measuring energy.

Choosing a Similar Word

In this type of questions, a group of three or four words is given, followed by four other words as alternatives. The candidate is required to choose the alternative, which is similar to the given words.

Example 60
Iron : Copper : Zinc
(a) Ceramic (b) Carbon
(c) Nickel (d) Mercury

Solution
Answer is (c). All are solid metals.

Example 61
Potato : Carrot : Radish
(a) Tomato (b) Spinach
(c) Sesame (d) Groundnut

Solution
Answer is (d). All of these crops/vegetables grow underground.

Alphabet Analogy

In this type of questions, two groups of letters related to each other in some way are given. The candidate is required to find out this relationship and then choose either a letter-group that is related in the same way to a third group provided in the questions or a pair consisting of similarly related letter-groups.

Example 62
BEGK is related to ADFJ in the same way as PSVM is related to …….?
(a) LOQT (b) ROUX
(c) OTUZ (d) ORUL

Solution
Clearly, each letter of the first group in a pair is moved one step backward to obtain the corresponding letter of the second group.

B	E	G	K
–1	–1	–1	–1
A	D	F	J

Similarly,

P	S	V	M
–1	–1	–1	–1
Q	R	U	L

Answer: (d).

Example 63
ABCD : LNPR : : FGHI : ?

Solution
Clearly, the first, second, third, and fourth letters of the first group are moved 11, 12, 13, and 14 steps forward, respectively, to obtain the corresponding letters of the second group.

A	B	C	D
+11	+12	+13	+14
L	N	P	R

Similarly,

F	G	H	I
+11	+12	+13	+14
Q	S	U	W

Number Based

Under this category, the following types of questions can be asked:

1. Choosing a number related to a given number in the same manner as the two numbers of another given pair are related to each other.
2. Choosing a similarly related pair as the given number pair on the basis of relationship between the numbers in each pair.
3. Choosing a number similar to a group of numbers on the basis of certain common properties that they possess.
4. Choosing a number set similar to a given number set.

Example 64

9 : 14 : : 26 : ?

(a) 2 (b) 13 (c) 15 (d) 31

Solution

Answer is (d). The relationship is $x : (x + 5)$.

Example 65

8 : 28 : : 27 : ?

(a) 55 (b) 63 (c) 64 (d) 85

Solution

Answer is (d). The relationship is $x : (3x + 4)$.

Example 66

42 : 56 : : 72 : ?

(a) 81 (b) 90 (c) 96 (d) 100

Solution

The ratio between 42 and 56 is 3 : 4. Similarly; 72 : 96 depicts the ratio 3 : 4.

Answer: (c).

Blood Relations

The questions that are asked in this section depend upon relation. The candidate should have a sound knowledge of the blood relations in order to solve the questions.

To remember easily, the relations may be divided onto two sides as given below in Table 5.4.

Table 5.4 Blood Relations of Paternal and Maternal Sides

Relations of paternal side	
Father's father	Grandfather
Father's mother	Grandmother
Father's brother	Uncle
Grandfather's Son	Father or Uncle
Grandfather's only son	Father
Father's sister	Aunt
Children of uncle	Cousin
Wife of uncle	Aunt
Children of aunt	Cousin
Husband of aunt	Uncle
Sister's husband	Brother-in-Law
Wife's brother	Brother-in-Law
Brother's son	Nephew
Brother's wife	Sister-in-law
Brother's daughter	Niece
Grandson's or granddaughter's daughter	Great granddaughter
Mother's or father's son/ daughter	Brother/sister
Son's wife	Daughter-in-law
Relations of maternal side	
Mother's father	Maternal grandfather
Mother's mother	Maternal grandmother
Mother's brother	Maternal uncle
Mother's sister	Aunt
Children of maternal uncle	Cousin
Wife of maternal uncle	Maternal aunt
Others	
Children of same parents	Siblings
Common term for husband and wife	Spouse

Developing a Family Relationship Tree

To develop a blood relation tree, some standard symbols may be used to tell about the relationships among the family members.

Suppose M is male and N is female. Some authors use the sign of + and – for indicating male and female. Cousin is a common gender; it means that this relationship can be used for both male and female.

Condition	Sign
When M is Male	+M
When N is Female	–N
M and N are married to each other	M = N
P and Q are siblings	P ⟷ Q
A is the child of B	A ↓ B
When A has two children B and C	A ↙ ↘ B C

Approach to Draw the Family Relations Diagram

To draw a family tree,

1. First of all identify the males and the females; then, according to generation, try to put each member at the appropriate position in the tree.
2. Draw the diagram with relationships among family members using notations.
3. Once the diagram is filled, the candidate can answer the given questions.

Example 67

X and Y are brothers. C and D are sisters. X's son is D's brother. How is Y related to C?

(a) Uncle (b) Grand Father
(c) Father (d) None of the above

Explanation

Y is the brother of X; X's son is D's brother. This implies that D is the daughter of X. As C and D are sisters, C is also the daughter of X. Hence, Y is the uncle of C.

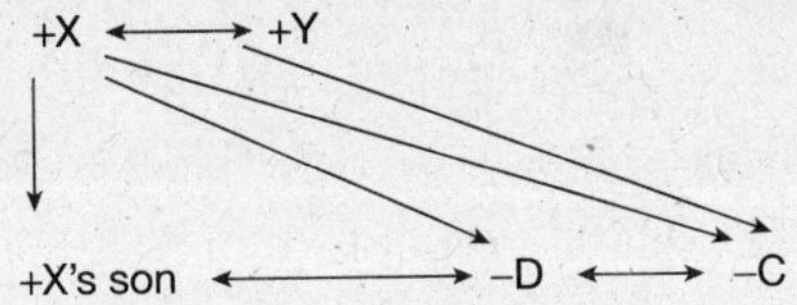

OR

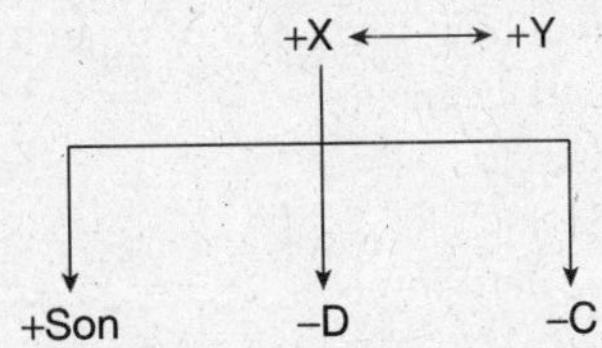

As per the statement and family tree, X's son, D, and C are siblings. Y is the uncle of C.

Example 68

'A' is the father of 'C', and 'D' is the son of 'B'. 'E' is the brother of 'A'. If 'C' is the sister of 'D', how is 'B' related to 'E'? *(NET June 2007)*

(a) Daughter (b) Husband
(c) Sister-in-law (d) Brother-in-law

Answer: (c)

Explanation

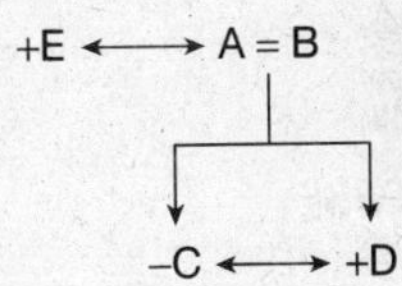

Thus, B is the sister in-law of E.

Example 69

E is the son of A; D is the son of B, E is married to C, C is the daughter of B. How is D related to E? *(NET June 2010)*

(a) Brother (b) Uncle
(c) Father-in-law (d) Brother-in-law

Answer: (d)

Explanation

Family Tree

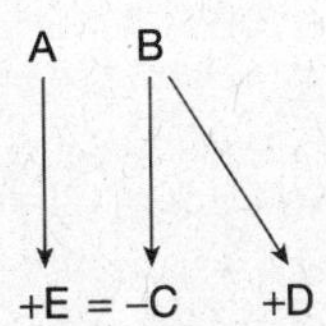

OR

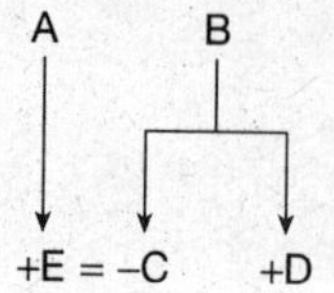

Hence, D is the brother-in-law of E.

Example 70

If B is the only child of C's grandfather's only daughter, then how is C's father related to B?

(a) Maternal uncle
(b) Father
(c) Paternal uncle
(d) Can't be determined

Answer: (a)

Explanation

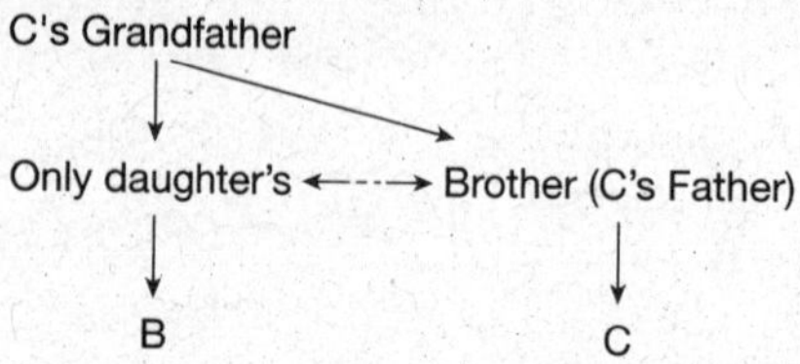

As B is the only child, C can't be the sister of B. On the other hand, B's mother is the only daughter of her parents, so she can have a brother. Hence, C's father is maternal uncle of B.

Direction Sense

There are four main directions: East, West, North, and South as shown below.

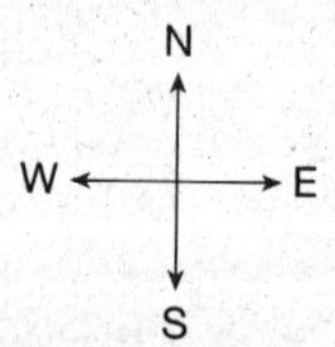

There are four cardinal directions: north-east (NE), north-west (NW), south-east (SE), and south-west (SW) as shown below.

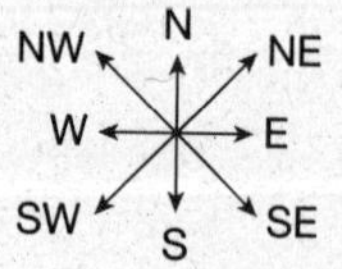

Few Important Points

1. At the time of sunrise, if a man stands facing the east, his shadow will be towards west.
2. At the time of sunset, the shadow of an object is always in the east.
3. If a man stands facing north, at the time of sunrise his shadow will be towards his left, and at the time of sunset, it will be towards his right.
4. At 12:00 noon, the rays of the sun are vertically downward; hence, there will be no shadow.

Example 71

Prakash walked 30 m towards west, took a left turn, and walked 20 m; he again took a left turn and walked 30 m. Then, he took right turn and stopped. He is now facing

(a) South (b) North (c) East (d) West

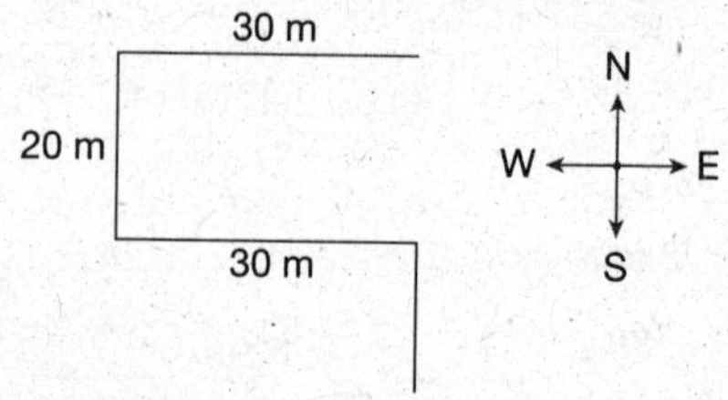

Answer: (a)

Example 72

If south-east direction becomes North, north-east direction becomes West, and so on, what will West become?

(a) North-west (b) North-east
(c) South-east (d) South-west

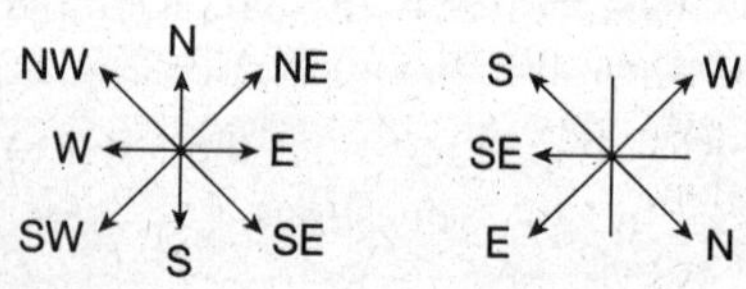

Answer: (c)

Example 73

Atul walks 20 m towards south; turning to the left, he walks 30 m. Then, turning right, he walks 10 m, and then, turning right, he walks 40 m; then, turning right, he walks 30 m and stopped. In which direction is he standing with respect to his starting point?

(a) East (b) West (c) North (d) South

Explanation

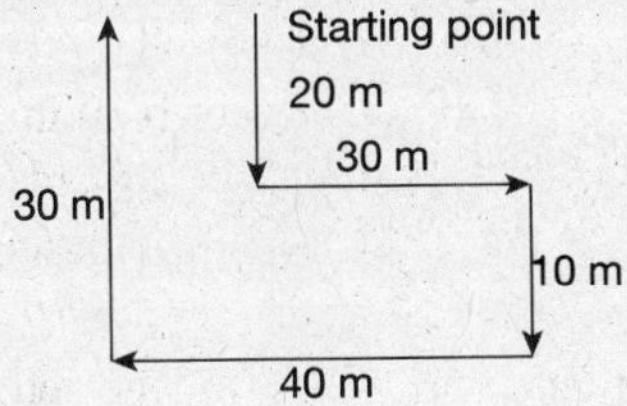

Answer: (c)

SEATING ARRANGEMENT

Example 74

Among six members P, Q, R, G, S, and M sitting along a circle facing the centre.

I R is between G and P.

II M is between P and S.

What is the position of Q

(a) To the immediate left of G
(b) To the immediate right of S
(c) Can't be determined
(d) None of the above

Explanation

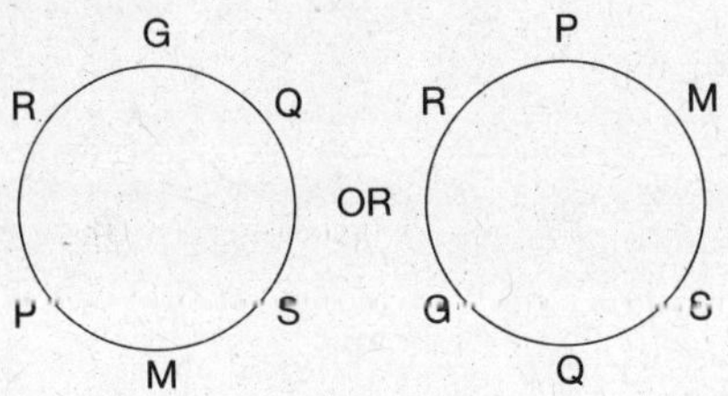

Q is between G and S, this is 100%; whether right or left, it requires more information. Therefore, position of Q cannot be determined with the available information. Hence, (c) is the right option.

Answer: (c)

Example 75

Among M, N, T, R, and D, each has a different height; T is taller than D, but shorter than M. R is taller than N, but shorter than D. Who among them is the tallest?

(a) R (b) M
(c) D (d) None of the above

Solution

$$M > T > D > R > N$$

Hence, M is the tallest.

Answer: (b)

Example 76

A, B, C, D, E, and F are sitting in a row facing north. A is the neighbour of B and D; E is the neighbour of C and F, and D is the neighbour of C. How many members are there between A and E?

(a) Two (b) One (c) Three (d) Four

Answer: (a)

Explanation

The sitting arrangement is **B A D C E F**. Between A and E, there are two members D and C.

BASIC ARITHMETIC

Here, few basic arithmetic topics such as percentages, averages, time and distance, and time and work have been covered. These questions are as per NET Paper I pattern though there are large varieties in these topics.

Percentage

There are two to three questions asked directly from percentage topic, and one or two questions may be asked indirectly. For solving the questions from data interpretation, the knowledge of concept of percentage is helpful. Per cent in the simplest sense means per cent, that is, per hundred. For example, $15\% = \frac{15}{100} = 0.15$.

1. To convert any per cent as a part or multiple of 1, divide it by 100. Examples: 4% = 0.04, 40% = 0.4, and 400% = 4
2. Conversely, to write any number in the per cent form, multiply it with 100 and append a % symbol. Example: 2 = 200%, 0.2 = 20%, 0.02 = 2%, and 0.002 = 0.2%

As seen above, x% is nothing but a fraction with numerator x and denominator 100. Identifying certain percentages in the reduced form of the fractions can be very useful. For example, whenever we have to calculate 20%, we can calculate $\frac{20}{100} = \frac{1}{5}$. Similarly, the ratio $\frac{3}{5}$ can be expressed as $\frac{60}{100}$, that is, 60%.

If we assume that 1 is equal to 100%, $\frac{1}{2}$ = 50%, $\frac{1}{3}$ = 33.33%, $\frac{1}{4}$ = 25%, $\frac{1}{5}$ = 20%, $\frac{1}{6}$ = 16.66%, $\frac{1}{8}x$ = 12.5%, $\frac{1}{12}$ = 8.33%, $\frac{1}{16}$ = 6.25%, $\frac{1}{20}$ = 5%, and so on.

If we were to convert 3/8 to percentage; simply multiply its percentage equivalent of 1/8 by 3. Then, we get an answer 3 × 12.5% = 37.5%.

Ratio, Proportion, and Percentage

Ratios can also be expressed as fractions. They represent the basic relationship between two quantities. Proportions are in comparison to the whole.

In a mixture of 20 *l* of milk and 30 *l* of water, the ratio of milk and water is 2 : 3. This can be converted to fraction of milk in the solution as 2 : 5 or $\frac{2}{5}$ th.

As seen, $\frac{2}{5}$ is nothing but $\frac{2}{5} \times 100 = 40\%$.

Example 77

What percentage of 180.50 is 36.1?

(*December 1997*)

(a) 20 (b) 25
(c) 20.50 (d) None of the above

Solution

Lets x% of 180.5 = 36.1
x% = 36.1/180.5
x = 36.1/180.5 × 100 = 20%

Concept of Base in Percentage Calculations

If it is said that India won 50% of the matches it played, neither does it means that India won 50 matches nor does it means that India won 0.5 matches. It means that India played 100 matches, it won 50 matches.

Now assume that India won 40% of matches that it played in 2015. We have to calculate how many matches it actually won, and for that, we ought to know the total matches played, say, for example, 25 matches. Thus, if India had played a total of 25 matches, it would have won 40% of 25 = $\frac{40}{100} \times 25$ = 10 matches.

Basic Examples

A candidate needs to be familiar with following basics of percentage.

Examples	Solution approach
Express 12% as a fraction	$x\% = \frac{x}{100} = \frac{12}{100} = \frac{3}{25}$
Express $\frac{3}{8}$ as percentage	Multiply the fraction by 100 to convert it to percentage. $= \frac{3}{8} \times 100 = 37.5\%$
A's income is 60% of B's income. If B's income is ₹ 15,000. What is A's income?	$A = \frac{x}{100} \times B$ $= \frac{60}{100} \times 15{,}000 = ₹9{,}000$
X's income is 25% more than Y's. By how much % is Y's income less than X's income?	As comparison is with X's income, it will be taken as a base. Difference = $\frac{r}{100+r} \times 100$ (where r is the percentage difference) $= \frac{25}{125} \times 100 = 20\%$
X's income is 20% less than Y's. By how much % is Y's income more than X's income?	Again as comparison is with X's income, it should be taken as base. Difference = $\frac{r}{100+r} \times 100$ $= \frac{20}{80} \times 100 = 25\%$
The price of petrol increases by 50%. By how much %, its consumption should be reduced so as to keep the expenditure same?	Expenditure = price × consumption Decrease = $\frac{r}{100+r} \times 100 =$ $\left(\frac{50}{150}\right) \times 100 = 33.33\%$

Calculation of Change in Quantities in Percentage Terms-Direct Formula

Suppose a quantity (such as price or salary) increases or decreases first by $x\%$, and then by $y\%$, what is the net increase or decrease in the price?

Net increase $= x + y + xy/100$. This formula is used where 'two' quantities are to be multiplied as per formula or requirement of the question, and one or both of these quantities may increase or decrease.

Example 78
The price of a commodity increases first by 20% and then by 10%. What is the net increase in the price?

Solution
Let original price = 100
Price after 1st increase = 100 + 20 = 120
Price after 2nd increase = 120 + (10% of 120) = 132.
Net increase = 132 − 100 = 32%
Direct formula = 20 + 10 + (20 × 10)/100 = 32%

Example 79
A retailer offers two successive discounts of 20% and 30%. What is the net decrease in the price?

Solution
Let original price = 100
Price after 1st discount = 100 − 20 = 80
Price after 2nd discount = 80 − (30% of 80) = 56.
Net discount = original price − discount = 100 − 56 = 44
Direct formula = (−20) + (−30) + (−20) × (−30)/100 = −50 + 6 = −44%. Negative sign shows the decrease.

Example 80
The price of a commodity is first increased by 40% and then reduced by 20%. What is the net increase or decrease in the price?

Solution
Let the original price = 100
Price after increase = 100 + 40 = 140
Price after decrease = 140 − (20% of 140) = 112
Net increase in price = 112 − 100 = 12%
Direct formula = 40 − 20 + (40 × −20)/100 = 12%

Example 81
A's income is 70% of B's. B's income is 50% of C's. If C's income is ₹1,00,000, what is A's income?

Solution

$$\text{B's income} = \left(\frac{50}{100}\right) \times 1{,}00{,}000 = ₹50{,}000$$

$$\text{A's income} = \left(\frac{70}{100}\right) \times 50{,}000 = ₹35{,}000$$

Alternative method
A's income = 70% of 50% of 1,00,000 = ₹35,000

Example 82
In an exam, a student scored 50% of the maximum marks and yet failed by 15 marks. If he had scored 10% more than what he scored, he would have just managed to get the pass percentage. What are the maximum marks of the paper?

Solution
Let maximum passing marks = 100
Actual marks obtained = 50

Had he scored 50 + 10% of 50, that is 55 marks, he would have scored passing marks. In this situation, difference between actual and passing marks is 5.
Actual difference = 15
5% of maximum marks = 15
Maximum marks = 15 × 100/5 = 300

Example 83
In a basket of fruits, 60% are mangoes and remaining are apples. In that, 25% of the apples are green and the rest are red. Of the mangoes, 80% are red and the rest of the mangoes are green. What percentage of the green fruits are mangoes?

Solution
Let us assume that total number of fruits is 100, 60 are mangoes and 40 are apples.

Green apples = 25% of 40 = 10
Green mangoes = 20% of 60 = 12

Total number of green fruits = 10 + 12 = 22

Thus, required percentage = 12/22 × 100 = 54.5%

Example 84

If the milk to water ratio in a mixture is 2 : 3, what is the percentage of milk in the mixture?

Solution

There are 5 parts in total, that is, 2 parts of milk and 3 parts of water.

Then percentage of milk in the mixture $= 2/5 \times 100 = 40\%$

Example 85

If two-third of residents in a housing society own cars, and furthermore, one-half of car owners own a Swift car, what percentage of residents own Swift cars?

Solution

The fraction of residents owning a Swift car = 1/2 of 2/3 = 1/2 × 2/3 = 1/3

Converting it into percentage $1/3 \times 100 = 33.33\%$

Example 86

Neeru's expenditure and savings are in the ratio 3 : 2. Her income increases by 10%. Her expenditure increases by 12%. By what percentage does her savings increase?

Solution

Let Neeru's income = 100

Expenditure = 3/(2 + 3) × 100 = 60

Saving = 100 – 60 = 40

New income after 10% increase = 110

New expenditure after 12% increase = 60 + 12% of 60 = 67.2%

New saving = 110 – 67.2 = 42.8

Percentage increase in saving

= (42.8 – 40)/40 × 100 = 2.8/40 × 100 = 7%

Per cent of a per cent = 20% of 30% will be nothing but $\frac{20}{100} \times \frac{30}{100} = 6/100$

6/100 is equal to 6%.

Example 87

What is 20% of 30% of 40%?

Solution

The value is $= \left(\frac{20}{100}\right) \times \left(\frac{30}{100}\right) \times 40\% = 2.4\%$

Arithmetic Mean

The arithmetic mean, or simply 'average' or 'mean' of a group of values, is the sum of the values divided by the total number of values. It is one of the measures of central tendencies. It is denoted by $\overline{X}$, where X is the variable such as height, weight, score, etc.

Average of n observations = sum of observations/n $= \sum x/n$

Combined average: $N_1X_1 + N_2X_2 + \cdots + N_nX_n / (N_1 + N_2 + \cdots + N_n)$ where $N_1, N_2, \cdots N_n$ are the respective numbers of observations in different groups, and $X_1, X_2, \cdots X_n$ are the averages.

Average Speed

Suppose a man covers a certain distance at x kmph and an equal distance at y kmph or x and y are the speeds in going to a station and coming back, then the average speed during the whole journey is

$$\frac{2xy}{x+y} \text{ kmph}$$

Example 88

If a candidate scores 5, 15, 25, 10, and 15 marks in different subjects, calculate the mean marks scored by the candidate.

Solution

$$\text{Mean marks} = \frac{5+15+25+10+15}{5} = \frac{70}{5} = 14$$

Example 89

The average age of 30 boys in a class is 15 years. If the age of teacher is also included, the new average age becomes 16 years. What is the age of teacher?

Solution

Here, average age = total age/number

Total age = average age × number

Total age = 15 × 30 = 450 years

New total age = 16 × 31 = 496

The new total age is higher because the age of teacher is also included in it.

Age of teacher = 496 – 450 = 46 years

Example 90

India scores 52 runs in first 10 overs in a 50-over one-day cricket match against Pakistan. What should be the run rate in the remaining 40 overs to reach the target of 252 runs?

Solution

The score required in 40 overs = 252 − 52 = 200 runs

Average required run rate in 40 overs = 200/40 = 5

Example 91

The average monthly income of A and B is ₹5,050. The average monthly income of B and C is ₹6,250 and the average monthly income of A and C is ₹5,200. The monthly income of A is

(a) 3,500 (b) 4,000
(c) 4,050 (d) 5,000

Solution

Total of A and B = (5,050 × 2) = 10,100 (i)
Similarly, total income of B and C = (6,250 × 2) = 12,500 (ii)
And total of A and C = (5,200 × 2) = 10,400 (iii)
Adding (i), (ii), and (iii), we get, 2(A + B + C) = 33,000
Or A + B + C = 16,500

But B + C = 12,500 from equation (ii)

Hence, A = 16,500 − 12,500 = 4,000

Answer: (b)

Time and Distance

Speed, Time, and Distance

If speed, time, and distance are denoted by S, T, and D, respectively, then $S = D/T$; $D = S \times T$, and $T = D/S$

To convert from km/h to metre/second (m/s), multiply by 5/18.

To convert m/s to km/h, multiply by 18/5.

If the ratio of the speeds of A and B is $a : b$, then the ratio of the time taken by them to cover the same distance is $1/a : 1/b$ or $b : a$.

Suppose a man covers a certain distance at x kmph and an equal distance at y kmph. Then, the average speed during the whole journey = $2xy/(x + y)$ kmph (also covered under the section Arithmetic Mean).

Example 92

A man covers 60 km in 4 hrs. Find the speed.

Solution

Speed = distance/time = 60/4 = 15 kmph

Note: Depending upon the answer choices, the kmph can also be converted into m/s by multiplying by 5/18.

Speed (in m/s) = 15 × 5/18 = $4\frac{3}{18}$ m/s

Example 93

A man covers 20 km in 2½ hours. Find the distance covered in 9 hrs.

Solution

Speed = D/T = 20 km/2½ hours = 8 kmph

Distance covered in 9 hours = $S \times T$ = 8 × 9 = 72 km

Example 94

A car completes a journey in 4 hours, the first half at a speed of 40 kmph and second at 60 kmph. Find the total distance covered.

Solution

As the total journey is divided into equal parts, the average speed can be calculated by the formula $2xy/(x + y) = 2 \times 40 \times 60/(40 + 60)$ = 48 kmph.
Distance = $S \times T = 48 \times 4 = 192$ km

Example 95

A student walks from his house at a speed of 3 kmph and reaches the school 10 minutes late. If he walks at a speed of 4 kmph, he reaches the school 10 minutes earlier. What is the distance between his school and his house?

Solution

Let the distance = x km

Difference between timings of reaching the school at different speeds = 10 + 10 = 20 minutes or 20/60 or 1/3 hrs.

Now the difference between timings = $x/3 - x/4 = 1/3$

$$= \frac{4x - 3x}{12}$$

$$x = 4 \text{ km}$$

Calendar Questions

In NET examination, usually one calendar question is asked and that is usually simple. We need to be familiar with few concepts.

It is necessary to know the concept of 'odd days' to solve calendar problems. We are supposed to find the day of the week on a given date.

Odd days: In a given period, the number of days more than the complete weeks is called odd days.

Leap year: A leap year has 366 days. Every year divisible by 4 is a leap year, if it is not a century. Only every 4th century is a leap year, and no other century is a leap year.

Examples

Each of the years such as 1880, 1988, 2004, 2012, and so on is a leap year.

Each of the years such as 400, 800, 1200, 1600, 2000, and so on is a leap year, but 1700, 1800, 1900, and so on are not leap years.

Ordinary year: The year that is not a leap year is called an ordinary year. An ordinary year has 365 days.

Counting of Odd Days

01 January 0001 is assumed to be Monday.

1 ordinary year = 365 days = 52 weeks + '1 day'. That one extra day is counted as odd day.

1 leap year = 366 days = (52 weeks + 2 days)

1 leap year has 2 odd days.

100 years = 76 ordinary years + 24 leap years = $(76 \times 1 + 24 \times 2)$ odd days = 124 odd days = (17 weeks + 5 days). It means 5 odd days.

Therefore, number of odd days in 100 years is 5.

Number of odd days in 200 years = (5×2) = 10 days. If further divided by 7, it gives us 3 odd days.

Number of odd days in 300 years = (5×3) = 15 days, which means '1 odd day'.

Number of odd days in 400 years = $(5 \times 4 + 1)$ = 0 odd days

Similarly, each one of 800th year, 1,200th year, 1,600th year, 2,000th year, 2,400th year, and so on has 0 odd days.

Day of the Week Related to Odd Days

We usually count days from Sunday.

For example, if as per our calculation, the number of 'odd days' is 2, it means that the answer will be Tuesday.

Day	Sunday	Monday	Tuesday	Wednesday	Thursday	Friday	Saturday
Number	0	1	2	3	4	5	6

Solved Examples

Example 96

What was the day of the week on January 1, 2001?

(a) Friday (b) Tuesday
(c) Sunday (d) Wednesday

(*June 2009*)

Answer: (b)

Explanation

By the end of centuries 400, 800, 1200, 1600, 2000, 2400, and so on, there are no extra days left. It means that the last year 2000 was Sunday. As per convention, the week starts with Monday, and hence, the next day after last day of year 2000 that is January 1, 2001, is Monday.

Example 97

January 1, 1995 was a Sunday. What would be the day of the week on January 1, 1996?

(a) Sunday (b) Monday
(c) Wednesday (d) Saturday

(*December 2009*)

Answer: (b)

Explanation

There is increase of 1 day (odd day) in the subsequent year. In case of leap year (if the day is after February), then there will be increase of two days.

Although 1996 is a leap year, the day in question is in January month, so there will be increase of one day. Thus, January 1, 1996 is Monday.

Example 98

On January 12, 1980, it was a Saturday. The day of week on January 12, 1979 was

(a) Thursday (b) Friday
(c) Saturday (d) Sunday

Answer: (b)

Explanation

Although 1980 is a leap year, it would not have any impact on the calculation as the date in the question is in January month (and before 28th February). Thus, it is assumed as a normal year.

There is a gain of one day in the next year. However, here we will do backward calculation, subtract 1 day from the year 1980. If it was Saturday, then the same day in the previous year was to be Friday.

Example 99

If 1st October is Monday, then 1st November will be

(a) Thursday (b) Friday
(c) Sunday (d) Monday

Answer: (a)

Explanation

October has 31 days. 1st, 8th, 15th, 22nd, and 29th dates of October will be Mondays. Thus, 1st November will be Thursday.

Example 100

If the first day of the month is Sunday, what date will be three days after the fourth Wednesday in the month? (*June 1998*)

(a) 24 (b) 29 (c) 27 (d) 30

Answer: (b)

Explanation

First Wednesday of the month will be on 4th day of the month, 2nd will be on 11th; 3rd Wednesday on 18th; and 4th Wednesday on 25th. Now three days after 25th means 25 + 4 = 29th day of the month.

Example 101

If the first day of the ordinary year (other than the leap year) was Friday, then which was the last day of that year?

(a) Wednesday (b) Thursday
(c) Friday (d) Sunday

Answer: (c)

Explanation

An ordinary year has 365 days. Week starting with Friday will end in Thursday. Hence, the 364th day (end of complete 52 weeks) will be Thursday. The 365th day will be Friday. Thus, first and last day of an ordinary year are same.

Example 102

It was Monday on January 1, 2007. What was the day of the week on January 1, 2011?

(a) Sunday (b) Saturday
(c) Friday (d) Wednesday

Answer: (b)

Explanation

Odd days in 2007 = 1 (2007 is an ordinary year; and we are doing calculation from January 1)
Odd days in 2008 = 2 (2008 is a leap year)
Odd days in 2009 = 1 (ordinary year)
Odd days in 2010 = 1 (ordinary year)

Thus, January 1, 2011, will be Monday plus 5 days, that is, Saturday.

Example 103

If the fourth Saturday of a month is the 22nd day, what day is the 13th day of the month?

(a) Tuesday (b) Wednesday
(c) Thursday (d) Friday

Answer: (c)

Explanation

The earlier three Saturdays are on 15th, 8th, and 1st. If 15th is Saturday, hence, Thursday falls on 13th. 13th is Thursday.

Venn Diagrams

In NET Paper I examinations, one or two questions are asked about Venn diagrams almost every time. While the circles or figures (also called sets) deal with individual data items, the number shown in rectangle is the total number (rectangle is also called as universal set).

There can be other shapes like triangles, squares, etc. to represent data. The following examples will help in better understanding on how to solve the questions on Venn Diagrams.

Venn Diagrams and Relationships

The main aim of this section is to test your ability about the relation between some items of a group by diagrams. In these questions, some figures of circles and some words are given. You have to choose a figure that represents the given words.

Some critical examples are given below.

1. If all the words are of different groups, then they will be shown by the diagram as given below.

Dog, Cow, and Horse

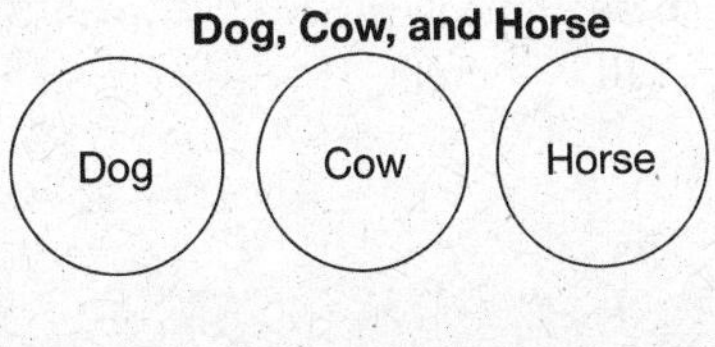

All these three are animals but of different groups; there is no relation between them. Hence, they will be represented by three different circles.

2. If few words belong to a common group

Cow, Horse, and Mammals

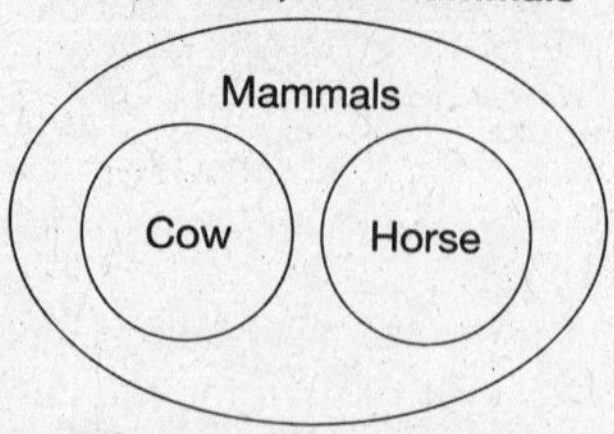

3. If one word belongs to a second group that further belongs to the third group.

Cow, Mammals, and Animal Kingdom

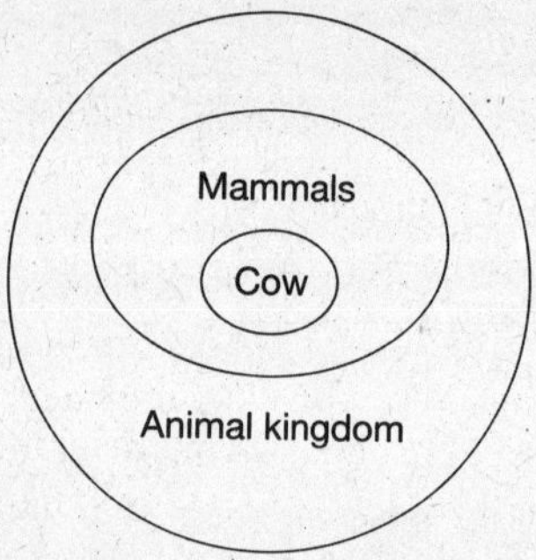

4. If there is some relation between two items and these two items are completely related to a third item, then they will be shown as given below.

Men, Brother, and Father

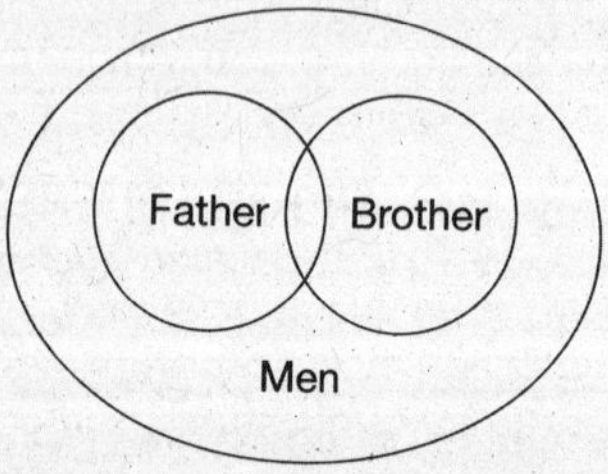

Some brothers may be fathers and vice versa. Similarly, some fathers may not be bothers and vice versa. But all the fathers and all the brothers belong to men group.

5. Two items are related to a third item to some extent but not completely and first two items are totally different.

Students, Boys, and Girls

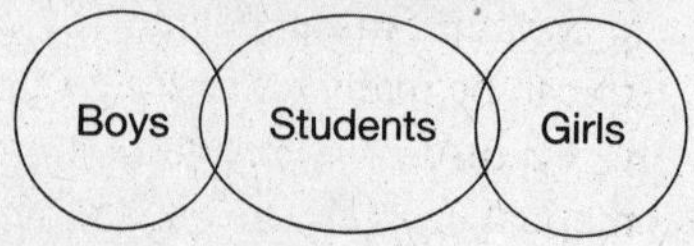

The boys and girls are different items while some boys may be students. Similarly, among girls, some may be students.

6. All the three items are related to one another but to some extent and not completely.

Boys, Students, and Athletes

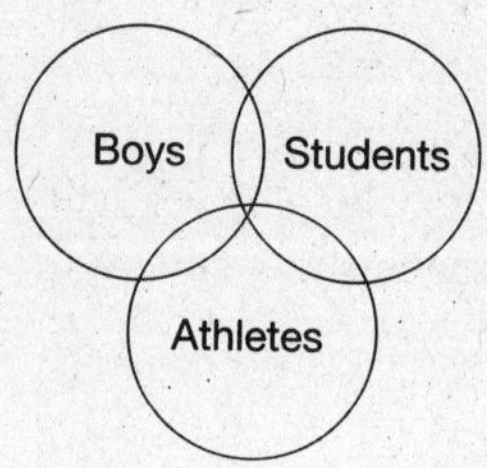

Some boys may be students and vice-versa. Similarly, some boys may be athletes and vice-versa. Some students may be athletes and vice-versa.

7. Two items are related to each other completely and third item is entirely different from the first two.

Lions, Carnivorous, and Cows

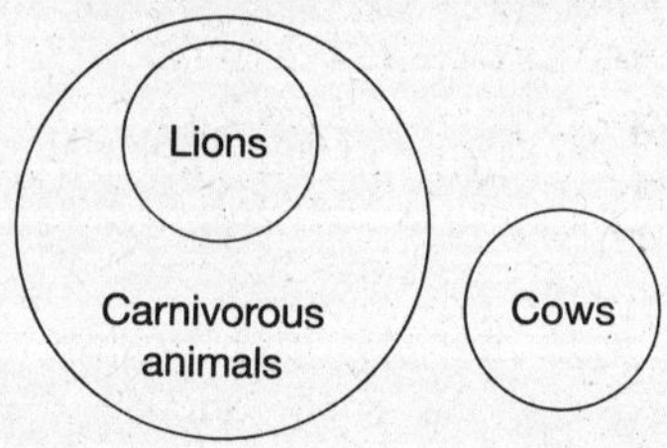

All lions are carnivorous but no cow is lion or a carnivore.

8. First item is partially related to second, but third is entirely different from the first two.

Dogs, Flesh eaters, and Cows

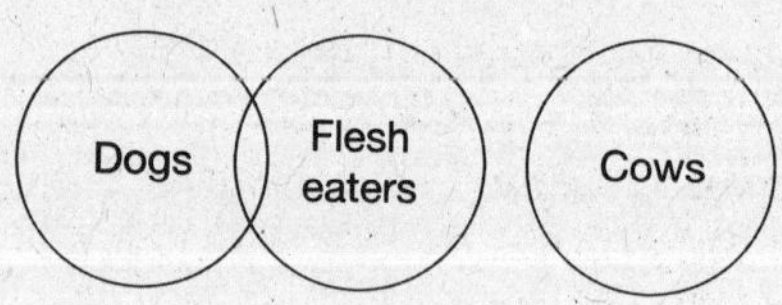

Some dogs are flesh eaters but not all, whereas any dog or any flesh eater cannot be cow.

There can be many other situations too.

Now, we discuss Venn diagram to solve mathematical problems. This can be used as an easier approach to solve problems, which can be practised by students from non-mathematical background also.

Example 104

In a class, there are:

(A) 8 students who play football and hockey

(B) 7 students who do not play football or hockey

(C) 13 students who play hockey

(D) 19 students who play football

How many students are there in the class?

Solution

Step I

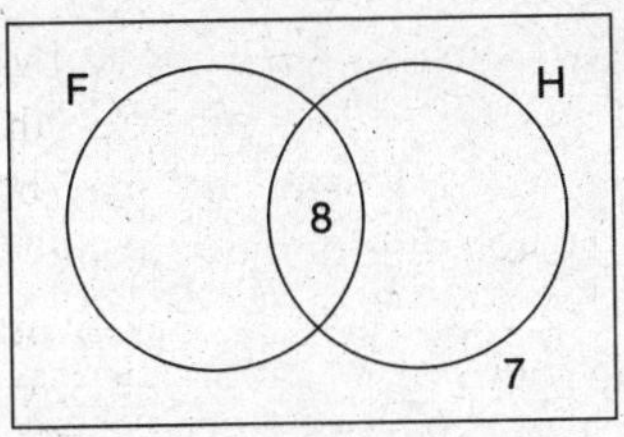

The 8 students who play both hockey and football go inside the intersection because they need to be in both circles. The 7 students who do not play either of the two sports go outside because they should not be in either of the circles.

Step II

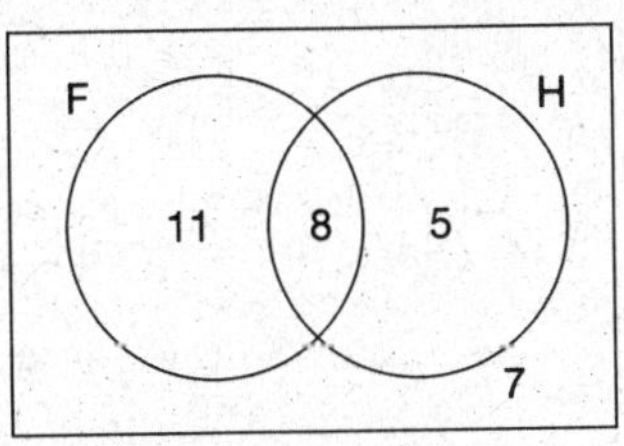

There are 13 students who play hockey, so the numbers in the hockey circle should add up to 13.

There are 8 students in the intersection, so there must be 5 who play hockey but not football.

Similarly, there are 19 students who play football. The students who play football but not hockey must be $19 - 8 = 11$.

Thus, the total number of students in the class $= 11 + 8 + 5 + 7 = 31$

There are 31 students in the class.

Example 105

In a class, there are 30 students.

(A) 21 students like Maths

(B) 16 students like English

(C) 6 students don't like Maths or English

How many students like both Maths and English?

Step I

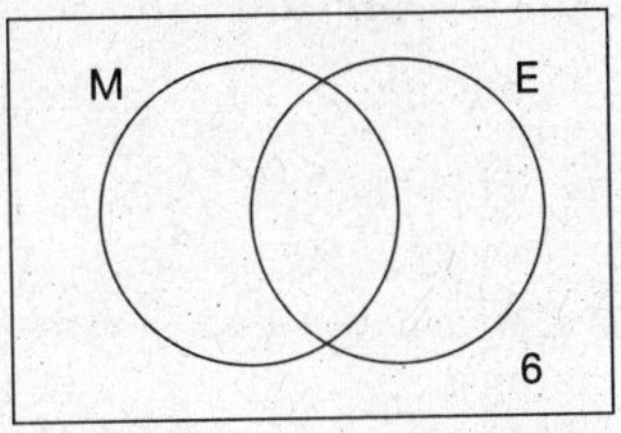

The 6 students who do not like either of the two subjects go outside because they should not be in either circles. We know that the total in the maths circle needs to be 21, but we cannot put this in because we don't know how many should go inside the intersection (if they like both subjects) and how many should go on the left (if they like only Maths).

Step II

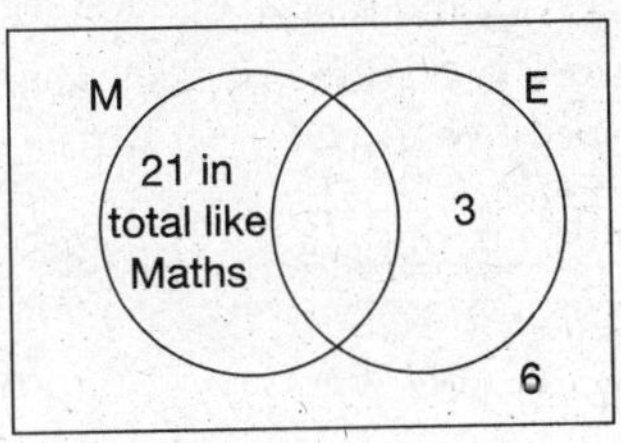

There are 30 students in the class, and if there are 6 students outside the circles, then the other three sections must add up to 24.

Furthermore, there are 21 students who like Maths, so the middle and left section must add up to 21. This leaves 3 on the right as $24 - 21 = 3$.

Step III

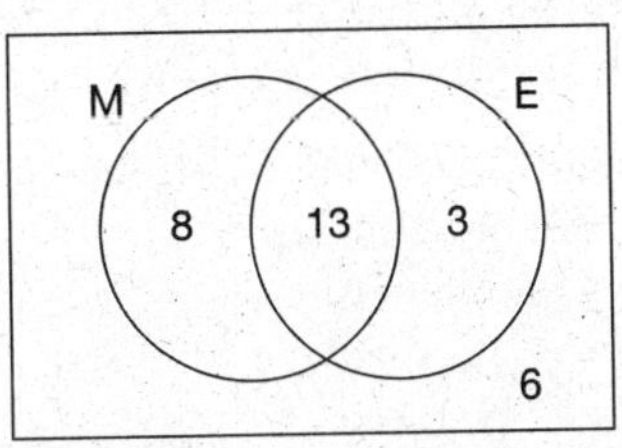

There are 16 students who like English. Hence, the two parts of the English circle should add up to 16 and so we can find the number in the intersection by doing 16 – 3 = 13.

There are 21 students who like Maths. There are 8 (got by 21 – 13) who like Maths but not English. If we check all the four given facts, we see that they are all true.

There are 13 students who like both Maths and English.

Practice Questions

Number Series Completion

1. Find the missing number in the following series.
8, 24, 12, ?, 18, 54 (*December 2005*)
(a) 26 (b) 24 (c) 36 (d) 32

2. Find the missing number in the following series.
28, 33, 31, 36, ?, 39
(a) 30 (b) 32 (c) 33 (d) 34

3. Find the missing number in the following series.
1, 3, 4, 8, 15, 27, ?
(a) 45 (b) 50 (c) 55 (d) 60

4. Find the missing number in the following series.
2/3, 4/7, ?, 11/21, 16/31 (*December 2008*)
(a) 10/8 (b) 6/10 (c) 5/10 (d) 7/13

5. Find the missing number in the following series.
4, 16, 8, 64, ?, 256 (*June 2008*)
(a) 16 (b) 24 (c) 32 (d) 20

6. Find the missing number in the following series.
512, 256, 128, ?, 32, 16, 8 (*June 1997*)
(a) 52 (b) 61 (c) 64 (d) 56

7. Find the missing number in the following series.
2, 7, 17, 32, 52, 77, ? (*June 1997*)
(a) 107 (b) 91 (c) 101 (d) 92

8. Find the missing number in the following series.
15, 18, 24, ?, 45 (*June 1997*)
(a) 27 (b) 30 (c) 33 (d) 36

9. Find the wrong number in the sequence.
125, 127, 130, 135, 142, 153, 165
(a) 130 (b) 142 (c) 153 (d) 165

10. Find the missing number in the following series.
3, 10, 101,?
(a) 10,101 (b) 10,201
(c) 10,202 (d) 11,012

11. Find the missing number in the following series.
1, 1, 4, 8, 9, 27, 16, ?
(a) 32 (b) 64 (c) 81 (d) 256

12. Find the missing number in the following series.
3, 5, 13, 43, 177, ?
(a) 891 (b) 713 (c) 885 (d) 899

13. Fill in the missing number in the following arrangement based on some principle. (*June 2002*)

8	6	4
3	?	7
14	16	18

(a) 4 (b) 5 (c) 6 (d) 8

14. Find the missing number in the following series.
3, 4, 7, 7, 13, 13, 21, 22, 31, 34, ?
(a) 41 (b) 43 (c) 45 (d) 47

15. Find the missing number in the following series.
10, 24, 52, ?, 220, 44, 892
(a) 104 (b) 98 (c) 112 (d) 108

16. What is the number that comes next in the sequence?

12, 20, 100, ?, 8,900, 88,900, 8,88,900

(*June 2007*)

(a) 1,000 (b) 900 (c) 800 (d) 400

17. Which of the following will not be a number of the series 1, 8, 27, 64, 125,?
(a) 256 (b) 512 (c) 729 (d) 1,000

18. Find the missing number in the following series.
13, 32, 24, 43, 35, ?, 46, 65, 57, 76
(a) 45 (b) 52 (c) 54 (d) 55

19. Find the missing number in the following series.
23, 33, 46, 62, 81, 103,?
(a) 126 (b) 130 (c) 133 (d) 128

20. Find the wrong number in the sequence.
10, 26, 74, 218, 654, 1,946
(a) 26 (b) 74 (c) 218 (d) 650

Letter Series Completion

21. Find the missing letters in the following series.
QAR, RAS, SAT, TAU, ________
(a) UAV (b) TAS (c) UAT (d) TAT

22. Find the missing letters in the following series.
FTG, GTF, HTI, ITH, ________
(a) JTK (b) HTL (c) HTK (d) JTI

23. Find the missing letters in the following series.
SCD, TEF, UGH, ________, WKL
(a) CMN (b) UJI (c) VIJ (d) IJT

24. Find the missing letters in the following series.
JAK, KBL, LCM, MDN, ________
(a) OEP (b) NEO (c) MEN (d) PFQ

25. Find the missing letters in the following series.
AK, EO, IS, ________, QA, UE

(*December 2002*)

(a) LV (b) MW (c) NX (d) LW

26. Find the missing letters in the following series.
ELFT, GLHT, ILJT, ________, MLNT
(a) OLPT (b) LLMT
(c) KLMT (d) KLLT

27. Find the missing letters in the following series.
WE, SG, PJ, LN, ________
(a) IS (b) SI (c) PT (d) QT

28. Find the missing letters and numbers in the following series.
C2A, E5D, G8G, I11J, ________
(a) K14M (b) M14K
(c) L14M (d) M14L

29. Find the missing letters in the following series.
QAR, RAS, SAT, TAU, ________
(a) UAV (b) UAT (c) TAS (d) TAT

30. Find the next pair in the sequence.
C – 3, E – 6, G – 12, I – 24, K – 48, ________
(a) S – 48 (b) M – 96
(c) L – 96 (d) O – 48

Coding and Decoding

1. If 'CERTAIN' is coded as 'XVIGZRM' in a particular code language, then how 'MUNDANE' be coded in that language?

(*December 2000*)

(a) NFMWZMX (b) VMZWMFN
(c) NFMWZMV (d) MIMXZMV

2. If 'EDUCATION' is coded as NOITACUDE, then 'RED FORT' will be coded as
(a) TROFDER (b) FORTRED
(c) TROFRED (d) FORTDER

3. In a certain code, 'MOTHER' is written as 'OMHURF'. How will 'ANSWER' be written in that code?
(a) NBWRRF (b) MAVSPE
(c) NBWTRD (d) NAWTRF

4. In a certain code, 'COMPUTER' is written as 'RFUVQNPC'. How is 'PRINTER' written in the same code?
(a) R F U O J S P (b) P F U O J S R
(c) P S J O U F P (d) R S J O U F P

5. BF is related to DH in the same way as PS is related to
(a) SU (b) SV (c) RV (d) RU

6. CLAIM : DNDMR : : CHARGE : ?
(*December 2000*)
(a) DJDVLK (b) DIDWLL
(c) DJCVMK (d) DIDWKL

7. COLD : FSQJ : : HEAT : ?
(*December 2000*)
(a) XJFY (b) KIGZ
(c) KIFZ (d) YIGY

8. In a certain code, 'PAPER' is written as 'SCTGW'. How is 'MOTHER' written in that code?
(a) POXJJT (b) ORVLGW
(c) PQXKJV (d) PQVJGT

9. If HE = 13 and MOVER = 73, then BASIC = ?
(a) 55 (b) 34 (c) 50 (d) 49

10. In a certain code, 15789 is written as XTZAL and 2346 is written as NPSU. How is 235491 written in that code?
(a) NPTSL (b) NPTUL
(c) NBTSL (d) PNTSL

11. If A stands for 5, B for 6, C for 7, D for 8, and so on, what do the following numbers stand for 22, 25, 8, 22, and 5?
(*December 2004*)
(a) PRIYA (b) NEEMA
(c) MEENA (d) RUDRA

12. If 'CALENDAR' is coded as 'CLANAEDR', then the code for CIRCULAR is
(a) LACANDER (b) CRIUCALR
(c) CLANADER (d) None of the above

13. In a code sign, 'DRLAL' is coded as 62014314. How is 'CAMEL' coded?
(a) 5315714 (b) 35729310
(c) 5313613 (d) None of the above

14. If 'LIGHT' is coded as 'GILTH', then find the code for 'RAINY'.
(a) IARYN (b) ARINY
(c) NAIRY (d) RINAY

15. If all the letters in the word 'ARGUMENT' are rearranged in alphabetical order and substituted by the letter immediately following it in English alphabet, then what will be the new arrangement of letters?
(a) BFHNOSUV (b) BFHONSWV
(c) BFHNOUSV (d) BFHNOQUV

16. Which of the following pairs have the same relationship as OFTEN : FOTNE?
(a) HEART : TRAHE
(b) OPENS : SNEOP
(c) RISKY : IRSYK
(d) FIRST : IFRST

17. If water is called food, food is called tree, tree is called sky, and sky is called wall, on which of the following a fruit grows?
(a) Water (b) Food (c) Sky (d) Tree

18. If red means blue, blue means green, green means orange, orange means pink, and pink means black, then what is the colour of clear sky?
(a) Orange (b) Green
(c) Blue (d) None of the above

19. In a certain code, 'bi nie pie' means 'some good jokes', 'nie bat lik' means 'some real stories', and 'pie lik tol' means 'many good stories'. Which word in that code means 'jokes'?
(a) bi (b) nie
(c) pie (d) None of the above

20. If 'table' is called 'chair', 'chair' is called 'cupboard', 'cupboard' is called 'chalk', 'chalk' is called 'book', 'book' is called 'duster', and 'duster' is called 'table', then what does the teacher use to write on the black board?
(a) Book (b) Cupboard
(c) Table (d) Duster

21. In a certain code language,
(A) 'pit dar na' means 'you are good'.
(B) 'dar tok pa' means 'good and bad'.
(C) 'tim na tok' means 'they are bad'.
In that language, which word stands for 'they'?
(a) na (b) tok (c) tim (d) pit

22. In a certain code language, '743' means 'mangoes are good', '657' means 'eat good

food', and '934' means 'mangoes are ripe'. Which of the following digit in that code means 'ripe'?
(a) 9 (b) 4 (c) 5 (d) 7

23. In a certain code, '256' means 'you are good', '637' means 'we are bad', and '358' means 'good and bad'. Which of the following digit in that code means 'and'?
(a) 2 (b) 5 (c) 8 (d) 3

24. In a certain code language, '526' means 'sky is blue', '24' means 'blue colour', and '436' means 'colour is fun'. Which of the following digit in that language means 'fun'?
(a) 5 (b) 4
(c) 3 (d) 2
(e) None of the above

25. In a certain code language, '123' means 'hot filtered coffee', '356' means 'very hot day', and '589' means 'day and night'. Which of the following digit in that language means 'very'?
(a) 9 (b) 5 (c) 8 (d) 6

Choose Odd Word

1. Choose the word that is least like the other words in a group.
(a) Moon (b) Sun
(c) Universe (d) Planets

2. Choose the word that is least like the other words in a group.
(a) Chemistry (b) Geography
(c) Zoology (d) Botany

3. Choose the word that is least like the other words in a group.
(a) Mechanic (b) Mason
(c) Blacksmith (d) Architect

4. Choose the word that is least like the other words in a group.
(a) Sister (b) Friend
(c) Brother (d) Father

5. Choose the word that is least like the other words in a group.
(a) Zinc (b) Aluminium
(c) Copper (d) Mercury

6. Choose the word that is least like the other words in a group.
(a) Lion (b) Cheetah
(c) Bear (d) Tiger

7. Choose the word that is least like the other words in a group.
(a) Sheet (b) Cot
(c) Spain (d) Pillow

8. Find the odd word among the following:
(a) Kiwi (b) Eagle
(c) Penguin (d) Ostrich

9. Find the odd word among the following:
(a) Lake (b) Sea
(c) River (d) Pool

10. Find the odd word among the following:
(a) Arrow (b) Axe
(c) Knife (d) Dagger

Odd Pairs

11. Find the odd pair of words.
(a) Mason : Wall (b) Cobbler : Shoe
(c) Farmer : Crop (d) Chef : Cook

12. Find the odd pair of words.
(a) Bottle : Wine (b) Cup : Tea
(c) Pitcher : Water (d) Racket : Shuttle

13. Find the odd pair of words.
(a) Lion : Roar (b) Snake : Hiss
(c) Frog : Bleat (d) Bees : Hum

14. Find the odd pair of words.
(a) Daring : Timid
(b) Beautiful : Pretty
(c) Clarity : Ambiguity
(d) Youth : Adult

15. Find the odd pair of words.
(a) Room : House (b) Atom : Electron
(c) Car : Engine (d) Milk : Water

16. Find the odd number.
(a) 13 (b) 53 (c) 63 (d) 23

17. Find the odd number.
(a) 51 (b) 144 (c) 64 (d) 121

18. Find the odd number.
(a) 15 (b) 21 (c) 24 (d) 28
(e) 30

19. Find the odd number
    (a) 324 (b) 244 (c) 136 (d) 352
20. Find the odd number.
    (a) 25 (b) 27 (c) 125 (d) 343

Choose the Odd Number Pair or Group

21. Find the odd number pair.
    (a) 95 : 82 (b) 69 : 56
    (c) 55 : 42 (d) 48 : 34
22. Find the odd number pair.
    (a) 2 : 8 (b) 3 : 27
    (c) 4 : 32 (d) 5 : 125
23. Find the odd number pair.
    (a) 80 : 9 (b) 64 : 8
    (c) 36 : 6 (d) 7 : 49
24. Find the odd number pair.
    (a) 3 : 5 (b) 5 : 3 (c) 6 : 2 (d) 7 : 3
25. Find the odd number pair.
    (a) 1 : 0 (b) 3 : 8
    (c) 6 : 35 (d) 7 : 50
26. Find the odd number pair.
    (a) 23 : 29 (b) 19 : 25
    (c) 13 : 17 (d) 3 : 5
27. Find the odd number pair.
    (a) 343 : 7 (b) 243 : 9
    (c) 512 : 8 (d) 216 : 6
28. Find the odd number pair.
    (a) 13 : 21 (b) 19 : 27
    (c) 15 : 23 (d) 16 : 24
29. Find the odd number pair.
    (a) 14 : 56 (b) 12 : 36
    (c) 23 : 92 (d) 15 : 35
30. Find the odd number pair.
    (a) 5 : 26 (b) 6 : 37
    (c) 7 : 49 (d) 8 : 65

Choose the Odd Letter Group

31. Find the odd letter group.
    (a) ACE (b) PRT
    (c) UWY (d) MNO
32. Find the odd letter group.
    (a) RTW (b) QOM
    (c) IKG (d) BDF
33. Find the odd letter group.
    (a) KOM (b) LPN (c) BFD (d) GLI
34. Find the odd letter group.
    (a) BHE (b) DJG (c) SYV (d) JPM
35. Find the odd letter group.
    (a) BCD (b) MNO (c) KLM (d) PQR
36. Find the odd letter group.
    (a) BYX (b) LPO (c) EVU (d) FUT
37. Find the odd letter group.
    (a) CHM (b) HMR (c) DIN (d) LPU
38. Find the odd letter group.
    (a) XUW (b) DAC (c) PMN (d) HEG
    (e) TQS
39. Find the odd letter group.
    (a) RAT (b) SAT (c) CAT (d) MAT
    (e) GET
40. Find the odd letter group.
    (a) OTP (b) ABA (c) SZX (d) UVB
    (e) YQR

Analogy

It is important to note that the analogy questions also cover many aspects of 'relationships'. Relationships have been specifically mentioned in NET Paper 1 syllabus.

Simple Analogy

1. As boxing is to 'Ring', tennis is to
   (a) Pool (b) Court
   (c) Arena (d) Ground
2. 'Doctor' is related to 'Patient' in the same way as 'Consultant' is related to
   (a) Customer (b) Accused
   (c) Magistrate (d) Client
3. 'Easiness' is related to 'Difficulty' in the same way as 'Comfort' is related to
   (a) Hardship (b) Rest
   (c) Poverty (d) Difficulty
4. As 'Pen' is related to 'Ink', 'Needle' is related to
   (a) Thread (b) Cloth
   (c) Stitching (d) Art

5. 'Chef' is related to 'Kitchen' in the same way as 'Scientist' is related to
(a) Medicine (b) Pharmacy
(c) Laboratory (d) Chemist

6. 'Engineer' is related to 'Production' in the same way as 'Doctor' is related to
(a) Cure (b) Hospital
(c) Body (d) Surgery

7. As 'Design' is related to a 'Structure', 'Rhythm' is related to
(a) Music (b) Art
(c) Kathak (d) Dance

8. 'Drama' is related to 'Director' in the same way as 'Magazine' is related to
(a) Story (b) Editor
(c) Reader (d) Printer

9. 'Demonstrator' is related to 'Laboratory' in the same way as 'Leader' is related to
(a) Podium (b) Assembly
(c) Parliament (d) State

10. 'Author' is related to 'Book' in the same way as 'Choreographer' is related to
(a) Drama (b) Dance
(c) Masque (d) Opera

11. 'Starvation' is related to 'Nutrition' in the same way as 'Exhaustion' is related to
(a) Energy (b) Bravery
(c) Freshness (d) Courage

12. 'Science' is related to 'Laboratory' in the same way as 'Astronomy' is related to
(a) Observatory (b) Telescope
(c) Space (d) Station

13. 'Bibliophile' is related to 'Books' in the same way as 'Patriot' is related to
(a) Defence (b) Country
(c) Mankind (d) Society

14. 'Ancestor' is related to 'Descendant' in the same way as 'Beautiful' is related to
(a) Gloomy (b) Handsome
(c) Girl (d) Ugly

15. 'Bee' is related to 'Hive', in the same way as 'Rat' is related to
(a) Burrow (b) Nest
(c) Hole (d) Stab

Completing the Analogous Pair

In each of the following questions, there is a certain relationship between two given words on left side of ::, one word is given on right side of ::, whereas another word is to be found from the given alternatives having the same relation with this word as the words of the given pair. Now choose the correct alternatives for the questions given below.

16. Terrible : Serene : : Roof : ?
(a) Door (b) Floor
(c) Walls (d) Pillars

17. Man : Biography : : Nation : ?
(a) Democracy (b) Constitution
(c) Geography (d) History

18. Victory : Encouragement : : Failure : ?
(a) Bad (b) Defeat
(c) Anger (d) Frustration

19. Dilatory : Expeditious : : Direct : ?
(a) Tortuous (b) Circumlocutory
(c) Straight (d) Curved

20. Foundation : Edifice : : Constitution : ?
(a) Government (b) State
(c) Nation (d) Cabinet

21. Taxonomy : Classification : : Pedology : ?
(a) Nature (b) Farming
(c) Soil (d) Mountain

22. Monotony : Variety : : Crudeness : ?
(a) Refinement (b) Raw
(c) Sobriety (d) Simplicity

23. Interview : Job : : Armistice : ?
(a) War (b) Treaty
(c) Amnesty (d) Agreement

24. Wizard : Witch : : Monk : ?
(a) Madam (b) Widow
(c) Nun (d) Virgin

25. Burglar : House : : Pirate : ?
(a) Sea (b) Ship
(c) Sailor (d) Crew

26. Bird : Chirp : : Horse : ?
(a) Bray (b) Neigh
(c) Race (d) Stable

27. Insert : Extract : : Mighty : ?
(a) Thin (b) Strong
(c) Frail (d) Feeble

28. Ornithologist : Birds : : Anthropologist : ?
(a) Plants (b) Animals
(c) Mankind (d) Environment

29. Oxygen : Burn : : Carbon dioxide : ?
(a) Isolate (b) Foam
(c) Extinguish (d) Explode

30. Seismograph : Earthquake :: Tachometer: ?
(a) Volcanoes (b) Resistance
(c) Landslides (d) Strains

Blood Relations

1. If F is the brother of A, C is the daughter of A, K is the sister of F, and G is the brother of C, then who is the uncle of G?
(a) F (b) K
(c) C (d) None of the above

2. Ravi said to Seeta, 'Your mother is the daughter of my grandmother'. How are Ravi and Seeta related?
(a) Uncle–niece (b) Father–daughter
(c) Cousin (d) None of the above

3. A has three children. B is the brother of C, and C is the sister of D; E, who is the wife of A, is the mother of D. There is only one daughter of the husband of E. What is the relation between D and B?
(a) B is brother of D
(b) B is not related to D
(c) D is sister of B
(d) None of the above

4. Dinesh said to Naveen, 'The person playing this game is the youngest of the two brothers of the daughter of my father's wife'. How is the person playing the game related to Dinesh?
(a) Cousin (b) Brother
(c) Son (d) Brother-in-law

5. Pointing to a picture of a boy, Somesh said, 'He is the son of the only son of my mother'. How is Somesh related to that boy?
(a) Brother (b) Uncle
(c) Cousin (d) Father

6. Introducing a woman, Namrata said, 'She is the daughter-in-law of the grandmother of my father's only son'. How is the woman related to Namrata?
(a) Grandmother (b) Sister-in-law
(c) Sister (d) Mother

7. Pointing to a photograph Raveena says, 'He is the son of the only son of my grandfather'. How is the man in the photograph related to Raveena?
(a) Uncle (b) Brother
(c) Cousin (d) None of the above

8. Vinita, who is the sister-in-law of Amit, is the daughter-in-law of Kamni. Deepak is the father of Sandy who is the only brother of Amit. How is Kalyani related to Ashok?
(a) Mother-in-law (b) Aunt
(c) Wife (d) None of the above

9. Pointing to a woman in a picture, Amit said, 'Her granddaughter is the only daughter of my brother'. How is the woman related to Amit?
(a) Sister (b) Grandmother
(c) Mother-in-law (d) Mother

10. X and Y are siblings. C and D are wife and husband, respectively; X is the only son of C. F is sister of D. How is Y related to F?
(a) Niece (b) Nephew
(c) Uncle (d) Cousin

Direction Sense

1. Raman travels a distance of 5 km in south direction. He turns to his right. After walking 3 km, he turns to the left and walks 5 km. Now in which direction is he from the starting place?
(a) West (b) South
(c) South-west (d) North-east

2. Ravilefthomeandcycled10kmtowardssouth. He, then, turned right and cycled 5 km, and then again turned right and cycled 10 km. After this, he turned left and cycled 10 km. How many kilometres will he have to cycle to reach his home straight?
(a) 15 (b) 20 (c) 25 (d) 30

3. Chintan walked 15 km towards west, and then, he turned left and walked for 20 km. Then, he moved towards east and walked 25 km, and finally, turning left, he covered 20 km. How far was he from his starting point?

(a) 20 km (b) 30 km
(c) 10 km (d) None of the above

4. Vijay starts walking towards north. After walking some distance, he turns to his right. Then, walking for a while, he turns to his left and walks for one kilometre, and then, he turns to his left again. In which direction is he moving now?
(a) North (b) South (c) West (d) East

5. Rashi travelled 20 km towards north. Then, she turned right and travels 30 km. Then, she turns right and travels a distance of 35 km. Then, she turns left and walks 15 km. Finally, she turns left and walks 15 km. In which direction and how many metres is she from the starting position?
(a) 5 km west (b) 30 km east
(c) 30 km west (d) 45 km east

6. Kumar walked 5 m towards north; took a left turn and walked for 10 m. He then took a right turn and walked for 20 m, and again took right turn and walked 10 m. How far is he from the starting point?
(a) 20 m (b) 15 m (c) 25 m (d) 30 m

7. Shalini walked 15 m towards south, took right turn, and walked 3 m. She took a right turn again and walked 15 m before stopping. Which direction did Shalini face after stopping?
(a) West (b) South
(c) East (d) North

8. Town D is 12 km towards the north of town A. Town C is 15 km towards the west of town D. Town B is 15 km towards the west of town A. How far and in which direction is town B from C?
(a) 15 km towards north
(b) 12 km towards south
(c) 3 km towards south
(d) 12 km towards south

9. Read the following carefully and answer the question given below.
I. Point B is 4 m towards the north of Point A.
II. Point E is 8 m towards the east of Point B.
III. Point C is 5 m towards the east of Point A
IV. Point D is 9 m towards the west of Point C.

How far should one walk from Point A in order to reach Point D.
(a) 4 m (b) 9 m (c) 5 m (d) 14 m

10. Rahul started from Point A and travelled 8 km towards the north to Point B; he then turned right and travelled 7 km to Point C, and from Point C, he took the first right and drove 5 km to Point D. Then, he took another right and travelled 7 km to Point E, and finally, he turned right and travelled for another 3 km to Point F. What is the distance between Points F and B?
(a) 1 km (b) 2 km (c) 3 km (d) 4 km

Seating Arrangement

1. A, P, R, X, S, and Z are sitting in a row. S and Z are in the centre. A and P are at the ends. R is sitting to the left of A. Who is to the right of P?
(a) S (b) X
(c) Z (d) None of the above

2. A, B, C, D, and E are sitting on a bench. A is sitting next to B; C is sitting next to D, and D is not sitting with E who is on the left end of the bench. C is on the second position from the right. A is to the right of B and E. A and C are sitting together. In which position A is sitting?
(a) Between B and D
(b) Between B and C
(c) Between E and D
(d) Between C and E

3. P, Q, R, S, T, U, V, and W are sitting around a circle and are facing the centre.
I. P is second to the right of T who is the neighbour of R and V.
II. S is not the neighbour of P.
III. V is the neighbour of U.
IV. Q is not between S and W. W is not between U and S.

Which two of the following are not neighbours?

(a) R and V (b) U and V
(c) R and P (d) Q and W

4. J, D L, H, and F are travelling to a station; each one reaches at a different time. L reaches only after J and D reaches only before F. Who among them is third to reach?
(a) F (b) L (c) D (d) H

5. P, Q, R, S, and T are sitting in a straight line facing north. P sits next to S but not to T. Q is sitting next to R, who sits on the extreme left corner. T does not sit next to Q. Who sits to the left of S?
(a) P (b) Q (c) R (d) S

Basic Percentage Calculations

1. The price of cooking oil has increased by 25%. The percentage of reduction that a family should effect in the use of cooking oil so not to increase the expenditure on this account is
(a) 25 (b) 30% (c) 20% (d) 15%

2. In an organization, 40% of the employees are matriculates, 50% of the remaining employees are graduates, and the remaining 180 are postgraduates. How many employees are graduates?
(a) 360 (b) 240 (c) 300 (d) 180

3. In a town, 96% of the population is 23,040. The total population of the town is
(a) 32,256 (b) 24,000
(c) 24,936 (d) 25,640

4. If 75% of the students in a school are boys and the number of girls is 420, then the number of boys is
(a) 1,176 (b) 1,350 (c) 1,260 (d) 1,125

5. A man spends ₹3,500 and saves $12\frac{1}{2}$% of his income. His monthly income (in rupees) is
(a) 3,937.50 (b) 4,000
(c) 4,250 (d) 4,160

6. The price of an item is increased by 20% and then decreased by 20%. The final price as compared to the original price is
(a) 20% less (b) 20% more
(c) 4% more (d) 4% less

7. X's salary is half that of Y. If X got a 50% rise in his salary and Y got a 25% rise in his salary, then the percentage increase in combined salaries of both is
(a) 30% (b) 33.33%
(c) 37.5% (d) 75%

8. A mixture of 40 *l* of milk and water contains 10% water. How much water should be added to it so that water may be 20% in the new mixture?
(a) 5 *l* (b) 4 *l* (c) 6.5 *l* (d) 7.5 *l*

9. A man spends 75% of his income. His income is increased by 20%, and he increased his expenditure by 10%. His savings are increased by
(a) 10% (b) 25%
(c) 37.5% (d) 50%

10. If A's income is 25% more than B's and B's income is 20% more than C's, by what per cent is A's income more than C's?
(a) 15% (b) 25%
(c) 33.5% (d) 50%

11. If the price of a television set is increased by 25%, then by what percentage should the new price be reduced to bring the price back to the original level?
(a) 15% (b) 20% (c) 25% (d) 30%

12. A dealer marks his goods 20% above cost price. He then allows some discount on it and makes a profit of 8%. The rate of discount is
(a) 4% (b) 6% (c) 10% (d) 12%

13. As the price of mangoes decreased by 25%, I can purchase 4 mangoes more for ₹60. What is the new price of one mango?
(a) ₹5 (b) ₹4
(c) ₹3.75 (d) None of the above

14. If the length of a rectangle increases by 10%, by what per cent should the breadth decrease to maintain the same area?
(a) 10 (b) 20 (c) 9.11 (d) 5

15. If the price of potatoes increased first by 20% and subsequently by 40%, what is the final price per kilogram, if the original price was ₹25 per kg?
(a) 40 (b) 42 (c) 45 (d) 48

16. The radius of a circle has increased by 20%. By what percentage does the circumference increase?
(a) 20% (b) 40% (c) 44% (d) 48%

17. The radius of a circle has increased by 20%. By what percentage does its area increase?
(a) 33% (b) 44%
(c) 55% (d) None of the above

18. If the side of a square is increased by 25%, then its area is increased by how much per cent?
(a) 25% (b) 50%
(c) 62.5% (d) None of the above

19. The length and breadth of a rectangle are 20 cm and 10 cm, respectively. The length is increased by 10% and the breadth is increased by 20%. What is the new area of the rectangle?
(a) 240 (b) 254 (c) 264 (d) 280

20. The number of seats in an auditorium are increased by 25%. The price on a ticket is also increased by 12%. What is the effect on the revenue collected?
(a) 37 (b) 40
(c) 42 (d) None of the above

Arithmetic Mean

1. The average weight of 8 persons increases by 2.5 kg when a person weighing 60 kg is replaced by a new person. What might be the weight of the new person?
(a) 76 kg (b) 76.5 kg
(c) 80 kg (d) Data inadequate

2. The average weight of 8 articles is 25 kg. If the average weight of 3 of them is 20 kg, what is the average weight of rest of the 5 articles?
(a) 26 kg (b) 27 kg
(c) 28 kg (d) None of the above

3. The average speed of a taxi car from Town A to Town B is 35 kmph and return journey is 42 kmph. What is the average speed of the whole journey?
(a) 35.5 kmph
(b) 36 kmph
(c) 38.17 kmph
(d) Cannot be determined

4. A car owner buys petrol at ₹8 and ₹10 for two successive years. What approximately is the average cost per litre of petrol if he spends ₹4,000 each year?
(a) ₹9 (b) ₹9.90
(c) ₹8.88 (d) None of the above

5. The average age of a husband and wife was 22 years when they were married five years back. What is the present average age of the family if they have a three-year-old child? (*December 2002*)
(a) 19 years (b) 25 years
(c) 27 years (d) 28.5 years

6. A train runs for 2 hrs at a speed of 35 kmph. It runs for 3½ hrs at the speed of 60 kmph and then runs for 2½ hrs at the speed of 70 kmph. Find the average speed of the train (*June 2002*)
(a) 50 kmph (b) 55 kmph
(c) 80 kmph (d) 56.87 kmph

7. A man's monthly income is ₹1,400. What should be his average monthly expenditure so that he is able to save 3,600 in a year?
(a) 1,000 (b) 1,100
(c) 1,150 (d) 1,200

8. A question is followed by two statements I and II that contain certain data. Tell by selecting one of the answer choices given, whether the data given in the statements are sufficient for answering the question.
(a) If statement I alone is sufficient
(b) If statement II alone is sufficient
(c) If both statements I and II taken together are sufficient
(d) If none of the statements is sufficient

Question: A horse ran 100 miles without stopping. What was the average speed in miles per hour?

Statements

I. The horse ran 20 miles per hour for the first 50 miles.
II. The entire journey starts from 8 pm on day one to 4 am the following day.

(*June 1997*)

9. The average of A, B and C is 50. If D is 10, what is the average of A, B, C and D?
(a) 15 (b) 40 (c) 30 (d) 60

10. A and B start from the same destination and take the same route. A starts at 8 am and drives at a speed of 40 kmph. B starts at 9 am and drives at a speed of 50 kmph. If the destination is 350 km away from the starting point, how far will A be from the destination when B reaches there? (*December 1997*)
(a) 20 km (b) 30 km
(c) 50 km (d) 70 km

Speed, Time, and Distance

1. A person crosses a 1,200 m long street in 10 minutes. What is his speed in kmph?
(a) 7.2 kmph (b) 8 kmph
(c) 9 kmph (d) None of the above

2. A person completes a journey of 48 km in 2 hrs. How much time will he take to cover a distance of 252 km?
(a) 10 hrs (b) 11 hrs
(c) 10½ hrs (d) None of the above

3. A train completed half a trip at 30 miles per hour and the other half at 60 miles per hour. If the whole trip was 20 miles, how much time did the train take to complete the trip? (*June 2002*)
(a) 90 min (b) 60 min
(c) 45 min (d) 30 min

4. A person performs half of his journey by train, one-third by bus and the rest 5 km by auto rickshaw. Find his total journey.
(a) 30 (b) 36 (c) 40 (d) 45

5. Excluding stoppages, the speed of a bus is 54 kmph, and including stoppages, it is 45 kmph. For how many minutes does the bus stop per hour?
(a) 9 (b) 10 (c) 12 (d) 20

6. A man completes a journey in 10 hrs. The first-half of the journey is covered at the speed of 21 km per hour and second-half at 24 km per hour. The total distance covered during the journey is.
(a) 220 km (b) 224 km
(c) 230 km (d) 234 km

7. A man on tour travels first 320 km at 64 kmph and the rest at 80 kmph. The average speed for the entire 640 km of the tour is
(a) 35.55 kmph (b) 36 kmph
(c) 71.11 kmph (d) 71 kmph

8. A person travelled a distance of 610 km in 9 hrs. He travelled the first phase at a speed of 40 kmph and the rest at 90 kmph. The distance travelled during the first phase is
(a) 140 km (b) 150 km
(c) 160 km (d) 170 km

9. A train whose length is 320 m is running at a speed of 36 kmph. How much time will it take to pass a pole?
(a) 30 s (b) 32 s (c) 36 s (d) 40 s

10. A 280 m train is moving at a speed of 80 kmph. How much time will it take to pass a bridge that is 120 m long?
(a) 30 s (b) 32 s (c) 36 s (d) 40 s

Calendar

1. The year next to 1991 will have the same calendar as that of the year 1991.
(a) 1992 (b) 1995
(c) 1996 (d) 1997

2. What was the day of the week on May 28, 2007?
(a) Thursday (b) Friday
(c) Saturday (d) Monday

3. What was the day of the week on 16 June, 1999?
(a) Monday (b) Tuesday
(c) Wednesday (d) Thursday

4. What will be the day of the week on 16 August, 2010?
(a) Sunday (b) Monday
(c) Tuesday (d) Friday

5. It was Wednesday on 15 August, 2012. What should be the day on November 15, 2013?
(a) Wednesday (b) Thursday
(c) Friday (d) None of the above

6. If it is Sunday today, what will be the day after 60 days?
(a) Sunday (b) Thursday
(c) Tuesday (d) Friday

7. If 22 April, 2013, is Monday, what was the day of the week on April 22, 2012?
(a) Sunday (b) Saturday
(c) Tuesday (d) Wednesday

8. What was the day of week on 1 April, 2001?
(a) Sunday (b) Saturday
(c) Tuesday (d) Friday

9. The last day of a century cannot be
(a) Monday (b) Wednesday
(c) Tuesday (d) Friday

10. 10 February, 2005, was Thursday. What was the day of the week on 8 February, 2004?
(a) Tuesday (b) Monday
(c) Sunday (d) Wednesday

Venn Diagrams

1. Out of 40 students, 14 are taking English composition and 29 are taking Chemistry. If 5 students are in both classes, how many students are in neither class? How many are in either class?
(a) 2 (b) 3 (c) 4 (d) 5

2. How many numbers are there between 1 and 100 that are not divisible by 3 and 5?
(a) 47 (b) 43 (c) 53 (d) 58

3. In an examination, 52% of the candidates failed in English, 42% in Mathematics, and 17% in both. The number of those who passed in both the subjects is
(a) 83% (b) 23%
(c) 64% (d) 55.5%

4. In a group of 40 people, 25 speak English and 20 speak both Hindi and English. All the people speak at least one of the two languages. How many people speak Hindi?
(a) 15 (b) 20 (c) 25 (d) 30

5. If 40% of the people read newspaper X, 50% read newspaper Y, and 10% read both the papers, what percentage of the people read neither of the newspaper?
(a) 10% (b) 15% (c) 20% (d) 25%

6. Which of the following diagrams indicate the best relation between a teacher, writer, and an artist?

(a)  (b) 

(c)  (d) 

7. Which of the following diagrams indicate the best relation between travellers, train, and taxi?

(a) 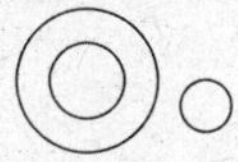 (b) 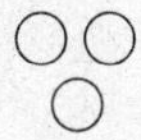

(c) 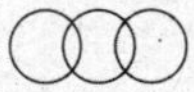 (d) 

8. Which of the following diagrams indicate the best relation between teacher, parents, and guardians?

(a) 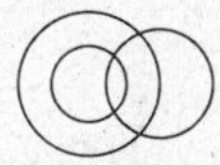 (b) 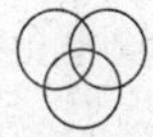

(c)  (d) 

9. Which of the following diagrams indicate the best relation between professors, doctors, and men?

(a) 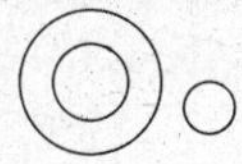 (b) 

(c) 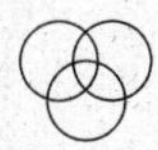 (d) 

10. Which of the following diagrams indicate the best relation between mercury, zinc, and metal?

(a) 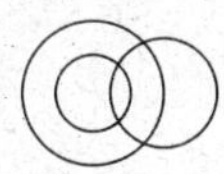 (b) 

(c) 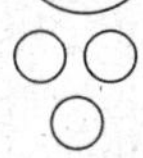 (d) 

Questions 11–15: Study the diagram given below and answer each of the following questions.

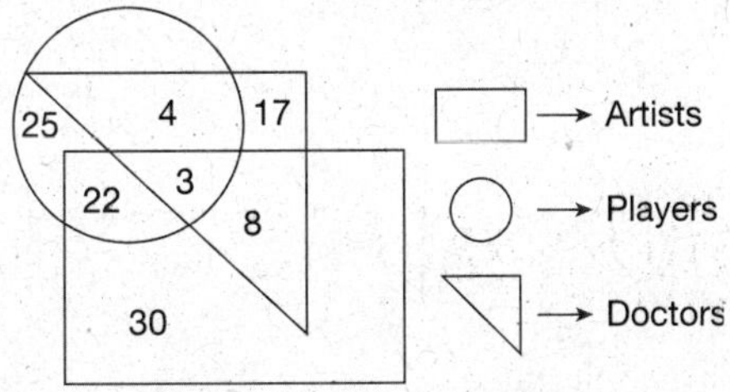

11. How many doctors are neither artists nor players?
(a) 17 (b) 5 (c) 10 (d) 30

12. How many doctors are both players and artists?
(a) 22 (b) 8 (c) 3 (d) 30

13. How many artists are players?
(a) 5 (b) 8 (c) 25 (d) 16

14. How many players are neither artists nor doctors?
(a) 25 (b) 17 (c) 5 (d) 10

15. How many artists are neither players nor doctors?
(a) 10 (b) 17 (c) 30 (d) 15

Solution

Number Series Completion

1. (c): Multiply first by 3 and divide the number so obtained by 2. This is to be done alternatively for all other numbers.
2. (d): The pattern is +5, –2, +5, –2, ... Hence, the missing term = 36 – 2 = 34.
3. (b): The sum of any three consecutive terms of the series is given to the next term. Hence, missing number = 8 + 15 + 27 = 50.
4. (d): The numerator increases by addition of 2, 3, 4, and 5. The denominator increases by addition of 4, 6, 8, and 10.
5. (a): The second number is the square of the first number; fourth number is the square of third number. Similarly, the sixth number should be the square of fifth. Hence, the answer is 16, that is, square root of 256.
6. (c): Each number is half of its preceding number.
7. (a): +5, +10, +15, +20, +25, +30
8. (c): +3, +6, +9, +12
9. (d): Prime number (numbers that are divisible by 1 and themselves only) starting with 2 are being added to each number to get the subsequent numbers.

   Thus, the sequence of numbers can be read as 125, 125 + 2, 127 + 3, 130 + 5, 135 + 7, 142 + 11, and 153 + 13. Hence, the last number should be 166.
10. (c): Each term in the series is obtained by adding 1 to the square of the preceding term.

    Hence, the missing term $= (101)^2 + 1 = 10{,}202$.
11. (b): It is a question of mixed series.
    (i) Numbers at 1st, 3rd, 5th, and 7th places are squares of 1, 2, 3, and 4.
    (ii) Numbers at 2nd, 4th, 6th, and 8th places are cubes of 1, 2, 3, 4, and 5. Hence, the answer is $4^3 = 64$.
12. (a): The pattern is

    $3 \times 1 + 2 = 5$

    $5 \times 2 + 3 = 13$

    $13 \times 3 + 4 = 43$

    $43 \times 4 + 5 = 177$

    $177 \times 5 + 6 = 891$

    Hence, (a) is the answer.
13. (b): In first row, it is –2; in second row, it is +2, and in third row, it is +2.
14. (b): The given sequence is a combination of two series:

    (i) 3, 7, 13, 21, 31, ? and (ii) 4, 7, 13, 22, 34

    The pattern in (i) is + 4, + 6, + 8, + 10, ...

    The pattern in (ii) is + 3, + 6, + 9, + 12, ...

    Hence, the missing term = 31 + 12 = 43.
15. (d): $10 \times 2 + 4 = 24$;

    $24 \times 2 + 4 = 52$;

    $52 \times 2 + 4 = 108$;

    and so on.
16. (b): × 10 – 100, × 10 – 100, and so on
17. (a): The given series consists of cubes of natural numbers only. The number 256 is not the cube of any natural number.

18. (c): The given sequence is a combination of two series.

    Ist Series - 13, 24, 35, 46, and 57

    IInd Series - 32, 43, ?, 65, and 76

    The pattern in both series is + 11. Hence, the missing term = 43 + 11 = 54.

19. (d): 23 + 10 = 33, 33 + 13 = 46, 46 + 16 = 62, and so on

20. (d): $10 \times 3 - 4 = 26$;

    $26 \times 3 - 4 = 74$;

    $74 \times 3 - 4 = 218$;

    $218 \times 3 - 4 = 650$;

    $650 \times 3 - 4 = 1,946$

Letter Series Completion

21. (a): The third letter is repeated as the first letter of the next segment. The middle letter, A, remains static. The third letters are in alphabetical order beginning with R.
22. The middle letter T is fixed. First and third letters are swapping their position in second and fourth terms. The first letters are in alphabetical order: F, G, H, I, and J. The missing segment begins with a new letter J.
23. (c): For first letter of each triplet, the series is STUVW. The remaining two letters of the series goes like CD, EF, GH, IJ, KL.
24. (b): This is an alternating series in alphabetical order. The middle letters follow the order ABCDE. The first and third letters of the triplets are in alphabetical order beginning with J. The third letter is repeated as a first letter in each subsequent three-letter segment.
25. (b): If we look at the alphabetic series given in Table 5.1, the difference between first letters of all pairs is three. Moreover, the difference between two letters in each pair is ten. Hence, MW is the answer.
26. (d): The second and forth letters in the series, L and T, are static. The first and third letters consist of an alphabetical order beginning with the letter E.
27. For 1st Letter: W – 4 = S; …I

    For 2nd Letter: E + 2 = G; … S
28. (a): This series is just like the above series. However, the middle letter of each term is replaced by a number.
29. (a): The third letter is repeated as the first letter of the next segment. The middle letter, A, remains static. The third letters are in alphabetical order beginning with R.
30. (b): There is a gap of one letter in the successive terms. Numbers are doubled.

Coding and Decoding

1. (c): Refer to Tables 5.1 and 5.2.

   For example, C is ranked 3 in Table 5.1. The same rank denotes 'X' in Table 5.2. Thus X is coded for C.

   Thus CERTAIN has been coded as XVIGZRM. Similarly, MUNDANE can be coded as NFMWZMV.

2. (a): Here, the code is the reverse of the given word. The answer is TROFDER, which is the reverse of RED FORT.

3. (d)

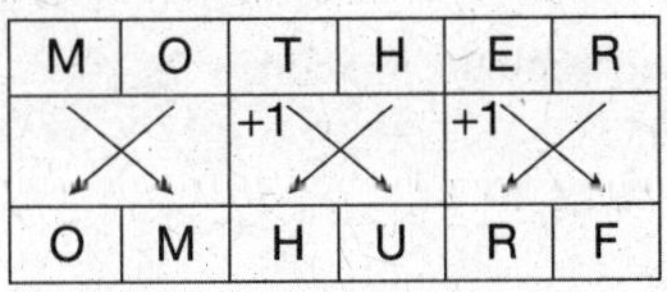

Similarly,

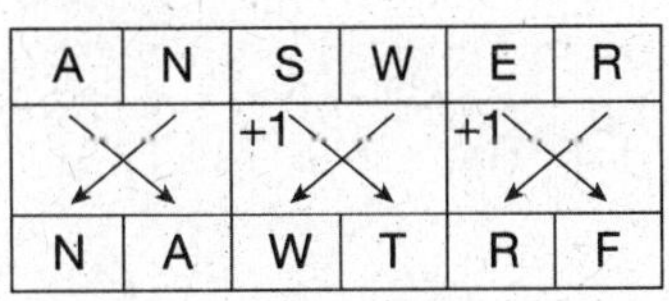

4. (a): The first and the last letters of the word swap their positions. All other letters are moved one place and get placed in the reverse manner.

5. (d)

6. (a)

C	L	A	I	M
+1	+2	+3	+4	+5
D	N	D	M	R

C	H	A	R	G	E
+1	+2	+3	+4	+5	+6
D	J	D	V	L	K

7. (c)

C	+3	F
O	+4	S
L	+5	Q
D	+6	J

Similarly,

H	+3	K
E	+4	I
A	+5	F
T	+6	Z

8. (c): The letters at the odd positions are moved three, four, and five steps forward, whereas the letters at the even positions are each moved two steps forward to get the corresponding letters of the code.

9. (b): Please refer to alphabetic series table and add the number of alphabets in the given word.

10. (a): The numbers are coded as

1	3	7	8	9
X	T	Z	A	L

2	3	4	6
N	P	S	U

That is, 2 as N, 3 as P, 5 as T, 4 as S, and 9 as L. Thus, 23549 coded as NPTSL.

11. (d)

A	B	C	D	E	F	G	H	I	J	K
5	6	7	8	9	10	11	12	13	14	15

L	M	N	O	P	Q	R	S	T	U
16	17	18	19	20	21	22	23	24	25

Now,

22	25	8	22	5
R	U	D	R	A

12. (b)

C	A	L	A	N	D	E	R
↓	⤫		⤫		⤫		↓
C	L	A	N	A	E	D	R

C	I	R	C	U	L	A	R
↓	⤫		⤫		⤫		↓
C	R	I	U	C	A	L	R

13. (a)

Letters	D	R	L	A	L
Position	4	18	12	1	12
Change	+2	+2	+2	+2	+2
Code	6	20	14	3	14

Hence, the code for DRLAL is 62014314

Letters	C	A	M	E	L
Position	3	1	13	5	12
Change	+2	+2	+2	+2	+2
Code	5	3	15	7	14

Hence, the code for CAMEL is 5315714

14. (a)

L	I	G	H	T
⤫			⤫	
G	I	L	T	H

R	A	I	N	Y
⤫			⤫	
I	A	R	Y	N

15. (a): First rearrange the letters of the word 'ARGUMENT' in alphabetical order and then substitute each letter by the letter immediately following it.

A	E	G	M	N	R	T	U
+1	+1	+1	+1	+1	+1	+1	+1
B	F	H	N	O	S	U	V

16. (c): All words in the answer choices consist of five letters. The first two and last two letters interchange their positions.

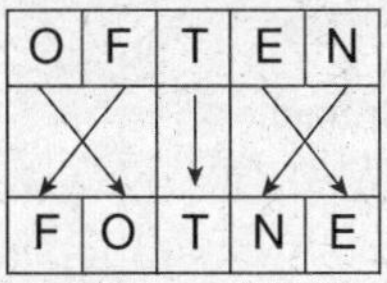

Similarly,

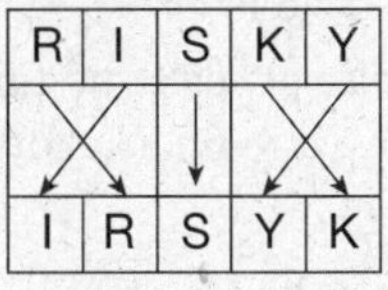

17. (c): The fruits grow on a 'tree', and 'tree' is called 'sky'. Hence, the fruits grow on the 'sky'.
18. (b): The colour of sky is blue; here, blue is called Green.
19. (a): In the first and second statements, the common code word is 'nie' and the common word is 'some'. Thus, 'nie' means 'some'.

    In the first and third statements, the common code word is 'pie' and the common word is 'good'. Thus, 'pie' means 'good'. Hence, 'jokes' is denoted by 'bi'.
20. (a): Teacher uses chalk to write on the blackboard. Here, chalk has been called book.
21. (c): In the first and third statements, the common word is 'na' and the common word is 'are'. Hence, 'na' means 'are'.

    In the second and third statements, the common code word is 'tok' and the common word is 'bad'. Hence, 'tok' means 'bad'. Thus, in the third statements, 'tim' stands for 'they'.
22. (a): In the first and third statements, the common code digits are '4' and '3' and the common words are 'mangoes' and 'are'.

    Hence, '4' and '3' are the codes for 'mangoes' and 'are', respectively. Thus, in the third statements, '9' means 'ripe'.
23. (c): In the first and third statements, the common code digit is '5' and the common word is 'good'. Hence, '5' means 'good'.

    In the second and third statements, the common code digit is '3' and the common word is 'bad'. Thus, '3' means 'bad'.

    Thus, in third statement, '8' means 'and'.
24. (c): In the first and third statements, the common code digit is '6' and the common word is 'is'. Thus, '6' means 'is'.

    In the second and third statements, the common code digit is '4' and the common word is 'colour'. Thus, '4' means 'colour'.

    Thus, in the statement, '3' means 'fun'.
25. (d): In the first and second statements, the common code digit is '3' and the common word is 'hot'. Thus, '3' means 'hot'.

    In the second and third statements, the common code digit '5' and the common word is 'day'. Thus, '5' means 'day'.

    Thus, in the second statements, '6' means 'very'.

Choose the Odd Word

1. (c): All, except universe, form a part of the universe.
2. (b): All, except Geography, are branches of science.
3. (a): All, except mechanic, help in building a house.
4. (b): All others denote blood relations.
5. (d): Mercury is the only liquid metal in the group.
6. (c): All, except bear, belong to the cat family
7. (b): All others are parts of bed spread.
8. (b): All, except eagle, are flightless birds.
9. (c): All, except river, contain stagnant water.
10. (a): All, except arrow, are used while holding hand.

Odd Pairs

11. (d): In all other pairs, second is prepared by the first.
12. (d): In all other pairs, first is used to contain the second.
13. (a): In all other pairs, second is the noise produced by the first.
14. (b): In all other pairs, the two words are antonyms of each other.
15. (a): In all other pairs, second is a part of the first.
16. (c): Each of the numbers except 63 is a prime number.
17. (a): Each of the number except 51 is a perfect square.
18. (d): Each of the numbers except 28 is divisible by 3.
19. (a): Sum of the digits in each other number is 10.
20. (a): All other numbers are cubes of odd numbers.

Choose the Odd Number Pair or Group

21. (d): In all other pairs, first number is 13 more than the second.
22. (c): In all other pairs, second number is the cube of the first.
23. (a): In all other pairs, one number is the square of the other.
24. (d): In all other pairs, the sum of two numbers is 8.
25. (d): In all other pairs, the second number is one less than the square of the first number.
26. (b): All other pairs consist of prime numbers only.
27. (b): In all other pairs, first number is the cube of the second.
28. (d): All other pairs consist of odd numbers only.
29. (d): In all other pairs, second is the multiple of first.
30. (c): In all other pairs, it is square of first term + 1.

Choose the Odd Letter Group

31. (d): All other groups contain alternate letters from left or right.
32. (a): All other groups contain alternate letters of the alphabet.
33. (d): First letter is moved two places forward to obtain the third letter. Then third letter is moved two positions forward to obtain the middle letter.
34. (d): In all other groups, the third and second letters are 3 steps ahead of the first and third letters, respectively.
35. (b): Only (b) contains a vowel.
36. (b): In all other groups, the first and second letters occupy the same position in the alphabet from the beginning and the end, respectively. The second letter is moved one step backward to obtain the third letter.
37. (d): In all other groups, four intervening letters are skipped.
38. (c): In all other groups, the second letter is moved 2 steps forward to obtain the third letter, which then is moved 1 step forward to obtain the first.
39. (d): All other groups end with AT.
40. (b): There is no repetition of any letter in any other group.

Analogy

Direct or Simple Analogy

1. (b): Second word denotes the place where the sport is held.
2. (d): First works for and earns from the second.
3. (a): The words in each pair are antonyms of each pair.
4. (a): Second is required by the first to function.
5. (c): Second is the working place of the first.
6. (a): The prime job of the first is to do the second.
7. (a): Second is made according to the first.

8. (b): First is prepared as per the directions of the second.
9. (a): Second is the place for the first to perform on.
10. (b): First composes the second.
11. (a): First denotes the lack of second.
12. (a): Scientific experiments are conducted in a laboratory. Similarly, astronomical observations are made in an observatory.
13. (b): Bibliophile is a lover of books. Similarly, patriot is a lover of one's country.
14. (d): The words in each pair are antonyms of each other.
15. (d): Second is the dwelling place of the first.

Completing the Analogous Pair

16. (b): The words in each pair are antonyms of each other.
17. (d): Second contains the story of the first.
18. (d): First causes the second.
19. (b): The words in each pair are antonyms of each other.
20. (c): First forms the basis of the second.
21. (c): Taxonomy is the science dealing with classification. Similarly, pedology deals with study of soils.
22. (a): The words in each pair are antonyms of each other.
23. (b): First is followed by the second.
24. (c): Second is the feminine gender of the first.
25. (b): First robs the second.
26. (b): Second is the sound produced by the first.
27. (d): The words in each pair are antonyms of each other.
28. (b): Ornithologist specializes in the study of birds. Similarly, anthropologist specializes in the study of mankind.
29. (c): Oxygen supports burning, whereas carbon dioxide extinguishes fire.
30. (d): Seismograph measures the intensity of earthquakes. Tachometer measures strains.

Blood Relations

1. (a)

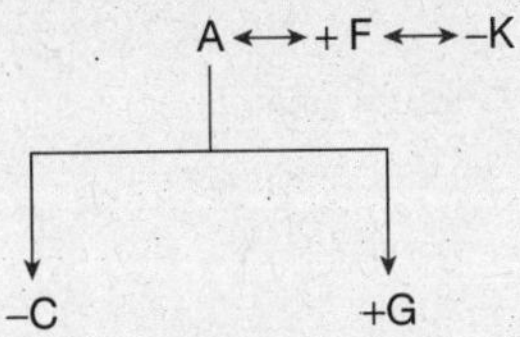

Hence, F is the uncle of G.

2. (c)

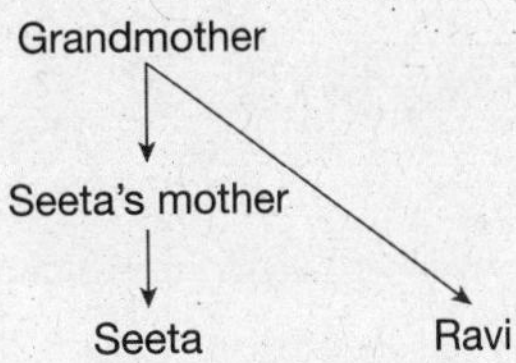

The maternal grandmother of Seeta and grandmother of Ravi is the same person. Hence, Seeta and Ravi are cousins.

3.

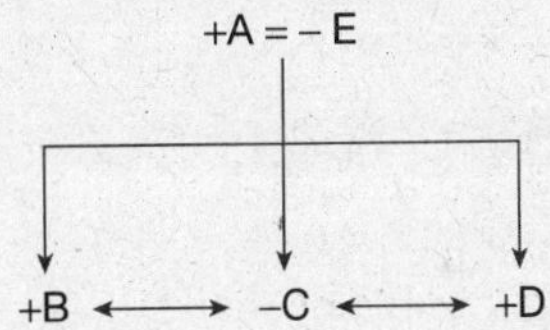

Therefore, D is a boy because there is only one daughter of E (or husband of E as given in the question statement).

Here + and − has been used for male and female, respectively. = sign has been used to show husband–wife relationship and for ↔ sibling relationship. Hence, B is the brother of D.

4. (b)

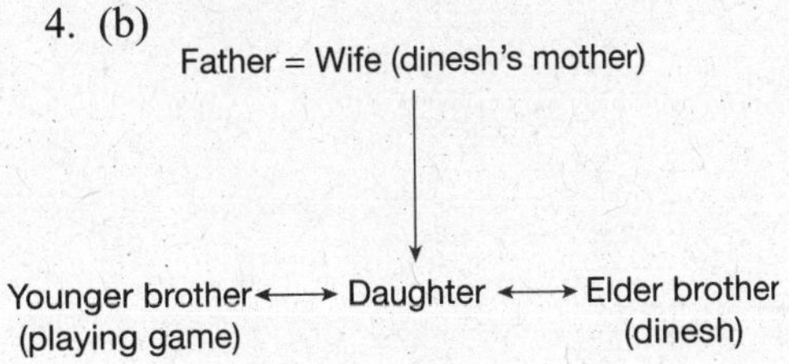

As per the question, the person playing game is different from Dinesh. The person playing game is brother of Dinesh.

5. (d)

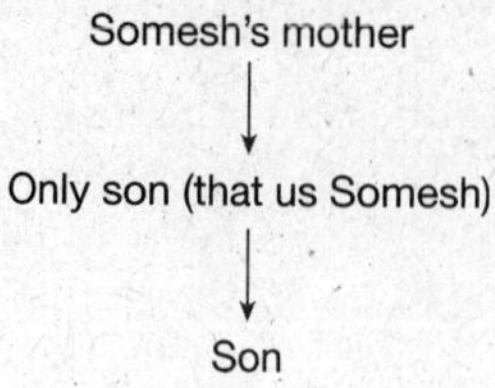

6. (d)

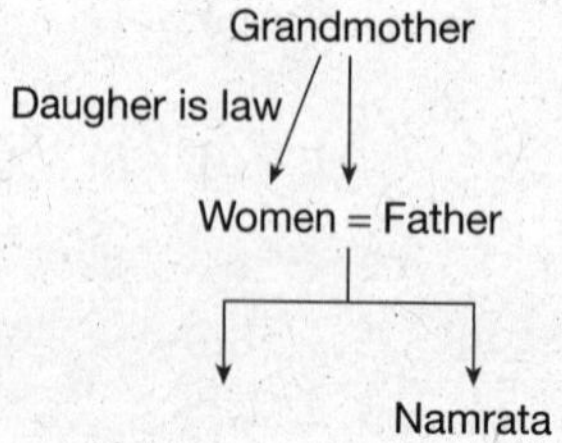

7. (b)

The man in the photograph is the son of the only son of Raveena's grandfather. Thus, the man is the son of Raveena's father. Hence, he is the brother of Raveena.

8. (d)

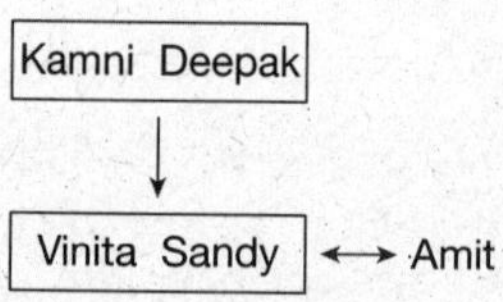

Amit is the only brother of Sandy, and Vinita is the sister-in-law of Amit. Hence, Vinita is the wife of Sandy. Kamni is the mother-in-law of Vinita. Kamni is the mother of Amit.

9. (d)

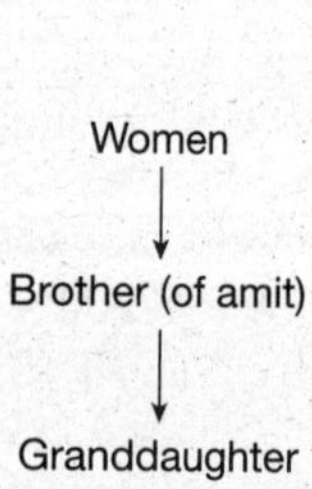

Hence, the woman in the picture is the mother of Amit.

10. (a)

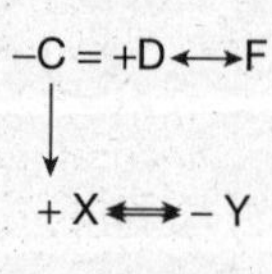

As X is the only son of C (and D), Y is female.

Looking at the family tree, we can say that Y is niece of F.

Direction Sense

1. (c)

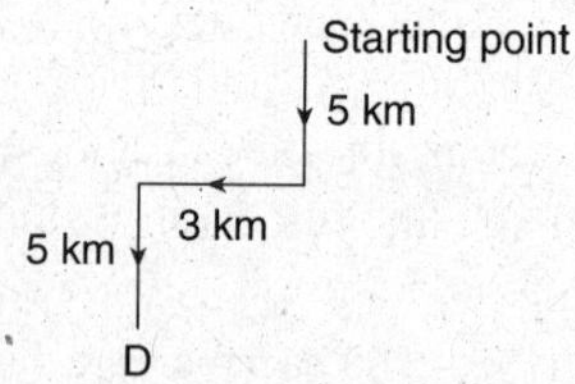

2. (a)
3. (c)

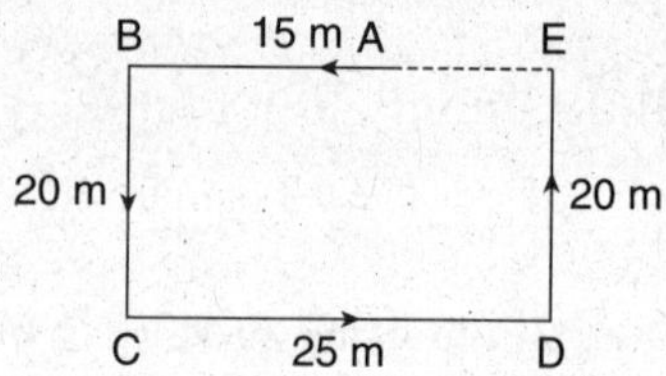

4. (c)

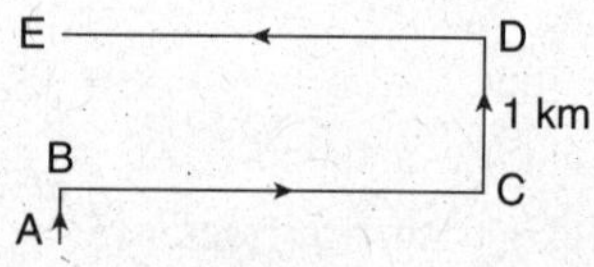

He is moving in the west direction now.

5. (d)

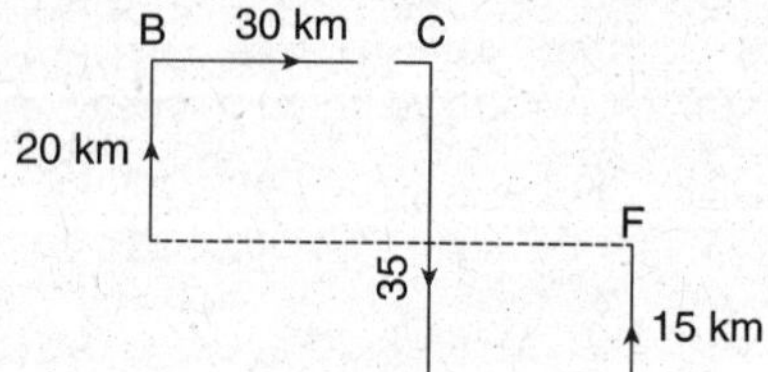

Required distance = AF

= 30 + 15

= 45 km

6. (c)
7. (d)
8. (d)
9. (a)
10. (b)

SEATING ARRANGEMENTS

1. (b)

   The seating arrangement is as follows:

   ● ● ● ● ● ●

   P X S Z R A

   Therefore, right of P is X.

2. (b)

   ● ● ● ● ●

   E B A C D

   Therefore, A is sitting in between B and C.

3. (a)

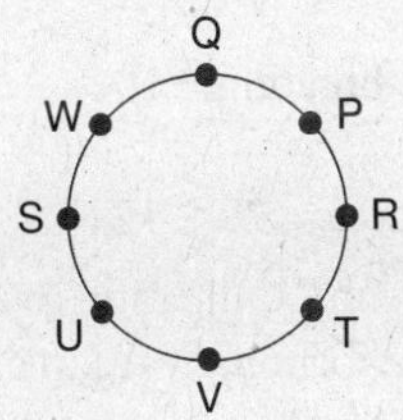

4. (d)

   J > L and D > F. Hence, J > L > H > D > F

   Hence, H is the third to reach.

5. (a)

   North

   R Q P S T

BASIC PERCENTAGE CALCULATIONS

1. (c): Let original price = 100

   Original quantity = 100

   Total expenditure = 100 × 100

   New price = 100 + 25 = 125

   New quantity = Q

   As expenditure is to be kept same,

   100 × 100 = 125 × Q

   Q = (100 × 100)/125 = 80.

   % reduction in quantity = 100 – 80 = 20.

2. (d): Let total employees = 100

   Matriculates = 40

   Remaining = 100 – 40 = 60

   Graduates = 50% of remaining 60 = 30

   Postgraduates = 100 – 40 – 30 = 30

   Graduates = Postgraduates

   Hence, graduates are also 180.

3. (b): 96% of total population = 23,040

   Hence, total population = 23,040 × 100/96 = 24,000

4. (c): Ratio between boys: girls = 75%: 25% = 3 : 1

   Hence, number of boys = 3 × 420 = 1,260

5. (b): (100 – 12.5)%, i.e., 87.5% of total income = 3,500, total income = 3,500 × 100/87.5 = 4,000

6. (d): +20 – 20 + (–20) × (+20)/100 = –4%.

7. (b): Let Y's salary = 100, then X's salary = 50

   X's new salary = 50 × 3/2 = 75

   Y's new salary = 100 × 5/4 = 125

   Combined old salary = 100 + 50 = 150

   New combined salary = 75 + 125 = 200

   Increase in combined salary = 50

   Percentage increase = 50/150 × 100 = 33.33%

8. (a): Let x water to be added to make water 20% of new mixture.

   Water in old mixture = 10% of 40 = 4 l

   Water in new mixture to make it 20% = $(4 + x)\ l$

   Now 20% of $(40 + x)\ l = 4 + x$

   Solving equation, we get $x = 5\ l$.

9. (d): Let income = 100

   New income = 120

   New expenditure = 75 + 10% of 75 = 82.5%

   New savings = 120 – 82.5 = 37.5

   Old saving = 25,

   Percentage increase in savings

   = (37.5 – 25)/25 × 100

   = 12.5/25 × 100 = 50%

10. (d): Let C's income = 100

    B's income = 100 + 20 = 120

    A's income = 125% of 120 = 150

    Thus, A's income is 50% higher than that of C.

11. (b): Let original price = 100

Increased price = 100 + 25 = 125

Now 125 is to be brought to 100; Say it is multiplied by x.

$125 \times x = 100$

$x = 100/125 = 4/5$ that is equivalent to 80%. Hence, the price should be reduced by 20%.

12. (c): Let cost price = 100

Net selling price = 100 + 8 = 108

Now 120 – (x% of 120) = 108

$x = 10$

13. (c): Discount on ₹60 = 25% of ₹60 = ₹15

Assume that the retailer offers a discount of ₹15 or 4 extra mangoes.

New purchase price of 4 mangoes = ₹15

Purchase price of one mango = 15/4 = ₹3.75

14. (c): Suppose both length and breadth are 100.

Hence, area = 100 × 100

New length = 100 + 10 m = 110

As area is to be kept same,

110 × new breadth = 100 × 100

New breadth = 100 × 100/110 = 1,000/11

Decrease in breadth = 100 – 1,000/11 = 100/11 = 9.11%

As breadth was assumed to be 100, no additional calculation is required for percentage figure.

15. (b): Using the formula: $x + y + xy/100$, Net percentage increase = 20 + 40 + (20 × 40)/100 = 68%

Increased price = ₹25 + 68% of 25 = 25 + 17 = ₹42

Alternatively: Using the multiplier factor concept, we get the final price as

$$25 \times \left(\frac{6}{5}\right) \times \left(\frac{7}{5}\right) = ₹42$$

16. (a): Circumference of a circle = $2pr$. As r increase by 20%, the circumference also increases by 20%.

17. (b): Area of a circle = πr^2

As $r^2 = r \times r$ and as r increases by 20%, r^2 increases by $20 + 20 + \frac{(20 \times 20)}{100} = 44\%$

18. (d): Let side of square = 100

Area = 100 × 100 = 10,000

New side = 100 + 25 = 125

New area = 125 × 125 = 15,625

Percentage increase = {(15,625 – 10,000)/ 10,000}× 100 = 56.25

Alternatively = $x + x + x^2/100$ = 25 + 25 + 25 × 25/100 = 56.25%

19. (c):Increased length = $20 \times \frac{11}{10} = 22$ cm

Increased breadth = $10 \times \frac{120}{100} = 10 \times \frac{6}{5} =$ 12 cm

The new area = 22 × 12 = 264 sq. cm

As there is multiplication of two quantities in the area formula, we can use the method $a + b + \frac{ab}{100}$ to calculate the percentage increase in area also.

20. (b): We can use the formula $x + y + \frac{xy}{100}$ to calculate the net increase.

25 + 12 + (25 × 12)/100 = 40%

Arithmetic Mean

1. (c): Total increase in weight = (8 × 2.5) kg = 20 kg

Weight of new person = (60 + 20) kg = 80 kg

2. (c): Total weight of 8 articles = 200 kg

Total weight of 3 articles = 3 × 20 = 60 kg

Total weight of rest of 5 articles = 200 – 60 = 140 kg

Average weight of 5 articles = 140/5 = 28 kg

3. (c): As the distance is not mentioned, LCM of 35 and 42, that is, 210 can be assumed to be the total distance.

Time taken from A to B = 210/35 = 6 hrs

Time taken from B to A= 210/42 = 5 hrs

Total Time taken = 11 hrs

Average speed = (210 + 210)/(6 + 5) = 420/11 = 38.17 kmph

Alternatively, by applying direct formula

$= \frac{2xy}{x+y}$

$= (2 \times 35 \times 42)/35 + 42 = 38.17$ kmph

4. (c): Petrol consumed during 1st year = 4,000/8 = 500

   Petrol consumed during 2nd year = 4,000/10 = 400

   Total expenditure = 4,000 × 2 = 8,000

   Total petrol consumed = 500 + 400 = 900

   Average cost per litre = 8,000/900 = ₹8.88

   Note: The answer won't be ₹9 as many have thought because calculation of average also depends upon quantity consumed.

5. (a): The present total age of husband and wife = 2 × (22 + 5) = 54 years

   Total age of family (including child) = 54 + 3 = 57 years

   Average age of family = 57/3 = 19 years

6. (d): Distance travelled in 2 hrs = 35 × 2 = 70 km

   Distance travelled in next 3½ hrs = 60 × 3.5 = 210 km

   Distance travelled in next 2½ hrs = 70 × 2.5 = 175 km

   Total distance = 70 + 210 + 175 = 455 km

   Average speed = total distance/total time taken

   = (70 + 210 + 175)/(2 + 3.5 + 2.5) = 455/8 = 56.87 kmph

7. (b): Monthly saving = 3,600/12 = ₹300

   Hence, monthly expenditure = income – saving = 1,400 – 300 = ₹1,100

8. (b): First Statement is not sufficient to answer the question because speed of the second half of the distance is not given here but statement II can answer as information to calculate average speed = distance/time is given in the statement.

9. (b): The total of a, b, and c = 3 × 50 = 150

   d = 10

   Total of a, b, c, and d = 150 + 10 = 160

   Average of a, b, c, and d = 160/4 = 40

10. (b): Time taken by B to reach destination = 350/50 = 7 hrs

    If A has a head start of 1 hr. the distance travelled by A when B reaches destination

    = 40 × (7 + 1) = 320 km

    Hence, A has to still travel 30 km while B has reached the destination.

Speed, Time, and Distance

1. (a): Speed = distance/time = 1,200 m/600 s = 2 m/s. Speed in kmph = 2 × 18/5 = 7.2 kmph

2. (c): Here, Speed = 48/2 = 24 kmph

   Time taken = 252/24 = 10½ hrs

3. (d): Average speed = 2 × 30 × 60/(30 + 60) = 2 × 30 × 60/90 = 40 mph

   Time taken by train to complete the trip = distance/speed = 20/40 = ½ hr = 30 min.

4. (a): The distance covered by auto-rickshaw

   = 1 – (1/2 + 1/3) = 1/6

   1/6 of total journey = 5 km

   Total journey = 6 × 5 = 30 km

5. (b): Due to stoppages, it covers 9 km less.

   Time taken to cover 9 km = 9/54 × 60 min = 10 min

6. (b): Average speed = (2 × 21 × 24)/(21 + 24) = 22.4 kmph

   Distance = time × speed = 22.4 × 10 = 224

7. (c): As the distance in both ways is same, we can apply the formula $2xy/x + y$.

   Average speed = (2 × 64 × 80)/(64 + 80) = 71.11 kmph

8. (c): Let the distance travelled in first phase be x km.

   Then, distance travelled in second phase = $(610 - x)$ km.

Hence, $x/40 + (610 - x)/90 = 9$ hrs

$\Rightarrow x = 160$ km

9. (b): Distance to be travelled = 320 m

Speed = 36 kmph = 36 × 5/18 = 10 m/s

Time taken = D/S = 320/10 = 32 s

10. (c): Total distance to be travelled = 280 + 120 = 400 m

Speed should be converted into m/s.

Speed = 40 kmph = 40 × 5/18 = 100/9 m/s

Time = D/S = 400/100/9 = 36 s

Calendar

1. (d): There are two conditions for two years having the same calender: both having same length in terms of number of days and first day starting with same day of the week.

The year 1991 has 365 days, that is, 1 odd day, year 1992 has 366 days, that is, 2 odd days, year 1993 has 365 days, that is, 1 odd day. The years 1994, 1995, and 1996 have 1 odd day each.

The sum of odd days so calculated from year 1991 to 1996.

(1 + 2 + 1 + 1 + 1 + 1) = 7 odd days.

Hence, the year 1997 will have the same calendar as that of the year 1991.

2. (d): 28th May, 2007 = (2000 years + 6 years + period from 1.1.2007 to 28.5.2007)

Odd days in 2000 years = 0

Odd days till 2006 = (5 ordinary years + 1 leap year) = (5 × 1 + 1 × 2) = 7 odd days

Jan	Feb	March	April	May	Total
31	28	31	30	28	148

148 days = (21 weeks + 1 day) ⇒ 1 odd day

Total number of odd days = (2000 years + 6 years + period from 1.1.2007 to 28.5.2007) = (0 + 7 + 1) = 8 odd days, that is, again 1 odd day. Hence, Monday is the answer.

3. (c) 16th June, 1999 = (1900 years + 98 years + period from 1.1.1999 to 16.6.1999)

Now first deal with 1998 complete years; how many odd days are there in 1998 years?

Odd days in 1600 years = 0

Odd days in 300 years = (5 × 3) = 1

98 years have 24 leap years + 74 ordinary years.

Number of odd days in 98 years (24 × 2 + 74) = 122 = 3 odd days.

Now come to calculation of odd days in period from 1.1.1999 to 16.6.1999.

Months	Jan	Feb	March	April	May	June	Total
Odd days	31	28	31	30	31	16	167

167 days = 23 complete weeks plus 6 odd days (this result is obtained by dividing 167 days by 7).

Total number of odd days = (0 + 1 + 3 + 6) = 10 ⇒ 3 odd days

Thus, the day asked in the question is Wednesday.

4. (b): 16th August, 2010 = (2000 + 9 years + period 1.1.2010 to 16.8.2010)

Odd days in 2000 years = 0

9 years = (2 leap years + 7 ordinary years) = (2 × 2 + 7 × 1) = 11 odd days

11 can be divided by 7 ⇒ 4 odd days

Months	Jan	Feb	March	April	May	June	July	Aug	Total
Odd days	31	28	31	30	31	16	31	16	228

The odd days can be calculated for each month separately and then added up. This can save some time in calculation. Such as

January has 3 odd days (31 divided by 7 gives remainder of 3 and so on).

Now, 228 days = 32 complete weeks + 3 extra days, it means 3 odd days.

Total number of odd days = (0 + 0 + 4 + 4) = 8; it means 1 odd day.

Thus, 16th August, 2010, was Monday.

5. (c): From August 15, 2012, till August 15, 2013, there is one extra day. In the rest of 16 days of August, there are 2 odd days. In September, there are 2 odd days, and in October, 3 odd days. In first 15 days of November, there will be 1 odd day. Thus, the total number of odd days is 1 + 2 + 2 + 3 + 1 = 9; it means 2 extra (odd) days. Hence, November 15, 2013, was Friday.

6. (b): Each day of the week is repeated after 7 days.
Assuming that first day is Sunday, 8th, 15th, 22nd, 29th, 36th, 43rd, 50th and 57th days will be Sundays. Hence, 58th day is Monday, 59th is Tuesday, 60th is Wednesday. Hence, day after 60 days will be Thursday.

7. (a): The year 2012 is a leap year. Thus, it has 2 odd days.

   But as calculation is to be done from April 22, 2012, till April 22, 2013, so it has 1 odd day only. As the calculation is to be done backwards, thus April 22nd was one day less. Thus, it was Sunday.

   Note: Had the question been about April 22, 2014, the answer would have been Tuesday. If the same question is framed for April 22, 2016, the answer would have been Friday as 2016 is a Leap year.

8. (a): 1st April, 2001 = (2000 years + period from 1.1.2001 to 1.4.2001)

   Odd days in 2000 years = 0

   Now, calculate the odd days for the year 2001.

Jan	Feb	March	April	Total
31	28	31	1	91

   91 divided by 7 gives 0 as remainder, so, odd days can be counted as 0.

   Total number of odd days = (0 + 0) = 0

   On 1st April, 2001, it was Sunday.

9. (c): 100 years contain 5 odd days.

   Last day of 1st century is Friday.

   200 years contain (5 × 2) = 3 odd days

   Last day of 2nd century is Wednesday.

   300 years contain (5 × 3) = 15 odd days that is, equal to 1 odd day.

   Last day of 3rd century is Monday.

   400 years contain 0 odd days.

   Last day of 4th century is Sunday.

   This cycle is repeated.

   Last day of a century cannot be Tuesday or Thursday or Saturday.

10. (c): The year 2004 is a leap year. It has 2 odd days.

   Hence, February 10, 2004, was Tuesday and February 8, 2004, must be Sunday.

Venn Diagrams

1. (a)

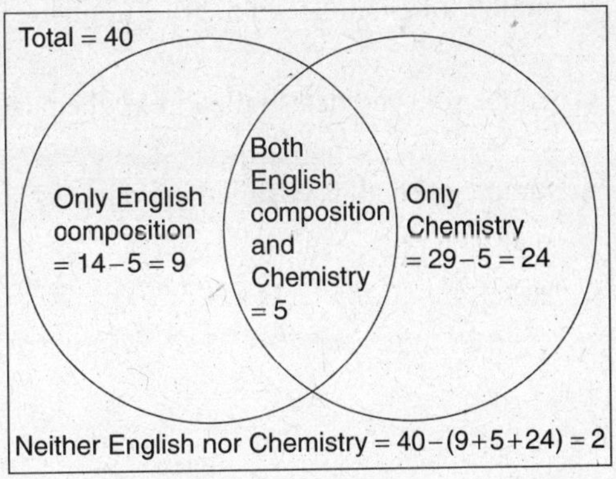

   Alternatively: Students taking either English composition or Chemistry = 14 + 29 − 5 = 38

   Hence, students not taking any class = 40 − 38 = 2

2. (c): Let us draw a Venn diagram with the information given in the question.

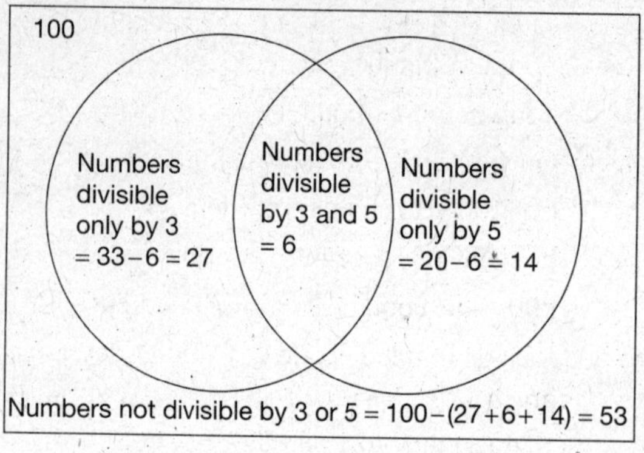

Numbers divisible by 3 (3, 6, 9, and so on) = 33

Numbers divisible by 5 (5, 10, 15, and so on) = 20

Numbers which are divisible by both 3 and 5 (15, 30, 45, 60, 75, and 90) = 6

Numbers divisible by 3 or 5 or both 3 and 5 = 27 + 6 + 14 = 47 (alternatively, 33 + 20 − 6 = 47)

Numbers neither divisible by 3 nor by 5 = 100 − 47 = 53

3. (b)

Number of candidates failed in English = 52%

Number of candidates failed in Mathematics = 42%

Number of candidates failed in both = 17%

Total failed = 52 + 42 − 17 = 77%

Passed in both the subjects = 100 − 77 = 23%

4. (a)

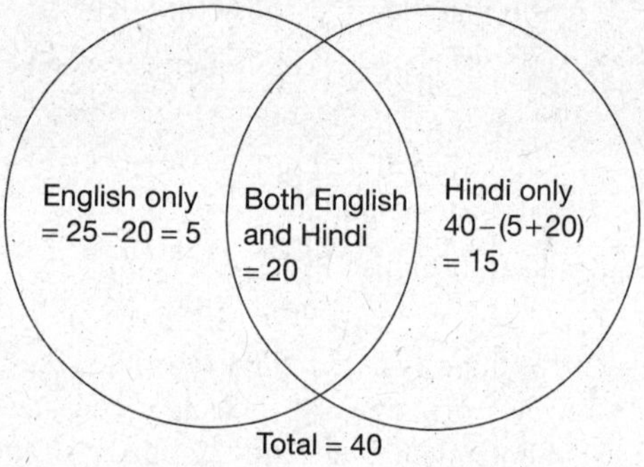

5. (c): People studying newspaper X or Y = 40 + 50 − 10 = 80

Hence, people studying neither X nor Y = 100 − 80 = 20

(Candidates can try to solve this question with Venn diagram also.)

6. (a): A teacher can be an author; an author can be an artist, and so on. Some person can be a teacher, an author, and artist also.
7. (d): A traveller can travel by both taxi and train.
8. (b): Same explanation as in 6.
9. (c): Same explanation as in 6.
10. (b): Mercury is also a metal, although it exists in liquid state.
11. (a)
12. (c)
13. (c)
14. (a)
15. (c)

6

LOGICAL REASONING

INTRODUCTION

Reasoning is an important section in aptitude tests and students need to master it necessarily. They aim to check our thinking capability. We always seek explanation of objects, events, subjects, and phenomena that occur around us. To seek accurate explanation, we have to apply logic. Then, what is logic? Logic is applying principles of reasoning to obtain valid inferences. Logical reasoning is largely about adopting complete rational approach to solve a problem, with no chance for ambiguity.

On the contrary, analytical reasoning is the act of carefully considering a problem, claim, question, or situation in order to determine the best solution. Applying analytical reasoning also means seeing things from your view point, and there may be some subjectivity also.

The purpose of using reasoning skills is to always justify your decisions and actions.

The first part of the unit deals with logical reasoning and the second part deals with analytical reasoning.

In Unit II on research aptitude, we have seen that there are basically two approaches to solve a problem—inductive and deductive. Continuing with the same idea, reasoning is basically of two types—deductive and inductive.

Deductive Reasoning

Premise: All dogs have long ears.
Premise: Hound is a dog.
Conclusion: Therefore, Hound has long ears.

In deductive reasoning, conclusion is guaranteed to be true if the premises are true. Therefore, in the deductive inference, the conclusion cannot be more general than premise(s). Given the premises that all dogs have long ears and Hound is a dog, it is logical to assume that Hound has long ears. After all, in this example, having long ears are an inherent quality of dogs. This argument is valid. Does it mean it is also true?

The conclusions are based on the premises and one of the premises is not true, it follows that the conclusion is not true, even though it is valid. If one of the premises is not true, then the conclusion is also not true.

Deductive inference is further categorized into immediate (where conclusion is drawn from a single statement) and mediate (where conclusion is drawn from two statements, called syllogism). Syllogism has been discussed further in this unit.

Deductive is akin to analysis (separating any material or abstract entity into its constituent elements).

Inductive Reasoning

Inductive reasoning is the process of making generalized decisions after observing, or witnessing, repeated specific instances of something. Inductive reasoning, while not 100% accurate 100% of the time, is still a relatively quick way to make decisions. Sometimes, saving time is as important as being accurate.

Over the course of our lifetime, we have witnessed hundreds of instances when animals eat, whether it is a cow, an elephant, or a horse. Inductive reasoning tells us that all animals must eat to survive. Have we ever witnessed every animal on earth eat? Of course, the answer is no.

However, by basic biology and common experience, we know that all animals must eat to survive. That is called inductive reasoning. Inductive is akin to synthesis (combining parts to form a whole).

The following example also help in differentiating between deductive and inductive reasonings.

Deductive Reasoning

Statement I: All vegetables contain vitamins.
Statement II: Carrot is a vegetable.
Conclusion: So carrot contains vitamins.

Inductive Reasoning

Statement I: Most vegetables contain vitamins.
Statement II: Carrot is a vegetable.
Conclusion: So carrot contains vitamins.

Types of syllogism: On the basis of proposition, syllogism is of four types:

1. **Categorical:** Here, the relationship between the subject and the predicate is without any condition.
   Example: I. All trains are planes. II. All dogs are animals.
   Within syllogism, our focus is on categorical syllogism.
2. **Hypothetical:** The relationship between the subject and the predicate is asserted conditionally. For example, if it rains he will not attend.
3. **Disjunctive:** In a disjunctive proposition, the assertion is of alteration.
   Example: I. Either he is courageous or he is strong.
4. **Relational:** Here, the relation between the various terms is shown in an order:
   Example: a > b > c > d; so a > d (conclusion).

Following types of questions appear regularly in the NET Exam. Candidates need to go through Previous Years' Papers section for more such questions.

1. In a deductive argument, conclusion is (*June 2009*)
   (a) Summing up of the premises
   (b) Not necessarily based on premises
   (c) Entailed by the premises
   (d) Additional to the premises
   Option (c) is the correct one.
2. Inductive reasoning is based on or presupposes
   (a) Uniformity of nature
   (b) God created the world
   (c) Unity of nature
   (d) Laws of nature
   Option (a) is the correct one.

The analytical method to solve syllogism problems has been discussed in the later part of the chapter.

Structure of Arguments

An argument, in general, is a form of communication that tries to persuade its audience to adopt a particular position about a topic. Arguments have three main parts: a claim that states the position to be argued; reasons that logically explain why the claim should be accepted; and evidence that supports the reasons with facts, anecdotes, statistics, expert testimony, and examples.

Reasoning has to be systematic and logical. There are two main components of reasoning—arguments (also known as premises, statements, or propositions) and conclusion. Structure of arguments deals with basic terms, validity of arguments, converting sentences into their logical form depending on the requirement, and then application of rules follows so as to arrive at a conclusion. In previous NET examinations, many questions have been asked about basic concepts and terms relating to structure of arguments, so candidates should be well versed with these concepts and terms before they attempt practical problems.

Validity of Arguments

Deductive arguments may be either valid or invalid. If an argument is valid, it is a valid deduction, and if its premises are true, the conclusion must be true. *A valid argument cannot have true premises and a false conclusion.*

The validity of an argument depends, however, not on the actual truth or falsity of its premises and conclusion, but solely on whether the argument has a valid logical form or not. The validity of an argument is not a guarantee of the truth of its conclusion. Under a given interpretation, a valid argument may have false premises that render it inconclusive. The conclusion of a valid argument with one or more false premises may be either true or false.

The following question was asked in June 2009 NET Exam:

(a) Premises are false and conclusion is true.
(b) Premises are false and conclusion is also false.
(c) Premises are true and conclusion is false.
(d) Premises are true and conclusion is also true.

The answer is (d).

Logic seeks to discover the valid forms, the forms that make arguments valid. A form of argument is valid if and only if the conclusion is true under all interpretations of that argument in which the premises are true. Since the validity of an argument depends solely on its form, an argument can be shown to be invalid by showing that its form is invalid. This can be done by giving a counterexample of the same form of argument with premises that are true under a given interpretation, but a conclusion that is false under that interpretation. In informal logic, this is called a counterargument.

Certain examples would help in better clarification about validity of arguments.

1. *Some Indians are logicians; therefore, some logicians are Indians.*

   Valid argument: It would be self-contradictory to admit that some Indians are logicians but deny that some (any) logicians are Indians.

2. *All Indians are human and all humans are mortal; therefore, all Indians are mortal.*

   Valid argument: If the premises are true, the conclusion must be true.

3. *Some Indians are logicians and some logicians are tiresome; therefore, some Indians are tiresome.*

   Invalid argument: For example, the tiresome logicians might all be Chinese.

4. *Either we are all doomed or we are all saved; we are not all saved; therefore, we are all doomed.*

   Valid argument: The premises entail the conclusion.

Remember that this does not mean the conclusion has to be true; it is only true if the premises are true, which they may not be.

The following examples would help to clarify this aspect about structure of arguments:

Premises

I: Some men are lawyers.

II: Some lawyers are rich.

Conclusion: Some men are rich.

This argument is invalid. There is a way where you can determine whether an argument is valid and give a counterexample with the same argument form.

Note: Logical strength and soundness are properties of arguments. Truth (or falsity) is a property of statements (or premises or conclusions). Never say that 'argument is false' or that 'premise is logically strong'.

What is a counterexample? *In logic, a counterexample is an exception to a proposed general rule. For example, 'All students are lazy' makes the claim that a certain property (laziness) holds for all students, even a single example of a diligent student will prove it false. Thus, any hardworking student is a counterexample to 'all students are lazy'. More precisely, a counterexample is a specific instance of the falsity of a universal quantification.*

Structure of logical argument is based on

(a) Formal validity
(b) Material truth
(c) Linguistic expression
(d) Aptness of examples

The correct answer is (a). As discussed, an argument is valid if and only if truth of its premises entails the truth of its conclusion, and each step, sub-argument, or logical operation in the argument is valid.

Analogous arguments: These are basically inductive reasoning. The analogies are not arguments. However, analogies are often used in arguments. To argue by analogy is to argue that because two things are similar, what is true of one is also true of the other. Such arguments are called 'analogical arguments' or 'arguments by analogy'. For example, like the Earth, Europa has an atmosphere containing oxygen; it means that there might be life on Europa because it has an atmosphere that contains oxygen just like the Earth.

In December 2009 Exam, the following question has been asked:
Which of the following is an analogous statement?

(a) Man is like God.
(b) God is great.
(c) Gandhi is the father of the nation.
(d) Man is a rational being.

Proposition

A proposition is a sentence that makes a statement and gives a relation between two or more terms. In logical reasoning, any statement is termed as a proposition.

A proposition is assumed to be true and from which a conclusion can be drawn. The statement, 'All cats are lemons' is assumed to be true as a proposition (or premise), but actually we all know that cats and lemons are entirely different entities. Proposition consists of the following four parts:

1. *Quantifier:* All, no, and some. They specify a quantity. 'All' and 'no' are universal quantifiers and 'some' is a particular quantifier.
2. *Subject (S):* About which something is being said.
3. *Predicate (P):* Something that affirms or denies about the subject.
4. *Copula:* Relation between subject and predicate.

   Quantifier + Subject + Copula + Predicate

Examples
All bats are boys
Some players are doctors.

Quality: Categorical propositions can have one of the two qualities—affirmative or negative that has been clarified through 'classification of proposition'.

Classification of Propositions

Propositions are basically of two types, namely universal and particular. Universal proposition is further divided into two parts:

1. *Universal positive or affirmative (A):* It denotes inclusion.

   Form: All S is P, where S is the subject and P is the predicate.

   Example: 'All cats are animals'. It is basically about inclusion.

   Distribution: It distributes the subject only. In the above statement, cats are distributed in animals.

   Predicate is not interchangeable with the subject while maintaining the validity of a proposition. We cannot say that all animals are cats.

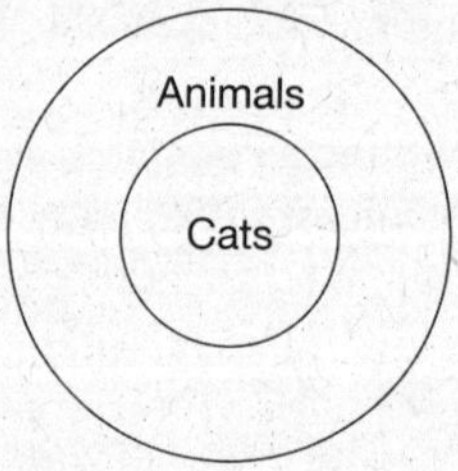

2. *Universal negative (E):* It denotes exclusion.

   Form: No S is P.

   Example: 'No fish are birds' would be a universal negative.

   Distribution: Both subject and predicate. Here, an entire class of predicate term is denied to the entire class of the subject term.

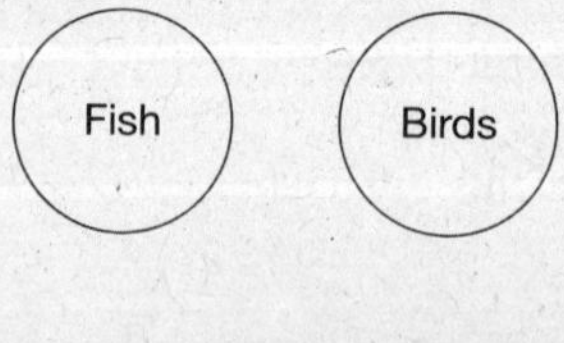

Particular proposition: A particular proposition can also be divided into two parts.

1. *Particular positive (I):* It denotes 'partial inclusion'.
   Form: Some S is P.
   Example: Some men are foolish.
   Distribution: Neither the subject nor the predicate. In the example, subject term, men is used not for all but only for some men and similarly the predicate term, foolish is affirmed for a part of subject class. So, both are undistributed.

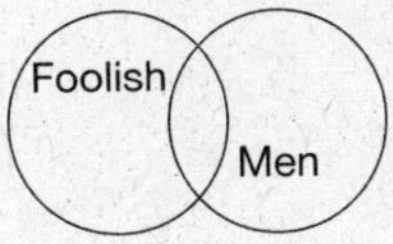

2. *Particular negative (O):* It denotes partial exclusion.
   Form: Some S is not P or not every S is P.
   Example: 'Some birds are not carnivores'.
   Distribution: Only of predicate.

Table 6.1 will help the candidates in comparing major aspects of different forms of a proposition.

Table 6.1 Types and Main Characteristics of Propositions

Sign	Statement form	Examples	Quantity	Quality	Distributed
A	All S are P	All politicians are liars	Universal	Positive	Only subject
E	No S are P	No politicians are liars	Universal	Negative	Both subject and predicate
I	Some S are P	Some politicians are liars	Particular	Positive	Neither subject nor predicate
O	Some S are not P	Some politicians are not liars	Particular	Negative	Only predicate

Parts of Categorical Propositions

There are three parts of statements in categorical syllogism—major premise, minor premise, and conclusion. Each of the premise has one term in common with the conclusion.

Parts	Example
Major premise	All humans are mortal
Minor premise	All Greeks are humans
Conclusion	All Greeks are mortal

1. *Major premise:* Predicate of the conclusion is called as the major term. The premise containing major term is called major premise. In the example, mortal is the major term.
2. *Minor premise:* Subject of the conclusion is called minor term. The premise containing minor term is called minor premise. In the example, Greeks is the minor term.
3. *Middle term:* One term common in both the premises is called middle term. It is not a part of conclusion. In the example, humans is the middle term.

For practical purpose, we can put statements in the following form:

Statement 1:

A - - ➔ B
B - - ➔ C

Conclusion:

A - - ➔ C

According to our above discussion, A is the minor term, C is the major term, B is the middle term.

4. *Conclusion:* In conclusion statement, first term or (subject) is the subject of the first proposition and second term (or predicate) is the predicate of the second proposition.

Converting Common Language Statements into their Logical Forms

In logical reasoning or syllogism problems, the common language sentences may have to be converted into their logical form before we apply logic rules on them to draw a conclusion. For example, in a previous NET examination, statements (i) 'only graduates are eligible for this post' and (ii) 'most rickshaw pullers are graduates' were given. These types of statements need to be converted to their logical form, that is, quantifier + subject + copula + predicate, as discussed earlier. The rules of reduction help in solving these problems.

The rules of reduction can help in solving these types of questions.

1. *A-type propositions:* Statements starting with words 'each', 'every', 'any', etc. are to be treated as A-type propositions (starting with all).

Original sentence	**Logical form**
Every man is liable to commit error	All men are persons who are liable to commit mistakes
Each student participated in the event	All students are persons who participated in the event
Any one of the Indians is laborious	All Indians are laborious
Only Indians are students of this college	All students of this college are Indians
The honest alone are successful	All successful persons are honest

Note: Sentences with singular term or definite singular term without the sign of negation are also to be treated as A-type proposition. For example, Ram is mortal.

2. *E-type propositions:* Sentences with singular term or definite singular term with the sign of negation are to be treated as E-type propositions. Sentences beginning with the words like 'no', 'never', and 'none' are to be treated as E-type propositions.

   'Never men are perfect' is 'No men are perfect' in its logical form.

3. *I-type propositions:* Affirmative sentences with words like 'a few', 'certain', 'most', and 'many' are to be treated as I-type propositions.

Sentence	**Logical form**
A few men are present	Some men are present
Most of the students are laborious	Some students are laborious
Few men are not selfish	Some men are selfish
Certain books are good	Some books are good
Many Indians are religious	Some Indians are religious
All students of my class, except a few, are well prepared	Some students of my class are well prepared
The poor may be happy	Some poor people are happy

4. *O-type propositions:* A negative sentence that begins with a word like 'every', 'any', 'each', or 'all' is to be treated as an O-type proposition.

Sentence	**Logical form**
Every man is not rich	Some men are not rich
Certain books are not readable	Some books are not readable
Most of the students are not rich	Some students are not rich
Some men are not above temptation	Few men are above temptation

5. *Exclusive proposition*
   (a) In exclusive propositions, the subject is qualified with words like 'only', 'alone', 'none but', or 'no one else but'.
   (b) Here, the quantity is not explicitly stated.
   (c) They can be reduced to A, E, or I types by first interchanging the subject and the predicate, and then replacing the words like 'only' or 'alone' with 'all'.

If the exception is definitely specified as in case of, 'All metals except mercury are solid', then the proposition is to be treated as universal (All non-mercury metals are solid.). In case, the exception is indefinite, as in case of, 'All metals except one is solid', the proposition is to be treated as particular.

The nature of proposition depends upon context also. For example, 'Students are present' is reduced to, 'Some students are present' (I type).

In certain cases, the predicates are qualified by words like 'hardly', 'scarcely', 'seldom', but quantity is not specified. Such propositions should be treated as particular negative. For example, 'Businessmen are seldom honest' is an irregular proposition. It is reduced to, 'Some businessmen are not honest'.

If such a proposition contains the sign of negation, then this proposition is to be treated as an I-type proposition.

For example, 'Businessmen are not seldom honest' is to be reduced to 'Some businessmen are honest', which is an I type proposition. This is so because it involves a double negation which is equivalent to affirmation.

Deductive Inference and Syllogism

As we discussed earlier, deductive inference problems are basically of two types, namely immediate inference and mediate inference.

Immediate Inference

Here, the conclusion is drawn only from one given proposition. Two important cases of immediate inference have been discussed as given below:

1. *By implication:* If a given proposition is A type, then it also implies that I type conclusion must be true.

Statement	Implication of statement
All chairs are tables (A type).	Some chairs are tables (I type).
No chair is table (E type).	Some chairs are not tables (O type).

Looking at the proposition again, when we say that 'All chairs are tables', it implies that 'Some chairs (we are presently concerned with) are tables'. This is based on our knowledge that some is a part of all.

Similarly, we can say that an E-type proposition also implies an O-type conclusion. If we say that 'No chair is table', we are absolutely sure that 'Some chairs are not tables'.

The immediate inferencing by implication is quite similar to the concept of sub alternation also discussed under Squares of Opposition.

2. *By conversion:* First of all, let us be familiar with few terms.

Convertend – The original proposition

Converse – The new proposition

Conversion – The process itself

The process consists of two steps. The first step is interchanging the subject and predicate—subject will become the predicate, and predicate will become the subject.

The second step is to change the type of the given proposition to the pattern given in Table 6.2.

Table 6.2 Conversion Table

Types of statements	Valid conversion
Universal **Positive (A)** All chairs are tables.	**Only Particular Positive (I)** Some tables are chairs. Some chairs are tables.
Universal **Negative (E)** No chairs are tables.	**Universal Negative (E)** No tables are chairs.
Particular **Positive (I)** Some chairs are tables.	**Only Particular Positive (I)** Some tables are chairs.
Particular **Negative (O)** Some chairs are not tables.	No conversion

These conversion rules are helpful not only for immediate inference but also for mediate inference, depending on the nature of the problem and answer choices. So candidates are expected to learn the conversion rules by heart.

Important note: In NET examination, many times the question is asked only about conversion.

For example, what can be concluded from the given statement, 'Some men are honest'. Which of the following is true?

(a) Some honest people are not men.
(b) All honest people are not men.
(c) Some honest people are men.
(d) None of the above

Solution: This statement is particular positive statement. Hence, according to Table 6.3, it can be converted into PP only.

Table 6.3 Answer Choices and Justification as per Conversion Table

Answer choices	Justification
(a) Some honest people are not men.	Particular Negative, hence eliminate
(b) No honest people are men.	Universal Negative, hence eliminate
(c) Some honest people are men.	PP, hence this is correct answer
(d) None of the above	Not applicable because C is the correct answer

Mediate Inference

There are basically two approaches to solve a syllogism problem, namely (i) analytical method and (ii) Venn diagram.

Most of the candidates prefer Venn diagram method to analytical method as they find it easier. In this book, there are many illustrations using both the methods. . As many times the questions are asked from analytical method in NET examination, the candidates should be well versed with analytical method as well. Here, we have focused mainly on the analytical method with Venn diagram just as a supplementary solution.

Candidates are advised not to rely exclusively on Venn diagrams as they can be ambiguous at times. As many questions based on theory are expected, analytical method can reinforce our understanding about the concepts.

Analytical Method for Mediate Inference Problems

The basic steps to solve syllogism problem are (i) the alignment of statements and (ii) drawing conclusions. Depending on the nature of the problem, it can entail two additional steps also. Table 6.4 shows the steps needed in analytical method for mediate inference.

Table 6.4 Steps in Analytical Method for Mediate Inference Problems

Step I	Alignment of the propositions—standard format
Step II	Draw conclusion by use of table
Step III	Check for immediate inferences
Step IV	Check for complementary pair if steps II and III fail

The requirement of steps I, III, and IV depends upon the question.

Step I: Alignment of the Propositions

This consists of two steps—firstly, make sure that there are exactly three terms given in both the statements. In case, the number of terms is different, we need not go further, as there will be no conclusion. Secondly, we check whether the propositions are in standard form or not.

For practical purposes, the following format can be used as a standard.

Minor (or first) term	A→B
Middle term (major or third) term	B→C

A, B, and C used above denote the first, second and the third term, just for quick representation of terms while solving practical questions. Please note that this A (used for first term) is different from A used for universal affirmative.

As discussed earlier, in the conclusion statement, first term (subject) is the subject of the first proposition and second term (predicate) is the predicate of the second proposition. This fact becomes the basis for the alignment of propositions.

In case, the problem is in the standard form, we can directly move to Step II.

If one or both propositions are not given in the standard format, align them by (i) converting the first or second statement or both and (ii) changing the order as will be clear through the following examples.

Note: It is important to remind at this stage that sometimes the words 'mostly', 'generally', 'only', and so on are mentioned in one or both the statements; first, we convert them into logical form before doing their alignment, if required. This has been discussed separately under 'Converting common language statements into their logical Form' on Page 6.5.

Example 1
Statements

1. Intelligent alone are laborious.
2. Most of the girls are intelligent.

These statements should first be converted into logical forms according to the rules for logical form.

1. All intelligent are laborious. This is in the form B to C.
2. Some girls are intelligent. This is in the form A to B.

Just by changing their order, we can align them. After alignment is done, we move to Step II.

Example 2
Statements

1. Some pens are books.
2. Some stationary are books.

As books are the common term, they are in the form A to B and C to B. The first statement does not require any change. As the second statement is in particular positive (I type), this can be changed to I type only according to conversion table given earlier: The second statement will become, 'Some books are stationary'.

Now, propositions are properly aligned, that is, 'Some pens are books' and 'Some books are stationary'. We now move to Step II.

Example 3
Statements

1. No van is house.
2. All boxes are house.

Here, the common term, house, is the predicate in both propositions. Here, we have to alter the first proposition and also change the order to bring it to the form A to B and B to C.

1. All boxes are house.
2. No house is van.

Now, the predicate of first proposition is the subject of the second statement.

Example 4
Statements

1. All boys are tigers.
2. Some tigers are coward.

Solution: Here, the middle term, tiger, is the predicate in first proposition and subject of the second proposition. No alignment is required.

After aligning the statements among themselves, we can move to Step II.

IEA Rule

There can be confusion while aligning a pair of statements—which statement should be given priority in terms of conversion. For example, if there are two statements, A type and I type, which should be converted so that our purpose of getting the standard form is achieved. The IEA rule helps in such decision-making.

If first statement given is of A type and second is of I type, then as per IEA rule, I type statement should be given priority for conversion. Similarly, in case of confusion between E type and A type, E type should be given priority over A type.

Step II: Applying Syllogism Rules

After ensuring that propositions are in a standard format, we apply syllogism rules to draw conclusions.

Table 6.5 Rules of Syllogism

Proposition I (A to B)	Proposition II (B to C)	Conclusion	Summarized form
Universal Positive (A)	Universal Positive (A)	Universal Positive (A)	A + A = A
	Universal Negative (E)	Universal Negative (E)	A + E = E
Universal Negative (E)	Universal Positive (A)	Particular Negative (O)	E + A = O*
	Particular Positive (I)	Particular Negative (O)	E + I = O*
Particular Positive (I)	Universal Positive (A)	Particular Positive (I)	I + A = I
	Universal Negative (E)	Particular Negative (O)	I + E = O

*In this case, the flow is from C to A, and not from A to C as in all other cases. (Please refer Table 6.5. A, B, and C stand for first, middle, and second terms, respectively.)

After aligning the statements, as per our discussion in Step I, conclusion may be drawn by using Table 6.5 where the rules of syllogism are mentioned.

No definite conclusion can be drawn for other combinations like A + I or O + A, which have not been mentioned in the above table. In general, we can say that two negatives (E + E, E + O, O + E, or O + O) do not lead to any conclusion.

Two particulars also do not lead to any conclusion.

Statements:

I. All chairs are tables. (A type)
II. All tables are furniture (A type)

Conclusion:

All chairs are furniture. (A + A = A).

Now, consider Example I discussed in Step I.

1. Some pens are books. (I type)
2. Some books are stationary. (I type)

No conclusion as I + I = No conclusion.

Now, consider some examples from NET previous years' exams. In each of the following questions (1–3), two statements are followed by two conclusions, A and B. Assuming that the given statements are true even if they are at variance with commonly known facts, pick up one of the following answer choices which you think is correct.

(a) If only conclusion A follows
(b) If only conclusion B follows
(c) If both A and B follow
(d) If neither A nor B follows

Question 1

Statements

1. Some doctors are fool.
2. He is a doctor.

Conclusions

A. He is a fool.
B. Some fools are doctors.

Solution

No conclusion can be drawn from the two particular affirmative propositions. So (A) does not follow. Second conclusion is the converse of first statement, so (B) follows. Hence, (B) is the answer.

Question 2

Statements

1. All birds are men.
2. All crows are birds.

Conclusions

A. All crows are not men.
B. Some men are not crows.

(*June 1997 and June 2001*)

Explanation

Step I: The middle term is birds. A close observation reflects that the statements are in the form B to C and A to B. After swapping, the statements will be 'All crows are birds' and 'All birds are men'.

Step II: The conclusion should be A + A = A (universal positive). The conclusion is 'All crows are men'. So (d) is the answer.

Question 3

Statements

1. All boats are boys.
2. All boys are lamps.

Conclusions

A. All lamps are boats.

B. All boats are lamps. (*December 2002*)

Solution

Step I: Statements are in the standard form A to B and B to C. The common term, boys, is the predicate of the first proposition and subject of the second proposition. So no alignment is required.

Step II: A + A ⇒ A

The subject of the conclusion will be the subject of first statement, and predicate of the conclusion will be the predicate of second statement. The common terms will disappear. So conclusion is 'All boats are lamps'. Thus, only conclusion 2 follows and (B) is the answer.

Now solving the problem through Venn diagram solution:

According to Statement I—'All boats are boys'.

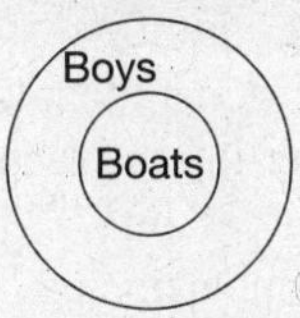

According to Statement I and Statement II, the Venn diagram looks as given below

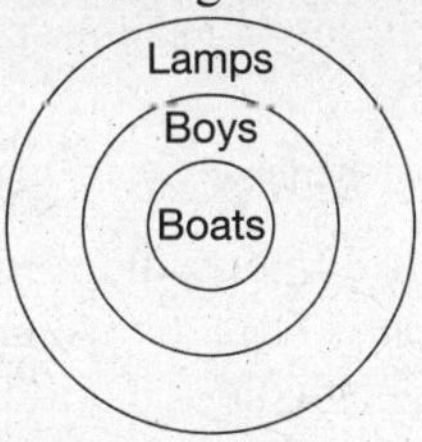

Looking at the Venn diagram, we can say that second conclusion, 'All boats are lamps' is correct.

Question 4

Statements

1. All lemons are balls.
2. No bats are lemons.

Conclusions

A. Some balls are not bats.

B. Some bats are lemons.

Solution

By changing the order of the statements itself, we can align the sentences. The aligned pair is

No bats are lemons. So (a) is the answer

All lemons are balls.

E + A = O*. So the conclusion is, 'Some balls are not bats'.

Note: In all the questions discussed previously, Step III and Step IV are not required as per the answer choices.

Step III: Checking for Immediate Inferences (If Required)

We can check the conclusion (or even statements) for immediate inference as per answer choices. Usually, in this case, there are more than two conclusions. Even in case of two conclusion questions, we can go for this step.

Let us discuss one comprehensive example:

Statements

1. Some tables are chairs.
2. Some chairs are furniture.

Conclusions

I. Some chairs are tables.

II. Some furniture is chair.

III. All tables are furniture.

Choices

(a) I and II are valid.

(b) II and III are valid.

(c) I and III are valid.

(d) None of the above.

Solution

I + I = No conclusion

(two particulars do not lead to any conclusion), but after immediate inference, we find that (i) and (ii) are valid. So (a) is the answer.

Step IV: Checking for Complementary Pair (If Required)

Check for complementary pair if Steps II and III fail. Complementary pair is a pair of contradictory statements, both cannot be true simultaneously.

We can call a pair as a complementary pair if

1. The subject and predicate of both the sentences are the same.
2. They are I + O or A + O or I + E type pairs which have been discussed below:

I + O type	A + O type	I + E type
Some chairs are tables.	All chairs are tables.	Some chairs are tables.
Some chairs are not tables.	Some chairs are not tables.	No chair is a table.

Note: Sometimes, the converse of the derived conclusions is among answer choices.

A Snap Shot—Golden Rules of Syllogism

To sum up all the discussion, some golden rules have emerged to solve the syllogism problems. These are in continuity with the earlier discussion.

1. Every deduction should contain exactly three terms.
2. The middle term (present in both the premises) must be distributed at least once.
3. If one of the premises is negative, the conclusion must be negative (will have the word 'no' or 'not'.
4. If one of the premises is particular, the conclusion must be particular (will have the words 'some', 'few', 'many', etc.).
5. If both the premises are particular, no conclusion can be drawn from the given premises.
6. If both the premises are negative, no conclusion can be drawn from the given premises.
7. A term that is not distributed in the premises cannot be distributed in the conclusion.

Comprehensive Example of Mediate and Immediate Inference as per the CBSE UGC-NET Exam Pattern

Statements

1. All movies are stories.
2. All stories are surprises.

Conclusions

A. All movies are surprises.

B. Some surprises are movies.

First, let us consider only the statements. The sentences are already aligned.

Since A + A = A, the conclusion will be 'All movies are surprises'. Till this point, it is a question of mediate inference.

If we convert this conclusion (immediate inference), we get, 'Some surprises are movies'. Hence, both the conclusions given in the question are true.

Statements

1. Some rooms are lamps.
2. Some lamps are tubes.

Conclusions

A. Some rooms are tubes.

B. Some lamps are rooms.

We know that from a combination of I + I, no conclusion can be drawn.

On converting the first statement, we get 'Some lamps are rooms', that is, conclusion (B).

Also, on converting the second statement, we get 'Some tubes are lamps'. This proposition is not given in the conclusion part. So in this example, conclusion (B) alone is true.

Thus, we can see the importance of immediate inferences in solving syllogism problems.

Squares of Opposition

The categorical propositions having same subject and predicate terms may differ in quality and quantity or in both. This differing is called opposition.

There were few questions in previous years' exams, where understanding terms such as contradictory, contrary, subalternation, and subcontrary may help in finding solutions.

By which of the following propositions, the proposition, 'Some men are not honest' is contradicted?

(a) All men are honest.
(b) Some men are honest.
(c) No men are honest.
(d) All of the above

1. Two propositions that have the same subject and predicate terms but different in quality are:
   (a) Contradictory
   (b) Contrary
   (c) Subaltern
   (d) Subalternation *(June 2008)*
2. 'No men are mortal' is contradictory to
   (a) Some men are mortal.
   (b) Some men are not mortal.
   (c) All men are mortal.
   (d) No mortal is man.

The understanding of squares of opposition can help candidates in attempting these types of questions.

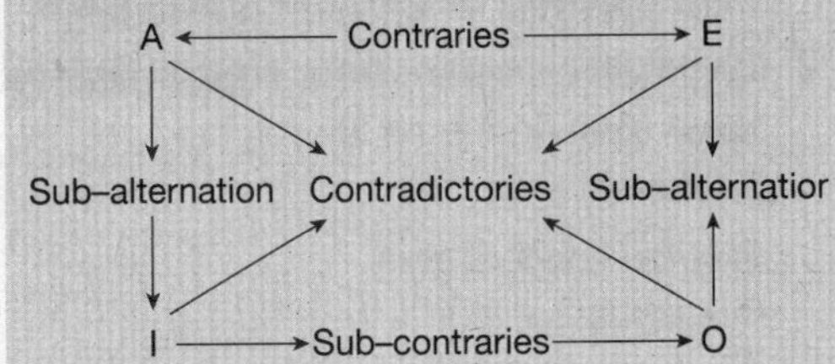

1. *Contradictories:* Contradictory opposition is the relation between two propositions having the same subject but differing in both quality and quantity.

   Relation between A and O and E and I is called contradictory.

   A ⟶ O
   E ⟶ I

A type	O type
All diamonds are precious stones.	Some diamonds are not precious stones.
All men are honest.	Some men are not honest.

E type	I type
No diamonds are precious stones.	Some diamonds are precious stones.
No men are honest.	Some men are honest.

In order to refute the truth of the proposition 'All men are honest', it would be enough to show that some men (or even one man) are not honest. One exception would disprove the truth of the universal affirmative proposition.

2. *Contraries:* Contrary opposition exists between two propositions when both have universal quantity but one affirms and the other denies its predicate of the subject. The relationship between A and E is called contraries.

   A ⟶ E

   Examples
   (A) All men are honest. (E) No men are honest.
   (A) All judges are lawyers. (E) No judge is lawyer.
3. *Sub contraries:* The relation between two particular propositions having the same subject and predicate but differing in quality is sub contrary opposition. The relation between particular affirmative (I) and particular negative (O) is called sub contraries.

   I ⟶ O

   Example: I: Some judges are lawyers. O: Some judges are not lawyers.
4. *Sub alternation:* Sub alternation opposition is the relation between two propositions having the same subject and predicate but differing in quantity only.

   If universal is true, then particular must be true. What is true about the whole population, is true about its part also.) If universal is false, then particular may be undecided. Relation between 'A and I' and 'E and O' is called sub alternation.

A ⟶ I

E ⟶ O

A: All Indians are spiritual. I: Some Indians are spiritual.
E: No Indians are spiritual. O: Some Indians are not spiritual.

Structure of Arguments: Additional Concepts

There are other perspectives or dimensions of structure of arguments (relational arguments, symmetry, transitivity, reflexiveness, and connexity), squares of opposition (contradictions, contraries, sub contraries, and sub alternations), definitions (stipulative, lexical, precising, operational, etc.), and other terms such as prejudices, facts, opinions, and advice that suggest more about the structure of arguments. The questions have been asked regularly in NET paper examination. The types of questions have been mentioned during the course of discussion as well as in practice questions theory. Candidates are expected to go through these topics. There is one example taken from NET previous years' paper.

Example: In the expression, 'Nothing is larger than itself', the relation 'is larger than' is

(a) Antisymmetric (b) Asymmetrical
(c) Intransitive (d) Irreflexive

Relational Arguments

In relationship arguments, both premises and their conclusions are relational proposition. There are two characteristics of a relation—relation to itself and to others. Deductive reasoning is also sometimes dependent on the validity of relational arguments. In NET examination, questions have been asked on relational arguments. These are quite easy to understand.

Symmetry

1. Symmetrical relationship

   Example

   A is equal to B.

   So, B is equal to A—valid.

   It is a 'symmetrical relationship'.

2. Asymmetrical relationship

   Example

   A is greater than B.

   So, B is greater than A—invalid.

3. Non-symmetrical relationship

   Example

   A is the sister of B.

   So, B is the sister of A—may or may not be valid. B may be the brother of A.

Transitivity

1. *Transitive relation:* It implies that a relation travels from A to C via B.

   Example

   A is equal to B.

   B is equal to C.

   So, A is equal to C—valid.

   In transitive relations, the premises are true and conclusion is also valid. 'Younger to', 'precedes', 'succeeds', and 'ancestor of' are other examples of transitive relationships.

2. *Intransitive relation:* Here, relation does not travel from A to C via B.

   Example

   A is the father of B.

   B is the father of C.

   So A is the father of C—invalid (false conclusion)

   Relations such as 'son of' also fall in the category of intransitive relations.

3. *Non-transitive relation:*

   Example

   A is an enemy of B.

   B is an enemy of C.

   So, A is an enemy of C—invalid or false conclusion.

   The relations such as 'friend of' and 'neighbour of' are examples of non-transitive relationships.

Reflexiveness

1. Reflexive relationship is between a term and itself. Examples are, 'is equal to itself,

'resembles itself', 'as old as', and 'as young as'.

2. Partial reflexiveness means establishing a relationship with some other thing. Its examples are, 'A is as tall as B; B is as tall as C'. Hence A is as tall as B.
3. *Irreflexive:* This type of relationship cannot be held between a term and itself. A is smaller (or greater) than itself. A is west (or east) of itself, and so on.
4. *Non-reflexive:* This may or may not be held between a term and itself. Example is, 'A loves itself'. This may or may not happen.

CONNEXITY

This type of relationship is valid between any two terms. For example, 3 is greater than 2 but less than 4.

Types of Definition

A definition is a comprehensive description of a concept by means of known concepts expressed mainly by verbal means. The purpose of a definition is as follows:

1. To describe a concept at a given level of abstraction;
2. To distinguish a concept from related concepts;
3. To establish a relationship between the concept in question and the other concept in order to determine the position of the concept in the system;
4. To delimit a concept for the purpose of normative terminological work.

The definition should be the starting point for selecting and analysing the term. When selecting or seeking an appropriate term for a concept, it is necessary to start with a clear definition of the concept. For clarifying the concept, its intension and its extension have to be determined.

In NET examination, many times questions have been asked on the definition of the following terms:

1. *Intensional definition:* Specifying the properties or features and also the meaning of a term. For example, water in chemistry is defined as a compound of hydrogen and oxygen and in physics as a liquid with freezing point of 0°C and boiling point of 100°C.
2. *Extensional definition:* Specifying the class members of the term. For example, the planets of the solar system are Mercury, Venus, Earth, Mars, Jupiter, Saturn, Uranus, Neptune, and Pluto.
3. *Lexical definition:* It is also termed as reportive definition. Lexical definition is the dictionary meaning of a term, the common vocabulary of a given language, for example, defining book, chair, and so on.
4. *Stipulative definition:* It is an arbitrary, specified definition. It is not used to explain the existing meaning of a term. It is used to assign a new meaning to a term, whether or not the term has already got a meaning. Examples are idioms and slangs used in English language.
5. *Precising definition:* A definition developed to clarify a vague or ambiguous term. It is often used in legal, scientific, or medical settings. For example, a virus is an infectious agent that causes small pox.
6. *Persuasive definition:* A persuasive definition is any definition that attaches an emotive, positive, or derogatory meaning to a term where it has none. This may be used as a rhetoric tool in a debate or discussion. For example, someone against abortion might offer the definition of 'abortion' as the murder of an innocent person during pregnancy. This definition carries a negative connotation, as the term murder suggests that abortion is wrongful killing, and it also assumes that the aborted foetus is already a person. Such a definition is surely not appropriate in a fair debate on the moral legitimacy of abortion, even though it might be useful as a rhetorical tool.
7. *Operational definition:* A definition that provides a meaning to a term by specifying a measurement procedure.
8. *Functional definition:* A definition that specifies the purpose or use of the items denoted by the term.

9. *Ostensive definition:* A definition developed by showing someone an object and attaching a word to it.

   This type of definition is often used where the term is difficult to define verbally, either because the words will not be understood (as with children and new speakers of a language) or because of the nature of the term (such as colours or sensations). For example, defining red by pointing out red objects—apples, stop signs, roses, etc.—is giving ostensive definition, as is naming.

10. *Analogous definition:* This definition has analogy; corresponding in some particular: A brain and a computer are analogous.
    In biology, there is corresponding in function but of different origins and having evolved separately, as the wings of birds and insects.

Connotative and Denotative Meanings

Words are not limited to one single meaning. Most words have multiple meanings, which are categorized as either denotative or connotative. The denotation of a word is its explicit definition as listed in a dictionary. Let us consider the word home as an example. The denotative or literal meaning of home is 'a place where one lives; a residence'. The expressiveness of a language, however, comes from the other type of word meaning—connotation, or the association or set of associations that a word usually brings to mind. The connotative meaning of home is a place of security, comfort, and family. The quote 'East or west, home is the best' does not refer to denotative meaning of home, but the emotions the word home evokes in most of us. By definition, synonyms have the same denotation or literal meaning, but almost always have different connotations.

Fact, Opinion, Belief, and Prejudice

In these types of questions, a statement is given; the candidate has to answer whether the statement is a fact, a prejudice, a belief, or just an opinion.

In the past, many questions have been based upon the understanding of these terms.

Statement

English is an invaluable asset in international communication.

Mark

(a) If the statement is a fact
(b) If the statement is an advice
(c) If the statement is an opinion
(d) If the statement is a prejudice

Similarly, there were statements

(i) Decline of the British Empire should have resulted in the decline of English.
(ii) Persons educated through a foreign language are sure to be unpatriotic.

Facts

A fact is verifiable. We can determine whether it is true by researching the evidence. Facts are as follows:

1. Things known for certain to have happened.
2. Things known for certain to be true.
3. Things known for certain to exist.

This may involve numbers, dates, testimony, and so on. For example, India got independent on 15 August, 1947. Facts provide crucial support for the assertion of an argument.

Opinion

An opinion is a judgment based on facts, an honest attempt to draw a reasonable conclusion from factual evidence. Opinions are as follows:

1. Things believed to have happened.
2. Things believed to be true.
3. Things believed to exist.

For example, we know that lakhs of people go without proper medical care in India, and so someone forms the opinion that the country should institute national health insurance even though it would cost few thousand crores of rupees. An opinion is potentially changeable, depending on how the evidence is interpreted. Opinions are debatable; facts usually are not.

Prejudice

Another kind of assertion that has no place in serious argumentation is prejudice, a half-baked opinion based on insufficient or unexamined evidence (e.g. women are bad drivers). Unlike a belief, a prejudice is testable, it can be contested and disapproved on the basis of facts. We often form prejudices or accept them from others—family, friends, media, and so on—without questioning their meaning or testing their truth.

Belief

Unlike an opinion, a belief is a conviction based on cultural or personal faith, morality, or values. Statements such as 'capital punishment is a legalized murder' are often called opinions because they express viewpoints, but are not based on facts or other evidence. They cannot be disapproved or even contested in a rational or logical manner. Since beliefs are inarguable, they cannot serve as the thesis of a formal argument.

Analytical Reasoning

Analytical reasoning is considered to be the recent form of logic in which almost all classical terms are covered. Here, a sentence, a group of sentences, a short argumentative paragraph covering concepts, facts, theories, figures and so on may be given and questions are asked with regard to arguments, conclusion, inferences, implications, and so on. In dealing with these questions, methods generally used include inductive reasoning, deductive reasoning, quoting authorities, and facts, findings, and illustrations.

Solution Approach

1. Underline the important assumptions in the case of passage. Note the inferences—both inductive and deductive
2. Identify the supporting arguments
3. Note the premises of supporting argument
4. See the nature of questions

Nature of Questions

Based on the given information, the types of questions to be asked include the following:

1. Assumptions and statements
2. Force of argument
3. Assertion and reasoning
4. Statements (situation) and course of action

They have been discussed below.

Assumptions and Statements

Assumptions are unstated or even unknown, but implied by the associated theory or argument. Thus, an assumption can be termed as an implied premise. An assumption is defined as something which is assumed, supposed, or taken for granted. In practical life, if something is to be conveyed, it is not put in words. Many things may not be said, but are taken for granted which may be defined as an assumption. Implicit means hidden; therefore implicit assumptions are those assumptions which are hidden. A typical question on implicit assumptions goes like:

Directions (Questions 1–5): In each of the questions below, a statement is followed by two assumptions numbered I and II. An assumption is something that is supposed or taken for granted. You have to consider the statement and the following assumptions and decide which of the assumptions is implicit in the statement.

(a) Only assumption I is implicit.
(b) Only assumption II is implicit.
(c) Both I and II are implicit.
(d) Neither I nor II is implicit.

Example 1

Statement

A to B – 'In my opinion, you should undergo a training under an expert in order to be successful in your career'.

Assumptions

I. B sought advice from A.

II. Experts are more competent to guide a person to be successful in their career.

Explanation

There are many instances in life when we get an advice from a person without asking it. I is not definitely valid.

Only assumption II is implicit. Otherwise, A would not have advised B to get training from an expert. Therefore, it is correct to assume that experienced people make better guides.

Example 2

Statement

'This multimedia CD-ROM offers you active help as you learn yoga without an instructor' says a newspaper advertisement.

Assumptions

I. Everyone may not be able to get active help from a yoga instructor.

II. Aerobic exercises can be learnt with the help of a CD-ROM.

Explanation

In the above, both I and II are valid. The multimedia CD-ROM intends to teach yoga in the absence of an instructor. This means that the absence of an instructor is a distinct possibility for many people. Therefore, I is valid. The advertiser has come out with a CD-ROM on yoga; it definitely implies that aerobic exercises can be learnt by CD-ROMs. Hence, II is also valid.

Example 3

Statement

'If you keep creating indiscipline in class, I will have to take a strict action against you'. A teacher warns his student.

Assumptions

I. With the warning, the student may stop creating indiscipline in the class.

II. All students are basically naughty.

Explanation

The teacher warns his students in anticipation that he would stop troubling him. So I is implicit. The general nature of children cannot be derived from the statement. So II is not implicit.

Example 4

Statement

Of all the newspapers published in India, 'The Hindu' has the largest number of readers.

Assumptions

I. The volume of readership of all newspapers in India is known.

II. No newspaper in India other than 'The Hindu' has a large readership.

Explanation

It is on the basis of data that we can say that 'The Hindu' has the largest number of readers. So assumption I is implied. But it is not possible to say that no other newspaper in India has a large readership. We need to define large readership as well. So assumption II is not implicit.

Such decisions as given in the statement are taken only after taking the existing vacancies into consideration. So I is implicit while II is not.

Force of Arguments

Argument: Earlier also we discussed about the validity of arguments. An argument is a set of two or more premises leading to a conclusion. An argument can be said to be valid if the premises, if true, definitely lead to a conclusion.

All scientists are intelligent persons. Raman is a scientist. So Raman is an intelligent person (valid).

All scientists are genius. Raman is an intelligent person. So Raman is a scientist (invalid).

The second argument is invalid as there is no premise which states that all intelligent persons are scientists.

Validity is the property of an argument.

Assertion and Reasoning

Introduction: Assertion and reasoning-type questions have one assertion (A) and one reason (R). We must first determine whether the statement is true. If statement is true, we must next determine whether the reason correctly explains the assertion. There is one option for each

possible outcome. These types of questions are followed by four options:
(a) A is true but R is false.
(b) A is false but R is true.
(c) Both A and R are true and R is not the correct explanation of A.
(d) Both A and R are true and R is the correct explanation of A.

Few examples have been discussed as given below:

Example 1

Assertion (A): Most of the prominent places in ancient civilizations grew near rivers.

Reason (R): Rivers provide water for irrigation and also work as means of transportation.

Explanation: Here, we can use our basic general knowledge or commonly known facts. We know that most of the ancient civilizations grew near rivers, so A is correct. In the example, R is also simple and true. So (a) is the answer.

Example 2

Assertion (A): Tides indicate the regular and periodic rise and fall in sea level.

Reason (R): Tides are caused by the gravitational pull of the moon and sea level.

Explanation: In this case also, the concept of tides is the reason for their origination. Both A and R are true, so (c) is the answer.

Example 3

Assertion (A): Mercury is the farthest planet from the sun.

Reason (R): Mercury is the smallest planet in the entire solar system.

Explanation: Here, A is false as mercury is the closet to sun. R is correct.

Example 4

Assertion (A): Carbon monoxide when inhaled causes death.

Reason (R): Carbon monoxide combines with haemoglobin.

Explanation: The chemical composition of oxygen and carbon monoxide is the same. Carbon monoxide combines with haemoglobin and reaches different parts of the body and causes death. Hence, (a) is the correct answer.

Statements and Courses of Action

Introduction: A course of action is a step or administrative decision to be taken for improvement, follow-up, or further action in regard to the problem, policy, and so on. On the basis of the information given in the statement or situation, the candidate has to assume everything in the statement to be true and then decide which of the suggested courses of action logically follow for pursuing.

Example 1

Situation: The incessant rains that have been continuing for past several days have created the problem of deluge; that is, because the river bed is full of silt and mud.

Courses of actions

I. The people living close to the river should be transferred to a safer place.
II. People should be given information about the imminent danger on radio or television.
III. Immediately after the reduction of water level of the river, the silt and mud should be removed from the river body.
(a) Only I and II follow
(b) Only II and III follow
(c) None of these follow
(d) All of these follow

Explanation: Actions I and II are immediately required as they are crucial in saving precious lives of the people. It may not be practicable for authorities to remove silt and mud from the river body. So only I and II follow, and hence, (a) is the answer.

Example 2

Indicate which of the following actions are the most appropriate in the situation given below:

Situation: Two to three students in the class of a sincere and devoted teacher frequently disturb him in the class while teaching. He is fed up with them.

Courses of actions

(a) He tells the students of the class that he will not hold the classes if the disturbing students continue doing that.

(b) He suspends the disturbing students from attending his class in the interest of the whole class.

(c) He talks to the disturbing students to find out what makes them behave that way and what could become about them.

(d) He reports against them to the principal with the recommendation to take strong action against them.

Explanation: (c) suggests long-term approach to deal with the issue of indiscipline in the class.

Theory Questions

1. The process by which conclusion is arrived at on the basis of other propositions is termed as
(a) Concept (b) Inference
(c) Connotation (d) Conference

2. Propositions that support the conclusion of an argument are called
(a) Inferences
(b) Premises
(c) Concepts
(d) None of the above

3. That proposition which is affirmed on the basis of premises is called
(a) Major term (b) Concept
(c) Conclusion (d) Syllogism

4. Deduction and induction are two main forms of
(a) Beliefs (b) Concepts
(c) Reasoning (d) Assumptions

5. A reasoning where we start with certain particular statement and conclude with a universal statement is called a
(a) Deductive reasoning
(b) Inductive reasoning
(c) Abnormal reasoning
(d) Transcendental reasoning

6. With which of the following terms, deduction inference can be identified?
(a) Synthetic
(b) Analytic
(c) Both (a) and (b)
(d) None of the above

7. Which of the following can be defined as group of statements that have common conclusion?
(a) Proposition (b) Argument
(c) Concept (d) Fallacy

8. The premises provide conclusive grounds for conclusion in
(a) Inductive reasoning
(b) Deductive reasoning
(c) Intuitive reasoning
(d) None of the above

9. The defining feature of a valid deduction is its
(a) Vagueness (b) Uncertainty
(c) Indefiniteness (d) Certainty

10. Inductive arguments are typically
(a) Analytic (b) Synthetic
(c) Intuitive (d) Aesthetic

11. The relationship between premises and conclusion in a deductive argument is basically of
(a) Cause–effect
(b) Analytic–synthetic
(c) Implication–entailment
(d) None of the above

12. In inductive reasoning, the conclusion is
(a) Probable (b) Certain
(c) Definite (d) Predictable

13. Certainty is
(a) An objective fact
(b) Emotionally satisfying
(c) Logical
(d) Ontological (*June 2010*)

14. Inductive arguments are properly characterized as

(a) Valid–invalid
(b) Strong–weak
(c) Definite–indefinite
(d) Certain–uncertain

15. In logical reasoning, truth or falsehood is usually associated with
(a) Arguments (b) Inferences
(c) Propositions (d) Syllogism

16. Validity or invalidity may be predicted of
(a) Deductive arguments
(b) Propositions
(c) Terms
(d) Concepts

17. The falsehood of a valid deductive argument's conclusion guarantees that
(a) The argument is sound
(b) At least one of the premise is false
(c) Premises are true
(d) The validity is uncertain

18. To be critical, thinking must be
(a) Practical
(b) Socially relevant
(c) Individually satisfying
(d) Analytical

19. Deductive argument involves
(a) Sufficient evidence
(b) Critical thinking
(c) Seeing logical relation
(d) Repeated observation

20. A fallacy is a
(a) True argument
(b) False argument
(c) Valid argument
(d) Invalid argument

21. Inductive reasoning is based on
(a) Uniformity of nature
(b) God created the world
(c) Unity of nature
(d) Laws of nature

22. If it is possible for the premises of a deductive argument to be true and its conclusion to be false that argument is
(a) Valid (b) Invalid
(c) Indescribable (d) Sound

23. Consider the following propositions:
A is human and mortal
B is human and mortal
C is human and mortal
D is human and mortal
Therefore, 'All humans are mortal' is an example of
(a) Deductive argument
(b) Inductive argument
(c) Syllogistic argument
(d) None of the above

24. Which of the following describes a valid deductive argument with true premises?
(a) Sound (b) Unsound
(c) Fallacious (d) Ambiguity

25. A deductive argument is sound if and only if it is
(a) Valid and all its premises are true
(b) Invalid and all its premises are true
(c) Is valid and one of the premise is false
(d) Is valid and its conclusion is false

26. Lakshmana is a morally good person because
(a) He is religious. (b) He is educated.
(c) He is rich. (d) He is rational

27. In terms of nature, both the premises and conclusion of an argument are
(a) Commands (b) Propositions
(c) Exclamations (d) Questions

28. Which of the following denotes a statement of relation between two terms?
(a) Proposition
(b) Denotation
(c) Syllogism
(d) None of the above

29. Structure of a logical argument is based on
(a) Formal validity
(b) Material truth
(c) Linguistic expression
(d) Aptness of examples

30. In a deductive argument, conclusion is
(a) Summing up of the premises
(b) Not necessarily based on premises
(c) Entailed by the premises
(d) Additional to the premises

31. Syllogistic reasoning is
    (a) Deductive (b) Inductive
    (c) Experimental (d) Hypothetical

32. A syllogism must have
    (a) Three terms (b) Four terms
    (c) Six terms (d) Five terms

33. The two kinds of propositions are
    (a) Connotative–denotative
    (b) Categorical–conditional
    (c) Both (a) and (b)
    (d) None of the above

34. Which of the following denotes relation between two terms?
    (a) Subject (b) Predicate
    (c) Object (d) Copula

35. A deductive argument is valid if
    (a) Premises are false and conclusion is true
    (b) Premises are false and conclusion is also false
    (c) Premises are true and conclusion is false
    (d) Premises are true and conclusion is true

36. Which of the following statements are false?
    I. Inductive arguments always proceed from the particular to the general
    II. A cogent argument must be inductively strong
    III. A valid argument may have a false premise and a false conclusion
    IV. An argument may legitimately be spoken of as true or false
    Codes:
    (a) II, III, and IV (b) I and III
    (c) II and IV (d) I and II

37. The sum total of the objects to which the term can be applied is its
    (a) Connotation (b) Denotation
    (c) Meaning (d) Function

38. Denotation is the same as
    (a) Extension (b) Intension
    (c) Value (d) Dictionary

39. The function of suggesting qualities possessed by the objects is known as
    (a) Evaluating (b) Denoting
    (c) Connoting (d) Meaning

40. Connotation is the same as
    (a) Intension (b) Extension
    (c) Value (d) Meaning

41. In a categorical proposition, the predicate is either affirmed or denied of the subject
    (a) Unconditionally
    (b) Conditionally
    (c) Emotionally
    (d) None of the above

42. The proposition 'if you work hard you will succeed' is an example of
    (a) Categorical proposition
    (b) Conditional proposition
    (c) Negative proposition
    (d) Pre-emptive proposition

43. A disjunctive proposition is a type of
    (a) Conditional proposition
    (b) Unconditional proposition
    (c) Categorical proposition
    (d) Imperative proposition

44. Inductive logic studies the way in which a premise may (*December 2011*)
    (a) Support and entail a conclusion
    (b) Not support but entail a conclusion
    (c) Neither support nor entail a conclusion
    (d) Support a conclusion without entailing it

45. Which of the following statements are true?
    I. Some arguments while not completely valid are almost valid
    II. A sound argument may be invalid
    III. A cogent argument may have a probably false conclusion
    IV. A statement may be true or false
    Codes:
    (a) I and II (b) I, III, and IV
    (c) IV alone (d) III and IV

46. Affirmative or negative is the classification of propositions on the basis of
    (a) Quantity (b) Quality
    (c) Validity (d) Truth

47. Universal or particular is the classification of the propositions on the basis of

(a) Quantity (b) Quality
(c) Validity (d) Truth

48. A proposition in which the predicate refers to all individual objects denoted by the subject is called
(a) Particular (b) Negative
(c) Disjunctive (d) Universal

49. A proposition in which the predicate belongs only to a part of the denotation of the subject is called
(a) Particular (b) Negative
(c) Disjunctive (d) Universal

50. Individual propositions are to be regarded as
(a) Universal
(b) Particular
(c) Negative
(d) None of the above

51. The proposition 'all men are mortal' is an example of
(a) Universal affirmative
(b) Universal negative
(c) Particular affirmative
(d) Particular negative

52. The proposition 'no men are perfect' is an example of
(a) Universal affirmative
(b) Universal negative
(c) Particular affirmative
(d) Particular negative

53. 'Some flowers are green' is an example of
(a) Universal affirmative
(b) Universal negative
(c) Particular affirmative
(d) Particular negative

54. The proposition 'some Indians are not spiritual' is an example for
(a) Universal affirmative
(b) Universal negative
(c) Particular affirmative
(d) Particular negative

55. When a term is used in its entire extent, referring to the objects denoted by the term, it is said to be
(a) Undistributed (b) Excluded
(c) Distributed (d) Verified

56. When a term refers only to a part of the class of things denoted by the term that term is said to be
(a) Undistributed (b) Unexcluded
(c) Distributed (d) Verified

57. Universal affirmative proposition distributes
(a) Subject
(b) Predicate
(c) Both subject and predicate
(d) Neither subject nor predicate

58. Universal negative proposition distributes
(a) Subject
(b) Predicate
(c) Both subject and predicate
(d) Neither subject nor predicate

59. Particular affirmative proposition distributes
(a) Subject
(b) Predicate
(c) Both subject and predicate
(d) Neither subject nor predicate

60. Particular negative proposition distributes
(a) Subject
(b) Predicate
(c) Both subject and predicate
(d) Neither subject nor predicate

61. The process of passing directly from a single proposition to a conclusion is
(a) Immediate inference
(b) Mediate inference
(c) Definition
(d) Classification

62. Which of the following asserts the agreement or disagreement of a subject and predicate after having compared each with middle term?
(a) Immediate inference
(b) Mediate inference
(c) Definition
(d) Classification

63. Which of the following shows the relationship between two universal propositions having the same subject but differing in quality only?

(a) Contrary opposition
(b) Contradictory opposition
(c) Subaltern
(d) Sub contrary

64. Which of the following terms show the relationship between two propositions having the same subject, but differing in both quality and quantity?
(a) Contrary opposition
(b) Contradictory opposition
(c) Sub alternation
(d) Sub contrary

65. The relation between two particular propositions having the same subject and predicate but differing in quality is
(a) Contrary (b) Contradictory
(c) Sub alternation (d) Sub contrary

66. Which of the following shows that an opposition is the relation between two propositions having the same subject and predicate but differing in quantity only?
(a) Contrary (b) Contradictory
(c) Subaltern (d) Sub contrary

67. If one of the contraries is true, the truth value of the other is
(a) True
(b) Partially true
(c) False
(d) Neither true nor false

68. If one of the contraries is false, the truth value of the other is
(a) True
(b) False
(c) Neither true nor false
(d) Doubtful

69. If one of the contradictories is true, the other must be
(a) True
(b) False
(c) Doubtful
(d) Neither true nor false

70. Both the contrary propositions cannot be
(a) True (b) False
(c) True and false (d) Doubtful

71. Of the two sub contraries if one is false, the other is necessarily
(a) True
(b) False
(c) Doubtful
(d) Neither true nor false

72. If one of the two sub contraries is true, then the other one is
(a) True
(b) False
(c) Doubtful
(d) Neither true nor false

73. Between subalternations, if the universal is true, the particular is
(a) True
(b) False
(c) Doubtful
(d) Both true and false

74. If the particular proposition of a subalternation relation is false, its corresponding universal proposition will be
(a) True
(b) False
(c) Both true and false
(d) Doubtful

75. If the particular proposition of a subalternation relation is true, the truth value of the universal proposition is
(a) True
(b) False
(c) Both true and false
(d) Doubtful

76. The proposition, 'Chanakya is wise', is an example of
(a) Negative proposition
(b) Singular proposition
(c) Emotive proposition
(d) Invalid proposition

77. The quantity of the proposition is determined by the extension of the
(a) Subject
(b) Predicate
(c) Both subject and predicate
(d) Copula

78. In a conditional proposition, the part which expresses the condition by 'if' or its equivalent is
(a) Antecedent (b) Consequent
(c) Opposite (d) Meaning

79. Which of the following terms describe the syllogism?
(a) Mediate and deductive
(b) Immediate and deductive
(c) Mediate and inductive
(d) Immediate inductive

80. The major term is the
(a) Subject of the conclusion
(b) Copula
(c) Predicate of the conclusion
(d) Predicate of the minor premise

81. The minor term is the
(a) Subject of the conclusion
(b) Predicate of the conclusion
(c) Subject of the major premise
(d) Predicate of the major premise

82. That term which occurs in the premises and not in the conclusion is
(a) Major term
(b) Minor term
(c) Middle term
(d) None of the above

83. Which of the following performs the function of an intermediary?
(a) Major term (b) Middle term
(c) Minor term (d) Copula

84. How many times each term occurs in the syllogism?
(a) Once (b) Twice
(c) Thrice (d) Four times

85. All Indians are hardworking. All Punjabis are Indians. Therefore, all Punjabis are hardworking.
The above argument is
(a) Invalid (b) False
(c) Valid (d) True

86. If one premise is negative, the conclusion must be
(a) Negative
(b) Positive
(c) Both negative and positive
(d) Neither negative nor positive

87. Combination of which of the following two types of premises yields no valid conclusion.
(a) Universal (b) Particular
(c) Affirmative (d) Categorical

88. No conclusion is possible from two
(a) Universal premises
(b) Affirmative premises
(c) Negative premises
(d) Categorical premises

89. If one premise is particular, the conclusion must be
(a) Universal (b) Negative
(c) Affirmative (d) Particular

90. Which one of the following is not an argument?
(a) If today is Tuesday, tomorrow will be Wednesday
(b) Since today is Tuesday, tomorrow will be Wednesday
(c) Ram insulted me so I punched him in the nose
(d) Ram is not at home so he must have gone to town

91. Which one of the following statements is completely nonsensical?
(a) He was a bachelor but he married recently
(b) He is a bachelor but he married recently
(c) When he married, he was not a bachelor
(d) When he was a bachelor, he was not married

92. Which of the following statements say the same thing? *(December 2006)*
I. 'I am a teacher' (said by Arvind)
II. 'I am a teacher' (said by Binod)
III. My son is a teacher (said by Binod's father)
IV. My brother is a teacher (said by Binod's sister)
V. My brother is a teacher (said by Binod's only sister)
VI. My sole enemy is a teacher (said by Binod's only enemy)

Codes:
(a) I and II
(b) II, III, IV, and V
(c) II and VI
(d) V and VI

93. Which of the following are the correct ways of arguing? (*December 2006*)
I. There can be no second husband without a second wife
II. Anil is a friend of Bob, Bob is a friend of Raj, hence Anil is a friend of Raj
III. A is equal to B, B is equal to C, hence A is equal to C
IV. If everyone is a liar, then we cannot prove it
Codes:
(a) III and IV
(b) I, III, and IV
(c) II, III, and IV
(d) I, II, III, and IV

94. Which of the following is an analogous statement? (*December 2009*)
(a) Man is like God
(b) God is great
(c) Gandhi is the father of the nation
(d) Man is a rational being

95. Venn diagram is a kind of diagram to
(a) Represent and assess the truth of elementary inferences with the help of Boolean Algebra of classes
(b) Represent and assess the validity of elementary inferences with the help of Boolean Algebra of classes
(c) Represent but not assess the validity of elementary inferences with the help of Boolean Algebra of classes
(d) Assess but not represent the validity of elementary inferences with the help of Boolean Algebra of classes

96. 'A is true because B is true; B is true because A is true'. This type of argument is termed as
(a) Inductive argument
(b) Deductive argument
(c) Circular argument
(d) None of the above

97. Which of the following is an example of circular argument?
(a) God created man in his image and man created God in his own image
(b) God is the source of scripture and the scripture is the source of our knowledge of God
(c) Some of the Indians are great because India is great
(d) Rama is great because he is Rama

98. All students are not geniuses (*June 2003*)
(a) Many students are not genius
(b) All geniuses are students
(c) No student is a genius
(d) None of the above

99. Determine the nature of the following definition, 'poor' means having an annual income of ₹1,000.
(a) Persuasive (b) Precising
(c) Lexical (d) Stipulative

100. In the expression, 'Nothing is larger than itself', the relation 'is larger than' is
(a) Antisymmetric (b) Asymmetrical
(c) Intransitive (d) Irreflexive

101. Determine the nature of the following definition, 'Abortion means the ruthless murdering of innocent beings'
(a) Lexical (b) Persuasive
(c) Stipulative (d) Theoretical

102. Which one of the following is not an argument?
(a) Abhimanyu does not eat in the day so he must be eating at night
(b) If Abhimanyu is growing fat and if he does not eat during the day, he will be eating at night
(c) Abhimanyu eats in the night so he does not eat during the day
(d) Since Abhimanyu does not eat in the day, he must be eating in the night

103. If P is true, Q is true. If P is false, Q is false. The relation of this proposition is
(a) Independent (b) Equivalent
(c) Sub contrary (d) Contradictory

104. Two propositions with the same subject and predicate terms but different in quality are
(a) Contradictory (b) Contrary
(c) Subaltern (d) Sub contraries

105. 'No men are mortal' is contradictory to
(a) Some men are mortal
(b) Some men are not mortal
(c) All men are mortal
(d) No mortal is man (*June 2009*)

106. Which of the following statements are always true?
I. A wooden table is a table
II. Now, it is raining or not raining
III. The sun rises in the East every day
IV. A chicken comes out of hen's egg.
Codes:
(a) I and III (b) I, III, and IV
(c) I and II (d) II and III

107. Persons educated through a foreign language are sure to be unpatriotic. Mark
(a) If the statement is a fact
(b) If the statement is an advice
(c) If the statement is an opinion
(d) If the statement is a prejudice

108. ***Statement:*** 'Decline of British Empire should have resulted in decline of English language'. Mark
(a) If the statement is a fact
(b) If the statement is an advice
(c) If the statement is an opinion
(d) If the statement is a prejudice

109. If 'X loves Y', what can be inferred about 'Y loves X'. It is
(a) True
(b) False
(c) May be true
(d) None of the above

110. 'Honesty is the best policy' because
(a) God rewards those who follow this maxim
(b) It leads to recognition in the society
(c) It facilitates cohesiveness in society
(d) It leads to material prosperity and spiritual awakening

111. Consider the following statements:
I. The sunset is beautiful
II. Mahatma Gandhi believed in non-violence
III. Do not tell the world what you can do, just do it
IV. Those who own a car are rich
Which one of the following is correct?

	Fact	Opinion	Advice	Assumption
(a)	I	IV	III	II
(b)	II	III	IV	I
(c)	IV	II	I	III
(d)	II	I	III	IV

112. Education and socio-economic development are
(a) Related in a direct proportion
(b) Related in an indirect proportion
(c) Sometimes related and sometimes not related
(d) Not related

113. Bats are mammals because bats suckle their young and
(a) All those who suckle their young are mammals
(b) All mammals suckle their young
(c) Some of those who suckle their young are mammals.
(d) All of the above

114. 'A single shelf of a good European Library is worth the whole native literature of India and Arabia'. This statement is
(a) Factual (b) Logical
(c) Opinion (d) Reactionary

115. Consider the following statements:
I think
Thinking things exist
Therefore, I am (i.e. I exist as a thinking thing)
This argument is
(a) Valid (b) Invalid
(c) Doubtful (d) Cannot be said

116. Which one of the following statements follow from the statement 'only goods trains stop at this station'?
(a) Some goods trains stop at this station
(b) All goods trains stop at this station

(c) Some goods trains do not stop at this station
(d) All trains that stop at this station are goods trains

117. Evaluate the following statements in terms of whether each is a fact, opinion, prejudice, or advice.
   I. Women are not suitable for police service
   II. In a democracy no party should be in power for too long
   III. Have proper rest, even during the examination time
   IV. Obesity is a risk factor for coronary heart disease

Which one of the following is correct?

	Opinion	Prejudice	Fact	Advice
(a)	II	III	IV	I
(b)	II	I	IV	III
(c)	III	I	IV	II
(d)	II	IV	III	I

118. ***Information:*** NET test is conducted for post graduates.
Inferences:
(a) Kumar is a post graduate, so she should have undertaken the test
(b) Kamal is a graduate. She cannot take the NET examination
(c) All post graduates can take the NET examination
(d) No other agency can take the NET examination

119. For a proposition to be true, it is necessary that it should have all the following characteristics EXCEPT
(a) It must be objective
(b) It must be in tune with accepted beliefs
(c) It must be consistent
(d) It must be testable

120. Four inferences are drawn from the statement given below, which one can be the correct inference?
Statement
People in Australia generally speak English.
Inferences
(a) Rosy speaks English. So she is from Australia
(b) Rahim knows English. That is why he is going to Australia next month
(c) Rahul has been living in Australia, most probably he can speak English
(d) Ramesh does not know English. He cannot talk to anyone if he goes to Australia (*December 98*)

Directions (Questions 121–135): In each of the questions below, a proposition is followed by four answer choices. Match the proposition with one of the choices that seems to be the most justified or applicable.

121. The spread of the Internet for higher education is premised on (*June 2000*)
(a) Research and development is vital
(b) Browsing encourages critical thinking
(c) Easy management and dissemination of knowledge
(d) India should be second to none in the world

122. World Trade Organization believes in Intellectual Property and Liberalized Trade Regime (*June 2000*)
Their belief is based on the assumption that
(a) Modern economy bestows equal benefits
(b) Knowledge-based economy and globalization is a reality
(c) All countries are well suited for modern trade
(d) Rich countries will always help the poor countries

123. The essence and justification to beauty contests is that (*June 2000*)
(a) Women have standard features on which they can be rated
(b) Beautiful women have a vision and role to play in social upliftment
(c) They symbolize eternal freedom for women
(d) They provide an opportunity for beautiful women of the world to come on one platform

124. This worker is a graduate. No one else in the factory is a graduate.

(a) All workers in the factory are graduates
(b) Everybody in the factory has a graduation certificate
(c) Some of the factory workers have higher qualification
(d) Only one worker in the factory is a graduate

125. All that glitters is not gold
(a) Many things that shine are other than gold
(b) Whatever shines is other than gold
(c) Gold is not the only glittering substance
(d) All of the above (*June 2003*)

126. Most dresses in that market are expensive means
(a) There are no cheap dresses available in that market
(b) There are some cheap dresses also in that market
(c) Some dresses in that market are expensive
(d) None of the above

127. Every library has books
(a) Books are only in library
(b) Libraries are meant for books only
(c) No library is without books
(d) Some libraries do not have readers

128. The electronic media convinces its viewers that the likelihood of their becoming the victim of a violent crime is extremely high; at the same time by its very nature, it persuades viewers to passively accept whatever happens to them
(a) Exposure to electronic media promotes criminal behaviour
(b) The users of electronic media are more vulnerable to become victims of violence than others
(c) Electronic media promotes a feeling of helpless vulnerability in viewers
(d) None of the above

129. This book can help because all good books help
(a) This is not a good book
(b) This is a good book
(c) No good book helps
(d) Some good books help

130. Soldiers serve their country
(a) Men mostly serve their country
(b) The persons who serve their country are soldiers
(c) Some persons who are soldiers serve their country
(d) Women usually do not serve their country as they are not soldiers

131. To pass any competitive exam, one must work hard
(a) Getting good grades in exam needs hard work
(b) All those who work hard, pass
(c) The candidates who work hard overcome anxiety in the competitive exam
(d) Without hard work, one does not pass the competitive exams

132. All the books written by Professor Bhardwaj are textbooks. Some of his books are published by India Publishing House
(a) India Publishing House publishes textbooks only
(b) Some textbooks written by Professor Bhardwaj are published by publishers other than M/s India Publishing House
(c) All the books published by M/s India Publishing House have been written by Professor Bhardwaj
(d) None of the above

133. All students in my class are bright. Mehtab is not bright
(a) Some students are not bright
(b) Mehtab is not a student of my class
(c) Mehtab must change the school
(d) No student is dull

134. Which one of the following is NOT correct? A belief becomes a scientific truth when it
(a) is established experimentally
(b) is arrived logically
(c) is accepted by many people
(d) can be replicated

135. Child labour can best be eradicated if the following is done for the concerned children
   (a) Schools are opened and free lunch is provided
   (b) Employment is provided to parents and free education given to children
   (c) Appropriate laws are enacted and enforced
   (d) Employers of child labourers are punished and children are sent to school

Practical Problems

***Directions (Questions 136–150)*:** In each of the questions below, two statements are followed by two conclusions I and II. Assuming that the given statements are true even if they are at variance with the commonly known facts, pick up one of the following answer choice which you think is correct.

(a) If only conclusion I follows
(b) If only conclusion II follows
(c) If both I and II follow
(d) If neither I nor II follows

136. ***Statements***

Some tables are golden.

All teaks are tables.

Conclusions

I. Some teaks are golden.

II. Some golden are teak.

137. ***Statements***

No man is a tiger.

Karan is a man.

Conclusions

I. Karan is not a tiger.

II. All men are not Karan.

138. ***Statements***

All boys are men.

All men are fathers.

Conclusions

I. Some men are boys.

II. All boys are fathers.

139. ***Statements***

All teachers are girls.

No girl is dull.

Conclusions

I. No boy is a teacher.

II. No teacher is dull.

140. ***Statements***

All poets are inspiring.

All artists are inspiring.

Conclusions

I. All artists are poets.

II. Some inspiring persons are not artists.

141. ***Statements***

No villagers own a car.

Shankar owns a car. (*December 2002*)

Conclusions

I. Shankar lives in a town.

II. Shankar owns a car.

142. ***Statements***

Some teachers are women.

No teacher is absent.

Conclusions

I. There are no male teachers.

II. All women teachers are present.

143. ***Statements***

Some benches are chairs.

Hammer is a bench.

Conclusions

I. Some chairs are benches.

II. Hammer is not a chair.

144. ***Statements***

All books are stones.

All stones are papers. (*December 2002*)

Conclusions
I. Some papers are books.
II. Some papers are stones.

145. ***Statements***

Only graduates are eligible for this post.

Most rickshaw pullers are graduates.

Conclusions
I. Some rickshaw pullers are eligible for this post.
II. All those eligible for this post are graduates.

146. ***Statements***

All grapes are oranges.

Some apples are not oranges.

Conclusions
I. All apples are grapes.
II. Some apples are grapes.

147. ***Statements***

All students are ambitious.

All ambitious persons are hardworking.

Conclusions
I. All students are hardworking.
II. All hardly working people are not ambitious.

148. ***Statements***

All horses are donkeys.

All donkeys are monkeys.

Conclusions
I. All horses are monkeys.
II. All monkeys are horses.

(*December 1998*)

149. ***Statements***

All garden are schools.

All schools are colleges.

Conclusions
I. All gardens are colleges.
II. Some gardens are not colleges.

150. ***Statements***

No tree is bottle.

No bottle is unbreakable.

(*NET June 1997 and June 2001*)

Conclusions
I. No tree is unbreakable.
II. Nothing unbreakable is tree.

***Directions (Questions 151–167)*:** In each of the questions below, there are two statements followed by three to four conclusions numbered I, II, III, and IV. You have to take the given statements to be true even if they seem to be at variance with commonly known facts and then decide which of the given conclusions logically follow from the given statements.

151. ***Statements***

All magic are women.

All women are crazy.

Conclusions
I. All magic are crazy.
II. All crazy are magic.
III. Some crazy are magic.
IV. Some crazy are women.

Choices
(a) Only I, III, and IV follow
(b) Only II and III follow
(c) All conclusions follow
(d) None of the conclusions follow

152. ***Statements***

All cats are mammals.

No tigers are cats.

Conclusions
(a) No tiger is a mammal.
(b) No mammals are tigers.
(c) Cats are tigers.
(d) None of the above

153. ***Statements***

Some boxes are round.

All rounds are spheres.

Conclusions
I. Some boxes are spheres.
II. Some spheres are boxes.
III. Some spheres are round.
IV. All spheres are round.

Choices
(a) I, II, and III follow
(b) II, III, and IV follow
(c) I, III, and IV follow
(d) I, II, and IV follow

154. ***Statements***

All books are clocks.

Some clocks are chips.

Conclusions

I. Some clocks are books.

II. No clocks are books.

III. Some books are chips.

IV. No books are chips.

Choices
(a) I and III follow
(b) Only I follows
(c) Either I or II follows
(d) Either III or IV and I follows

155. ***Statements***

Some tables are TVs.

Some TVs are radios.

Conclusions

I. Some tables are radios.

II. Some radios are tables.

III. All radios are TVs.

IV. All TVs are tables.

Choices
(a) Only I and III follow
(b) Only II and IV follow
(c) All follow
(d) None follows

156. ***Statements***

Some rabbits are bears.

No goats are bears.

Conclusions

I. Some rabbits are not goats.

II. All rabbits are goats.

III. Some goats are not rabbits.

IV. All goats are rabbits.

Choices
(a) Only I follows
(b) Only III follows
(c) Either I or II follows
(d) Either III or IV and I follow

157. ***Statements***

No systems are desks.

All desks are books.

Conclusions

I. Some systems are books.

II. Some systems are not books.

III. Some books are systems.

IV. Some books are not systems.

Choices
(a) Only II follows
(b) Only IV follows
(c) I and IV follow
(d) Either I or II and IV follow

158. ***Statements***

All branches are flowers.

All flowers are trees.

Conclusions

I. All branches are trees.

II. All trees are branches.

III. All flowers are branches.

IV. Some trees are branches.

Choices
(a) Only I and IV follow
(b) Only II and III follow
(c) All follow
(d) None follows

159. ***Statements***

Some bags are pockets.

No pocket is a pouch.

Conclusions

I. No bag is a pouch.

II. Some bags are not pouches.

III. Some pockets are bags.

IV. No pocket is a bag.

Choices

(a) Only I and III follow
(b) Only II and III follow
(c) Only either I or IV follows
(d) None follows

160. ***Statements***

All politicians are honest.

All honest are fair.

Conclusions

I. Some honest are politicians.

II. No honest is politician.

III. Some fair are politicians.

IV. All fair are politicians.

Choices

(a) None follows
(b) Only I follows
(c) Only I and II follow
(d) Only I and III follow

161. ***Statements***

All the students passed the examination.

Some students are girls.

Conclusions

I. Some boys passed the examination.

II. All the girls failed the examination.

III. None of the boys passed the examination.

IV. None of the girl students failed the examination.

Choices

(a) Only I and II follow
(b) Only II and III follow
(c) Only I, II, and III follow
(d) None of the above

162. ***Statement***

Most of the Indian states existed before independence

Conclusions

I. Some Indian states existed before independence.

II. All Indian states did not exist before independence.

Choices

(a) Only I is implied
(b) Only II is implied
(c) Both I and II are implied
(d) Neither I nor II is implied

163. ***Statement***

Most teachers are hardworking.

Conclusions

I. Some teachers are hardworking.

II. Some teachers are not hardworking. *(June 2006)*

Choices

(a) Only I is implied
(b) Only II is implied
(c) Both I and II are implied
(d) Neither I nor II is implied

164. ***Proposition***

No teacher is on time for the class. *(June 2002)*

Conclusions

I. No persons who are on time for their classes are teachers.

II. Some teachers are not late for their classes.

III. Most teachers come to their classes on time.

IV. Few teachers come on time for their classes.

165. ***Statement***

Necessity is the mother of all inventions.

Conclusions

I. There can be no invention without there being a mother.

II. Mother is a necessity. *(June 2002)*

Choices

(a) Only I is implied
(b) Only II is implied
(c) Both I and II are implied
(d) Neither I nor II is implied

166. ***Statement***

No man is infallible.

Conclusions

I. All men are fallible.

II. No infallible persons are men.

Choices

(a) Only inference I is correct
(b) Only inference II is correct
(c) Both inferences I and II are correct
(d) Neither inference I nor inference II is correct

167. ***Statements***

All aeroplanes are trains.

Some trains are chairs.

Conclusions

I. Some aeroplanes are chairs.

II. Some chairs are aeroplanes.

III. Some chairs are trains.

IV. Some trains are aeroplanes.

Codes:

(a) None follows
(b) Only I and II follow
(c) Only II and III follow
(d) Only III and IV follow

Statements and Assumptions

Directions (Questions 168–187): In each of the questions below, a statement is followed by two assumptions I and II. An assumption is something that is supposed or taken for granted. You have to consider the statement and the following assumptions and decide which of the assumptions is implicit in the statement.

(a) Only assumption I is implicit.
(b) Only assumption II is implicit.
(c) Both I and II are implicit.
(d) Neither I nor II is implicit.

168. ***Statement:*** Apartment building owners argue that rent control should be abolished as it will increase housing supply in the long run.

Assumptions

I. Abolishing rent control will increase investment in housing sector.

II. Greater supply leads to lower prices.

169. ***Statement:*** The government has decided to discontinue the telegram services which were provided at post offices across country.

Assumptions

I. There were hardly any users of this service to keep it financially viable.

II. The government wanted to force people to switch to alternative means of communication.

170. ***Statement:*** An appointment letter was issued to a recently passed out engineering graduate, 'You are hereby appointed as a Network Engineer with a probation period of one year. The confirmation is subjected to performance review at the end of the year'.

Assumptions

I. This will help to manipulate the behaviour of the employee more effectively.

II. This acts as a motivational factor to perform better.

171. ***Statement:*** The automobile companies decreased prices of their products, besides offering many attractive financing schemes.

Assumptions

I. This will boost the market demand that is now sluggish.

II. There is high competition in the market.

172. ***Statement:*** The new environmental law has been passed in our parliament with two-third majority.

Assumptions

I. Protecting the environment has become a very important issue in our society.

II. This will absolve the government of its responsibility for any further damage to the environment.

173. ***Statement:*** The Delhi government has made it mandatory for all commercial vehicles to switch over to CNG in order to improve air quality.

Assumptions

I. There is sufficient domestic supply of CNG.

II. This will reduce carbon emissions in the air which are the major pollutants.

174. ***Statement:*** Government started the Mid-day Meal Scheme across states in the country in order to reduce absenteeism and dropout ratio in the schools.

Assumptions

I. Many poor parents are not able to afford food for their school-going children.

II. This will help the government in making optimum use of food grains stored in warehouses.

175. ***Statement:*** The government has decided to disinvest large chunks of its equity in select public sector undertakings to reduce fiscal deficit that is well above the targeted figure.

Assumptions

I. The money generated out of the disinvestment process may reduce substantially the mounting fiscal deficits.

II. There is a large public demand in the market for the shares of these undertakings.

176. ***Statement:*** The government has enacted anti-rape laws in the Parliament in wake of rise in such incidents in the recent years.

Assumptions

I. Strict law is the only and only way to deal with such incidents.

II. This will help to strengthen the vote bank of the ruling party in the centre.

177. ***Statement:*** An advertisement by a bank— We offer higher deposit rate in comparison to other banks.

Assumptions

I. The different banks offer different deposit rates.

II. There is competition in the market to attract customers.

178. ***Statement:*** As a result of climate change and global warming, there has been an increase in the number and intensity of hurricanes, flash floods, and so on, which cause extensive damage.

Assumptions

I. We ought to know the causes so as to minimize the damage.

II. There should be public awareness about the complete inevitability of impending dangers as a consequence of climate change and global warming.

179. ***Statement:*** His recent investment in the shares of Company A is very risky.

Assumptions

I. More risk more gain.

II. He may incur huge losses on his investment.

180. ***Statement:*** To maintain law and order in India, police works under high pressure and tension.

Assumptions

I. The police of other countries works without any interferences.

II. We expect that functions of the police should be free from any interferences.

181. ***Statement:*** The new education policy envisages major changes in the educational system to meet our national objectives.

Assumptions

I. The present education system needs improvement as it is not meeting our objectives.

II. The present education system is not consistent with the manifesto of the ruling political party.

182. ***Statement:*** The 'Right to Information Act (2005)' has been implemented almost in all departments dealing with the public.

Assumptions

I. The government felt that employees in various departments can be made more accountable by providing services to public.

II. This was required to keep the government employees busy.

183. ***Statement:*** Teaching through TV is to help the students learn without a teacher.

Assumptions

I. Students want to study without a teacher.

II. Teachers are incapable of teaching.

184. ***Statement:*** If you lose after competing hard, that is fine. If you lose without trying hard, that is what disappoints me.

Assumptions

I. Losing after trying hard is excusable.

II. Losing without effort is regrettable.

185. ***Statement:*** Trade union leadership is in the hands of politicians.

Assumptions

I. Trade unions have leaders.

II. Leaders are generally politicians.

186. ***Statement:*** A prominent university has started the practice of putting results on its website rather than in newspapers.

Assumptions

I. Most of the students have access to the Internet these days.

II. Students use both website and newspapers to see their results.

187. ***Statement:*** The state government has decided to appoint 4,000 primary school teachers during the next financial year.

Assumptions

I. There are enough schools in the state to accommodate 4,000 additional primary school teachers.

II. The eligible candidates may not be interested to apply as the government may not finally appoint such a large number of primary school teachers.

Force of Arguments

188. ***Statement:*** Should there be a common entrance exam for admissions into medical colleges in India?

Arguments

I. Yes, this will help candidates in focussing on a single test in the best possible manner and also save lot of hassle and cost of appearing in many examinations.

II. No, this will deny candidates the opportunities to try their luck in other entrance exams, in case they are not able to perform in one particular exam.

189. ***Statement:*** Should there be a world government? *(June 2003)*

Arguments

I. Yes, it will help in eliminating tension among nations.

II. No, then also the developed countries will dominate the government.

190. ***Statement:*** Should political parties be banned? *(June 2003)*

Arguments

I. Yes, it is necessary to teach a lesson to the politicians.

II. No, it will lead to an end of democracy.

191. ***Statement:*** Should India's foreign trade policy focus on increasing exports, when India has limited supplies for domestic market.

Arguments

I. Yes, through exports we can earn foreign exchange to pay for our imports.

II. No, even export of selective commodities would lead to shortages.

192. ***Statement:*** Should our government allow medicines patented and manufactured in other countries for sale to general public only after conducting field trials?

Arguments

I. Yes, the genetic make-up and physical and geographical conditions of Indian population are different from other parts of the world.

II. No, this is just not feasible and hence cannot be implemented.

193. ***Statement:*** Should government focus on spending money on research to develop technologies to harness alternative energy resources to fulfil its energy requirements?

Arguments

I. Yes, most of the energy resources such as fossil fuels are exhaustible in near future at the present rate of consumption.

II. No, the outcome of research is always uncertain, so spending money on research may be a wasteful expenditure.

194. ***Statement:*** Is nuclear family system better than joint family system?

Arguments

I. Yes, nuclear families enjoy greater freedom.

II. No, joint families offer physical, psychological, and financial security and better division of work.

195. ***Statement:*** Should government stop spending huge amounts of money on international sports?

Arguments

I. Yes, this money can be utilized for the socio-economic development of the country.

II. No, lack of sports infrastructure will discourage players and they will not get international exposure.

196. ***Statement:*** Should there be compulsory medical examination of both the men and the women before they marry each other?

Arguments

I. Yes, this will substantially reduce the risk of giving birth to children with serious ailments.

II. No, this is an intrusion into the privacy of an individual and hence cannot be tolerated.

197. ***Statement:*** Should there be a ban on product advertising?

Arguments

I. Yes, the money spent on advertising is very huge and it inflates the cost of the product.

II. No, it is an age of advertising; unless your advertisement is better than your other competitors, the product will not be sold.

198. ***Statement:*** Should sex determination test during pregnancy be completely banned?

Arguments

I. Yes, this leads to indiscriminate female foeticide and eventually leads to social imbalance.

II. No, people have a right to know about their unborn child.

199. ***Statement:*** Should persons convicted of criminal offences in the past be allowed to contest elections in India?

Arguments

I. Yes, it is a democracy—let people decide whom to vote.

II. No, such persons cannot serve the cause of the people and the country.

200. ***Statement:*** Should cutting of trees be banned altogether?

Arguments

I. Yes, it is very much necessary to do so to restore ecological balance.

II. No, a total ban would harm timber-based industries.

Explanation

Clearly, trees play a vital role in maintaining ecological balance and so must be preserved. So argument I holds true. Also, trees form the basic source of timber and a complete ban on cutting of trees would harm the timber-based industries. So only a controlled cutting of trees should be allowed and the loss replenished by planting more trees. So argument II is also valid.

201. ***Statement:*** Should there be a restriction on the migration of people from one state to another in India?

Arguments

I. Yes, this is the way to effect an equitable distribution of resources across the states in India.

II. No, any Indian citizen has the basic right to stay at any place of his/her choice and hence they cannot be stopped.

Explanation

Clearly, argument I holds strong, while argument II is vague.

202. ***Statement:*** Should India create a huge oil reserve like some Western countries to face difficult situations in future?

Arguments

I. Yes, this will help India withstand shocks of sudden rise in oil prices due to unforeseen circumstances.

II. No, there is no need to block huge amount of foreign exchange and keep the money idle..

Explanation

Oil, being an essential commodity, must be kept in reserve in our country. So argument I is vague, while argument II holds true as it provides a substantial reason for the same.

203. ***Statement:*** Should there be more than one High Court in each state in India?

Arguments

I. Yes, this will help reduce the backlog of cases pending for a very long time.

II. No, this will be a sheer wastage of taxpayers' money.

204. ***Statement:*** Should an open book examination system be introduced in India?

Arguments

I. Yes, this will help in eliminating rote memory method.

II. No, the students may not take the study seriously.

205. ***Statement:*** Should an advisory be issued to women in metropolitan cities that they should not travel alone at night in view of increasing incidences of rape and sexual abuse?

Arguments

I. Yes, providing security at every place is not possible.

II. No, this may send a wrong message to the people that government is not able to provide security to women.

206. ***Statement:*** Should there be a restriction on number of limited matches in India so as to fix the problem of match fixing?

Arguments

I. Yes, the high number of such matches offers more opportunities to anti-social elements to indulge in match fixing.

II. No, these will discourage sports culture in the country.

207. ***Statement:*** Should the teenagers be denied access to social media sites?

Arguments

I. Yes, they waste a lot of precious time that can be used for studies.

II. No, this will deny them of the useful information.

208. ***Statement:*** Should there be a ban on the use of plastic bags in metro cities?

Arguments

I. Yes, the excessive use of plastic bags chokes drainage system and causes water logging.

II. No, instead, the thickness of plastic bags should be specified that will cause minimal damage to the environment.

209. ***Statement:*** Should smoking be completely banned in India?

Arguments

I. Yes, this will improve the health of the nation.

II. No, this will drive thousands of people out of jobs.

210. ***Statement:*** Should social media sites be banned by the Government?

Arguments

I. Yes, this will check the misuse of social media against government.

II. No, this will curtail the expression of power.

211. ***Statement:*** Should there be capital punishment for persons found guilty of committing heinous crimes against women and children?

Arguments

I. Yes, this kind of exemplary punishment can work as deterrence against committing such type of crimes.

II. No, this can also lead to misuse of law by miscreants.

212. ***Statement:*** We should privatize higher education. (*June 2004*)

Arguments

I. Yes, because the government institutes are not working properly.

II. No, as this will deprive the poor of education.

III. Yes, because education in private institutions is of high quality.

Which of these arguments is weighty and correct?

(a) Only I
(b) Only II
(c) Both I and II
(d) Both II and III

Assertion and Reason

Directions (Questions 213–232): Assertion and reasoning type questions have one assertion and one reason. The question is followed by four options.

(a) A is true but R is false.
(b) A is false but R is true.
(c) Both A and R are true and R is not the correct explanation of A.
(d) Both A and R are true and R is the correct explanation of A.

213. ***Assertion (A):*** Hindi should be the official language of India.

Reason (R): Majority of people living in India are Hindus. (*December 1998*)

214. ***Assertion (A):*** In India, people elect their own representatives for Parliament and State Assemblies.

Reason (R): India is a democratic country.

215. ***Assertion (A):*** In India, cotton crop is grown mainly in alluvial soils.

Reason (R): Alluvial soils are very fertile.

216. ***Assertion (A):*** The Indian Constitution came into force with effect from 26 January 1950.

Reason (R): 26 January is celebrated as Republic Day.

217. ***Assertion (A):*** Robert Clive defeated Siraj-ud-daulah in the Battle of Plassey.

Reason (R): The army of Clive was the best and it followed the best strategic policy. (*December 2000*)

218. ***Assertion (A):*** The Hoysala sculptures have highly detailed descriptions and ornamentation.

Reason (R): Hoysala sculptures are soft; these have been created in Chloristic Schism.

219. ***Assertion (A):*** Akbar abolished *jizya* in 1564 but reimposed it subsequently.

Reason (R): As a young man he was quite liberal and tolerant but became orthodox and reactionary as he matured.

220. ***Assertion (A):*** Gupta period is described as the Golden Age of Indian History.

Reason (R): Guptas issued a large number of gold coins.

221. ***Assertion (A):*** Most of the Himalayan rivers are perennial.

Reason (R): They are fed by melting snow.

222. ***Assertion (A):*** Earthworms are not good for agriculture.

Reason (R): Earthworms break down the soil into fine particles and make it soft.

223. ***Assertion (A):*** The Greek influence on the Indian art manifested itself in the form of Gandhara School of Art and moved from Taxila to Mathura and Sarnath.

Reason (R): During Gupta period, art became entirely and truly Indian.

224. ***Assertion (A):*** Heavy water is used as a moderator in nuclear reactor.

Reason (R): Thermal neutrons are used for fission reactions in a reactor.

225. ***Assertion (A):*** The 'Green Belt' represents a planning concept for controlling the physical expansion of large cities.

Reason (R): 'Green Belt' is an integral component of a planned city.

226. ***Assertion (A):*** The import of Chinese toys was recently banned by the Government of India.

Reason (R): The plastic materials used to make the toys are not biodegradable.

227. ***Assertion (A):*** Conversion of coal to diamond is a physical change.

Reason (R): Physical change does not change the composition of materials.

228. ***Assertion (A):*** Caste involves a system consisting of many castes arranged in a hierarchy of rank and status.

Reason (R): The hierarchical ordering of castes is based on the distinction between purity and pollution as per ancient literature.

229. ***Assertion (A):*** Seasonal employment results in large-scale migration of agricultural labourers from agriculturally backward regions to that of developed regions.

Reason (R): In seasonal unemployment, once the seasons are over, the agricultural workers, especially landless labourers and marginal farmers, remain unemployed.

230. ***Assertion (A):*** Intensive cultivation accelerates land degradation.

Reason (R): Second Green revolution emphasizes on the improvement of mechanism to stop land degradation.

231. ***Assertion (A):*** Division of work is the separation of work processes into a number of tasks with each task performed by a separate person or a group of persons.

Reason (R): Division of labour is a complex web of independent and isolated work.

232. ***Assertion (A):*** One of the important decisions of the framers of the constitution of India was to guarantee every adult citizen in India the right to vote.

Reason (R): The universal adult franchise is not consistent with the principle of equality.

Statements and Courses of Actions

In each of the questions below (233–242), a statement followed by two courses of action numbered I and II. Mark the answer:

(a) If only course of action I follows
(b) If only course of action II follows
(c) If both courses of action I and II follow
(d) If neither course of action I nor course of action II follows

233. ***Statement:*** According to a report, not even a single institution of higher learning in India has appeared in the top 200 institutions of the world.

Courses of action

I. Government should privatize higher education.

II. The regulatory agencies must do introspection and work hard to raise the standard of education in higher learning institutions.

234. ***Statement:*** Mobile phone users have found that billing is not done according to advertised tariff plans by telecom companies and complained to regulatory authority about the same.

Courses of action

I. The regulatory authority should direct telecom companies to be transparent on the tariff structure of all plans.

II. The government should restrict the number of foreign telecom companies operating in the country.

235. ***Statement:*** A report states—an increasing number of engineering graduates produced by Indian universities are not employable in the industry.

Courses of action

I. The engineering colleges should be given greater autonomy to decide the course content as per the demand of the industry.

II. World-class foreign universities should be encouraged to set up campuses in India.

236. ***Statement:*** Most of them who passed from premier engineering colleges in India have migrated to developed nations for better career prospects.

Courses of action

I. It should be made mandatory for students to sign the bond at the time of admission to the effect that they will serve in India at least for 10 years after they complete their graduation.

II. The government should take measures to provide suitable opportunities within the country that motivates them to stay in the country.

237. ***Statement:*** A number of school children in the local schools have fallen ill after consumption of subsidized meals provided by the school authorities.

Courses of action

I. This kind of government scheme should be discontinued with immediate effect.

II. The government should put in place a more effective system to check the quality of meal provided to the students.

238. ***Statement:*** According to the latest census report, the gender ratio has fallen further in India.

Courses of action

I. Government should conduct another census to verify the results.

II. Government should immediately start an awareness campaign through its public relations department about the effects of low gender ratio and encourage them to improve it.

239. ***Statement:*** According to a survey report—majority of school teachers are not familiar with the need and importance of environmental education and also of their role in its promotion.

Courses of action

I. Environmental education programme should be included in the college curriculum.

II. Orientation programme should be conducted for teachers on population education.

240. ***Statement:*** The frequency of natural disasters such as hurricanes and flash floods has increased during the past two decades due to global warming.

Courses of action

I. Action should be taken at the community levels.

II. The governments of the world should work together as factors and its effects are not confined to a single nation.

241. ***Statement:*** India is facing continuous military threats from its neighbouring countries.

Courses of action

I. India should strengthen military presence at the border.

II. India should engage its neighbours into a serious dialogue to reduce the tension at its borders.

242. ***Statement:*** The users of social media sites have expressed their anguish at government's inability to deal with cases of violence against women in a prompt manner.

Courses of action

I. Government should ban the use of social media websites.

II. Government should try to devise measures to ensure the safety of women.

Previous Year's Questions

One interrogative sentence is followed by two arguments, one beginning with 'yes' and other with 'no'. Pick up the correct answer choice from the answer choices given below for each of the questions from 243 to 245.

Directions (Questions 243–245): One interrogative sentence is followed by two arguments, one beginning with 'yes' and the other with 'no'. Pick up the correct answer choice from the answer choices given below for each of the questions from 243 to 245.

(a) If only argument I is forceful

(b) If only argument II is forceful

(c) If both arguments are forceful

(d) If neither argument I nor II is forceful

243. Should old age pension be introduced in India?

I. Yes, because it is the most important social necessity.

II. No, because it will increase financial burden on the state

Explanation

Old age pension is still not considered as the most important social necessity in India; family support system is still intact. If it is introduced in India, it will increase the financial burden on the state. So, only II is more forceful.

244. Should free education be imparted in Indian schools?

I. Yes, because India is a democratic country.

II. No, because free education will lead to unemployment of educated people.

Explanation

Argument I is not strong as it is not incumbent on a democratic setup to provide free education to its populace. Argument II is also not strong because in the statement, there is nothing to link free education with the employment of people.

245. Should reservation of seats for SC/ST candidates be discontinued?

I. Yes, because reservation serves no purpose except for support to the political parties.

II. No, because the backward sections of the society must be helped.

Explanation

Argument I is not forceful because reservation is not being extended to SC/ST candidates to gain support from political parties. Argument II is strong as SCs/STs need reservation so that they get some help in this manner.

Miscellaneous

246. Which of the following statements are mutually inconsistent?
    I. Mostly poets are not egoistic.
    II. Mostly poets are humble.
    III. Some poets are egoistic.
    IV. Some poets are not non-egoistic.

    Codes:
    (a) I and IV (b) II and III
    (c) I and III (d) III and IV

247. ***Statement***
    If all men are mortal, and if Rama is a man, Rama is also mortal
    (a) The premise is true and the conclusion is true.
    (b) The premise is false and the conclusion is false.
    (c) The premise is false and the conclusion is true.
    (d) The premise is true and the conclusion is false.

248. If 'no politician is dishonest' is false, then the statement 'some politicians are dishonest' shall be
    (a) True (b) False
    (c) May be true (d) None of the above

249. If the statement 'some men are cruel' is false, which of the following statement/s is/are true?
    I. All men are cruel.
    II. No men are cruel.
    III. Some men are not cruel.

    Codes:
    (a) I and III (b) I and II
    (c) II and III (d) III only

250. ***Proposition***
    No teacher is on time for the class.
    (*June 2000*)

    Conclusions
    (a) No persons who are on time for their classes are teachers.
    (b) Some teachers are not late for their classes.
    (c) Most teachers come to their classes on time.
    (d) Few teachers come on time for their classes.

251. Which of the following statements are mutually contradictory? (*December 2006*)
    I. All flowers are not fragrant.
    II. Most flowers are not fragrant.
    III. None of the flowers are fragrant.
    IV. Most flowers are fragrant.

    Codes:
    (a) I and II (b) I and III
    (c) II and III (d) III and IV

***Directions (Questions 252 and 253)*:** In each of the questions below, two statements are given followed by an inference. Mark (A) if the inference is definitely true, mark (B) if the inference is definitely false, mark (C) if the inference is probably false or true, and mark (D) if the inference cannot be drawn.

252. ***Statements***
    1. Glass is brittle.
    2. This substance is not brittle.

    Inference
    This substance is not glass.

253. ***Statements***
    1. Some intelligent people are happy.
    2. Some intelligent people are rich.

    Inference
    Some who are rich are happy. (*June 2003*)

ANSWER KEYS

Theory Questions

1. (b) 2. (b) 3. (c) 4. (c) 5. (b)
6. (b) 7. (a) 8. (b) 9. (d) 10. (b)
11. (c) 12. (a) 13. (c) 14. (b) 15. (c)
16. (a) 17. (b) 18. (d) 19. (c) 20. (b)
21. (a) 22. (b) 23. (b) 24. (a) 25. (a)

26. (d) 27. (b) 28. (a) 29. (a) 30. (c)
31. (a) 32. (a) 33. (b) 34. (d) 35. (d)
36. (c) 37. (a) 38. (a) 39. (c) 40. (a)
41. (a) 42. (b) 43. (a) 44. (d) 45. (d)
46. (b) 47. (a) 48. (d) 49. (a) 50. (a)
51. (a) 52. (b) 53. (c) 54. (d) 55. (c)
56. (a) 57. (a) 58. (c) 59. (d) 60. (b)
61. (a) 62. (b) 63. (a) 64. (b) 65. (d)
66. (c) 67. (c) 68. (d) 69. (b) 70. (a)
71. (a) 72. (c) 73. (a) 74. (b) 75. (d)
76. (b) 77. (a) 78. (a) 79. (a) 80. (c)
81. (a) 82. (c) 83. (b) 84. (b) 85. (c)
86. (a) 87. (b) 88. (c) 89. (d) 90. (a)
91. (b) 92. (b) 93. (a) 94. (a) 95. (b)
96. (c) 97. (b) 98. (a) 99. (b) 100. (d)
101. (b) 102. (b) 103. (c) 104. (d) 105. (b)
106. (b) 107. (d) 108. (c) 109. (c) 110. (c)
111. (d) 112. (a) 113. (a) 114. (d) 115. (a)
116. (d) 117. (b) 118. (c) 119. (b) 120. (c)
121. (c) 122. (b) 123. (a) 124. (d) 125. (d)
126. (c) 127. (c) 128. (c) 129. (b) 130. (c)
131. (d) 132. (b) 133. (b) 134. (c) 135. (b)

Practical Problems

136. (d): ***Explanation:***

Step I: First, we check that there are three terms—tables, golden, and teak. Here, **table** is the middle term.

Then, we see whether it is in the form: A to B and B to C. It is not; so alignment is required. For alignment, we just need to change the order in this case.

After alignment:

All teak are **tables**.

Some **tables** are golden.

Step II: This is 'A + I'. (Please refer to 'syllogism rule table'. No conclusion can be drawn.

So (d) is the answer.

Venn diagram solution:

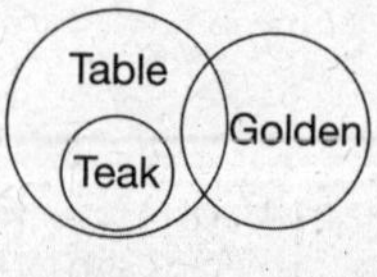

Or

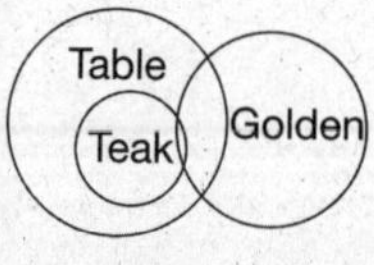

Conclusion I: Some teak may or may not be golden, ambiguity is there. Conclusion I does not follow.

Conclusion II: Similarly, some golden may or may not be teak.

As there is ambiguity in both cases, none follows. (d) is the answer.

137. (a): First check the number of terms. It is three. Ok. Now look at alignment.

Now, the common term 'man' is not in the form A to B and B to C. So alignment is required.

Align this pair as 'Karan is a man' and 'No man is a Tiger'.

Here, it is important to mention that statement 'Karan is a Tiger' is considered as A type.

Now, A + E = E. So conclusion I 'Karan is not a Tiger' follows.

Alternative solution:

Venn diagram solution:

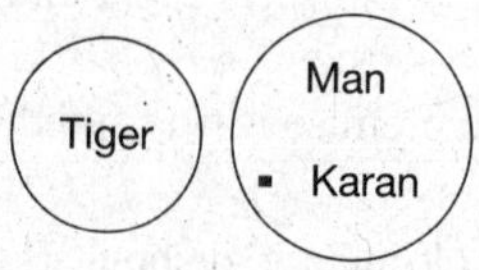

138. (c): There are three terms. No alignment is required as it is in the standard format.

A + A = A. The conclusion is 'all boys are fathers'. Conclusion II follows.

By applying immediate reference to (converting) statement I, we can say that all some men are boys. Conclusion I also follows. Both I and II follow.

Venn diagram solution:

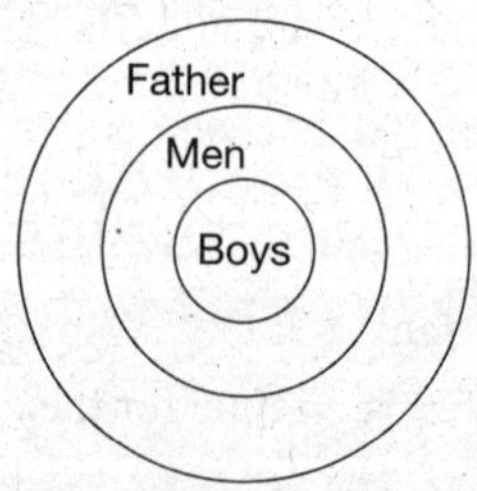

139. (b): Three terms—Teacher, girls, and dull. Next, it is in proper format. No alignment is required.

Now, A + E = E. That is 'No Teacher is dull'. Conclusion II follows. Boys is not mentioned as a term. So nothing can be said about conclusion I.

Venn diagram solution:

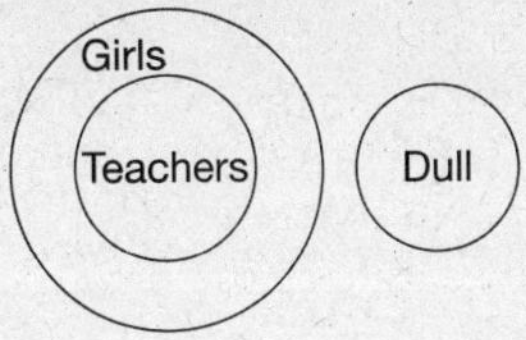

140. (d): There are three terms—poets, inspiring, and artists.
All poets (A) are inspiring (B).
All artists (C) are inspiring (B).
A to B.
C to B.
So alignment is required as it should be in the form A to B and B to C.
After converting second statement.
All poets are inspiring (A type).
Some inspiring persons are artists (I type).
It contradicts second conclusion also.
A + I = No conclusion.
So (d) is the answer.

Venn diagram solution:

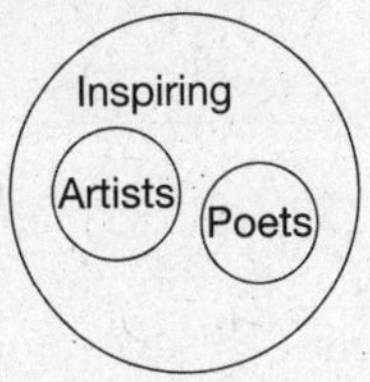

141. (d): Town is not mentioned in statements. So conclusion I cannot follow. Premise and conclusion cannot be the same. So (d) is the answer.

142. (d): If we look at conclusions directly, the term 'male teacher' in the first conclusion and 'women teachers' and 'present' in the second conclusion are not mentioned in statements.
So (d) is the answer. Here, it is important to mention the syllogism propositions—the opposite of 'absent' is not 'present'.

143. (a): The aligned pair is 'Hammer is a bench' and 'Some benches are chairs'. There is no definite conclusion for A + I-type pair. But conversion of statement I implies conclusion I.

144. (c): The condition of three terms is satisfied. No alignment is required.
A + A = A, conclusion is 'All books are papers'. The immediate inference of conclusion is 'Some papers are books'. So conclusion I follows.
The immediate inference of second statement is 'some papers are stones'; that is also conclusion 2. So (c) is the answer.

Venn diagram solution:

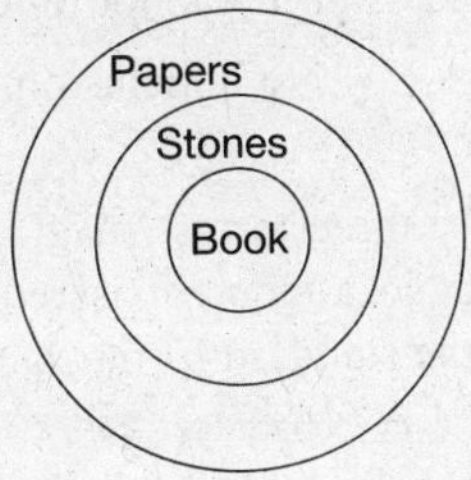

145. (c): This is a comprehensive question, covering all major aspects of syllogism. Please look at the solution carefully.
We need to bring the statements to their logical form before checking them for alignment.
All those eligible for the post are graduates.
Some rickshaw pullers are graduates.
There are three terms—eligible, graduates, and rickshaw pullers. 'Graduates' is the common term.
The statements are not in the form: A to B and A to B.
According to IEA, second statement should be given priority for conversion:
'Some graduates are rickshaw pullers'.
Now the statements are to be brought to A to B and B to C form.
'All those eligible for the post are graduates' (A type)
'Some graduates are rickshaw pullers' (I type)
A + I = No conclusion.

146. (d): there are three terms—grapes, oranges, and apples.
A + O = No conclusion.
We do not get any conclusion through immediate inference (conversion) also. So (d) is the answer.

147. (a): A + A = A, so conclusion I follows. In conclusion II, the term 'hardly working' is not mentioned in the statements. So it does not need any consideration.

148. (a): A + A = A, only statement I follows, so (a) is the answer.

149. (a) Since, both the premises are affirmative, the conclusion must be affirmative, the conclusion II cannot follow.

150. (d): E + E = No conclusion. So (d) is the answer.

151. (c) Only three terms (magic, women, and crazy). No alignment is required as they are in the standard format.
Now A + A = A.

Conclusion: All magic are crazy. So statement I is correct. Its immediate inference is 'Some crazy are magic'. It means third statement is true.
The converse of second statement 'All women are crazy' is 'Some crazy are women'. So fourth conclusion is also true. Thus, (c) is the answer.

152. (d): There are three terms. After alignment,
Some mammals are cats.
No cats are tigers.

If we look at conclusions directly, the term 'male teacher' in the first conclusion and 'women teachers' and 'present' in the second conclusion are not mentioned in statements. So (d) is the answer.

153. (a): I + A = I. The conclusion is some boxes are spheres which is I. This can be converted to some spheres are boxes, which is II. Conclusion III follows after converting all rounds are spheres. So (a) is the answer.

Venn diagram solution:

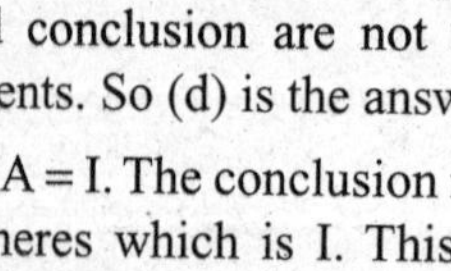

154. (b): They are in desired format A to B and B to C.
All books are clocks (A-type)
Some clocks are chips (I-type)
A + I = No conclusion.
Now, we can check first statement after immediate inference—Some clocks are books.
Second statement after immediate inference—Some chips are clocks.
So only conclusion I follows. (b) is the answer.

155. (d): Since both the premises are particular, no definite conclusion follows.

156. (d): It has three terms.
After alignment—'no goats are bears' and 'some bears are rabbits'.
E + I = O. So the conclusion is Some rabbits are not goats. Hence, I follows. III and IV also make a complementary pair.

157. (d): E + A = O*. Hence, the conclusion is 'Some books are not systems'. Again, I and II are complementary pair.

158. A + A = A, 'All branches are trees'. Conclusion I follows. The immediate inference of 'All branches are trees' is 'Some trees are branches', that is, conclusion IV. So option (a)' is valid.

159. (b)

160. (c)

161. 'd'. The opposites of 'passed' and 'girls' are not 'failed' and 'boys'. Failed and boys are not mentioned in the statements. So no conclusion is valid.

162. (d): The logical form of 'Most of Indian states existed before independence' is 'Some Indian states existed before independence'. It is same as conclusion I. Statement and conclusion cannot be the same. Conclusion II is also not implied. So (d) is the answer.

163. (b): 'Most teachers are hardworking' is 'Some teachers are hardworking' in its logical form. Both statement and conclusion cannot be the

same. So conclusion I is not implied. However, conclusion II 'Some teachers are not hardworking' is complimentary of I, so only II is implied. (b) is the answer.

164. (a): After converting statement I, we can say that 'a' is true. 'On time' does not mean 'not late' in case of propositions. (c) and (d) also not converse of (a).

165. (d): The contextual meaning and logical meanings are different for both the terms. So (d) is the answer.

166. (a): The immediate inference of 'No man is infallible' is 'No infallible (persons) are men'. So conclusion II is right. In logical form, the opposite of infallible may not be fallible. So inference may not apply. So (a) is the answer.

167. (d): Since the middle term 'trains' is not distributed even once in the premises, no definite conclusion follows. However, III is the converse of the second premise while IV is the converse of the first premise. So, both of them hold.

Statements and Assumptions

168. (c)

169. (a)

170. (b)

171. (c)

172. (a): Absolving government could never be the motive of any legislation.

173. (c): Even if there is no sufficient domestic supply, the import can be an option as India already is importing fossil fuels.

174. (a)

175. (c)

176. (d): Despite enactment of strict laws, their implementation and changes in psychology of people are other aspects. So I does not follow. Assumption II seems to be a narrow approach. This also does not follow. So (d) is the answer.

177. (c)

178. (c)

179. (c): The investment is being stated to be risky as it may incur huge losses.

180. (b)

181. (a)

182. (a)

183. (d): Students want to learn, sometimes this may be without any teacher. So assumption I is not implicit. Assumption II is not implicit; teaching through TV may be required because of other reasons.

184. (c)

185. (a): Leadership does not always mean political leadership. There can be leaders from religious, social, and business entities also.

186. (c)

187. (a): The government will appoint teachers only if has requisite vacancies.

Force of Arguments

188. (c): Both

189. (c): As we can see from our experience of United Nations, that is also a semblance of world government and that is dominated by developed countries.

190. (b)

191. (a): Mostly, countries export their surplus production. Recently, exports include intangible items also, such as software. Resources generated through exports pay for imports. So only argument I holds.

192. (a): Health of the citizens is an issue of major concern for any government. So drugs must be first studied and tested in the Indian context before giving licence for its sale. So only argument I holds strong.

193. (a): Developing alternative sources of energy helps us in long run. Argument II is invalid as research is crucial for finding solution to existing problem.

194. (c): There is more security in joint family system, as many responsibilities shared. So argument I holds. In nuclear families, with lesser number of people, there are

lesser responsibilities and more freedom. Thus, II also holds.

195. (b): Argument I does not hold. Clearly, spending money on sports cannot be avoided merely because it can be spent on socio-economic problems. Also, sports culture helps in better health and will help in reducing medical expenses, and rather help in socio-economic development of nation. Argument II holds as with the lack of sports facilities, our country will lag behind in the international sports competitions.
196. (b): Such a step would help to prevent the growth of diseases such as AIDS. So only argument II is strong.
197. (b): It is the advertisement that helps company to generate higher sales which means economies of scale actually may bring down the cost of production. It also makes customer aware of the qualities of the product. So argument I is not valid. Only argument II holds strong.
198. (a): Sex determination tests have led to skewed gender ratio. So argument I holds. People have a right to know only about the health aspect of unborn child. So argument II does not hold strong.
199. (b): There should be a check on these kinds of elements at first place itself.
200. (c): Both I and II are valid. Only a limited ban should be imposed.
201. (b): Clearly, argument I holds strong, while argument II is vague.
202. (a): Oil, being an essential commodity, must be kept in reserve in our country; even for war-like situations.
203. (b): Creating more than one High Court may make sense only for big states. The number of pending cases should be dealt with more number of judges in existing high courts, not with increased number of high courts. Only argument II holds.
204. (c): Both I and II are valid arguments. So (c) is the answer.
205. (b): The government cannot absolve itself of the responsibility of providing security to its citizens—men or women, though women may need to be more cautious while moving at night. Argument II is more forceful.
206. (c): Both I and II are forceful.
207. (c): Both are strong.
208. (c): Both I and II are equally strong.
209. (a): Health is more important than any other issues. So I is more forceful.
210. In a democratic society like ours, everybody has the right of expression, even if it is against government. So argument I is not valid. Argument II is valid.
211. (c)
212. (b): The private institutions usually charge higher fees which poor people in India might not be able to afford.

Assertion and Reason

213. (c): Hindi should be the official language, but not on the basis of religion. There are many Hindu-dominated areas where Hindi is not being spoken, though Hindi is being spoken by almost half of our population.
214. (d): Only in democratic setup, people elect their own representatives.
215. (b): In India, cotton is mainly raised in the black soil that is found in Maharashtra. Alluvial soil is very fertile, found in Northern plains.
216. (d): Republic Day celebrates the coming into force of its constitution.
217. (a): The army of Clive won the battle of Plassey; he bribed Mir Jafar, Siraj-ud-daulah's Army Chief.
218. (a)
219. (c)
220. (c)
221. (d)
222. (b)
223. (c)
224. (c): Basically heavy water is used as a moderator in a nuclear reactor. It is used to

slow down the neutrons being directed at the fissionable material.

225. (c): The idea is for a ring of countryside where urbanization will be resisted for the foreseeable future, maintaining an area where agriculture, forestry, and outdoor leisure can be expected to prevail.

226. (c): The Chinese toys were banned for other concerns. The plastic used in toys made in India or for that matter anywhere else is not biodegradable. Thus, though reason statement is right but not in support of assertion.

227. (c)

228. (d)

229. (d)

230. (d)

231. (a)

232. (a): The words universal and equality conform to each other.

Statements and Courses of Action

233. (b)

234. (a)

235. (c)

236. (b): First course of action is not desirable as an individual is free to take any decision about one's career. Even if there is mandatory signing of bond, one cannot be forced to give productive work. The second course of action is a long-term solution.

237. (b)

238. (b): Census is a very detailed survey; it leaves very little scope for any kind of error. Second course of action is a pragmatic approach.

239. (c)

240. (c): Both I and II represent—think global and act local.

241. (c): For the protection of our nation, we have to adopt a combination of proactive and defensive approaches.

242. (b): The second approach is a solution-oriented approach. The first measure will be perceived as suppression of power of expression.

Miscellaneous

246. The logical form of statement I is 'some poets are not egoistic'.
The opposite of egoistic is not 'humble' or 'not egoistic'.
So I and III are mutually inconsistent.

247. (a)

248. (a): Please refer to 'square of opposition'. If a statement is false, its contradictory is taken to be true. The contradictory of 'No politician is dishonest' (E type) is 'Some politicians are dishonest' (I type). So it is true.

249. (d)

250. (a): As there is single proposition, we can apply immediate inference to draw conclusion. This is an E type proposition with 'teacher' as subject and '(persons) on time for the class' as the predicate which can conclude only E type. After conversion 'persons who are on time' becomes subject and teacher becomes predicate. So (a) is the answer.

251. (d): According to squares of opposition: The logical form of 'None of the flowers is fragrant' is 'No flower is fragrant' (i.e., E type). It can be converted only to I type, that is statement IV (the logical form of 'Most flowers are fragrant' is 'Some flowers are fragrant').

252. (a)

253. (d): There are three terms. Both are I type, even after conversion for alignment purpose, they will be of I type as shown below.
'Some intelligent people are happy', we get
Some who are happy are intelligent (I type)—first statement.
Some intelligent people are rich (I type)—second statement.
I + I = No inference. So (d) is the answer.

7

DATA ANALYSIS AND INTERPRETATION

DATA INTERPRETATION

Data interpretation is one of the easiest sections of NET Paper I. It is basically about drawing conclusions and inferences from a comprehensive data presented numerically in a tabular or graphical form by means of an illustration, namely, graphs, pie charts, and so on. Therefore, the act of organizing and interpreting data to get meaningful information is known as data interpretation. The important aspects of data sources, their acquisitions, and interpretation have been covered in Unit II on Research Aptitude. In this unit, the focus is on solving practical problems as per questions asked in the NET pattern.

Data interpretation needs some mathematical and statistical skills. It needs good knowledge of concepts of percentage, ratio, proportion, average, etc. The other main input required is to practice a few problems.

Familiarity with graphical representation of data such as Venn diagrams, graphs, pie charts, histogram, and polygon is helpful. Once the data is grasped well, questions based on tables and graphs take little time.

Sometimes, data is presented in more than one table or graph. The aim is to test not only the quantitative skills but also relative, comparative, and analytical abilities.

Tables

A table is a systematic arrangement of data into vertical columns and horizontal rows. The process of arranging data into rows and columns is called tabulation.

PURPOSE

The purpose of tabulation is to present the data in such a way that it becomes more meaningful and can be easily understood by a common man. However, in case of voluminous data, it may require closer reading than graphs of charts and hence is difficult and time consuming to interpret.

ESSENTIAL PARTS OF A TABLE

A statistical table is divided into following eight parts:

1. *Title of the table:* A title is a heading at the top of the table describing its contents. It mainly reflects upon the nature of the data, where the data is, what time period the data covers, and how the data is classified.
2. *Caption:* The headings for various columns and rows are called column captions and row captions, respectively.
3. *Box head:* The portion of the table containing column caption is called box head.

4. *Stub:* The portion of the table containing row caption is called stub.
5. *Body of the table:* The body of the table contains the statistical data that has to be presented in different rows and columns.
6. *Prefatory notes or head notes:* Prefatory notes appear between the title and the body of the table and are enclosed in brackets. They may throw some light on units of measurements.
7. *Footnote:* A footnote is always given at the bottom of the table but above the source note. A footnote is a statement about something which is not clear from headings, title, stubs, captions, and so on.
8. *Source note:* A source note is placed immediately below the table but after the footnote. It refers to the source from where information has been taken.

The Title

PREFATORY NOTES

----Box head----	
----Row Captions----	**----Column Captions----**
----Stub entries----	----The body----

Footnotes:

Source notes:

Example

	POPULATION (BOX HEAD)					
	State A			**State B**		
Census (Stub)	**Male**	**Female**	**Total**	**Male**	**Female**	**Total**
2001	1,550	1,450	3,000	640	620	1,260
2011	1,900	2,000	3,900	780	750	1,530

Footnote: All areas including Union Territory

Source note: Census report 2001 and 2011

Solved Questions on Tables (Examples 1–10)

***Directions*:** Study the table given below and answer questions 1–5. (The table consists of marks obtained by candidates in different subjects. Numbers in the brackets give the maximum marks in each subject.)

MARKS OBTAINED IN DIFFERENT SUBJECTS BY VARIOUS CANDIDATES

	Subjects (maximum marks)					
Students	**Maths**	**Chemistry**	**Physics**	**Geography**	**History**	**Computer Science**
	(150)	**(130)**	**(120)**	**(100)**	**(100)**	**(100)**
Ayush	90	50	90	60	70	80
Aman	100	80	80	40	80	70
Sajal	90	60	70	70	90	70
Rohit	80	65	80	80	60	60
Muskan	80	65	85	95	50	90
Tanvi	70	75	65	85	40	60
Tarun	65	35	50	77	80	80

1. What is the average of marks obtained by Aman for all subjects?
   (a) 72 (b) 75 (c) 80 (d) 85
   Ans.: (b): Average marks

$$= \left[\frac{100+80+80+40+80+70}{6}\right] = \left[\frac{450}{6}\right] = 75$$

2. What is the approximate percentage of marks obtained by Ayush?
   (a) 62.8 (b) 72.5 (c) 75 (d) 74
   Ans.: (a): Percentage marks

$$= \left[\frac{90+50+90+60+70+80}{150+130+120+100+100+100}\times 100\right]$$

$$= \left[\frac{440}{700} \times 100\right] = 62.8\%$$

3. What is the average of marks obtained by all candidates in Physics?
   (a) 62.85 (b) 74.28
   (c) 78.52 (d) None of the above
   Ans.: (b): Average marks in Physics =
   $$\left[\frac{90+80+70+80+85+65+50}{7}\right] = \left[\frac{520}{7}\right]$$
   $$= 74.28$$
4. Who among the following has obtained the highest aggregate marks?
   (a) Ayush (b) Aman
   (c) Sajal (d) Muskan
   Ans.: (d): Aggregate marks Ayush – 440, Aman – 450, Sajal – 450, and Muskan – 465.
5. Who among the following has secured the highest percentage marks in Physics, Chemistry, and Mathematics?
   (a) Ayush (b) Aman
   (c) Rohit (d) Muskan
   Ans.: (b): As the denominator is same for the calculation of percentage of marks in all the cases, there is no need to calculate the percentage figures. Simply the aggregate marks of three subjects will provide the answer.
   Ayush – 230, Aman – 260, Rohit – 225, and Muskan – 230.

Directions: Study the table given below and answer questions 6–10. (The table consists of number of candidates who appeared and qualified in a competitive examination from different states from 2007 to 2011.)

6. What is the percentage of candidates who qualified during 2007 for all states combined?
   (a) 12% (b) 14%
   (c) 15% (d) None of the above
   Ans.: (b):
   $$= \left[\frac{(780+1{,}170+1{,}200+1{,}320+1{,}350)}{(5{,}200+7{,}800+8{,}000+8{,}800+9{,}000)} \times 100\right]$$
   $$= \left[\frac{4{,}900}{35{,}000} \times 100\right] = 14\%$$
7. What is the average percentage of candidates who qualified from State M for all the years?
   (a) 12% (b) 14% (c) 15% (d) 16%
   Ans.: (c): Percentage of candidates qualified
   $$= \frac{\text{Number of candidates qualified}}{\text{Number of candidates appeared}} \times 100$$
   $$= \left[\frac{(780+\ldots)}{(5{,}200+\ldots)} \times 100\right]$$
   $$= \left[\frac{5{,}820}{38{,}800} \times 100\right] = 15\%$$
   If we look at all the figures for individual years, we can see that the result has been consistent at 15% for all these years.
8. What is the average number of candidates who appeared from State Q during the given years?
   (a) 8,660 (b) 9,260 (c) 9,560 (d) 9,660
   Ans.: (b): Average number of candidates appeared
   $$= \left[\frac{(8{,}100+9{,}000+9{,}200+10{,}000+10{,}000)}{5}\right]$$
   $$= \left[\frac{46{,}300}{5}\right] = 9{,}260$$

Number of Candidates Who Appeared and Qualified in a Competitive Examination

State	2007		2008		2009		2010		2011	
	App.	Qual.	App.	Qual.	App.	Qual.	App.	Qual.	App.	Qual.
M	5,200	780	7,800	1,170	8,000	1,200	8,800	1,320	9,000	1,350
N	7,500	750	8,500	850	8,600	860	9,200	920	8,800	880
P	6,400	960	8,800	1,100	9,000	900	9,200	920	10,000	1,100
Q	8,100	850	9,000	1,350	9,200	1,480	10,000	1,200	10,000	1,280
R	7,800	1,560	7,600	760	9,800	700	10,000	1,250	11,200	1,650

9. What is the average number of candidates who qualified from State N during all these years?
(a) 702 (b) 852 (c) 862 (d) 902

Ans.: (b):

$$\text{Average} = \left[\frac{(750+850+860+920+880)}{5}\right]$$

$$= \left[\frac{4,260}{5}\right] = 852.$$

10. What is the percentage increase in candidates who appeared between 2007 and 2011?
(a) 35% (b) 40% (c) 45% (d) 50%

Ans.: (b): Total number of candidates in 2007 = 35,000 (as calculated in Question 6)
Total number of candidates in 2011
= 9,000 + 8,800 + 10,000 + 10,000 + 11,200
= 49,000
Increase = 49,000 – 35,000 = 14,000
Percentage increase = 14,000/35,000 × 100
= 40%

Graphs

A graph is a pictorial form of representing data. If there is large volume of data, then it is better to use graphs as it shows trends also. The tables may become unwieldy in this case.

A basic graph consists of two parameters—variables and axes. Variables are plotted on a graph with the help of axes. In two-dimensional graphs, there are two axes—'X' and 'Y'. X axis is horizontal and Y axis is vertical. The variable shown along the X axis is independent variable such as time and that shown along the Y axis is dependent.

The common methods of graphical representation are as follows:

1. Simple line graph
2. Circle graph (or pie chart)
3. Bar graph

These have been discussed as given below:

Simple Line Graph

Line graphs are used to show how a quantity changes continuously. If the line moves up, the quantity is increasing; if the line slopes downwards, the quantity is decreasing; if the line is horizontal, the quantity is constant.

Solved Examples on Simple Line Graph (Questions 11–20)

Directions: Study the following graph carefully and answer questions 11–15 given below it. It depicts profits earned by a company during various years. Profit earned in lakhs (Profit = revenue – expenditure).

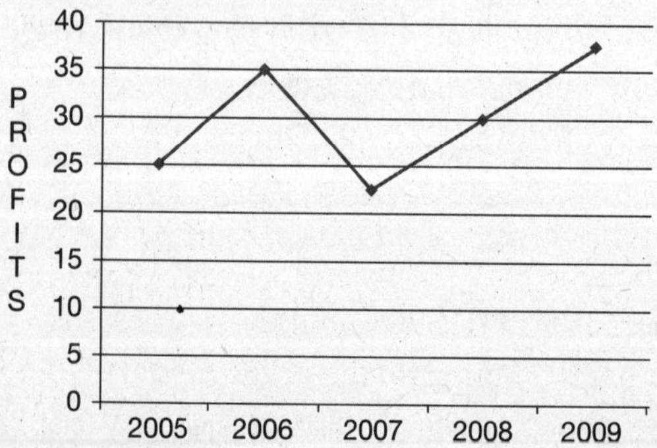

11. What is the average profit earned by the company over the years?
(a) ₹26 lakhs (b) ₹28 lakhs
(c) ₹30 lakhs (d) ₹32 lakhs

Ans.: (c): Total profit earned over 5 years = (25 + 35 + 22.5 + 30 + 37.5) = 150 lakhs
Average profit = 150/5 = ₹30 lakhs

12. If the expenditure of the company in 2009 was ₹28 lakhs, then what was the revenue of the company in that year?
(a) ₹65.5 lakhs
(b) ₹72.5 lakhs
(c) ₹75 lakhs
(d) None of the above

Ans.: (a): Revenue in 2009 = Profit + Expenditure = ₹65.5 lakhs

13. What is the approximate percent increase in the profit of the company in 2008 in comparison to the previous year?
(a) 28 (b) 30 (c) 36 (d) 40

Ans.: (b): Percentage increase = (30 – 23)/23 × 100 = 30.43 ~ 30%

14. What is the ratio of profit earned by the company in 2005 to the profit earned in 2009?

(a) 1 : 3 (b) 2 : 3 (c) 3 : 5 (d) 1 : 2

Ans.: (b): The required ratio = 25 : 37.5 = 2 : 3

15. If the revenue of the company in 2007 was ₹45 lakhs, then what was the expenditure of the company in that year?

(a) ₹20.5 lakhs (b) ₹22.5 lakhs
(c) ₹24.5 lakhs (d) ₹25.5 lakhs

Ans.: (b): Expenditure in 2007 = 45 – 22.5 = ₹22.5 lakhs

Directions: Study the following graph carefully and answer questions 16–20. The graph consists of data about the number of vehicles manufactured by two companies over the years.

Number of Vehicles Manufactured by Two Companies Over the Years

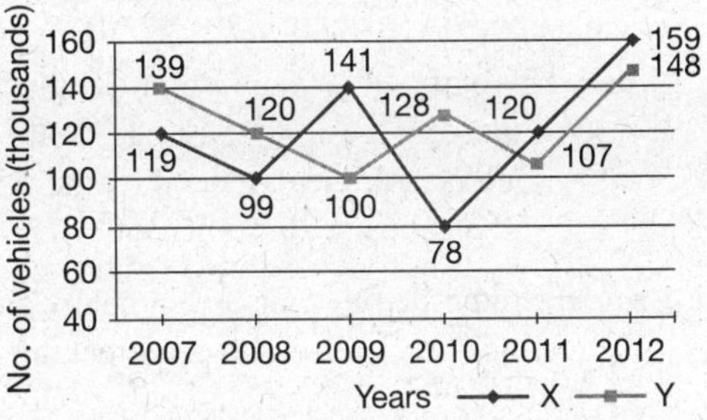

16. What is the difference between the number of vehicles manufactured by Company Y in 2010 and 2011?

(a) 50,000 (b) 42,000
(c) 33,000 (d) 21,000

Ans.: (d): Difference = 1,28,000 – 1,07,000 = 21,000

17. What is the difference between the total production of the two companies in the given years?

(a) 19,000 (b) 22,000
(c) 26,000 (d) 28,000

Ans.: (c): Total production of Company X from 2007 to 2012 (in thousands) = 119 + 99 + 141 + 78 + 12 + 159 = 716. Total production of Company Y from 2007 to 2012 (in thousands) = 139 + 120 + 100 + 128 + 107 + 148 = 742. Difference = (742 – 716) thousands = 26,000.

18. What is the average numbers of vehicles manufactured by Company X over the given period?

(a) 1,19,333 (b) 1,17,166
(c) 1,12,778 (d) 1,11,223

Ans.: (b): Average number of vehicles manufactured by Company X = (119 + 99 + 141 + 78 + 107 + 159)/6 = 1,17.166 (in thousands) = 1,17,166

19. In which of the following years, the difference between the productions of Companies X and Y was the maximum?

(a) 2007 (b) 2008 (c) 2009 (d) 2010

Ans.: (d): The differences between the productions of Companies X and Y in various years are (all figures in thousands):

For 2007 (139 – 119) = 20
For 2008 (120 – 99) = 21
For 2009 (141 – 100) = 41
For 2010 (128 – 78) = 50
For 2011 (120 – 107) = 13
For 2012 (159 – 148) = 11

Hence, maximum difference was in 2010.

20. The production of Company Y in 2010 was approximately what percent of the production of Company X in the same year?

(a) 173 (b) 164 (c) 132 (d) 97

Ans.: (b): As the comparison is with Company X, its production figure will appear as denominator.

Required percentage = (1,28,000/ 78,000) × 100 = 164%

Circle Graphs (or Pie Charts)

Circle graphs are used to show how various sectors are in the whole. Circle graphs are popularly called pie charts. Circle graphs usually give the percent that each sector receives.

In such representation, the total quantity in question is distributed over a total angle of 360°. While using pie chart to find the ratios of various sectors, there is no need to find the amounts each sector received and then the ratio of the amounts. Find the ratio of the percents, which is much easier.

If some percent figure is to be converted into degrees of angles extended at the centre, then multiply it by 3.6. For example, if some category is 20%; in degrees equivalent, it is 72°, that is (20 × 3.6). Conversely, if degree data are to be converted into percent figure, then divide it by 3.6.

Solved Examples on Pie Charts (Questions 21–30)

***Directions*:** Study the pie chart given below and answer questions 21–25. It gives the breakup of expenses of an educational institute.

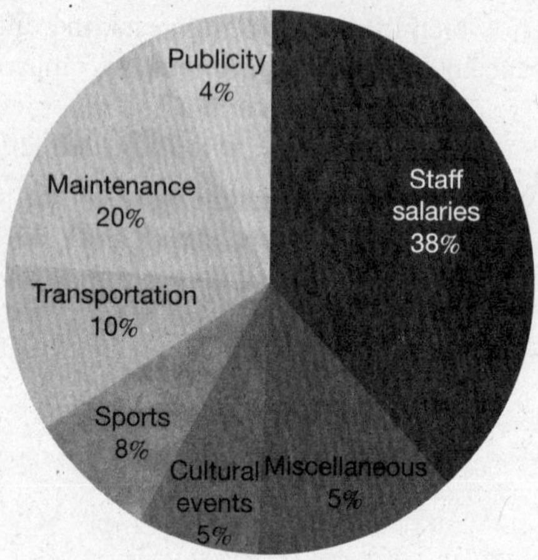

21. If total expenditure during a year is ₹65 lakhs, then what are the expenses on cultural events (in lakhs)?
(a) 1.67 (b) 2.65 (c) 3.25 (d) 4.25
Ans.: (c): 5% of ₹65 lakhs = ₹3.25 lakhs

22. What is the approximate angle extended by staff salaries at the centre (in degrees)?
(a) 132 (b) 137 (c) 142 (d) 145
Ans.: (b): Angle extended by staff salaries at the centre = 38 × 3.6 = 137°

23. The total of which of the following heads is equal to salary expenses?
(a) Miscellaneous, transportation, and cultural events
(b) Maintenance, transportation, and sports
(c) Maintenance, publicity, and miscellaneous.
(d) None of the above
Ans.: (b): maintenance + transportation + sports = 38%.

24. If the teachers' salaries are increased by 20%, then what will be the new angle extended at the centre (in degrees)?
(a) 45.6
(b) 43.6
(c) 56
(d) Cannot be determined
Ans.: (d): No separate data is given for teachers' salary. Hence, it cannot be determined. so new angle extended may not be determined.

25. What is the angle extended at the centre by a combination of miscellaneous and cultural events expenses at the centre (in degrees)?
(a) 65 (b) 72 (c) 78 (d) 84
Ans.: (b):Total of Misc. and Cultural percentages = 15 + 5 = 20%. Hence, angle extended by them at the centre = 20/100 □ 360 = 72°.

***Directions*:** Study the pie chart given below and answer questions 26–30. It gives the breakup of expenses incurred in publishing a book.

Expenditure Incurred in Publishing a Book

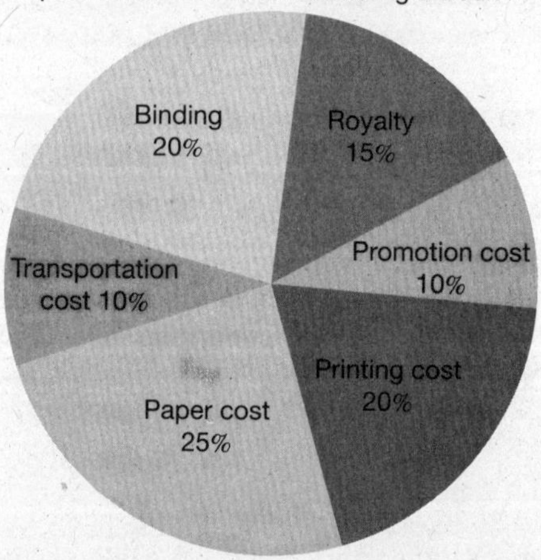

26. If the publisher has to pay ₹61,200 as the printing cost for production of a certain quantity of books, then what will be the amount of royalty to be paid for these books?

(a) ₹22,950 (b) ₹45,000
(c) ₹45,900 (d) ₹48,900

Ans.: (c): The ratio between printing cost and royalty = 20 : 15 or 4 : 3.
Let royalty is denoted by R
Then 4 : 3 = 61,200 : R
R × 4 = 61,200 × 3
R = (61,200 × 3)/4 = ₹45,900

27. If the cost price of the book is ₹150, then what is the combined printing and binding cost for a single copy of the book?
(a) 60 (b) 75
(c) 80 (d) None of the above

Ans.: (a): Total of printing and binding cost = 20 + 20 = 40%
Printing and binding cost = 40% of cost price = 40% of 150 = ₹60

28. What is the central angle of the sector corresponding to the expenditure incurred on royalty?
(a) 48 (b) 54 (c) 60 (d) 72

Ans.: (b): Central angle corresponding to royalty = (15% of 360)° = 15/100 × 360 = 54°

29. What is the difference between promotion and printing cost if we assume that total cost is ₹200
(a) ₹10 (b) ₹20
(c) ₹30 (d) None of the above

Ans.: (b): Difference in percentage terms = 20 – 10 = 10%
10% of ₹200 = ₹20

30. If 1000 copies are published and the transportation cost on them amounts to ₹15,000, then what should be the selling price per book so that the publisher can earn a profit of 20%?
(a) 150 (b) 160 (c) 180 (d) 200

Ans.: (c): To calculate the selling price of a single book, we need to total cost. Let us calculate it first.
Transportation cost per book = 15,000/1,000 = ₹15
As transportation cost is 10% of total cost, thus ₹15 = 10% of total cost
Total cost of printing a copy = 15 × 100/10 = ₹150
Now selling price = total cost + profit
150 + 20% of 150 = 150 + 30 = ₹180

Simple Bar Graphs

Bar charts are one of the easiest, graphically attractive, and hence most commonly used methods of presenting all types of data. Given quantities can be compared by the height or length of a bar graph. A bar graph can either have vertical or horizontal bars.

The width of the bars is largely inessential and is used only for clarity of presentation. We can compare different quantities or the same quantity at different times.

In bar graphs, the data is discrete. Presentation of data in this form makes comparative evaluation easier.

Solved Examples on Simple Bar Graphs (Questions 31–40)

Directions: Study the bar graph given below and answer the questions 31–35. It consists of data on sales of cellular phones during 2007–2012.

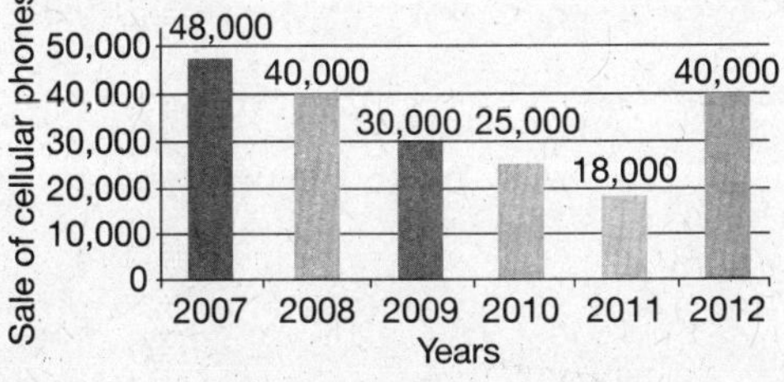

31. The difference in the sales of cellular phones for the years 2007 and 2009 is
(a) 500 units (b) 1,000 units
(c) 5,000 units (d) 18,000 units

Ans.: (d): The difference = 48,000 – 30,000 = 18,000 units

32. The two years between which the rate of change of cellular phones is minimum are
(a) 2007 and 2008
(b) 2009 and 2010
(c) Both option (a) and (b)
(d) 2011 and 2012

Ans.: (c): Percentage changes over years
2007 and 08 = 8,000/48,000 × 100 = 16.66%
2008 and 09 = 10,000/40,000 × 100 = 25%
2009 and 10 = 5,000/30,000 × 100 = 16.66%
2010 and 11 = 7,000/25,000 × 100 = 28%
2011 and 12 = 22,000/18,000 × 100 = 122.22%

33. The sum of sales of cellular phones in the years 2009 and 2011 is equal to that in
(a) 2007 (b) 2008
(c) 2010 (d) 2012

Ans.: (a): Combined sales of 2009 and 2011 = 30,000 + 18,000 = 48,000
It tallies with sales figure of 2007.

34. The percentage increase in sales from 2011 to 2012 was
(a) 115% (b) 128%
(c) 122% (d) 118%

Ans.: (c): It has been calculated in question 32.

35. What is the average sales figure of all the years?
(a) 32,000 units (b) 33,500 units
(c) 34,500 units (d) 35,000 units

Ans.: (b): Average = 2,01,000/6 = 33,500 units

Directions: Study the bar graph given below and answer questions 36–40. It consists of data on number of students passed (in thousands) from two universities over years 2003–08.

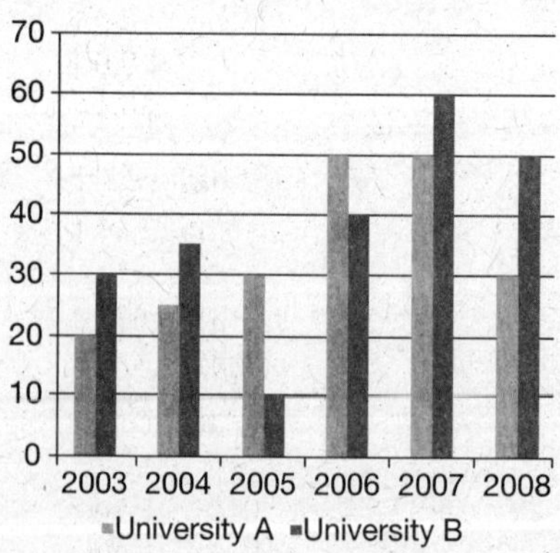

36. What is the sum of students passing from University B in 2003, 2005, and 2006 together?
(a) 75,000 (b) 80,000
(c) 88,000 (d) 90,000

Ans.: (b): Required number of students = (30 + 10 + 40) thousands = 80,000

37. What is the ratio of students passed from University A in year 2007 and number of students passed from University B in year 2004?
(a) 7 : 10 (b) 10 : 7
(c) 4 : 5 (d) 5 : 4

Ans.: (b): Required ratio = 50 : 35 = 10 : 7

38. The number of students from University B in the year 2008 is approximately what percentage of total number of students passed from University A over the years?
(a) 20 (b) 22
(c) 28 (d) 30

Ans.: (b): Required percentage = 50/225 × 100 = 22.22% ~ 22% apprx.

39. What is the ratio between the number of students passed in the years 2007, 2008, and 2005 from University A?
(a) 3 : 5 : 5 (b) 5 : 3 : 3
(c) 5 : 3 : 2 (d) 5 : 2 : 2

Ans.: (b): Required ratio = 50 : 30 : 30 = 5 : 3 : 3

40. What is the difference between the total number of students passed from both the universities together in 2007 and the total number of students passed from both the universities together in the year 2005?
(a) 70,000 (b) 80,000
(c) 85,000 (d) 90,000

Ans.: (a): Total number of students passed in 2007 = 110 (in thousands)
Total number of students passed in 2005 = 40 (in thousands)
Required difference = 110 – 40 = 70 (in thousands)

Practice Questions

Directions: Study the table given below and answer questions 1–5. The table shows the populations of three states over the years 2002–2007.

Population (in Lakhs) of Three States Over the Years

State/ Year	2002	2003	2004	2005	2006	2007
A	4.5	4.8	5.2	5.4	5.8	6.2
B	3.2	3.6	3.4	3.8	4.1	4.4
C	5.6	5.5	5.8	6.3	6.6	6.9

1. What is the average population of State B for all the years together (in lakhs)?
   (a) 3.5 (b) 3.6 (c) 3.75 (d) 3.8
2. What is the percentage increase in population of State A between 2002 and 2003?
   (a) 5 (b) 5.25 (c) 6.67 (d) 7.5
3. What was the difference between combined populations of all the three states for the years 2004 and 2005?
   (a) 90,000
   (b) 1,00,000
   (c) 1,10,000
   (d) None of the above
4. What was the average population of all the three states in 2006?
   (a) 5.5 (b) 5.8 (c) 6.1 (d) 6.3
5. What is the ratio between combined populations of all the three states in 2004 and 2005?
   (a) 155 : 144 (b) 144 : 155
   (c) 144 : 165 (d) 165 : 144

Directions: Study the following table carefully and answer questions 6–10. It consists of data on the number of candidates who appeared from five schools in the board exams over 2004–2008.

	Schools				
Year	**A**	**B**	**C**	**D**	**E**
2004	650	760	820	800	780
2005	700	740	860	780	740
2006	800	820	940	750	730
2007	750	880	920	840	790
2008	850	840	900	860	770

6. The number of students who appeared from School E in 2004 is approximately what percent of total number of students who appeared from all the schools together in that year?
   (a) 16% (b) 18%
   (c) 20% (d) 25%
7. What is the average number of students who appeared from School B for all the years?
   (a) 676 (b) 787 c) 808 (d) 818
8. The number of students who appeared in 2006 from School A is what percent of the total number of students who appeared from School A for all the years together?
   (a) 25.25 (b) 21.33
   (c) 22.45 (d) 23.45
9. What is the ratio between the total numbers of students who appeared in 2004 and 2005 from Schools C and D, respectively?
   (a) 84 : 79 (b) 79 : 84
   (c) 84 : 89 (d) 89 : 84
10. What is the average number of students who appeared from the given schools in 2007?
    (a) 825 (b) 836 (c) 845 (d) 863

Directions: Study the following table carefully and answer questions 11–15. It consists of data on the graduates and postgraduates living in various towns.

Towns	Graduates	Postgraduates
A	10,200	8,000
B	25,250	18,000
C	15,150	10,500
D	20,200	16,250
E	24,000	20,000
F	16,500	18,450

11. What is the difference between the number of graduates and the number of postgraduates in town C?
    (a) 4,500 (b) 4,600
    (c) 4,650 (d) 4,560
12. What is the average number of postgraduates in all the towns together?
    (a) 15,000 (b) 15,500
    (c) 16,250 (d) 15,200

13. What is the ratio of the number of graduates from towns A and B together to the number of postgraduates from towns A and E together?
(a) 709 : 580
(b) 709 : 560
(c) 560 : 709
(d) None of the above

14. What is the total number of graduates and postgraduates in towns A, D, and F together?
(a) 85,500 (b) 88,600
(c) 89,600 (d) 90,600

15. The number of graduates in town F is approximately what percent of the number of postgraduates in the same town?
(a) 84 (b) 89 (c) 92 (d) 95

Directions: Study the following bar graph carefully and answer questions 16–20. It consists of data on exports and imports of IT and electronics industry over a period.

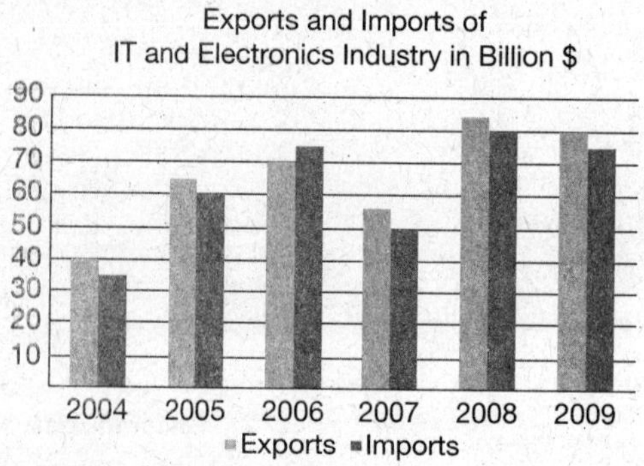

16. For how many years, the exports are at least 10% higher than the imports?
(a) 1 (b) 2 (c) 3 (d) 4

17. In which year, the exports have shown the highest growth in percentage terms in comparison to preceding year?
(a) 2005 (b) 2006 (c) 2007 (d) 2008

18. What are the average exports (in billion $) for the period 2004–2009?
(a) 60.35 (b) 65.83 (c) 70.20 (d) 75.36

19. By how much percentage, total exports are higher than total imports over 2004–2009?
(a) 4.15 (b) 5.33 (c) 6.33 (d) 7.58

20. What is the percentage increase in imports between the years 2004 and 2009?
(a) 110 (b) 114 (c) 125 (d) 135

Directions: Study the following bar graph carefully and answer questions 21–25. It consists of data on student enrolment in different states.

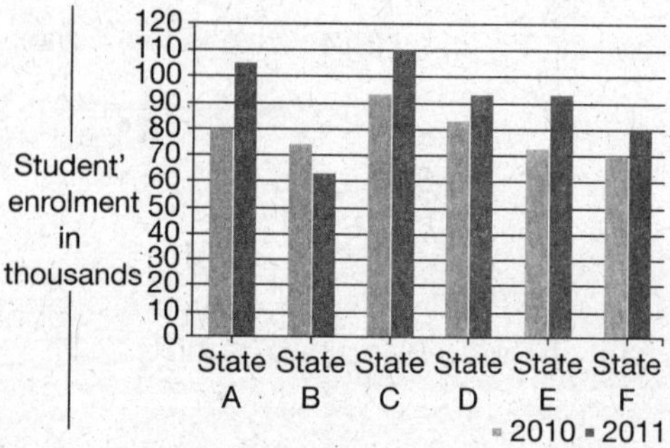

21. What is the ratio of the total enrolment of State B for years 2010 and 2011 to the total enrolment of State D for both the years combined?
(a) 7 : 9 (b) 4 : 5
(c) 3 : 5 (d) 2 : 3

22. What is the percentage of total enrolment of State C in comparison to enrolment of State E for years 2010 and 2011?
(a) 73 (b) 126
(c) 137 (d) 145

23. By what percent the enrolment in the year 2011 is higher than that of 2010 for all the states combined?
(a) 12 (b) 15
(c) 18 (d) 20

24. Which of the following states has shown the highest increase in student enrolment from years 2010 to 2011?
(a) A (b) C (c) E (d) F

25. What is the average enrolment for all the states for the year 2010?
(a) 80 (b) 85
(c) 90 (d) 95

Directions: The bar graph given below shows the percentage distribution of the total expenditures of a company under various expense heads during 2003. Study it and answer questions 26–30.

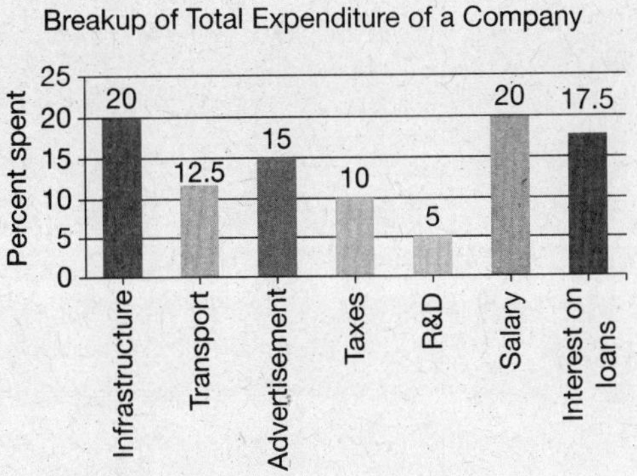

26. The total amount of expenditure of the company is how many times the expenditure on research and development?
(a) 27 (b) 20
(c) 18 (d) 8

27. If the expenditure on advertisement is 2.10 cr, then the difference between the expenditure on transport and taxes is?
(a) ₹1.25 cr
(b) ₹95 lakhs
(c) ₹65 lakhs
(d) ₹35 lakhs

28. What is the ratio of the total expenditure on infrastructure and transport to the total expenditure on taxes and interest on loans?
(a) 5 : 4 (b) 8 : 7
(c) 9 : 7 (d) 13 : 11

29. If the interest on loans amounted to ₹2.45 cr, then the total amount of expenditure on advertisement, taxes, and research and development is?
(a) ₹7 cr (b) ₹5.4 cr
(c) ₹4.2 cr (d) ₹3 cr

30. The expenditure on the interest on loans is by what percent more than the expenditure on transport?
(a) 5% (b) 10%
(c) 20% (d) 40%

Directions: Study the following pie chart carefully and answer questions 31–35. It consists of data about subscription from different sources for Bharat Bonds issued by Government of India.

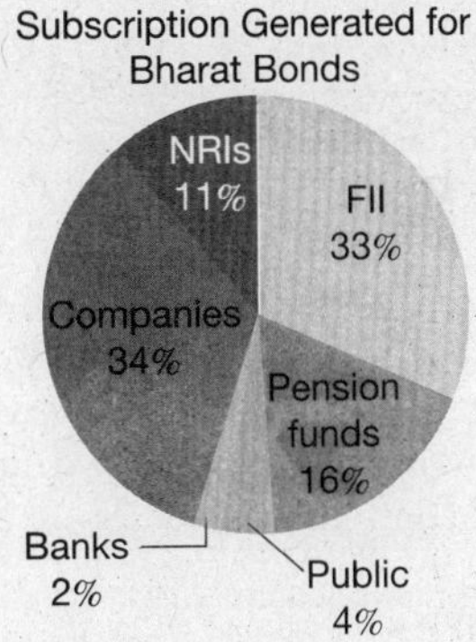

31. If the investments by NRIs is ₹8,000 cr, then the combined investment of companies and FIIs into Bharat Bonds is
(a) ₹48,726 cr
(b) ₹48,000 cr
(c) ₹50,827 cr
(d) Insufficient information

32. If the total investment is 55,000 cr, then the combined investment by pension funds and public is
(a) ₹10,000 cr (b) ₹10,200 cr
(c) ₹10,500 cr (d) ₹11,000 cr

33. If the funds contributed by FIIs is 33,000 cr, then the funds contributed towards subscription of Bharat Bonds by NRIs is
(a) ₹10,000 cr
(b) ₹11,000 cr
(c) ₹12,000 cr
(d) ₹12,500 cr

34. If total subscription is ₹55,000, then the difference between funds invested by banks and public is
(a) ₹550 cr (b) ₹1,100 cr
(c) ₹1,050 cr (d) ₹1,650 cr

35. If the difference between funds contributed by public and banks on one hand and pension funds on the other is ₹5,000 cr, then the total funds subscribed for Bharat Bonds are
(a) ₹25,000 cr
(b) ₹50,000 cr
(c) ₹55,000 cr
(d) ₹1,10,000 cr

Directions: Study the following pie chart carefully and answer questions 36–40. It consists of data on tourist arrival from different countries.

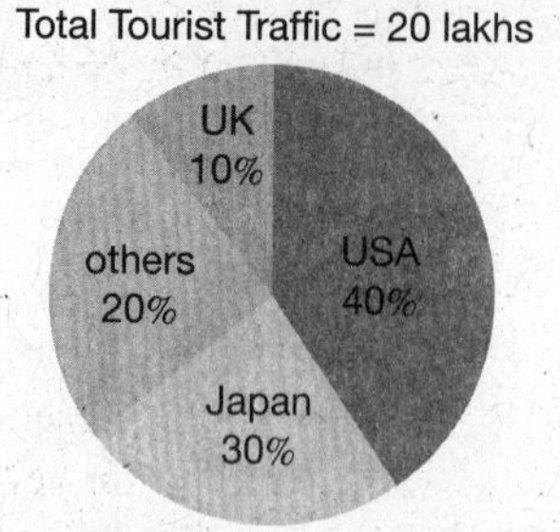

36. The difference between tourist numbers from USA and Japan is
    (a) 2 lakhs (b) 3 lakhs
    (c) 4 lakhs (d) 5 lakhs
37. The angle extended at the centre by sector of tourists from USA is
    (a) 108° (b) 118°
    (c) 144° (d) 165°
38. If the number of tourists from UK doubles up while the total remains the same, then the new angle extended by tourists from UK will be
    (a) 60° (b) 72° (c) 90° (d) 120°
39. If the total number of tourists doubles up while the absolute number of tourists from 'others' remains the same, then the new angle extended by 'others' at the centre will be
    (a) 36°
    (b) 72°
    (c) 108°
    (d) None of the above
40. If the tourist traffic from USA shows a growth of 50% while the total number of tourists remains the same, then the new percentage from USA is
    (a) 40%
    (b) 45%
    (c) 50%
    (d) None of the above

Directions: Study the following table carefully and answer questions 41–45. It consists of breakup of expenses of a company over different years.

Year	Items of Expenditure ₹ (in lakhs)				
	Salary	Fuel and Transport	Bonus	Interest on Loans	Taxes
1998	288	98	3.00	23.4	83
1999	342	112	2.52	32.5	108
2000	324	101	3.84	41.6	74
2001	336	133	3.68	36.4	88
2002	420	142	3.96	49.4	98

41. What is the average amount of interest per year which the company had to pay during this period?
    (a) ₹32.43 lakhs (b) ₹33.72 lakhs
    (c) ₹34.18 lakhs (d) ₹36.66 lakhs
42. The total amount of bonus paid by the company during the given period is approximately what percent of the total amount of salary paid during this period?
    (a) 0.1% (b) 0.5% (c) 1% (d) 1.25%
43. Total expenditure on all these items in 1998 was approximately what percent of the total expenditure in 2002?
    (a) 62% (b) 66% (c) 69% (d) 71%
44. The total expenditure of the company over these items during year 2000 is
    (a) ₹544.44 lakhs (b) ₹501.11 lakhs
    (c) ₹446.46 lakhs (d) ₹478.87 lakhs
45. The ratio between the total expenditure on taxes for all the years and the total expenditure on fuel and transport for all the years, respectively, is approximately
    (a) 4 : 7 (b) 10 : 13
    (c) 15 : 18 (d) 5 : 8

Directions: Study the following bar graph carefully and answer questions 46–50. It consists of data on students' enrolment in different vocational courses in A, B, C, D, and E institutes.

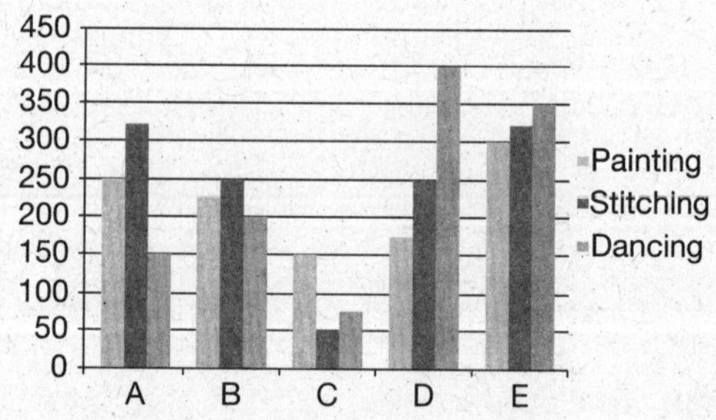

46. What is the respective ratio of the total number of girls enrolled in painting in Institutes A and C together to those enrolled in stitching in Institutes D and E together?
(a) 14 : 23 (b) 16 : 23
(c) 18 : 23 (d) 8 : 12

47. The number of girls enrolled in stitching in Institute B forms approximately what percent of the total number of girls enrolled in stitching in all the institutes put together?
(a) 19 (b) 21
(c) 23 (d) 25

48. What is the respective ratio of the total number of girls enrolled in painting and stitching from all the institutes put together?
(a) 11 : 12 (b) 12 : 11
(c) 11 : 14 (d) 12 : 17

49. The number of girls enrolled in dancing in Institute A forms what percent of the total number of girls enrolled in all the vocational courses together in that institute?
(a) 20.7 (b) 25.5
(c) 28.2 (d) 29.5

50. What is the total number of girls enrolled in painting from all the institutes together?
(a) 1050 (b) 1100
(c) 1150 (d) 1200

Directions: Study the following line graph carefully and answer questions 51–55. It consists of profit data of a company for 2003 and 2004.

Profit (₹ in crores) Earned by Companies During 2003 and 2004 (Profit = income – expenditure)

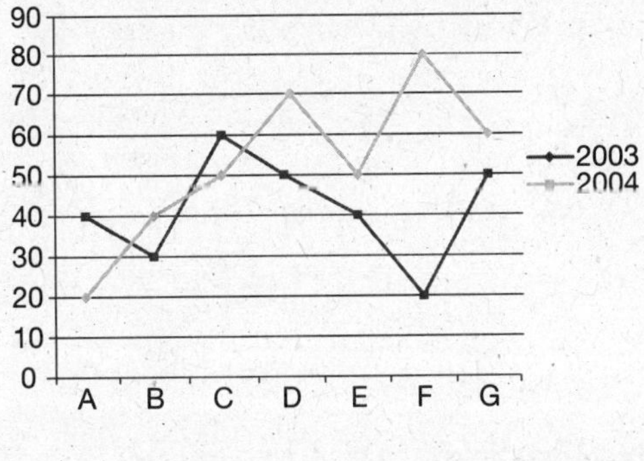

51. What is the ratio between the profits earned by Company A in 2004 and Company B in 2003?
(a) 4 : 3 (b) 3 : 2
(c) 3 : 4 (d) 1 : 1

52. What is the difference between the total profit earned by Companies E, F, and G together in 2003 and 2004 (₹in crores)?
(a) 70 (b) 72
(c) 78 (d) 80

53. What is the ratio between the profit earned by Company C in 2003 and 2004 together and the profit earned by Company E in the same two years mentioned above?
(a) 11 : 9
(b) 10 : 11
(c) 9 : 11
(d) None of the above

54. What is the approximate average profit earned by all the companies in year 2003 (₹in crores)?
(a) 53 (b) 58
(c) 62 (d) 68

55. The profit earned by Company B in 2004 is what percent of profit earned by the same company in 2003?
(a) 60 (b) 75
(c) 125 (d) 133.33

Directions: Study the following pie charts carefully and answer questions 56–60. It consists of data on admission in graduate and postgraduate courses in different institutions.

Postgraduate Admissions
(Percentage Breakup)

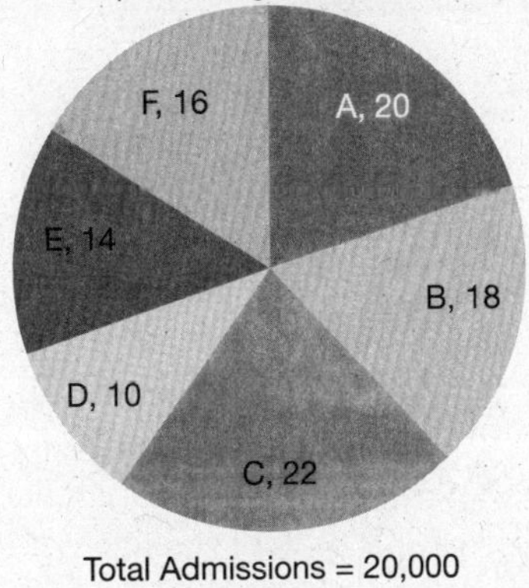

Total Admissions = 20,000

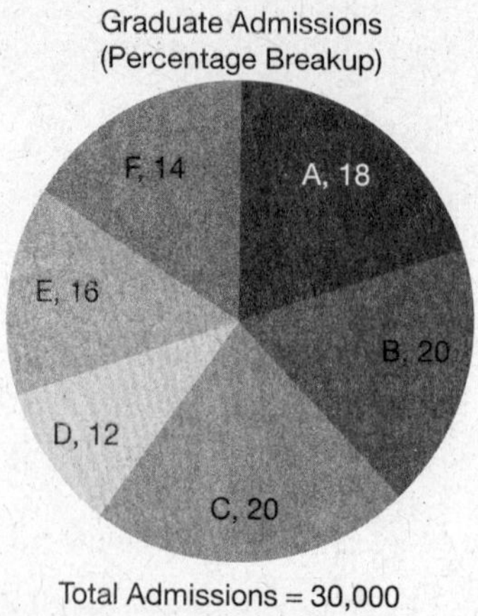

56. What are the total admissions in College B for both graduate and postgraduate courses?
(a) 9,600
(b) 9,800
(c) 10,200
(d) 10,500

57. What is the difference in graduate and postgraduate courses in College A?
(a) 1,400 (b) 1,600
(c) 1,800 (d) 2,000

58. By what percent are admissions in graduate courses higher than postgraduate courses in case of College F?
(a) 31.25 (b) 25.50
(c) 33.33 (d) 35.50

59. What is the difference between the highest admissions in graduate and the highest admissions in postgraduate courses in any combination of the colleges?
(a) 1,200 (b) 1,500
(c) 1,600 (d) 2,000

60. By what percent are postgraduate admissions lower than graduate admissions in case of College D?
(a) 45 (b) 55
(c) 70 (d) 80

Directions: The bar graph given below shows the foreign exchange reserves of a country (in million USD) from 1991–1992 to 1998–1999.

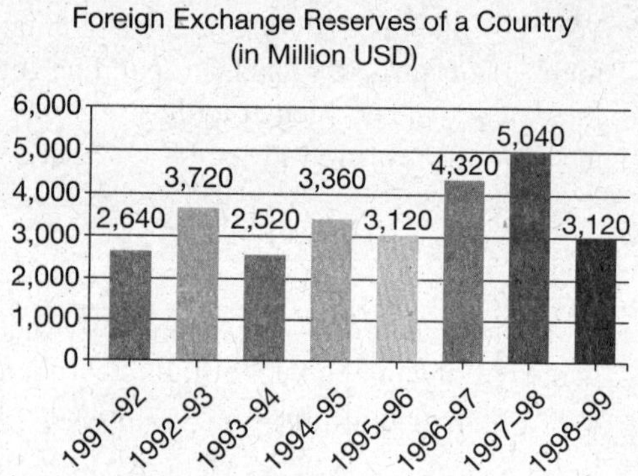

61. The ratio of the number of years, in which the foreign exchange reserves are above the average reserves, to those in which the reserves are below the average reserves is
(a) 2 : 6 (b) 3 : 4
(c) 3 : 5 (d) 4 : 4

62. The foreign exchange reserves in 1997–98 were how many times of that in 1994–95?
(a) 0.7 (b) 1.2
(c) 1.4 (d) 1.5

63. For which year the percent increase in foreign exchange reserves over the previous year is the highest?
(a) 1992–93
(b) 1993–94
(c) 1994–95
(d) 1996–97

64. The foreign exchange reserves in 1996–97 were approximately what percent of the average foreign exchange reserves over the period under review?
(a) 95%
(b) 110%
(c) 115%
(d) 125%

65. What was the percentage increase in the foreign exchange reserves in 1997–98 over 1993–94?
(a) 100 (b) 150
(c) 200 (d) 250

Directions: Study the bar graph given below and answer questions 66–70.

66. Which year witnessed the maximum growth in sales turnover in absolute terms?
(a) 2008 (b) 2009
(c) 2010 (d) 2011

67. Which year witnessed the maximum growth in sales turnover in percentage terms?
(a) 2008 (b) 2009
(c) 2010 (d) 2011

68. What is the average sales turnover during all the years (₹ in crores)?
(a) 17,000
(b) 18,000
(c) 19,000
(d) None of the above

69. What is the approximate percentage growth between 2007 and 2011?
(a) 400 (b) 500
(c) 525 (d) 600

70. How many years witnessed more than average growth?
(a) 1
(b) 2
(c) 3
(d) None of the above

Miscellaneous

71. Census is conducted after every
(a) 5 years (b) 10 years
(c) 11 years (d) 15 years

72. Match List I with List II.

List I (Event)		List II (Year)	
A	Statistical abstract of British India	I	1868
B	Agricultural statistics of British India	II	1886
C	First census	III	1881
D	Central Statistical Organization	IV	1952

Codes:

(a) A-I, B-II, C-III, D-IV
(b) A-I, B-III, C-II, D-IV
(c) A-IV, B-III, C-II, D-I
(d) A-IV, B-II, C-III, D-I

73. National Sample Survey (NSS) came into being to collect information through sample surveys on a variety of socioeconomic aspects in the year
(a) 1950 (b) 1952
(c) 1956 (d) 1962

74. Indian Statistical Institute is located in
(a) New Delhi (b) Kolkata
(c) Mumbai (d) Hyderabad

75. How many divisions are there in Central Statistical Organization?
(a) 2 (b) 3 (c) 4 (d) 5

76. National Statistical Commission was set up in the year
(a) 2000 (b) 2003 (c) 2005 (d) 2008

77. Which of the following methods is best suited to show on map the types of crops grown in a region?
(a) Choropleth (b) Chorochromatic
(c) Choroschematic (d) Isopleth

78. Which of the following sources of data is not based on primary data collection?
(a) Census of India
(b) National Sample Survey
(c) Statistical Abstracts of India
(d) National Family Health Survey

79. Which of the following is not a source of data?
(a) Administrative Records
(b) Population Census

(c) GIS
(d) Sample Survey

80. Which of the following is the oldest archival source of data in India?
(a) National Sample Survey
(b) Agricultural Statistics
(c) Census
(d) Vital Statistics

Answer Keys

1. (c)	10. (b)	19. (b)	28. (d)	37. (c)
2. (c)	11. (c)	20. (b)	29. (c)	38. (b)
3. (c)	12. (d)	21. (a)	30. (a)	39. (a)
4. (a)	13. (b)	22. (c)	31. (a)	40. (c)
5. (b)	14. (c)	23. (b)	32. (d)	41. (d)
6. (c)	15. (b)	24. (a)	33. (b)	42. (c)
7. (c)	16. (b)	25. (a)	34. (b)	43. (c)
8. (b)	17. (a)	26. (b)	35. (b)	44. (a)
9. (a)	18. (b)	27. (d)	36. (a)	45. (b)

46. (b)	51. (d)	56. (a)	61. (c)	66. (d)
47. (b)	52. (d)	57. (a)	62. (d)	67. (d)
48. (a)	53. (a)	58. (a)	63. (a)	68. (c)
49. (a)	54. (a)	59. (c)	64. (d)	69. (b)
50. (b)	55. (b)	60. (d)	65. (a)	70. (b)

Miscellaneous

71. (b)	73. (a)	75. (d)	77. (a)	79. (d)
72. (a)	74. (b)	76. (c)	78. (c)	80. (b)

Solution

1. (c): Required average
$$= \left[\frac{3.2+3.6+3.4+3.8+4.1+4.4}{6}\right]$$
$$= \left[\frac{22.5}{6}\right] = 3.75 \text{ lakhs}$$

2. (c): Required percentage = (4.8 – 4.5)/4.5 × 100 = 0.3/4.5 × 100 = 6.67%

3. (c): Combined population in 2004 = 5.2 + 3.4 + 5.8 = 14.4 lakhs
Combined population in 2005 = 5.4 + 3.8 + 6.3 = 15.5 lakhs
Difference = 15.5 – 14.4 = 1.1 lakhs = 1,10,000

4. (a): Average population in 2006 = (5.8 + 4.1 + 6.6)/3 = 16.5/3 = 5.5 lakhs

5. (b): Total population in 2004 = 5.2 + 3.4 + 5.8 = 14.4 lakhs
Total population in 2005 = 5.4 + 3.8 + 6.3 = 15.5 lakhs
Required ratio = 14.4 : 15.5 = 144 : 155

6. (c): Total candidates appeared in 2004 = 3,810
Percentage of students from School E = 780/3,810 × 100 = 20.47 ~ 20%

7. (c): Required average = (760 + 740 + 820 + 880 + 840)/5 = 4,040/5 = 808

8. (b): Total no. of students appeared from School A during 2004–2008 = (650 + 700 + 800 + 750 + 850) = 3,750
Required percentage = 800/3,750 × 100 = 21.33%

9. (a): Required ratio = (820 + 860) : (800 + 780) = 1,680 : 1,580 = 84 : 79

10. (b): Required average
$$= \left[\frac{(750+880+920+840+790}{5}\right] = \left[\frac{4,180}{5}\right]$$
= 836

11. (c): Number of graduates in C = 15,150
Number of postgraduates in C = 10,500
Difference = 15,150 – 10,500 = 4,650

12. (d): Required average
$$= \left[\frac{(8,000+18,000+10,500 +16,250+20,000+18,450)}{6}\right]$$
$$= \left[\frac{91,200}{6}\right] = 15,200$$

13. (b): Total no. of graduates from A and B = 10,200 + 25,250 = 35,450
Total No. of postgraduates from A and E = 8,000 + 20,000 = 28,000

Required ratio = 35,450 : 28,000 = 709 : 560

14. (c): Total No. of graduates in A, D, and F = 46,900
Total No. of postgraduates in A, D, and F = 42,700
Required total = 46,900 + 42,700 = 89,600

15. (b): Required percentage = 16,500/18,450 × 100 = 89.43 ~ 89%

16. (b): As the comparison is with the imports, imports will appear as denominator.
The formula to calculate the percentage figure for higher exports vis-à-vis imports is
Difference/imports × 100
In 2004, exports = 40 > 35
Required percentage figure = 5/35 × 100 ~ 14%
Similarly, for the year 2005, required percentage = [(65 – 60)/60] × 100 = 8.33%
For 2006, imports > exports, so no calculation is required.
For 2007, 5/50 × 100 = 10%
For 2008, 5/80 × 100 = 6.25%
For 2009, 5/75 × 100 = 6.66%
Thus, for years 2004 and 2007, the exports are at least 10% higher than imports.

17. (a): The required formula = increase/exports in preceding year × 100
In 2005, percentage increase in exports = (65 – 40)/40 × 100 = 25/40 × 100 = 62.5%
In 2006, percentage increase in exports = 5/65 × 100 = 7.69%
In 2007, exports have actually declined over preceding year, so no calculation is required.
In 2008, percentage increase in exports = [(85 – 55)/55] × 100 = 54.54%
In 2009, exports declined in comparison to 2008, again no calculation is required.

18. (b): Average export = (40 + 65 + 70 + 55 + 85 + 80)/6 = 395/5 = 65.83 billion $

19. (b): Total exports = 395 billion $
Total imports = 375 billion $
Difference = 20 billion $
Percentage difference = 20/375 × 100 = 5.33%
As the comparison is with imports, imports will appear as denominator.

20. (b): The imports have increased from 35 in 2004 to 75 in 2009. Hence, %age increase in imports is to be calculated by taking 2004 as base year.
Required %age = [(75 – 35)/35] × 100 = 114.28 ~ 114%

21. (a): The required ratio is
(65 + 75)/(85 + 95) = 140/180 = 7 : 9

22. (c): As the comparison is with State E, it will appear as denominator.
The required ratio = [(95 + 110)/(70 + 80)] × 100 = 136.66% ~ 137%

23. (b): Total enrolments for the year 2010 = 80 + 75 + 95 + 85 + 75 + 70 = 480
Total enrolments for the year 2011 = 105 + 65 + 110 + 95 + 95 + 80 = 550
Percentage difference = [(550 – 480)/480] × 100 = 14.58% ~ 15%

24. (a): For State A, percentage increase = [(105 – 80)/80] × 100 = 31.25%
For State C, percentage increase = [(110 – 95)/95] × 100 = 15.78%
For State E, percentage increase = [(95 – 75)/75] × 100 = 26.66%
For State F, percentage increase = [(80 – 70)/70] × 100 = 14.28%

25. (a): Average enrolments for 2010 = 480/6 = 80

26. (b): Expenditure on R & D is 5% of total expenditure.
It means it is 1/20th of total expenditure.

27. (d): Advt. expenditure is 15% of total expenditure.
Given, 15% of total Expenditure = 2.10 cr
Hence, total expenditure = 2.10 × 100/15 = 14 cr
Transport cost = 12.5% of 14 cr = 1.75 cr
And taxes = 10% of 14 cr = 1.4 cr
So, the difference between transport and taxes = 1.75 – 1.40 = 0.35 cr = 35 lakhs

28. (d): Total of infrastructure and transport:total of taxes and interest on loans
= (20 + 12.5) : (10 + 17.5)

= 32.5 : 27.5
= 13 : 11

29. (c): As interest on loan is 10% of total expenses,
17.5% of total expenditure = ₹2.45 cr
Total expenditure = (2.45 × 100)/17.5 = 14 cr
Advertisement + Taxes + R&D = 15 + 10 + 5 = 30%
30% of ₹14 cr = ₹4.2 cr

30. (a): Difference = 17.5 – 12.5 = 5%

31. (a): Combined investment by companies and FIIs = 67/11 × 8,000 = ₹48,726 cr

32. (d): (16 + 4)/100 × 55,000 = ₹11,000 cr.

33. (b): FIIs contribute 33% and NRIs contribute 11% of total funds.
Hence, funds contributed by NRIs = 11/33 × 33,000 = ₹11,000 cr.

34. (b): Percentage difference = 4 – 2 = 2%
Given that 2% of ₹55,000 cr = (2/100) × 55,000 = ₹1,100 cr

35. (b): Difference in percentage terms = 16 – (2 + 4) = 10%
10% of total funds = ₹5,000 cr
Hence, total funds = 5,000/10% = 5,000 × 100/10 = ₹50,000 cr

36. (a): Difference = 40 – 30 = 10
Now 10% of 20 lakhs = 2 lakhs
Hence, option (a) is the answer.

37. (c): 40/100 × 360 = 144°

38. (b): Old number = (10/100) × 20 = 2 lakhs
New number = 2 × 2 = 4 lakhs
New angle extended at centre = 4/20 × 360 = 72°

39. (a): Old number from 'others' = 20% of 20 lakhs = 4 lakhs
New total of tourists = 20 × 2 = 40 lakhs
So, new angle extended at centre by 'others' = 4/40 × 360 = 36°

40. (c): Old number of tourists from USA = 40% of 20 lakhs = 8 lakhs
Increase of 50% = 50% of 8 lakhs = 4 lakhs
New traffic figure from USA = 8 + 4 = 12 lakhs
New total number from all countries = 20 + 4 = 24 lakhs
Revised percentage of tourist traffic from USA = 12/24 × 100 = 50%

41. (d): Average Interest =

$$= ₹\left[\frac{23.4+32.5+41.6+36.4+49.4}{5}\right]\text{lakhs}$$

$$= ₹\left[\frac{183.3}{5}\right]\text{lakhs} = ₹36.66\text{ lakhs}$$

42. (c): Required percentage

$$= \left[\frac{(3.00+2.52+3.84+3.68+3.96)}{(288+342+324+336+420)}\times 100\right]\%$$

$$= \left[\frac{17}{1710}\times 100\right]\% = 1\%$$

43. (c): Required percentage

$$= \left[\frac{(288+98+3.00+23.4+83)}{(420+142+3.96+49.4+98)}\times 100\right]\%$$

$$= \left[\frac{495.4}{713.36}\times 100\right]\% = 69.45\%$$

44. (a): Total expenditure during 2000
= ₹ (324 + 101 + 3.84 + 41.6 + 74) lakhs
= ₹ 544.44 lakhs

45. (b): Required ratio

$$= \left[\frac{(83+108+74+88+98)}{(98+112+101+133+142)}\right]$$

$$= \left[\frac{451}{586}\right] = \frac{10}{13} = 10:13$$

46. (b): Total no. of girls enrolled in painting in A and C = 250 + 150 = 400
Total number of girls enrolled in stitching in D and E = 250 + 325 = 575
Required ratio = 400 : 575 =16 : 23

47. (b): Total number of girls enrolled in stitching in all institutes = 325 + 250 + 50 + 250 + 325 = 1,200
Number of girls enrolled in stitching in B = 250
Required percentage = 250/1,200 × 100 = 21%

48. (a): Total girls enrolled in painting = 250 + 225 + 150 + 175 + 300 = 1,100
Total enrollment in stitching course stitching = 1,200 (calculated in earlier question)
And in dancing = 150 + 200 + 75 + 400 + 350 = 1,175
Required ratio = 1,100 : 1,200 = 11 : 12

49. (a): Total enrolments of girls in A = 250 + 325 + 150 = 725
No. of girls enrolled in dancing in A = 150
Required percentage = 150/725 × 100 = 20.69 ~ 20.7%

50. (b): Solution is done as in Question 48.

51. (d): Profit earned by Company A in 2004 = ₹40 cr
Profit earned by Company B in 2003 = ₹40 cr
Required ratio = 40 : 40 = 1 : 1

52. (d): Total profits earned by Companies E, F, and G in 2003 = 50 + 80 + 60 = ₹190 cr
Total profit earned by Companies E, F, and G in 2004 = 40 + 20 + 50 = ₹110 cr
Required difference = 190 – 110 = ₹80 cr

53. (a): The profit earned by Company C in 2003 and 2004 = 50 + 60 = ₹110 cr
Profit earned by Company E in 2003 and 2004 = 40 + 50 = ₹90 cr
Required ratio = 110 : 90 = 11 : 9

54. (a): Required average = (20 + 40 + 50 + 70 + 50 + 80 + 60)/7 = 370/7 = 52.86 ~ ₹53 cr

55. (b): Profit earned by Company B in 2004 = ₹30 cr
Profit earned by Company B in 2003 = ₹40 cr
Required ratio = 30/40 × 100 = 75%.

56. (a): Postgraduate admissions in College B = 18% of 20,000 = 3,600
Graduate admissions in College B = 20% of 30,000 = 6,000
Total admissions = 3,600 + 6,000 = 9,600

57. (a): Admissions in postgraduate courses in College A = 20% of 20,000 = 4,000
Admissions in graduate course = 18% of 30,000 = 5,400
Required difference = 5,400 – 4,000 = 1,400

58. (a): Admissions in postgraduate courses in College F = 16% of 20,000 = 3,200
Admissions in graduate courses in College F = 14% of 30,000 = 4,200
Difference = 4,200 – 3,200 = 1,000
Percentage difference = 1,000/3,200 × 100 = 31.25%

59. (c): The highest admissions were in College C for graduate as well postgraduate college.
Admission in postgraduate courses in College C = 22% of 20,000 = 4,400
Admission in graduate courses in College C = 20% of 30,000 = 6,000
Difference = 6,000 – 4,400 = 1,600

60. (d): Admission in postgraduate courses in College D = 10% of 20,000 = 2,000
Admission in graduate courses in College C = 12% of 30,000 = 3,600
Difference = 3,600 – 2,000 = 1,600
As the comparison is with admissions in graduate courses, 3,600 will be taken as denominator.
Percentage difference = 1,600/3,600 × 100 = 44.5% ~ 45%

61. (c): Average Foreign Exchange Reserves (FER) over the given period = 3,480 mn USD.
The country had reserves above 3,480 mn USD during the years 1992–93, 96–97, and 97–98, that is for 3 years and below 3,480 mn USD during the years 1991–92, 93–94, 94–95, 95–56, and 98–99, that is for 5 years. Hence, required ratio = 3 : 5.

62. (d): Required ratio = 5,040/3,360 = 1.5

63. (a): There is an increase in foreign exchange reserves during the years 1992–93, 94 95, 96–97, and 97–98 as compared to previous year (as shown by bar graph).
The percentage increases in reserves during these years compared to previous years are:
For 1992–93,

$$=\left[\frac{(3,720-2,640)}{2,640}\times 100\right]\% = 40.91\%$$

For 1994–95,

$$= \left[\frac{(3,360 - 2,520)}{2,520} \times 100\right]\% = 33.33\%$$

For 1996–97,

$$= \left[\frac{(4,320 - 3,120)}{3,120} \times 100\right]\% = 38.46\%$$

For 1997–98,

$$= \left[\frac{(5,040 - 4,320)}{4,320} \times 100\right]\% = 16.67\%$$

Clearly, the percentage increase over previous years is highest for 1992–93.

64. (d): Average FER over the given period
= (2,640 + 3,720 + 2,520 + 3,360 + 3,120 + 4,320 + 5,040 + 3,120)/8
= 3,480 mn USD
FER in 1996–1997 = 4,320 mn USD
According to question, let's assume
FER for 1996–1997 = x% of average FER
Thus, 4,320 = x% of 3,480
x% = 4,320/3,480 × 100 = 124.1% ~ 125%

65. (a): As the FER doubled from 2,520 in 1993–1994 to 5,040 in 1997–1998, there is an increase of 100%.
Alternatively, it can be calculated very easily.
Increase = 5,040 – 2,520 = 2,520
Increase percentage = (2,520/2,520) × 100 = 100%

66. (d): Growth in 2008 = 10,500 – 6,300 = 4,200 cr
Growth in 2009 = 15,000 – 10,500 = 4,500 cr
Growth in 2010 = 25,300 – 15,000 = 10,300 cr
Growth in 2011 = 37,900 – 25,300 = 12,600 cr

67. (d): % age growth in 2008 = (4,200/6,300) × 100 = 66.66%
%age growth in 2009 = (4,500/10,500) × 100 ~ 43%
% age growth in 2010 = (10,300/15,000) × 100 ~ 69%
% age growth in 2011 = (12,600/25,300) × 100 ~ 50%

68. (c): Total turnover = 6,300 + 10,500 + 15,000 + 25,300 + 37,900 = 95,000 cr
Average = 95,000/5 = 19,000 cr

69. (b): Increase between 2007 and 2011 = 37,900 – 6,300 = 31,600 cr
Percentage growth = 31,600/6,300 × 100 = 500%

70. (b): Years 2010 and 2011 witnessed higher than average sales turnover figures.

8

INFORMATION AND COMMUNICATION TECHNOLOGY

INTRODUCTION

The education sector is facing many challenges because of two main factors in India. The first factor is a continuous increase in population. The population is increasing by geometric progression and every year, more and more students are seeking admissions in educational institutions to educate themselves; hence, more institutes are required. Then, there is an additional challenge to appoint more trained teachers. All these require more financial resources. The second dimension is knowledge explosion. In almost every subject, the knowledge is accumulative. This actually turns out to be a challenge for teachers as more knowledge is to be imparted within the available time, though the curriculum may remain unchanged.

Today, from the time we wake up the morning to the time we sleep, we are surrounded by media, such as newspapers, radio, television (TV), and computers. Sometimes, we are not even aware that we are surrounded by these media. Knowing and using information and communication technology (ICT) tools is important in today's fast changing society; however, we are very often confused about what these media are.

The optimum use of ICTs in India's higher education system can propel the country to become a knowledge superpower. The innovative use of information technology (IT) in higher education addresses the three fundamental challenges that are access, equity, and quality.

MEANING OF INFORMATION AND COMMUNICATION TECHNOLOGIES

According to United Nations Development Programme (UNDP) definition, ICTs are basically information-handling tools—a varied set of goods, applications, and services that are used to produce, store, process, distribute, and exchange information.

ICT includes both old and new tools. Old ICT tools mainly include radio, TV, and telephone. New ICT tools mainly include computers, satellite, wireless technology, and the Internet. These different tools are now able to work together and combine to form our networked world—a massive infrastructure of interconnected telephone services, standardized computing hardware, the Internet, radio, and TV, which reaches into every corner of the globe.

ICTs not only refer to the latest computer and the Internet-based technologies but also refer simple audio–visual aids such as transparencies, slides, cassette and video recorders, radio, television, and film.

These older and more familiar technologies are referred under the collective heading of analogue media, while the newer computer and the Internet-based technologies are called the digital media. The differentiation between the old ICT and new ICT is subjective to some extent.

ICT AND EDUCATION

Liberalization, privatization, and globalization (LPG) coupled with the advancement in IT, have opened up a new demand for skilled manpower, especially in the services sector. In this kind of scenario, education has been identified as one of the 12 main services under General Agreement on Trade in Services (GATS), which needs to be opened up for free flow of trade between countries. Knowledge is expected to become a tradable commodity; and it will be essential that Indian educators keep pace with the change, or else perish in the face of competition from multinational forces in all fields of education and learning, including adult learning.

According to Cross and Adam, the four basic rationales behind introducing ICT in education are as follows:

Table 8.1 Basic Rationales for Introducing IT in Education

Rationale	Basis
Social	Keeping in view the role that technology now plays in society, students need to learn technology.
Vocational	Now, most of the jobs require technological orientation.
Catalytic	To enhance teaching effectiveness with the help of technology.
Pedagogical	To make use of technology in enhancing learning, flexibility, and efficiency in the course of delivery.

The various kinds of ICT products available and having relevance to education, such as teleconferencing, e-mail, audio conferencing, TV lessons, radio broadcasts, interactive radio counselling, interactive voice response system, audiocassettes, and compact disc read-only memory (CD-ROM) have been used in education for different purposes.

The objective must be clear while deciding to use ICTs. There are three ways in which ICT in education is considered in current thinking. There is ICT education, ICT-supported education, and ICT-enabled education.

1. *ICT education:* It refers to the creation of trained manpower to meet the IT needs of knowledge society. The motivation is to train people in order to meet the manpower requirements of IT industry in both software and hardware. The role of ICT in the education policy of a government is to equip students with IT skills.
2. *ICT-supported education:* It is sometimes termed as multimedia education. Nowadays, many distance education universities and institutions use ICT to supplement of printed study materials. Here, ICT mainly includes broadcast media, such as radio and TV programmes, audio and video tapes. Multimedia contents such as lessons are offered on CDs.
3. *ICT-enabled education:* In this case, the whole of the educational programme is purely delivered through ICTs, that is, using them as the basic medium for the teaching–learning process; it requires ICT access.

Target Community of IT in India

As far as India's demographic profile is concerned, almost half of India's population is below 25 years of age, 70% people live in rural areas, literacy rate is around 60%, and people speak 15 major languages. The demand for education outstrips the conventional system's ability to provide it, leaving no alternative for the use of technology in education.

Urban-rural divide (sometimes termed as digital divide) still exists in terms of access, equity, and resources.

In the new educational system, there are likely to be four levels of learners.

1. *First level:* The learners in this category can afford the high cost of education for the sake of its quality.
2. *Second level:* It consists of intelligent and competent students, who are not able to afford the cost of education, so prefer the existing public institutions and would soon be competing with the first level.
3. *Third level:* It consists of the academically and financially poor students, who seek access to education from not so qualitative institutions of higher learning.
4. *Fourth level:* It consists of the illiterate and the poor.

Objectives of Using ICT in Higher Education

The objectives of using ICT are the following:

1. Improving access to the system through online education.
2. Improving the quality of teaching, especially across remote locations.
3. Increasing transparency and strengthening systems, processes, and compliance norms in higher education institutes.
4. Measuring the students' learning participation and effectiveness.
5. Analysing students' behaviour to maximize students' involvement, optimizing retentions, and improving placements.
6. Analysing students' performance, placement, application volume, website analytics, and social media metrics for brand audit.

Strengths and Limitations of ICTs

Strengths of ICT

Some of the strengths of ICTs are as follows:

1. *Individualization of learning:* Individualization of learning means that people learn as individuals and not as a homogenous group. ICTs may offer flexibility to each individual to relate to the medium and its content. The concept of self-paced learning helps in this process.
2. *Interactivity:* Through interactivity feature, the learner can relate to the content more effectively, go forward and backward in the content, and start at any point, depending upon prior knowledge and experience. It is not always necessary that the learner should move in a sequential manner.
3. *Distance and climate insensitive:* Teaching and learning could be taken out of the conventional education system of schools and colleges. Teaching can be individualized, and geo-climatic conditions (a combination of geographical distances and climatic conditions) can be overcome as a result of ICT.
4. *More economical, higher speed of delivery and wider reach:* With increase in number of learners, the unit overhead cost comes down, though the initial investment may be higher. The speed of delivery of contents is instantaneous.
5. *Multiple teaching functions and diverse audiences:* ICTs, especially the computer and the Internet-based can be useful in drills and practices; to help diagnose and solve problems, for accessing information and knowledge about various related themes.
6. *Uniform quality:* If content is well produced and is of good quality, the same quality can be delivered to the rich and the poor, the urban and the rural equally, and at the same low cost. This way of using ICTs can be a great equalizer.

Limitations of ICT

ICTs also have weaknesses which we must understand. Some of the weaknesses depend upon the use of ICTs. These include the following:

1. *High infrastructure and start-up costs:* It costs money to build ICT systems and to maintain them. The cost of hardware and software can be very high.
2. *Little attention towards individual differences in order to achieve economies of scale:* The higher the quantity, the lower will be the cost. To keep the cost low, we make the content common. We do not take into

account the individual differences among students.

It may create a digital divide within the class as students who are more familiar with ICT reap more benefits and learn faster than those who are not familiar with the technological aspects.

3. *Accessibility issue:* Not everyone has equal access; therefore, not everyone benefits equally from the use of ICTs. A 100% reach of radio or a 90% reach of TV does not mean that all the listeners or viewers have access to the medium. Timing of broadcast, electricity supply, socio-cultural factors, poverty, illiteracy, time constraints, mobility, and relevance are the key factors influencing access.
4. *ICT is basically a delivery system:* A medium is different from the content; ICTs are essentially meant only to deliver content, they are not expected to major attitudinal or behavioural changes.
5. *Difficulty in performance evaluation:* Learning from ICTs is usually multidimensional in nature and with long-term perspective. Thus, it may take longer time to assess performance in comparison to classroom assessment which is spontaneous.
6. *Continuous training requirement:* As technologies change, there is a continuous need to train the trainers which may sometimes be resisted by them. Also, since not all teachers are experts with ICT, they may be lax in updating the course content online which can slow down the learning among students. In fact, there is a need to train all stakeholders in ICT.
7. *Call for attitudinal change to understanding of teaching and learning:* These are different media and have a different way of teaching from what we are accustomed to—therefore, they need different ways of understanding what teaching and learning is all about. It may shift attention from the primary goal of the learning process to developing ICT skills, which is the secondary goal. Higher dependence on ICTs affects the bonding process between the teacher and the student as ICTs become a communication tool rather than face-to-face conversation and thus the transactional distance increases.

The potential threat of plagiarism is high as students can copy information rather than learning and developing their own skills.

Synchronous and Asynchronous Media

Based upon their characteristics, media technologies can be grouped into two categories, namely synchronous and asynchronous.

Synchronous media requires all participants to be together at the same time even though they are in different locations. Asynchronous media allows participants in the learning process to be at different times and at different places.

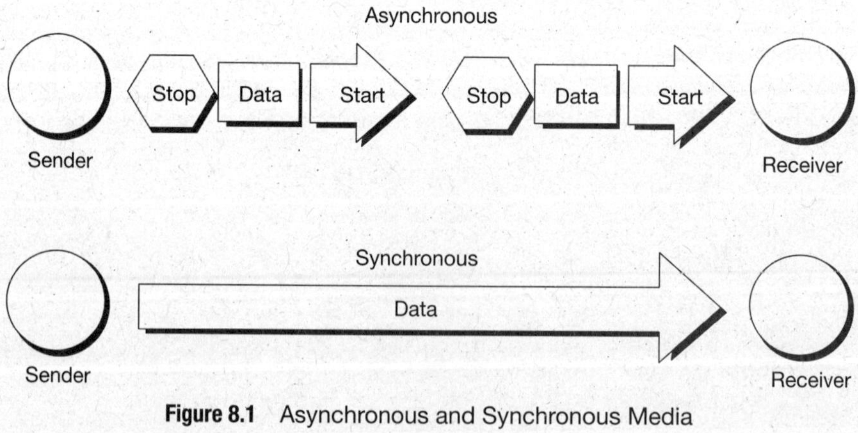

Figure 8.1 Asynchronous and Synchronous Media

Major ICT Learning Categories

In view of ICT, education can be classified into three main categories:

1. E-learning
2. Blended learning
3. Distance learning

In addition, there are face-to-face, self-paced, and online collaborative learning under major ICT learning categories.

E-LEARNING OR ELECTRONIC LEARNING

It is also known as online learning and is commonly associated with the field of advanced learning technology (ALT), which deals with both the technologies and associated methodologies in learning using networked and/or multimedia technologies. Distance education provided the base for e-learning's development. E-learning can be 'on demand'. It overcomes timing, attendance, and travel difficulties. It also allows higher participation and greater interaction.

BLENDED LEARNING

It is a combination of multiple approaches to learning. It is usually used to define a situation where different delivery methods are combined together to deliver a particular course. These methods may include a mixture of face-to-face learning, self-paced learning, and online classrooms.

FACE-TO-FACE LEARNING

It refers to learning that occurs in a traditional classroom setting where a faculty member delivers instructions to a group of learners. This could include lectures, workshops, presentations, tutoring, conferences, and so on.

SELF-PACED LEARNING

It provides the flexibility to learn according to the availability of learners' own time and pace. It occurs in a variety of ways, such as reading-specific chapters from the text book, studying the course material presented through web-based or CD-based courses, attending pre-recorded classes or sessions, reading articles referred by the faculty members, working on assignments and projects, and searching and browsing the Internet.

ONLINE COLLABORATIVE LEARNING

It involves interaction between the learners and the faculty members through the web. This interaction can occur in one of the following modes (i) synchronous interaction and (ii) asynchronous interaction, which have been discussed earlier.

DISTANCE LEARNING

It is a type of education, where students work on their own at home or at office and communicate with the faculty and other students via e-mail, electronic forums, video conferencing, chat rooms, instant messaging, and other forms of computer-based communication. It is also known as open learning. Most distance learning programmes include a computer-based training (CBT) system and communications tools to produce a virtual classroom. As the Internet and World Wide Web (WWW) are accessible from virtually all computer platforms, they are increasingly serving as the foundation for many distance learning systems.

ICTs also allow for the creation of digital resources like digital libraries where the students, teachers, and professionals can access research material and course material from any place at any time. Such facilities allow the networking of academics and researchers; hence sharing of scholarly material leads to quality enhancement in teaching and learning.

Recent ICT Initiatives in Higher Education

1. National Mission on Education through Information and Communication Technology (NMEICT): NMEICT is a centrally sponsored scheme to realize the potential of ICT in teaching/learning process for benefit of all the learners in higher education institutions anytime and anywhere. Content

generation and connectivity along with provision for access devices for institutions and learners are the main objectives. Nearly, 400 universities have been provided 1 Gbps connectivity or have been configured under the scheme and more than 14,000 colleges have also been provided VPN (virtual private network) connectivity.

A-view software has been developed under the NMEICT for teacher training. This could become the basis for successful implementation of the proposed National Mission on Teachers.

Under the N-list program of INFLIBNET (under NMEICT), lakhs of e-books and thousands of high-quality paid e-journals have been made available to colleges and universities with a view to inculcate research culture in teachers and students. The model needs to be scaled up for maximizing coverage and for productive usage of the available resources.

2. National Programme on Technology Enhanced Learning (NPTEL)
3. National Knowledge

Major Initiatives in India for Providing E-content for Different Courses

1. *Lekhika 2007:* It was developed by the Centre for the Development of Advanced Computing (C-DAC) under India's IT Ministry and Israel's FTK Technologies. The objective of this project is to spread computer literacy to the masses in India who do not know English.
2. *National Programme on Technology Enhanced Learning (NPTEL):* It is a joint initiative of the IITs (Indian Institute of Technology and IISc (Indian Institute of Science) to provide e-learning through online web and video courses in engineering, science, and humanities streams, aiming to enhance the quality of engineering education in the country by providing free online courseware.
3. *National Knowledge Network (NKN) and Connected Digital:* An initiative has been undertaken to cover 1000 institutions besides providing digital campuses, video-conference classrooms, wireless hotspots, laptops/desktops to all students of professional/science courses, and Wi-Fi connectivity in hostels.
4. *Centre for Distance Engineering Education Program (CDEEP):* CDEEP is an emulated classroom interaction programme by using real-time interactive satellite technology. This was launched by the Indian Institute of Technology (IIT)-Bombay.
5. *EDUSAT:* The launch of EDUSAT brought satellite connectivity to large parts of rural India. Indira Gandhi National Open University (IGNOU) is leveraging satellite, TV, and the Internet technologies to offer online courses.
6. *IIMs:* IIM-C, IIM-B, IIM-K, XLRI, and other management institutes have started offering courses (in association with private players like Hughes Global Education, Reliance, NIIT, and so on.) after the Distance Education Council (DEC) allowed them to do so in 2007.
7. *Brihaspati:* This open source e-learning platform has been developed by IIT-Kanpur.
8. *Private players:* An increasing number of private players like Hughes Global Education, Manipal Education Group, Centum Learning, UEI Global, Shiv Nadar University, and so on are offering online education courses in association with leading central and state universities having with good ICT infrastructure.
9. *Digitization of books (e-text books):* There is an increased trend towards creation of a digital repository of books to create a digital learning environment for students. The digital version of the books embedded with text, pictures along with video, simulations, and visualizations help the students to learn the concepts in an interactive way. The National Mission on Education, through ICT, plans to generate a new online course content for

UG, PG, and Doctoral education. Efforts are already underway to prepare the course content for 130 courses (UG and PG).

10. *Content delivery using IT/ICT:* Higher education is purely a content-driven play where educational content is delivered through innovative use of ICT. There is an increased trend in higher education institutes to render content through radio, TV, and satellite.

11. *Open education resources:* Many Indian universities are contemplating technology-enabled free access to educational resources. All India Council for Technical Education-Indian National Digital Library in Engineering and Technology (AICTE-INDEST) is a consortium set up by the Ministry of Human Resource to enhance greater access and generate annual savings in access of bibliographic databases. UGC has also launched its Digital Library Consortium to provide access to peer reviewed journals and bibliographic databases covering subjects such as arts, humanities, technology, and sciences.

12. *Virtual Technical University (VTU):* The National Mission on Education through ICT is working hard to establish a VTU to impart training to UG/PG students along with new teachers. It focuses on science, technology, management, and other related areas.

13. *Gyan Darshan:* Launched in 2000, Gyan Darshan is a joint effort of IGNOU and the IITs. It is a bouquet of channels that broadcasts educational programmes for school kids, university students, and adults. Courses are contributed by IGNOU, UGC Consortium for Educational Communication (UGC – CEC), IITs, and so on. CEC is an inter-university centre of UGC.

14. *Gyan Vani:* It is a bouquet of frequency modulation (FM) radio channels which broadcast programs contributed by institutions such as IGNOU and IITs. Under UGC Countrywide Classroom initiative, education programmes are telecast on Gyan Darshan and Doordarshan's National Channel (DD1) every day.

15. *E-Gyankosh:* It is a knowledge repository launched by IGNOU in 2005 which aims at storing and preserving digital learning resources. Almost 95% of IGNOU's printed material has been digitized and uploaded on the repository.

16. *Education and Research Network (ERNET):* It is promoted by the Department of Information Technology, Government of India. It provides communication infrastructure and services to academic research institutions in India. It is undertaking networking projects such as AICTE-Net, Indian Council of Agricultural Research (ICAR)-Net and UGC-Infonet to provide the Internet and intranet facilities.

17. *Sakshat Portal:* Launched in 2006, Sakshat is a one-stop education portal for addressing all the education and learning related needs of students, scholars, teachers, and lifelong learners. It has been developed at IGNOU. The portal, developed by NIC, provides links to vast knowledge resources, educational news, examination alerts, sample papers and other useful links available on the web. It has an in-built repository of educational resources and online testing facility.

18. *GRID GARUDA:* It is India's first national grid bringing together academic, scientific and research communities for developing their data and other applications. It is connected with National Knowledge Network (NKN).

19. *Shruti-Drishti:* It is basically for visually impaired women empowerment (VIWE).

20. *IIT Madras:* It has been assigned the task to develop e-contents for 996 courses. These courses belong to engineering, sciences, technology, humanities, and management.

21. *Consortium for Educational Communication:* It has been tasked with creation of e-content for 87 undergraduate courses (UGC). UGC has cleared a proposal to publish e-content for 77 postgraduate courses (PGC).

Mobility

Now, the mobile phones are rich in the feature that they provide more than just voice calls. Smartphones, iPhones, Kindle, etc., which have the Internet access, allow students and faculty to perform a wide range of assignments. Tasks like administration, sharing class notes, downloading lectures, instant messaging, and so on, are possible wherever cell phone services are available.

Mobile phones can now access computer files from remote locations. With services like Soonr, students who forget to bring an assignment to class can use their cell phone to access the completed work on their home computer and show it to the professor.

Concept of Social Learning

Web 2.0, social networking such as blogs and wikis, YouTube, iTunes, and Big Think are influencing a new trend in higher education. The emergence of smartphones such as the iPhone and other intelligent devices has enhanced mobile learning (referred to as m-learning). These technologies create new channels for content delivery, online video expansion, and podcasting. The adoption of virtual reality websites such as Second Life has provided the higher-education institutions with new venues for virtual class learning.

A combination of Web 2.0 tools such as blogs, wikis, podcasts, mashups, and social networking communities have made traditional learning more social and personalized. To begin with, the initial learning management systems (LMS) like Blackboard, Sakai, Moodle, or Web CT (Course tool) were course-centred and teacher-driven. Off late it is becoming more and more learner-centric.

E-journal Consortia

1. AICTE-INDEST is a consortium set up by the Ministry of Human Resource to enhance greater access and generate annual savings in access of bibliographic databases.
2. UGC has also launched its Digital Library Consortium to provide access to peer reviewed journals and bibliographic databases covering subjects such as arts, humanities, and sciences.

Key Challenges in IT/ICT Adoption in Indian Universities

The key challenges affecting the utilization of IT/ICT in Indian Higher Education fall broadly into the following categories:

1. Lack of desired level of knowledge and technology readiness. Low technology and people's readiness in order to realize the true potential of ICT in higher education with penetration of computers and the Internet, especially in the rural areas being extremely poor.
2. Poor implementation.
3. Linguistic barriers.

PAL, NTSC, and SECAM

There are three video formats used in the world, each one incompatible with the other. These are PAL, NTSC, and SECAM.

1. *Phase Alternating Line (PAL):* PAL is a video signal standard. Its increased bandwidth allows for better picture quality. It is the analogue TV format used in much of western Europe and other major areas such as China, India, Australia, and South America.
2. *National Television System Committee (NTSC):* It is mainly used in the North American countries such as USA and Canada. This was the first coloured TV broadcast system. NTSC is also used in Asia, including Japan.
3. *Sequential Couleur Avec Memoire (SECAM):* It is also known as sequential colour with memory. It is used mainly in France and many other western European countries. SECAM uses the same bandwidth as PAL but transmits the colour information sequentially.

Frequency Modulation

Frequency Modulation (FM) is a form of modulation that conveys information over a carrier wave by varying its frequency (contrast this with amplitude modulation, in which the amplitude of the carrier is varied while its frequency remains constant).

Prasar Bharati

It is a statutory autonomous body established under the Prasar Bharati Act. The Board came into existence in 1997. Prasar Bharati is the public service broadcaster of the country. The objective of public service broadcasting is achieved through All India Radio (AIR) and DD which were earlier working as independent media units under the Ministry of Information and Broadcasting (MoIB).

All India Radio (AIR)

Broadcasting started in India in 1927 with two privately owned transmitters, one at Bombay and the other at Calcutta, which were taken over by the Government in 1930. These operated under the name Indian Broadcasting Service until 1936 when it was given the present name AIR. It came to be known as Akashwani from 1957 onwards.

The AIR network comprises the national channels, regional stations, local radio stations, Vividh Bharati centres, FM stereo services, external services, and north-eastern services.

Doordarshan

The experimental telecast started in Delhi in September 1959 with a small transmitter and a makeshift studio. The regular daily transmission started in 1965. The TV service was extended to a second city, Bombay, only in 1972. Till 1975, only seven cities were covered by the TV.

TV was separated from radio in 1976 and DD came into existence, National programme was introduced in 1982 and from then onwards, there has been a steady progress in DD. Swasth Bharat is the world's biggest health communication initiative launched on DD.

Indian Space Programme

Indian Space Research Organization (ISRO) has established two major space systems. Firstly, it is Indian National Satellite System (INSAT) that is Geo-stationary satellites for communication, TV broadcasting. Secondly it is Indian Remote Sensing Satellites, used for resource monitoring. A transponder is a wireless communication device that picks up and responds to incoming signals. India's first EDUSAT (GSAT-3) was launched in 2004. Ku bandwidth (12-18 Ghz) is mostly used for satellite TV and VSAT systems. Ka-bandwidth (26.5-40 GHz) is used in high-definition satellite TV. D Band has the highest bandwdith and L-Band has the lowest bandwidth. India's first moon mission Chandrayan-I was launched in the year 2003. Meteorological satellites (METSAT-I, II ,etc.) have been named after Kalpana Chawla. (Kalpana-I, Kalpana–II).

Community Radio Stations

In December 2002, the Government of India approved a policy for the grant of licenses for setting up of community radio stations to well-established educational institutions including the IITs and IIMs.

eduroam®

It is a global service that enables students, researchers, and staff from the participating institutions to obtain the internet connectivity across campuses and when visiting other participating institutions, by simply opening their laptop or activating their smartphone or other portable device through Wi-Fi.

The Internet Protocol Television (IPTV)

It is a digital TV (and not PC) that is delivered through high-speed Internet (broadband) connection. In this service, channels are encoded in IP format and delivered to the TV through a set-top box that is required at the customer's location.

IPTV services also include video on demand (similar to watching video CDs/DVDs using a VCD/DVD player).

The quality of digital video and audio is much better compared to the traditional analogue TV. With additional features, it can become interactive as well.

1. *Doordarshan:* Being one of the largest TV networks, it started its services in 1959 in Delhi with the transmission of educational and developmental programmes. The second TV centre was started in 1972. DD is presently operating 31 TV channels besides free direct-to-home (DTH) services. DD National is the largest terrestrial network in the world and also the flagship channel of DD. Satellite transmission of all 31 DD channels is in digital mode. DD's DTH service called DD Direct Plus was started in 2004. DD also started mobile TV service (DVB-H transmission) in Delhi in 2007.
2. *Headend in the Sky (HITS):* It is Comcast's satellite multiplex service that provides cable channels for cable TV operations. At a traditional cable TV headend, multitudes of satellite dishes and antennas are used to grab cable stations from dozens of communication satellites. In contrast, HITS combines cable stations into multiplex signals on just a few satellites; cable TV companies can then pull in hundreds of channels at the local headend with relatively little equipment; the HITS feed effectively replaces the more complex traditional headend operations.

Press and Print Media

Registrar of Newspapers for India (RNI)

The office of RNI came into being in 1956. It is mandatory for all newspapers and magazines to get them registered with RNI. Its head office is in New Delhi.

Press Information Bureau (PIB)

It is the nodal agency of the Government of India to disseminate information to the print and electronic media on government policies, programme initiatives, and achievements. It has its headquarters in New Delhi and has eight regional offices. Activities of PIB can be classified into three categories—Information, Education, and Communication, abbreviated as, I.E.C and mean publicity. Apart from these, feedback, accreditation, etc., are other services dealt by PIB. The National Media Centre is located in New Delhi. PIB also has seven sister websites in seven different languages—Tamil, Malayalam, Kannada, Telugu, Bengali, Marathi, and Mizo.

Public Information Campaigns (PICs)

PICs are held to disseminate information directly to the target beneficiaries on the flagship programmes of the Union Government.

Main News Agencies in India

Questions have been asked earlier about the news agencies in UGC NET Paper I Exam.

Press Trust of India (PTI): PTI was founded in 1947 and started its services in 1949. PTI is a non-profit sharing co-operative owned by the country's newspapers with a mandate to provide efficient and unbiased news to all the subscribers.

United News of India (UNI): UNI was incorporated in 1959 and started its functioning in 1961. It started its first news agency in India, a full-fledged Hindi wire service called Univarta in 1982 and also started the first-ever service in Urdu. UNI distributes world news from Reuters—the world's largest information company.

Press Council of India (PCI): PCI is a quasi-judicial authority mandated by the Parliament to preserve the freedom of press and maintain and improve the standard of newspapers and news agencies in India. PCI Act, 1978, provides for the reconstitution of the council in every three years.

NAM News Network (NNN): NNN is the Internet-based news and photograph-exchange arrangement of news agencies of non-aligned movement countries.

Basic Computer Terms

A computer is a programmable machine. It allows the users to store all sorts of information and then process that information, or data, or carry out actions with the information, such as calculating numbers or organizing words.

A computer can be defined as an electronic device that is capable of (i) accepting, storing, and logically manipulating data or text that is input and (ii) processing and producing output (results or decisions) on the basis of stored programs of instructions. Some computers are also capable of processing graphics, video, and voice input. Most computers include a keyboard for text entry, a central processing unit (CPU), one or more disk drives, a display screen, and a printer—these components are referred to as the hardware.

Types of Computers

The computers are classified according to (i) generation, (ii) functionality, and (iii) size.

According to Generation

Generation refers to the time period during which a computer has been developed. The different generations of computer are as follows:

First Generation (1940–1956)

1. Used vacuum tubes for circuitry and magnetic drums for memory.
2. High electricity consumption.
3. Programming in machine language

Examples: Mark 1, ENIAC

Second Generation (1956–1963)

1. Transistors were used.
2. First operating system and core memory were developed.
4. Programming was in machine language and assembly language.
5. Magnetic tapes and discs were used.
6. Example: early versions of COBOL and FORTRAN, IBM 1401, IBM_1402, PDP-1

Third Generation Features (1964–1971)

1. Integrated circuits developed.
2. Low-power consumption
3. Small-scale integration (SSI) and medium-scale technology (MSI) was used
4. High-level languages (HLL) was used
5. The main examples are PDP-8, ICL 2900, IBM-360, and IBM-370.

Fourth Generation (1971–Present)

1. Large-scale integration (LSI) and very large-scale integration (VLSI) technology used
2. Development of portable computers
3. Use of RAID (Redundant Array of Inexpensive Disks) technology for data storage
4. Used in virtual reality multimedia, and simulation
5. Computers started in use for data communication

Examples: IBM –PC, Apple Macintosh

Fifth Generation (Present and Beyond)

These computers are used in parallel processing, speech recognition, intelligent robots, and artificial intelligence.

According to Function

The computers are of following types according to the function:

There are three different types of computers according to the principles of operation and are as follows:

1. Analogue computers
2. Digital computers
3. Hybrid computers

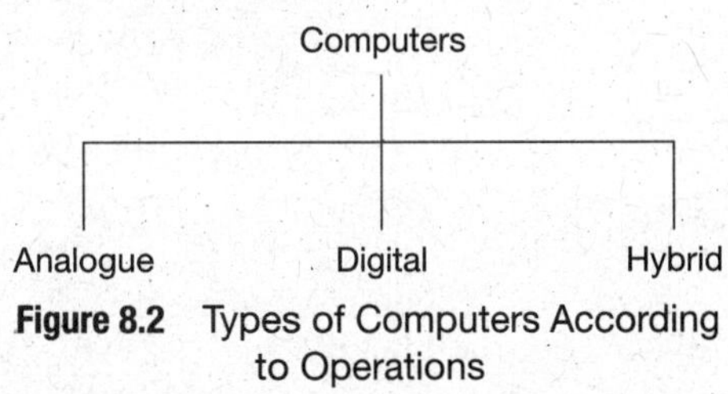

Figure 8.2 Types of Computers According to Operations

Analogue Computers

Analogue computers are that in which data varies continuously, that is, the movement of data is continuous. It is generally meant to measure physical variables such as voltage, pressure, temperature, speed, and so on. It is mainly used for communication and broadcast transmission.

Digital Computers

Digital computers are those computers in which data flow in discrete form. These are high-speed programmable electronic devices that perform mathematical calculations, compare values, and store the results. It uses binary number system in which there are only two digits 0 and 1 (each one called a bit). The digital computer is designed using digital circuits in which there are two levels for an input or output signal. These two levels are known as logic 0 and logic 1. Digital computers give more accurate and faster results.

Digital computer is better suited for solving complex problems in science, engineering, and technology. Hence, they are increasingly used in the field of design, research, and data processing.

Based on the purpose, digital computers can be further classified as follows:

1. General-purpose computers
2. Special-purpose computers

General-purpose computers are used for any type of applications. Most of the computers are general-purpose computers. Special-purpose computer is one that is built for a specific application.

Hybrid Computers

A hybrid computer combines the desirable features of analogue and digital computers. They combine the speed of analogue computers and accuracy of digital computers. Now, analogue-to-digital and digital-to-analogue converters are used for transforming data into suitable form for either type of computation.

For example, in a hospital's intensive care unit (ICU), analogue devices might measure a patient's temperature and blood pressure. These analogue measurements may then be converted into numbers and supplied to digital components in the system for better monitoring. Hybrid computers are mainly used for specialized tasks.

According to Size and Configuration

There are four different types of computers when classified based on their size and configuration:

1. Super computers
2. Mainframe computers
3. Mini computers
4. Microcomputers

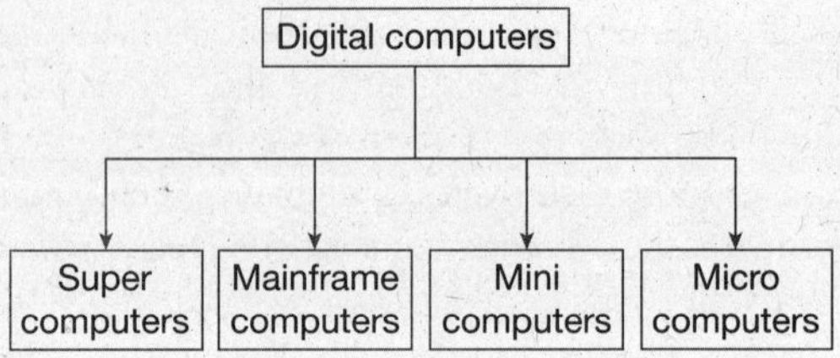

Figure 8.3 Types of Computers According to Size and Configuration

Super Computers

They are mostly used for applications that require intensive numerical computations such as stock analysis, weather forecasting, nuclear energy research, electronic design, and for analysing geological data. They can process billions of instructions per second. The best known super computer manufacturer is Cray Research. Some of the companies which produce super computers are Cray, IBM, HP, and so on. PARAM is India's first super computer. Tata's EKA is also an example of super computer.

Mainframe Computers

Mainframe computers can also process data at very high speed (million instructions per second — MIPS). Mainframe computers are large-sized, powerful, multi-user computers that can support concurrent programs. They can accommodate more than 1,000 workstations simultaneously. Normally, they are used in banking, airlines, railways, and so on for their applications.

The technique that allows many people at the terminals to access the same computer concurrently is called time sharing.

Mini Computers

Mini computers have lesser speed and storage capacity in comparison to mainframe computers. Hence, their performance also is less than that of mainframes. They are mid-sized multi-processing computers. They can perform several actions at the same time and can support 4 to 200 users simultaneously. Some of the features of mainframes are not available in minicomputers.

In recent years, the distinction between minicomputers and small mainframes has blurred. Often the distinction depends upon how the manufacturer wants to market his machines.

Workstations

Workstations are powerful, single-user computers. They have the capacity to store and process large quantities of data, but they can only be used by one person at a time. They are typically linked together to form a computer network called a local area network (LAN), which means that several people, such as staff in an office, can communicate with each other and share electronic files and data. In terms of computing power, workstations lie in between personal computers and mini computers. Workstations commonly support applications that require relatively high-quality graphics capabilities and a lot of memory, such as desktop publishing, software development, and engineering applications.

A workstation is similar to a personal computer but is more powerful and often comes with a higher-quality monitor.

Microcomputers

A microcomputer is also called a personal computer (PC). It is a small and relatively inexpensive computer, commonly consisting of a display screen, a keyboard, a CPU (central processing unit), one or more disk drives, and a printer, with limited storage, based upon a microprocessor. It is designed for an individual user.

The invention of microprocessor (single chip CPU) gave birth to the much cheaper micro-computers. They are further classified into the following:

1. Desktop computers
2. Laptop computers
3. Hand-held computers (PDAs)

Computer Hardware

It is the physical equipment required to create, use, manipulate, and store electronic data. The hardware of a computer system can be classified into CPU and peripherals.

Central Processing Unit: Central processing unit (CPU) is a microprocessor that controls the execution of program instructions {microprocessor is programmable while integrated circuits (ICs) perform predetermined tasks only}. The CPU performs the following functions:

(a) Arithmetic operations
(b) Logical operations
(c) Input/output operations
(d) Data manipulations

Main CPU Components: To carry out the functions as mentioned earlier, CPU has the following components:

(a) *Arithmetic Logic Unit (ALU):* It performs various calculations such as addition, subtraction, division, multiplication, comparison, and so on.

(b) *Control Unit:* It coordinates the operation of hardware, the flow and execution of data, and instructions that are fed into memory or main storage via CPU.

(c) *Memory Unit (main storage):* It holds data instructions, intermediate results, and final results ready for output. The data and instructions are passed from the main store into ALU or to and from storage device under the control of control unit (CU).

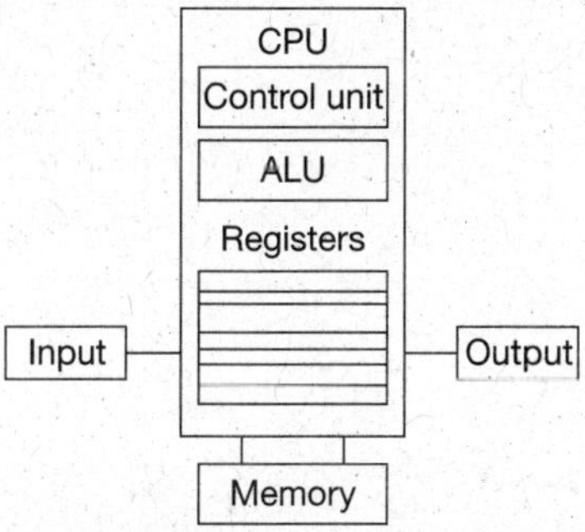

Now computers hold megabytes or even gigabytes of data. A megabyte is a unit of one million bytes; a gigabyte is one billion bytes, and a terabyte is one trillion bytes. If a computer has a memory of 64 megabytes, then it can hold 64 million bytes of information.

Set of Registers: Within CPU, there are a number of high speed, special purpose, memory units called registers. These registers carry out critical functions in the execution of programmes. They are used for storing small information.

Motherboard: The computer's main circuit board, which contains the CPU, the memory, and expansion slots for additional circuit boards are called adapters or cards.

Buses: A set of parallel wires for connecting the CPU of a computer to all other input-output devices. Data can be transmitted in two directions, from and to the CPU.

Peripheral Devices

A peripheral device is any device that can be connected to a computer. This term includes monitors, keyboards, mouse, webcams, drawing pads, joystick, modems, printers, scanners, interactive whiteboards, drive wheel, and so on.

Input Devices

Any device that is capable of inputting information into a computer system, for example, keyboard, microphone, mouse, scanner, webcam and so on.

Output Devices

Output devices are basically meant for anything that comes out of a computer after being processed. These include monitor, headphone, printers, speakers, plotters, and VDUs (visual display units).

Storage Devices

Computer data storage, often called memory, refers to computer components and recording media which retains the digital data. Memory refers to the temporary internal storage areas within a computer. The term memory is usually used as a shorthand for physical memory, which refers to the actual chips capable of holding data. Some computers also use virtual memory, which expands physical memory onto a hard drive.

MEMORY

Memory is that part of a computer which stores information.

1. *Random Access Memory (RAM):* It is also termed as the main memory. It is the temporary memory (volatile) that allows information to be stored randomly and accessed quickly and directly (without the need to go through intervening data).

   A computer can both write data into RAM and read data from RAM. Every time a user turns on his/her computer, a set of operating instructions is copied from the hard disk into RAM. These instructions, which help control basic computer functions, remain in RAM until the computer is turned off. As soon as the power is turned off, whatever data was in RAM disappears.
2. *Read-only Memory (ROM):* It is the permanent memory of a computer; a set of instructions that has been built into the computer by the manufacturer and cannot be accessed or changed by the user. It only permits the user to read data. Computers almost always contain a small amount of ROM that holds instructions for starting up the computer.
3. *Programmable Read-only Memory (PROM):* A PROM is a memory chip on which you can store a program. Once the PROM has been used, you cannot wipe it clean and use it to store something else. Like ROMs, PROMs are non-volatile.
4. *Erasable Programmable Read-only Memory (EPROM):* An EPROM is a special type of PROM that can be erased by exposing it to ultraviolet light.
5. *Electrically Erasable Programmable Read-only Memory (EEPROM):* An EEPROM is a special type of PROM that can be erased by exposing it to an electrical charge. It is also termed as flash memory.

Memory is also classified as (i) primary storage and (ii) secondary storage

(i) *Primary storage:* It consists of RAM and ROM. In primary memory, data are not stored permanently, but temporarily. After getting off data are erased from the memory of computer. These are considered as short-term memory.

(ii) *Secondary storage:* It is also termed as auxiliary storage. Secondary memory/storage is the slowest and the cheapest form of memory. It cannot be processed directly by the CPU. It must first be copied into primary storage (RAM).

Secondary memory devices include magnetic disks like hard drives and floppy disks; optical disks such as CDs and CD-ROMs; and magnetic tapes, which were the first forms of secondary memory. In computer disk storage, a sector is a subdivision of a track on a magnetic disk or optical disc. Each sector stores a fixed amount of user-accessible data, traditionally 512 bytes for hard drives and 2048 bytes for CD-ROMs and DVD-ROMs.

Storage devices can be divided into two categories:

1. *Internal:* They reside within a computer. Hard disk is an example of a magnetic disk on which computer data can be stored. They usually hold more data and are conventionally faster.
2. *External:* They are portable and usually removable storage devices. USB flash drive (commonly termed as pen drive), CD, digital video disk (DVD), Blu-ray Disc, are certain examples.

USB flash drives look like a small flat pen. They may have large storage capacity and they can be plugged into any computer with a USB socket. Flash drives are also commonly referred to as **pen drives or memory sticks.**

Computer Software

Software is a set of programs, procedures, algorithms, and associated documents that provide instructions for telling a computer what to do, when to do, and how to do. It can also be defined as computerized instructions that operate a computer, manipulate the data, and execute particular functions or tasks.

When software is stored in a hardware that cannot be easily modified (such as BIOS, ROM in a PC), it is called a firmware to indicate that it falls into an area somewhere between the software and the hardware.

System Software

System software provides the basic functions for computer usage and helps to run the computer hardware and system.

It includes a combination of devices, drivers, operating systems, servers, utilities, and Windows systems. It manages hardware devices. It is also responsible for resource allocation. The operating system and utility software are the two major categories of system software.

Types of System Software

1. *Compilers:* It converts source code (written in programming language) into another computer language called object code). Examples are ALGOL compilers, BASIC compilers, C++ compilers, FORTRAN compilers.
2. *Operating System (OS):* An operating system controls all other resources of a computer system. It can be 16-bit, 32-bit, or 64-bit.

The main categories of operating system are as follows:

(a) *Unix/BSD:* Unix system V, AIX, HP-UX, Solaris, IRIX, BSD distros

(b) *GNU/Linux:* Linux, Google Chrome OS

(c) *Windows:* 2000, XP, Vista, 7, CE

(d) *Mac OS:* Mac OS X

(e) *Embedded and Real-Time OS*

(f) *Experimental:* Oberon/Bluebottle, Amoeba, Plan 9 (Bell Labs)

Windows was developed in 1985 as an add-on to MS-DOS in response to the growing interest in graphical user interfaces (GUIs). Mac OS was the previous operating system that used a GUI. The most recent client version of Windows after Vista is Windows 8. Linux was developed by Linus Torvalds. It is a freely available multi-tasking and multi-user operating system. Since the very beginning, Linux was placed under General Public License (GPL).

Utility Software

It is a system software designed to help, analyse, monitor, configure and optimize settings, and maintain the computer. Skins that customize the media player's looks and DVD burners are examples of utility software.

The utility software is classified as follows:

1. *Anti-virus software:* Anti-virus is a protective software designed to defend your computer against malicious software (malware).
2. *Desktop widgets:* Interactive virtual tools that provide single purpose vehicles showing the latest news, time, calendar, dictionary, map, calculator, and so on.
3. *Backup software:* The backup softwares are back-up files, cleaning up hard disk,and shredding files. Examples are Windows Backup and restore centre and Net Backup made by Symantec.

Application Software

It helps the user to perform singular or multiple related tasks. It can be further classified into productivity software (word processors, spreadsheets, schedulers, DBMS, desktop publishing, ERP, Mozilla Firefox) or collaborative software (also referred to as groupware. Examples include Facebook application, Etherpad).

Software can be either proprietary (also called closed) or open. Proprietary software is privately owned and controlled. The specifications of such software are not divulged in order to prevent other companies from duplicating it.

Users usually prefer using open software, which is publicly accessible. Anyone can create add-on products for it because they can understand how it was designed. Freeware is the software that can be copied and used without payment to the author(s), although there may be some restrictions on distribution.

Programming Languages

These are the rules, conventions, and specific commands used to write a computer program. Most programs must be converted into machine language or binary code so that the instructions can be performed on a specific computer platform.

1. *Machine language:* Machine language is the only language understood by a computer. Each statement in a machine language program is a sequence of bits. Each bit may be set to 0 or 1. Series of bits represent instructions that a computer can understand. While easily understood by computers, machine languages are almost impossible for humans to use because they consist entirely of binary numbers. Programmers, therefore, use either a high-level programming language or an assembly language. Machine language is also known as the first-generation language.
2. *Assembly language:* An assembly language is also known as the second-generation language. It contains the same instructions as a machine language, but the instructions and variables have names instead of being just numbers. The advantage of assembly language is that its instructions are readable. For example, assembly language statements like MOV and ADD are more recognizable than sequences of 0's and 1's.
3. *High-level language (HLL):* High-level languages are what most programmers use. Languages such as C++ and Java are all HLLs. One advantage of HLLs is that they are very readable. The statements in these languages are in English. Programs written in HLLs are translated into assembly language or machine language by a compiler. Assembly language programs are translated into machine language by a program called an assembler.

Every CPU has its own unique machine language. Programs must be rewritten or recompiled, to run on different types of computers.

Program

A program is a set of instructions for performing a particular task. These instructions are just like English words. The computer interprets the instructions as 1's and 0's. A program can be written in assembly language as well as in HLL. This written program is called the source program. The source program is to be converted to the machine language, which is called an object program. A translator is required for such translation.

Language Processors

1. *Assembler:* This language processor converts the program written in assembly language into machine language.
2. *Interpreter:* This language processor converts a HLL program into machine language by converting it line-by-line. If there is any error in any line, it reports it at the same time and program execution cannot resume until the error is rectified.
3. *Compiler:* It also converts the HLL program into machine language. It converts the entire HLL program in one go, and reports all the errors of the program along with the line numbers. After all the errors are removed, the program is recompiled, and after that the compiler is not needed in the memory as the object program is available.

How Does a Computer Process Information?

When data are put into a computer, the numbers or words we understand are translated into a binary number system. Binary language is the language of computers.

Everything you type, input, output, send, retrieve, draw, and so on is, in the end, converted to the computer's native language—binary.

Binary Number System

It is a numerical system wherein each digit stands for a power of two. The binary system uses only two symbols, 0 and 1, to represent values.

In the decimal system, commonly used in most countries, each digit represents a value of 10. For example, the number 107 would break down as follows:

$$1 \times 100 = 100, 0 \times 10 = 0, 7 \times 1 = 7$$

As computers use the binary system, powers of 2 play an important role. This is why everything in computers seems to come in 8s (2 to the 3rd power), 64s (2 to the 6th power), 128s (2 to the 7th power), and 256s (2 to the 8th power). Therefore, in the binary system, the number 103 would break down as follows:

$1 \times 64 = 64$, $1 \times 32 = 32$, $0 \times 16 = 0$, $0 \times 8 = 0$, $1 \times 4 = 4$, $1 \times 2 = 2$, $1 \times 1 = 1$ and $(1100111)_2 = 103$

The values in a binary system—the 0's and 1's—are called binary digits or bits.

Computers use base 2 because they can only recognize two values, 1 or 0. This is simulated electronically by using a device, such as a switch, which is either on (1) or off (0). When data are typed into a computer, the keyboard converts each keystroke into a binary character code.

8 bits = 1 byte
1024 bytes = 1 kilobyte
1024 kilobytes = 1 megabyte
1024 megabytes = 1 gigabyte
1024 gigabytes = 1 terabyte.

In large computers, the number of bits can be 16, 32 or 40 bits.

Binary Digit (Bit)

It is a digit within the binary number system. A bit is the smallest unit of information held in a computer. In order to make the bits useful, they are combined into bytes of information.

Byte

A combination of bits that represent one character. A byte is usually composed of 8 bits.

ASCII (American Standard Code for Information Interexchange)

It assigns a specific pattern of bits to each character, as described earlier. Another code that may be found, especially in IBM-brand mainframe computers, is EBCDIC.

EBCDIC (Extended Binary Coded Decimal Interchange Code)

The important point to remember about these codes is that their main value is to store information so that it is readable by other computers. By using ASCII or EBCDIC, it is possible for people to retrieve and use someone else's data using a different type of hardware or software. The main disadvantage of using ASCII is that the formatting or other special qualities of computerized information may be lost.

Computer Networks

1. *Network:* A network is a system of interconnected computers. There are a number of types of computer networks.
2. *Local Area Networks (LANs):* LANs use cable to connect a number of computers within the same location or in close proximity.
3. *Wide Area Networks (WANs):* WANs use telephone lines or other telecommunication devices to link computers in widely separated locations.
4. *Wireless Local Area Network (WLAN):* WLAN links two or more devices using some wireless distribution method and provides connection through an access point to the wider Internet.
5. *Personal Area Network (PAN):* PAN is a computer network used for communication among computers and different IT devices close to one person.
6. *Metropolitan Area Network (MAN):* A network of computers located at different sites within a large fixed area, such as a city.
7. *Campus Area Network (CAN):* CAN is a network of multiple interconnected local area networks (LAN) in a limited geographical area. A CAN is smaller than a WAN or MAN.
8. *Storage Area Network (SAN):* Is also known as Storage Area Network or Server Area Network.
9. *Internet:* The Internet is a system that links existing networks into a worldwide network.
10. *Intranet:* A private network inside a company or an educational organization and used over its LAN. This can be taken as akin to local Internet. It is under single administrative set-up.
11. *Extranet:* A technology that permits users of an organization's intranet to enter portions of another organization's intranet in order to conduct business transactions or collaborate on joint projects.
12. *Virtual Private Network (VPN):* It is a computer network in which some of the links between the nodes are carried out by open connections or virtual circuits in some larger ,network (e.g., the Internet) instead of by physical wires.

Topology: The physical topology of a network refers to the configuration of cables, computers, and other peripherals or simply as arrangement of computers. Here, workstation or node refers to computer systems which are in the network. The topology can be

(i) *Bus topology:* Here, every computer is connected to a main (single) cable like a bus.
(ii) *Star topology:* There is a hub or switch box to which all workstations are directly connected.
(iii) *Ring topology:* Here, every device has exactly two neighbours.
(iv) *Mesh topology:* Every computer is connected to another, so messages can take any path.
(v) *Tree topology:* It is a combination of two or more star networks.

Computer virus: These are the programs that spread across computers by attaching a copy of itself to the files on the infected computer. Thus, they spread from one computer to another by attaching itself to other programs. When the user runs the infected file, the virus get into action. A virus is usually harmful, and can corrupt data, overwrite files, or use up system resources. They are usually written by programmers to cause trouble. Some viruses act to cause a humorous message to appear on the screen, some cause minor glitches, but others may cause serious damage to a computer's memory or disks, some flood an organization's web site, interrupt or entirely prevent access to the organization's customers.

The Internet Basics

The **Internet** is a global system of interconnected computer networks that use the standard Internet protocol suite (TCP/IP) to serve millions of users worldwide. It is probably the largest WAN in the world.

The Internet dates back to the group of interconnected networks that evolved from the ARPANET of the late 1960s and early 1970s. It has grown from a handful of interconnected networks into a huge network of millions of computers. The main Internet services of interest to language teachers are e-mail and WWW (World Wide Web).

Working of the Internet

A computer network allows sharing of resources. The software resources exist in the form of files of data, which need to be moved between two specific computer systems for the purpose of sharing. For such type of communication, we require (i) address for communication (ii) a secure means for moving data in the form of electronic signals. For secure movement, we need rules (protocols) for sending and receiving files. There are basically two sets of rules (protocols) for the purpose—transmission control protocol (TCP) and the Internet protocol (IP). transmission control protocol (TCP) and the Internet protocol (IP). TCP divides the data into data packets for the purpose of sending and receiving data. In addition, the rules for reassembling data and damage-free delivery are also specified. The role of IP here is to put destination—addressing information on such packets. The address can be typically written as user@host.domain. The user is the name of the Internet account holder. The name must be the same which is used by the user while logging in. Hosts are individual machines at a particular location. Resources of host machine are normally shared and used by any Internet user.

Intranet and Extranet

Intranet: A network that is accessible to computers which are not physically a part of an organization's own private network, but is not accessible to the general public. For example, allowing vendors and business partners to access a company web site. Often an intranet makes use of a VPN.

Extranet: A technology that permits users of an organization's network to enter portions of another organization's network in order to conduct business transactions or collaborate on joint projects.

Hardware Requirements for the Internet

1. *Modem (Modulator and Demodulator):* Modem is a device or program which converts computer data to a signal that can be transmitted over a telephone line. It can also reconvert a signal coming into a computer via a telephone line so that it can be understood by the computer. Modems are used to connect computers with the Internet.

2. *Hub:* A hub is a place of convergence where data arrives from one or more directions and is forwarded out in one or more directions. A hub is a common connection point for networked computers and other devices. Hubs are used to connect devices in a LAN.

3. *Bridge:* A bridge is a network device that connects two or more networks such as one LAN to another LAN that use the same protocol (Ethernet or token ring).

4. *Router:* Router is a device (or software in some cases) that determines the next network point to which data packet should be forwarded towards its destination. It is a hardware device that connects computers to

a network or that connects one network with another network. Routers are now available at low prices and can be used for connecting two or more computers together in home networks, so that the data can be exchanged between the computers and all the computers in the network can access the Internet.

5. *Gateway:* A gateway is a node on a network that serves as an entrance to another network. The computers that control traffic within an organization or at the Internet service provider (ISP) are gateway nodes.

Apart from the above requirements, connector, cables, adapter, circuits, switches, leased lines are other hardware requirements. In transmission media, twisted wires, coaxial cables, and fibre optics can be used.

Software Requirements for the Internet

The Internet protocol (IP) is the method or protocol by which data is sent from one computer to another on the Internet. They can be of different types:

(i) *Hypertext Transfer Protocol (HTTP):* It defines the format for communication between web browsers (web clients) and web servers.

(ii) *Internet Message Access Protocol (IMAP):* It defines the format for communication between e-mail servers and clients.

(iii) *Secure Sockets Layer (SSL):* A protocol developed by Netscape for transmitting private documents via the Internet.

(iv) *Transfer Control Protocol/Internet Protocol (TCP/IP):* It is the main data transfer protocol used in the Internet. It manages all the information that moves across the Internet. It consists of multiple protocols, each of which transfers data across the network in a different format and with different options.

(v) *File Transfer Protocol (FTP):* A set of guidelines or standards that establish the format in which files can be transmitted from one computer to another.

(vi) *Trivial File Transfer Protocol (TFTP):* This protocol allows transferring of files between the network devices.

(vii) *Simple Mail Transfer Protocol (SMTP):* Network-based e-mail was initially exchanged on the ARPANET in extensions to the FTP, but it is now carried by the SMTP.

(viii) *Telnet:* A protocol that allows a computer to connect with a remote host computer on the Internet. The use of Telnet has diminished as the Web's HTTP has become the dominant protocol.

(ix) *Hypertext Markup Language (HTML):* It is a formatting language used to establish the appearance of a web page. It thus helps in creating pages on the World Wide Web. HTML also enables us to insert hypertext links within one web page or to other pages anywhere on the web.

(x) *Standardized General Markup Language (SGML):* A meta-language that can be applied to documents in order to maintain their structure and context is called SGML.

(xi) *Uniform Resource Locator (URL):* It is an address for a specific document found on the web. It can also be termed as the location of a resource on the Internet. A URL specifies the address of the computer where the resource is located, which may be the homepage of a website.

It is made up of several components like a domain name, the directories, and subdirectories of the site, and the extension. It is also known as the web address.

Internet Service Provider (ISP): A company that provides a subscription service to enable the user or organization to access the Internet is ISP. An ISP has a network of computers permanently linked to the Internet. Dedicated lines are also provided by some ISPs. ISPs also give you an e-mail address and space on the World Wide Web for setting up one's own website.

Main Internet Connection Options

To be specific, the following technological options are available to us for accessing the Internet:

1. *Dial-up connection:* It uses an analogue telephone line for establishing a temporary communication. For that, computer's digital signals must be converted into analogue signals. ISDN (integrated services digital network) is a type of digital telephone service, used for transferring large chunks of data to and from the Internet without a modem. It is termed as wired Ethernet.
2. *Cable TV connections:* Households with cable TVs have the option of cable modem Internet access.
3. *Digital Subscriber Line (DSL):* It works over POTS (plain old telephone service), that is, copper telephone lines. ADSL (asymmetric digital subscriber line) is the type of DSL that provides different bandwidths in the upstream and downstream directions, while SDSL (symmetric digital subscriber line) provides the same bandwidth in both the directions.
4. *Satellite connection:* It is akin to getting TV signals directly from satellite.
5. *Bluetooth:* Bluetooth is an open wireless technology for data exchange over short distances. It is a protocol that permits wireless exchange of information between computers, cell phones, and other electronic devices within a radius of about 30 feet.
6. *Broadband:* Broadband Internet access is a high-speed Internet access—typically contrasted with dial-up access over a modem. Broadband technologies supply a minimum speed of 256 Kbps. The term broadband refers to any type of transmission technique that carries several data channels over a common wire.

   In home networking, broadband constitutes any form of high-speed Internet access using this transmission technique. Both DSL and cable modem are common broadband Internet technologies. Wired Ethernet/integrated service digital network (ISDN) is high-speed digital access for the Internet. Connection speed is usually measured in Kbps (kilobytes per second) and Mbps (megabytes per second). Typically, a home user will have a broadband connection using an ADSL telephone line running at 2 Mbps up to 8 Mbps.

Other Important Internet-related Terms

World Wide Web (www)

The component of the Internet that combines audio, video, and graphics with text is also called the web or simply the www. It is a subset of the Internet and is a collection of documents and applications residing on the Internet servers around the world.

www was the brainchild of Tim Berners-Lee, who in 1989 invented the HTML coding language that is the basis of the web. www became a public service in 1993. It opened the Internet to millions of people interested in finding information. It is a huge collection of resources of information, including learning materials, which is accessed by means of a computer program known as a browser. www is only a part of the Internet, but many people treat both the terms as synonyms.

www consists of documents called web pages that contain information on a particular topic. A web page might also contain one or more links that point to other web pages.

A website is a location on the www.

Web Browsers

A web browser is a software that permits a user, with the click of a mouse, to locate, display, and download text, video, audio, and graphics stored in a host computer on the web.

A browser helps in opening up pages and in their navigation as well. It acts as an interface between the user and the inner working of the Internet, specifically the www. There are different browsers for different platforms and with multiple features. Some popular browsers are enlisted as below:

1. Internet Explorer
2. Mozilla Firefox 3.5

3. Opera
4. Safari 4.0

Cross–platform browsers: They can operate on more than one platform such as Windows, Mac, Linux etc. Sea Monkey, Flock, K-Melon are different examples of cross-platform browsers.

A browser can be (i) graphical or (ii) text based. The main examples of graphical browsers are Microsoft Internet Explorer, Netscape Navigator, Mosaic, and Opera. Lynx can be taken as an example of text-based browser.

Here, it is important to mention that web browsing or the Internet surfing is the process of visiting different websites on the Internet.

The web browser can also store a list of favourite sites, often called bookmarks, to permit the user to jump directly to the site they wish to see instead of having to enter its URL every time.

Domain Name

It is the unique name that identifies an Internet site or web site. Domain names always have two or more parts, separated by dots. The part on the left is the most specific, and the part on the right is the most general. A given machine may have more than one domain name but a given domain name points to only one machine.

Domain names are the alphabetical names used to refer to computers on the Internet. The suffix indicates what type of an organization is hosting the site. There are six main categories which are follows:

1. *.com:* Commercial institutions or organization
2. *.edu:* Educational institutions
3. *.gov:* Government sites
4. *.mil:* Military sites
5. *.net:* Gateways and administrative hosts
6. *.org:* Private organizations

Domain Name Server

A special type of Internet computer which converts a website's domain name into a unique numerical IP address that identifies the computer where the website is stored. When you try to connect to a website with a domain name such as **hull.ac.uk** (University of Hull), a request is first made to a name server to resolve this name into an IP address, which is then used to locate the computer where the website is stored and to establish a connection with it.

Internet Protocol Address (IP Address)

It is the unique numerical address of a computer on the Internet, expressed as four sets of numbers (maximum 3 digits each) separated by dots, for example, **150.237.176.24**. Computers on the Internet are nearly always referred to by more memorable domain names, which are mapped onto their IP addresses by special Internet computers known as name servers.

Home Page

The main page of a website is its home page. Typically, the home page serves as an index or table of contents to other documents stored at the site (i.e., the address). A home page is similar to the title page and table of contents in a book. It identifies the site and contains links to other pages at the site called Microsoft Explorer.

Hyperlink

An element in a hypertext document that is highlighted by means of underlining or the use of a different colour. When highlighted element is clicked, the user is connected with another element in the same document or another document.

Firewall

A firewall is a software package that sits between the computer and the Internet connection, keeping an eye on the traffic going to and fro. If anything suspicious appears, such as an unauthorized attempt from a remote computer to write information to the hard disc or to send information from one's computer to a remote computer, it will block it and warn the user.

Firewalls have become essential these days because of the frequent attempts being made by hackers to grab confidential information from computers all around the world, for example, one's bank or credit card details, which may be stored in a file somewhere on one's computer. Any computer is vulnerable when connected to the Internet.

Voice Over the Internet Protocol (VoIP)

It is another name for the Internet telephony.

Search Engine

It is a program that searches documents for specified keywords and returns a list of documents where the keywords were found.

The most popular search engines are Google and Yahoo. Baidu is a search engine developed by China. A meta search engine is a search tool that sends user requests to several other search engines and/or databases and aggregates the results into a single list or displays them according to their source.

The Internet search system which locates documents that contain the keywords specified by the user is termed as wide-area information server (WAIS).

Electronic Mail

Commonly referred to as email or e-mail since approximately 1993, it is a paperless method of sending messages, notes, or letters from one person to another or even many people at the same time via the Internet. E-mail is very fast compared to the normal post. E-mail messages usually take only a few seconds to arrive at their destination. One can send messages anytime of the day or night and it gets delivered immediately. Modern e-mail operates across the Internet or other computer networks. Today's e-mail systems are based on a store-and-forward model. E-mail servers accept, forward, deliver, and store messages. Neither the users nor their computers are required to be online simultaneously; they need to connect only briefly, typically to an e-mail server, for as long as it takes to send or receive messages. When sender sends an e-mail, it leaves the computer and travels first to ISP; then it may travel through many host computers to reach its final destination.

Historically, the term electronic mail was used generically for any electronic document transmission. For example, several writers in the early 1970s used the term to describe fax document transmission. As a result, it is difficult to find the first citation for the use of the term with the more specific meaning that it has today.

The Internet e-mail message consists of three components such as

1. Message envelope
2. Message header
3. Message body

The message header contains control information, including, minimally, an originator's e-mail address and one or more recipient addresses. Usually, descriptive information is also added, such as a subject header field and a message submission date or time stamp.

An e-mail predates the inception of the Internet and was in fact a crucial tool in creating it, but the history of modern, global Internet e-mail services reaches back to the early ARPANET. Standards for encoding e-mail messages were proposed as early as 1973. Conversion from ARPANET to the Internet in the early 1980s produced the core of the current services. An e-mail sent in the early 1970s looks quite similar to a basic text message sent on the Internet today.

Glossary of ICT and the Internet Terms

Address book: Usually, it is supplied as part of your e-mail software. An address book in this sense is used to keep a record of all the e-mail addresses of people whom you may wish to contact by e-mail.

Adware: Adware is a software that may have been installed on your computer by a remote computer, that is, via the web.

AJAX (combination of asynchronous java script and XML): Web programming tool (or rather a set of tools) which makes it possible to create interactive web applications AJAX is a programming tool that is used extensively in what are known as web 2.0 applications.

Apache: It is the most popular web server software on the www. Apache mainly runs on UNIX systems.

Applet: It is a small program written in the Java programming language and embedded in a web page. When you use your browser to access a web page, an applet may run inside the web page, as it were, to perform an interactive animation, make a calculation or carry out another simple task.

Archive: Used to describe documents or files that are not immediately needed but which should not be completely discarded. An archive may be stored on an external hard disc, CD-ROM, DVD, or other storage devices.

Attachment: It is a term used in connection with an e-mail. An attachment can be a file of almost any kind—a document file, an image file, a sound file, or a video clip—that you can add, that is, attach, to an e-mail.

Audio conferencing: It is a computer-based communication system that allows a group of computer users at different locations to conduct a virtual conference in which the participants can hear one another, as if they were in the same room participating in a real conference. Unlike video-conferencing, audio-conferencing systems do not allow the participants to see one another.

Authoring package/authoring program/ Authoring tool: These terms describe content-free software packages that allow the teacher to develop interactive learning and teaching materials without having to have a detailed knowledge of a computer programming language. These terms may also be applied to software packages used for creating web pages, for example, **FrontPage** or **Dreamweaver**.

Bandwidth: It is the amount of data that can be sent from one computer to another through a particular connection in a certain amount of time, for example, via a computer to the Internet and vice versa. The more the bandwidth, the faster is the access to information. Bandwidth is usually measured in Kbps or Mbps.

Baud: It is a unit of measurement at which data can be transferred (i.e., the baud rate), for example, over a telephone line via a modem or from a computer to an external device such as a printer. Baud is rarely used nowadays, as transfer rates are normally expressed in Kbps or Mbps.

Blog: A blog (short form for web log) is an online diary in which an individual records and publishes his/her thoughts on one or more subjects. A blog can contain news items, short essays, annotated links, documents, graphics, and multimedia. These posts are usually in reverse chronological order and often take the form of a journal or diary. Blogger refers to someone who blogs, that is, who regularly writes blogs.

Conferencing: Computer conferencing is a development of e-mail designed to support many-to-many communication, whereby computer users in different locations can take part in a virtual conference. A conference usually consists of a group of participants who have a common interest in the conference subject matter. Computer conferencing software enables organizing, storing, structuring, and retrieving of messages.

Cookie: A piece of information stored on a user's computer by a web browser, when the user visits a website for the first time. Websites use cookies to recognize users who have previously visited them. The next time the user visits that site, the information in the cookie is sent back to the site so that the site can tailor what it presents to the user, for example, tastes in music or shopping habits.

Course Management System (CMS): It is a type of virtual learning environment (VLE), for example, Moodle.

Crawler: A crawler is a program that searches the web for new links, new content, and changes in order to keep the search engine results up to date. A crawler may also be called a bot (short form for robot) or spider. Crawlers, within the search engines, perform a useful indexing function, but there are also crawlers or bots that have more sinister motives, such as gathering addresses to be targeted by spammers.

Executable: This describes a program which has been converted (compiled) into binary machine code. If you double-click on an executable program name in Windows Explorer, it will immediately execute itself—that is, run. Executables usually have the Extension .exe or .com.

Extension: In computer jargon, an extension is an optional addition, usually consisting of a dot plus three or four letters, to the name of a file. The extension to the filename helps the computer (and the user) recognize what type of file it is and what it may contain, for example, **.doc** is a Word document file, **.exe** is a computer program, **.jpg** or **.jpeg** is a picture file, and **.htm** or **.html** is a web page file.

Host: It refers to computer that provides services to other computers that are linked to it, via a local network or via the Internet.

Hypermedia: It is an extension of hypertext that integrates audio, video, and graphics with text (like multimedia).

Hypertext: It is the technology that links text in one part of a document with related text in other part of the document or in other documents. A user can quickly find the related text by clicking on the appropriate keyword, key phrase, icon, or button.

Interactive Whiteboard (IWB): A touch-sensitive projection screen that allows the teacher to control a computer directly by touching the screen, that is, the whiteboard, rather than using a keyboard or a mouse.

iPod: It is the name of a portable (mobile) media player designed and marketed by Apple.

Java: A programming language, invented by Sun Microsystems, that is specifically designed for writing programs which can be downloaded to one's computer through the Internet and immediately executed. Java is a programming language designed for programs or applets used over the Internet.

JPEG (Joint Photographic Experts Group): A format for storing complex graphics in compressed form.

Mashup: A mashup is a web page that brings together the data from two or more web services and combines the data into a new application with added functionality.

Microblogging: It is an approach to blogging in which very short texts are posted containing snippets of information about events, websites, and other sources.

Moodle: Moodle is an open source software, which means one is free to download, use modify, and even distribute it.

Netbook: A netbook is a small, lightweight computer, smaller than a laptop computer, with a long battery life, and ideal for travelling. Netbook computers have built-in Wi-Fi and are optimized for browsing the web and e-mail.

Open Source: It is used to describe a software that is provided free of charge, along with the original source code used to create it, so that anyone can modify, improve and work in ways that reflect their own preferences. Moodle is the typical example of an open source software.

Optical Character Recognition: Optical character recognition (OCR) software is used in conjunction with a scanner to convert the printed text into a digital format.

Personal Digital Assistant (PDA): It is a hand-held device that combines computing, audio communication, browsing, and networking features and serves as an organizer for personal information.

Portable Network Graphics: Portable network group (PNG) is a graphics format specifically designed for use on the www. PNG enables compression of images without any loss of quality, including high-resolution images.

Pixel: A contraction of picture element.

Podcast: The term podcast takes its name from a combination of iPod and broadcasting. Podcasts can simply be downloaded to a computer and played using a standard media player program.

Pop-up: It is a small window that appears within a program or over the top of a web page to deliver additional information. Pop-ups on the web can be annoying as they are often used for unwanted advertising material.

Portal: It is a web page, website, or service that acts as a link or entrance to other websites on the Internet. Typically, a portal includes an annotated catalogue of websites and may also include a search engine, e-mail facilities, a forum, and other services.

Public Domain: It is a material that is either copyright free, or whose copyright has expired, or which cannot be copyrighted. Many people think that because something is on the web, it must be in the public domain. This is not so. A work is in the public domain only if it is explicitly stated to be so.

RSS: It is a development in the Internet technology that enables the users to subscribe to websites that change or add content regularly, for example, news sites (such as the BBC) and sites containing blogs, nings, podcasts, and Wikis. RSS makes use of software that presents new additions.

Smiley: In e-mail messages, a facial expression constructed sideways (for the lateral-minded) with standard characters is called a smiley. It is also referred to as an emoticon (emotions with icons).

Server: It is a computer which provides services to other computers, known as clients.

Smartphone: A smartphone is an advanced mobile phone that offers a wide range of applications. In addition to functioning as a mobile phone, smartphones can be used as a media player, a camera, a GPS navigation device, and a web browser—and in many other ways. Apple's iPhone is a typical example of a smartphone, using a touchscreen for typing and to run applications.

Social Media: It is a term used to describe a variety of web 2.0 applications that enable people to share images, audio recordings, and video recordings via the web and also initiate discussions about them.

Social Networking: It is a term applied to a type of website where people can seek other people who share their interests, find out what's going on in their areas of interest, and share information with one another.

Spam: These are unsolicited e-mail advertisements, the Internet equivalent of junk mail.

Splog: The splog site creator (i.e., a splogger) begins by finding a subject that attracts lot of visitors. Then, the splogger sets up a blog that plagiarizes content from other sites dealing with this subject. Splogs may consist of hundreds of blogs with plagiarized content, containing multiple links to selected websites.

Simultaneous Peripheral Operations Online (SPOOL): Using this technique, the output is not directly sent to the printer. It is first transferred to an intermediary storage medium such as a disk file. Output can be stored in separate files and printed at a later stage depending upon the availability of time and storage.

Spyware: It is a term that may be used synonymously with adware but implies more sinister motives on the part of the person who has dumped it onto your computer, for example, with a view to steal private information such as bank account numbers, credit card numbers, passwords, and so on.

Tablet Computer: A tablet computer is a compact portable computer that makes use of a touchscreen instead of a keyboard for typing and running applications. Apple's iPad is a typical example of a tablet computer.

Tag: Tagging has become more common in recent years as a result of widespread use of social media for sharing images, audio recordings, video recordings, website references, and so on. Tags are labels that briefly describe what the media or references are all about and help other people find them quickly. Tags are also used in HTML, to define how the onscreen text is rendered by the browser.

Tandem Learning (Buddy Learning): A form of learning in which two language learners pair up in order to learn each other's language. This may take place face-to-face or via the Internet, including using virtual worlds such as second life.

Text File or Textfile: A data file consisting entirely of printable ASCII characters, that is, plain unformatted text. Text files often have a .txt extension after the filename (e.g., readme .txt) and their contents can be viewed using programs such as Windows Notepad. The term text file is also used to describe files, that is, texts, created by authoring packages such as Fun with Texts, which then manipulates the texts into a set of activities for completion by the learner.

Video Conferencing: A computer-based communication system that allows a group of computer users at different locations to conduct a virtual conference in which the participants can see and hear one another as if they were in the same room participating in a real conference.

Vodcast: It is the short form of video podcast. This podcast incorporates video as well as audio features.

Voice over Internet Protocol (VoIP): It is audio communication using the Internet instead of telephones. Skype and Ventrilo are examples of VoIP.

Wireless Application Protocol (WAP): A system that enables users to browse online services such as information about the weather, traffic conditions, shopping, and so on via a special type of mobile phone. WAP is the mobile phone equivalent of www. Newer mobile phones include WAP browser software to allow users access to WAP sites.

Website: An area on the www where an organization or individual stores a collection of pages of material—web pages. The pages are usually interlinked with one another and with other websites. Every website has a unique web address or URL.

Wi-Fi: Wireless fidelity, also known as high frequency wireless local area network. Wi-Fi systems use high-frequency radio signals to transmit and receive data over distances of several hundred feet. Many hotels, educational institutions, railways, and airports offer Wi-Fi access to people using laptops.

Wiki: A website or a similar online resource which allows anyone to set up a resource in which the content can be created collectively. It allows anyone who views the wiki to add or to edit the existing content. Wiki also refers to the software used to create such website.

Wikipedia: It is the best known example of a wiki. It is a collaboratively written encyclopaedia.

Worldwide Web Consortium (W3C): An international non-profit organization which acts as a resource centre for the www, and is active in setting technical standards.

Zip Drive: A type of disc drive that accepts portable zip discs. Zip drives themselves are also portable and can be connected to almost any computer.

Zip: Used as a verb to describe the process of compacting files or programs in order to cut down the amount of storage space they require by compressing them into one tightly-packed file and thus to make it easier for them to be transported on floppy discs or transmitted electronically to other locations, for example, via the Internet. Proprietary programs, such as WinZip or WinRar, can be used to zip data and files. Zipped files are recognized by the Extension .zip or .rar (for files created with WinRar) and have to be unzipped before they can be used, again using proprietary programs.

ICT Basics

1. ICT stands for (*December 2004*)
   (a) Information and communication technology
   (b) Information controlled technology
   (c) Information capable technology
   (d) None of the above
2. Which of the following is also termed as multimedia education?

(a) ICT supported education
(b) ICT enabled education
(c) ICT education
(d) None of the above

3. Information and communication technology includes (*December 2006*)
(a) Online learning
(b) Learning through the use of EDUSAT
(c) Web-based learning
(d) All of the above

4. Which of the following is the appropriate definition of Information Technology? (*December 2004*)
(a) Information technology refers to the use of hardware and software for proccssing information.
(b) Information technology refers to the use of hardware and software for distribution of useful information.
(c) Information technology refers to the use of hardware and software for storage, retrieval, processing, and distributing information of many kinds.
(d) Information technology refers to the use of principles of physical sciences and social sciences for processing of information of many kinds.

5. CBT stands for
(a) Central basic training
(b) Computer-based training
(c) Computer basic test
(d) None of the above

6. NPTEL stands for
(a) National programme on technology enhanced learning
(b) National programme on technology enabled learning
(c) National programme on technology enhanced lessons
(d) National programme on technology embedded learning

7. The ERNET stands for
(a) Engineering and research network
(b) External and regulated network
(c) Educational and research network
(d) None of the above

8. At which of the following institutions ERNET is used to connect computers?
(a) IISCs
(b) IITs
(c) National Centre for Software Technology
(d) All of the above

9. Which of the following is not included in the four basic dimensions of ICT?
(a) Skills (b) Infrastructure
(c) Attitude (d) Personnel

10. Which of the following open source e-learning platform has been developed by IIT-Kanpur?
(a) e-Gyan
(b) e-Sarawati
(c) Brihaspati
(d) None of the above

11. Recording a television programme on a VCR is an example of
(a) Time-shifting
(b) Content reference
(c) Mechanical clarity
(d) Media synchronization

12. Which of the following is/are the main challenge/s in ICT adoption in Indian universities?
(a) Lack of technological readiness
(b) Poor implementation of ICT initiatives
(c) Linguistic barrier
(d) All of the above

13. Which of the following parameter is/are used for expansion of higher education?
(a) Access (b) Equity
(c) Resources (d) All of the above

14. TKDL stands for
(a) Traditional knack digital library
(b) Traditional knowledge digital library
(c) Transfer knowledge desktop literature
(d) Transfer knowledge digital library

15. Sending and receiving messages/signals occurring at the same time is denoted by
(a) Synchronous
(b) Asynchronous
(c) Both a and b
(d) None of the above

16. Video conferencing is an example of
    (a) Synchronous technologies
    (b) Asynchronous technologies
    (c) Both synchronous and asynchronous
    (d) None of the above
17. Which of the following terms can be used in the context of education through CDs?
    (a) Synchronous
    (b) Asynchronous
    (c) Both a and b
    (d) None of the above
18. Digital divide is the term used in context of differentiation in use of IT/ICT?
    (a) Developed and developing nations
    (b) Urban and rural India
    (c) Both (a) and (b)
    (d) None of the above
19. In the hypermedia database, information bits are stored in the form of (*December 2005*)
    (a) Signals (b) Cubes
    (c) Nodes (d) Symbols
20. Communication bandwidth that has the highest capacity and is used by microwave, cable, and fibre optics lines is known as (*December 2005*)
    (a) Hyper link (b) Broadband
    (c) Bus width (d) Carrier wave
21. An electronic bill board that has a short text or graphical advertising message is referred to as (*December 2005*)
    (a) Bulletin (b) Strap
    (c) Bridge line (d) Banner
22. The concept of connect intelligence is derived from (*June 2006*)
    (a) Virtual reality
    (b) Fuzzy logic
    (c) Bluetooth technology
    (d) Value-added networks
23. The function of mass communication of applying information regarding the processes, issues, events, and societal developments is known as (*June 2006*)
    (a) Content supply (b) Surveillance
    (c) Gratification (d) Correlation
24. Information that is a combination of graphics, text, sound, video, and animation is called (*December 2008*)
    (a) Multiprogramme
    (b) Multifacet
    (c) Multimedia
    (d) Multiprocess
25. Which of the following institutions launched a knowledge repository e-Gyankosh in 2005 that aims at storing and preserving digital learning resources?
    (a) IIT-Kanpur
    (b) IGNOU
    (c) Allahabad University
    (d) Delhi University
26. The institution promoted by the Department of IT to provide communication infrastructure and services to academic research institutions in India is
    (a) INFLIBNET
    (b) UGC
    (c) ERNET
    (d) None of the above
27. The bouquet of FM radio channels which broadcast programs contributed by institutions such as IGNOU and IITs is
    (a) Gyan Vani
    (b) Gyan Darshan
    (c) EDUSAT
    (d) None of the above
28. Which of the following institutions has been working in the direction to develop a Virtual Technical University in India?
    (b) IGNOU (c) UGC
    (d) NMCEIT (e) AICTE
29. The joint initiative of the IITs and IISc to provide e-learning through online web and video courses in many streams, specifically engineering in the country, by providing free online courseware is
    (a) National Programme on Technology Enhanced Learning
    (b) AICTENET
    (c) NMCEIT
    (d) None of the above

30. Which organization has been assigned the task to develop e-content of 996 courses belonging to engineering, sciences, technology, humanities, and management?
    (a) IIT-Madras (b) BITS Pilani
    (c) IIT Mumbai (d) None of the above
31. 'A-View', the software that has been developed under the NMEICT is basically developed for
    (a) Teacher's Training
    (b) Technical training
    (c) Students' Training
    (d) All of the above
32. Web 2.0 tools have made traditional learning more social and personalized. Which of the following can be referred to as Web 2.0 tools?
    (a) Blogs and Wikis
    (b) Podcasts and Mashups
    (c) Social networking communities
    (d) All of the above
33. Which of the following services can help students to access computer files from remote locations though mobile phones?
    (a) Facebook (b) Renren
    (c) Soonr (d) Twitter
34. The satellite communication works through
    (a) Transponder (b) Radar
    (c) TV (d) Fibre optics cable

Computer Terms

35. Which of the following is the appropriate definition of a computer? (*December 2006*)
    (a) Computer is a machine that can process the information
    (b) Computer is an electronic device that can store, retrieve, and quickly process both quantitative and qualitative data quickly and accurately.
    (c) Computer is an electronic device that can store, retrieve, and quickly process only quantitative data.
    (d) Computer is an electronic device that can store, retrieve, and quickly process only qualitative data.
36. A computer consists of
    (a) A central processing unit
    (b) A memory
    (c) Input and output unit
    (d) All of the above
37. A typical modern computer uses
    (a) LSI chips (b) Vacuum tubes
    (c) Valves (d) All of the above
38. Which of the following is the correct statement? (*December 2004*)
    (a) Computers can be used for diagnosing the difficulty of a student in learning a subject.
    (b) Psychological testing can be done with the help of computer provided a software is available.
    (c) A set of instructions is called a programme.
    (d) All of the above
39. The pioneer organization in personal computer industry is
    (a) IBM (b) Apple
    (c) Compaq (d) Infosys
40. Which of the following terms is the most closely related to main memory?
    (a) Non-volatile (b) Permanent
    (c) Control unit (d) Temporary
41. Which of the following is used for manufacturing chips?
    (a) Control bus (b) Control unit
    (c) Parity unit (d) Semiconductor
42. Micro Processing is made for (*December 2008*)
    (a) Computer (b) Digital system
    (c) Calculator (d) Electronic goods
43. Group of instructions to direct the functioning of a computer is called
    (a) Storage (b) Memory
    (c) Program (d) Byte

44. The main component of first generation computer was
(a) Transistors
(b) Vacuum tubes and valves
(c) Integrated circuits
(d) None of the above

45. FORTRAN is the acronym for
(a) File translation
(b) Format translation
(c) Formula translation
(d) Floppy translation

46. Which of the following statements is not correct? (*December 2004*)
(a) Computer is capable of processing only digital signal.
(b) Computer is capable of analysing both quantitative and qualitative data.
(c) Appropriate software is required for processing the data.
(d) Computer is capable of processing digital as well as analogue signals.

47. Which of the following is not the characteristic of a computer? (*December 2005*)
(a) Computer is an electrical machine.
(b) Computer cannot think on its own.
(c) Computer processes an information error free
(d) Computer can hold data for any length of time.

48. In analogue computer
(a) Input is first converted to digital form
(b) Input is never converted to digital form
(c) Output is displayed in digital form
(d) All of the above

49. A hybrid computer
(a) Resembles a digital computer
(b) Resembles an analogue computer
(c) Resembles both a digital and analogue computer
(d) None of the above

50. In the latest generation computers, the instructions are executed
(a) Parallely only
(b) Sequentially only
(c) Both sequentially and parallely
(d) All of the above

51. Who designed the first electronics computer—ENIAC?
(a) Van-Neumann
(b) Joseph M. Jacquard
(c) J. Presper Eckert and John W. Mauchly
(d) None of the above

52. The hexadecimal number system consists of the symbols
(a) 0–7 (b) 0–9, A–F
(c) 0–7, A–F (d) None of the above

53. The binary equivalent of $(-15)_{10}$ is (two's complement system is used)
(a) 11110001 (b) 11110000
(c) 10001111 (d) None of the above

54. 1 GB is equal to
(a) 2^{30} bits (b) 2^{30} bytes
(c) 2^{20} bits (d) 2^{20} bytes

55. All computers—big, medium, or small must have
(a) ALU (b) Control unit
(c) Primary storage (d) All of the above

56. A byte consists of
(a) One bit (b) Four bits
(c) Eight bits (d) Sixteen bits

57. Which of the following is/are example/s of operating systems?
I. Unix/BSD
II. GNU/Linux
III. Windows
IV. Mac OS: Mac OS X
(a) I, II, and III (b) II, III, and IV
(c) I, III, and IV (d) All of the above

58. System software designed to help in analyzing, monitoring, configuring, optimizing settings, and maintaining the computer are called as
(a) Application software
(b) Utility software
(c) Groupware
(d) None of the above

59. The general term used for the software that can be copied and used without payment to the author(s), although there may be some restrictions on distribution is
(a) Spyware (b) Freeware
(c) Malware (d) None of the above

60. The silicon chips used for data processing are called
(a) RAM chips (b) ROM chips
(c) Microprocessors (d) PROM chips

61. The metal disks, which are permanently housed in sealed and contamination free containers are called
(a) Hard disks (b) Floppy disks
(c) Winchester disks (d) Flexible disks

62. All modern computers operate on
(a) Information (b) Floppies
(c) Data (d) Word

63. Instructions and memory address are represented by
(a) Character code (b) Binary codes
(c) Binary word (d) Parity bit

64. The computer size was very large in
(a) First generation
(b) Second generation
(c) Third generation
(d) Fourth generation

65. Microprocessors as switching devices are for which generation computers
(a) First generation
(b) Second generation
(c) Third generation
(d) Fourth generation

66. UNIVAC is
(a) Universal automatic computer
(b) Universal array computer
(c) Unique automatic computer
(d) Unvalued automatic computer

67. Which of the following programming languages is widely used in computer science, engineering and also in business?
(a) COBOL (b) FORTRAN
(c) PASCAL (d) LISP

68. The first electronic digital computer contained
(a) Electronic valves
(b) Vacuum tube
(c) Transistors
(d) Semiconductor memory

69. The name of Centre for Development of Advanced Computing's (C-DAC's) next generation high performance, scalable, computing cluster, breaking the barrier of computing power of one teraflop is
(a) PARAM (b) Chakra
(c) Shri (d) None of the above

70. Normally, these computers are used in banking, airlines, and railways etc. for their applications. They can accommodate more than 1,000 workstations simultaneously and can process data at a very high speed and can support concurrent programmes. These are
(a) Mainframe computers
(b) Micro computers
(c) Workstations
(d) Super computers

71. Which is used for manufacturing chips?
(a) Bus (b) Control unit
(c) Semiconductors (d) a and b only

72. Which of the following is the most powerful computer?
(a) Mini computer
(b) Microcomputer
(c) Mainframe computer
(d) Super computer

73. In which of the following languages, a source programme is written?
(a) English (b) Symbolic
(c) High level (d) Temporary

74. The set of computer programs that manage the hardware/software of a computer are called
(a) Compiler system
(b) Operation system
(c) Operating system
(d) None of the above

75. A software that converts a program in assembly language into the machine language is called
(a) Compiler (b) Assembler
(c) Interpreter (d) None of the above

76. A software which converts a high-level language program to machine language in one go is called
(a) Compiler (b) Assembler
(c) Interpreter (d) Loader

77. A computer program that converts an entire program into machine language is called a/an
(a) Interpreter (b) Simulator
(c) Compiler (d) Commander

78. A computer program that translates one program instructions at a time into machine language is called a/an
(a) Interpreter (b) CPU
(c) Compiler (d) Simulator

79. A small or intelligent device is so-called because it contains within it a
(a) Computer (b) Microcomputer
(c) Programmable (d) Sensor

80. Which of the following belongs to the first generation of computers?
(a) AC (b) IBM 1401
(c) IBM 8090 (d) UNIVAC

81. A collection of eight bits is called
(a) Byte (b) Word
(c) File (d) Folder

82. The brain of a computer which keeps peripherals under its control is called (*December 2007*)
(a) Common power unit
(b) Common processing unit
(c) Central power unit
(d) Central processing unit

83. Central processing unit consists of
(a) Input, output, and processor
(b) Input, output, processor, and browser
(c) Control unit, arithmetic logic unit, and primary storage
(d) Control unit, processor, and primary storage

84. ALU stands for
(a) Arithmetic Logic Unit
(b) Array Logic Unit
(c) Application Logic Unit
(d) None of the above

85. The ALU of a computer responds to the commands coming from
(a) Primary memory
(b) Control section
(c) External memory
(d) Cache memory

86. It contains buttons and menus that provide quick access to commonly used commands. It is a
(a) Menu bar (b) Toolbar
(c) Window (d) None of the above

87. The type of keys Ctrl, Shift, and Alt belong to is
(a) Adjustment (b) Function
(c) Modifier (d) Alphanumeric

88. Which of the following is a part of the central processing unit?
(a) Printer
(b) Keyboard
(c) Arithmetic logic unit
(d) None of the above

89. The instructions for starting the computer are set up on
(a) Random access memory
(b) CD-ROM
(c) Read-only memory chip
(d) All of the above

90. ALU of a computer normally contains a number of high-speed storage elements called
(a) Semiconductor memory
(b) Registers
(c) Hard disks
(d) Magnetic disk

91. A factor which would strongly influence a business person to adopt a computer is its
(a) Accuracy (b) Reliability
(c) Speed (d) All of the above

92. Keyboard of a computer is encoded in
(a) Baudot code (b) ASCII code
(c) BCDIC code (d) EBCDIC code

93. EBCDIC stands for
(a) Extended Binary Coded Decimal Interchange Code
(b) Extended Bit Code Decimal Interchange Code
(c) Extended Bit Case Decimal Interchange Code
(d) Extended Binary Case Decimal Interchange Code

94. EBCDIC can code up to how many different characters?
(a) 256 (b) 16 (c) 32 (d) 64

95. BCD is
(a) Binary Coded Decimal
(b) Bit Coded Decimal
(c) Binary Coded Digit
(d) Bit Coded Digit

96. ASCII stands for
(a) American Stable Code for International Interchange
(b) American Standard Case for Institutional Interchange
(c) American Standard Code for Information Interchange
(d) American Standard Code for Interchange Information

97. Which is the largest unit of storage among the following? (*December 2009*)
(a) Terabyte (b) Megabyte
(c) Kilobyte (d) Gigabyte

98. CD ROM stands for (*December 2007*)
(a) Computer Disk Read-only Memory
(b) Compact Disk Read-over Memory
(c) Compact Disk Read-only Memory
(d) Computer Disk Read-over Memory

99. Data can be saved on backing storage medium known as (*December 2007*)
(a) Compact disk recordable
(b) Computer disk rewriteable
(c) Compact disk rewritable
(d) Computer data rewritable

100. RAM means (*December 2007*)
(a) Random Access Memory
(b) Rigid Access memory
(c) Rapid Access Memory
(d) Revolving Access memory

101. In comparison to secondary storage, primary storage is
(a) Slower and lesser expensive
(b) Faster and more expensive
(c) Faster and lesser expensive
(d) Slower and more expensive

102. The two kinds of main memory are
(a) ROM and RAM
(b) Primary and secondary
(c) Floppy diskette and compact diskette
(d) None of the above

103. The act of retrieving existing data from memory is called
(a) Read-out (b) Read from
(c) Read (d) All of the above

104. RAM is used as short memory as it is
(a) Expensive (b) Small capacity
(c) Programmable (d) Volatile

105. The computer memory used for temporary storage of data and program is called
(a) ROM (b) RAM
(c) EROM (d) EPROM

106. The memory which is programmed at the time of its manufacturing is
(a) ROM (b) RAM
(c) PROM (d) EPROM

107. Which of the following is a secondary memory device?
(a) CPU
(b) ALU
(c) Floppy diskette
(d) None of the above

108. The most important advantage of a video disk is
(a) Compactness
(b) Potential capacity
(c) Durability
(d) Cost effectiveness

109. Floppy disks which are made from flexible plastic material are also called?
(a) Hard disks
(b) High-density disks
(c) Diskettes
(d) Templates

110. What is the latest write-once optical storage media?
(a) Digital paper
(b) Magneto-optical disk
(c) WORM disk
(d) CD-ROM disk

111. Regarding a VDU, which statement is more correct?
(a) It is an output device
(b) It is an input device
(c) It is a peripheral device
(d) It is hardware item

112. The two main memory types are:
(a) Primary and secondary
(b) Random and sequential
(c) ROM and RAM
(d) All of the above

113. Which of the following will happen when data is entered into a memory location?
(a) It will add to the content of the location
(b) It will change the address of the memory location
(c) It will erase the previous content
(d) It will not be fruitful if there is already some data at the location

114. A storage area used to store data to compensate for the difference in speed at which the different units can handle data is
(a) Memory (b) Buffer
(c) Accumulator (d) Address

115. Which of the following memories allow simultaneous read and write operations?
(a) ROM (b) RAM
(c) EPROM (d) None of the above

116. Which of the following memories has the shortest access times?
(a) Cache memory
(b) Magnetic bubble memory
(c) Magnetic core memory
(d) RAM

117. To locate a data item for storage is
(a) Field (b) Feed
(c) Database (d) Fetch

118. The magnetic storage chip used to provide non-volatile direct access storage of data and that has no moving parts is known as
(a) Magnetic core memory
(b) Magnetic tape memory
(c) Magnetic disk memory
(d) Magnetic bubble memory

119. The OCR stands for
(a) Operational Character Reader
(b) Optical Character Reader
(c) Only Character Reader
(d) None of the above

120. As compared to secondary memory, the primary memory of a computer is
(a) Large (b) Cheap
(c) Fast (d) Slow

121. Which of the following is a way to access secondary memory?
(a) Random access memory
(b) Action method
(c) Transfer method
(d) Density method

122. A CD-RW disk
(a) has faster access than other disks
(b) is a type of optical disk
(c) can be written only once
(d) can be erased and rewritten

123. EEPROM stands for
(a) Electrically Erasable Programmable Read-only Memory
(b) Easily Erasable Programmable Read-only Memory
(c) Electronic Erasable Programmable Read-only Memory
(d) None of the above

124. Which of the following statements is correct? *(December 2004)*
(a) Virus improves the speed of processing information through the computer
(b) The Internet does not allow a virus to spread
(c) Virus is a part of software
(d) Virus is an operating system

125. VGA denotes
(a) Video Graphics Array
(b) Visual Graphics Array
(c) Volatile Graphics Array
(d) Video Graphics Adapter

126. MSI stands for
(a) Medium Scale Integrated Circuits
(b) Medium System Integrated Circuits
(c) Medium Scale Intelligent Circuit
(d) Medium System Intelligent Circuit

127. WAN stands for
(a) WAP Area Network
(b) Wide Area Network
(c) Wide Array Net
(d) Wireless Area Network

128. MICR stands for
(a) Magnetic Ink Character Reader
(b) Magnetic Ink Code Reader
(c) Magnetic Ink Cases Reader
(d) None of the above

129. Which of the following devices can be used to directly image printed text?
(a) OCR (b) OMR
(c) MICR (d) All of the above

130. The output quality of a printer is measured by
(a) Dot per inch
(b) Dot per square inch
(c) Dots printed per unit time
(d) All of the above

131. Which printer is very commonly used for desktop publishing?
(a) Laser printer
(b) Inkjet printer
(c) Daisywheel printer
(d) Dot matrix printer

132. An output device that uses words or messages recorded on a magnetic medium to produce audio response is
(a) Magnetic tape
(b) Voice response unit
(c) Voice recognition unit
(d) Voice band

133. An error in software or hardware is called a bug. What is the alternative computer jargon for it?
(a) Leech (b) Squid
(c) Slug (d) Glitch

134. Errors in computer programme are called
(a) Follies (b) Mistakes
(c) Bugs (d) Spam

135. Modern computers are very reliable but they are not
(a) Fast (b) Powerful
(c) Infallible (d) Cheap

136. Personal computers use a number of chips mounted on a main circuit board. What is the common name for such boards?
(a) Daughter board (b) Motherboard
(c) Father board (d) Dash board

137. What is meant by a dedicated computer?
(a) Which is used by one person only
(b) Which is assigned one and only one task
(c) Which uses one kind of software
(d) Which is meant for application software

138. The system unit of a personal computer typically contains all of the following except:
(a) Microprocessor
(b) Disk controller
(c) Serial interface
(d) Modem

139. Programs designed to perform specific tasks are known as
(a) System software
(b) Application software
(c) Utility programs
(d) Operating system

140. Time during which a job is processed by the computer is
(a) Delay time (b) Real time
(c) Execution time (d) Down time

141. An approach that permits the computer to work on several programs instead of one is
(a) On-line thesaurus
(b) Multiprogramming
(c) Over-lapped processing
(d) Outline processor

142. The term gigabyte refers to
(a) 1024 bytes
(b) 1024 kilobytes
(c) 1024 megabytes
(d) 1024 gigabyte

143. Device that provides information, which is sent to the CPU is termed as
(a) Input (b) Output
(c) CPU (d) Memory

144. The type of media with varying capacities that is used in the storage subsystem in a microcomputer is

(a) Memory or video
(b) Magnetic or optical
(c) Optical or memory
(d) Video or magnetic

145. Which is considered a direct entry input device?
(a) Optical scanner
(b) Mouse and digitizer
(c) Light pen
(d) All of the above

146. The computer code for interchange of information between terminals is
(a) ASCII (b) BCD
(c) EBCDIC (d) All of the above

147. On the keyboard of a computer, each character has an ASCII value which stands for
(a) American Stock Code for Information Interchange
(b) American Standard Code for Information Interchange
(c) African Standard Code for Information Interchange
(d) Adaptable Standard Code for Information Interchange

148. Which part of the CPU performs calculations and makes decisions
(a) Arithmetic logic unit
(b) Alternating logic unit
(c) Alternate local unit
(d) American logic unit

149. Dpi stands for
(a) Dots per inch
(b) Digits per unit
(c) Dots pixel inch
(d) Diagrams per inch

150. The process of laying out a document with texts, graphics, headlines, and photographs is involved in
(a) Deck top publishing
(b) Desktop printing
(c) Desktop publishing
(d) Deck top printing

151. Transfer of data from one application to another line is known as
(a) Dynamic disk exchange
(b) Dodgy data exchange
(c) Dogmatic data exchange
(d) Dynamic data exchange

152. An application program that helps the user to change any number and immediately see the result of that change is
(a) Desktop publishing program
(b) Database
(c) Spreadsheet
(d) All of the above

153. CAD stands for
(a) Computer Aided Design
(b) Computer Algorithm for Design
(c) Computer Application in Design
(d) All of the above

154. Which of the following is required when more than one person use a central computer at the same time?
(a) Terminal (b) Light pen
(c) Digitizer (d) Mouse

155. Which of the following is used only for data entry and storage, and never for processing?
(a) Mouse
(b) Dumb terminal
(c) Microcomputer
(d) Dedicated data entry system

156. Which of the following will be required to produce high quality graphics?
(a) RGB monitor (b) Plotter
(c) Ink-jet printer (d) Laser printer

157. Magnetic tape can serve as
(a) Secondary storage media
(b) Output media
(c) Input media
(d) All of the above

158. If in a computer, 16 bits are used to specify address in a RAM, the number of addresses will be
(a) 216 (b) 65,536
(c) 64K (d) Any of the above

159. The two major types of computer chips are
(a) External memory chip
(b) Primary memory chip

(c) Microprocessor chip
(d) Both (b) and (c)

160. What is the responsibility of the logical unit in the CPU of a computer?
(a) To produce result
(b) To compare numbers
(c) To control the flow of information
(d) To do mathematical works

161. The secondary storage devices can only store data but they cannot perform
(a) Arithmetic operations
(b) Logical operation
(c) Fetch operations
(d) Either of the above

162. Which of the printers used in conjunction with computers use dry ink powder?
(a) Daisy wheel printer
(b) Line printer
(c) Laser printer
(d) Thermal printer

163. Which of the following produces the best quality graphics reproduction?
(a) Laser printer
(b) Ink jet printer
(c) Plotter
(d) Dot matrix printer

164. A 32-bit microprocessor has a word length equal to
(a) 2 byte (b) 32 byte
(c) 4 byte (d) 8 byte

165. An error in computer data is called
(a) Chip (b) Bug
(c) CPU (d) Storage device

166. A set of information that defines the status of resources allocated to a process is
(a) Process control
(b) ALU
(c) Register unit
(d) Process description

167. Any method for controlling access to or use of memory is known as
(a) Memory map
(b) Memory protection
(c) Memory management
(d) Memory instruction

168. The accounting software Tally was developed by
(a) HCL (b) TCS
(c) Infosys (d) Wipro

The Internet and E-mail

169. www represents (*December 2007*)
(a) Who What And Where
(b) Weird Wide Web
(c) Word Wide Web
(d) World Wide Web

170. What is the Internet?
(a) A hardware networking technique
(b) World Wide Web
(c) Computers that are all linked together in a network
(d) None of the above

171. Which of the following is the appropriate format of URL of e-mail?
(*December 2006*)
(a) www_mail.com
(b) www@mail.com
(c) WWW@mail.com
(d) www.mail.com

172. HTML is basically used to design
(*December 2008*)
(a) Webpage
(b) Website
(c) Graphics
(d) Tables and frames

173. Which of the following protocols manages the assembling of a message or file into smaller packets that are transmitted over the Internet and received by a layer that reassembles the packets into the original message. It also handles the address part of each packet so that it gets to the right destination?

(a) HTTP (b) TCP/IP
(c) FTP (d) All of the above

174. A set of guidelines or standards that establish the format in which files can be transmitted from one computer to another is
(a) TCP (b) IP
(c) FTP (d) All of the above

175. The protocol used specifically for exchange of e-mails is
(a) SMTP
(b) TCP
(c) IP
(d) None of the above

176. SMTP stands for
(a) Simplest Mail Transfer Protocol
(b) Simple Mail Transfer Protocol
(c) Sample Mail Transfer Protocol
(d) Separate Mail Transfer Protocol

177. In web search, finding a large number of documents with very little relevant information is termed (*June 2006*)
(a) Poor recall
(b) Web crawl
(c) Poor precision rate
(d) Poor web response

178. A word in a web page that, when clicked, opens another document is
(a) Anchor (b) URL
(c) Hyperlink (d) Reference

179. Which of the following identifies a specific web page and its computer on the web?
(a) Website (b) Website address
(c) URL (d) Domain name

180. Which of the following terms applies to all the web pages for Amazon.com?
(a) Top-level domain
(b) Website
(c) Website address
(d) Web domain

181. Softwares, such as Explorer and Firefox, are referred to as
(a) Systems software
(b) Utility software
(c) Browsers
(d) The Internet tools

182. Firewalls are used to protect a communication network against
(a) Unauthorized attacks
(b) Virus attacks
(c) Data-driven attacks
(d) Fire attacks

183. Use of an ordinary telephone as an Internet appliance is called (*June 2006*)
(a) Voice net (b) Voice telephone
(c) Voice line (d) Voice portal

184. Which of the following ISP is free of cost?
(a) CompuServe
(b) AOL
(c) NetZero
(d) None of the above

185. Which of the following is virtual reality website?
(a) First Life
(b) Second Life
(c) Gyanlife
(d) None of the above

186. Which of the following statements is correct? (*December 2006*)
(a) Modem is a software
(b) Modem helps in stabilizing the voltage
(c) Modem is an operating system
(d) Modem converts analogue signals into digital and vice versa

187. Which of the following refers to an educational website that allows its members to add or change its information?
(a) Educational or .edu
(b) Social networking site
(c) Wiki
(d) Web 2.0

188. If you want to create a broadcast that can be downloaded from the Internet, what would you create?
(a) IBroadcast (b) EShow
(c) Podcast (d) ICast

189. Video transmission over the Internet that looks like delayed livecasting is called
(a) Virtual video (b) Direct broadcast
(c) Video shift (d) Real-time video

190. It is a very high-speed data transmission line that provides networking facilities to relatively small but high-speed Internet service providers (including commercial, educational, military, government establishments) all around the world. It is called as
(a) Pathway
(b) Backbone
(c) Communication system
(d) Routers

191. Using websites to pour out one's grievances is called *(June 2006)*
(a) Cyberventing (b) Cyber ranting
(c) Web hate (d) Web plea

192. What type of telecommunication hardware allows you to access the web?
(a) Browser (b) Modem
(c) FTP protocol (d) IRC

193. VoIP technology converts voice calls from
(a) analogue to digital
(b) Digital to analogue
(c) It depends
(d) None of the above

194. What is the domain originally meant for non-profitable organizations
(a) .gov (b) .org (c) .net (d) .in

195. Which of the following is the Internet connection option?
(a) Dial-up Connection
(b) Digital Subscriber Line
(c) Broadband
(d) All of the above

196. Which of the following is not related to information security on the Internet? *(December 2009)*
(a) Data encryption
(b) Water marking
(c) Data hiding
(d) Information retrieval

197. Bit stands for *(December 2009)*
(a) Binary information term
(b) Binary tree
(c) Binary digit
(d) Bivariate theory

198. Which one of the following is not a linear data structure? *(December 2009)*
(a) Array (b) Binary tree
(c) Queue (d) CPU

199. A compiler is used to convert the following to object code which can be executed *(December 2009)*
(a) High level language
(b) Low level language
(c) Assembly language
(d) Natural language

200. Which of the following is not a network device? *(December 2009)*
(a) Router (b) Switch
(c) Hub (d) CPU

201. What is the full form of http?
(a) HyperText Transmission Protocol
(b) HyperText Transfer Protocol
(c) HyperTerminal Transport Protocol
(d) HyperTerminal Transfer Protocol

202. The protocol dealing with transfer of hypertext between two or more computers is
(a) HTML (b) FTP
(c) HTTP (d) TCP

203. IRC stands for
(a) Internet Related Chat
(b) Internet Relay Chat
(c) Internet Related Content
(d) None of the above

204. Line access and avoidance of collision are main functions of *(December 2005)*
(a) CPU
(b) Monitor
(c) Network protocols
(d) Wide area networks

205. Which of these are types of internet connections?
(a) SLIP (b) DIAS
(c) PPP (d) All of the above

206. Internet's initial development was supported by
(a) ARPANET (b) Bill Rogers
(c) Bill Gates (d) Microsoft

207. The Internet Explorer was invented and released by

(a) Microsoft
(b) WIPRO
(c) Sun Microsystems
(d) Infosys

208. Gopher protocol is used to
(a) distributing documents over the Internet
(b) searching documents over the Internet
(c) retrieving documents over the Internet
(d) All of the above

209. World Wide Web was proposed by
(a) Bill Gates
(b) ARPANET
(c) Tim Berners-Lee
(d) Bill Rogers

210. What are the uses of the Internet?
(a) Communication
(b) Information retrieval
(c) Presentation of information
(d) All of the above

211. .edu domain is used for
(a) Educational institution
(b) The Internet infrastructure and service providers
(c) International organizations
(d) None of the above

212. What is the full form of URL?
(a) Uniform Resource Library
(b) Uniform Resource Locators
(c) United Resource Library
(d) United Resource Locators

213. The main advantages an e-mail are?
(a) Speed
(b) Cost
(c) Record keeping
(d) All of the above

214. www provides standardized access to
(a) GOPHER (b) Telnet
(c) FTP (d) All of the above

215. Which of these is not an Internet browser?
(a) Netscape Navigator
(b) Chrome
(c) Drupal
(d) Opera

216. What is the World Wide Web?
(a) A computer game
(b) A software program
(c) Part of the Internet that enables information sharing via interconnected pages
(d) Another name for the internet

217. Which one of the following is a search engine?
(a) Macromedia Flash
(b) Google
(c) Netscape
(d) Librarians' Index to the Internet

218. What is a URL?
(a) A computer software program
(b) A type of UFO
(c) Address of a document or page on the www.
(d) An acronym for unlimited resources for learning

219. http://www.classzone.com is an example of what?
(a) URL (b) Access code
(c) Directory (d) Server

220. What is a browser?
(a) An HTML system
(b) A server
(c) Application software for accessing and viewing web pages
(d) None of the above

221. A chat program that allows people to communicate over the Internet in real time is called as
(a) Distant Messaging
(b) Instant Messaging
(c) Chatting room
(d) All of the above

222. The first page of a Website is called the
(a) Home page
(b) Index
(c) Menu bar
(d) None of the above

223. HTML is an acronym of
(a) High Tech Markup Language
(b) How To Markup Language

(c) Hyper Text Markup Language
(d) HoT MeaL

224. A machine that links two networks using two different protocols is called as
(a) Gateway (b) Protocol way
(c) e-way (d) Gate

225. E-mail is an abbreviation of
(a) Electronic mail
(b) Extra mail
(c) Enhanced mail
(d) None of the above

226. ISP is an acronym of
(a) Internal Service Provider
(b) Internet Service Procedure
(c) Internet Service Provider
(d) Instant Service Protocol

227. Web Server is a software for
(a) Analysing web traffic
(b) Serving web page upon user's request
(c) Crawling the web
(d) Unix operating system

228. FTP stands for
(a) Full Text Processing
(b) File Transfer Program
(c) File Transfer Process
(d) File Transfer Protocol

229. Telnet is
(a) A telephone network
(b) A teller network
(c) Standard Internet protocol for remote login
(d) Dialup program

230. LAN is an acronym of
(a) Local Area Network
(b) Logical Area Network
(c) Last Area Network
(d) None of the above

231. The term used to connect a number of computers within the same location or in close proximity is
(a) LAN (b) WAN
(c) PAN (d) All of the above

232. Ethernet is a family of protocols used in
(a) LAN
(b) The Internet
(c) Extranet
(d) None of the above

233. MAN is a network of computers located at different sites within a large fixed area, such as a city. It stands for
(a) Metropolitan Area Network
(b) Manual Area Network
(c) Marginal Area Network
(d) Maximum Area Network

234. A computer network in which some of the links between the nodes are carried by open connections or virtual circuits in some larger network such as an internet instead of physical wires is a
(a) Virtual private network
(b) Virtual public network
(c) Virtual private net
(d) Virtual public net

235. This type of computer networking is accessible to computers that are not physically part of an organization's own private network, but are also not accessible to the general public is
(a) The Internet
(b) Intranet
(c) Extranet
(d) None of the above

236. Name of the protocol that supports linking from one web page to another page
(a) HTML (b) IP
(c) HTTP (d) FTP

237. The first part of a complete URL that is required to access the web resource
(a) Address (b) Name
(c) Location (d) Protocol

238. An address for a specific document found on the web is termed as
(a) HTTP
(b) URL
(c) ISP
(d) Nonc of the above

239. Which of the following organizes the web into categories?
(a) Search engine (b) Encyclopaedia
(c) Archive (d) Directory

240. A large number of computers in a wide geographical area can be efficiently connected using
(a) Twisted pair lines
(b) Coaxial cables
(c) Communications satellites
(d) All of the above

241. A computer network allows sharing of resources. The software resources exist in the form of files of data, which need to be moved between two specific computer systems for the purpose of sharing
(a) Address for communication
(b) A secure means for moving data in the form of electronic signals
(c) Both (a) and (b)
(d) Either (a) or (b)

242. The hardware and software combinations that connect devices running different native protocols are called as
(a) Protocols (b) Models
(c) Gateways (d) Ports

243. USB stands for:
(a) United Serial Bus
(b) Universal Serial By-Pass
(c) Universal Serial Bus
(d) Universal System Bus

244. Which of the following denotes the Internet hardware requirements?
I. Modem
II. Hub
III. Bridge
IV. Router
V. Gateway
(a) I, II, III
(b) I, III, IV, and V
(c) I, IV, and V
(d) I, II, III, IV, and V

245. Network-based e-mail was initially exchanged on the
(a) ARPANET
(b) SMTP
(c) TCP/IP
(d) None of the above

246. The type of digital telephone service, used for transferring large chunks of data to and from the Internet without a modem is
(a) ISDN (b) MSDN
(c) TSDN (d) None of the above

247. The term/protocol used for open wireless technology for data exchange over short distances is
(a) ISDN (b) Bluetooth
(c) Wi-Fi (d) None of the above

248. ISDN stands for
(a) Integrated Services Digital Network
(b) Intelligent Services Digital Network
(c) Individual Services Digital Network
(d) Image Services Digital Network

249. Wired Ethernet is basically
(a) ADSL (b) ISDN
(c) Broadband (d) The Internet

250. The software that permits a user—with a click of mouse—to locate, display, and download text, video, audio, and graphics stored in a host computer on the web is a
(a) Web browser
(b) Domain
(c) URL
(d) None of the above

251. Which of the following are web browsers?
I. Internet Explorer
II. Mozilla Firefox
III. Opera
IV. Safari
(a) I, II, and III (b) II, III, and IV
(c) 1, III, and IV (d) All of the above

252. Which of the following domain name extension is used for gateways and administrative hosts?
(a) .gov (b) .mil (c) .net (d) .org

253. .com, .org, .net are popular as
(a) Top level domains
(b) Tax level domains
(c) Terrific level domains
(d) None of the above

254. The unique numerical address of a computer on the Internet (expressed as four sets of numbers and maximum 3 digits each,

separated by dots such as 150.237.176.24) is termed as

(a) Internet protocol address
(b) URL
(c) ISP
(d) None of the above

255. The term used for a search tool that sends user requests to several other search engines and/or databases and aggregates the results into a single list or displays them according to their source is

(a) Meta search engine
(b) Google
(c) Moodle
(d) None of the above

256. An Internet e-mail message consists of

I. Message envelope
II. Message header
III. Message body

(a) I and II (b) II and III
(c) I and III (d) All of the above

257. Which of the following symbols is in e-mail addresses to separate the username from the ISP?

(a) $ (b) @ (c) % (d) *

258. The size of the IPv4 is:

(a) 16 Bits (b) 32 Bits
(c) 64 Bits (d) 128 Bits

259. Which of the following can be used to send e-mails to a large group at one time?

(a) Listserv (b) Group
(c) Groupware (d) Mail server

260. Which of the following line gives an overview of message while sending an e-mail?

(a) To (b) Subject
(c) Contents (d) CC

261. Unsolicited commercial e-mail is usually referred to as

(a) Junk (b) Hoaxes
(c) Spam (d) Hypertext

262. Which of the following is used by news servers to distribute documents to readers?

(a) Network News Transfer Protocol (NNTP)
(b) Hypertext Transfer Protocol
(c) File Transfer Protocol
(d) None of the above

263. To search FTP archives for a file, the tool used is

(a) Gophe (b) Jughead
(c) Archie (d) Jalopy

264. Which of the following is often referred to as 'The CB of the Internet'?

(a) IRC (b) FTP
(c) e-mail (d) HTTP

265. Which of the following monitors postings and enforces the site's rules in context of discussion groups?

(a) Judge (b) Sysop
(c) Narrator (d) Censor

266. A message with replies on a newsgroup is often called a

(a) List (b) Thread
(c) Comment (d) Post

267. S/MIME in the Internet technology stands for

(a) Secure Multipurpose Internet Mail Extension
(b) Secure Multimedia Internet Mail Extension
(c) Simple Multipurpose Internet Mail Extension
(d) Simple Multipurpose Internet Mail Extension

268. A small text file that a web server stores on a user hard drive when the user visits certain web sites is called

(a) Cookie
(b) History
(c) Logjam
(d) None of the above

269. Which of the following software allows users to surf the Internet?

(a) Search engine
(b) Internet service provider
(c) Multimedia
(d) Browser

Misc MCQs on ICT

270. Which of the following pair is not correctly managed? (*December 2004*)
(a) Aaj Tak—24 hours news channel
(b) P. M Stations—radio
(c) National Geographic Channel—television
(d) Vir Sanghvi—India Today

271. Which is the oldest soap opera telecasted in India? (*December 2004*)
(a) Kahani Ghar Ghar Ki
(b) Buniyaad
(c) Hum Log
(d) Kyunki Saas Bhi Kabhi Bahu Thee

272. Which satellite channel uses the ad line, 'knowing is everything'? (*December 2004*)
(a) BBC World (b) Star
(c) Sony (d) Zee

273. Which is the first 'made in India' kids channel of television? (*December 2004*)
(a) Cartoon Network
(b) Walt Disney
(c) United Home Entertainment's Hungama TV
(d) Nick Jr.

274. The largest number of newspapers in India is published from the state of (*December 2005*)
(a) Kerala (b) Maharashtra
(c) West Bengal (d) Uttar Pradesh

275. The launch of satellite channel by IGNOU on 26th January 2003 for technological education for the growth and development of distance education is: (*December 2005*)
(a) Eklavya Technology channel
(b) Gyan Darshan channel
(c) Rajrishi channel
(d) None of the above

276. Networked media exist in interconnected: (*June 2006*)
(a) Social environment
(b) Economic environment
(c) Political environment
(d) Technological environment

277. The combination of computing, telecommunication and media in a digital atmosphere is referred to as (*June 2006*)
(a) Online communication
(b) Integrated media
(c) Digital combine
(d) Convergence

278. A dialogue between a human being and a computer programme that occurs simultaneously in various forms is described as
(a) Man-machine speak
(b) Binary chat
(c) Digital talk
(d) Interactivity

279. Which is the 24 hours English business news channel in India? (*December 2006*)
(a) Zee News (b) NDTV 24 × 7
(c) CNBC (d) India News

280. Which of the following pair is not correctly matched? (*December 2006*)
(a) N Ram : The Hindu
(b) Barkha Dutt : Zee News
(c) Prannoy Roy : NDTV 24 × 7
(d) Prabhu Chawla : Aaj Tak

281. 'Because you deserve to know' is the punch line used by (*December 2006*)
(a) The Times of India
(b) The Hindu
(c) Indian Express
(d) Hindustan Times

282. Press Council of India is located in (*June 2007*)
(a) Chennai (b) Mumbai
(c) Kolkata (d) Delhi

283. DTH service was started in India in the year (*December 2007*)
(a) 2000 (b) 2002
(c) 2004 (d) 2006

284. National Press Day is celebrated on (*December 2007*)
(a) 16th November (b) 19th November
(c) 21st November (d) 30th November

285. The total number of members in the Press Council of India is (*December 2007*)
(a) 28 (b) 14 (c) 17 (d) 20

286. The right to impart and receive information is guaranteed in the Constitution of India by Article (*December 2007*)
(a) 19 (2) (a) (b) 19 (16)
(c) 19 (2) (d) 19 (1) (a)

287. Use of radio for higher education is based on the presumption of (*December 2007*)
(a) Enriching curriculum-based instruction
(b) Replacing a teacher in the long run
(c) Everybody having access to a radio set
(d) Other means of instruction getting outdated

288. The first Indian satellite for serving the education sector is known as
(a) SATEDU (b) INSAT B
(c) EDUSAT (d) INSAT C

289. Exclusive educational channel of IGNOU is known as
(a) Gyan Darshan (b) Gyan Vani
(c) Doordarshan (d) Prasar Bharati

290. Community radio is a type of radio service that caters to the interests of
(a) Local audience (b) Education
(c) Entertainment (d) News

291. Orkut is a part of
(a) Intrapersonal communication
(b) Mass communication
(c) Group communication
(d) Interpersonal communication

292. The biggest news agency of India is (*June 2008*)
(a) PTI (b) UNI
(c) NANAP (d) Samachar Bharti

293. Which broadcasting system for TV is followed in India (*June 2008*)
(a) NTSE (b) PAL
(c) SECAM (d) NTCS

294. All India Radio, before 1936, was known as (*June 2008*)
(a) Indian Radio Broadcasting
(b) Broadcasting Service of India
(c) Indian State Broadcasting Service
(d) All Indian Broadcasting Service

295. Prasar Bharti was launched in India in the year
(a) 1995 (b) 1997
(c) 1999 (d) 2001

296. Eklavya Technology channel, started in 2003, is a distant-learning joint initiative between
(a) IIT and IGNOU
(b) IIIT and IGNOU
(c) UGC and AICTE
(d) IIT and AICTE

297. Virtual education refers to imparting instructions in a learning environment where the teacher and the students are separated by
(a) Time only
(b) Space only
(c) May be both (a) and (b)
(d) None of the above

298. Which of the following technology is mostly used by a teacher in virtual education?
(a) Course management applications
(b) Multimedia resources
(c) The Internet
(d) Video-conferencing

299. In which of the following years community radio started in India?
(a) 2001 (b) 2002
(c) 2003 (d) 2004

300. The number of bits that makes one nibble is
(a) 8 (b) 16
(c) 4 (d) None of the above

301. Which of the following is the only flash memory?
(a) RAM (b) EEPROM
(c) PROM (d) EPROM

302. SIMM is
(a) Serial in Memory Module
(b) Serial Input Memory Module
(c) Synchronous In Memory Module
(d) Synchronous Input Memory Module

303. Which of the following is not an example of primary memory?
(a) RAM (b) ROM
(c) Cache Memory (d) Magnetic Tape

304. Which of the following memory has the highest capacity?
(a) USB (b) Virtual Memory
(c) Hard Disk (d) None of the above

305. Which of the following figure depicts normal size of cache memory?
(a) 8 KB (b) 8 MB
(c) 8 GB (d) None of the above

306. Central processing unit performs read or write operations directly with
(a) ROM (b) RAM
(c) Hard Disk (d) Registers

307. The algorithm is basically
(a) Solution of a program
(b) Random idea about a program
(c) The logical flow of a program
(d) None of the above

308. The file extension of MS Window sound file is
(a) .m (b) .c
(c) .wav (d) None of the above

309. The file extension of Excel spread sheet is
(a) .doc (b) .txt
(c) .xls (d) .ppt

310. The XML stands for
(a) Extensible Markup Language
(b) External Makeup Language
(c) External Markup Logic
(d) External Magnitude Language

311. The standard size of IP address is
(a) 16 bits (b) 32 bits
(c) 48 bits (d) 64 bits

312. Multimedia is basically a/an
(a) Animation feature
(b) Programming language
(c) Technology
(d) All of the above

313. What do you need to put your web pages on the www?
(a) A connection to the Internet
(b) A web browser
(c) A web server
(d) All of the above

314. Which is the largest unit of storage among the following?
(a) Terabyte (b) Megabyte
(c) Kilobyte (d) Gigabyte

315. Which of the following is not a linear data structure?
(a) Array (b) Binary tree
(c) Queue (d) Stack

316. Which of the following is not a network device?
(a) Router (b) Switch
(c) Hub (d) CPU

317. Which one of the following represents the binary equivalent of the decimal number 23?
(a) 01011
(b) 10111
(c) 10011
(d) None of the above

318. Computers on the Internet are identified by
(a) e-mail address
(b) Street address
(c) IP address
(d) None of the above

319. An example of asynchronous medium is
(a) Radio (b) Television
(c) Film (d) Newspaper

320. A message beneath a message is labelled as
(a) Embedded text (b) Internal text
(c) Inter-text (d) Sub-text

321. In analogue mass communication, stories are
(a) Static (b) Dynamic
(c) Interactive (d) Exploratory

Answer Keys

ICT Basics

1. (a) 2. (a) 3. (d) 4. (c) 5. (b)
6. (a) 7. (c) 8. (d) 9. (c) 10. (c)
11. (a) 12. (d) 13. (d) 14. (b) 15. (a)
16. (a) 17. (b) 18. (c) 19. (a) 20. (b)
21. (b) 22. (d) 23. (b) 24. (c) 25. (b)
26. (c) 27. (a) 28. (d) 29. (a) 30. (a)
31. (a) 32. (d) 33. (b) 34. (a)

Computer Terms

35. (b) 36. (d) 37. (a) 38. (d) 39. (a)
40. (d) 41. (d) 42. (a) 43. (c) 44. (b)
45. (c) 46. (d) 47. (a) 48. (b) 49. (c)
50. (c) 51. (c) 52. (b) 53. (a) 54. (b)
55. (d) 56. (c) 57. (d) 58. (b) 59. (b)
60. (c) 61. (a) 62. (c) 63. (b) 64. (a)
65. (d) 66. (a) 67. (c) 68. (d) 69. (a)
70. (a) 71. (c) 72. (d) 73. (c) 74. (c)
75. (b) 76. (a) 77. (c) 78. (a) 79. (d)
80. (d) 81. (a) 82. (d) 83. (c) 84. (a)
85. (b) 86. (b) 87. (b) 88. (c) 89. (c)
90. (b) 91. (d) 92. (b) 93. (d) 94. (a)
95. (a) 96. (c) 97. (a) 98. (c) 99. (c)
100. (a) 101. (b) 102. (a) 103. (d) 104. (d)
105. (b) 106. (a) 107. (c) 108. (b) 109. (c)
110. (d) 111. (c) 112. (c) 113. (c) 114. (b)
115. (b) 116. (a) 117. (d) 118. (d) 119. (b)
120. (c) 121. (a) 122. (d) 123. (a) 124. (c)
125. (a) 126. (a) 127. (b) 128. (a) 129. (a)
130. (a) 131. (a) 132. (a) 133. (d) 134. (c)
135. (c) 136. (b) 137. (b) 138. (d) 139. (b)
140. (c) 141. (c) 142. (c) 143. (a) 144. (b)
145. (d) 146. (a) 147. (b) 148. (a) 149. (a)
150. (c) 151. (d) 152. (c) 153. (a) 154. (a)
155. (b) 156. (b) 157. (d) 158. (b) 159. (d)
160. (b) 161. (d) 162. (c) 163. (c) 164. (c)
165. (b) 166. (d) 167. (b) 168. (b)

The Internet and E-mail

169. (d) 170. (c) 171. (b) 172. (a) 173. (b)
174. (c) 175. (a) 176. (b) 177. (a) 178. (c)
179. (d) 180. (b) 181. (c) 182. (a) 183. (c)
184. (c) 185. (b) 186. (d) 187. (c) 188. (c)
189. (d) 190. (b) 191. (a) 192. (b) 193. (a)
194. (b) 195. (d) 196. (d) 197. (b) 198. (b)
199. (a) 200. (d) 201. (b) 202. (c) 203. (b)
204. (c) 205. (d) 206. (a) 207. (a) 208. (d)
209. (d) 210. (d) 211. (a) 212. (b) 213. (d)
214. (d) 215. (c) 216. (c) 217. (b) 218. (c)
219. (a) 220. (c) 221. (b) 222. (a) 223. (c)
224. (a) 225. (a) 226. (c) 227. (b) 228. (d)
229. (a) 230. (a) 231. (a) 232. (a) 233. (a)
234. (a) 235. (b) 236. (c) 237. (d) 238. (b)
239. (d) 240. (c) 241. (c) 242. (c) 243. (c)
244. (d) 245. (a) 246. (a) 247. (b) 248. (a)
249. (b) 250. (a) 251. (d) 252. (c) 253. (a)
254. (a) 255. (a) 256. (d) 257. (b) 258. (b)
259. (c) 260. (b) 261. (c) 262. (a) 263. (b)
264. (a) 265. (b) 266. (b) 267. (a) 268. (a)
269. (d)

Misc MCQs on ICT

270. (d) 271. (c) 272. (a) 273. (c) 274. (d)
275. (a) 276. (d) 277. (d) 278. (d) 279. (c)
280. (b) 281. (d) 282. (d) 283. (c) 284. (a)
285. (a) 286. (d) 287. (c) 288. (c) 289. (a)
290. (a) 291. (c) 292. (a) 293. (b) 294. (c)
295. (b) 296. (a) 297. (c) 298. (c) 299. (b)
300. (c) 301. (b) 302. (a) 303. (d) 304. (c)
305. (b) 306. (b) 307. (c) 308. (c) 309. (c)
310. (a) 311. (b) 312. (c) 313. (d) 314. (a)
315. (b) 316. (d) 317. (b) 318. (c) 319. (d)
320. (d) 321. (a)

9

PEOPLE AND ENVIRONMENT INTERACTION

INTRODUCTION

This unit deals with people and environment, so first of all we need to get familiar with basic definitions. Population is a near permanent group of interbreeding individuals of a species found in a space or geographical area at a particular point. It is called local population or deme. Metapopulation is a complex of local populations connected by dispersing individuals.

The main factors affecting population are as follows:

1. Natality (birth rate)
2. Mortality (death rate)
3. Population dispersal (emigration, immigration, and migration)
4. Age distribution (pre-reproductive, reproductive, and post-reproductive)
5. Population growth rate
6. Carrying resources mainly food, water, space - there are limited resources to support all life forms.

Population density is number of individuals divided by space (such as per square km).

The term environment is derived from the French word *environner*. It means 'to surround'. According to the Environment (Protection) Act, 1986, environment includes all the physical and biological surroundings of an organism and their interactions. Environment is defined as the sum of water, air, and land, and the interrelationships that exist among them and with the human beings, other living organisms, and materials.

The flora, fauna, microorganisms and the man-made structures in our surroundings have a bi-directional interaction with us, directly or indirectly. The totality of all these components and their interactions constitute the environment. Air, water, and land constitute our environment and influence us directly. We too exert an influence on our environment due to over use or over-exploitation of resources or due to discharge of pollutants in the air, water, and land.

In context of relation between people and environment, concept of 'environmental determinism' developed in 19th century Europe - a belief that environment determines how a culture develops. For example, white European nations believed that people from warmer climates were lazier because they did not have to work as hard to survive. In the first half of the 20th century, though, environmental determinism was replaced with environmental possibilism, which is the belief that the environment puts limits on people, but that it does not determine how they will behave.

ECOLOGY

The term ecology was coined by Ernst Haeckel in 1869. Ecology deals with the study of organisms in their natural home.

It is the scientific study of the relations that living organisms have with respect to each other and their natural environment the ecosystems.

It is present at three levels, which are as follows:

1. The individual organism (how individuals are affected by the environment and how they, in turn, affect the environment)
2. The population
3. The community

Ecology is defined as the study of ecosystems.

> **Ecological Footprint:** The ecological footprint measures human consumption of natural resources in comparison to Earth's ecological capacity to regenerate them. Calculation of the footprint takes into account our consumption habits both at (i) micro (individual) level and (ii) macro (area or nation) level. The objective of its calculation is also to educate people about the need to change our consumption behaviour to make it more sustainable. Ecological footprint is measured in global hectares (*gha*).

Species, Population, and Community

The organisms in this world can be divided into different species; just as human beings are a species, so are the roses and neem trees.

A species is a set of organisms that resemble each other in certain features. The members of a species living together and interacting with each other are called a population. The members of a population live within a given area.

SPECIES DIVERSITY

- It is an important attribute of biotic community, which is determined by total number of species and their relative abundance.
- Greater species diversity indicates higher number of niches and greater stability of the community.

KEYSTONE SPECIES

- It is a species that has a significant and disproportionately large influence on the community structure and characteristics.
- It has often considerably low abundance and biomass as compared to dominant species.

CRITICAL LINK SPECIES

- They are species that play an important role in supporting network species as pollinators, dispersal agents, absorption or circulation of nutrients, etc. Mycorrhizal fungi help the vascular plants in obtaining inorganic nutrients from soil and organic residues.

COMMUNITY

A community is an assemblage of all the interacting populations of different species in a geographical area. It is a complex interacting network of plants, animals, and microorganisms. Each population has a defined role in the community.

ECOSYSTEM

The term ecosystem was defined by Arthur Tansley in 1935. Ecosystem is a self-regulating community of living organisms (populations of species), interacting with each other and their non-living, physical environment, for example, forest ecosystem and ocean ecosystem. Even a clump of bushes can be an ecosystem. All ecosystems on the planet are interconnected and interdependent; and together, they make up the biosphere.

There is also exchange of matter and energy with physical environment. In an open ecosystem, there is free exchange of energy and matter with the outside world. In a closed ecosystem, there is no or very limited exchange.

> **ECOTONE**
>
> An ecotone is the transitional area of vegetation between two different plant communities, such as forest and grassland. The influence of the two bordering communities on each other is known as the edge effect.

Ecosystems show large variations in their size, structure, composition, and so on. However, all the ecosystems are characterized by certain basic structural and functional features, which are common. There can be different types of ecosystems such as forest ecosystem, marine ecosystem, and desert ecosystem.

Composition and organization of communities and physical components decide the structure of an ecosystem. Thus, ecosystems have basically two types of components, namely biotic and abiotic.

Biotic Components (Living Components)

Living components in an ecosystem are either the producers or the consumers. They are also called the biotic components. Producers produce organic components, for example, plants produce starch, carbohydrates, and cellulose by a process called photosynthesis.

Different living organisms constitute the biotic component of an ecosystem and belong to the following categories:

1. *Producers (or Autotrophs):* These produce their own food. Green plants produce food through photosynthesis, by combining carbon dioxide and water with the help of energy in the form of sunlight.
2. *Consumers:* Consumers depend upon producers for their food, for example, human beings and other animals. These organisms get their food by feeding on other organisms. They are of the following types:
   (a) Herbivores feed on plants, for example, rabbit and insects.
   (b) Carnivores are those animals that eat other animals. They are of two types:
      (i) Secondary carnivores feed on herbivores, for example, a frog and a small fish.
      (ii) Tertiary carnivores feed on other carnivores for example, a snake and a big fish.
   (c) Omnivores feed on both plants and animals, for example, humans, rats, and many species of birds.
   (d) Detritivores feed on dead organisms, for example, earthworms, crabs, and ants. The living beings that feed on dead or decayed organic matter are also called saprophytes. They are fungi and bacteria, which does not contain any chlorophyll and are dependent on dead organisms for their food.

   The parasites depend on living organisms for food. They can be (i) endoparasites, which live inside the body, such as liver flukes and tapeworms and (ii) ectoparasites, which live on the exterior, such as fleas and lice.
3. *Decomposers:* These are microorganisms that break down organic matter into inorganic compounds and in this process, derive their nutrition. They play a very important role in converting the essential nutrients from unavailable organic form to free inorganic form which is available for use by plants, for example, bacteria, fungi, and so on.

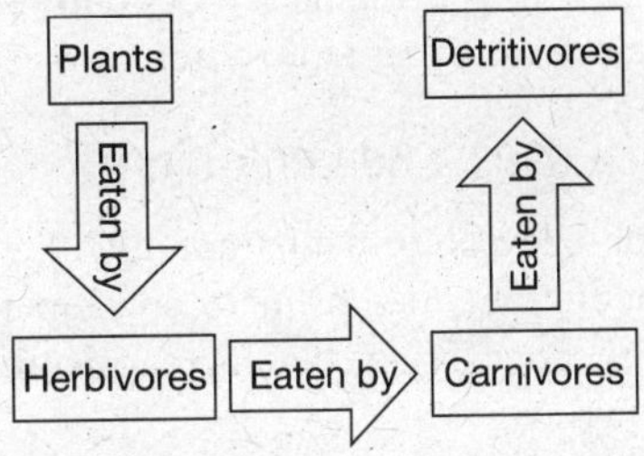

Abiotic Components

In ecology, abiotic components are non-living chemical and physical factors in the environment that affect the ecosystems.

Examples are water, light, wind, soil, humidity, minerals, and gases. They affect the ability of organisms to survive and reproduce. They also help determine the types and numbers of organisms able to exist in an environment.

Functions of Ecosystem

Every ecosystem performs the following important functions:

1. It has different food chains and food webs. Food chain is the sequence of eating and being eaten.

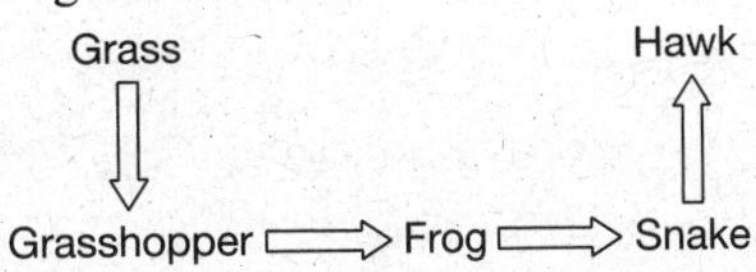

Food chains are generally found to be interlinked and interwoven as a network and hence known as a food web. There are several options of eating and being eaten in a food web. Hence, these are more stable.

2. There is unidirectional flow of energy. It flows from sun and then after capture by primary producers (green plants), flows through the food chain or the food web.
3. Materials (nutrients) in an ecosystem move in a cyclic manner. The cycling of nutrients takes place between the biotic and abiotic components.
4. Every ecosystem functions to produce and sustain some primary production (plant biomass) and secondary production (animal biomass).
5. Every ecosystem regulates and maintains itself. This self-regulation or control system is known as cybernetic system.

Trophic Levels and Ecological Pyramids

The trophic levels form a pyramid, with producers at the bottom, then primary consumers (herbivores), secondary consumers (carnivores), and tertiary carnivores.

Ecological Pyramids - Trophic Levels

The concept of ecological pyramid was developed by Charles Elton. All ecological pyramids begin with producers like plants at the bottom and proceed through various trophic levels such as herbivores (consume plants), carnivores (prey on herbivores), and so on. The highest level is at the top of the food chain.

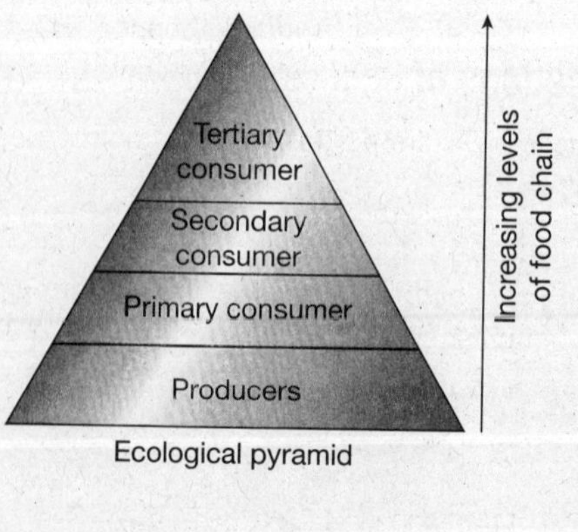

Ecological pyramid

There are three types of ecological pyramids, which are as follows:

- Pyramid of energy
- Pyramid of numbers
- Pyramid of biomass

1. Pyramid of Energy

The pyramid of energy or the energy pyramid describes the overall nature of the ecosystem. During the flow of energy from one organism to other, there is considerable loss of energy in the form of heat. In primary producers like the autotrophs, large amount of energy is available. The least energy is available in the tertiary consumers. Therefore, shorter food chain has more amount of energy available even at the highest trophic level.

- The energy pyramid is always upright and vertical.
- This pyramid shows the flow of energy at different trophic levels.
- It depicts the energy is minimum at the highest trophic level and is maximum at the lowest trophic level.
- At each trophic level, there is successive loss of energy in the form of heat, respiration, etc.

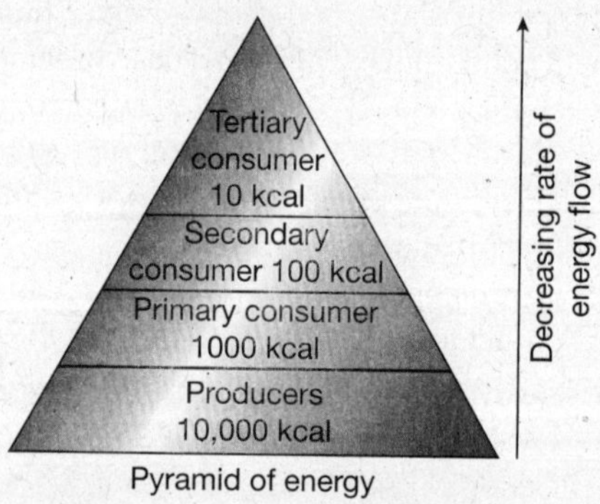

Pyramid of energy

2. Pyramid of Numbers

The pyramid of numbers depicts the relationship in terms of the number of producers, herbivores, and the carnivores at their successive trophic levels. There is a decrease in the number of individuals from the lower to the higher trophic levels. The number pyramid varies from ecosystem to ecosystem. There are three types of pyramid of numbers, which are as follows:

- Upright pyramid of number
- Partly upright pyramid of number
- Inverted pyramid of number

Upright Pyramid of Number This type of pyramid number is found in the aquatic and grassland ecosystems. In these ecosystems, there are numerous small autotrophs that support lesser herbivores, which in turn support smaller number of carnivores, and hence, this pyramid is upright.

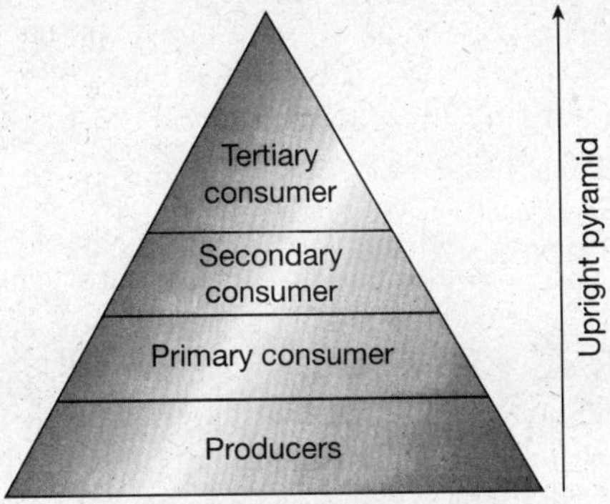

Pyramid of number

Partly Upright Pyramid of Number It is seen in the forest ecosystem where the number of producers are lesser in number and support a greater number of herbivores and which in turn support a fewer number of carnivores.

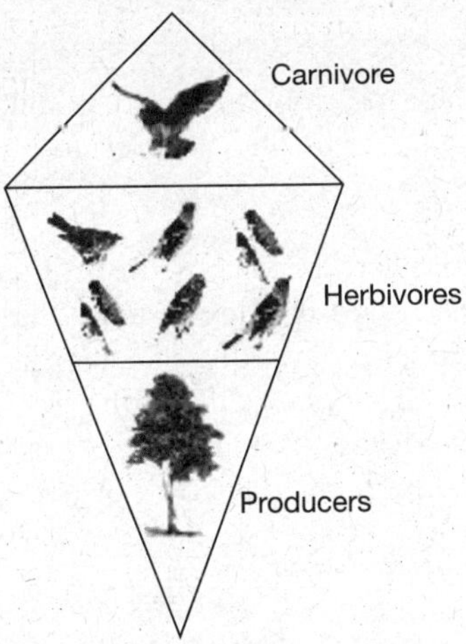

Partly upright
Pyramid of number

Inverted Pyramid of Number This type of ecological pyramid is seen in parasitic food chain where one primary producer supports numerous parasites, which in turn support more hyperparasites.

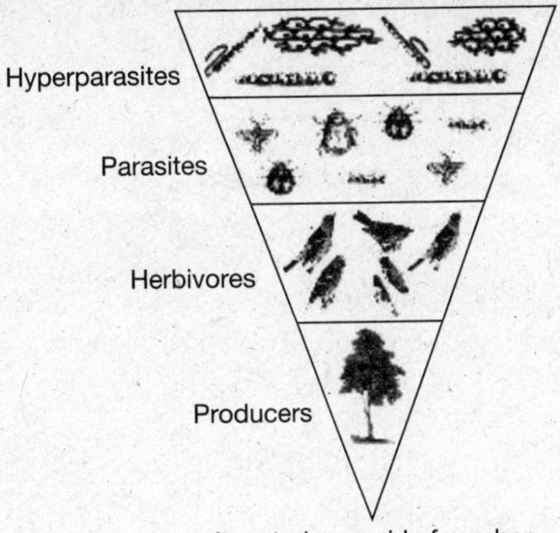

Inverted pyramid of number

3. Pyramid of Biomass

The pyramid of biomass is more fundamental. They represent the quantitative relationships of the standing crops. In this pyramid, there is a gradual decrease in the biomass from the producers to the higher trophic levels. In simple terms, biomass here represents the net aggregate weight of dried organisms collected from each feeding level. This dry weight is the biomass, and it represents the amount of energy available in the form of organic matter of the organisms. In this pyramid, the net dry weight is plotted to that of the producers, herbivores, carnivores, etc.

There are two types of pyramid of biomass, which are as follows:

- Upright pyramid of biomass
- Inverted pyramid of biomass

Upright Pyramid of Biomass This occurs when the larger net biomass of producers support a smaller weight of consumers, e.g., forest ecosystem.

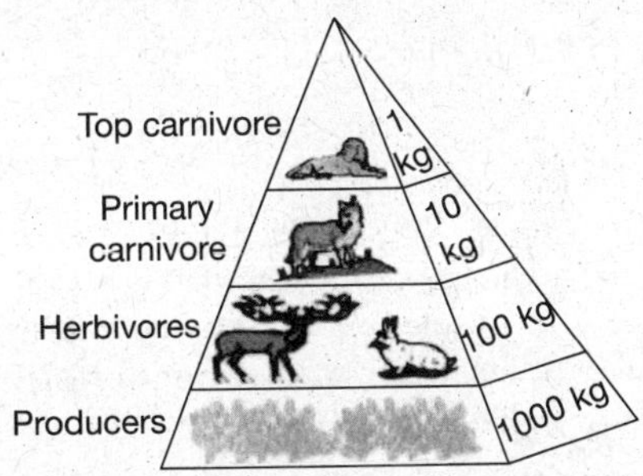

Upright pyramid of biomass in a terrestrial ecosystem

INVERTED PYRAMID OF BIOMASS This happens when the smaller weight of producers support consumers of larger weight, e.g., aquatic ecosystem.

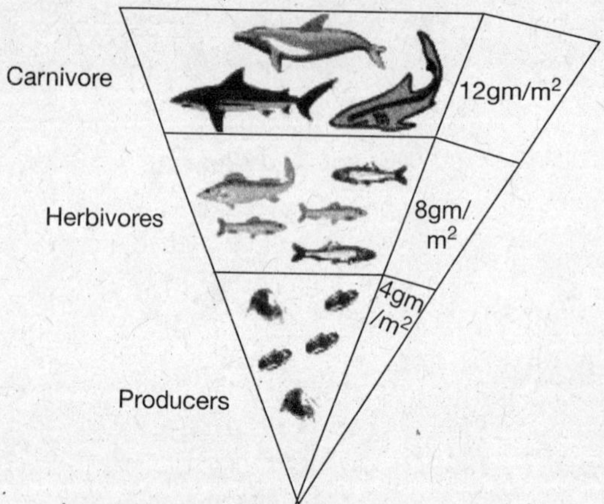

Inverted pyramid in an aquatic ecosystem

The trophic levels are linked through food chains, and these food chains form interlocking patterns called food webs.

> RELATED TO TROPHIC LEVELS
>
> **Eutrophic:** Water bodies having good quantity of minerals and hence supra optimum growth of plants.
>
> **Oligotrophic:** Water bodies deficient in minerals and organic growth.
>
> **Dystrophic:** Water bodies rich in undecomposed organic matter, e.g., bogs and marshy lakes.

BIOSPHERE

There are different types of ecosystems around us, which involve living organisms and non-living things. If we combine all the ecosystems present on earth, it is called biosphere.

BIOMES

The terrestrial portion of biosphere is divided into biomes. They usually have distinct climates and life forms adapted to that climate. Deserts, grasslands, tropical forests, and rain forests are the main examples of biomes.

HABITAT

The area or natural environment in which an organism or population normally lives is called habitat. A habitat is made up of physical factors such as soil, moisture, range of temperature, and availability of light as well as biotic factors such as availability of food and the presence of predators.

When organisms of different species live together, it is called as cohabitat.

A habitat is not necessarily a geographic area. When particular organism/s live in a small and specific part/s of a habitat, it is called as micro-habitat. For example, within the forest habitat, certain organisms live beneath the bark of a tree; a parasite may live in the body of the host.

Four Spheres of Earth

The area near the surface of the earth can be divided into four interconnected geospheres, namely the lithosphere, hydrosphere, biosphere, and atmosphere. Scientists can classify life and material on or near the surface of the earth to be in any of these four spheres.

The names of the four spheres are derived from the Greek words for stone (*litho*), air (*atmo*), water (*hydro*), and life (*bio*).

LITHOSPHERE

The lithosphere is the solid, rocky crust covering the entire planet. This crust is inorganic and is composed of minerals. It covers the entire surface of the earth from the top of Mount Everest to the bottom of the Mariana Trench.

HYDROSPHERE

The hydrosphere is composed of all the water on or near the earth. This includes the oceans, rivers, lakes, and even the moisture in the air. Ninety-seven per cent of the earth's water is present in the oceans. The remaining 3% is freshwater; Furthermore three quarters of freshwater is in the form of ice sheets and glaciers, hardly one per cent is left for human consumption.

BIOSPHERE

The biosphere is composed of all the living organisms. Plants, animals, and one-celled organisms are all part of the biosphere. Most of the planet's life is found from 3 metres below the ground to 30 metres above it and in the top 200 metres of oceans and seas.

Atmosphere

We live at the bottom of an invisible ocean called the atmosphere, which is a layer of gases surrounding our planet. Nitrogen and oxygen account for 99 per cent of the gases in dry air, with argon, carbon dioxide, helium, neon, and other gases making up minute portions. Water vapour and dust are also part of earth's atmosphere. Other planets and moons have very different atmospheres, and some have no atmospheres at all. The different layers of atmosphere are discussed below.

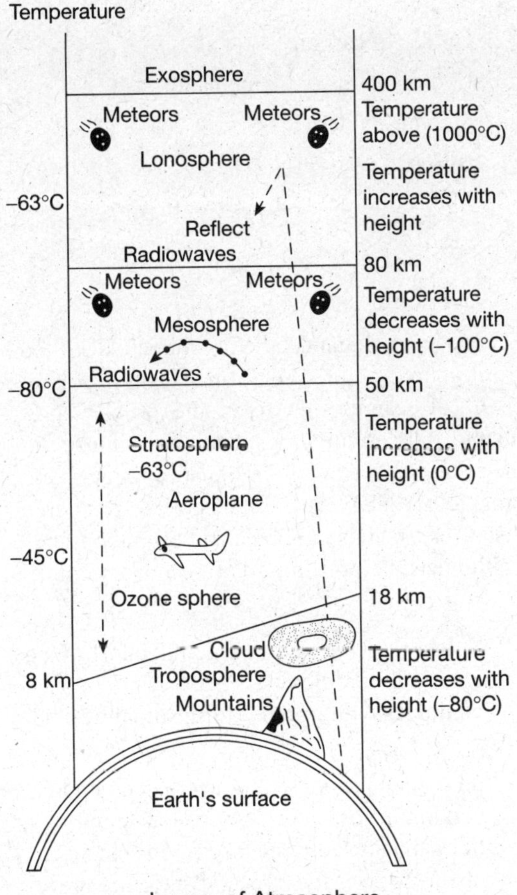

Layers of Atmosphere

Troposphere

It is the lowest layer of atmosphere and contains about four-fifths of the Earth's air, but extends only to a height of 18 km at equator and 8 km at poles during winter. Almost all weather developments occur in the troposphere. Air in the troposphere thins as altitude increases, and the temperature also decreases. The rate at which temperature decreases is called as lapse rate; it is 6.4° per km. Fast-moving, high-altitude winds called jet streams occur at the top level of the troposphere that helps aeroplanes to fly at high speeds.

This layer also absorbs heat that is reflected back from the ground in a process called the greenhouse effect.

Stratosphere

The stratosphere extends from the tropopause, the upper boundary of the troposphere, to about 50 km above the Earth's surface. It is characterized by the following:

1. Strong horizontal winds blowing in the stratosphere that is ideal for planes that can fly in this part of the atmosphere.
2. The stratosphere is crucial to life on Earth because it contains small amounts of ozone, a form of oxygen that prevents harmful UV rays from reaching the Earth.

Mesosphere

The mesosphere extends up to 80 km above the surface of the Earth. This layer is characterized by the following:

1. It has the coldest temperatures in the atmosphere, dipping as low as –100°C.
2. The phenomenon of 'shooting stars' also occur in this layer.

Ionosphere

It extends to about 690 kilometres and is extremely thin. It is generally considered as a part of outer space. This atmospheric layer conducts electricity. It is characterized by the following:

1. The ionosphere—a layer of free electrons and ions, reflecting radio waves.

2. It is broken into distinct layers, called the D, E, F1, and F2 layers. The lower D layer absorbs high-frequency radio waves.
3. It also reflects particles from solar wind, which is a stream of highly charged particles called aurora ejected by the sun in the polar regions.

Thermosphere

Temperatures in the thermosphere can rise well above 1000°C, up to 1,500°C. This layer is characterized by:

1. It is the thickest (most vertical expansion) layer in the atmosphere.
2. Hubble Space Telescope and the International Space Station (ISS) orbit the Earth in the thermosphere.

Exosphere

The exosphere expands and contracts as it comes into contact with solar storms (solar flares and coronal mass ejections). Hydrogen and trace amounts of helium, carbon dioxide, oxygen, and other gases are present. Many weather satellites orbit Earth in the exosphere.

Pollution and Its Types

Pollution is a negative/undesirable change in the environment, usually the addition of something hazardous or detrimental. Generally, degradable or non-persistent pollutants such as domestic sewage, discarded vegetables are broken down by natural processes. Some persistent or non-biodegradable pollutants do not get destroyed and are our source of worry. The different types of pollution such as air pollution, water pollution, noise pollution, and radiation pollution have been discussed in the ensuing paragraphs.

Air Pollution

Clean, dry air contains 78.09% nitrogen by volume and 20.94% oxygen. The remaining 0.97% is made of gaseous mixture of carbon dioxide, helium, krypton, argon, xenon, nitrous oxide, and very small amounts of other organic and inorganic gases.

It is also known as atmospheric pollution. The degradation of air quality of natural atmospheric conditions due to pollutants is known as air pollution. World Health Organization defined it as the presence of materials in the air, which are harmful to the living beings, once they cross their threshold concentration levels. The foreign bodies, gases, and so on act as air pollutants. It is the most extensive and worst form of pollution.

Types of Air Pollution

There are two types of air pollutants, namely primary and secondary.

Primary Pollutants

Primary pollutants enter the atmosphere directly from the source. Some important primary pollutants are as follows:

1. Suspended particulate matter (SPM)
2. Oxides of carbon
3. Hydrocarbons (e.g., methane)
4. Sulphur oxides (SOx)
5. Nitrogen oxides (NOx)
6. Chlorofluorocarbons (CFCs)
7. Lead

Secondary Pollutants

Secondary pollutants are not directly emitted from sources; they are formed as a result of chemical reactions between the primary pollutants and certain atmospheric constituents, in the presence of sunlight. Sulphates, nitrates, and organic particles can be transported over large distances, such as hundreds and even thousands of kilometres. Some important secondary pollutants are as follows:

1. *Sulphur trioxide:* It is a compound formed when sulphur dioxide reacts with oxygen. It combines with water to form sulphuric acid.
2. *Smog formation:* Smog is an odd combination of smoke and fog. The effect of smog is maximum just before sunrise as smog particles that are entrapped between cold air are unable to rise. Two types of smog are prevalent as per records:

(a) *Sulphurous or London smog:* It affected London for a very long time, hence its name. It is also termed as 'reducing smog' as its mixture of components is chemically reducing in nature. This is due to the presence of sulphur dioxide in air. It is more prevalent during the morning hours of winter season when the relative humidity is high and air near the ground is also cooler. London smog causes throat irritation and difficulty in breathing.

(b) *Photochemical or Los Angeles smog:* This type of smog is due to the presence of oxides of nitrogen in the atmosphere, formed as a result of vehicular exhaust. It is formed due to chemical reactions involving ozone, nitrogen oxide, hydrocarbons and peroxyacetyl nitrate (PAN) in the presence of sunlight. This phenomenon mainly occurs during warm sunny days as sunlight is required to carry out photochemical reaction in seasons when the sky is clear. Photochemical smog consists of brown hazy fumes. It irritates the eyes and lungs, causes cracking of rubber, and extensive damage to plant life.

(c) *Ground level ozone:* Tropospheric or ground-level ozone is formed from photo-chemical reaction between two major classes of air pollutants--volatile organic compounds (VoCs) and nitrogen oxides.

3. *Acid rain:* Acid rain is caused by a chemical reaction that begins when compounds like sulphur dioxide and nitrogen oxides are released into the air. These substances can rise very high into the atmosphere, where they mix and react with water, oxygen, and other chemicals to form more acidic pollutants known as acid rain.

Effects:

1. Acid rain has many ecological effects, but none is greater than its impact on lakes, streams, wetlands, and other aquatic environments. Acid rain makes water acidic and causes them to absorb aluminium.
2. Acid rain also damages forests, especially those at higher elevations. It erodes the soil of essential nutrients and releases aluminium in the soil, which makes it hard for trees to take up water.
3. The effects of acid rain, combined with other environmental stressors, leave trees and plants less able to withstand cold temperatures, insects, and disease. The pollutants may also inhibit trees' ability to reproduce.

Air Pollution and Aerosols

- Aerosols - They are stable suspensions of solid or liquid particles in air. Aerosols affect the weather conditions by blocking solar radiations. Deposition of aerosols on leaves affects the process of photosynthesis.
- Mist - Aerosols consisting of liquid droplets
- Dust - Aerosols consisting of solid particles
- Fume - Aerosols consisting of hot vapours of metals
- Smoke is also an aerosol—mixture of liquid and solid particles as a result of burning
- Plume - geometrical form of smoke

Smog is the mixture of smoke and fog (discussed separately)

The following are the major government initiatives to monitor air pollution:

1. National Air Quality Monitoring Programme
2. National Ambient Air Quality Standards
3. System of Air Quality and Weather Forecasting

1. **National Air Quality Monitoring Programme** - Central Pollution Control Board is executing a nation-wide programme of ambient air quality monitoring known as National Air Quality Monitoring Programme (NAMP).

National Air Quality Index (NAQI) was launched on 17 October 2014 to disseminate

Table 9.1 Major Air Pollution-Related Chemical Substances

Pollutants	Source	Pathological effect on human beings
Ozone (Ground Level)	Vehicular exhaust	Lung Function – aggravation of asthma, emphysema, and chronic bronchitis
Lead	Leaded Petrol (used as anti-knocking agent)	Central Nervous System, interference with development of RBCs
Sulphur Dioxide	Thermal power plant and industries	Severe respiratory problem, reduces exchange of gases from lung surface
Nitrogen Oxides	Thermal Power Plant	Heart and lung problems Bronchitis, asthma, and also carcinogenic
Carbon Monoxide	Incomplete combustion of fossil fuels, wood stoves, cigarette smoking	Reduces oxygen-carrying capacity of blood, breathing problems
Hydrogen sulphide	Oil refineries, chemical industries	Nausea, irritation of eyes and throat
Hydrogen cyanide	Blast furnace, fumigation, and chemical industry	Headache, dry throat, indistinct vision, and dysfunction of nerve cells
Ammonia	Fertiliser industry, dye making, bleaching, and explosives	Acidification of water bodies at high level
Phosgene	Chemical and dye-making industry	Pulmonary oedema
Volatile organic compounds	Vapourize easily, examples are gasoline, benzene, etc.	Smog formation
Arsenic	Arsenic soldering	Damage red blood cells, kidneys, and cause jaundice
SPM*	Incinerators, and basically manufacturing processes	Emphysema, respiratory system problems-asthma, chronic bronchitis

*Suspended Particulate Matter (SPM) or Particulate Matter (PM) includes soot, smoke, dust, fibres, pesticides, metals (such as mercury, lead, and copper), dust mites, and pollen.
Some of the pollutants fall under categories of both air and water pollutants, such as heavy metal cadmium.

information on air quality in an easily understandable form for the general public. The measurement of air quality is based on the pollutants mentioned below:

1. PM10 – Particulate matter (size less than 10 μm)
2. PM2.5 – Particulate matter (size less than 2.5 μm)
3. NO_2
4. SO_2
5. CO
6. Ozone
7. Ammonia
8. Lead

The unit of measurements in case of pollutants mentioned above is microgram per cubic metre except in the case of CO where it is milligram.

The AQI is classified along one of the six categories:

1. Good (0–50)
2. Satisfactory (51–100)
3. Moderately polluted (101–200)
4. Poor (201–300)
5. Very Poor (301–400)
6. Severe (401–500).

The formulation of the index was an initiative under Swachh Bharat Mission (Cleanliness Mission) based on the recommendations of IIT Kanpur and the expert Group formed in this regard.

2. **National Ambient Air Quality Standards -** It may be noted that ambient air quality standards are specified separately in India for around 12 pollutants including the 8 that constitute the NAQI. The additional four pollutants are Arsenic, Nickel, Benzene, and Benzopyrene. PM2.5 is particularly dangerous and can cause adverse health effects owing to its greater penetrability into the human respiratory system and eventual accumulation in human organs and blood. PM concentrations are higher in winter season and are lower during monsoon months.

   SO_2 levels are within the prescribed National Ambient Air Quality Standards in residential areas of all the cities. Decreasing trend may be due to various interventions that have taken place in recent years such as reduction of sulphur in diesel, use of cleaner fuel such as CNG in Delhi, implementation of Bharat Stage-III emission norms. In addition, there has been a change in use of domestic fuel from coal to LPG, which may have contributed to reduction in ambient levels of SO_2.

   NO_2 levels are within the prescribed National Ambient Air Quality Standards in residential areas of most of the cities. The reasons for low levels of NO_2 may be various measures taken such as banning of old vehicles, better traffic management, etc. Despite an increase in number of vehicles, CO levels have reduced during last few years. The decrease may be attributed to measures such as conversion of three wheelers of CNG.

3. **System of Air Quality and Weather Forecasting** – Ministry of Earth Sciences

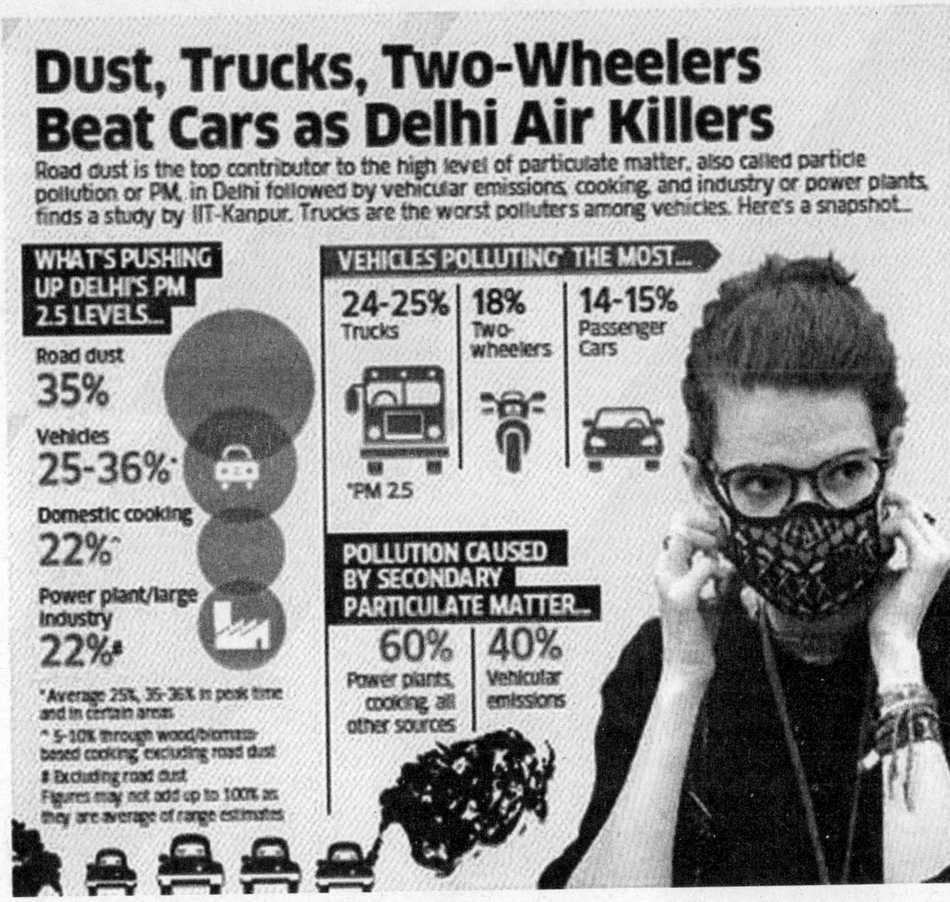

(MoES), Govt. of India, has introduced a major national initiative, "System of Air Quality and Weather Forecasting and Research" known as "SAFAR" for greater metropolitan cities of India to provide location-specific information on air quality in near real-time and its forecast 1–3 days in advance for the first time in India. It has been combined with the early warning system on weather parameters. The SAFAR system is developed by Indian Institute of Tropical Meteorology, Pune.

WHO has its own standards. World over, most of the emissions that reach the atmosphere come from coal (43%), followed by oil (33%).

Odd Even Formula in Delhi

Pollution situation became so alarming in Delhi that it was declared as a 'gas chamber' by the Delhi High Court in 2015. Delhi Government started a pilot project 'Odd Even Formula' on January 1, 2016 to bring down the air pollution levels amidst reports that Delhi is the most polluted city in the world. Accordingly, odd number cars were to ply on city roads on odd dates and even numbered cars on even days for 15 days. The similar schemes have been tried at Mexico City, Bogota (Capital of Columbia), and Beijing.

The odd even scheme showed mixed results. Although the percentage effect could be small, but given the concentrations as high as in Delhi, the absolute reductions in PM 2.5 concentrations are 'significant' as it can help reduce health impacts. The scheme brought 'considerable' additional benefits including reducing on road congestion, increase of average car speeds, reduced fuel usage, and made significant impact on public awareness levels on air pollution and its impacts on human health.

Indoor Air Pollution

The major reasons for indoor air pollution are inefficient burning of inferior fuels during cooking or heating such as cow dung, agricultural residue, and coal and fuel wood, along with poor ventilation systems inside the house. The problem aggravates during winters when the doors and windows of the houses, especially in rural areas, are kept shut. The smokeless chullahs were introduced as a solution to the problem of indoor air pollution. However, they could not make much impact.

Water Pollution and Its Causes

Water covers about 70% of earth's surface. Water is an important resource for the people and the environment. Water is the basis of life; it makes up to 60–95% of the total weight of any functioning living cell.

Although 70% of earth's surface is covered with water, only 0.00192% of the water is available for human consumption. Less than 3% of the world's water is fresh—the rest is seawater and undrinkable. Of this 3%, over 2.5% is frozen as glaciers, which are locked up in the Arctic and Antarctica regions, and are not available to man. Thus, humanity must rely on the remaining 0.5% for all of man's and ecosystem's fresh water needs.

The sector wise breakup of water withdrawal in India is agriculture and livestock—91%, Municipalities—7%, and Industry—2%. Pollution of water affects drinking water, lakes, river, and oceans all over the world.

Water pollution is the presence of harmful substances in a water body, thus making its water unfit for intended use.

Types of Water Pollution

According to the sources of pollution, there are two types of water pollution, namely point source and non-point source pollution.

Point Source Solution

The discharge of harmful substances by specific sources into a water body leads to point source pollution. Industrial wastewater and hot water from thermal power plants cause point source pollution. The discharge of pollutants into a water body from large areas leads to non-point source pollution. Construction runoff and acid rain cause non-point source pollution.

The major sources of this type of water are as follows:

1. *Industrial wastewater:* Both small and large industrial units produce wastewater, which has a variety of organic and inorganic pollutants. This is the major reason for river pollution in India.
2. *Hot water:* Industries, such as thermal power plants and oil refineries, use water as coolant.
   When this water discharged into the water body, its temperature is higher by 15°C. The warmer temperature decreases the solubility of oxygen and increases the metabolism of fish. This changes the ecological balance of the river.

Non-point Source Pollution

Non-point source pollution is caused by the following pollutants:

1. *Municipal wastewater:* Wastewaters from domestic sources, such as kitchen and toilet are sometimes discharged into a river or large water body nearby. This is the major reason for river pollution in India, and world over.
2. *Surface run-off:* The practices followed in agriculture affect the groundwater quality. Intensive cultivation causes fertilizers and pesticides to seep into the groundwater; this process is known as leaching. Irrigation run-off from agricultural fields causes high nitrate content in ground water. The problem is aggravated if industries are located in that area.
3. *Oil spills:* An oil spill is the accidental discharge of petroleum into the ocean or estuaries, leading to the pollution of marine ecosystem. Oil spills are caused due to capsized oil tankers or offshore oil mining and oil explorations.

Impact of Water Pollution on Life

Water pollution affects all types of organisms, from microorganism to humans. Let us take a look at the harmful effects of water pollution on various forms of life.

Oxygen Depletion in Water Bodies

High levels of organic wastes increase the rate of decomposition by bacteria, which use oxygen for this process. This causes a drop in dissolved oxygen in water. In other words, the biochemical oxygen demand (BOD) of water increases. A high BOD indicates a low level of dissolved oxygen in water. This destruction leads to the destruction of sensitive organisms such as phytoplankton, molluscs, and fish.

Biomagnification

The accumulation of a toxic chemical in the bodies of organisms as we move from producers, to primary consumers, to secondary consumers etc. is called biomagnification. It occurs when a chemical becomes more and more concentrated as we move up a food chain. This is specifically true in case of nonbiodegradable chemicals or pollutants. The classic example is DDT. It is eaten first by planktons, then by small fish, then by big fish. The fish are eaten by birds and so on. At each level, its concentration goes up. The consumption of DDT by birds causes thinning of their eggs, which rupture prematurely during their warming by birds; and babies dying a premature death. The process of biomagnification is also called bioaccumulation.

Eutrophication

The inorganic nutrients in the run-off from agricultural fields reaching a water body increase the nutrient content of the water body. These nutrients cause the profuse growth of algae (algal bloom) in it. This growth eventually causes the death of small fish and organisms in them.

Effect of Water Pollution on Human Life

Water contamination due to domestic sewage containing pathogens, such as viruses, bacteria, parasitic protozoa, and worms, can cause diseases such as jaundice, cholera, typhoid, and amoebiasis. This type of contamination renders the water unfit for drinking, bathing, swimming, and even irrigation.

Contamination of Water by Heavy Metals

Heavy metals are commonly defined as those having a specific density of more than 5 g/cm^3. The main threats to human health from heavy metals are associated with exposure to lead, cadmium, mercury, and arsenic (a metalloid). Heavy metal contamination of water bodies and groundwater due to industrial wastewater affects health in a number of ways. Industrial effluents containing lead, fluorides, nitrates, and arsenic pose a grave danger to human beings.

1. *Mercury:* Mercury compounds in wastewater are converted by bacterial action into extremely toxic methyl mercury. Fish accumulate this poison in their bodies. The consumption of such fish can cause numbness of limbs, lips and tongue, deafness, blurring of vision, and mental derangement. This syndrome is called Minamata disease since it was first noticed in Japan in 1950s, where people developed it after consuming fish from the Minamata Bay. It can also cause gingivitis.
2. *Pesticides:* Organophosphates and carbonates present in pesticides that get washed off into water bodies damage the nervous system and can cause cancer.
3. *Fluoride:* Excess fluoride can cause yellowing of teeth and damage to the spinal cord.
4. *Nitrates:* Drinking water contaminated with nitrates can prove fatal, especially to infants feeding on formula milk made with this water. Nitrates restrict the amount of oxygen that reaches the brain, causing blue baby syndrome.
5. *Chromium:* Chromium is a known carcinogen.
6. *Arsenic:* Earlier it was widely used as an insecticide, rodenticide, for wood preservation, and medical preparation. It has many industrial applications. Different fungi and microorganisms convert arsenic to dimethyl arsenic in water, which gets detected in natural water, bird egg shells, sea shells, and human urine. Arsenic poisoning through water can cause damage to the liver, nervous system disorders, vascular disease, skin cancer (dermatitis), and bronchitis.
7. *Cadmium:* Cadmium compounds are mainly used in re-chargeable nickel–cadmium batteries. Cadmium is also used in making fusible alloys, electroplating, and as control rods in nuclear reactors.

   Cigarette smoking is a major source of cadmium exposure. In non-smokers, food is the most important source of cadmium exposure. It damages the heart, liver, lungs, reproductive organs, and also causes kidney damage. The itai-itai disease in Japan was due to cadmium pollution; it causes bone defects and fractures.
8. *Cyanide:* It is used in extraction of gold and silver metals, metal painting, and in pesticides. Its consumption leads to nausea and death.
9. *Manganese:* It is abundant in nature. Higher concentration of manganese causes cramps, tremors, hallucinations, manganic pneumonia, and renal degeneration.
10. *Iron:* The excessive presence of iron in human body can aggravate thalassaemia that is basically a genetic disorder. This has an adverse impact on red blood corpuscles (RBCs) count and haemoglobin. Water bodies also become foul due to abundance of iron-oxidizing microbes.

Effect of Water Pollution on Marine Life

Marine oil spills is also a type of water pollutant and has direct impact on marine life. It is accidental release of petroleum products into the ocean or coastal waters.

1. *Tanker spills:* Even small amounts of oil spread across large areas of water and prevents oxygen in the air from dissolving in water, thus making it difficult for organisms to breathe.
2. *Oil coating:* Oil coating results in poisoning of marine birds such as seagull. The oil coating reduces their body temperature and makes it impossible for them to survive the cold temperature of the ocean.

Soil and Its Pollution Causes

The soil is a thin covering over the land consisting of a mixture of minerals, organic materials (carbon compounds, generally derived from organisms), living organisms, air, and water.

Mature soil is arranged into series of zones called soil horizons (Table 9.2).

Table 9.2 Layers of Soil

Layer	Description
O-Horizon	Freshly fallen leaves, twigs, animal waste, fungi, and so on
A-Horizon	Partially decomposed organic matter (humus) and some inorganic mineral particles
B-Horizon	Called subsoil, has less organic matter and fewer organisms than A-Horizon soil
C-Horizon	Helps to determine the pH of soil; determines the soil's rate of water absorption and retention

Different types of soils vary in content of clay (very fine particles), silt (fine particles), sand (medium sized particles), and gravel (coarse particles). In combination, they determine the soil texture.

The following are the different causes of soil pollution:

1. *Industrial waste:* Heavy metals and toxic chemicals
2. *Municipal and medical wastes:* Some wastes are non-biodegradable.
3. *Radioactive wastes*
4. *Agrochemicals:* Pesticides, weedicides, and excess inorganic fertilizers.
5. *Opencast mining:* Digging the earth's surface for extraction of mineral ores degrades the top soil of earth.
6. *e-waste:* Used computers, mobile phones, TV, etc. simply dumped into landfills. Since these are of toxic nature, they affect the quality of soil. The toxins may leach from landfills and also spoil the groundwater.
7. *Pesticides and fertilizers:* Temperature, light, and carbon dioxide levels affect photosynthesis. Farmers use fertilisers, pesticides, and biological control to increase crop yields. Excessive use of fertilizers reduces the population of soil-born organisms, the crumb structure of the soil, and productivity of the soil.

   This can cause the problem of water logging. The plant roots cannot respire due to excess water in soil profile. Nitrogen is lost from waterlogged soils due to leaching and denitrification (degassing). Denitrification leads to the gaseous loss of nitrous oxide (N_2O) into the atmosphere, which is the major greenhouse gas, and adds to the phenomenon of global warming.
8. *Other pollutants:* Many air pollutants (acid rain) and water pollutants ultimately become a part of soil pollution.

Soil Types in India

Alluvial Soil

It is formed as a result of flooding of plain areas, especially in lower courses of rivers. The alluvial soil is very fertile. These are basically sedimentary rocks. They lack humus and nitrogen. They have high potassium content. They are suitable to grow paddy, sugarcane, and so on. In India, they are found in the Indo-Gangetic Plains.

Red Soil

They are rich in iron, hence red in colour. They are formed as a result of breakdown of igneous and metamorphic rocks. The soil is found in areas of India with low rainfall, in Madhya Pradesh, South Karnataka, Maharashtra, and Rajasthan. Crops such as red gram, groundnut, and castor seed are grown in red soil.

Laterite Soil

Laterite soil is formed from a mixture of clay and red soil and also as a result of leaching process. They are rich in minerals such as aluminium and iron and are found in hot and wet tropical areas. It has very low fertility and becomes hard when exposed to air, so it is used as a building material. Crops such as coffee, coconut, and cashew are capable of growing in laterite soil.

Regur Soil

It is also known as black soil or cotton soil and found in the Deccan trap. Black soil is rich in nutrients such as calcium, potassium, and magnesium, but has poor nitrogen content. Black soil is appropriate for growing crops such as cotton, tobacco, oil seeds, and maize.

Apart from these, other varieties of soil are desert soil (coarse or sandy texture) and mountain soil (formed from deposition of organic matter from woodlands and forests).

Soil Degradation

A good quality soil can support vegetation; without which life on earth cannot be sustained. It may take up to 1,000 years to form an inch of soil, and building-up of organic matter can also take a very long time. Even soil makes a dynamic ecosystem to sustain itself. For example, though nitrogen is the major gas in the atmosphere, it can be absorbed in the form of nitrates, which is carried out by nitrifying bacteria present in the soil. Soil exchanges gases with the environment; soil breaks down the organic wastes and recycles the nutrients back to the plants.

1. Soil ecosystem is disturbed by deforestation.
2. The use of heavy machinery results in soil compaction or pressing, which reduces the porosity of soil and also its water-holding capacity.
3. Sewage water is used to irrigate the fields or sewage sledge is used as a fertilizer, which increases the heavy metal content in the soil.
4. With intensification of agriculture as a result of green revolution, the same type of crop is raised again and again, which deprives the soil of a particular type of nutrient. To prevent this, crop rotation should be followed as a regular process.

   High-yielding varieties of food grains demand use of more water and fertilizers.
5. Use of water with high salt content to raise crops may result in high salinity of soil. Salt makes the layer at the top impermeable, which does not allow water to seep into the soil and thus results in the problem of water logging.
6. Excessive use of pesticides and fertilizers to increase land productivity also degrades the quality of soil and ultimately these fertilizers and pesticides enter into our ecological system.
7. The overexploitation of ground water results in fall of water table and ultimately in desertification.

Noise Pollution

Noise pollution may be defined as environmental noise that causes physiological or psychological damage if the volume is high or exposure is prolonged. Noise is also defined as unwanted sound; it is an irritant and a source of stress. The hair cells in the ear are damaged to an extent that cannot be repaired or replaced. The intensity or loudness of sound is felt in the form of pressure waves and affects our eardrums. Just like any other form of pollution, noise pollution too has serious impact on the working of our vital organs.

Measurement of Sound

Sound is measured in decibel (dB). The unit was chosen in honour of Alexander Graham Bell, who invented the telephone. It is not a linear scale, but a logarithmic scale. For example, a change from 40 dB to 80 dB represents a 10,000-fold increase in loudness. A modified scale called as decibel-A takes into account the pitch as well. The permitted noise level is 125 dB as per the Environment Protection Rules, 1999.

Sources of Noise Pollution

The following are the common sources of noise pollution:

1. Industries
2. Vehicles
3. Sound amplifiers (music system and loudspeakers)
4. Crackers
5. Passenger aircrafts and fighter jets

The permissible sound levels and typical average decibel levels are provided in Tables 9.3 and 9.4.

Table 9.3 Permissible Sound Levels

Area	Day (dB)	Night (dB)
Industrial	75	65
Commercial	65	55
Residential	50	45
Silence Zones	50	40

Table 9.4 Typical Average Decibel Levels

Source	dBA
Threshold of hearing	0
Quiet whisper	30
Normal conversation	60
Loud singing	75
Automobile	80
Jet plane	130

Effects of Noise Pollution on Human Health

WHO has included noise as one of the most hazardous factors that affect living conditions in crowded cities.

Hearing Loss

The intensity, frequency, and duration of noise have a proportionate impact on our body. The threshold of human hearing is 0 dB. Persistent exposure to intensity of noise in the range of 71–85 dB or even below can cause permanent loss of hearing. When noise level reaches around 130 dB, it even causes physical pain.

Masking

It is the inability to hear important environmental cues and animal signals.

Noise affects the heart rate, peripheral circulation, and breathing patterns. Persistent noisy environment can cause irritability, headache, and sleeplessness, thus decreasing productivity.

Radioactive Pollution

Radiation is defined as transmission of energy in the form of waves through space or a material medium. Radiation is of two kinds—ionising and non-ionising. Ionising radiation or high energy radiation like X-rays or gamma rays can alter DNA and can be harmful.

Non-ionising radiation is low energy radiation as emitted by mobile phones or radio towers and tends to generate heat.

Radiation can be natural or can arise from human activities. Most radiation exposure is from natural sources—rocks, earth's crust and cosmic among other sources. Radon is the most prominent example of natural radiation. Human activities typically accounts for up to 20% of our radiation exposure on an average.

Radiation particularly associated with nuclear medicine and the use of nuclear energy, along with X-rays, is 'ionizing' radiation, which means that the radiation has sufficient energy to interact with matter, especially the human body, and produce ions.

Effects of Radioactive Pollution

Some of the ultraviolet (UV) radiations from the sun are considered as ionizing radiation and provide a starting point in considering its effects. UV from sunlight is important in producing vitamin D in humans, but too much exposure produces sunburn and, potentially, skin cancer. The skin tissue gets damaged, and the damage to DNA (though mutation) could not be repaired properly, and hence, over time, cancer develops and could be fatal. The depletion of ozone layer may increase our exposure to UV rays and thus can cause skin cancer.

Genetic abnormalities occur in children of parents who had significant exposure to radiation.

Natural Hazards and Mitigation

Hazard may be defined as a dangerous condition or event, which threatens or has the potential for causing injury to life or damage to property or the environment.

Natural hazards are hazards that are caused by natural phenomena (hazards of meteorological, geological, or even biological origin). Examples of natural hazards are cyclones, tsunamis, earthquakes, and volcanic eruptions, which are exclusively of natural origin. Landslides, floods, drought, fires, are socionatural hazards since their causes are both natural and man-made. For example, flooding may be caused due to heavy rains, landslides, or blocking of drains with human waste.

Earthquake

It is the sudden shaking of earth's crust. The impact of an earthquake is sudden and there is hardly any warning, making it impossible to predict. Seismology is the study of earthquakes and seismic waves that move through and around the earth.

Causes of Earthquake

Earth's crust is not one piece but consists of portions called plates, which vary in size from a few hundred to thousands of kilometres. According to the Theory of Plate Tectonics, when these plates contact each other, stress arises in the crust. The plates may pull away from each other, push against each other, or slide sideways. If plates get locked together, they are unable to move. It results in stress in areas around the plate boundaries called faults. When this reaches a maximum point, the fault rupture generates vibration called seismic waves, which radiate in all directions from the focus (Figures 9.1 and 9.2). To put simply, focus can also be defined as underground origin of an earthquake.

Seismic Waves

These are waves of energy that travel through the earth's layers. There are two main types of Seismic Waves

1. Body waves
2. Surface waves

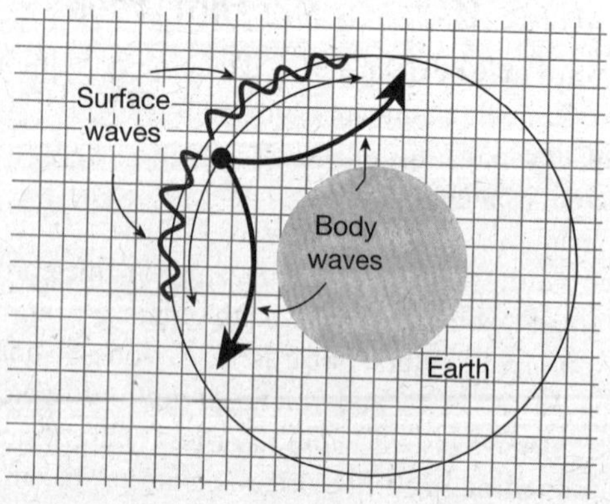

Figure 9.1 Body Waves and Surface Waves

Body Waves

These are called body waves as they pass through the body of earth. They are further categorized as follows:

1. Primary or compressional waves, also popular as P waves.
2. Secondary or transverse waves, also popular as S waves.

Primary waves travel faster than the secondary waves; thus, they are the first to reach the seismograph stations.

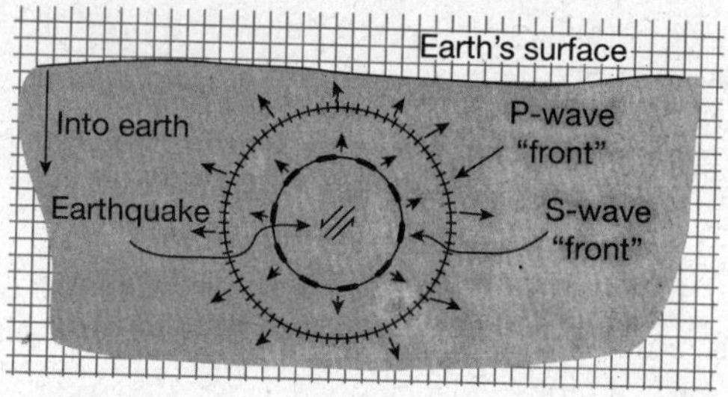

Figure 9.2 P (Primary) Waves and S (Secondary) Waves

Surface Waves

They travel along the earth's crust and vibrate the ground horizontally and vertically. They are more dangerous than the body waves and destroy buildings and highways, which come in their path. Their amplitude decreases with increasing depth into the earth. These are further categorized as (i) Love waves and (ii) Rayleigh waves.

Love waves move the ground from side-to-side. Confined to the surface of the crust, Love waves produce entirely horizontal motion.

Rayleigh moves the ground up and down, and side-to-side. Love waves are faster than Rayleigh waves.

The earthquakes can be shallow (less than 60 km), medium (60–300 km), and deep (300–600 km). Shallow-focus earthquakes are the most damaging because of the proximity to the surface.

Measurement of Intensity of Earthquakes

There are manly two techniques available to measure the intensity of earthquakes. These are:

1. *Richter scale:* Earthquake's magnitude or amount of energy released is determined by the use of a seismograph, which is an instrument that continuously records ground vibrations. An earthquake with a magnitude 7.5 on the Richter scale releases 30 times more energy than the one with 6.5 magnitude and will also have a shaking amplitude of 10 times higher. Similarly, an earthquake that measures 5.0 on the Richter scale has a shaking amplitude 10 times larger than one that measures 4.0, and corresponds to a 30 times larger release of energy. An earthquake of magnitude 3 is the smallest that is normally felt by humans.
2. *Modified Mercalli scale:* It expresses the intensity of earthquake's effect on people, structure, and the earth's surface on scale from I to XII.

Earthquake Prone Zones in India

India has been recently divided into four seismic zones by Ministry of Earth Sciences, Government of India, on the basis of Modified Mercalli (MM) intensity scale.

Broadly, Zone-V comprises entire north-eastern India, parts of Jammu and Kashmir, Himachal Pradesh, Uttaranchal, Rann of Kutch in Gujarat, parts of North Bihar, and Andaman & Nicobar Islands.

Zone-IV covers remaining parts of Jammu & Kashmir and Himachal Pradesh, Union Territory of Delhi, Sikkim, northern parts of Uttar Pradesh, Bihar, and West Bengal, parts of Gujarat and small portions of Maharashtra near the west coast, and Rajasthan.

Zone-III comprises Kerala, Goa, Lakshadweep islands, and remaining parts of Uttar Pradesh, Gujarat, and West Bengal, parts of Punjab, Rajasthan, Madhya Pradesh, Bihar, Jharkhand, Chhattisgarh, Maharashtra, Orissa, Andhra Pradesh, Tamil Nadu, and Karnataka.

Zone-II covers the remaining parts of the country.

Furthermore, as a part of pre-disaster preparedness measure, Government of India has also completed seismic microzonation studies of some of the major cities in the country such as, Jabalpur, Guwahati, Bangalore, greater Bharuch in Gujarat, Jammu in Jammu & Kashmir, Shillong in Meghalaya, Chennai in Tamil Nadu, and Sikkim state.

Mitigation of Earthquakes

Planning

The Bureau of Indian Standards has published certain building codes and guidelines for safe construction of buildings against earthquakes. Before the buildings are constructed, the building plans have to be checked by the municipality, according to the rules laid down by the law.

Public Education

Educating the public on causes and characteristics of an earthquake and preparedness measures helps to a certain extent in mitigating the natural disaster.

Engineered Structures

Buildings need to be designed and constructed as per the laws to withstand ground shaking. Architectural and engineering inputs need to be put together to improve building design and construction practices. The soil type needs to be analysed before construction.

Tsunami

The term tsunami has been derived from a Japanese term *Tsu* meaning harbour and *nami* meaning waves.

A tsunami is a series of ocean waves with very long wavelengths (typically hundreds of kilometres) caused by large-scale disturbances of the ocean, such as the following:

1. Earthquakes
2. Landslide
3. Volcanic eruptions
4. Explosions
5. Meteorites

These disturbances can either be from below (e.g., underwater earthquakes with large vertical displacements and submarine landslides) or from above (e.g., meteorite impacts).

Tsunamis can have wavelengths ranging from 10 to 500 km and wave periods of up to an hour. As a result of their long wavelengths, tsunamis act as shallow-water waves. A wave becomes a shallow-water wave when the wavelength is very large compared to the water depth. Tsunamis may reach a maximum vertical height onshore above sea level, often called a run-up height, of tens of metres.

Tsunamis can result in massive destruction when they arrive onshore; it can cause severe coastal erosion, which is wearing away of coastal land or beaches. The power of water can wash away vegetation, making it hard to establish the shoreline. As tsunamis are triggered by sudden events, there may be little time to warn coastal residents of its arrival.

This fact became evident in March of 2011 when Japan was struck by a large tsunami that was triggered by a 9.0 magnitude earthquake, which damaged several nuclear power plant reactors followed by massive radioactive pollution. Tsunami originated in Indian Ocean caused massive damage in Indonesia and India.

Volcanoes

A volcano is an opening, or rupture, in the earth's surface or crust, which allows hot magma, volcanic ash, and gases from within the earth to reach the surface. Most volcanoes have a volcanic crater at the top. When they are active, materials pour out of it. This includes lava, steam, gaseous compounds of sulphur, ash, and broken rock pieces.

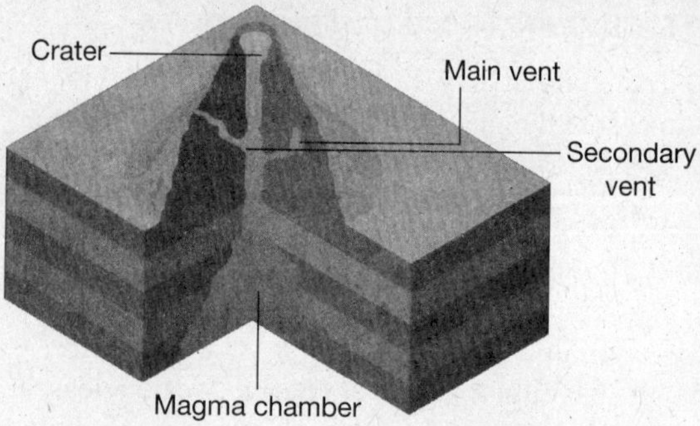

Volcanoes are generally found where tectonic plates diverge or converge. Subduction zones are places where two plates, usually an oceanic plate and a continental plate, collide; as is the case with earthquakes as well. Volcanoes tend to exist along the edges between tectonic plates, massive rock slabs that make up earth's surface. About 90 per cent of all volcanoes exist within the 'Ring of Fire' along the edges of the Pacific Ocean.

Eruption of volcanoes away from the subduction zone is referred to as mantle plumes, also called as 'hotspots'. These are columns taking out the magma from the deep interior of the earth.

Erupting volcanoes can pose many hazards. Volcanic ash can be a threat to aircraft, especially jet aircrafts.

Large eruptions can affect temperature as ash and droplets of sulphuric acid obscure the sun and cool the earth's lower atmosphere or troposphere.

Cyclone

Cyclone is a region of low atmospheric pressure surrounded by high atmospheric pressure, resulting in swirling atmospheric disturbances, accompanied by powerful winds blowing in anti-clockwise direction in the northern hemisphere and in clockwise direction in the southern hemisphere. They occur mainly in the tropical and temperate regions of the world. Cyclones are called by various names in different parts of the world. Cyclones in India are moderate in nature. Some of the general features of a typical cyclone are as follows:

1. Strong winds
2. Exceptional rain
3. Storm surge

Cyclones are called by different names such as typhoons and hurricanes (Caribbean and Gulf of Mexico), tropical cyclones (India), willie (Australia), and tornadoes (South America).

Damage by Cyclones

First, in a sudden, brief onslaught, high winds cause major damage to infrastructure and housing, particularly in fragile constructions. They are generally followed by heavy rains and floods and, in flat coastal areas, by storm surge riding on tidal waves and inundating the land over long distances of even up to 15 km inland. There can be loss of life due to flooding and flying elements and contamination of water supplies may lead to viral outbreaks, diarrhoea, and malaria.

Mitigation of Cyclones

Green belt plantation along the coastal line in a scientific, interweaving pattern can reduce the effects of hazard. Providing a cover through green belt sustains less damage. Forests act as a wide buffer zone against strong winds and flash floods. The roots of the plants and trees keep the soil intact and prevent erosion and slow runoff to prevent or lessen flooding.

Flood

Flood is a state of high water level along a river channel or on the coast that leads to inundation of land, which is not usually submerged. There are different types of floods, namely flash flood, riverine flood, and urban flood.

Flash Floods

These are rapid inland floods due to intense rainfall. A flash flood describes sudden flooding within a short duration. In sloped terrains, the water flows rapidly with a high destruction potential. In flat terrains, the rainwater cannot infiltrate into the ground or run-off (due to small slope) as quickly as it falls. Flash floods are typically associated with thunderstorms. A flash flood can occur at virtually any place.

Causes of Flash Floods

1. Heavy rainfall in a short span of time.
2. Heavy siltation of the river bed reduces the water carrying capacity of the rivers or stream.
3. Blockage in the drains leads to flooding of the area.
4. Landslides blocking the flow of the stream.
5. Construction of dams and reservoirs
6. In areas prone to cyclone, strong winds accompanied by heavy downpour along with storm surge leads to flooding.

The understanding of the concept of catabatic (also termed as katabatic) and anabatic winds can help further to understand the phenomenon of flash floods. The term catabatic wind is used for downslope winds flowing from high elevations of mountains, plateaus, and hills, down their slopes, to the valleys or planes below. This happens during the night time. The concept of anabatic winds is just opposite to catabatic winds, which flow up the hill, specifically during the daytime. The catabatic winds cause occurrence of flash floods.

Cloudbursts

A cloudburst is an extreme amount of precipitation, sometimes with hail and thunder, which normally lasts no longer than a few minutes but is capable of creating flood conditions. Colloquially, the term cloudburst may be used to describe any sudden heavy, brief, and usually unforecasted rainfall.

The heavy rainfall, flash floods, landslides, and cloudbursts in June 2013 caused havoc in Uttarakhand, causing death of thousands of people.

Drought

Drought is either the absence or deficiency of rainfall from its normal pattern in a region for an extended period of time leading to general suffering in the society. It is an interplay between the demand that people place on natural supply of water and the natural event that provides water in a given geographical region. The state of Kerala, which receives more than 3,000 mm of rainfall every year, was declared drought-affected in the past as it was insufficient to have two good crops. The more the imbalance in supply, the higher is the drought. The following explains this general definition further.

1. It is the slow on set of disaster and is difficult to demarcate the time of its onset and the end.
2. Any unusual dry period that results in shortage of useful water.

Although drought is basically caused by rainfall deficit, which is a meteorological phenomenon, it manifests into different spheres because of various vulnerability factors associated with it. Some of these factors are induced by humans.

Although drought is a natural disaster, its effects are made worst in developing countries due to overpopulation, overgrazing, deforestation, soil erosion, excessive use of ground and surface water for growing crops, and loss of biodiversity. The four types of droughts are as follows:

1. *Meteorological drought:* It is simply the absence or deficit of rainfall. It is the least severe form of drought and is identified by sunny days and hot weather.
2. *Hydrological drought:* It leads to reduction of natural stream flows or ground water levels, plus stored water supplies. The main impact is on the water resource systems.
3. *Agricultural drought:* This form of drought occurs when moisture level in the soil is insufficient to maintain average crop yields. Initial consequences are reduced seasonal output of crops and other related production. An extreme agricultural drought can lead to a famine, which is prolonged shortage of food in a restricted region causing widespread disease and death from starvation.
4. *Socio-economic drought:* It correlates the supply and demand of goods and services with the three above-mentioned types of drought.

Wildfire

A wildfire is any uncontrolled fire in combustible vegetation that occurs in the countryside or a wilderness area. A wildfire differs from other fires by its extensive size, the speed at which it can spread out from its original source, its potential to change directions unexpectedly, and its ability to jump gaps such as roads, rivers, and fire breaks.

Landslides

The term landslide includes all varieties of mass movement of hill slopes and can be defined as the downward and outward movement of slope-forming materials composed of rocks, soils, artificial fills, or a combination of all these materials along surfaces of separation by falling, sliding and flowing, either slowly or quickly from one place to another. Although the landslides are primarily associated with mountainous terrains, these can also occur in areas where activities such as surface excavation for highways, buildings, and open-pit mines take place. Landslides take place in conjunction with earthquakes, floods, and volcanoes. At times, prolonged rainfall causing landslide may block the flow of river for quite some time. The formation of river blocks can cause havoc to the settlements downstream on its bursting.

Causes of Landslides

1. *Geologically weak material:* Weakness in the composition and structure of rock or soil
2. *Erosion:* Erosion of slope top due to cutting down of vegetation and construction of roads
3. *Intense rainfall:* Intense rainfalls, heavy melting of snow in the hilly terrains
4. *Human excavation:* Mining, deforestation, irrigation
5. *Earthquake*
6. *Volcanic eruption*

Exploitation of Natural Resources

There are basically two approaches in context of man–environment interaction. These are as follows: environmental determinism and possibilism.

According to determinism, our earth is the creation of nature and not just a matter of chance. It is the conditions in the environment that tell us what we are capable of doing. Man is subservient to nature. According to pragmatic possibilism, anything is possible. Man is intelligent and has the necessary knowledge, skills, technology, and money to manage the environment.

The exploitation of natural resources is a key factor in economic growth and development, but it is not without serious negative environmental and socio-economic impacts.

Main Reasons for Exploitation of Natural Resources

In last few decades, the developing nations are trying to develop a model which the developed countries did in the past. Deforestation is on going and is shaping the climate and geography. In fact, the demand for natural mineral and energy sources is coming from newly industrialized nations and emerging economies such as China and India.

The exploitation of natural resources has intensified during the last few decades because of the following reasons:

Rapid Industrialisation, Urbanisation, and Increase in Population

All our gadgets run on electricity, generated mainly from thermal power plants, which further run on fossil fuels (coal). Manufacturing industries are primarily located in urban areas, which create jobs; and people have moved from rural areas to the cities over the years. This process is continuing even today.

During the twentieth century, world population increased by four and a half times, from 1.5 billion to 6.2 billion, but urban population grew 13 times from 225 million to 3.4 billion or 47% of the total population. By 2030, the figures are likely to increase to 4.9 billion or 60%. By 2015, the number of megacities (with 10 million plus population) is likely to increase to 23 (with 15 in Asia). Urban areas cover just 3–4% of the world's land surface, and accommodate half of the world's population, but consume around 80% of global energy supply and thus emit the bulk of greenhouse gases (GHGs).

Transport vehicles also run mainly on petrol or diesel, both of which are fossil fuels. Natural resources are being used extensively for construction, industries, transport, and consumption. Consumer cult, coupled with manifold increase in population, has created mountains of waste. Large quantities of plastic waste, which do not decay, also damage the environment. Use of huge quantities of paper in educational institutes and offices, for which millions of trees have to be cut each year, is also one of the culprits. Timber is used in large quantities for construction of houses.

As land area available for agriculture, to feed the population, is limited, high-yielding varieties of crops have been developed to increase the agricultural output, which requires large quantities of fertilizers; and more fertilizers means more emission of nitrous oxide, both from the field into which it is applied and the fertilizer industry that produces it. Pollution also results from runoff of fertilizers into water bodies. Further, available land area is actually shrinking as a result of ecological degradation.

Availability of Technology

Increase in sophistication of technology enables quick and efficient extraction of natural resources. For example, rates of deforestation have increased greatly due to electric saws.

Intensive Agricultural Practices

To meet the food requirements of large population, more and more land has been brought under cultivation.

Culture of Consumerism

Excessive demand leads to a mad scramble for resources and conflicts.

Non-equitable Distribution of Resources

The raw material for finished goods is available in underdeveloped or developing nations. To earn foreign exchange and taxes, the governments allow the exploitation of resources, however, without a long-term approach to replenish them or mitigate the after effects.

Natural Resources—Our Mineral Wealth

India is rich in metallic minerals of ferrous groups such as iron, manganese, chromite, and titanium. However, petroleum and some non-ferrous minerals such as copper, lead, zinc, tin, and graphite are not adequate.

Iron

Iron ores have been categorized into three grades, namely, (1) haematite, also known as red ore, which contains up to 68% iron; (2) magnetite (60%, known as black ore); and (3) lignite contains between 35 and 50% iron. Pure iron is soft, but hardened because of metallurgical processes. A certain proportion of carbon is required in ferrous to make it steel. Chromite is essential for the manufacture of stainless steel and high-temperature alloys.

India has deposits of high-grade iron ore, that is, haematite and magnetite. India is the second largest producer of iron ore after Brazil. The mineral is found mainly in Jharkhand, Odisha, Chhattisgarh, Madhya Pradesh, Goa, Maharashtra, and Karnataka. In Goa, there are open cast iron ore mines, which are mechanized.

Bauxite

Bauxite is an aluminium ore. Aluminium is used in manufacturing of aeroplanes, electrical gadgets, and so on. India is the third largest producer of bauxite in the world. Major bauxite producing areas are Jharkhand, Odisha, Chhattisgarh, Madhya Pradesh, Gujarat, Maharashtra, and Tamil Nadu.

Mica

India is the largest producer and exporter of mica in the world. Mica deposits mainly occur in Bihar, Jharkhand, Andhra Pradesh, and Rajasthan. It is used for manufacturing of electrical fittings.

Copper

It is a ductile metal with very high thermal and electrical conductivity. Pure copper is soft and malleable. It is mainly produced in Rajasthan, Madhya Pradesh, Jharkhand, Karnataka, and Andhra Pradesh.

Manganese

India is the third largest producer of manganese after Russia and South Africa. India's manganese deposits lie in Maharashtra, Madhya Pradesh, Chhattisgarh, Odisha, Karnataka, and Andhra Pradesh.

Limestone

Limestone with high silica content is used for the manufacture of white cement. Major limestone-producing states in India are Bihar, Jharkhand, Odisha, Madhya Pradesh, Chhattisgarh, Rajasthan, Gujarat, and Tamil Nadu.

Gold

Kolar in Karnataka has deposits of gold in India. These mines are among the deepest in the world which makes mining of this ore a very expensive process.

Salt

It is obtained from seas, lakes, and rocks. India is one of the world's leading producers and exporters of salt.

Coal

Coal is used as a raw material in chemical and fertilizer industries. It is found in two regions: (i) Gondwana and (ii) extra-peninsular areas such as Assam and other north-east states. There are high lignite reserves in Tamil Nadu.

Petroleum

Petroleum exists in anticlines and fault traps. In India, it is found in sedimentary rocks.

Uranium and Thorium

Uranium is embedded in igneous and metamorphic rocks in Bihar (Jaduguda in Singhbhum district of Bihar), Rajasthan, and Andhra Pradesh.

USA, Australia, and India have particularly large reserves of thorium. In India, thorium is found in monazite sands across the coasts of Kerala.

More About the Effects of Chromium Intake on Human Health

Chromium is a mineral that aids in the body's ability to use insulin to convert carbohydrates to energy. It is used in many industries as well.

Naturally occurring trivalent chromium is essential for good health and the normal intake from eating foods is 70–80 μg per day and is considered safe.

Hexavalent chromium does not occur naturally but is produced by certain industrial processes. It is the most toxic form of chromium and is shown to cause lung cancer when workers are exposed to high levels for longer time periods.

Breathing chromium dust or fume is the main route for exposure to chromium.

Plants can absorb chromium and it can be passed on to those who eat the plants.

Contact with contaminated soil can result in exposure to chromium.

Exploitation of Forest Resources

Deforestation is clearing the earth's forests on a massive scale, resulting in damage to the quality of land. The world's rain forests will completely vanish in about hundred years at the current rate of deforestation.

Expansion of Agriculture

The major direct cause of deforestation is agriculture, with subsistence farming responsible for 48% of deforestation, commercial agriculture for 32%, and fuel wood for 5%.

Shifting Cultivation

Farmers cut forests to provide more room for planting crops or grazing livestock. Many small farmers clear a few acres to feed their families by cutting down trees and burning them in a process known as slash and burn agriculture. It is still practiced in Assam and Madagascar (Indian Ocean) for subsistence farming.

Shifting cultivation has occurred due to poor fertility of soil. In this cultivation, a small patch of tropical forests is cleared; vegetation is destroyed and burned. Crops are grown as long as the soil is productive, after which the cultivation is abandoned, and cultivations move on to fresh patch of land.

Timber Harvesting

Logging (for world's wood and paper products) is responsible for 14% of deforestation. Timber resource is an important asset for the prosperity of the country. Commercial wood is found readily in national as well as international markets. Countries such as Myanmar, Malaysia, Indonesia, Brazil, Argentina, and many African countries are examples.

Extension of Cultivation on Hill Slopes

This is termed as contour farming. Although agriculture has always been concentrated on planes and floors of valleys, farming on narrow flat steps cut one after another across the slope or terrace is an age old practice. There are many medicinal plants, which should better be raised in hilly areas.

Wild Fires

Not all deforestation is intentional. Some is caused by a combination of human and natural factors such as wildfires and subsequent overgrazing, which may prevent the growth of young trees. However, in the last decade, the intensity and frequency of wild fires has increased because of global warming.

Negative Effects of Deforestation on the Environment

Globalization is viewed as another root cause of deforestation. The degradation of forest ecosystems has been traced to economic incentives that make forest conversion appear more profitable than forest conservation. The forest cover, which helps in absorbing Green House Gas, has shrunk from 4.7 billion hectares in 1949 to 714.9 million hectares in 2015.

Climate Change

Deforestation is the main driver of climate change. Conventionally, trees play a critical role in absorbing the Green House Gases (GHGs) that are the main cause of global warming.

Now, deforestation or less tree cover means more quantities of GHGs being released into the atmosphere. This has increased the severity of global warming (the concept of GHGs has been discussed separately).

Tropical deforestation is responsible for approximately 20% of world's GHG emissions. According to Intergovernmental Panel on Climate Change (IPCC) reports, deforestation accounts for up to one-third of total anthropogenic carbon dioxide emissions in tropical areas.

Other plants remove carbon (in the form of carbon dioxide) from the atmosphere during the process of photosynthesis and release oxygen back into the atmosphere during normal respiration. Only when actively growing, can a tree or forest remove carbon over an annual or longer time frame. Both the decay and burning of wood release much of this stored carbon back into the atmosphere.

A GHG is a gas in the atmosphere that absorbs and emits radiation within the thermal infrared range. This process is the fundamental cause of greenhouse effect. The primary GHGs in the earth's atmosphere are water vapour, carbon dioxide, methane, nitrous oxide, and ozone. GHGs greatly affect the temperature of the earth; without them, the earth's surface average would be about 33°C colder than the present average of 14°C.

Forests are effective as carbon sinks or biodiversity reserves.

Reduced Moisture Content in the Environment

Forest soils are moist, but without protection from sun-blocking tree cover, they quickly dry out. Trees also help perpetuate the water cycle by returning water vapour back into the atmosphere. Without trees to fill these roles, many former forest lands can quickly become barren deserts.

Effects of Deforestation on Water Cycle

Deforestation changes the quantity of water on surface, in soil, or in the atmosphere. This in turn changes the erosion rates and the availability of water, either for ecosystem functions or for human services.

Decrease in Water Precipitation

Trees extract groundwater through their roots and release it into the atmosphere. When trees are removed, there will not be any evaporation, resulting in a much drier climate. Thus, trees help in perpetuating the water cycle by returning water vapour back into the atmosphere. Without trees to fill these roles, it would result in reduced rainfall and many former forest lands would quickly become barren deserts. Deforestation reduces the content of water in the soil and groundwater as well as the atmospheric moisture. 99% of the water absorbed by the roots moves up to the leaves and transpires. Forest cover brings down the temperature of the area, which is crucial for rainfall.

Soil Erosion Tree roots bind soil together, and if the soil is sufficiently shallow, they act to keep the soil in place by binding with the underlying bedrock. Tree removal on steep slopes with shallow soil increases the risk of landslides, which threatens the people living nearby. The quicker transport of surface water translates into flash flooding and more localized floods than those which would occur with the forest cover.

Deforestation generally increases the rate of soil erosion, by increasing the amount of runoff and reducing the protection of soil from tree litter. Yellow River is an example. Its yellow colour is caused by the downstream carriage of loess and causes flooding of river in lower reaches (hence the river's nickname China's sorrow).

Desertification and deforestation are linked closely. Desertification is a systemic phenomenon resulting from excessive felling of trees. It is the degradation of land in any dry land. Dry land ecosystems are already very fragile, and can rarely sustain the increased pressures that result from intense population growth. Many of these areas are inappropriately opened to development, when they cannot sustain human settlements.

1. The most common cause of desertification is the over cultivation of desert lands. Over-cultivation causes nutrients in the soil to be depleted faster than they are restored. Improper irrigation practices result in salinated soils, and depletion of aquifers.
2. Vegetation plays a major role in determining the biological composition of soil. The soil erosion and water runoff decreases with increased vegetation cover. Overgrazing removes vegetation, causing erosion and loss of topsoil.
3. Forests cause precipitation and maintain humidity of an area. Air humidity not only results in less penetration of solar heat to ground during the day but also checks heat escape to outer atmosphere during the night. Forests thus tend to provide seasonal stability to the terrain.
4. As result of deforestation, there is higher wind velocity, which increases the rate of soil erosion.

Exploitation of Mineral Resources

A mineral is any substance that is present naturally in the earth's crust and is not made of any animal or vegetable matter. Mining is the process of extracting and processing minerals. The minerals include metals such as gold, iron, aluminium, copper; and non-metals such as stone, sand, and salt.

The earth's geological processes have taken millions and billions of years to form the minerals and they are non-renewable.

In the entire history of human civilization, such an unusually high demand has never been placed on natural resources of our planet. The consequences of this overexploitation of mineral wealth will be serious, drastic and enormously damaging to the entire biosphere. These can be summed up as follows:

1. *Fast depletion of high-grade mineral deposits:* Overexploitation of mineral resources is depleting our good quality deposits. The ever increasing demand is compelling miners to dig lower and lower grades of ore. For example, about few centuries ago, copper was extracted from ores containing 8–10% of metal. Now, the ore has come down to a level of 0.35%.
2. *Wastage and dissemination of mineral wealth:* Generally, ore deposit consists of complex mixture of many elements. Thus, many minerals are left open as waste materials, many of which may be in short supply. This wastage rises as more and more ores are extracted and processed.
3. *Pollution of environment from mining and processing wastes:* Mining, especially opencast mining, is a dirty industry. It destroys vegetation cover. Large craters may be left behind. It has created some of the largest environmental disaster zones in the world.

   Each step in mining and processing operations produces large quantities of waste materials.
4. *Pollution caused by heavy energy requirement of mining industry:* Moving huge amounts of sand particles, silt, and clay needs massive energy. Many power projects are undertaken because of this requirement. Energy is required at every step, namely, concentration, smelting, and refining. Electrolytic process used for refining of some metals, such as aluminium, requires energy.
5. *Lack of skilled labour:* As skilled labour to mine may not be available from local

communities, they usually come from outside and there can be a problem linked with migration of communities from their natural habitats as a result of mining activities. There is loss of land, livelihood, and even culture for the local communities. Due to mechanization, there is less requirement of manual labour.

Our Energy Sources

Energy is the capacity to do work. It is the basic requirement for a living being, machine, and matter to move, function, or perform any kind of work. The whole development of civilization is based on the availability of energy. Energy is present in different forms; and it has been further modified from time to time to suit the requirements of mankind. The common forms of energy are as follows:

1. Mechanical energy of a body is the energy it possesses by virtue of its motion or its position. When a body is in motion, it possesses kinetic energy. Potential energy is the energy possessed by a body due to its position. For example, energy stored in a compressed spring is an example of potential energy.
2. Thermal energy is the energy a substance or system has in relation to its temperature, that is, the energy of moving or vibrating molecules.
3. Chemical energy is stored in the form of molecular bonds.
4. Nuclear energy is the mass converted into energy.
5. There can be a few other forms of energy such as radiant energy or light energy.

Law of Conservation of Energy

The total amount of energy in the universe remains constant. It changes from one form to another. For example, when water is stored in a dam at a height, it possesses potential energy. However, when water falls on the turbine, it possesses kinetic energy.

Primary Energy and Secondary Energy

Primary energy form is directly found in nature such as coal and sunlight. This can be renewable or non-renewable. When primary energy form is converted into some convenient form of energy, it is called as secondary energy. For example, coal or sunlight is converted into electrical energy, which can be consumed in homes or industry.

Non-renewable Energy Sources

A non-renewable resource is a natural resource that cannot be reproduced, grown, generated, or used on a scale, which can sustain its consumption rate; once depleted there is no more available for future needs. Resources that are consumed much faster than nature can create them are also considered as non-renewable. They basically consist of fossil fuels.

Fossil Fuels

Fossil fuels consist of oil and coal. They are preferred for the following main reasons:

1. They have high calorific value.
2. The technology is available to exploit these resources.

The market is well developed for trading of the fossil fuels. Our conventional infrastructure and transport systems, which are fitted with combustion engines, remain prominent throughout the globe.

The main disadvantages of use of fossil fuels are in terms of harm to environment:

1. *Global warming:* The continued use of fossil fuels at the current rate will increase global warming and cause more severe climatic change. The SO_2 and CO_2 produced during the burning of fossil fuels contribute towards global warming and acid rains.
2. *Health hazards:* Fly ash and other particulate matter cause health hazards such as asthma and tuberculosis.
3. *Oil spills:* They are a threat to marine life and our ecosystem.

Eventually, fossil-based resources will become too costly to harvest and humanity will need to shift its reliance to other sources of energy.

As fossil fuels are non-renewable and thus finite, that will eventually run out of stock, they have become too expensive or too environmentally damaging to retrieve. In contrast, many types of renewable energy resources, such as wind and solar energy, are constantly replenished and will never run out. At present, the main energy source used by humans are non-renewable fossil fuels as they meet 80% of our energy needs.

Petroleum Oil

Oil occurs in rock formations in the earth, which before getting processed in refineries is called crude oil—a mixture of hydrocarbons. It is processed by fractional distillation and transported to points of consumption.

Coal

Coal is a black or brown carbonaceous sedimentary rock formed by combustion of partially decomposed plant material. It takes millions of years to form from decayed plants. The process of formation of coal is termed as coalification.

Coal provides 30.3% of global primary energy needs and generates 42% of the world's electricity. In India, 70–80% of electricity is produced by burning coal. The amount of energy in coal is expressed in British Thermal Units per pound (a BTU is the amount of heat required to raise the temperature of one pound of water by one degree Fahrenheit.) Higher the carbon content, higher is its calorific value and its quality.

The grading of coal is done on the basis of the carbon contents:

1. *Peat:* Peat is not a typical variety of coal. The carbon content is 50–60%. Under conditions of temperature and pressure, it converts into lignite, bituminous, and subsequently into anthracite. The carbon contents increase in subsequent stages.
2. *Lignite or brown coal:* It contains 70% carbon and is found in geologically young mines, the lowest rank of coal with high moisture content.
3. *Bituminous coal:* It is also termed as soft coal; it contains around 80% carbon.
4. *Anthracite coal:* It is the best quality coal and contains 90–95% carbon and around 5% volatile matter; therefore, its burning gives very little smoke.

When bituminous coal is heated at extremely high temperature, the residual matter is called coke. Different types of coal have different uses. Steam coal, also known as thermal coal, is mainly used in power generation. Coking coal, also known as metallurgical coal, is mainly used in steel production. It is composed primarily of carbon and hydrocarbons. Its extraction causes environmental hazards. Air pollution (mainly suspended particulate matter) due to burning of coal causes respiratory problems. Thermal power stations produce waste in the form of fly ash; large dumps are required to dump this waste material. Burning coal causes smog, soot, acid rain, global warming, and toxic air emissions.

Coal is the most abundantly available fossil fuel, which at current rate of consumption may last up to 200 years. China, USA, India, Australia, and Indonesia are the five major coal producers in the world.

Coal deposits in India belong to Gondwana age. Nearly three-fourths of coal deposits are situated in Damodar Valley.

An unconventional form of gas formed during coalification process and found on the internal surfaces of coal is called 'coal bed methane'.

Natural Gas

1. Natural gas mainly comprises of methane, butane, ethane, and propane, and has very high calorific value.
2. Some of the organic material was changed by heat and pressure into oil and coal while natural gas was trapped within the earth's crust.
3. It was formed from decaying plants and animals, millions of years ago, and is found near oil deposits.

It is obtained in three forms:

1. *Compressed Natural Gas (CNG):* It mainly contains methane with traces of butane, propane, ethane, and so on. Clean burning of fuel with very less emission of GHGs is possible. It is ideal for public transport vehicles.
2. *Liquefied Natural Gas (LNG):* It contains 98% methane. It is obtained by cooling natural gas into a liquid and is suitable for long distance travelling vehicles.
3. *Liquefied Petroleum Gas (LPG):* It mainly contains propane, which turns to liquid when compressed. It is widely used as cooking gas and can be easily transported over long distances. A strong foul-smelling substance called ethyl mercaptan (C_2H_5SH) is added to LPG to detect its leakage as LPG is an odourless gas.

Shale Gas and Shale Fuel

Although we have long known about huge gas resources trapped in shale rock formations, technology was not available. However, in the last decade, two technologies namely, hydraulic fracturing and horizontal drilling, were combined to successfully unlock this resource. Shale rock formations are basically sedimentary rocks.

USA is the top shale energy producing nation in the world. It is tipped to be the top oil-producing nation in the world followed by Saudi Arabia and Russia, as its total oil production has doubled considerably since 2008 due to shale oil exploitation. Before 2014, the price of oil had been steadily increasing for a decade. Since then, the price of oil has been falling, and the trend may continue for sometime.

Concept of Extreme Energy

Klare formulated the concept of extreme energy. Extreme energy is a range of technique for the production of energy from unconventional resources, which share the characteristics of being environmentally damaging or risky. Examples include exploitation of oil sands and shale oil, deepwater drilling, hydraulic fracturing, mountaintop removal mining, petroleum exploration in the Arctic, and natural gas hydrates.

Nuclear Energy

Earlier, we discussed about the law of conservation of energy in which energy can be changed from one form into another. The source of nuclear energy is the mass of the nucleus and energy generated during a nuclear reaction is due to conversion of mass into energy (Einstein's theory). The energy produced is given by $e = mc^2$, where m is the mass and c is the speed of light. This equation was developed by Einstein. There are two ways to obtain nuclear energy, namely, nuclear fission and nuclear fusion.

In a nuclear fission reaction, the nucleus of a heavy radioactive element such as uranium, plutonium, or thorium splits up into smaller nuclei, when bombarded with low-energy neutrons. A huge amount of heat is generated in this process. At this point, carbon dioxide in gas form is pumped into the reactors with uranium, removing heat from the system. The gas turns very hot, and this heat is used to convert water into steam. The steam created from this process drives the turbines, which in turn drive the generators that produce nuclear energy.

Nuclear fusion reaction involves the combination or fusion of two light elements such as hydrogen to form a heavier element, resulting in the release of uncontrollable energy. Thus, it cannot be used to generate electricity and cannot be commercialized as is case with fission reaction. Sun's energy is generated by nuclear fusion reaction. The heat and light that we receive from sun is all due to the continuous fusion reactions going on inside it.

The nuclear power reactor that creates all these reactions is controlled through rods of boron, known as control rods. These boron rods absorb the neutrons. The rods are lowered into the reactor to absorb neutrons and slow down the process of fission. To generate more power, the rods are raised again to allow even more neutrons to crash into the atoms of uranium.

Advantages

1. Nuclear energy is more cost-effective compared to coal.
2. It does not use as much fuel in the process.
3. It produces less waste and does not produce carbon dioxide or smoke; thus, nuclear energy does not contribute to environmental hazards or greenhouse effect.
4. Nuclear power stations are usually very compact compared to the thermal stations. Although the initial capital cost of building a nuclear plant is high, the maintenance and running costs are relatively low.

Limitations

Creating nuclear energy is a complex chemical process that can be very dangerous.

1. There is a great deal of radiation danger associated with nuclear energy. It is capable of causing genetic disorders. Thus, if someone is once exposed to these radiations, it can affect the generations to come adversely.
2. Storage of nuclear wastes can lead to disastrous effects if not disposed or stored in a proper manner.
3. Once it was assumed that the supply of nuclear fuel will not be a problem. However, that appears to be a fallacy now. Nuclear power is not a renewable source of energy. Uranium is a metal that is mined from the ground in much the same way as coal is mined. It is a scarce metal and the supply of uranium will one day run out, making all the nuclear power plants obsolete.
4. Radioactive minerals are unevenly distributed around the world and are found in limited quantities.
5. Starting a nuclear plant requires huge capital investment and advanced technology.
6. There have been instances of proliferation of nuclear technology and number of restrictions by international community for use of nuclear technology. There are many moral groups opposing production of nuclear energy, in the wake of nuclear accidents.

There have been many nuclear accidents in the last five decades such as Three Miles (1979, USA) and Chernobyl (1987, Ukraine). The most recent nuclear mishap was the Fukushima Accident in Japan in March 2011. It was caused by an earthquake-generated tsunami. Germany declared that it would phase out all the nuclear power plants in near future.

Fast Breeder Reactors (FBR): A breeder reactor is a nuclear reactor capable of generating more fissile material than it consumes. It uses uranium-238 or thorium-232 as fuel. Breeders were at first considered superior because of their superior fuel economy compared to the light water reactors. India is focusing on using thorium as an alternative fuel to uranium in nuclear reactors. There is a growing interest in developing a thorium-fuel cycle due to its safety benefits, absence of non-fertile isotopes, and its higher occurrence and availability when compared to uranium. India has the world's largest reserves of thorium in the world.

Renewable Energy Resources

Most renewable energy comes either directly or indirectly from the sun. Sunlight, or solar energy, can be used directly for heating and lighting homes and other buildings, for generating electricity, and for hot water heating, solar cooling, and a variety of commercial and industrial uses.

The sun's heat also drives the winds, whose energy, is captured with wind turbines. Then, the winds and the sun's heat cause water to evaporate. When this water vapour turns into rain or snow and flows downhill into rivers or streams, its energy can be captured using hydroelectric power.

At least 40% of India's total power capacity will come from renewable sources by 2030. This ambitious target will help India offer the global community a 35 per cent reduction in the greenhouse gas emission intensity of its economy below 2005 levels by 2030 as part of its Intended Nationally Determined Contributions (INDCs) under the Paris agreement.

Biomass

Organic matter that makes up the plants is known as biomass. Biomass is derived from sources such as by-products from timber industry, agricultural crops, forest waste, household waste, and municipal waste dumps. Biomass can be used to produce electricity, transportation fuels, or chemicals. The use of biomass for any of these purposes is called bioenergy.

For example, Indian sugar mills are rapidly turning to bagasse, the leftover of cane after it is crushed and its juice extracted, to generate electricity.

Advantages

1. It is renewable, cost-effective, and less polluting source of energy.
2. It provides manure for agriculture and gardens.
3. There is tremendous potential to generate biogas energy.
4. Growing biomass crops use carbon dioxide and produce oxygen.

Limitations

1. Initial cost of construction of biogas plant is high.
2. Continuous supply of biomass is required to generate biomass energy.
3. Difficult storage and transportation
4. Many food crops such as corn and wheat are being diverted to make ethanol, which may lead to high food inflation.

Biofuel

Biofuels are renewable liquid or gaseous fuels made from living organisms or the wastes that they produce. Bioethanol and biodiesel are the two main types of biofuel that are currently commercially produced. This oil is extracted and mixed with diesel and is used as fuel. Bioethanol is produced from sugar beet, sugar cane, and corn. The biofuels are divided into two categories.

First-generation or Traditional Biofuels

Other source of biofuels is oil extracted from seeds of plants such as Jatropha and Pongamia which have good calorific value. They are less sustainable as they have an adverse impact on the supply of food for the human population and hence are less preferred. The food prices increase as a result.

Second- and Third-generation Biofuels

They are generated from non-food crops. Microbes play a key role in the development of these biofuels. They are more sustainable than first-generation biofuels, as they produce higher yields, reduce GHG production, and do not compete with crops grown for food. Example is oil extracted from seeds of plants such as Jatropha and Pongamia, which have good calorific value.

In the beginning of 2013, it was recommended that 5% ethanol blending is mandatory for petrol whereas in 2007, it was recommended to be as low as 10% by the Group of Ministers.

Biogas

1. Bacterial action is introduced in digesters with sewage of human beings and animal (animal dung).
2. The decomposition of sewage produces methane, which is used for cooking and fuel.
3. The leftover matter called slurry is used as manure in agriculture fields.

Biomass fuels used in India account for about one-third of the total fuel used in the country, being the most important fuel used in over 90% of the rural households and about 15% of the urban households.

Biomass can be used in briquettes form, which is used directly as fuel instead of coal in the traditional *chulhas* and furnaces. Alternatively, gasifier converts solid fuel into a more convenient-to-use gaseous form of fuel called producer gas.

Hydrogen

1. It is the most abundant element on the earth and has the highest calorific value.
2. It does not occur naturally as a gas.
3. As it is highly reactive, it combines with other elements such as oxygen to form water.
4. Once separated from other elements, hydrogen can be burned as a fuel or converted into electricity.
5. As it burns completely, it does not result in atmospheric pollution and in greenhouse effect.

Fuel Cells

Fuel cells use hydrogen as a fuel. Fuel cells convert the chemical energy of a fuel directly and efficiently into electricity and heat. Thus, they are electrochemical devices. There is no combustion, as in the case of fossil fuels. Hydrogen or a mixture of compounds containing hydrogen is used as a fuel. It consists of two electrodes, with electrolyte in between. Oxygen passes over one electrode and hydrogen over the other, and they react electrochemically to generate electricity, water, and heat.

The fuel cells have been used in space flights as well. Electric vehicles using fuel cells for their energy requirements are the best options available to dramatically reduce urban air pollution. Not all renewable energy resources come from the sun.

A hybrid car is a petrol and electricity driven vehicle, a car starting with petrol engine and switching to electric motor at low speed.

Wind Energy

Wind, that is, moving air, possesses some kinetic energy due to its high speed. It can produce mechanical or electrical energy by using wind mills. Wind is a result of solar energy, as heating of land results in the movement of air. Wind energy has been used for hundreds of years for sailing, grinding grains, and for irrigation. Wind energy systems convert the kinetic energy of winds to other forms of energy or to generate electric power. Windmills for water pumping have been installed in many countries, particularly in the rural areas.

To generate electricity on a large scale, a number of windmills are set up over a large area, called a wind energy farm. Such areas need a wind speed of 15 kmph.

Advantages

1. Inexhaustible source of energy
2. No pollution and emission of GHGs
3. Possibility of large-scale production
4. Scope of direct use as mechanical energy
5. Land, around wind turbines, can be used for other purposes, for example, farming.

Limitations

1. Requires expensive storage during peak production time
2. Winds are uncertain and unpredictable
3. The visual aesthetic impact is not good.
4. Large open areas are required for setting up wind farms
5. Noise pollution
6. Possible threat to wildlife
7. High maintenance cost.

A total capacity of 22,465 MW has been established up to December, 2014, mainly in Tamil Nadu, Gujarat, Maharashtra, Andhra Pradesh, Karnataka, and Rajasthan. India now ranks 5th in the world after China, USA, Germany, and Spain in grid connected wind power installations.

The Netherlands is called 'The Land of Windmills'.

Geothermal Energy

The core of the earth is very hot and so it is possible to make use of this geothermal energy. These are areas where water and steam gush out in the form of hot springs and geysers, which may be used to run turbines to produce electricity. The water can be pumped from underground hot water deposits and used to heat people's houses.

Tidal Energy

Tides are the waves caused due to the gravitational pull of the moon (and to a smaller extent of the sun also). The rise is called high tide and fall is called low tide. This building up and receding of waves happens twice a day and causes enormous movement of water.

The height of the tidal waves makes it possible to trap water in reservoirs behind dams. Tidal dams are built near shores for this purpose. During high tide, the water flows into the dam and during low tide, the water is released in the same manner in hydroelectric power plants.

In addition to tidal energy, the energy of the ocean's waves can also be used to produce electricity. Ocean waves are driven by both tides as well as winds. Sun also warms the surface of the ocean more than its depth, thus creating a temperature difference. It can be used as an energy source. All these forms of ocean energy can be used to produce electricity.

Advantages

1. It is an inexhaustible source of energy.
2. High-energy efficiency, as compared to solar and wind energy, and high-energy density.
3. Although initial cost is high, maintenance and operational cost is low.
4. They follow high prediction as rise and fall of tides is quite predictable.
5. No emission of GHGs as no fuel is required.

Limitations

1. High cost of construction.
2. Few ideal locations for construction of plants that are too close to coastal regions; therefore, transmission loss can be quite high.
3. Intensity of sea waves is unpredictable and there is apprehension of damage to power generation units.
4. Influences aquatic life adversely.
5. The tides only happen twice a day; therefore, electricity can be produced only for that time.

Hydroelectric Power

1. It is electricity generated using the force of running water from a height. The water may be stored in the form of dams. The potential energy is converted into kinetic energy.
2. It is the second largest source of electricity.
3. Heavily dependent on rainfall and melting of snow in the mountainous regions.
4. It entails heavy investment for construction of dams, but per unit cost of electricity is low.

Risk factors include the following:

1. As a huge water body is created, the release during heavy rainfall may cause floods and loss of biodiversity.
2. Dams impede the migration of fish along the river. The silt pile-up may threaten the structure and decrease the life of the dam.

Solar Energy

Solar energy is the ultimate source of energy for almost all living organisms. It is the heat and light energy produced as a result of nuclear fusion and fission reactions taking place inside the sun.

The producers (discussed earlier) produce food by photosynthesis. Energy from the sun is responsible for all the weather phenomena in nature such as the wind, storms, rain, and sea waves.

Now, scientists are devising methods to make optimum use of solar energy in routine lives in the form of solar cooker, water heater, and solar cells, which can be used in multiple devices. Many advanced nations have come up with concepts such as energy-efficient green buildings.

Advantages

1. Readily available, inexhaustible, clean, uninterrupted, and continuous source of energy.
2. Solar devices can be installed in remote, inaccessible areas such as small villages in interior regions, forests, deserts, mountains, off-shore platforms, and remote oceanic islands.

3. It is possible to produce solar energy in large quantities across many regions in the world, especially tropical regions.

Limitations

1. Can be produced in tropical and sub tropical areas only that too in specific seasons.
2. Technology is still expensive and involves high installation cost.
3. Difficult to store and run heavy machines.
4. Solar panels consume land, as power generation per square unit is low.
5. Silicon, used in production of SPV (solar photo voltaic) cells is a pollutant.

National Solar Mission: National Solar Mission is one of the eight missions set up of National Action Plan on Climate Change (NAPCC) that was released on 30 June 2008.

Government stepped up India's solar power capacity target under the Jawaharlal Nehru National Solar Mission (JNNSM) by five times, reaching 1,00,000 MW by 2022. The new targets were approved in June 2015. The target will principally comprise 40 GW Rooftop and 60 GW through Large and Medium Scale Grid Connected Solar Power Projects. With this ambitious target, India will become one of the largest Green Energy producers in the world, surpassing several developed countries. During recent times, with improvement in technology and scaling up production capacities, solar energy has become cost competitive and targets seem to be more viable now.

The total installed capacity of solar power in India crossed the milestone of 5000 MW on January 15, 2016, total being 5130 MW. The leading Solar energy producing states are Rajasthan (1264 MW), Gujarat (1024 MW), Madhya Pradesh (679 MW), Tamil Nadu (419 MW), Maharashtra (379 MW), and Andhra Pradesh (357 MW).

Climate Change and Global Warming

Climate change is the most important issue of the twenty-first century with potential direct adverse impact on global economy and civilization. It is a long-term change in the average weather patterns. It may occur over a period of time, which may range from a decade to millions of years. Climate change may be limited to a specific region, or may occur across the whole earth.

Paleoclimatology or Palaeoclimatology is the study of climatic changes, taken on a scale of the entire history of earth. It makes use of data from ice sheets, tree rings, sediments, corals, shells, and rocks.

Global warming is the progressive increase in the average temperature of earth's near-surface air and oceans during the last few decades, and its likely continuation in future as well. This is mainly because of emission of heat-retaining GHGs into the atmosphere, which results from human activities such as burning of fossil fuel and deforestation. One of its main effects is a shift in the global weather patterns, referred to as climate change. Here, it is important to mention that global warming is closely associated with climate change and both terms may be used interchangeably.

Causes of Climate Change

They can be divided into two types of factors, namely natural and anthropogenic.

Natural Causes

The main natural factors are as follows:

1. *Continental drift:* A glance at the map shows how South America fits snugly into Africa's Bight of Benin. Almost all continents on the globe appear to fit into each other like the components of a jigsaw puzzle. Continents were formed when parts of a large landmass called Pangaea began drifting apart gradually around 200 million years ago. There are many similarities between plant and animal fossils and rocks on the two continents.
2. *Volcanoes:* Large volumes of SO_2, water vapour, dust, and ash are thrown out into the atmosphere during volcanic eruption. SO_2 can reach the upper levels of atmosphere (called stratosphere) where they combine

with water to form tiny droplets of sulphuric acid. These small droplets and dust particles reflect sunlight and partially block the incoming rays of the sun, leading to cooling in lower levels of atmosphere (troposphere). Winds in stratosphere carry the aerosols rapidly around the globe in either an easterly or a westerly direction. This gives some idea of cooling, which is brought about for a few years after a major volcanic eruption.

3. *Earth's tilt:* Earth makes one revolution around the sun in 365 days. It is tilted at an angle of 23.5° to the perpendicular plane of its orbit, which causes seasonal variations. Furthermore, earth's orbit is somewhat elliptical, which means that the distance between the earth and the sun varies during the course of a year.
4. *Ocean currents:* Oceans cover about 71% of the earth and absorb about twice as much of the sun's radiation as the atmosphere. Ocean currents transfer vast amounts of heat across the planet, which causes temperature difference and climatic changes.

Human Causes (Anthropogenic Factors)

Beyond a point, human activities and consumption styles are considered as human interference in nature. Urbanization and industrialization have been powered by fossil fuels and thus contribute to global warming and climate change. All our gadgets run on electricity, which is generated mainly from thermal power plants that further run on fossil fuels (coal).

The Science of Climate Change

The greenhouse effect like a greenhouse keeps things warm for us, here on earth. The greenhouse effect works hand-in-hand with the sun's radiation. Without greenhouse gases, the planet would be much colder. Greenhouse gases act like a blanket for earth; this blanket can be found in the troposphere layer of the atmosphere. Greenhouse gases have kept the planet warm by trapping radiation from the earth for billions of years. The only thing is, greenhouse gases are very picky about which kind of radiation they will absorb.

The whole process begins when the sun heats the earth. Shortwave solar radiation passes through the atmosphere and this energy makes the atoms of the earth vibrate faster (heat up). The earth then radiates long-wave radiation or infrared radiation back into the space. This infrared radiation heats the atmosphere and some of it is trapped by the greenhouse gases. After the greenhouse gases trap the infrared radiation, it is re-radiated back to the earth, thereby warming the air.

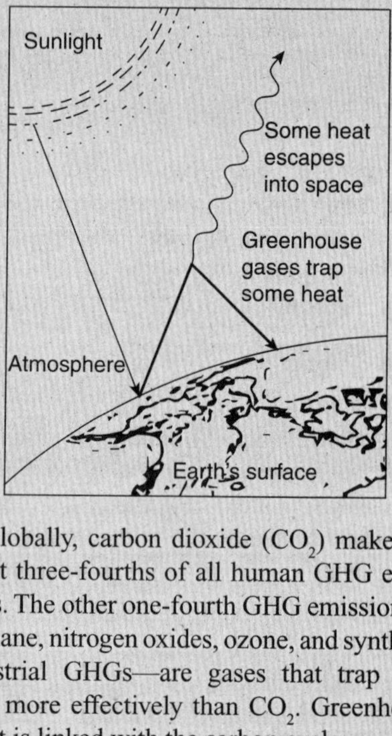

Globally, carbon dioxide (CO_2) makes up about three-fourths of all human GHG emissions. The other one-fourth GHG emissions—methane, nitrogen oxides, ozone, and synthetic industrial GHGs—are gases that trap heat even more effectively than CO_2. Greenhouse effect is linked with the carbon cycle.

The following are all greenhouse gases in order from strongest to weakest. Notice how all of these gases contain three or more atoms.

1. Methane (CH_4) is the strongest greenhouse gas because it has the most atoms. This is why it is the best at trapping radiation, and it has more atoms to do so. Even though it is the strongest greenhouse gas, it is one of the least abundant.

2. Carbon dioxide (CO_2) is the second strongest and one of the most abundant greenhouse gases. It is the second strongest because it has the most mass, which helps it to trap heat more efficiently.
3. Nitrous oxide (NO_2) is the third strongest greenhouse gas because it only has three atoms and does not have as much mass as CO_2. It is not as efficient as CO_2 and CH_4 at trapping infrared radiation, but it is stronger than water vapour.
4. Water vapour (H_2O) is the weakest because it is the lightest of the greenhouse gases. It often changes into liquid and solid forms as well. Hence, it is the least effective at trapping infrared radiation.

Here, we need to get familiar with the term 'Global Warming Potential' (GWP). CO_2 is considered as the main GHG because of its volume; otherwise, its GWP is very less in comparison to methane and nitrous oxide. CO_2 is chosen as the reference gas because it has 100 year's GWP of 1, and all other gases' GWP is measured against this. The 100 year's GWP of methane and nitrous oxide is, respectively, 21 and 310.

Because of industrialization, CO_2 has increased in the atmosphere from about 280 to more than 400 parts per million and the GHG emissions are increasing continuously and steadily.

Combustion of fossil fuels (coal, oil, and natural gas) oxidizes carbon present in the long-buried ancient plants to form the greenhouse gas CO_2. As our chief source of energy for generating electricity, heating buildings, and operating vehicles, fossil fuels contribute most of the CO_2 we emit. Some ancient carbon has been sequestered chemically; for example, as calcium carbonate in limestone rock; these compounds convert to CO_2 when the rock is heated to make cement.

Deforestation and land use change release the carbon stored more recently in trees and soils. Besides adding significant CO_2 to the atmosphere's GHG load, deforestation diminishes the biosphere's present and future capacity to remove CO_2 from the atmosphere.

Humans' massive infusion of CO_2 has unbalanced Earth's carbon cycle by adding more carbon than natural processes can remove.

Effects of Climate Change and Global Warming

Cyclonic Storms

Both the intensity and frequency of tropical storms have increased in the past decade. They are caused by evaporation of water from oceans. Coriolis effect causes the storms to spin, and a hurricane is declared when this spinning mass of storms attains a wind speed greater than 119 km/hour.

An ice storm is a particular weather event in which precipitation falls as ice due to atmospheric conditions.

Loss of Biodiversity

The most dramatic impact is the loss of habitat for millions of species.

1. Seventy per cent of earth's land animals and plants live in forests, and many cannot survive the loss of their natural habitat. Deforestation results in decline in biodiversity and in the extinction of many species.
2. Forests support biodiversity, providing habitat for wildlife; moreover, forests foster medicinal conservation. With forest biotopes being an irreplaceable source of new drugs (such as taxol), deforestation can destroy genetic variations (such as crop resistance) irretrievably.
3. It was only during Earth Summit in 1991 or 1992 that these figures came out, which equates to 50,000 species a year.

Sea-level Rise and Small Islands

Role of oceans in global warming is very complex. They serve as a sink for CO_2, taking up much that would otherwise remain in the atmosphere, but increased levels of CO_2 have led to the acidification of oceans. Furthermore, as the ocean temperature rises, their ability to absorb excess CO_2 decreases. Global warming is projected to have a number of effects on the oceans. The on-going effects include rising sea levels due to thermal expansion and melting of glaciers and ice sheets, and warming of the ocean surface leading to increased temperature stratification. Other possible effects include large-scale changes in oceanic circulation.

Bleaching of Coral Reefs

Coral reefs are a collection of biological communities forming one of the most diverse ecosystems of the world (termed as rainforests of the oceans). Corals are important for a variety of reasons. Some of these are as follows:

1. They provide habitat for a variety of organisms.
2. They prevent erosion of soil on beaches.
3. They function as carbon sink (help in absorption of CO_2).

They are found in shallow coastal areas of tropical and sub-tropical regions, where light can penetrate for synthesis of food. They feed on small fish and live in colonies; each coral is called a polyp. They enjoy a symbiotic relationship with algae. The increase in sea temperature, salinity of water, increased UV radiation, and so on will result in decreased photosynthesis activity and this in turn leads to loss of algae. Ultimately, the reefs become dead and lose their colour. This is called coral bleaching.

Melting of polar ice and migration of fish are other effects of climate change on marine life.

Runaway Climate Changes and Tipping Point

Runaway climate change is what happens when global warming becomes self-sustaining and beyond control of human beings. This may upset the normal system of checks and balances that keep the climate in equilibrium.

A global warming spiral kicks in if the following occur:

1. *The environment absorbs less CO_2:* About 50% of our current emissions are absorbed by the environment, that is, roughly half of that by the oceans and the other half by the plants on land. The uptake of CO_2 by the environment may already be in decline.
2. *Reflection of sunlight drops:* As snow covers in the form of glaciers are retreating (means they are shrinking in terms of geographical extent), dark grounds and darker water are exposed, which absorb less sunlight and that has caused further increase in global warming.
3. *Emission of CO_2 and methane:* More CO_2 and methane are emitted from nature. Soils, forests, peat, seas, organic deposits in permafrost, and methane clathrates, all emit some amount of CO_2 and methane. As the environment warms, natural emissions increase.

Tipping point is a small amount of warming that may set off unstoppable and irreversible changes. The best example is the melting of ice caps. Once the temperature goes up by certain degrees, then all ice caps may melt (even though, complete melting of ice at the Arctic and Antarctic may take thousands of years). The tipping point in many scientists' view is a 2°C rise in temperature. European Union has adopted that as the maximum limit that mankind can risk. Beyond that point, there is possibility of runaway climate change.

Key Developments in the Context of Climate Change and Global Warming

1. Jean Baptiste Joseph Fourier (1824) was the first to describe that without the presence of GHGs the earth would have been cooler by 33°C. When the radiations from the sun enter the atmosphere of the earth, they are of short wavelength and when emitted by earth

they are of longer wavelength. GHGs do not allow these radiations to escape into the outer atmosphere and hence are reflected back to the earth. This causes the heating of the earth.

2. In 1896, Svante Arrhenius claimed that fossil fuel combustion may eventually result in enhanced global warming. As much as 25% of CO_2 emissions are naturally absorbed by the ocean and another 25% are absorbed by the biosphere such as trees, plants, and soil. 50% of the CO_2 emissions are not absorbed by nature and accumulate in the atmosphere.
3. The World Meteorological Organization (WMO) was set up in 1950 in Geneva to promote international exchange of weather reports and other weather-related services.
4. In the 1950s and 1960s, aerosol pollution called smog became a serious local problem in many cities, causing dimming and fall in temperature to such an extent that many scientists talked about the return of Ice Age. The phenomenon of London Smog in 1954 is a prominent example.
5. Keeling curve is a graph, which has been showing the variations in the concentration of atmospheric CO_2 since 1958. It is based on continuous measurements taken at the Mauna Loa Observatory in Hawaii.
6. Roger Randall Dougan Revelle suggested that earth's oceans would absorb excess CO_2 generated by humanity at a much slower rate, thereby contributing to the greenhouse effect and global warming. Revelle factor is a measure of resistance to the absorption of atmospheric CO_2 by ocean surface layer due to different factors.
7. The UN's first major initiative was the UN Conference on Human Environment (also known as the Stockholm Conference) held in Sweden in the year 1972. WMO sponsored a conference on the long-term climatic fluctuations at the University of East Anglia at Norwich in 1975.
8. Wallace S. Broecker was the first person to use the term global warming in 1975.
9. The first World Climate Conference took place in Geneva in 1979.
10. World Commission on Environment and Development was convened by the UN in 1983, named after its Chairman Gro Harlem Brundtland, also known as the Brundtland Commission. It was recognized by the UN that as environmental problems were global in nature, there was a need to decide common policies for sustainable development.
11. Intergovernmental Panel on Climate Change (IPCC) was set up in 1988 by two organizations of UN, that is, the World Meteorological Organization (WMO) and the UN Environment Programme (UNEP), to assess the risk of human-induced climatic change, its impact and to suggest alternatives solutions. Its reports have generated good awareness about climate changes and forced the governments worldwide into action. IPCC shared the Nobel Peace Prize 2007 with the former US Vice President Al Gore who also wrote 'The Inconvenient Truth' about climatic changes and global warming. Five Assessment Reports have been presented by IPCC so far.
12. United Nations Framework Convention on Climate Change (UNFCCC) is an international environmental treaty produced at the UN Conference on Environment and Development, (also known as the Earth Summit), held in Rio de Janeiro (Brazil) in June 1992. Its objective is to stabilize GHG concentrations in the atmosphere at a level that would prevent dangerous anthropogenic interference with climate system.
13. UNFCCC was opened for signature on 9 May, 1992. After having received over 50 countries' instruments of ratification, it entered into force on 21 March, 1994. By December 2009, UNFCCC had 192 parties.

14. Agenda 21 is an action plan of the UN related to sustainable development and was an outcome of the Earth Summit. It is a comprehensive blueprint of the actions that need to be taken globally, nationally and locally by organizations of the UN, governments, and major groups in every area in which humans directly affect the environment.

Benchmarking

In the context of UNFCCC, benchmarking is the setting up of emission reduction commitment, as measured against a particular base year. The only quantified target set in the original UNFCCC (Article 4) was for the developed countries to reduce their GHG emissions to 1990 levels as against the original 2000.

Emissions by Countries

Country	Percentage share in global annual emissions	CO_2 emissions per capita (tonnes/person)
World	100%	4.9
China	28.6%	7.1
United States	15.1%	16.4
European Union	10.9%	7.4
India	**5.7%**	**1.6**
Russia	5.1%	12.4
Japan	3.8%	10.4

Source: Press Information Bureau (PIB).

Conferences of the Parties

Since UNFCCC entered into force, parties have been meeting annually in Conferences of the Parties (COPs) to assess the progress in dealing with climatic changes. The meeting is held every year from the last week of November to the first week of December. In the month of June, a lower level meeting of civil servants is held to assess the progress and to prepare the ground for next meeting. Kyoto Protocol has been a major achievement so far.

Kyoto Protocol: CO_2 is recognized as the key GHG that contributes to climatic changes and for which the developed countries are principally responsible for the high levels of GHG emission currently in the atmosphere, due to more than 150 years of industrial activity. Kyoto Protocol places a heavier burden on the developed nations under the principle of common but differentiated responsibilities.

Kyoto Protocol entered into force on 16th February, 2005.

The targets cover emission of six main GHGs—carbon dioxide (CO_2), methane (CH_4), nitrous oxide (N_2O), hydrofluorocarbons (HFCs), perfluorocarbons (PFCs), and sulphur hexafluoride (SF_6).

The following terms are worth mentioning in this context:

1. *Carbon footprints:* Using coal, natural gas, or oil for electricity, heat, or transportation, releases CO_2 into the atmosphere. Their daily CO_2 emissions make up the carbon footprint of any business unit.
2. *Carbon credit:* One carbon credit is equal to one tonne of CO_2, or its equivalent gases. For example, any business unit avoiding one tonne of CO emission will be issued a certificate of one carbon credit that can be traded in national or international market. Thus, any firm helping in avoiding CO_2 can actually make money.

The Kyoto mechanisms are as follows:

1. Emissions trading (known as the carbon market).
2. Clean development mechanism (CDM)
3. Joint implementation (JI)

Paris Agreement on Climate Change: The Paris Agreement is an agreement under UNFCCC, which was adopted by 195 nations on 12 December 2015 at the 21st COP. This agreement shows a shift from Kyoto Protocol—from

Table 9.5 Summary of Main COPs

Main COPs	Place of meeting	Key developments
COP 1	Berlin, Germany (1995)	First Meeting - Commitment for Subsidiary Body for Scientific and Technological Advice
COP 3 (1997)	Kyoto, Japan	Kyoto Protocol Annexe I parties commit to binding reduction targets
COP 8	New Delhi, India (2002)	Call for transfer of technologies to developing nations to minimise the impact of climate change on developing nations
COP 11	Montreal, Canada (2005)	Montreal Action Plan is an agreement to 'extend the life of the Kyoto Protocol beyond its 2012
COP 13	Bali, Indonesia (2007)	Discussion about post 2012 scenario
COP 15	Copenhagen, Denmark (2009)	Voluntary mitigation pledges
COP 16	Cancun, Mexico (2010)	Establishing a Green Climate Fund
COP 18	Doha, Qatar (2012)	The Kyoto Protocol has been extended till 2020.
COP 19 and 20	Warsaw (Poland) and Lima (Peru)	Intended Nationally Determined Contribution (INDC)
COP 21	Paris	Discussed separately

mandatory and binding targets towards voluntary targets, set by nations themselves. It focuses on climate justice and sustainable lifestyles. 22nd session of Conference of the Parties is to be held in Marrakesh, Morocco from 07 Nov to 18 Nov 2016.

Paris Agreement brings for the first time all nations into a common cause based on their historic, current, and future responsibilities to combat climate change. Agreement's main aim is to keep global temperature rise, in this century, well below 2°C and to drive efforts to limit the temperature increase even further to 1.5°C above pre-industrial levels.

The Paris Agreement includes the following aspects:

1. Mitigation (reducing emissions)
2. Transparency system and global stock take (accounting for climate action)
3. Adaptation (enhancing the capacity of countries to deal with climate impacts)
4. Loss and damage (strengthening ability to recover from climate impacts)
5. Support including finance, for nations to build clean, resilient futures

The Paris Agreement is different from its predecessor—Kyoto Protocol—in the sense that nations settled on a bottom-up approach in this agreement allowing each nation to submit its own national plans to reduce greenhouse gas emissions rather than trying to follow a top-down approach.

Before and during the Paris conference, countries submitted comprehensive national climate action plans (INDCs). These are not yet enough to keep global warming below 2°C.

India' INDC

In its INDC, India has pledged to improve the emissions intensity of its GDP by 33 to 35 per cent by 2030 below 2005 levels. It has also pledged to increase the share of non-fossil fuels-based electricity to 40 per cent by 2030. It has agreed to enhance its forest cover which will absorb 2.5 to 3 billion tonnes of carbon dioxide by 2030.

The agreement traces the way to achieving this target.

Natural Resources—Biodiversity

Biodiversity is the number of living organisms (both plants and animals) present in an ecosystem.

Any loss in species in the food chain means breaking a link in the chain, which in turn affects all those who benefit from the chain. The diversity can be divided as follows:

1. *Genetic diversity:* Variation of genes in species that is a single population.
2. *Species diversity:* It is the most basic way to keep an account of biodiversity as it includes all forms of life from single cell organisms such as amoeba and virus to multi-cellular organisms such as plants and animals.
3. *Ecosystem diversity:* It differentiates between different habitats, ecological processes, and ecosystems in which the species exist. This can be a forest ecosystem marine ecosystem, desert ecosystem, and so on.

Endemic species are likely to develop on biologically isolated areas such as islands. Due to their geographical isolation, endemics can easily become endangered or extinct if their habitat changes, not only due to human actions, but also due to the introduction of new organisms. The opposite of endemic species is cosmopolitan species.

India is one of the richest countries in the world in terms of biodiversity. Due to many factors such as deforestation, urbanization, industrialization, and climate changes (including global warming), many species have lost their habitat and even become extinct. International Union for Conservation of Nature and Natural Resources (IUCN) has categorized wild flora and fauna into eight categories (known as the Red List). This includes (i) extinct, (ii) extinct in wild, (iii) critically endangered, (iv) endangered, (v) vulnerable, (vi) lower-risk, (vii) data-deficient, and (viii) not evaluated.

Schedule I of Wildlife (Protection) Act, 1972 defines endangered species in a formal manner. So far 38 species of birds, 18 of amphibians and reptiles, and 81 of mammals have been labelled as endangered. There are 47 critically endangeredspecies in India.

Biological Hotspots in India

A biodiversity hotspot is a biogeographical region with a significant reservoir of biodiversity that is under threat from humans. India is a country rich in biological diversity. It is home to 7.31% species of fauna and 10.78% species of flora. Among the 34 hotspots of the world, two are located in India and then extending to the neighbouring countries These are Eastern Himalayas and Western Ghats (and Sri Lanka). Eastern Himalayas is home to 163 globally threatened species including Asian elephants, one-horned rhinoceros (*Rhinoceros unicornis*), wild water buffalos, and panthers and tigers. Earlier, Eastern Himalayas was clubbed with Indo-Burma biodiversity hotspot. The Agasthyamalai Hills in Western Ghats is home to the highest level of plant biodiversity.

Conservation of Biodiversity

The process of conservation can be divided into two types:

1. *In situ conservation:* When conservation is attempted at the natural habitat of the species by creating national parks, sanctuaries, and biosphere reserves, it is called *in situ* conservation.
2. *Ex situ conservation:* This is done in case of complete degradation of natural habitat. The endangered species is kept under total human supervision such as in zoos, botanical gardens, and seed banks. Manas National Park has been declared a World Heritage Site. The other world heritage sites (natural) in India are Kaziranga National Park (Assam), Manas Wildlife Sanctuary (Assam), Keoladeo National Park (Rajasthan), Sundarbans National Park (West Bengal), and Nanda Devi National Park (Uttar Pradesh). These world heritage sites are recognized by UNESCO.

There are 27 tiger reserves in India under Project Tiger. Other prominent reserves are Bandipur (Karnataka), Corbett (Uttaranchal), Kanha (Madhya Pradesh), Ranthambore Sariska (Rajasthan), and Sundarbans (West Bengal).

Concept of Threatened Species

Threatened species (T)

These species are likely to become extinct if immediate steps are not taken to ensure that they have proper food, proper habitat, protection from predators, and exotic species so that they are able to realise their biotic potential.

A record of threatened species of plants and animals is maintained by **International Union for Conservation of Nature and Natural Resources (IUCN),** Morges, Switzerland. It is called **Red Data Book.** For conservation purpose, the following four criteria have been used for this categorisation:

(i) *Distribution:* Present, past, continuous, or discontinuous distribution, area and degree of decline, if available

(ii) *Population:* Decline in population in course of time

(iii) *Natural habitat:* Abundance and quality

(iv) *Importance:* Potential value and biology of the species, IUCN has identified four categories of threatened species.

Endangered species (E)

These are threatened species or taxa which are in danger of extinction if the current causal factors continue to operate.

Examples: Lion-tailed Macaque - *Macaca silenus*

Asiatic Wild Ass - *Asinus hemionus Khur*

Vulnerable species (V)

Vulnerable species or taxa have sufficient population at present, but at the same time, they deplete fast (hence, **depleted species**) so that they are likely to enter the category of endangered species if the factors bringing about depletion are allowed to continue.

Examples: Golden langur - *Presbytis geei*

Leopard cat - *Felis bengalensis*

Rare species (R)

The populations of species or taxa are small, either localized or thinly scattered.

Example: Hawaiian monk seal - *Monachus schauinslandi*

Slow loris - *Nycticebus coucangg*

Biosphere Reserves

Biosphere reserves protect larger areas of natural habitat in comparison to national parks or animal sanctuaries. Biosphere reserves are the areas of terrestrial and coastal ecosystems which promote the conservation of biodiversity with its sustainable use. UNESCO's Man and Biosphere (MAB) was launched in 1971. There are over 500 biosphere reserves world over in more than 100 countries. National parks, wild life sanctuaries, conservation reserves and community reserves are the four types of protected areas under The Wildlife Protection Act, 1972. Biosphere reserves are considered akin to national parks, usually larger than national parks. The primary criteria for the selection of biosphere reserves are effective protection and minimally disturbed core area. The secondary criteria include (i) having rare and endangered species (ii) diversity of soil and microclimatic conditions, and (iii) preservation of tribal/rural life. As on 1st April 2016, the total number of biosphere reserves in India was 18. Ten of these are a part of UNESCO's MAB Programme list.

Biosphere reserves are large areas of biodiversity where flora and fauna are protected. These regions of environmental protection roughly correspond to IUCN Category V Protected areas. The Indian Government has established 18 Biosphere Reserves of India, which protect larger areas of natural habitat (than a National Park or Wildlife Sanctuary).

Biosphere Reserves of India often include one or more national parks or sanctuaries, along with buffer zones that are open to some economic uses. Protection is granted not only to the flora and fauna of the protected region but also to the human communities who inhabit these regions and their ways of life.

List of Biosphere Reserves of India

S. No.	Year	Name	State	Type	Key fauna
1	2008	Great Rann of Kutch	Gujarat	Desert	Indian Wild Ass
2	**1989**	**Gulf of Mannar**	**Tamil Nadu**	**Coasts**	**Dugong or Sea Cow**
3	**1989**	**Sundarbans**	**West Bengal**	**Gangetic Delta**	**Royal Bengal Tiger**
4	2009	Cold Desert	Himachal Pradesh	Western Himalayas	Snow Leopard
5	**1988**	**Nanda Devi**	**Uttarakhand**	**Western Himalayas**	**NA**
6	**1986**	**Nilgiri Biosphere Reserve**	**Tamil Nadu, Kerala and Karnataka**	**Western Ghats**	**Nilgiri Tahr, Lion-tailed macaque**
7	1998	Dihang-Dibang	Arunachal Pradesh	Eastern Himalaya	NA
8	**1999**	**Pachmarhi Biosphere Reserve**	**Madhya Pradesh**	**Semi-Arid**	**Giant Squirrel, Flying Squirrel**
9	2010	Seshachalam Hills	Andhra Pradesh	Eastern Ghats	NA
10	**1994**	**Simlipal**	**Odisha**	**Deccan Peninsula**	**Gaur, Royal Bengal Tiger, Wild elephant**
11	**2005**	**Achanakmar -Amarkantak**	**Madhya Pradesh, Chhattisgarh**	**Maikal Hills**	**NA**
12	1989	Manas	Assam	East Himalayas	Golden Langur, Red Panda
13	2000	Khangchendzonga	Sikkim	East Himalayas	Snow Leopard, Red Panda
14	**2001**	**Agasthyamalai Biosphere Reserve**	**Kerala, Tamil Nadu**	**Western Ghats**	**Nilgiri Tahr, Elephants**
15	**1989**	**Great Nicobar Biosphere Reserve**	**Andaman and Nicobar Islands**	**Islands**	**Saltwater Crocodile**
16	**1988**	**Nokrek**	**Meghalaya**	**East Himalayas**	**Red Panda**
17	1997	Dibru-Saikhowa	Assam	East Himalayas	Golden Langur
18	2011	Panna	Madhya Pradesh	Ken River	Tiger, Chital, Chinkara, Sambhar, and Sloth bear

*Agasthyamala Biosphere Reserve has been added in World Network of Biosphere Reserves (UNESCO's MAB) in March 2016.

Biosphere Reserves of India in World Network of Biosphere Reserves

Ten of the 18 biosphere reserves of India are a part of the World Network of Biosphere Reserves, based on the UNESCO Man and the Biosphere (MAB) Programme list. They are given in 'bold' in the above list.

Main difference between Biosphere Reserves, National Park, and Wild Life Sactuaries

Biosphere reserves are the biggest entity among the three. The level of restriction in the increasing order is biosphere reserves, wildlife sanctuaries, and national parks. The Indian Government has established 18 Biosphere Reserves of India, roughly corresponding to IUCN Category V Protected Areas. India has over 441 animal sanctuaries, referred to as Wildlife Sanctuaries (IUCN Category IV Protected Area). The National Parks of India are IUCN Category II Protected Areas. As of July 2015, there were 105 national parks in India.

Important Legislations and Terms Relating to Environment, Pollution, Forests, and Wildlife

1. *The Factories Act, 1948:* This Act aims at providing information on hazardous processes taking place inside the factory to its workers, local residents, and government officials.
2. *The Insecticides Act, 1968:* It aims to regulate import, manufacture, sale, transport, distribution, and use of insecticides to prevent risk to human and animal life.
3. *The Water (Prevention and Control of Pollution) Act, 1974:* This Act defines what water pollution is and determines its penalties.
4. *The Air (Prosecution and Control of Pollution) Act, 1981:* This Act controls and regulates emissions from automobiles and industrial plants.
5. *The Forest Conservation Act, 1980:* It mainly prohibits the state governments from declaring any reserve forest as non-reserve without approval of the central authority.
6. *The Wildlife Protection Act, 1972:* It aims to provide necessary protection against serious threat to wildlife (both animals and birds) by the expansion and advancement of agriculture, industry, and urbanization. The Indian Board of Wildlife was set up in 1952. Various projects have been launched for the protection of endangered species such as lions (1972), tigers (1973), crocodiles (1974), and brown antlered deer (1981). India became a party to the Convention of International Trade in Endangered Species of Fauna and Flora (CITES) in 1976. India also started a national component of United Nations Educational, Scientific and Cultural Organization's (UNESCO) Man and Biosphere (MAB) programme in 1971.
7. *The Environment Protection Act, 1986:* It lays down the standards for emission and discharge of pollutants, restricting areas for certain industries, and laying down safeguards for prevention of industrial accidents.
8. *Mashelkar Committee Recommendations:* The Auto Fuel Policy suggested by the expert committee headed by Dr. R. A. Mashelkar includes recommendations on auto fuel's quality, vehicular emission norms, and related issues for the country as a whole. It also recommended introduction of low-sulphur diesel, unleaded petrol, and low-benzene gasoline in a phased manner along with promotion of alternative fuels such as compressed natural gas (CNG).

   The policy is modelled on the pattern of Euro norms of European Union. Emission norms were introduced such as Bharat I, II, III, and IV for different vehicles with different schedules for its implementation across India. Bharat III norms were introduced for all new passenger cars across India and Bharat IV norms were introduced in 12 major cities. With effect from February 2000, lead has been phased out of automobile fuel.

The Union Ministry of Transport is going to implement Bharat Stage V and Bharat Stage VI emissions standards to 2019 and 2021, respectively. They mainly aim at reducing sulphur levels in the air.

9. *National Green Tribunal (NGT):* The tribunal was been established on 18 October 2010 under the National Green Tribunal Act 2010 for effective and expeditious disposal of cases related to environmental protection and conservation of forests and other natural resources. It is a specialized body equipped with the necessary expertise to handle environmental disputes involving multi-disciplinary issues.
10. *Environment Impact Assessment (EIA):* It is a widely recognized study to assess the environmental impact of development projects. It is basically cost-benefit analysis in context of the environment. Environmental risk assessment (ERA) is a fact-finding stage where EIA indicates the potential hazards. In India, the Department of Environment and National Council of Environmental Planning (NCEP) have adopted a preliminary procedure to prepare EIA.
11. *Precautionary principle:* The precautionary principle is a moral and political principle, which aims to prevent any action that can cause damage to the public or society at large. For example, the Supreme Court of India ordered the shifting of industries outside Delhi a few years back. In the Earth Summit held in Rio de Janeiro in 1992, a precautionary approach was codified for the first time at a global level, to protect the environment in the form of Principle 15 of Agenda 21. It emphasizes that every state should apply the principle according to its capabilities and lack of full scientific knowledge should not be used as a reason for not taking action. This is necessary to check the possibility of any irreversible damage to the environment. There are two popular terms associated with precautionary principle.
    (a) *Polluter Pays Principle (PPP):* This idea first originated in the Organization for Economic Cooperation and Development where pollution control costs are to be financed by the polluter alone.
    (b) *Beneficiary Pays Principle (BPP):* It suggests that funding for environmental improvement should be obtained from its beneficiaries. This method of financing would generate larger revenue for the government as the rich are willing and capable of paying more for environmental enrichment. Imposing carbon tax is an example.
12. *ISO 14000:* After the success of ISO 9000 Quality Management System, which focuses on continual improvement of the processes and quality of goods and services, International Standards Organisation (ISO) introduced ISO 14000 series of Environmental Management System in 1996. It specifically deals with environmental aspects of processes in products and services.
13. *Emissions trading:* It is an administrative approach to deal with the issue of pollution control by providing financial incentives for achieving reduction in carbon emission. An organization earns one carbon credit if it is able to avoid emission of one tonne of carbon dioxide or its equivalent. The carbon credits thus earned can be sold to other companies for whom it is mandatory to cut carbon emissions. It is also termed as cap and trade.
14. *Carbon trading:* The idea of carbon trading is a part of Kyoto Protocol, which was signed in 1997 and came into force in 2002.

Few Important International Conventions on Environment and Biodiversity

Convention on International Trade in Endangered Species of Wild Fauna and Flora (CITES), 1973: The objective is to control international commercial trade in endangered species or products derived from them.

Montreal Protocol, 1987: The main objective is to reduce consumption and production of ozone-depleting substances, specifically chlorofluorocarbons (CFCs). Vienna Convention for the Protection of Ozone Layer was adopted in 1985.

Basel Convention, 1989: The main aim is to minimize transboundary movement of hazardous wastes.

UN Framework Convention on Climate Change (UNFCCC), 1992: The main aims are to stabilize emission of greenhouse gases and to check reasons for global warming and climate change.

Convention on Biological Diversity (CBD), 1992: The main aims are conservation of biodiversity, sustainable use of biological resources, and equitable sharing of benefits.

Nagoya Protocol: It is a supplementary agreement to the Convention on Biological Diversity. The Nagoya Protocol on Access and Benefit Sharing (ABS) was adopted on 29 October 2010 in Nagoya, Japan.

Stockholm Convention: It was adopted in 2001 and enforced in 2004; it deals with reducing and eliminating the production and use of persistent organic pollutants.

Ramsar Convention: It was signed in Iranian city of Ramsar in 1971 and enforced in 1975; it deals with conservation and use of wetlands.

A Snap Shot of Main Environmental Movements in India

Chipko Movement: It was started in 1973 in Chamoli District of Uttarakhand. It entailed embracing the trees upon seeing an axe coming near the tree to cut it. Its main leader was Shri Sunderlal Bahuguna.

Appiko Movement: It was started in 1983 in the villages of Western Ghats in Uttar Kannada region of Karnataka. The main purpose was to prevent commercial felling of trees. It became a symbol for people's power for their rights of natural resources vis-à-vis the state.

Tehri Dam Movement: This movement was spearheaded by Baba Amte against submergence of land by construction of dams,population displacement among other environmental concerns. It started in 1970s and continued until a decade ago.

Save Silent Valley Movement: It was started in Palakkad district of Kerala in 1973 to save the Silent Valley Reserve Forest from being flooded by a hydroelectric project. The valley was declared as Silent Valley National Park in 1985.

Narmada Bachao Andolan: It was launched to protect the population from the adverse effects of Narmada Valley Project, that is, two mega projects—Sardar Sarovar Project and Narmada Sagar Project in Madhya Pradesh. This interstate project involving Madhya Pradesh, Maharashtra, and Gujarat has been constructed on Narmada River. Its main leader is Medha Patkar. The main issues involved are related to displacement of population, submerging of forest land.

Taj Trapezium Zone: Sulphur dioxide gas released by Mathura Oil Refinery and other industries (combined with oxygen and moisture to form sulphuric acid) caused extensive damage to Taj marbles. It corroded the marble and formed fungus, also referred as 'marble cancer'. A lawyer Mahesh Chander Mehta filed a case before Supreme Court in 1984. The court ruled in 1996 to relocate and shift certain industries.

Key Institutions for Environment in India

Bombay Natural History Society, Mumbai

World Wide Fund for Nature-India, New Delhi

Centre for Science and Environment, New Delhi

CPR Environmental Education Centre, Chennai

Centre for Environment Education (CEE), Ahmedabad

The Botanical Survey of India (BSI), Kolkata

Zoological Survey of India (ZSI), Kolkata

National Environment Engineering Research Institute, Nagpur

Important Days Linked with Environment

Table 9.6 Important days related to environment

Dates	Important days	Dates	Important days
January 30	World Leprosy Day	June 27	International Diabetes Day
February 2	World Wetlands Day	July 11	World Population Day
February 25	World Sustainable Energy Day	July 28	World Nature Conservation Day
March 20	World Sparrow's Day	July 29	World Tiger Day
March 21	World Forestry Day	August 6	Hiroshima Day
March 22	World Water Day	October 3	World Nature Day
April 22	World Earth Day	October 4	World Animal Day
April 25	World Malaria Day	December 2	World Pollution Prevention Day
May 31	World No Tobacco Day	December 14	World Energy Day
June 5	World Environment Day	December 29	International Biodiversity Day
June 8	World Oceans Day		

People and Environment Interaction

1. The term ecosystem was coined by
   (a) Arthur Tansley
   (b) Al Gore
   (c) Arrhenius Svante
   (d) Mobius
2. Who first used and defined Ecology in 1866?
   (a) H. Reiter (b) Haeckel
   (c) Charles Elton (d) Odum
3. In the study of man–environment interaction, the statement of Miss Semple that 'the humans are slowly the product of their environment' is *(December 2004)*
   (a) An opinion
   (b) A prejudice
   (c) A fact
   (d) A widely accepted phenomenon
4. A habitat is
   (a) An area inhabited by a community
   (b) A small part of ecosystem
   (c) A particular area inhabited by plants and animals
   (d) The number of different organisms living in a specific area
5. Biome is a natural community of
   (a) Plants in a geographical area
   (b) Animals in a geographical area
   (c) Plants and animals in a geographical area
   (d) Plants in the Arctic region
6. If we combine all the ecosystems present on earth, it is called
   (a) Biome (b) Biosphere
   (c) Habitat (d) Ecology

7. All the energy in a food chain originates from
   (a) Plants (b) Sea
   (c) Sun (d) All of the above

8. A food web is to show
   (a) How feeding relationships are interlinked
   (b) How several food chains are connected together
   (c) Who eats what
   (d) All of the above

9. In the analysis of man–environment relationship pragmatic possibilism implies that *(December 2004)*
   (a) There is no limit for man to exploit the resources of earth
   (b) There are limited possibilities to explore the Earth's resources
   (c) The man has to watch and assess the situation and then go ahead with resource utilization
   (d) The man has to keep in mind only his basic needs while planning to harness the potential of resourceful Earth

10. Which of the following are included in the biosphere?
    (a) Hydrosphere (b) Lithosphere
    (c) Atmosphere (d) All of the above

11. Interlocking of two or more types of food chains at different trophic levels is called
    (a) Food chain
    (b) Food web
    (c) Succession
    (d) Ecological pyramid

12. The transfer of food energy through a chain of organisms from one trophic level to another is called
    (a) Energy chain (b) Food chain
    (c) Trophic chain (d) Organism chain

13. A keystone species is characterized by its
    (a) Disproportionate large impact on ecosystem
    (b) Very less impact on ecosystem
    (c) No impact at all
    (d) None of the above

14. A population that is at equilibrium is
    (a) Steadily decreasing
    (b) Steadily increasing
    (c) Its number is almost stable over a period of time
    (d) Intermixing rapidly with other populations

15. Which of the following are considered as producers in a food chain?
    (a) Autotrophic plants
    (b) Herbivores
    (c) Carnivores
    (d) Decomposers

16. Which of the following are directly dependent on producers for living?
    (a) Carnivores (b) Decomposers
    (c) Scavengers (d) Herbivores

17. The animals which feed only on other animals are called as
    (a) Omnivores (b) Carnivores
    (c) Herbivores (d) Autotrophs

18. The green plants, which can make their own food with the help of process of photosynthesis, are termed as
    (a) Herbivores
    (b) Carnivores
    (c) Autotrophs
    (d) None of the above

19. The various levels through which energy passes into an ecosystem are called
    (a) Consumers (b) Autotrophs
    (c) Trophic levels. (d) None of the above

20. The transitional area between two ecosystems is termed as
    (a) Ecoline (b) Ecotourism
    (c) Ecotone (d) None of the above

21. Population consists of
    (a) Organisms in a species that are capable of reproducing among themselves
    (b) Different species that can interbreed
    (c) Collective members of a species living and interacting across the biosphere
    (d) Some organisms that may not belong to any species

22. Which of the following is not an abiotic condition?
(a) Water (b) Soil
(c) Temperature (d) Bacteria

23. The existence of atmosphere on the earth is due to
(a) The revolution of the earth around the sun
(b) The rotation of the earth
(c) The gravitational force of the earth
(d) None of the above

24. Match the following:

List I		List II	
A	Troposphere	I	Dust particles
B	Stratosphere	II	Ozone layer
C	Ionosphere	III	Meteors
D	Exosphere	IV	Aurora

Codes:
(a) A-I, B-II, C-III, D-IV
(b) A-II, B-I, C-III, D-IV
(c) A-IV, B-II, C-III, D-I
(d) None of the above

25. Which of the following is the basis for all food chains?
(a) Consumers (b) Producers
(c) Decomposers (d) None of the above

26. Total organic matter in an ecosystem is called
(a) Biome (b) Biotic community
(c) Plants (d) Biomass

27. Energy pyramid is
(a) Always inverted
(b) Always horizontal
(c) Sometimes diagonal
(d) None of the above

28. As a result of biomagnification, the secondary consumers will be
(a) The most toxic (b) The least toxic
(c) Not toxic at all (d) None of the above

29. Which of the following gases is not harmful as a natural component of the atmosphere?
(a) Carbon dioxide (b) Hydrogen
(c) Nitrogen (d) Water vapours

30. Two main components of an ecosystem are
(a) Plants and animals
(b) Biotic and abiotic
(c) Earth and its surroundings
(d) Macro and microorganisms

31. Cloudy nights are warmer compared to clear nights (without clouds) during winters. This is because (*December 2005*)
(a) Clouds radiate heat towards the earth
(b) Clouds prevent cold waves from the sky descending on the earth
(c) Clouds prevent escaping of heat radiation from the earth
(d) Clouds being at great heights from earth absorb heat from the sun and send them towards the earth

32. The urbanization process accounts for the wind in the urban centres during nights to remain (*December 2006*)
(a) Faster than that in rural areas
(b) Slower than that in rural areas
(c) The same as that in the rural areas
(d) Cooler than that in rural areas

33. If population growth follows a logistic curve, the maximum sustainable yield (*June 2008*)
(a) Is equal to half the carrying capacity
(b) Is equal to the carrying capacity
(c) Depends on growth rates
(d) Depends on the initial population

34. The structure of earth's system consists of the following:
Match the following: (*June 2008*)

List I (Zone)		List II (Chemical character)	
A	Atmosphere	I	Inert gases
B	Biosphere	II	Salt, fresh water, snow, and ice
C	Hydrosphere	III	Organic substances
D	Lithosphere	IV	Light silicates

Codes:
(a) A-II, B-III, C-I, D-IV
(b) A-I, B-III, C-II, D-IV
(c) A-II, B-I, C-III, D-IV
(d) A-IV, B-II, C-III, D-I

35. Earth is often struck by solar eruptions, which comprise energetic particles that are hurled away from the Sun into space. Which of the following statements reflect the effect on earth?
   1. When these eruptions interact with the magnetic field, they cause beautiful auroras.
   2. They breakdown radio communication and power supplies.
   3. They don't affect life support system on earth.

   Codes:
   (a) 1 only (b) 1 and 2 only
   (c) 2 and 3 only (d) 3 only

36. A temperature inversion is a condition when the air
   (a) Near the ground is lighter
   (b) Near the ground is cooler than air at the higher altitudes
   (c) Near the ground is hotter than that at higher altitude
   (d) None of the above

37. Beginning from the surface of earth, what is the sequence of different layers of atmosphere?
   (a) Stratosphere, Troposphere, Ionosphere, Exosphere
   (b) Troposphere, Stratosphere, Ionosphere, Exosphere
   (c) Troposphere, Stratosphere, Ionosphere
   (d) None of the above

38. The most dynamic layer of the atmosphere in terms of climatic and weather conditions is
   (a) Troposphere (b) Ionosphere
   (c) Stratosphere (d) Mesosphere

39. In which of the following layers of the atmosphere, ozone (O_3) gas is present?
   (a) Stratosphere (b) Mesosphere
   (c) Troposphere (d) None of the above

40. In which of the following atmospheric layers Ionosphere occurs?
   (a) Mesosphere (b) Exosphere
   (c) Stratosphere (d) Troposphere

41. In an ecotone, the species which become abundant are called:
   (a) Keystone species
   (b) Endemic species
   (c) Edge species
   (d) Foster species

Sources of Pollution, Pollutants and Their Impact on Human Life

42. The air pollutants are mainly classified as
   (a) Point source and non-point source
   (b) Primary and secondary pollutants
   (c) Natural or anthropogenic pollutants
   (d) None of the above

43. The main difference between primary air pollutants and secondary air pollutants is
   (a) Former contains water molecules, while secondary pollutants do not
   (b) Primary air pollutants have more direct effect on human health
   (c) Former are released directly into the atmosphere, while the latter are formed by chemical reactions in the atmosphere
   (d) Primary air pollutants are formed through photochemical reactions in the sunlight, while the secondary air pollutants are not

44. Which of the following can be considered as the best example of primary air pollutants?
   (a) Carbon dioxide released from burning of coal
   (b) Sulphur trioxide
   (c) Ozone produced in photochemical smog
   (d) Carbon dioxide released through photosynthesis

45. Which of the following best illustrates a secondary air pollutant?
(a) CO_2 released from the burning of coal
(b) NO_2 released from the burning of oil
(c) Ozone produced in photochemical smog
(d) None of the above

46. The common features between NO_2, SO_2, CO, and SPM is that all of them
(a) Are classified as primary pollutants
(b) Are classified as secondary pollutants
(c) Have equal role in causing acid rain
(d) Are greenhouse gases

47. How are nitrogen oxides, sulphur oxides, and carbon oxides related?
(a) All of them are secondary air pollutants that contribute to global warming.
(b) All of them are primary air pollutants that contribute to acid deposition.
(c) All are air pollutants formed by combustion of fossil fuels.
(d) All of them are air pollutants that result in respiratory diseases in humans.

48. Atmospheric pollutants are mainly present in
(a) Ionosphere
(b) Stratosphere
(c) Mesosphere
(d) Troposphere and lower stratosphere

49. Lead is used as anti-knocking agent (tetraethyl lead) in petrol. It affects our
(a) Central nervous system
(b) Respiratory system
(c) Cardiac system
(d) Skeletal system

50. Match the following:

List I (Metal)		List II (Effects)	
A	Chromium	I	Thalassaemia
B	Arsenic	II	Itai-Itai
C	Cadmium	III	Dermatitis
D	Iron	IV	Carcinogen

Codes:
(a) A-IV, B-III, C-II, D-I
(b) A-IV, B-II, C-III, D-I
(c) A-I, B-III, C-II, D-IV
(d) A-I, B-II, C-III, D-IV

51. The chemical responsible for blue baby syndrome that is caused by restricted supply of oxygen to the brain is?
(a) Nitrates (b) Sulphates
(c) Fluorides (d) Oxides

52. Which of the following metal is responsible for Minamata disease?
(a) Mercury (b) Cadmium
(c) Chromium (d) Iron

53. Intake of lead may primarily cause damage of the
(a) Brain (b) Lung
(c) Liver (d) Kidney

54. Which of the following geographic area is the largest source of CO_2 emissions from burning of fossil fuel?
(a) China (b) Russia
(c) North America (d) European Union

55. Industries generating hazardous waste are classified as
(a) Brown (b) Green
(c) Yellow (d) Red

56. Which of the following greenhouse gases are entirely anthropogenic in origin?
(a) Water vapour (b) Carbon dioxide
(c) CFCs (d) Methane

57. Peroxyacyl nitrate (PAN) is a by-product of
(a) Photochemical smog
(b) London smog
(c) Sulphurous smog
(d) None of the above

58. Maximum soot is released from (*December 2009*)
(a) Petrol vehicles
(b) CNG vehicles
(c) Diesel vehicles
(d) Thermal power plants

59. The balance in oxygen level is maintained by
(a) Photosynthesis and cellular respiration
(b) Industrial emissions of gases
(c) Release of ozone in upper atmosphere
(d) None of the above

60. The problems caused by air pollutants basically affect
    (a) Circulatory and nervous system
    (b) Circulatory and respiratory system
    (c) Muscular system
    (d) None of the above

61. Arrange columns II in proper sequence so as to match it with column I and choose the correct answer from the code given below: (*December 2004*)

List I (Activity)		List II (Noise level (dB))	
A	Hearing	I	30
B	Whispering	II	1
C	Interference with sleep	III	60
D	Normal Talk	IV	30–50

Codes:
(a) A-I, B-II, C-III, D-IV
(b) A-II, B-I, C-IV, D-III
(c) A-IV, B-II, C-III, D-I
(d) A-III, B-I, C-II, D-IV

62. The inability to hear important environmental cues and animal signals is termed as
    (a) Masking
    (b) Tasking
    (c) Frisking
    (d) None of the above

63. Which of the following about peroxyacyl nitrates (PAN) is true?
    (a) They are secondary pollutants.
    (b) Produced when hydrocarbon radical reacts with nitrogen oxide
    (c) Cause respiratory diseases in human beings
    (d) All of the above

64. Which of the following is an indicator of water quality and presence of organic matter in water?
    (a) BOD
    (b) COD
    (c) Both (a) and (b)
    (d) None of the above

65. Match List I with List II

List I (Disease)		List II (Cause)	
A	Osteoporosis	I	Fluorine
B	Leukaemia	II	Sr-90
C	Lung Cancer	III	Benzopyrene

Codes:
(a) A-I, B-III, C-II
(b) A-III, B-I, C-II
(c) A-I, B-II, C-III
(d) A-III, B-II, C-I

66. Which of the following units is used to measure the intensity of noise? (*June 2008*)
    (a) Decibel (b) Hz
    (c) Phon (d) watts/m^2

67. Human ear is most sensitive to noise in the following frequency range (*June 2008*)
    (a) 1–2 kHz (b) 100–500 Hz
    (c) 10–12 kHz (d) 13–16 kHz

68. The plume rise in a coal-based power plant depends on
    I. Buoyancy
    II. Atmospheric stability
    III. Momentum of exhaust gases
    (*June 2007*)

Codes:
(a) (I) and (II) only (b) (II) and (III) only
(c) (I) and (III) only (d) (I), (II), and (III)

69. In the metro city of Kolkata, the major cause of air pollution is
    (a) Hydrocarbons
    (b) Carbon monoxide
    (c) Water vapours
    (d) None of the above

70. Which of the following is the main discharge from coal-based power plants (thermal plants)?
    (a) SPM
    (b) Fly ash
    (c) Smog
    (d) None of the above

71. Which of the following methods can be used to increase the supply of usable, good quality water?

(a) Chlorination (b) Metallurgy
(c) Cloud seeding (d) None of the above

72. Malaria is caused by (*December 2005*)
(a) Bacterial infection
(b) Viral infection
(c) Parasitic infection
(d) Fungal infection

73. Ozone depletion is caused due to increase in the level of
(a) Water vapour
(b) Chlorofluorocarbon
(c) Oxygen
(d) Carbon monoxide

74. What type of chemical weathering is enhanced by acid rain?
(a) Dissolution
(b) Hydrolysis
(c) Oxidation
(d) None of the above

75. What process causes the disintegration of rock at or near the earth's surface?
(a) Physical weathering
(b) Erosion
(c) Chemical weathering
(d) None of the above

76. Which of the following gas affects human health by reducing blood's ability to carry oxygen to different parts of the body?
(a) Carbon monoxide
(b) Sulphur dioxide
(c) Carbon dioxide
(d) Nitrous dioxide

77. Nitrogen oxide affects human health by
(a) Causing irritation to the eyes and skin
(b) Aggravating asthma problem
(c) Decreasing blood's ability to transport oxygen
(d) None of the above

78. Ozone is considered as a secondary air pollutant because it
(a) Is in the upper layers of the atmosphere
(b) Is formed by chemical reactions in atmosphere
(c) Is produced in industry
(d) Secondary role in causing pollution

79. Automobiles and trucks are not an important source of which of the following air pollutants?
(a) Carbon dioxide
(b) Hydrocarbons
(c) Nitrogen oxides
(d) Sulphur oxides

80. Sulphur dioxide is mainly released from
(a) Cars and trucks
(b) Photochemical reactions
(c) Factories
(d) None of the above

81. High concentration of oxides of nitrogen can cause
(a) Headache
(b) Dizziness and loss of consciousness
(c) Respiratory irritation
(d) All of the above

82. Excessive exposure to pesticides is mainly responsible for damage to
(a) Endocrine and immune system
(b) Respiratory system
(c) Muscular system
(d) Nervous system

83. Excessive exposure to pesticides mainly causes
(a) Malaria
(b) Diphtheria
(c) Cancer and neurological problems
(d) None of the above

84. The main chemical responsible for ozone depletion is
(a) PAN (b) Sulphur dioxide
(c) CO (d) CFCs

85. The process of dumping solid waste in a scientifically designated land area is called
(a) Dumping
(b) Waste disposal
(c) Sanitary landfill
(d) None of the above

86. The constituent of smog that causes irritation to the eyes is
(a) NO (b) PAN
(c) CO (d) None of the above

87. The pesticide directly affecting the nervous system is
    (a) DDT
    (b) Aldrin
    (c) Organic phosphates
    (d) None of the above
88. Which of the following pollutants, mainly released by burning of diesel fuel, is responsible for photochemical smog?
    (a) Oxides of sulphur
    (b) Oxides of nitrogen
    (c) Oxides of carbon
    (d) None of the above
89. Which of the following fuels are mainly responsible for release of lead into the environment?
    (a) Diesel (b) Petrol
    (c) Coal (d) All of the above
90. All hydrocarbons (except CH_4) contribute to the production of
    (a) Acid deposition
    (b) Greenhouse effect
    (c) Photochemical smog
    (d) None of the above
91. Carbon dioxide and methane are similar in terms of
    (a) Both being secondary air pollutants
    (b) Being responsible for respiratory diseases
    (c) Contribution to global warming
    (d) None of the above
92. What is the main source of pollutants of nitrogen oxides, sulphur oxides, and carbon oxides?
    (a) Photochemical reactions in the atmosphere
    (b) Burning fossil fuels at high temperatures
    (c) Industrial processes
    (d) All of the above
93. Why is photochemical smog typically worse in the summer?
    (a) There is more solar energy to drive photochemical reactions
    (b) People tend to travel more in summers.
    (c) Warm temperatures prevent the dissipation of pollutants
    (d) None of the above
94. How does photochemical smog form?
    (a) The release of primary air pollutants
    (b) Interaction occurs between chemicals such as CFCs and ozone
    (c) Reactions occur between secondary air pollutants and sunlight
    (d) The release of formaldehyde and radon inside buildings
95. Which of the following can help in reducing air pollution?
    (a) Small-sized cars
    (b) Removal of sulphur from coal
    (c) Lower ignition fuels
    (d) None of the above
96. Air pollution is an increasing problem in developing countries due to
    (a) Burning of more coal to produce electricity
    (b) Changing lifestyles
    (c) Unavailability of environment-friendly technologies
    (d) All of the above
97. Quality of resource not degraded due to pollution is
    (a) Sun (b) Sand
    (c) Water (d) Air
98. The main source of water pollution is
    (a) Sewage water
    (b) Acid rain
    (c) Industrial pollutants
    (d) None of the above
99. Which of the following ultimately causes oxygen depletion in water bodies?
    (a) Fish
    (b) Human beings
    (c) Micro-organisms
    (d) None of the above
100. Which of the following is a water-borne disease?
    (a) Blue baby syndrome
    (b) Meningitis
    (c) Diarrhoea
    (d) Cholera

101. The main pollutant of the Indian coastal water is (*December 2005*)
   (a) Oil spills
   (b) Municipal sewage
   (c) Industrial effluents
   (d) Aerosols

102. Tamil Nadu coastal belt has drinking water problem due to (*June 2006*)
   (a) High evaporation
   (b) Sea water flooding due to Tsunami
   (c) Over exploitation of ground water by tube wells
   (d) Seepage of sea water

103. Arrange column II in proper sequence so as to match it with column I and choose the correct answer from the code given below: (*December 2006*)

List I (Water quality)		List II (pH Value)	
A	Neutral	I	5
B	Moderately acidic	II	7
C	Alkaline	III	4
D	Injurious	IV	8

Codes:
(a) A-II, B-III, C-I, D-IV
(b) A-I, B-III, C-I, D-IV
(c) A-II, B-I, C-IV, D-III
(d) A-III, B-I, C-II, D-IV

104. The maximum emission of pollutants from fuel sources in India is caused by (*December 2006*)
   (a) Coal
   (b) Firewood
   (c) Refuse burning
   (d) Vegetable waste product

105. Which of the following is not a primary air pollutant? (*June 2006*)
   (a) Methane (b) Sulphur dioxide
   (c) Ozone (d) Asbestos

106. **Assertion (A):** Aerosols have potential for modifying climate.
   Reason (R): Aerosols interact with both the short waves and radiations. (*June 2006*)
   (a) Both A and R are true, and R is the correct explanation of A
   (b) Both A and R are true, but R is not the correct explanation of A
   (c) A is true but R is false
   (d) A is false but R is true

107. Which of the following statements is true with regard to noise and noise pollution?
   (a) Decibel is the linear scale of noise measurement
   (b) A jet plane is one of the highest decibel sources of noise
   (c) A change from 40 dB to 80 dB is exactly double in loudness
   (d) Noise cannot be shielded

108. Which of the following is the unit of measurement of noise pollution?
   (a) Pascal (b) Decibels
   (c) Hertz (d) All of the above

109. Zero decibel is the
   (a) Threshold point for hearing
   (b) Threshold point for physical pain
   (c) Where no sound waves can travel
   (d) None of the above

110. With which of following kinds of pollution, the term 'green muffler' is associated?
   (a) Water pollution
   (b) Air pollution
   (c) Nuclear pollution
   (d) Noise pollution

111. A natural phenomenon that becomes harmful due to pollution is
   (a) Global warming
   (b) Ecological balance
   (c) Greenhouse effect
   (d) Desertification

112. The pollutant responsible for ozone holes is
   (a) SO_2 (b) CO (c) CFC (d) CO_2

113. The best solution to get rid of non-biodegradable wastes is
   (a) Burning (b) Dumping
   (c) Burying (d) Recycling

114. Animal dung is
(a) Biodegradable
(b) Non-biodegradable
(c) Hazardous
(d) Toxic

115. Which of the following is non-biodegradable?
(a) Animal bones
(b) Nylon
(c) Wool
(d) Banyan tree leaves

116. Which of the following non-biodegradable waste has the potential of polluting earth to dangerous levels of toxicity, if not handled properly?
(a) DDT
(b) CFC
(c) Radioactive substances
(d) PAN

117. Which of the following is a non-point source of water pollution?
(a) Oil spill
(b) Sewage treatment plant
(c) Open cast mine
(d) Deep bore well

118. With the absorption and decomposition of CO_2 in ocean water beyond desired level, there will be (*December 2006*)
(a) Decrease in temperature
(b) Increase in salinity
(c) Growth of phytoplanktons
(d) Rise in sea level

119. BOD stands for
(a) Biological oxygen demand
(b) Basic oxygen dissolved
(c) Biological organic demand
(d) Biological oxygen decomposition

120. Which of the following statement is not a method of purifying water?
(a) Reverse osmosis
(b) UV radiation
(c) Distillation
(d) Evaporation from a water body

121. Which of the following statements is not true with regard to normal plastic waste?
(a) It lasts long
(b) It clogs the sewage system
(c) It is biodegradable
(d) Burning results in toxic fumes

122. Acid rain is formed by the
(a) Combination of chemical air pollutants with atmospheric water droplets
(b) Mixing of acid with rain
(c) Release of industrial pollutants in the atmosphere
(d) None of the above

123. Which of the following is not an impact of acid rain?
(a) Death of trees
(b) Loss of productivity of plants
(c) Soil alkalinity
(d) Death of fish in lakes and ponds

124. In a lake polluted with pesticides, which one of the following will contain the maximum amount of pesticides as a result of biomagnification?
(a) Small fish
(b) Microscopic animals
(c) Big fish
(d) Water birds

125. Which of the following is the most dangerous and long-lasting?
(a) Nuclear waste
(b) Volcano ash
(c) Mining waste
(d) Biomedical waste

126. Name the substance whose accumulation in pelicans of Lake Michigan led to the formation of thin shells of their eggs.
(a) CFC (b) PAN
(c) DDT (d) PAC

127. Name the process in which a harmful chemical enters the food chain and gets concentrated at each level in the food chain.
(a) Concentration
(b) Biomagnification
(c) Expansion
(d) Pollution

128. Combustion of most fuels releases
(a) CO_2 (b) SO_2 (c) NO_2 (d) O_2

129. The use of which of the following fuel can help in the reduction of air pollution?
(a) Petrol
(b) Diesel
(c) CNG
(d) None of the above

130. Which of the following organisms is the main indicator for sulphur dioxide pollution?
(a) Blue green algae
(b) Lichens
(c) *E. coli*
(d) None of the above

131. Petrol engines release gaseous oxides of
(a) Sulphur (b) Nitrogen
(c) Phosphorous (d) Carbon

132. Global warming during winter becomes more pronounced at the (*December 2004*)
(a) Equator
(b) Poles
(c) Tropic of Cancer
(d) Tropic of Capricorn

133. They are covered under Stockholm Convention; the toxic is also known as Agent Orange. It was sprayed by the US forces during Vietnam War to destroy the forest cover.

Which of the following chemicals is being referred to in the above statement?
(a) Dioxin
(b) Asbestos
(c) Benzene
(d) All of the above

134. Best extinguisher for inflammable materials is
(a) Water (b) SO_2
(c) CO_2 (d) CO

135. CO_2 is stored as a liquid in cylinder at
(a) High pressure
(b) Low pressure
(c) High temperature
(d) Low temperature

136. The best way to dispose plant waste is
(a) Burning
(b) Composting
(c) Dumping in a hilly area
(d) Incineration

137. Which of the following is not one of the major environment problems resulting from human interference in the nitrogen cycle?
(a) Global warming due to release of nitrous oxide
(b) Acid rain
(c) Eutrophication
(d) Ozone depletion

138. Which of the following is not a major greenhouse gas?
(a) Carbon dioxide
(b) Water vapour
(c) Methane
(d) Calcium carbonate

139. Montreal Protocol signed in 1987 was signed to
(a) Phase out the use of CFC's which cause depletion of the ozone layer
(b) Reduce the greenhouse effect
(c) Protect endangered species
(d) Ban nuclear testing in tropical oceans

140. Which of the following is not one of the prime health risks associated with greater UV radiation through the atmosphere due to depletion of stratospheric ozone?
(a) Increased skin cancer
(b) Reduced immune system
(c) Increased liver cancer
(d) Damage to eyes

141. Unburnt carbon particles causes
(a) Cardiac problem
(b) Respiratory problems
(c) Throat problems
(d) Skin infection

142. Which of the following statements are correct in the context of carbon monoxide emissions?
1. It is mainly due to incomplete combustion of fuel.
2. They are more evident in petrol engine.
3. Long-term exposure can cause nausea.

Codes

(a) 1 and 2 only (b) 1, 2, and 3
(c) 2 and 3 only (d) 1 and 3 only

143. Which of the following pairs regarding typical composition of hospitals wastes is incorrect? (*December 2008*)
(a) Plastics: 9–12%
(b) Metals: 1–2%
(c) Ceramic: 8–10%
(d) Biodegradable: 35–40%

144. Surface ozone is produced from (*December 2009*)
(a) Transport sector
(b) Cement plants
(c) Textile industry
(d) Chemical industry

145. According to WHO, maximum permissible level of chlorides in drinking water is
(a) 100 mg/l (b) 200 mg/l
(c) 600 mg/l (d) 800 mg/l

146. Which of the following body parts is most likely to be affected by nuclear radiation during the early stages of exposure?
(a) Skin
(b) Bones
(c) Bone marrow
(d) None of the above

147. Which of the following terms is used to describe phenomenon of removing carbon dioxide from nature by carbon sinks (natural or artificial)?
(a) Decomposition
(b) Bio-sequestration
(c) Emission trading
(d) None of the above

148. Which of the following terms is used to reflect the potential of a greenhouse gas to cause global warming?
(a) Warming potent
(b) Warming potential
(c) Global warming potential
(d) None of the above

149. The living organism that serves as an indicator of air pollution is
(a) Viruses (b) Fungi
(c) Bacteria (d) *E. coli*

150. The gas that is mainly responsible for global warming because of its quantity in the atmosphere is
(a) CFC (b) CO_2 (c) CH_4 (d) N_2

151. Which of the following statements are true in the context of particulate matter?
1. It is basically a mist, more prevalent during winter weather.
2. It is more prevalent in diesel engine vehicles.
3. Long-term exposure can harm respiratory track and lung functions.

Codes:

(a) 1 and 2 (b) 1, 2, and 3
(c) 2 and 3 (d) 1 and 3

152. Match List I with List II.

	List I (Act)		List II (Year)
A	Water (Prevention and Control of Pollution)	I	1974
B	Air (Prosecution and Control of Pollution)	II	1981
C	Wildlife Protection Act	III	1972
D	Environment Protection Act	IV	1986

Codes:

(a) A-I, B-II, C-III, D-IV
(b) A-I, B-III, C-II, D-IV
(c) A-IV, B-II, C-III, D-I
(d) A-IV, B-III, C-II, D-I

153. Which of the following elements is deposited into aquatic and terrestrial ecosystem when used in intensive agriculture practices?
(a) Nitrogen (b) Phosphorus
(c) Sulphur (d) None of the above

154. Discharge of industrial wastewater causes all except
(a) Depletion of dissolved oxygen
(b) Destruction of aquatic life
(c) Change in climate
(d) Impairment of biological activity

155. The rules pertaining to biomedical waste (India) are notified under
(a) Environmental (protection) Act, 1980
(b) Environmental (protection) Act, 1983
(c) Environmental (protection) Act, 1986
(d) Environmental (protection) Act, 1988

156. The following is not recommended for management of plastic waste.
(a) Incineration
(b) Deep burial
(c) Autoclave/hydroclave
(d) All of the above

157. Fertilizers can be washed into rivers by rain leading to
(a) Bioaccumulation
(b) Eutrophication
(c) Biodegradation
(d) Spontaneous combustion

158. Which of the following is not an air pollutant?
(a) Oxides of carbon
(b) Oxides of sulphur
(c) Oxides of nitrogen
(d) Oxides of hydrogen

159. The gradual build-up of concentration of chemicals as they transfer through higher levels of the food chain is called
(a) Biomagnification
(b) Biodegradation
(c) Bioconcentration
(d) None of the above

160. Stockholm Convention is a global treaty to protect environment and human health from
(a) Greenhouse gases
(b) Persistent organic pollutants
(c) Hospital acquired Infections
(d) None of the above

161. Presence of high algal content in water indicates that the water is
(a) Neutral
(b) Alkaline
(c) Acidic
(d) None of the above

162. When the fluoride concentration in water exceeds 1.5 mg/l or so, the disease that may be caused is
(a) Fluorosis
(b) Poliomyelitis
(c) Dental decay
(d) None of the above

163. The safe permissible limit of sulphate in domestic water supplies is
(a) 100 mg/l (b) 200 mg/l
(c) 400 mg/l (d) 300 mg/l

164. Silicosis is caused in the
(a) Textile industry
(b) Sugar industry
(c) Stone crushers
(d) All of the above

Exploitation of Natural and Energy Resources

165. The ultimate source of energy is
(a) Plants (b) Animals
(c) Bacteria (d) Sun

166. The source of energy of the sun is
(a) Nuclear fission
(b) Chemical reaction
(c) Nuclear fusion
(d) Photoelectric effect

167. Photosphere refers to
(a) The outermost layer of earth's atmosphere
(b) The visible surface of the sun from where the radiation emanates
(c) The outer space
(d) None of the above

168. According to the India State of Forest Report 2015, the total forest and tree cover is 24.16 percent of the India's total geographical area.

Which of the following states have shown maximum increase during the recent years as per report?

(a) Odisha
(b) West Bengal
(c) Madhya Pradesh
(d) Arunachal Pradesh

169. The maximum loss of forest lands in India is caused by (*December 2004*)
(a) River valley projects
(b) Industries
(c) Means of transportation
(d) Agriculture

170. Which one of the following is/are the main reason/s that solar energy could not become a viable alternative source of energy?
(a) It needs continuous solar radiation
(b) Solar power plants need a lot of space
(c) It is still very expensive
(d) All of the above

171. Deforestation leads to an increase in atmospheric carbon dioxide because
(a) Decaying trees release carbon dioxide
(b) Living trees remove carbon dioxide from the atmosphere via photosynthesis
(c) Burning wood releases carbon dioxide into the atmosphere
(d) All of the above

172. Thermal power generation in India is carried out by burning
(a) Natural gas (b) Coal
(c) Oil (d) All of the above

173. The fuel used in the conventional nuclear reactor is
(a) Cadmium (b) Radium
(c) Uranium (d) Thorium

174. Calorific value is basically about
(a) Fuel efficiency
(b) Amount of heat
(c) Amount of light
(d) None of the above

175. The nuclear fuel used in the fast breeder reactor is
(a) Cadmium (b) Radium
(c) Uranium (d) Thorium

176. Nuclear fusion reactions happens spontaneously in
(a) The core of the earth
(b) The commercial nuclear reactor
(c) The atmosphere of the sun
(d) The eruption of a volcano

177. Which one of the following is not a renewable energy source?
(a) Solar (b) Coal
(c) Wave (d) Wind

178. The world's largest producer of rare earth metals, which are used mainly in electronics industry is
(a) China (b) Japan
(c) India (d) Russia

179. Which of the following causes the least pollution when burnt?
(a) Petrol (b) Diesel
(c) Coal (d) Natural gas

180. With the help of photosynthesis, plants convert solar energy into
(a) Chemical energy
(b) Mechanical energy
(c) Kinetic energy
(d) Nuclear energy

181. Deforestation during the recent decade has led to (*December 2007*)
(a) Soil erosion
(b) Land slide
(c) Loss of biodiversity
(d) All of the above

182. In the sun, heat and light are produced by
(a) Chemical reactions
(b) Nuclear reactions
(c) Ionic reactions
(d) None of the above

183. Chemical weathering of rocks is largely dependent on (*June 2008*)
(a) High temperature
(b) Strong wind action
(c) Heavy rainfall
(d) Glaciation

184. In which of the following years, National Green Tribunal Act that intends to set up

environment courts in the country was enacted?
(a) 2003 (b) 2005
(c) 2008 (d) 2010

185. Which of the following types of energy resources can last indefinitely or for a very long time due to judicious use
(a) Non-renewable (b) Renewable
(c) Domestic (d) None of the above

186. Match the following:

List I (Type of coal)		List II (Carbon content)	
A	Peat	I	50–60%
B	Lignite (Brown)	II	70%
C	Bituminous	III	80%
D	Anthracite	IV	90–95%

Codes:
(a) A-I, B-II, C-III, D-IV
(b) A-I, B-III, C-II, D-IV
(c) A-IV, B-II, C-III, D-I
(d) A-IV, B-III, C-II, D-I

187. Bitumen is obtained from (*December 2005*)
(a) Forests and plants
(b) Kerosene oil
(c) Crude oil
(d) Underground mines

188. The increased water demand in the cities can be better met by
(a) Larger desalination plants
(b) Adoption of conservation measures
(c) Drilling more tube wells
(d) By sewerage treatment plants

189. Which of the following is a conventional source of energy?
(a) Coal (b) Wind energy
(c) solar energy (d) Natural gas

190. Which of the following is NOT an inexhaustible natural resource?
(a) Air (b) Water
(c) Solar energy (d) Natural gas

191. Which of the following is a non-conventional source of energy?
(a) Wood (b) Sun
(c) Coal (d) Petroleum

192. Biogas is produced as a by-product of anaerobic breakdown and fermentation of biomass. The main constituent of biogas is
(a) Methane (b) Ethane
(c) Propane (d) Butane

193. Biogas is
(a) 50–70% of methane
(b) 30–40% carbon dioxide
(c) Hydrogen and hydrogen sulphide
(d) All of the above

194. The tallest trees in the world are found in the (*December 2008*)
(a) Equatorial region
(b) Temperate region
(c) Monsoon region
(d) Mediterranean region

195. A geographic unit that collects, stores, and releases water is a
(a) Wasteland
(b) Watershed
(c) Wetland
(d) None of the above

196. Bog is a wetland that receives water from (*June 2009*)
(a) Nearby water bodies
(b) Melting
(c) Rainfall only
(d) Sea only

197. The biggest fresh water lake in India
(a) Wular (b) Sukhna Lake
(c) Dal Lake (d) Loktak Lake

198. The largest thorium reserves in the world are in
(a) India (b) USA
(c) Australia (d) None of the above

199. Freshwater achieves its greatest density at (*December 2008*)
(a) –4°C (b) 0°C
(c) 4°C (d) –2.5°C

200. Which one of the following non-conventional energy sources can be exploited most economically? (*December 2009*)
(a) Solar
(b) Wind
(c) Geothermal
(d) Ocean Thermal Energy Conversion (OTEC)

201. The largest soil group of India is (*December 2005*)
(a) Red soil (b) Black soil
(c) Sandy soil (d) Mountain soil

202. The regur soil refers to
(a) Black cotton soil (b) Laterite soil
(c) Desert soil (d) Alluvial soil

203. The soil's fertility can be increased by growing more of
(a) Food grains
(b) Leguminous plants
(c) Fibre crops
(d) None of the above

204. Which of the following soils is very hard to cultivate?
(a) Alluvial (b) Red soil
(c) Cotton soil (d) Sandy soil

205. Which of the following is true about laterite soils?
(a) They are formed as a result of leaching
(b) They are rich in minerals such as aluminium and iron
(c) They are found in hot and wet tropical areas
(d) All of the above

206. Which of the following layer of soil determines its pH value and also its rate of water absorption and retention?
(a) O-Horizon (b) A-Horizon
(c) B-Horizon (d) C-Horizon

207. Which of the following is measured by the porometer?
(a) Soil fertility (b) Soil salinity
(c) Soil acidity (d) All of the above

208. Which of the following states has forests rich in sandalwood?
(a) Andhra Pradesh
(b) Karnataka
(c) Kerala
(d) Madhya Pradesh

209. Soils in the Mahanadi Delta are less fertile than those in the Godavari Delta because of
(a) Erosion of top soil by annual floods
(b) Inundation of land by sea water
(c) Traditional agriculture practices
(d) The derivation of alluvial soil from red soil hinterland

210. In India, oil is mostly found in
(a) Anticlines and fault traps
(b) Sedimentary rocks
(c) Igneous rocks
(d) None of the above

211. CNG stands for
(a) Compressed Natural Gasoline
(b) Compressed Natural Gas
(c) Compressed Nitrogen Gas
(d) Calibrated Natural Gas

212. Which of the following are salt water wetlands?
(a) Marsh lands (b) Bogs
(c) Fish ponds (d) Estuaries

213. Hydroelectric power is
(a) Produced with the help of dams
(b) Renewable energy source
(c) Not contributing to global warming
(d) All of the above

214. The water suitable for drinking is
(a) Pure water (b) Portable water
(c) Potable water (d) Pungent water

215. Which of the following is a major pollutant causing acid rain?
(a) Carbon dioxide
(b) Sulphur dioxide
(c) Hydrogen peroxide
(d) Carbon monoxide

216. Which of the following is the main producer of carbon monoxide?
(a) Automobiles (b) Industry
(c) Dying industry (d) Domestic sector

217. Biodiesel is produced in India presently from
(a) Calotropis (b) Catharanthus
(c) Jatropha (d) Delonix

218. For harnessing ocean thermal energy, the temperature difference between water at the surface and water at depths up to 2 km should be more than
(a) 5°C (b) 10°C (c) 15°C (d) 20°C

219. Which of the following is not a biomass energy source?
(a) Wood (b) Gobar gas
(c) Nuclear energy (d) Biogas

220. The production of nuclear energy
(a) Follows Einstein's principle of conversion of mass into energy
(b) Is not ultimately derived from the sun's energy
(c) Both (a) and (b)
(d) None of the above

221. On which principle does a hydroelectric power plant work?
(a) Law of conservation of energy
(b) The conversion of potential energy into kinetic energy
(c) The conversion of mechanical energy into electrical energy
(d) All of the above

222. Which of the following is not a fossil fuel?
(a) Wood (b) Coal
(c) Petroleum (d) Natural gas

223. CBD stands for
(a) Coal bed methane
(b) Cheap bed methane
(c) Commercial bed methane
(d) None of the above

224. The energy source that eventually runs out of stock is known as
(a) Renewable resource
(b) Non-renewable resource
(c) Endangered resource
(d) None of the above

225. Which country is the leader in harnessing wind energy?
(a) Denmark (b) Germany
(c) India (d) USA

226. Which of the following country is a pioneer in the production of shale gas?
(a) China (b) USA
(c) Brazil (d) Saudi Arabia

227. Shale gas is basically entrapped in
(a) Igneous rocks
(b) Sedimentary rocks
(c) Metamorphic rocks
(d) None of the above

228. With which of the following sources of energy, the terms hydraulic fracturing or fracking associated with?
(a) Coal bed methane
(b) Conventional gas production
(c) Shale gas exploitation
(d) Hydroelectric power

229. Which of the following is a renewable source of energy?
(a) Uranium (b) Petroleum
(c) Coal (d) Biomass

230. Which of the following element is used in the making of solar cells?
(a) Platinum (b) Carbon
(c) Silicon (d) Silver

231. The metal used in a solar panel is
(a) Gold (b) Copper
(c) Silver (d) Nickel

232. Which one of the following is a renewable resource?
(a) Natural gas (b) Petroleum
(c) Ground water (d) Coal

233. Which of the chemical substances released into the environment while burning of fossil fuels can lead to acid rain?
(a) Oxides of sulphur
(b) Oxides of carbon
(c) Oxides of nitrogen
(d) All of the above

234. Which of the following is not a biomass source?

(a) Gobar gas (b) Coal
(c) Wood (d) Nuclear energy

235. The energy which is not derived from the sun is
(a) Biomass
(b) Fossil fuels
(c) Nuclear energy
(d) Geothermal energy

236. Harmful radiation emitted by the sun is
(a) Visible (b) Infrared
(c) Ultraviolet (d) Radio waves

237. Fuel formed under the earth's surface by the decomposition of organic matter is called
(a) Fossil fuel
(b) Inorganic fuel
(c) Biogas
(d) None of the above

238. The main constituent of LPG is
(a) Methane (b) Butane
(c) Hydrogen (d) Propane

239. The main constituent of CNG is
(a) Methane (b) Butane
(c) Ethane (d) Propane

240. Which of these is not a renewable source of energy?
(a) Solar energy
(b) Natural gas
(c) Wind energy
(d) Ocean tidal energy

241. Exposure to which of the following radiations can cause skin problem?
(a) Infrared
(b) Ultraviolet
(c) Gamma rays
(d) None of the above

242. Which of following gas has the highest calorific value?
(a) Butane (b) Methane
(c) Ethane (d) Hydrogen

243. A solar cell converts
(a) Heat energy into electrical energy
(b) Solar energy into electrical energy
(c) Heat energy into light energy
(d) Solar energy into light energy

244. Which of the following sources of energy makes use of floating generators for its exploitation?
(a) Tidal energy
(b) Wave energy
(c) Wind energy
(d) OTEC power plant

245. Which of the following term is used for the molten material mixed with gases in the mantle of earth?
(a) Litho (b) Lava
(c) Geyser (d) Magma

246. Production of electricity from waste material is called
(a) Pyrolysis
(b) Landfill
(c) Dumping
(d) None of the above

Natural Disasters and Their Mitigation

247. Which of the following is not an example of natural disaster?
(a) Tsunami (b) Heat waves
(c) Nuclear accident (d) Epidemic

248. Which of the following is true with regard to tsunami?
(a) It is a tidal wave
(b) It is caused by earthquake beneath the sea
(c) It moves very fast in the ocean water
(d) It is caused by the gravitation pull of the sun

249. What best describes an earthquake?
(a) Sudden movement along the surface of earth
(b) Collision of tectonic plates
(c) Any natural phenomenon causing destruction
(d) None of the above

250. What is the immediate energy source for earthquakes?
(a) Stored elastic energy in bent rock
(b) Stored elastic energy in compressed rock
(c) Stored heat energy from the earth's interior
(d) Stored heat energy from the sun

251. What does tsunami mean?
(a) Series of waves
(b) Any movement following earth quake
(c) Harbour wave
(d) None of the above

252. Which country is known for its frequent earthquakes?
(a) China (b) Philippines
(c) South Korea (d) Japan

253. What is a flood?
(a) The building up of large quantities of water
(b) Any obstruction in the water flow
(c) Rise in ground water level
(d) None of the above

254. Which place on earth is known as 'Ring of Fire' as it has the earth's most active volcanoes?
(a) Europe (b) Pacific Ocean
(c) South America (d) None of the above

255. What is the correct description for volcanic eruption?
(a) Vertical explosion of gas and ash
(b) Explosion or emission of lava, ashes, and toxic gases
(c) Both (a) and (b)
(d) None of the above

256. The most significant volcanic eruptions have been felt in the form of (*December 2006*)
(a) Change in weather
(b) Sinking of islands
(c) Loss of vegetation
(d) Extinction of animals

257. Tsunami occurs due to (*June 2007*)
(a) Mild earthquakes and landslides in the oceans
(b) Strong earthquakes and landslides in the oceans
(c) Strong earthquakes and landslides in the mountains
(d) Strong earthquakes and landslides in the deserts

258. Which of the following describes the build-up and release of stress during an earthquake?
(a) Modified Mercalli scale
(b) Elastic rebound theory
(c) The travel time difference
(d) None of the above

259. The amount of ground displacement in an earthquake is called the
(a) Epicentre (b) Dip
(c) Slip (d) Focus

260. The point where the movement that triggers an earthquake is
(a) Dip (b) Epicentre
(c) Focus (d) strike

261. Which of the following sequences correctly lists the different arrivals from first to last?
(a) P waves ... S waves ... Surface waves
(b) Surface waves ... P waves .... S waves
(c) P waves ... Surface waves ... S waves
(d) No fixed pattern

262. How many seismograph stations are needed to locate the epicentre of an earthquake?
(a) 1 (b) 2 (c) 3 (d) 4

263. What is the approximate percentage of earthquakes occurring at plate boundaries?
(a) 25% (b) 50% (c) 75% (d) 90%

264. Body waves consist of
(a) P waves only (b) S waves only
(c) P and S waves (d) Surface waves

265. In general, the most destructive earthquake waves are the
(a) P waves (b) S waves
(c) Surface waves (d) Q waves

266. Indian coastal areas experienced tsunami in the year (*June 2009*)
(a) 2005 (b) 2004
(c) 2006 (d) 2007

267. Match List I with List II:

Column – I		Column – II	
A	Rio Summit	1	1997
B	Johannesburg Earth Summit	2	1972
C	Kyoto Protocol	3	1992
D	Stockholm Conference	4	2002

Codes:

	A	B	C	D
(a)	3	4	1	2
(b)	1	2	3	4
(c)	4	3	2	1
(d)	2	1	4	3

268. What is the main cause for the occurrence of tsunamis?
(a) Because of ocean floor movement, induced by an earthquake and producing gigantic waves
(b) As a result of hurricane
(c) Volcanic eruption in the sea
(d) Nonc of thc above

269. The earthquake waves that have transverse movements are known as
(a) Primary waves
(b) Secondary waves
(c) Surface waves
(d) None of the above

270. Which of the following natural disaster can occur as a result of the earth's internal heat?
(a) Hurricanes (b) Floods
(c) Earthquakes (d) Tornadoes

271. Which of the following region is in the way of high risk zone of earthquakes? (*June 2009*)
(a) Central Indian Highland
(b) Coastal region
(c) Himalayan region
(d) Indian desert

272. The most recurring natural hazard in India is
(a) Earthquakes (b) Floods
(c) Landslides (d) Volcanoes

273. Which of the following is not associated with earthquakes? (*December 2008*)
(a) Focus (b) Epicentre
(c) Seismograph (d) Swells

274. For which of the following phenomenon, solar energy is primarily responsible?
(a) Precipitation
(b) Wind
(c) Erosion of earth materials
(d) All of the above

275. Which of the following can serve as a reliable safety hedge against coastal calamities?
(a) Coral reefs
(b) Mangroves
(c) Both (a) and (b)
(d) None of the above

276. The term used in context of landslides and basically the downslope movement of materials under the influence of gravity is
(a) Mass wasting
(b) Mass tracking
(c) Mass transfer
(d) None of the above

277. What is the correct order where you would find stream deposits starting at the headwaters and going towards the mouth across the course of the river?
(a) Gravel, sand, silt
(b) Sand, silt, gravel
(c) Silt, sand, grave
(d) None of the above

278. The majority of earth's water is in the form of
(a) Oceans
(b) Atmosphere
(c) Fresh water lakes and glaciers
(d) Rivers

279. Which of the following natural hazards has a big effect on the Indian people each year? (*June 2007*)
(a) Cyclones (b) Floods
(c) Earthquakes (d) Landslides

280. The point at which a fault first ruptures in the earth during earthquake is called
(a) Hypocentre
(b) Epicentre
(c) Mouth
(d) None of the above

281. A flash flood differs from a normal flood
(a) By sudden increase in the level of water
(b) As it is likely to cause much more damage
(c) Both (a) and (b)
(d) None of the above

282. Which of the following is a method to prevent flood?
(a) Levees
(b) Winding streams
(c) Efficient sewage systems
(d) All of the above

283. The Richter scale measures
(a) The number of deaths
(b) The size of its epicentre
(c) The energy released by an earthquake
(d) The body waves count

284. What are the three main components of the water cycle?
(a) Evaporation, sublimation, solidification
(b) Evaporation, condensation, precipitation
(c) Rain, snow, sleet
(d) Liquid, solid, gas

285. The almost identical basic phenomenon is known by different names across countries in the world.
Match the following:

List I (Phenomenon)		List II (Country)	
A	Cyclone	I	India
B	Hurricane	II	USA
C	Typhoon	III	China
D	Willy willy	IV	Australia

Codes:
(a) A-I, B-II, C-III, D-IV
(b) A-II, B-I, C-III, D-IV
(c) A-IV, B-II, C-III, D-I
(d) None of the above

286. What should you do to prepare for a hurricane?
(a) Prepare for a safety route
(b) Arrange for emergency food and water
(c) Both (a) and (b)
(d) None of the above

287. The main cause/s that tsunami waves lose some of its energy as they get closer to the shore is
(a) There is lesser depth/room for the tsunami
(b) Buildings on the beach
(c) Friction and turbulence from the beach
(d) None of the above

288. The main effect of volcanic eruptions is
(a) Flying of ash contents
(b) Mud slides
(c) Low temperatures on earth's surface
(d) All of the above

289. The loss of an entire animal species is referred to as
(a) Distinction
(b) Annihilation
(c) Genocide
(d) Extinction

290. Which of the following is true about ozone layer?
(a) It absorbs most of the UV-B radiation
(b) It screens out the UV-C radiation
(c) Its depletion leads to cancer
(d) All of the above

291. Which of the following is the main cause of global warming?
(a) Burning of fossil fuel
(b) Changes in carbon cycle
(c) Climate change
(d) None of the above

292. Which one of the following gases is not a greenhouse gas?
(a) Methane
(b) Hydrogen
(c) Carbon dioxide
(d) Sulphur hexafluoride

293. Volcanic eruptions can affect climate because
(a) They heat the atmosphere
(b) Volcanic dust and gas in the upper atmosphere reflects and absorbs solar radiation
(c) Volcanoes have no effect on the earth's climate
(d) None of the above

294. Which of the following is an effective protection against cyclones and tsunamis?
(a) Shrimp farms
(b) Building walls
(c) Mangrove forests
(d) None of the above

295. Comparative environment impact assessment study is to be conducted for *(June 2007)*
(a) The whole year
(b) Three seasons excluding monsoons
(c) Any three seasons
(d) The worst season

296. Sea level arises primarily as a result of *(June 2007)*
(a) Heavy rainfall
(b) Melting of glaciers
(c) Submarine volcanism
(d) Sea floor spreading

297. The main aim of Kyoto Protocol is to
(a) Require concessions from all countries involved equally in greenhouse gas emission
(b) Required increases in nuclear power generation
(c) Would have resulted in overall increases in greenhouse emissions
(d) Reduce emissions of six greenhouse gases to levels lower than those of 1990

298. Which of the following gas is released when rice is grown in the wet fields?
(a) Methane
(b) Nitrous oxides
(c) Ozone
(d) Carbon dioxide

299. El Niño and La Niña are responsible for producing
(a) Changes of opposite direction in global temperature
(b) Precipitation patterns
(c) Both (a) and (b)
(d) None of the above

300. The greenhouse effect involves warming of the earth's surface and the
(a) Troposphere
(b) Mesosphere
(c) Stratosphere
(d) Thermosphere

301. Tidal energy is also a potential renewable energy resource. Which of the following is the main cause for the formation of tidal waves?
(a) Gravitational pull of moon
(b) Gravitational pull of sun
(c) Gravitational pull of sun and moon
(d) None of the above

Miscellaneous Topics

302. Biodiversity is described as
(a) The range of different species in an environment
(b) The seasonal and daily changes in an environment
(c) The way species differ from one another
(d) The influence of physical factors on an environment

303. How an organism is suited to live in a particular place is called
(a) Competition (b) Adaptation
(c) Addition (d) Participation

304. Which of the following is termed as the Tiger State?
(a) Rajasthan
(b) Gujarat

(c) Madhya Pradesh
(d) Jammu and Kashmir

305. Match the following: (*December 2008*)

List I (National parks)		List II (States)	
A	Periyar	I	Orissa
B	Nandankanan	II	Kerala
C	Corbett National Park	III	Rajasthan
D	Sariska Tiger Reserve	IV	Uttarakhand

Codes:
(a) A-II, B-III, C-IV, D-III
(b) A-I, B-II, C-IV, D-III
(c) A-III, B-II, C-I, D-IV
(d) A-I, B-II, C-III, D-IV

306. The Great Indian Bustard bird is found in (*December 2009*)
(a) Thar Desert of Rajasthan
(b) Coastal regions of India
(c) Malabar coast
(d) Delta regions

307. The turpentine oil used in the manufacture of medicines is obtained from
(a) Acacia
(b) Chir pin
(c) Sunflower
(d) None of the above

308. The main characteristic of biodiversity hotspots is/are
(a) Threat from human beings
(b) Biogeographical region with a specified percentage of endemic species
(c) Both (a) and (b)
(d) Neither (a) nor (b)

309. The Sagarmatha National Park has been established to preserve the eco-system of which mountain peak? (*December 2009*)
(a) Kanchenjunga (b) Mount Everest
(c) Annapurna (d) Dholavira

310. Chipko Movement, basically to protect environment, originated in 1974 in
(a) Uttarakhand
(b) Bihar
(c) Madhya Pradesh
(d) None of the above

311. Solid waste treatment by pyrolysis refers to
(a) Heating in the absence of air
(b) No heating
(c) Heating in the presence of air
(d) Treating with chemicals before heating

312. Environmental Impact Assessment is an objective analysis of the possible changes in the (*June 2009*)
(a) Physical characteristics of the environment
(b) Biophysical characteristics of the environment
(c) Socio-economic characteristics of the environment
(d) All of the above

313. The main reason for global warming is
(a) Increased concentration of anthropogenic CO_2 in the air
(b) Decreased concentration of CO_2 in the air
(c) Increased water vapours in the atmosphere
(d) None of the above

314. The number of major GHGs identified for reduced emissions as per Kyoto Protocol are
(a) 4 (b) 5 (c) 6 (d) 8

315. The species those are especially likely to develop on biologically isolated areas such as islands are called
(a) Endemic species
(b) Extinct
(c) Wild
(d) None of the above

316. Ramsar Convention is related to the conservation of
(a) Tiger
(b) Elephants
(c) Crop genetic diversity
(d) Wetlands

317. The Great Indian Rhino has its natural home in
(a) Kaziranga National Park
(b) Corbett National Park
(c) Sunderbans
(d) Kanha National Park

318. Which of the following results in bioaccumulation and contamination of food chains?
(a) Pesticides
(b) Polychlorinated biphenyls
(c) PAN
(d) All of the above

319. Pollutants in the soil can be broken by micro-organisms. The process is called
(a) Probiotics
(b) Bioremediation
(c) Bioaugmentation
(d) None of the above

320. Match the following:

	List I		List II
A	Ozone depletion	I	Basel convention
B	CO_2 reduction	II	Kyoto Protocol
C	Sustainable development	III	Rio Summit
D	Hazardous waste	IV	Montreal Protocol

Codes:
(a) A-IV, B-II, C-III, D-I
(b) A-IV, B-III, C-II, D-I
(c) A-I, B-II, C-III, D-IV
(d) A-I, B-III, C-II, D-IV

321. The Lion Tail Macaque is endemic to
(a) Andaman and Nicobar Islands
(b) Lakshadweep
(c) Nilgiris
(d) Arunachal Pradesh

322. The most efficient method of biodegradable urban solid waste management is
(a) Landfills (b) Pelletization
(c) Gasification (d) Composting

323. Wild water buffalo or Asian Buffalo or Indian Buffalo is mostly found in
(a) Eastern Himalayas
(b) Western Ghats
(c) Aravali Hills
(d) Satpura Range

324. The status of World Heritage Site is assigned by the
(a) UN (b) UNESCO
(c) World Bank (d) UNHRC

325. Match the following:

	List I (Sanctuary)		List II (State)
A	Kaziranga National Park	I	Assam
B	Keolado National Park	II	Rajasthan
C	Sunderbans National Park	III	West Bengal
D	Nanda Devi National Park	IV	Uttar Pradesh

Codes:
(a) A-I, B-II, C-III, D-IV
(b) A-I, B-III, C-II, D-IV
(c) A-IV, B-II, C-III, D-I
(d) A-IV, B-III, C-II, D-I

326. As in beginning of 2016, the number of biosphere reserves in India was
(a) 15 (b) 18 (c) 20 (d) 22

327. MAB stands for
(a) Man and Biome
(b) Man and Biodiversity
(c) Man and Biosphere
(d) Man and Biosciences

328. As in 2016, the number of biosphere reserves in India as per UNESCO's MAB list is
(a) 10 (b) 9 (c) 11 (d) 12

329. UNESCO stands for
(a) United Nations Educational, Scientific, and Cultural Organization
(b) United Nations Engineering, Scientific, and Cultural Organization

(c) United Nations Educational, Social, and Cultural Organization
(d) United Nations Educational, Scientific Control Organization

330. How many biological hotspots are located in India?
(a) 1 (b) 2 (c) 3 (d) 4

331. In which city was the UN Conference on Environment, also termed as Earth Summit, held in 1992?
(a) Rio de Janeiro (b) Kyoto
(c) Stockholm (d) Copenhagen

332. One of the following is not an *in situ* conservation for biological resources.
(a) Biosphere reserve
(b) National parks
(c) Protected areas
(d) Breeding in confined areas

333. Mauna Loa, in Hawaii (USA), is famous for
(a) Botanical garden
(b) Monitoring sea-level rise since 1950
(c) Biggest collection of mammal fossils
(d) Continuous monitoring of atmospheric CO_2 levels since 1957

334. The Tehri Dam is located in
(a) Gujarat
(b) Madhya Pradesh
(c) Uttarakhand
(d) Uttar Pradesh

335. IUCN stands for
(a) International Union for Conservation of Nature and Natural Resources
(b) Indian Union for Conservation of Nature and Natural Resources
(c) Integrated Union for Conservation of Nature and Natural Resources
(d) None of the above

336. In which of the following cities the phenomenon of classical smog was observed for the first time?
(a) Japan (b) New York
(c) London (d) Los Angeles

337. While all rivers of Peninsular India flows into Bay of Bengal, Narmada, and Tapti flow into Arabian Sea because
(*June 2006*)
(a) These two rivers follow the slope of the rift valleys
(b) The general slope of Indian Peninsula is from east to west
(c) The Indian Peninsula, north of the Satpura Ranges, is tilted towards the west
(d) The Indian Peninsula, south of the Satpura Ranges, is tilted towards the east

338. The process of conversion of solid waste into organic fertilizers by making use of micro-organisms such as bacteria and fungi is called
(a) Disposal
(b) Remediation
(c) Composting
(d) None of the above

339. The Coriolis effect results from
(a) Earth's rotation
(b) The prevailing winds
(c) Heating of the earth near the equator and cooling near the poles
(d) Ocean currents

340. On which of the following day, Environment Day is celebrated?
(a) December 29
(b) May 15
(c) June 5
(d) None of the above

341. Which of the following is considered as the common indicator organism of water pollution?
(a) Coral reefs
(b) *Plasmodium*
(c) *Escherichia coli*
(d) None of the above

342. In which year India announced a National Action Plan on Climate Change (NAPCC)?
(a) 2008 (b) 2005
(c) 2003 (d) 1998

343. Match the following:

List I (Disease)		List II (Causes)	
A	Black Foot	I	Arsenic
B	Pulmonary Oedema	II	Nitrogen Oxides
C	Hay Fever	III	Allergy
D	Sariska Tiger Reserve	IV	Uttara-khand

Codes:
(a) A-II, B-I, C-III
(b) A-I, B-II, C-III
(c) A-III, B-II, C-I
(d) A-II, B-III, C-I

344. Which of the following region has the greatest biodiversity?
(a) Tropical rain forests
(b) Arctic region
(c) Sub-tropical region
(d) None of the above

345. Which National Park is situated at the highest altitude in the country?
(a) Corbett National Park
(b) Hemis National Park
(c) Silent Valley National Park
(d) Dachigam National Park

346. The Indian government has established around eighteen biosphere reserves in India. Ten of eighteen biosphere reserves are a part of the World Network of Biosphere Reserves, based on the UNESCO's Man and the Biosphere (MAB) Programme list. Which of the following has been added in 2016?
(a) Agasthyamala Biosphere Reserve
(b) Seshachalam Hills
(c) Achanakmar-Amarkantak Biosphere Reserve
(d) Great Nicobar

347. Which of the following pairs of Health problem and its causing pollutant is not correctly matched?
(a) Nervous System – Aldrin
(b) Neurological Disorders – Pesticides
(c) Loss of consciousness – Oxides of Nitrogen
(d) Skin Cancer – PAN

348. India exploded her first underground nuclear device at
(a) Kota (b) Ranchi
(c) Jaipur (d) Pokhran

349. Weeds compete with crops for resources. Farmers can get rid of weeds by using
(a) Insecticide (b) Fungicide
(c) Herbicide (d) Rodenticide

350. Organic food is supposed to be better for human health as
(a) It is raised on special chemicals
(b) It is more expensive
(c) It is grown without the use of artificial fertilizers and pesticides
(d) None of the above

351. The biggest impacts are made on the environment by
(a) The migration of species
(b) Human interference
(c) Competition
(d) None of the above

352. Maintaining balance between fulfilment of human needs and protection of environment is termed as
(a) Environmental development
(b) Sustainable development
(c) Economic development
(d) None of the above

353. The Rio Declaration on the Environment and Development and Agenda 21 encouraged people to
(a) Think global, act local
(b) Act global, think local
(c) Act as we are, think as we do
(d) Depends on situation

354. Which of the following would indicate a warming in the average global temperature?

(a) An expansion of glaciers around the world
(b) A rise in sea level
(c) Earlier freeze dates for major lakes
(d) Both (a) and (b)

355. A by-product of fossil fuel combustion is carbon dioxide. Which of the following is the cleanest with respect to the release of carbon dioxide?
(a) Coal (b) Oil
(c) Wood (d) Natural gas

356. Vermicomposting is a method of composting that involves
(a) Silkworms (b) Earthworms
(c) Bacteria (d) One of these

357. The method which can increase the supply of usable, good quality water is
(a) Chlorination
(b) Recharging of water
(c) Cloud seeding
(d) None of the above

358. Why would global warming lead to an increase in sea level?
(a) Melting of Polar ice
(b) Melting of glaciers
(c) An increase in water temperature would cause the water to expand
(d) All of the above

359. Which of the following is not considered to be a greenhouse gas?
(a) Methane
(b) Chlorofluorocarbons (CFCs)
(c) Hydrogen
(d) Ozone

360. Baba Amte was the leader of
(a) Appiko Movement
(b) Chipko Movement
(c) Narmada Bachao Andolan
(d) Tehri Dam Movement

361. An organization or entity is to get one carbon credit if it is able to avoid emission of
(a) One tonne of carbon dioxide or its equivalent
(b) One tonne of any greenhouse gas
(c) One tonne of hydrocarbon emissions
(d) One tonne of carbon monoxide

362. Using coal, natural gas, or oil for electricity, heat, or transportation releases CO_2 into the atmosphere. The daily CO_2 emissions make up the
(a) Carbon footprint
(b) Carbon dating
(c) Carbon credit
(d) None of the above

363. Which of the following is considered as the best quality of coal?
(a) Peat (b) Lignite
(c) Bituminous (d) Anthracite

364. Which of the following organizations has categorized wild flora and fauna into eight categories (known as Red List) such as extinct, critically endangered, and endangered?
(a) International Union for Conservation of Nature and Natural Resources
(b) UNESCO
(c) Conference on Biodiversity
(d) Kyoto Protocol

365. The small amount of warming that may set off unstoppable and irreversible changes is termed as
(a) Tipping point
(b) Inflection point
(c) Turning point
(d) None of the above

366. In which year was the Kyoto Protocol signed?
(a) 1997 (b) 1992
(c) 1995 (d) 2005

367. The endangered largest living lemur Idri idri is inhabitant of
(a) Nepal (b) Pakistan
(c) Madagascar (d) USA

368. Which of the following is the most productive agro ecosystem?
(a) Maize
(b) Wheat
(c) Sugarcane
(d) None of the above

369. In which year India announced National Action Plan on Climate Change?
(a) 2005 (b) 2008
(c) 2012 (d) 2013

370. The logo of WWF is
(a) Giant panda
(b) Lion
(c) Tiger
(d) None of the above

371. Greenhouse Gases Observing Satellite or GOSAT, also known as Ibuki, was launched by
(a) USA (b) Japan
(c) South Korea (d) China

372. Which of the following state has maximum of mangrove cover in India?
(a) Goa
(b) West Bengal
(c) Orissa
(d) Andaman and Nicobar Islands

373. On which of the following days Biological Diversity Day is celebrated?
(a) December 29
(b) June 5
(c) May 21
(d) October 22

374. Which of the following organizations have promoted Reducing Emissions from Deforestation and Forest Degradation (REDD+)?
(a) International Union for Conservation of Nature
(b) United Nations
(c) World Bank
(d) International Monetary Fund

375. Dachigam Sanctuary is associated with conservation of
(a) Hangul
(b) Tiger
(c) Lion
(d) Rhinoceros

376. Which of the following Indian States/UT has the maximum percentage of mangrove cover in the country?
(a) Gujarat
(b) West Bengal
(c) Andaman and Nicobar
(d) Orissa

377. 'India is graduating from megawatts to gigawatts in renewable energy production'. Which of the following is new target for the solar energy production in India by 2022?
(a) 20 GW (b) 40 GW
(c) 100 GW (d) 350 GW

378. Government of India submitted its Intended Nationally Determined Contribution (INDC) targets to United Nations Frame Work Convention on Climate Change.

Which of the following statements are true in this context?

1. To reduce the emissions intensity of its GDP by 33 to 35 per cent by 2030 from 2005 level.
2. To achieve about 40 per cent cumulative electric power installed capacity from non-fossil fuel-based energy resources by 2030.
3. To create an additional carbon sink of 2.5 to 3 billion tonnes of CO_2 equivalent through additional forest and tree cover by 2030.

Codes:
(a) 1 and 2 only
(b) 1 and 3 only
(c) 1, 2, and 3
(d) 2 and 3 only

Answer Keys

People and Environment Interaction

1. (a) 2. (b) 3. (c) 4. (c) 5. (c)
6. (b) 7. (c) 8. (d) 9. (c) 10. (d)
11. (b) 12. (b) 13. (a) 14. (c) 15. (a)
16. (d) 17. (b) 18. (c) 19. (c) 20. (a)
21. (c) 22. (d) 23. (c) 24. (a) 25. (b)
26. (d) 27. (a) 28. (a) 29. (b) 30. (b)
31. (c) 32. (b) 33. (a) 34. (b) 35. (b)
36. (b) 37. (b) 38. (a) 39. (a) 40. (a)
41. (c)

Sources of Pollution, Pollutants, and Their Impact on Human Life

42. (b) 43. (c) 44. (a) 45. (c) 46. (a)
47. (b) 48. (d) 49. (a) 50. (a) 51. (a)
52. (a) 53. (a) 54. (c) 55. (d) 56. (c)
57. (a) 58. (d) 59. (a) 60. (b) 61. (a)
62. (a) 63. (d) 64. (a) 65. (c) 66. (a)
67. (d) 68. (d) 69. (b) 70. (b) 71. (c)
72. (c) 73. (b) 74. (b) 75. (a) 76. (a)
77. (b) 78. (b) 79. (b) 80. (a) 81. (d)
82. (a) 83. (c) 84. (d) 85. (c) 86. (b)
87. (b) 88. (b) 89. (b) 90. (c) 91. (c)
92. (b) 93. (a) 94. (c) 95. (b) 96. (d)
97. (a) 98. (a) 99. (c) 100. (d) 101. (c)
102. (d) 103. (c) 104. (c) 105. (c) 106. (a)
107. (b) 108. (b) 109. (a) 110. (d) 111. (c)
112. (c) 113. (d) 114. (a) 115. (b) 116. (c)
117. (a) 118. (c) 119. (a) 120. (b) 121. (c)
122. (a) 123. (c) 124. (c) 125. (a) 126. (c)
127. (b) 128. (a) 129. (c) 130. (b) 131. (b)
132. (d) 133. (a) 134. (c) 135. (a) 136. (b)
137. (d) 138. (d) 139. (a) 140. (c) 141. (b)
142. (b) 143. (d) 144. (a) 145. (b) 146. (c)
147. (b) 148. (c) 149. (b) 150. (b) 151. (b)
152. (a) 153. (a) 154. (c) 155. (c) 156. (a)
157. (b) 158. (d) 159. (a) 160. (b) 161. (c)
162. (a) 163. (b) 164. (c)

Exploitation of Natural and Energy Resources

165. (d) 166. (c) 167. (b) 168. (b) 169. (d)
170. (d) 171. (d) 172. (b) 173. (c) 174. (a)
175. (d) 176. (c) 177. (b) 178. (a) 179. (d)
180. (a) 181. (d) 182. (b) 183. (a) 184. (d)
185. (b) 186. (a) 187. (c) 188. (b) 189. (a)
190. (d) 191. (b) 192. (a) 193. (a) 194. (a)
195. (b) 196. (c) 197. (a) 198. (a) 199. (c)
200. (a) 201. (a) 202. (a) 203. (b) 204. (b)
205. (d) 206. (d) 207. (b) 208. (b) 209. (a)
210. (b) 211. (b) 212. (d) 213. (d) 214. (c)
215. (b) 216. (a) 217. (c) 218. (d) 219. (c)
220. (c) 221. (d) 222. (a) 223. (a) 224. (b)
225. (b) 226. (b) 227. (b) 228. (c) 229. (d)
230. (c) 231. (c) 232. (c) 233. (d) 234. (d)
235. (c) 236. (c) 237. (a) 238. (b) 239. (a)
240. (b) 241. (b) 242. (d) 243. (b) 244. (b)
245. (d) 246. (a)

Natural Disasters and Their Mitigation

247. (c) 248. (b) 249. (b) 250. (a) 251. (a)
252. (d) 253. (a) 254. (b) 255. (c) 256. (a)
257. (b) 258. (b) 259. (c) 260. (c) 261. (a)
262. (c) 263. (d) 264. (c) 265. (c) 266. (b)
267. (a) 268. (a) 269. (b) 270. (c) 271. (c)
272. (b) 273. (d) 274. (d) 275. (b) 276. (a)
277. (a) 278. (a) 279. (b) 280. (a) 281. (c)
282. (d) 283. (c) 284. (b) 285. (a) 286. (c)
287. (a) 288. (a) 289. (d) 290. (d) 291. (a)
292. (b) 293. (b) 294. (c) 295. (a) 296. (b)
297. (d) 298. (a) 299. (c) 300. (a) 301. (c)

Other Important Miscellaneous Topics

302. (a) 303. (b) 304. (c) 305. (a) 306. (a)
307. (b) 308. (c) 309. (b) 310. (a) 311. (a)
312. (d) 313. (a) 314. (c) 315. (a) 316. (d)
317. (a) 318. (a) 319. (b) 320. (a) 321. (c)
322. (d) 323. (a) 324. (b) 325. (a) 326. (b)
327. (a) 328. (a) 329. (a) 330. (b) 331. (a)
332. (c) 333. (d) 334. (c) 335. (a) 336. (a)
337. (a) 338. (c) 339. (a) 340. (c) 341. (c)
342. (a) 343. (b) 344. (a) 345. (b) 346. (a)
347. (d) 348. (d) 349. (c) 350. (c) 351. (b)
352. (b) 353. (a) 354. (b) 355. (d) 356. (b)
357. (c) 358. (a) 359. (c) 360. (c) 361. (a)
362. (a) 363. (d) 364. (a) 365. (a) 366. (a)
367. (c) 368. (c) 369. (b) 370. (a) 371. (b)
372. (b) 373. (a) 374. (a) 375. (a) 376. (b)
377. (c) 378. (c)

10

Higher Education System: Governance, Polity, and Administration

Education is the manifestation of the perfection already in man

— Swami Vivekananda

Introduction to Higher Education

Higher education provides people with an opportunity to reflect on the critical, social, economical, cultural, moral, and spiritual issues facing humanity. It contributes to the national development through dissemination of specialized knowledge and skills. It is, therefore, a crucial factor for survival. Being at the apex of the educational pyramid, it also has a key role in producing teachers for the educational system. Higher Education is a key element in 'demographic dividend' and also that it intends to make optimum utilization of human resources specifically in age group of 15–59 years.

Indian higher education system, which includes technical education, is one of the largest in the world, just after the United States and China.

Formal education system can be categorized into three, namely primary, secondary, and tertiary education. Tertiary education is a wider term; it is higher education plus vocational education. According to the perspective of the NET Paper I, our focus is on higher education.

Secondary education begins to expose students to the varied roles of science, humanities, and social sciences, and also to vocational streams. This is also an appropriate stage to provide children with a sense of history and national perspective and give them opportunities to understand their constitutional duties and rights as citizens. Board of Secondary Education plays the main role in imparting this education. Elementary or primary education adopts child-centred approach. It continues up to 14 years.

There are three principle levels of qualification in higher education:

1. Undergraduate level leading to bachelor's degree
2. Postgraduate level leading to master's degree
3. Research level leading to Ph.D., Fellowship, or Post Doctorate

Some higher education institutes provide diplomas as well as Chartered Accountancy, PGDBA, and PGDCA. Most undergraduate courses take three years except for certain professional courses such as engineering and medicine. Postgraduate courses are generally of two-year duration.

Evolution of Higher Education System in India

The origin of education in India can be traced to the Vedic age. Our ancient literature, namely Vedas, Brahmanas, and Upanishads revealed the highest knowledge to mankind through our ancient rishis.

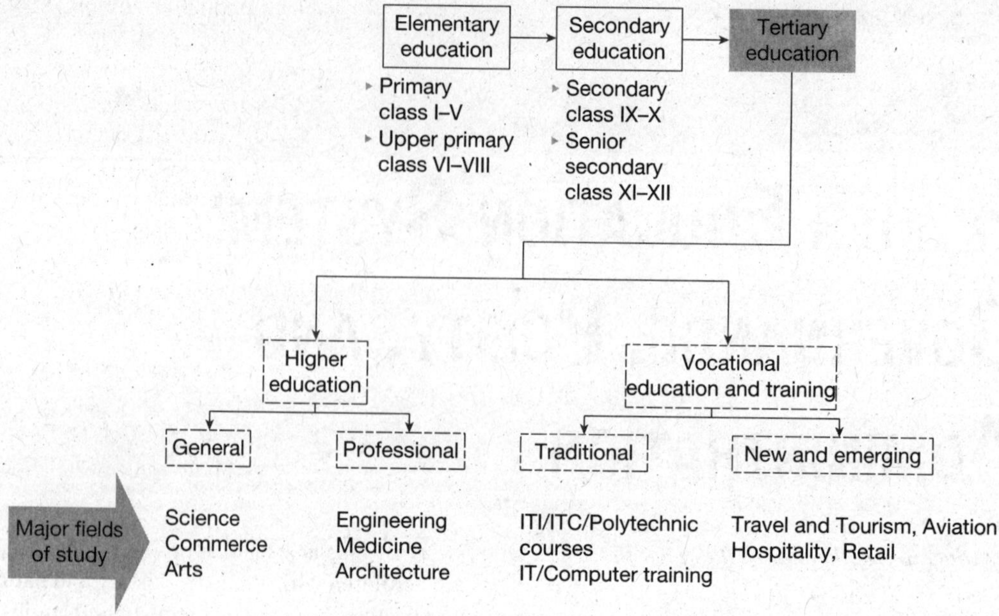

Overview of Education System in India

1. During the Gupta period, India became a centre of higher learning with Nalanda (all branches of knowledge), Takshila (study of medicine), and Ujjain (study of astronomy) among others.
2. During the advent of Buddhism, Sarnath University became a great centre of learning to study Buddhism. Ajanta was also a great place of learning art, architecture, and painting. Indian society thrived and its economy also dominated the world under this kind of education system.
3. Mughal education system consisted of primary and secondary schools, and even colleges. Colleges were established at Fatehpur Sikri, Agra, Delhi, and other places. Education system based on Hindu philosophy also existed side by side.
4. In 2006, Singapore, China, India, Japan, and other nations announced a proposed plan to restore and revive the ancient site as Nalanda International University.

Key Developments of Modern Education System

Indian higher education system has emerged as one of the largest in the world in terms of number of institutions as well as student enrolment. India is the third largest in the world in terms of student enrolment.

Our modern education system struck its roots during the British period. The British developed the system primarily to consolidate their rule in India and to get manpower for their routine administrative jobs.

Charter Act (1813)

The objective was to spread scientific knowledge in British India.

The Christian missionaries were allowed in the country to preach their religion. In 1817, Hindu College was established in Calcutta which later became Presidency College in 1855 and Presidency University in 2010.

Elphinstone Report (1823)

It recommended the appointment of District Examination Officers, School Supervisors, and training to teachers.

Elphinstone Institution was set up in 1834 in Bombay which marked the beginning of new developments in the field of higher education. It is one of the oldest colleges of Bombay University.

Macaulay's Minutes (1835)

It suggested diffusion of English education in the country. However, these initiatives were mainly directed at elementary and secondary education.

Lord Macaulay wanted to build an education system that was secular and scientific, free of age-old prejudices, and at par with the Western world. In this way, he played his part in building the modern India.

Wood Dispatch (1854)

It was the first policy measure regarding higher education. It recommended setting up of three universities, namely, at Madras, Calcutta, and Bombay, which were set up in 1857.

Hunter Commission (1882–1883)

It emphasized the segregation of primary education and higher education. It proposed that universities would have to manage the affiliated colleges.

Universities Commission (1902)

Lord Curzon was the first person to appoint a commission on university education. On January 27, 1902, the Indian Universities Act, 1904 - Indian University Commission was appointed under the Chairmanship of Sir Thomas Raleigh to enquire into the conditions and prospects of the universities established in British India and to consider and report upon the proposals for improving their constitution and working. The Commission recommended the reorganisation of university administration; a much more strict and systematic supervision of the colleges by the university; and the imposition of more exacting conditions of affiliation.

The Indian Universities Act of 1904, passed on March 21, was formulated on the basis of the recommendations of the Indian University Commission of 1902.

National Council of Education

After partition of Bengal in 1905, National Council of Education was set up by Swadeshi Nationalist leaders, which developed into Jadavpur University after independence.

For propagating learning of Indian traditions and culture along with modern values and developments in own national languages, Sri Rabindranath Tagore established a great education centre named Shantiniketan, and Satish Mukherjee started the Dawn Society.

Resolution on Educational Policy (1913)

This policy recommended that a university should be established for each province, the teaching activities of universities should be encouraged, and that the colleges located in mofussil towns should be developed into teaching universities in due course.

Saddler Commission (1917)

It is also popular as the Calcutta University Commission.

1. It recommended the separation of intermediate education from degree colleges and suggested a special selection committee for selection of university teachers. It is also known as the precursor to 10+2+3 system, which was started in India in 1975.
2. Calcutta University Commission suggested the setting up of Central Advisory Board of Education (CABE). CABE was set up in 1920 but was abolished in 1923 due to financial crisis.
3. Under the Government of India Act, 1919, education was made a provincial subject so as to minimise the control of central government in the education system.

Hartog Committee (1929)

The committee focused on improving the quality and standards of university-level education. It again recommended the setting up of CABE, which was again established in 1935 and has been in existence since.

Sapru Committee

The Committee appointed in 1934 by the United Province (largely present Uttar Pradesh) Government to enquire into the causes of unemployment in U.P. came to the conclusion that the system of education commonly prevalent prepared pupils only for examinations and degrees and not for any avocation in life.

Abbot-Wood Report (1937)

It proposed that English should be the medium of instruction at university level. It recommended vocational training through polytechnics and setting up of vocational teacher's training colleges.

Wardha Scheme of Education (1937)

It is also known as *Nai Talim* or Basic Education or *Buniyadi Talim (Shiksha)* or Basic Shiksha. The scheme is an outcome of the philosophy of Gandhiji. It was given a definite shape by the committee under the chairmanship of Dr Zakir Hussain who later on became the President of India. Gandhian philosophy of education is a dynamic concept. It provides for the fulfilment of men's needs at all levels—biological, social and psychological. He believed that education should bring development of the whole man. he emphasized free, compulsory, and universal education for age groups of 7 to 14 years; and also that education should be imparted in one's mother language.

Sargent Report (1944)

The Sargent Report is also called Scheme of Post War Educational Development in India. It recommended setting up of University Grants Commission (UGC) and proposed a three-year degree course.

Higher Education after Independence

Government of India took several initiatives to improve and promote higher education in the country after independence.

Radhakrishnan Commission (1948–1949)

Radhakrishnan Commission, also known as University Education Commission, suggested the integration of secondary education and higher education by setting up of UGC. It also recommended the setting up of rural universities.

Mudaliar Commission (1952–1953)

It is also popular as the Secondary Education Commission. It recommended introducing a three-year secondary and a four-year higher education system. It also advocated setting up of multipurpose schools and vocational training institutes.

Committee on Emotional Integration (1961)

It was set up under the chairmanship of Dr Sampurnanand to study the role of educational programmes for youth, in general, and students in schools and colleges, in particular, in order to strengthen the process of emotional integration.

Kothari Commission (1964–1966)

The commission was titled as 'Education and National Development' report. It is a very progressive report. It proposed a three-year degree course and a four-year honours degree course. Establishment of Indian Education Service (IES) to improve the quality of Indian higher education with emphasis on quality teaching faculties to vocationalize secondary education was recommended. It recommended that 6% of the national income should be spent on education.

Education Subject in Concurrent List (1976)

India has a federal setup and education is the concurrent responsibility of both the centre as well of states. Post-independence, education (including university education) was the responsibility of the states, while the centre was given the function of coordination and determination of standards. However, in 1976, through Entry 25 (42nd Constitutional Amendment) in the Concurrent List of the Constitution of India, the centre was also given the responsibility along with the states for all levels of education.

National Policy on Education

Kothari Commission was followed by the National Policy on Education (NPE) of 1968 and 1986. These emphasized on improving the quality of higher education level and also proposed imparting higher education by distance learning mode.

Both policies suggested that 6% of our national income should be spent on education.

Note: It is ironical that though the outlay of 6% of GDP was recommended almost 50 years ago, we are still far from reaching the mark in view of the present outlay not crossing even 4% of GDP. Education spending in India has been lower than the world average. Globally, 4.9% of GDP was spent on education in 2010, whereas India spent only 3.3% of GDP, according to World Bank data. In 2014–15 budget, the figure was 3.9%. If India has to realize its potential economic growth rate of 8–10% as envisaged in budget 2016–17, then it needs a skilled, trained, and educated workforce to make it possible.

Here, it is important to mention that the second generation economic reforms followed by market-oriented reforms started by the Government of India in 1991 also called for making changes in the education system of India.

Gnanam Committee (1993)

It recommended flexibility and autonomy for ensuring academic excellence and asked for restricting the unchecked growth of deemed universities. It emphasized the need for a National Commission on higher education and research to regulate the quality of education and to encourage research in university system.

Sam Pitroda Committee

It was set up in 2007. It is also popularly known as National Knowledge Commission (NKC). It recommended restructuring of curricula to meet the demand for multidisciplinary professionals and criteria-based resource allocation to ensure maintenance of standards and strategic preferences to promote excellence in higher education. It supported the entry of foreign universities and also favoured reducing the burden of affiliation of colleges on universities. NKC recommended increasing the number of universities to 1500 by 2015.

Yashpal Committee

It suggested scrapping of all higher education, regulatory or monitoring bodies and creation of a super regulator, that is, a seven-member Commission for Higher Education and Research (CHER). State Higher Education Councils would form the second tier of the system.

It also recommended that the deemed university status be abandoned and that all deserving deemed varsities be either converted into full-fledged universities or scrapped. The committee stressed the need for more attention to undergraduate programmes and a multidisciplinary approach to learning. Yashpal Committee also strongly recommended reducing the burden of affiliation of colleges on the universities and a GRE-like test be evolved for university education.

The recommendations of Yashpal Committee and the National Knowledge Commission emanated from the realization that fragmentation of various fields of knowledge in higher education led to inadequate growth of interdisciplinary learning.

Sharma Committee

Set up under Prof MM Sharma, it deliberated upon the development of science and technology education in India. The committee suggested establishment of Indian Institute of Science, Education, and Research (IISER). It also recommended expansion of technical education, assuring quality and providing access and affordability for technical education. The committee also recommended that ₹500 crores be spent on research in basic sciences every year by the UGC.

Dr Anil Kakodkar Committee

It was constituted to recommend strategies to improve technical education in the country. It recommended 2% budget in every institution to be earmarked for research.

K. B. Pawar Committee

Constituted by the UGC, the committee recommended four models of Public–Private Partnership (PPP) in higher education.

Regulatory and Policy Framework Structure of Higher Education in India

Education is in concurrent list where both central and state governments can legislate.

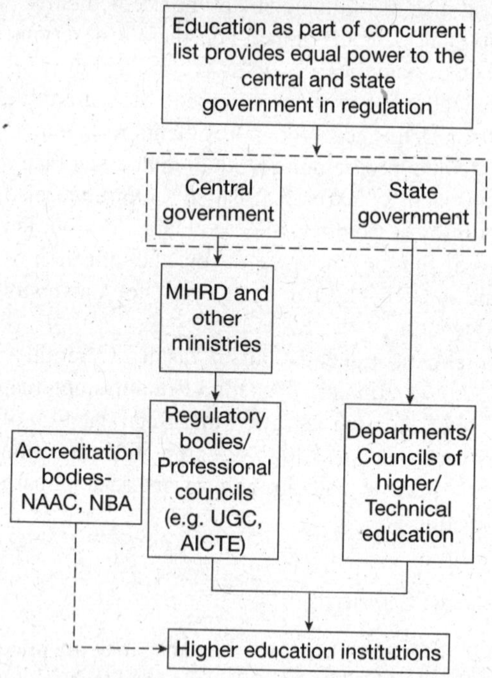

Regulatory Framework of Higher Education in India

While the centre coordinates and determines the standards in higher and technical education, school education is primarily the responsibility of the state. The key policy-making agencies for higher education are as follows:

1. *Central Government:* It lays down the National Policy on Education. It provides grants to the UGC and establishes Central Universities/Institutions of national importance in the country. It is also responsible for declaring an educational institution as 'Deemed-to-be University' on the recommendations of the UGC.
2. *State Government:* Many states have also set up state councils and advisory boards to provide guidelines for proper functioning of higher education institution in the states. State Councils for Higher Education coordinates the roles of government, universities, and apex regulatory agencies in higher education within the state.
3. *Central Advisory Board of Education (CABE)* was set up for coordination and cooperation between the union and the states in the field of education, including policy making.

Apex Level Bodies

There are eight Apex Level Bodies (Regulatory Bodies/Research Councils) under the Department of Higher Education, which are responsible for higher education in India. These bodies can be broadly divided into two categories (i) Regulatory Bodies and (ii) Research Councils.

Regulatory Bodies

There are three Regulatory Bodies—University Grants Commission, All India Council for Technical Education, and Council of Architecture—to regulate higher education in India.

University Education System in India

The word university is derived from the Latin word *Universitas*, which means specialized associations between students and teachers.

Universities are the seats of higher learning from where the society gets its leaders in Science, Arts and various other fields of national life. University education aims at providing knowledge and wisdom for developing personality.

The functions of the university mainly include providing instruction, conducting research and post-graduate studies, and giving affiliation and extension to the colleges under it.

In India, university means a university established or incorporated by or under a central act, a provincial act, or a state act and includes any such institution as may be recognized by the UGC in accordance with the regulations made under this Act.

Universities have degree-granting powers and are responsible for conducting examinations. They have autonomy in matters of fees and curriculum design. They also have affiliating powers for colleges within a particular geographical region.

On the other hand, degree-granting colleges have autonomy in admissions. However, they have to follow the fee, examination, and curriculum standards of the university they are affiliated to.

University Grants Commission

UGC governs universities in India and came into existence on 28 December 1953. It became a statutory organization established by an act of Parliament in 1956.

1. According to Section 12 of UGC Act, the main function of UGC is coordination, determination, and maintenance of standards in universities.
2. It also disburses funds within the university education system. Most importantly, it only acts as a recommendatory body since it does not have any power to establish or derecognize any university.
3. UGC consists of the Chairman, Vice-Chairman, and 10 other members appointed by the Central Government. Secretary is the Executive Head. It functions from New Delhi as well as its six regional offices located in Bangalore, Bhopal, Guwahati, Hyderabad, Kolkata, and Pune.
4. UGC also implements various schemes aimed at improving the quality of higher education like Universities with Potential for Excellence (UPE), Colleges with Potential for Excellence (CPE), Centre with Potential for Excellence and a Particular Area (CPEPA), Special Assistance Programme (SAP), Basic Scientific Research (BSR), etc.
5. Dr C. D. Deshmukh was the first Chairman of UGC.

Categorization of Universities

Universities can be set up only through legislation or the deemed route. At present, the main constituents of universities or university-level institutions are listed below.

Universities	Number
Central Universities	47
State Universities	365
Deemed Universities	122
Private Universities	269
Total Universities	803

Source: ugc.ac.in as on August 21, 2017.

In addition, there are many university level institutions.

Central Universities

A central university or a union university in India is established by Act of Parliament and are under the purview of the Department of Higher Education in the Union Human Resource Development Ministry. In general, universities in India are recognised by UGC, which draws its power from the University Grants Commission Act, 1956.

1. There are 47 central universities under the purview of MHRD. Out of them, 16 new central universities were established in 2009 by an Act of Parliament, namely, Central Universities Act, 2009.
2. IGNOU, New Delhi is funded directly by the MHRD.
3. President of India is the Visitor of all central universities. In that capacity, he nominates some members to important committees of the university for their effective functioning. He also exercises powers in various legal matters and relevant amendments.

The state/UT wise list of central universities is given below.

Arunachal Pradesh (1)

1. Rajiv Gandhi University, Itanagar (2007 - formerly Arunachal University)

Assam (2)

2. Assam University, Silchar (1994)
3. Tezpur University, Tezpur (1994)

Bihar (3)

4. Central University of South Bihar, Patna (est 2014 - territorial jurisdiction south of river Ganges in Bihar)
5. Mahatma Gandhi Central University, Patna (est 2014 - territorial jurisdiction north of river Ganges in Bihar)
6. Nalanda University, Rajgir, Nalanda (2010 - established under Central Act)

Chhattisgarh (1)

7. Guru Ghasidas Vishwavidyalaya, Bilaspur (2009, Converted from State University, originally set up in 1983)

Gujarat (1)

8. Central University of Gujarat, Gandhinagar (2009)

Haryana (1)

9. Central University of Haryana, Mahendragarh (2009)

Himachal Pradesh (1)

10. Central University of Himachal Pradesh, Dharamshala (2009)

Jammu & Kashmir (2)

11. Central of University of Kashmir, Srinagar (2009)
12. Central University of Jammu, Jammu (2011)

Jharkhand (1)

13. Central University of Jharkhand, Ranchi (2009)

Karnataka (1)

14. Central University of Karnataka, Gulbarga (2009)

Kerala (1)

15. Central University of Kerala, Kasargod (2009)

Madhya Pradesh (2)

16. Dr Harisingh Gour Vishwavidyalaya, Sagar (2009, converted from State University to Central University, originally set up in 1946)
17. Indira Gandhi National Tribal University, Amarkantak (2007)

Maharashtra (1)

18. Mahatma Gandhi Antarrashtriya Hindi Vishwavidyalaya, Wardha (1997)

Manipur (2)

19. Central Agricultural University, Imphal (1993)
20. Manipur University, Canchipur, Imphal (2005)

Meghalaya (1)

21. North Eastern Hill University, Shillong and TURA (1973)

Mizoram (1)

22. Mizoram University, Aizawl (2000)

Nagaland (1)

23. Nagaland University, Kohima (1994)

Odisha (1)

24. Central University of Orissa, Koraput (2009)

Punjab (1)

25. Central University of Punjab, Bathinda (2009)

Rajasthan (1)

26. Central University of Rajasthan, Ajmer (2009)

Sikkim (1)

27. Sikkim University, Gangtok (1997 - Dr M.S. Swaminathan, the Father of Green Revolution in India and first winner of World Food Prize, was the VC of Sikkim University)

Tamil Nadu (1)

28. Central University of Tamil Nadu, Thiruvarur (2009)

Tamil Nadu (1)

29. Indian Maritime University, Chennai (2008)

Telangana (3)

30. Hyderabad Central University, Hyderabad (1974)
31. Maulana Azad National Urdu University, Gachibowli, Hyderabad (1998)
32. The English and Foreign Languages University, Hyderabad (2007)

Tripura (1)

33. Tripura University, Agartala (2007)

Uttar Pradesh (5)

34. Aligarh Muslim University, Aligarh (Originally MAO College, was incorporated as a Central University by an Act of Parliament in 1920)

35. University of Allahabad, Allahabad (set up in 1887, it is one of the oldest universities in India)
36. Babasaheb Bhimrao Ambedkar University, Lucknow (1996)
37. Banaras Hindu University, Varanasi (1916, it is one of the oldest and largest central universities)
38. Rajiv Gandhi National Aviation University, Raebareli (2014)
39. Rani Lakshmi Bai Central Agricultural University, Jhansi (2014, under Department of Agricultural Research and Education)

Uttarakhand (1)

40. Hemwati Nandan Bahuguna Garhwal University, Srinagar (2009, converted from State University to Central University, originally set up in 1973)

West Bengal (1)

41. Vishwa Bharati, Shantiniketan (1951)

Nct Of Delhi (5)

42. University of Delhi, Delhi (1922)
43. Indira Gandhi National Open University, New Delhi (1985)
44. Jamia Millia Islamia, Jamia Nagar, New Delhi (1988)
45. Jawaharlal Nehru University, New Delhi (1969)
46. South Asian University, New Delhi (established under Central Act, sponsored by the eight Member States of the South Asian Association for Regional Cooperation (SAARC). The eight countries are Afghanistan, Bangladesh, Bhutan, India, Maldives, Nepal, Pakistan, and Sri Lanka)

Pondicherry (1)

47. Pondicherry University, Pondicherry (1985)

Note: Seven universities namely (i) Central Agricultural University, Imphal, (ii) Indira Gandhi National Open University, New Delhi, (iii) Indian Maritime University, Chennai (iv) Nalanda University, Bihar (v) Rajiv Gandhi National Aviation University, Raebareli, Uttar Pradesh, (vi) South Asian University, New Delhi and (vii) Rani Lakshmi Bai Central Agricultural University, Jhansi are not funded by UGC as these are directly funded by Government of India. Goa has no central university, as per the request of the state government.

Indian National Defence University (INDU) is a proposed university of defence of the Government of India, which will be established at Binola in Gurgaon, Haryana. The principle proposal was accepted by the Union Cabinet on 13 May 2010 and is expected to become functional by 2018–19.

State Universities

A university established or incorporated by a Provincial Act or by a State Act is called a state university.

The state universities are included in the List of 12 (B) of UGC Act, 1956 and are eligible for central assistance.

Although the development of state universities is the primary concern of state governments, development grants, including grants under special schemes, are provided to all eligible state universities. Such grants facilitate the creation, augmentation, and upgradation of infrastructural facilities that are not normally available from the state government or other sources of funds.

State universities dominate university education in India as they account for almost half the universities and also for 84% of total enrolment.

Private Universities

A university established through the state or central act by a sponsoring body, namely a society registered under the Societies Registration Act, 1860 or any other corresponding law for the time being in force, in a state or a public trust or a company registered under Section 25 of the Companies Act, 1956 is called a private university.

The private universities are competent to award degrees as specified by UGC under Section 22 of the UGC Act with the approval of the statutory councils, wherever required through their main campus.

The first private university set up in 1995 was the Sikkim Manipal University of Health, Medical and Technological Science, Gangtok.

Deemed to be University

A deemed to be university, commonly known as a deemed university, refers to a high-performing institution, as declared by the central government under Section 3 of the UGC Act, 1956.

Deemed universities can be approved only by an executive order after UGC recommendation. Although they enjoy all the powers of a university, they do not have the right to affiliate colleges.

1. Indian Institute of Science, Bangalore, and Indian Agricultural Research Institute, Delhi, were the first two institutes to be granted a deemed status. IISc was granted the status in 1958 though it was set up in the year 1908.
2. Manipal Academy of Higher Education (MAHE) was the first private institution to be declared a deemed university in 1976.

The following institutions of higher learning are few prominent examples of deemed to be university

1. National University of Educational Planning and Administration (NUEPA), New Delhi
2. Rashtriya Sanskrit Sansthan, New Delhi
3. Shri Lal Bahadur Shastri Rashtriya Sanskrit Vidyapeetha, New Delhi
4. Rashtriya Sanskrit Vidyapeetha, Tirupati
5. National Dairy Research Institute, Karnal
6. Tata Institute of Fundamental Research, Mumbai

The top ranking states in terms of total number of universities are Rajasthan, Uttar Pradesh, and Tamil Nadu.

The 11th Five year plan envisaged establishment of 14 world class central universities (renamed as innovative universities aiming at world-class standards).

Note: P.N. Tandon Committee in 2009 suggested blacklisting 44 deemed universities, saying they lacked the required quality. In 2015, UGC asked 10 deemed universities including BITS Pilani to shut their off-campus centres. In February 2016, UGC amended its regulation allowing private deemed universities to have up to six off-campuses. This ceiling won't apply in case of government-established and managed deemed universities.

Meta University and CIC Concepts

During the 12th Plan, UGC initiated a concept of Meta University. The main purpose of the Meta University is to share learning resources by different Universities by using latest technologies available in order to enable students to benefit from learning resources available in other institutions. Meta Universities represent 2nd Generation Universities, free from physical boundary conditions and able to operate in virtual space, taking advantage of the innovation and flexibility possible in such domains.

For the first time in India, University of Delhi and Jamia Millia Islamia, the two main universities of India, under the Meta University Concept have started a 2-year joint degree program 'Master of Mathematics Education' (equivalent to M.Sc Mathematics Education) from the academic session 2015.

Cluster Innovation Centre (CIC) is a Government of India funded institute established under the aegis of the University of Delhi. It was founded in 2011 and introduced Innovation as a credit-based course for the first time in India.

Other Higher Level Institutions

Inter-University Centres (IUCs)

UGC has established autonomous IUCs within the university system with an objective to provide common, advanced, centralized facilities, and services for universities, in order to offer the best expertise in each field to teachers and researchers across the country.

Nuclear Science Centre at New Delhi (now called Inter University Accelerator Centre) was the first such research centre established in 1994.

At present, there are six IUCs functioning within the university system. These are as follows:

1. Inter-University Accelerator Centre (IUAC), New Delhi
2. Inter-University Centre for Astronomy and Astro-Physics (IUCAA), Pune

3. UGC-DAE Consortium for Scientific Research (UGC-DAECSR), Indore
4. Information and Library Network (INFLIBNET), Ahmedabad
5. Consortium for Educational Communication (CEC), New Delhi.
6. National Assessment and Accreditation Council (NAAC), Bangalore

Association of Indian Universities

Association of Indian Universities (AIU) is a forum for administrators and academicians of member universities to exchange views and discuss matters of common concern. The idea originated during Vice Chancellors' Conference at Shimla in 1924 that was convened by Lord Reading.

It got its present name in 1973. The members include traditional universities, open universities, professional universities, institutes of national importance, and deemed to be universities. In addition, there is a provision of granting associate membership to universities of neighbouring countries.

It brings out a number of useful publications, including the Universities Handbook, research papers, and a weekly journal titled University News.

Institutions of National Importance

An institution is established by an act of Parliament and is declared as an Institution of National Importance, such as IITs and IIMs among others. Some institutions are established or incorporated by the State Legislature Act.

Research Councils

1. Indian Council of Social Science Research (ICSSR), New Delhi.
2. Indian Council of Philosophical Research (ICPR), New Delhi.
3. Centre for Studies in Civilizations, Project of History of Indian Science, Philosophy, and Culture (PHISPC)
4. Indian Council of Historical Research (ICHR), Guwahati.
5. National Council of Rural Institutes (NCRI), Hyderabad.

Rashtriya Uchchatar Shiksha Abhiyan (RUSA)

Rashtriya Uchchatar Shiksha Abhiyan is a Centrally Sponsored Scheme (CSS), which was launched in 2013. It aims at providing strategic funding to eligible state higher educational institutions. The central funding (in the ratio of 65:35 for general category states and 90:10 for special category states) would be norm based and outcome dependent. The funding would flow from the central ministry through the state governments/ UTs to the State Higher Education Councils before reaching the identified institutions. The funding to the states would be made on the basis of critical appraisal of State Higher Education Plans, which would describe each state's strategy to address issues of equity, access, and excellence in higher education.

RUSA is implemented and monitored through an institutional structure comprising the National Mission Authority, Project Approval Board, and the National Project Directorate at the centre, and the State Higher Education Council and State Project Directorate at the state level.

RUSA programme also seeks enhancement of intake capacity of the existing institutions of higher education. It is designed on the lines of the Sarva Shiksha Abhiyan with an aim to increase Gross Enrolment Ratio to 25%, which at present is just 17%. It proposes to set up 800 new colleges under central universities (40 central universities covering 20 colleges each), 400 new college cluster universities, and a set of other new universities under various categories.

According to UGC sources, promotion of evening colleges and universities would not only help in enhancing enrolment but would also provide opportunities to working class for improving their academic and professional qualifications. This would help in making optimum use of the existing infrastructure that remains unused for an average of 16–18 hours a day. The shift system of courses in colleges would be effectively supported by separate qualified teachers.

Technical Education Scenario in India

In India, technical education covers programmes in engineering, technology, management, architecture, town planning, pharmacy, applied arts and crafts, and hotel management and catering technology.

1. The first engineering college was established in Uttar Pradesh in 1847 for training of civil engineers at Roorkee. It conferred diplomas that were considered to be equivalent to degrees.
2. Three engineering colleges were opened by about 1856 in three presidencies, namely Calcutta, Bombay, and Madras.
3. In Bengal, the leaders of the Swadeshi Movement tried to start many institutions; however, only College of Engineering and Technology at Jadavpur survived.
4. Many technical courses were started at the University of Banaras with great efforts put by Pandit Madan Mohan Malaviya (1917).
5. Many other courses were also started at the Bengal Engineering College at Shibpur in the 1930s.
6. A number of engineering colleges started since 15 August 1947. It was due to the realization that India had to become a great industrial country and would require a large number of engineers than could be supplied by the older institutions.

All India Council for Technical Education

All India Council for Technical Education (AICTE) governs technical education in India. It was set up in 1945 as an advisory body and later on in 1987, was given a statutory status by an act of Parliament. AICTE grants approval for starting new technical institutions, for the introduction of new courses, and for variation in intake capacity in technical institutions.

The AICTE is headquartered in New Delhi and has seven regional offices located at Kolkata, Chennai, Kanpur, Mumbai, Chandigarh, Bhopal, and Bangalore. A new regional office at Hyderabad has been set up and is yet to be operational.

The council discharges its functions through an executive committee.

It is responsible for the maintenance of standards of technical education, which currently includes education research and training in:

1. Engineering
2. Technology including MCA
3. Architecture
4. Town planning
5. Management
6. Pharmacy
7. Hotel management and catering technology
8. Applied arts and crafts

Council of Architecture

The Council of Architecture (COA) was constituted by the Government of India under the provisions of the Architects Act, 1972, enacted by the Parliament which came into force on 1 September 1972. The Act provides for registration of architects and matters connected therewith.

MHRD-funded Institutions

Technical education system in the country can be broadly classified into three categories, namely central government-funded institutions, state government or state-funded institutions, and self-financed institutions. The centrally funded institution of technical and science education are as follows:

IITs	15	NITs	30
IIMs	13	IIITs	4
IISc, Bengaluru	1	NITTTRs	4
IISERs	5	Others	9

Indian Institute of Technology

These are the apex institutions for engineering education and research. At present, there are 15 Indian Institute of Technology (IITs).

IIT-Kharagpur (1951), IIT-Bombay (set up in 1958 with help from USSR and UNESCO),

IIT-Madras (1959), IIT-Delhi (1963) and IIT-Guwahati (1994) are governed by the Institutes of Technology Act, 1961 which has declared them as Institutions of National Importance.

In 2008, the government approved setting up of eight new IITs in Bihar (Patna), Rajasthan (Jodhpur), Odisha (Bhubaneswar), Andhra Pradesh (Hyderabad), Gujarat (Gandhinagar), Madhya Pradesh (Indore), Himachal Pradesh (Mandi), and Punjab (Ropar).

As part of the National Plan of Science and Technology, five Centres of Advanced Study and Research have been set up in the IITs in Energy Studies (Delhi), Material Science (Kanpur), Cryogenic Engineering (Kharagpur), Ocean Engineering (Madras), and Resource Engineering (Bombay).

Indian Institute of Management

Indian Institute of Management (IIMs) located at Ahmedabad, Kolkata, Bangalore, Lucknow, Indore, Kozhikode, and Shillong are institutions of excellence, established with the objectives of imparting high-quality management education and training, conducting research, and providing consultancy services in the field of management to various sectors of the Indian economy. All the IIMs are registered societies governed by their respective Board of Governors. IIM-Ahmedabad was set up in 1961.

During the 11th Five Year Plan, six new IIMs have been set up in Haryana (Rohtak), Chhattisgarh (Raipur), Jharkhand (Ranchi), Tamil Nadu (Tiruchirappalli, Uttarakhand (Kashipur), and Rajasthan (Udaipur) in 2010.

Indian Institute of Science (IISc), Bangalore

Indian Institute of Science (IISc), Bangaluru, was started in 1909 through the pioneering vision of J.N. Tata. The Institute has been engaged in higher learning and advanced research in the fields of science and engineering. As discussed earlier, IISc was the first deemed university in India.

Five new institutions devoted to science education and research have been set up as Indian Institutes of Science Education and Research (IISER) broadly on the pattern of IISc, Bangalore. These have been started at Kolkata, Pune, Mohali, Bhopal, and Thiruvananthapuram.

National Institute of Technology

On recommendations of Engineering Personnel Committee set up by the Planning Commission in 1955, eight Regional Engineering Colleges (two each in east, west, north, and south) were set up in early sixties. Gradually, the number increased to 17.

In 2003, Regional Engineering Colleges (RECs) were rechristened as National Institute of Technology (NITs) and taken over as fully-funded institutes of the central government. They were granted a deemed university status. Over a period, the total number of NITs has gone up to 30.

Indian Institute of Information Technology (IIITs)

IIITs were specifically set up to meet the man-power requirements of the IT sector. Central government established four IIITs at Allahabad, Gwalior, Jabalpur, and Kanchipuram. These institutions are meant to provide undergraduate as well as postgraduate education. The 11th Five Year Plan envisaged the establishment of 20 more IIITs in the country in the PPP mode.

List of IIITs

1. Indian Institute of Information Technology, Allahabad
2. Atal Bihari Vajpayee-Indian Institute of Information Technology and Management (ABV-IIITM), Gwalior
3. Pandit Dwarka Prasad Mishra-Indian Institute of Information, Technology, Design and Manufacturing (IIIT-D and M), Jabalpur
4. Indian Institute of Information Technology, Design and Manufacturing (IIIT-D and M), Kanchipuram

National Institute of Technical Teachers' Training and Research (NITTTRs)

Four National Institute of Technical Teachers' Training and Research (NITTTRs) located at

Bhopal, Chandigarh, Chennai, and Kolkata were established in mid-1960s for the training of polytechnic teachers to undertake activities in the areas of education, planning, and management.

Recent Government Initiatives

The present government aims at creating more institutions of higher learning and reducing the regional disparities as far as elite institutions of advanced studies are concerned. With this objective, the government has announced new institutes of excellence: two IIMs will come up in Jammu and Kashmir and Andhra Pradesh. One IIT will come up in Karnataka, and the second will be formed by upgrading the Indian School of Mines, Dhanbad, in Jharkhand to an IIT.

The Government has announced the setting up of new National Institutes of Pharmaceutical Education and Research (NIPERs) in Maharashtra, Rajasthan, and Jharkhand. Institutes of Sciences and Educational Research are to be set up at Odisha and Nagaland.

A Centre for Film Production, Animation and Gaming will be set up in Arunachal Pradesh. Apprenticeship Training Institutes for Women would come up in Haryana and Uttarakhand.

Externally Aided Projects in Technical Education

1. *Technical Education Quality Improvement Programme (TEQIP):* It was launched by MHRD in 2002 to upscale and support the ongoing efforts in improving the quality of technical education. TEQIP Phase I (2003–09) and TEQUIP Phase II were implemented with the assistance of World Bank.
2. *Technician Education Project-III:* It was launched with the help of World Bank, for the upgradation of polytechnics in the country.

Other Regulators in Higher Education: Specialized Professional Bodies

The professional regulatory bodies grant approval for establishment of institutes and determine standards for the same. Some of the specialized professional bodies are as follows:

1. Medical Council of India
2. Dental Council of India
3. India Nursing Council
4. Council of Architecture
5. Bar Council of India
6. Pharmacy Council of India
7. Indian Council of Agricultural Research (ICAR)
8. Rehabilitation Council of India
9. Central Council of Homeopathy
10. Central Council of Indian Medicine
11. Veterinary Council of India

Thus, a significant part of the Indian higher education system is regulated; however, there are certain areas that are not.

Language Universities

India has six language universities, out of which three are deemed to be universities and three are central universities. The deemed to be universities are for promotion of Sanskrit and the three central universities are, one each, for the promotion of English and foreign language, Hindi, and Urdu.

UGC is funding these language universities.

1. Shri Lal Bahadur Shastri Rashtriya Sanskrit Vidyapeetha, New Delhi
2. Rashtriya Sanskrit Vidyapeetha, Tirupati
3. English and Foreign Languages University, Hyderabad
4. Mahatma Gandhi Antarrashtriya Hindi Vishwavidyalaya, Wardha
5. Maulana Azad National Urdu University, Hyderabad
6. Rashtriya Sanskrit Sansthan, New Delhi

Classical Languages

Sanskrit, Tamil, Telugu, Kannada, Malayalam, and Odia are the six classical languages in India. Tamil was the first language to be assigned the status of classical language in 2004. Odia was the last one to be assigned the status in February 2014, but it is the first language from the Indo-Aryan linguistic group to be assigned the status.

Sahitya Academy's Expert Committee gave the following four criteria for a classical language:

1. The high antiquity of early texts/recorded history of over 1500 to 2000 years.
2. A body of ancient literature/texts that is considered a valuable heritage by generations of speakers.
3. The literary tradition should be original and not borrowed from another speech community.
4. The classical language and literature should be distinct from the modern and there may also be a discontinuity between the classical language and its later forms of offshoots.

The proposals are made by Ministry of Culture. Once a language is declared classical, it gets financial assistance for setting up a centre of excellence for the study of that language and also opens up an avenue for two major awards for scholars of eminence. Besides, the UGC can be requested to create—to begin with at least in Central Universities—a certain number of professional chairs for classical languages for scholars of eminence in that language.

The fathers of the Constitution conferred Sanskrit the special status by Article 351 as it was the primary source language for many languages including Hindi

Five languages in the world, namely Chinese, Sanskrit, Arabic, Greek, and Latin have been assigned the status of Classical languages.

Few Important Offices or Agencies in Higher Education

Subordinate Offices Under the Bureau of Language Education

1. *Central Hindi Directorate*, New Delhi, was set up in the year 1960 to develop Hindi as a link language throughout India, in pursuance of Article 351 of the Constitution of India. Its regional offices are located in Chennai, Kolkata, Hyderabad, and Guwahati.
2. *Commission for Scientific and Technical Terminology* was constituted to evolve and define scientific and technical terms in Hindi and in all Indian languages.
3. *Central Institute of Indian Languages*, Mysore, set up in 1969 to help in evolving and implementing the language policy of Government of India and to coordinate the development of Indian languages by conducting research in areas of language analysis, language pedagogy, language technology, and language use in the society.
4. *Regional Language Centres (RLC)* located at Bhubaneswar, Pune, Mysore, Patiala, Guwahati, Solan, and Lucknow work for the implementation of the three-language formula of the government and for preparation of instructional materials.
5. *National Testing Service (NTS)* was approved by the MHRD in 2006–2007 and implemented by the Centre of Testing and Evaluation (CT and E) under Central Institute of Indian Languages (CIIL), Mysore.
6. *Linguistic Data Consortium for Indian Languages (LDC-IL)*, a central sector scheme, was implemented by the Central Institute of Indian Languages (CIIL), Mysore from the financial year 2007–2008.
7. *National Translation Mission:* On the basis of recommendations of the National Knowledge Commission, MHRD set up the National Translation Mission (NTM) with the main objective of functioning as a clearing house for all translation activities, both theoretical and practical, in as many Indian languages as possible. Central Institute of Indian Languages (CIIL), Mysore is the nodal organization for operation of the scheme.
8. *National Book Trust*, was established in 1957 with the objective of promoting a culture of reading in the society by publishing good literature at affordable price in all major Indian languages including English and

by undertaking book promotion activities such as organization of seminars, workshops, book fairs, and book exhibitions in India and abroad.

Accreditation in Higher Education

Higher education sector ensures quality of the educational process with the help of accreditation agencies established for the purpose.

National Assessment and Accreditation Council (NAAC)

NAAC is an autonomous body established in 1994 by the UGC with its headquarters in Bangalore. It was established as per recommendations of NPE (1986).

The prime function of NAAC is to assess and accredit institutions of higher learning, universities and colleges or their departments, schools, institutions, programmes etc.

It regularly publishes manuals and promotion materials for assessment and accreditation.

National Board of Accreditation (NBA)

Set up in 1994, NBA is an autonomous body established by AICTE to conduct periodical evaluation of technical courses offered in India. It has the authority to recognize or derecognize institutions or programmes. The accreditation process is not linked to funding.

Accreditation Board (AB)

AB was set up by Indian Council of Agricultural Research in 1996 with a mandate to accredit agricultural institutions. Accreditation done by AB is generally valid for a period between 5–10 years and is linked to funding year wise number of institutions accredited

It is important to note that although accreditation is voluntary in India, some states such as Karnataka and Tamil Nadu have made it mandatory, especially for professional institutions. Despite this, only very few institutions are accredited. In fact, only 36% engineering and 10% management programs have been accredited by NBA.

Government is in the process of creating a single independent body to regulate various aspects of higher education. The same should be done at the earliest. However, due care needs to be taken to ensure that it gets adequate independence and autonomy.

Open and Distance Education

Defining Distance Education

Today, two terms that are being used almost interchangeably are 'Open Learning' and 'Distance Education', and they are often combined to be known as Open and Distance Learning (ODL). Open learning is a philosophy, whereas distance education is the mode used for translating it into reality as the two are complementary to each other.

Distance education (DE) is an umbrella term that describes all the teaching and learning arrangements in which the learner and the teacher are separated by space and time. In fact, it is a mode of delivering education and instruction to learners who are not physically present in a traditional classroom setting. Transaction of the curriculum is effected by means of specially prepared materials [self-study (learning) materials] which are delivered to the learners at their doorstep through various media such as print, television, radio, satellite, audio/video tapes, CD-ROMs, Internet, etc. In addition, a technological medium replaces the interpersonal communication of conventional classroom-based education that takes place between the teacher and the learners. Communication between the institution, teacher, and learners is mainly through electronic media (telephone, interactive radio counselling, teleconferencing, videoconferencing, chat sessions, email, website, etc.) and also through postal correspondence and limited face-to-face contact sessions held at Study Centres that are set up by the DE institutions as close to the learners' homes as possible.

Open learning, covers a wide range of innovations and reforms in the educational sector that advocates flexibility to the learner with regard to entry and exit, pace and place of study, method of study, choice and combination of courses; assessment, and course completion. The lesser the restrictions, the higher the degree of openness. The open learning system aims to redress

National Institutional Ranking Framework - IInd List - released on April 3rd, 2017

National Institutional Ranking Framework (NIRF) has been approved by the MHRD and launched on 29 September 2015. The first list was released in April 2016. This framework outlines a methodology to rank institutions across the country. The methodology draws from the overall recommendations and broad understanding arrived at by the Core Committee set up by MHRD, to identify the broad parameters for ranking various universities and institutions.

The following five parameters (weightages in brackets) were broadly considered:

1. Teaching, and Learning (0.30)
2. Research and professional practices (0.30)
3. Graduation outcomes (0.20)
4. Outreach and inclusivity (0.10)
5. Perception (0.10)

The 'India Rankings 2017' were put together with the participation of around 2800 private and public institutions. They were ranked by National Bureau of Accreditation (NBA). All institutions were judged based on self-disclosure.of information.

Although the ranking frameworks are similar, the exact methodologies are domain specific. Ranking methods have been worked out for these categories - (1) Overall (2) Universities (3) Colleges, (4) Engineering (5) Management and (6)Pharmaceuticals.

Top 10 Institutes - Overall

1. Indian Institute of Science, Bengaluru
2. Indian Institute of Technology, Chennai
3. Indian Institute of Technology, Mumbai
4. Indian Institute of Technology Kharagpur
5. Indian Institute of Technology New Delhi
6. Jawaharlal Nehru University, Delhi
7. Indian Institute of Technology Kanpur
8. Indian Institute of Technology, Guwahati
9. Indian Institute of Technology Roorkee
10. Banaras Hindu University, Varanasi

Top 10 Universities in India

1. Indian Institute of Science, Bangalore
2. Jawaharlal Nehru University, New Delhi
3. Banaras Hindu University, Varanasi
4. Jawaharlal Centre For Advanced Scientific Research, Bengaluru
5. Jadavpur University
6. Anna University
7. University of Hyderabad
8. University of Delhi
9. Amrita Vishwa Vidyapeetham
10. Savitribai Phule Pune University

Top 5 Management Institutes in India

1. Indian Institute of Management, Ahmedabad
2. Indian Institute of Management, Bangalore
3. Indian Institute of Management, Calcutta
4. Indian Institutes of Management, Lucknow
5. Indian Institute of Management, Kazhikode

Top Five Colleges in India

1. Miranda House, New Delhi
2. Loyola College, Chennai
3. Shri Ram College of Commerce,New Delhi
4. Bishop Heber College, Tiruchirapalli
5. Atma Ram Sanatan Dharma College, New Delhi

Top 5 Pharmaceutical Institutes in India

1. Jamia Hamdard, Delhi
2. National Institute of Pharmaceutical Education and Research, Mohali
3. University Institute of Pharmaceutical Sciences, Chandigarh
4. Institute of Chemical Technology, Mumbai
5. National Institute of Pharmaceutical Education and Research, Hyderabad

The top Five Engineering Colleges in India are all IITs - Chennai, Mumbai, Kharagpur, Delhi, Kanpur.

The top five Management Institutes are IIMs - Ahmedabad, Bengaluru, Kolkata, Lucknow and Kozikhode

source- www.nirfindia.org

social or educational inequality and to offer opportunities not provided by conventional colleges or universities. Educational opportunities are planned deliberately so that access to education is available to larger sections of the society.

Therefore, ODL is a term that accepts the philosophy of 'openness' and uses the 'distance mode' of learning.

ODL occupies a special place in the Indian higher education system because of its major contribution in enhancing the Gross Enrollment Ratio and democratization of higher education to large segments of the Indian population particularly to reach out to the unreached and to meet the demands of lifelong learning, which has become more of a necessity in the knowledge society.

The major objectives of DE system are as follows:

1. To democratize higher education to large segments of the population, in particular to the disadvantaged groups such as those living in remote and rural areas, working people, women, etc.
2. To provide an innovative system of university-level education, which is both flexible and open in terms of methods and pace of learning, combination of courses, eligibility for enrollment, age of entry, conduct of examination, and implementation of the programmes of study;
3. To provide an opportunity for upgradation of skills and qualifications;
4. To develop education as a lifelong activity to enable persons to update their knowledge or acquire knowledge in new areas.

India has one of the largest DE systems in the world, second only to China. There are **following types** of institutions offering DE.

1. National Open University
2. State Open Universities
3. Distance Education Institutions (DEIs) at:
   (a) Institutions of National Importance
   (b) Central Universities
   (c) State Universities
   (d) Deemed to be Universities
   (e) State Private Universities
4. DEIs at Stand alone Institutions
   (a) Professional Associations
   (b) Government Institutions
   (c) Private institutions

Historical Developments in Distance Education in India

The Expert Committee under the chairmanship of Dr D.S. Kothari in 1960s recommended the institution of correspondence courses in view of the greater flexibility, economic viability, and innovative methods of imparting education. The committee also suggested that correspondence courses in India should be administered by the universities only, and in the first instance, the initiative was done in the University of Delhi as a pilot project.

- Hence, in 1962, the University of Delhi's School of Correspondence Courses and Continuing Education was started. Subsequently, the Education Commission (1964–66), under the chairmanship of Dr. D.S. Kothari, also perceived correspondence education as an answer to the increasing pressure of numbers as well as the growing financial pressures on the universities.
- The next decade, that is, the 1970s, saw the growth and spread of the correspondence education system in India, by more conventional universities opening Correspondence Course Institutes (subsequently renamed as Directorates of Distance Education/Centres of Distance Education).
- The opportunity of access, affordability, and convenience offered by the DE system contributed to its increasing popularity and growth. However, again the DE system was plagued by the rigidities of the conventional system. The only flexibility was with regard to the larger number of seats. Education was still out of reach of the marginalized and the disadvantaged. It was realized that unless we open

educational opportunities to the deprived, unless we remove the structural rigidities in our educational system, and unless we integrate the educational system, with developments in communication technology, we cannot and will not make headway in realizing the uphill task of educating majority of the people and of catering to the diverse types of education that a modern society demands.

- Against this background, the government introduced the OUS system in the 1980s, with the objective to further democratize opportunities for higher education to large segment of the Indian population, particularly for those whom access was difficult or impossible such as those living in remote and rural areas, working people, women, and other adults who wish to acquire and upgrade their knowledge and skills through studies in various fields.
- The Ministry of Human Resource Development, in its National Policy on Education (NPE) 1986, gave prominence to an OU system as a means to 'augment opportunities for higher education and as an instrument of democratizing education'. Clearly, the vision was that OUs would be different from conventional universities.
- Therefore, a new chapter in DE system began with the establishment of Dr B.R. Ambedkar Open University in Hyderabad in 1982, followed by the establishment of Indira Gandhi National Open University at the national level by the Parliament of India in 1985. The idea was accepted by many states, and 1987 saw the emergence of two more Open Universities, namely Nalanda Open University (NOU) in Patna, Bihar, and Vardhman Mahaveer Open University (VMOU) in Kota, Rajasthan. Subsequently, Yashwantrao Chavan Maharashtra Open University (YCMOU) in Nashik, Maharashtra, was established in 1989.
- The major responsibility for the promotion and coordination of Open and DE was bestowed by the Parliament on the Indira Gandhi National Open University (IGNOU), instead of the UGC, which the statutory authority for regulating higher education India. Therefore, IGNOU became a unique institution as it was entrusted with a dual role of functioning like an Open University by offering programmes of education and training through distance mode and also acting as the promoter and coordinator of the Open and Distance Education system in the country and determining standards in such systems. To fulfil this particular mandate, the Distance Education Council (DEC) was set up by IGNOU in 1991 as a statutory mechanism under IGNOU Act, which became operational in February 1992. The DEC functioned within the broad framework and the policies laid down by the Board of Management of IGNOU while enjoying a significant measure of autonomy in its operations.
- As per the mandate of the DEC and the NPE 1986, which was revised in 1992, the DEC started interacting with the state governments for establishing the SOUs in the respective states. As a result of DEC initiatives, several state governments established open universities. As emphasized in the NPE of 1986 and subsequently in the Programme of Action in 1992, the OUs adopted a radically different approach to reach the disadvantaged by adopting a variety of media and delivery channels for dissemination of information and knowledge. As a result of this, they have been able to make a definite impact on society and more Indians have access to higher education than ever before.
- The DEC took several initiatives for promotion, coordination, and maintenance of standards of open and distance education system in the country. DEC has developed guidelines for regulating the establishment and operation of ODL institutions in the country.
- In August 2010, the Ministry of Human Resource Development constituted a Committee under the chairmanship of Prof. Madhava Menon in respect of regulation of standards of education imparted through distance mode.
- The Ministry of Human Resource Development accepted the Madhava Menon Committee's report and its recommendations for the creation of a new regulatory body for ODL

system, that is, the Distance Education Council of India (DECI). The Madhava Menon Committee also decided that as an interim measure, the DEC of IGNOU may be shifted to UGC.

- Subsequently, the MHRD, in an order dated 29 December 2012, transferred the regulatory authority of distance education from IGNOU to UGC, and UGC manages this function through Distance Education Bureau. This is an interim measure till such time an independent body, namely Distance Education Council of India, is created by the Parliament.

Indira Gandhi National Open University (IGNOU)

IGNOU was established in 1985 by an act of Parliament with dual responsibilities of (i) enhancing access and equity to higher education through distance mode and (ii) promoting, coordinating, and determining standards in open learning and distance education systems. Since then, IGNOU has undergone rapid expansion and emerged as an international institution in the field of open and distance learning.

IGNOU practices a flexible and open system of education with regard to methods and places of learning, combination of courses and eligibility for enrolment, age for entry and methods of evaluation, and so on. The university has adopted an integrated strategy for imparting instruction. This consists of providing print materials, audio–video, tapes, broadcast on radio and educational TV channels, teleconferencing, video conferencing and also face-to-face counselling, at its study centres located throughout the country. The university has adopted the method of continuous assessment and term-end examination for evaluation of performance of its students enrolled in various subjects.

About 10% of the Annual Plan Budget is used to extensively earmark the development of north-east region.

The university has established eight regional centres in the north-east region. The university has developed a number of programmes for women, and special study centres were established in the backward areas and districts with low female literacy rate.

IGNOU makes use of Information and Communication Technologies extensively for imparting education. In addition to self-instructional printed materials, the university utilizes audio–video programme tapes, teleconferencing, Gyan Vani (FM radio), Gyan Darshan (educational TV channels), and computer networks for imparting instructions. IGNOU has a large number of programmes, ranging from purely academic to technical, professional, and vocational at various levels leading to awarding of competency certificates, diplomas, bachelor's, master's, and doctor's degree to successful candidates. Many of these programmes are modular in nature.

International Activities

Besides presence in many countries, IGNOU is offering distance education programmes in collaboration with UNESCO and International Institute for Capacity Building in many parts of Africa. IGNOU plays an active role in SAARC consortium for Open and Distance Learning (SACODiL) and Global Mega Universities Network (GMUNET).

Sakshat

This one-stop education portal was launched on 30 October 2006 to facilitate lifelong learning for students, teachers, and employees or for those in pursuit of knowledge, free of cost. The content development task for Sakshat was looked after by the Content Advisory Committee (CAC). National Knowledge Network (NKN) interconnects all universities, libraries, laboratories, hospitals, and agricultural institutions for sharing data and computing resources across the country over a high-speed information network having gigabyte capabilities.

State Open Universities

Presently there are 13 state open universities in India, which are single-mode institutions. This means they provide education only in the distance mode. These universities cater to people who are unable to pursue regular courses due to various reasons. The list of the 13 SOUs is as follows:

1. Dr B. R. Ambedkar Open University, Hyderabad
2. Vardhman Mahaveer Open University, Kota, Rajasthan
3. Nalanda Open University, Patna, Bihar
4. Yashwantrao Chavan Maharashtra Open University, Nashik, Maharashtra
5. Madhya Pradesh Bhoj Open University, Bhopal, Madhya Pradesh
6. Dr Babasaheb Ambedkar Open University, Ahmedabad, Gujarat
7. Karnataka State Open University, Mysore, Karnataka
8. Netaji Subhas Open University, Kolkata
9. U.P. Rajarshi Tandon Open University, Allahabad
10. Tamil Nadu Open University, Chennai, Tamil Nadu
11. Pt. Sunderlal Sharma Open University, Bilaspur, Chhattisgarh
12. Uttarakhand Open University, Haldwani, Uttarakhand
13. Krishna Kanta Handique State Open University, Guwahati

Commonwealth of Learning

The Commonwealth of Learning (COL) is an intergovernmental organisation established by the Commonwealth countries in 1988 to encourage the development and sharing of open learning and distance education knowledge, resources, and technologies.

COL was hosted in Canada by the Government of Canada. The major voluntary contributors—currently Canada, India, New Zealand, Nigeria, South Africa, and the United Kingdom—are each entitled to seats on COL's Board of Governors. The following Indian organisations are partners of COL for different purposes:

1. Indira Gandhi National Open University
2. National Institute of Open Schooling
3. National Assessment and Accreditation Council

Value Education

From a broader perspective, the aim of value education is linked with the fundamental question of what education itself is meant for.

1. *Individual's perspective:* To enable students to achieve personal fulfilment for success in life and work.
2. *Societal perspective:* Education aims to prepare the youth to contribute to society, nation, and the world.

Plato wrote in The Republic, "The mark of an educated person is the willingness to use one's knowledge and skills to solve the problems of society.

Key Developments in Value Education

1. *National Commission of Secondary Education (1952–1953)* emphasized character building as the defining goal of education.
2. *University Education Commission (1962)* noted, 'If we exclude spiritual training in our institutions, we would be untrue to our whole historical development'.
3. *Education Commission of 1964–1966* put the spotlight on education and national development. Agreeing with the Sri Prakasa Committee Report 1959, it recommended direct moral instruction for which one or two periods a week should be set aside in the school time table.
4. *NPE (1986)* advocated turning education into a forceful tool for the cultivation of social and moral values. Education should foster universal and eternal values, oriented toward the unity and integration of our people.

5. *NPE—Programme of Action (1992)* tried to integrate the various components of value education into the curriculum at all stages of school education, including the secondary stage.
6. *Chavan's Committee Report (1999)* provided impetus to resume work on value orientation of education.
7. *The National Curriculum Framework for School Education (2000)* advanced a plea to integrate value education into the curriculum.
8. *National Curriculum Framework (2005)* articulates the need to reaffirm our commitment to the concept of equality amidst diversity, mutual interdependence of humans to promote values that foster peace, humaneness, and tolerance in a multicultural society. The NCF, 2005 particularly emphasizes education for peace as one of the national and global concerns.

Main Issues behind the Need for Imparting Value Education

Tradition versus Modernity

Developing societies, such as India, face a conflict between tradition and modernization. It is important to make young learners develop attitudes where they do not see everything in tradition as bad or everything in modernization as good. There are many things positive about our traditional culture, which needs to be appreciated and understood such as tolerance of dissonance, harmony rather than control over environment, collectivism and self-definition in a social context emphasizing modesty, cooperation, duty, acceptance, and so on.

Globalization

Globalization signifies an omnipresent culture. Societies have become less and less monocultural. Consequently, the pluricultural environment in which we live now is more complex and multiple with different cultures developing in such a way that it is no longer possible to think of adapting to a homogeneous environment.

Diversity

India is a multilingual, multicultural, and multireligious country. Universality and diversity may seem incompatible, but both have to co-exist in a democratic and diverse society such as ours, where values of democracy prevail along with the values of differences that are also fully recognized and respected.

Inclusivity

A healthy, happy society is one in which all its members feel included and do not feel excluded from the processes of the society because of their colour, culture, caste, religion, gender, or community.

Environment

Making children sensitive to the environment and the need for its protection is an immediate social concern. The reckless exploitation of environment, depletion of ozone layer, global warming, industrial pollution, deforestation, and soil erosion are few problems faced by humanity.

Exploding World of Science and Technology

It is very clear that the coming decades are going to see a greater explosion of science and technology, while we are still trying to cope with the present challenges of new technology. It has many good and bad unintended consequences. How science and technology are to be used is a question of values. Application of science and technology in a more humane and rationale way is related to moral and ethical responsibility.

Mass and Social Media

A major ubiquitous aspect of contemporary society is the intrusion of mass media into the day-to-day life of all societies. The values and attitudes that get transmitted, are rather contrary to the values desired by the family, society, or school. Propagating myths and derogatory images of women, for example, is likely to make the young learner grow up with prejudices that are injurious to women and society, rather than learning that all human beings are equal.

Values enshrined in our constitution such as justice, liberty, equality, and fundamental duties have been discussed in the later sections.

Key Trends in Higher Education System in India

1. General courses (arts, science, and commerce) account for majority (around 80%) of student enrolments. Engineering has increasingly strengthened its position as the most highly preferred professional course.
2. Degree-granting courses have seen greater enrolment vis-à-vis diploma and certificate courses; however, the relative enrolment of students in postgraduate programmes has declined as compared to enrolment in undergraduate courses.
3. The share of unaided private higher education institutions in the country has grown significantly in the last few years. The percentage of students in unaided private higher education institutions has also increased considerably.
4. There has been a rapid growth in the number of professional private higher education institutions. This growth is reflected in the dominant share of unaided private higher education institutions in professional courses.

All India Survey on Higher Education (AISHE)

To portray the status of higher education in the country, Ministry of Human Resource Development has endeavoured to conduct an annual web-based All India Survey on Higher Education (AISHE) since 2010–11. The survey covers all the institutions in the country engaged in imparting of higher education. Data are being collected on several parameters such as teachers, student enrolment, programmes, examination results, education finance, and infrastructure. Indicators of educational development such as Institution Density, Gross Enrolment Ratio, Pupil–teacher ratio, Gender Parity Index, and Per Student Expenditure will also be calculated from the data collected through AISHE. These are useful in making informed policy decisions and research for development of education sector.

The major findings of the AISHE 2014–15 and earlier surveys are as follows:

1. Increase in overall enrolment in higher education from 27.5 million in 2010–11 to 33.3 million in 2014–15.
2. Improvement in Gross Enrolment Ratio, which is a ratio of enrolment in higher education to population in the eligible age group (18–23 years), from 19.4% in 2010–11 to 23.6% in 2014–15.

   The target of 30 per cent GER by 2020 seems achievable, though it is very low in comparison to USA where GER is 84%.
3. Gender Parity Index (GPI), a ratio of proportional representation of female and male, has marginally improved from 0.86 to 0.93 in the corresponding period.

   GPI in higher education is calculated for 18–23 years of age group. The ratio of female to male in higher education measures progress towards gender equity and the level of learning opportunities available for women in relation to those available to men. It also serves as a significant indicator of the empowerment of women in the society. The data provides state-wise gender parity index for all categories, including SC and ST.
4. Number of institutions of higher education listed on AISHE portal has also increased significantly—universities from 621 to 757 and colleges from 32, 974 to 38,056 during the same period.
5. Eleven universities were exclusively started for women: 3 in Rajasthan, 2 in Tamil Nadu, and 1 each in Andhra Pradesh, Delhi, Haryana, Karnataka, Maharashtra, and Uttarakhand. In addition to 1 Central, 13 State Open Universities and 1 State Private Open Universities.

6. There are 116 dual mode Universities, which offer education through distance mode. Out of 116 dual mode Universities, the most (20 universities) are in Tamil Nadu.
7. The top 8 States in terms of highest number of colleges in India are Uttar Pradesh, Maharashtra, Karnataka, Rajasthan, Andhra Pradesh, Tamil Nadu, Telangana and Madhya Pradesh.
8. Bangalore district tops in terms of number of colleges with 911 colleges followed by Jaipur with 571 colleges. Top 50 districts have about 35% of colleges.
9. College density, that is, the number of colleges per lakh eligible population (population in the age group 18–23 years) varies from 7 in Bihar to 60 in Puducherry as compared to all India average of 26. Pupil–Teacher Ratio (PTR) in universities and colleges is 25.
10. In Union Territories of Andaman & Nicobar Islands, Dadra & Nagar Haveli, Daman & Diu, and Lakshadweep, there are no universities.
11. Among the major states, Andhra Pradesh and Telangana have more than 80% private-unaided colleges and Tamil Nadu has 76% private-unaided colleges, whereas Bihar and Assam each has only 9% private-unaided colleges.
12. Looking at the state-wise variation, out of the total reported enrolled students pursuing studies through distance education, in 6 states, around 61% of the total students receive higher education through distance mode. These are Delhi with 14.8% of students, Tamil Nadu with 14.0% of students, Maharashtra with 11.8%, Andhra Pradesh with 9.1%, Telangana with 5.5%, and Karnataka with 5.4%.

Key Issues Facing Spread of Higher Education in India

National Policy on Higher Education translated the vision of the Radhakrishnan Commission and the Kothari Commission into an actionable policy by setting five main goals for higher education, which are enumerated as follows:

1. *Access:* Greater access requires an enhancement of educational institutional capacity of higher education sector to provide opportunities to all who deserve and desire higher education.
2. *Equity:* Equity involves fair access to the poor and the socially disadvantaged groups to higher education.

   According to the report 'Intergenerational and Regional Differentials in Higher Education in India' authored by Abusaleh Shariff and Amit Sharma, access to education beyond higher secondary schooling is a mere 10% among the university-age population in India. The report says that a huge disparity exists—as far as access to higher education is concerned—across gender, socio-economic religious groups, and geographical regions.
3. *Quality and excellence:* This involves provision of education in accordance with accepted standards so that students receive available knowledge of the highest standards that helps them in enhancing their human resource capabilities.
4. *Relevance:* It involves promotion of education so as to develop human resources in order to keep pace with the changing economic, social, and cultural development of the country.
5. *Value-based education:* This involves inculcating basic moral values among the youth.

As per the UGC guidelines, the student–teacher ratio should be 30:1. However, in some of the states, the ratio is as high as 100:1. Rising enrolment and shortage of faculty has led to India's higher education system with the highest student–teacher ratio. Higher education institutions face an acute problem in terms of lack of academic and physical infrastructure.

Despite having one of the largest higher education systems in the world, few Indian institutions have earned global distinction. There is no Indian institute in the world's top 200.

New Government Initiatives

SWAYAM (Study Webs of Active-Learning for Young Aspiring Minds): SWAYAM is a Massive Open Online Courses (MOOCs) initiative on a national platform with a comprehensive academic structure. The integrated platform will offer courses covering Engineering, Humanities and Social Science, etc. to be used by learners at large. Formation of a Consortium of Premier Educational Institutions & Universities to offer flipped online courses instantaneously after due authentication and award of certification. On this platform, professors of centrally funded institutions like IITs, IIMs, central universities, among other elite institutions, could offer online courses that will be accessible to all Indians free of cost.

The IIM-Bangalore has become the first management school in the country to offer MOOC from this year. The MOOC courses would be made available over internet without charge to a very large number of people. Anyone, who decides to take a MOOC would have to simply log on to IIMB website, these courses are being offered under IIMBx.

GIAN Global Initiative for Academic Network: GIAN aims at tapping the talent pool of scientists and entrepreneurs, internationally, to encourage their engagement with the institutes of Higher Education in India so as to augment the country's existing academic resources, accelerate the pace of quality reform, and elevate India's scientific and technological capacity to global excellence. It is proposed to initiate the program under collaboration with various countries.

Skills Assessment Matrix for Vocational Advancement of Youth (SAMVAY): A credit framework—SAMVAY—is now in place which allows vertical and lateral mobility within vocational education system and between the current education systems. The strength of this framework is the seamless integration of pursuit of academic knowledge and practical vocational skills. Efforts like these will improve the employability of our educated youth.

Campus Connect: The National Mission on Education through Information and Communication Technology (NMEICT) Scheme aims to leverage the potential of ICT for teaching and learning processes. The mission has two major components: (a) content generation and (b) provide connectivity along with provision for access devices to the institutions and learners. Under the NMEICT Mission, connectivity to 419 Universities/University level Institutions and 25,000+ colleges and polytechnics in the country has been envisaged to be provided.

National E-Library: The National Digital Library of India is envisaged as a National knowledge asset that will provide ubiquitous digital knowledge source. It will support and enhance education, research, and innovation catering to the needs of all types of learner groups over the country. Developing and providing efficient access to quality e-content addressed to various learners with different backgrounds, expectations, and languages.

National Ranking Framework: A committee on National Ranking Framework under the chairmanship of Secretary (HE) was constituted to evolve a ranking framework for universities and institutions. Workshops were organized in coordination with the *Times Higher Education* World University Rankings (THER) and the Quacquarelli Symonds (QS) ranking agencies to address various ranking parameters. The MHRD and MHA are collaborating to address employment VISA requirements, which aims at increasing the number of foreign faculty. This will help improve the internationalization parameter in various ranking systems.

Mandatory Accreditation: National Assessment and Accreditation Council had submitted a project proposal to MHRD under Rashtriya Uchchatar Shiksha Abhiyan (RUSA). The major features of the National Quality Renaissance Initiative (NQRI) are (i) awareness building, popularization, and promotion of quality assurance mentoring higher education institutions, (ii) building collegium of assessors, and (iii) quality sustenance and enhancement initiatives.

Bachelor of Vocational Studies: The UGC has introduced the scheme for B.Voc degree with multiple exits at Diploma/Advanced Diploma under National Skill qualification Framework (NSQF).

The Objectives are (i) to enhance the employability of youth, (ii) to maintain their competitiveness through provisions of multi-entry multi-exit learning opportunities and vertical mobility, (iii) to fill the gap between educated and employable, and (iv) to reduce the drop-out rate at the secondary level. Currently, 2035 schools across 25 States are implementing the scheme.

Education Sector Skill Council: Education Sector Skill Council was constituted in September 2014 to consider job roles other than academic faculties and teacher qualifications.

Kaushal Kendras: One hundred 'Deen Dayal Upadhyay Centres for Knowledge Acquisition and Upgradation of Skilled Human Abilities and Livelihood' (KAUSHAL) will be set up. These Kendras will formulate courses at postgraduate level keeping in mind the need of (i) industry in specialized areas, (ii) instructional design, curriculum design, and contents in the areas of skills development, (iii) pedagogy, assessment for skills development education and training, (iv) trained faculty in the areas of skill development, and (v) entrepreneurship.

Unnat Bharat Abhiyan: IIT, IISER, and NIT to adopt villages and develop appropriate rural technologies for sustainable development through peoples' participation. The Abhiyan will enable processes that connect institutes of higher education with local communities. Focus on water management, organic farming, renewable energy, frugal technology, infrastructure, and livelihood.

Ishan Uday—Scholarship Scheme for Students of North East Region: The UGC has launched a Special Scholarship Scheme for students of North East Region, Ishan Uday, from the academic session 2014–15.

Ishan Vikas—Academic Exposure for North Eastern Students: The programme has been launched with a plan to bring selected college and school students from the North Eastern states into close contact with IITs, NITs, and IISERs during their vacation periods for academic exposure.

Saakshar Bharat—Adult Literacy and Pradhan Mantri Jan Dhan Yojna: Centrally Sponsored Scheme of Adult Education and Skill Development has a special focus on underprivileged groups. Four hundred and ten districts are covered under the programme.

PRAGATI—Scholarships for Girl Child for Technical education: PRAGATI aims at providing encouragement and support to girl child to pursue technical education.

Swami Vivekananda Scholarship for Single Girl Child: UGC has introduced the Swami Vivekananda Scholarship for Single Girl Child for research in Social Sciences with an aim to compensate direct costs of higher education especially for such girls who happen to be the only girl child in their family.

CIHEC (Council for Industry Higher Education Cooperation): This relates to creating linkages between the Industry and Academia. A nodal agency—potentially called the Council for Industry and Higher Education Collaboration (CIHEC)—would be established to promote and facilitate industry–higher education collaboration.

Nineteen New Higher Educational Institutions: Five IITs (one each in Andhra Pradesh, Jammu & Kashmir, Chhattisgarh, Goa, and Kerala); Six IIMs (one each in Himachal Pradesh, Andhra Pradesh, Punjab, Maharashtra, Bihar, and Odisha; Four New Central Universities—Andhra Pradesh (one Central University and one Tribal University), Bihar (Mahatma Gandhi Central University); One IISER in Andhra Pradesh; One NIT in Andhra Pradesh; One IIIT in Andhra Pradesh; and One Tribal University in Telangana.

Many new institutions that are in pipeline have been discussed under New Government Initiatives on page 10.14.

Budget 2016-17 : Education Funding Agency (HEFA)

Source: economictimes.indiatimes.com, accessed on March 1, 2016

Governance, Polity, and Administration

The topics, such as governance, polity, and administration, have their origins in the constitution of the country. In Net Paper 1 Exam, 3–4 questions are asked from constitution.

Defining Constitution

Constitution is a living document, an instrument that makes the government system work. The constitution of the United State of America, which was promulgated way back in 1787, became the world's first written constitution. Unlike most modern states, Britain does not have a codified constitution but an unwritten one formed of Acts of Parliament, court judgements, and conventions. Magna carta (origin UK) completed 800 years in 2015. It is considered as mother of all constitutions and fundamental rights.

Constitution is the supreme law of the land. All other laws have to conform to the constitution. It contains laws concerning the government and its relations with the people. We adopted many features from other constitutions of the world, which are as follows:

UK

1. Nominal head of state (President in India)
2. Cabinet system of ministers
3. Prime minister as the head of the government
4. Parliamentary system of government
5. Bicameral parliament with more powerful lower house (Lok Sabha)
6. Council of ministers responsible to lower house
7. Speaker in Lok Sabha

US

1. Written constitution
2. President being the supreme commander of the armed forces
3. fundamental rights
4. Supreme court—independent judiciary and judicial review
5. Preamble

USSR

1. Fundamental Duties
2. Five Year Plans

Australia

1. Concurrent List
2. Language of the Preamble

Japan

1. Law on which the Supreme Court functions

Weimar Constitution of Germany

1. Suspension of fundamental rights during emergency

Canada

1. Scheme of federation with a strong centre, distribution of powers between the centre and the states and placing residuary powers with the centre.

Ireland

1. Concept of Directive Principles of States Policy
2. Method of election of President
3. Nomination of members in the Rajya Sabha by the President

Development of Constitution

Government of India Act (1935): It introduced provincial autonomy, that is, a responsible government at the provinces with elected Indians in charge of the administration, and responsible to the elected legislatures. A federal government was proposed, though it did not come into effect. At the centre, diarchy was introduced.

Note: 2015 was celebrated as 800th year of magna carta.

Constituent Assembly

1. The idea to have a constitution was given by M. N. Roy, a political philosopher.
2. Constituent Assembly of India (1946) to write the Constitution of India under the Cabinet Mission Plan. It took place on 9 December 1946. Dr Sachchidananda Sinha was elected as its ad hoc Chairman.
3. On 11 December 1946, Dr Rajendra Prasad was elected as the permanent chairman of the Constituent Assembly.
4. On 13 December 1946, Objective Resolution was introduced by J. L. Nehru, which later became the basis of Preamble to our constitution.
5. Dr Bhim Rao Ambedkar was elected as the Chairman of Drafting Committee.
6. Constituent Assembly approved the constitution on 11 November 1949, and the constitution came into effect on 26 January 1950. The Constituent Assembly took 2 years, 11 months and 8 days to complete the constitution.
7. India became republic on the same day.
8. Initially, it had 395 articles in 22 parts and 8 schedules, which are presently 12.
9. G.V. Mavalankar became the first speaker of the Legislative Assembly.
10. Constituent Assembly was to comprise of 389 members, of which as many as 296 of them were to be elected from British India and 93 of them were to be the representatives of the Native States.

Salient Features of the Constitution

In making the constitution, the Assembly was inspired by several sources such as the Preamble, which was inspired by the French Declaration of the Rights of Man and Citizen, the Fundamental Rights by the American Bill of Rights, the Directive Principles by the Irish Constitution, and the federal setup by the American Government as well as the Act of 1935.

The following are some of the prominent features of our constitution:

1. *Federal (dual) polity:* India has both central and state governments. They have their separate spheres of functioning and are not subordinate to each other. For a federal setup to work, there must be a written, supreme, and a rigid constitution, with a powerful and independent Supreme Court. India has all this. It is federal in form (in normal times) but unitary in spirit (in emergencies).

2. *Lengthiest constitution in the world:* Our constitution is the lengthiest in the world. It contains details of both the central and the state governments.
3. *Sovereign, socialist, and democratic republic:* India is sovereign because its government is not subject to any outside authority. It is socialist because it has mixed economy and is secular as there is no state religion. The state treats all religions equally. It is democratic as its rulers are elected by the people and are responsible to them, and it is republic as it has an elected head of state.
4. *Parliamentary form of government:* India has a parliamentary form of government. This means the executive (Prime Minister and his council of ministers) is responsible to the legislature (parliament). The three constituents of parliament are President, Lok Sabha, and Rajya Sabha. The president of the union is the constitutional head of the state. The prime minister is considered the head of the government.
5. *Blend of flexibility and rigidity:* Usually, the process of amendment of the Indian constitution is simple and requires only a majority in the parliament. However, in cases involving the government of the states, the process of amendment is more complicated and requires the consent of at least half the state legislatures.
6. *Fundamental rights:* These are contained in Part III of the constitution. The fundamental rights are in the form of restrictions on the power of the government. They are protected by the Supreme Court.
7. *Directive Principles of State Policy:* These principles are in the spirit of Modern Welfare State. These are contained in Part IV and define the aims of the government. They aim to set up a socialistic state in India, in which all the basic needs are met by the government. However, they are not enforceable by the Supreme Court. The different schemes launched by the government are actually inspired by the Directive Principles.
8. *Universal adult suffrage (franchise):* Franchise or suffrage means the right to vote. In India, anybody above the age of 18 years can vote without qualifications of sex, property, taxation, or literacy.
9. *Independent judiciary:* The Indian Supreme Court is independent and impartial. It safeguards the fundamental rights and settles disputes between the centre and the states.
10. *Single citizenship:* Single citizenship states that any person who voluntarily acquires the citizenship of any other country is not an Indian citizen any longer.
11. *Fundamental duties:* These were introduced by the 42nd Amendment in 1976. They are intended to balance the fundamental rights. However, they are also not justiciable.

Preamble to the Constitution

The draft of the Preamble was prepared by Jawaharlal Nehru and is based on the American model. The Preamble states:

'We, the People of India, having solemnly resolved to constitute India into a sovereign, socialist, secular, democratic, republic, and to secure to all its citizens:

1. *Justice* in terms of social, economic, and political
2. *Liberty* of thought, expression, belief, faith, and worship
3. *Equality* of status and of opportunity and to promote them among all
4. *Fraternity* by assuring the dignity of the individual and the unity and integrity of the nation

In our Constituent Assembly, 26 November 1949, do hereby adopt, enact, and give to ourselves this constitution'.

Through the 42nd Amendment in 1976, the words secular and socialist were added to the constitution.

The 42nd amendment is termed as the Mini constitution as many amendments were effected in the constitution.

The below Table 10.1 gives us a snapshot of our constitution.

Table 10.1 A Snapshot of Our Constitution

Part	Articles	Deals in
Part I	1–4	Territory of India, admission, establishment or formation of new states
Part II	5–11	Citizenship
Part III	12–35	Fundamental Rights
Part IV	36–51	Directive Principles of State Policy
Part IV A	51A	Duties of a citizen of India. It was added by the 42nd Amendment in 1976
Part V	52–151	Government at the union level
Part VI	152–237	Government at the state level
Part VII	238	States in Part B of First Schedule were repealed by 7th Amendment in 1956
Part VIII	239–241	Administration of Union Territories
Part IX	242–243	Territories in Part D of the First Schedule
Part X	244–244A	Scheduled and tribal areas
Part XI	245–263	Relations between the union and states
Part XII	264–300	Finance, property, contracts, and suits
Part XIII	301–307	Trade, commerce, and travel within the territory of India
Part XIV	308–323	Services under the union and states
Part XIV A	323A–323B	Added by the 42nd Amendment—administrative tribunals for settling disputes
Part XV	324–329	Election and election commission
Part XVI	330–342	Special provision to certain classes ST/SC and Anglo Indians
Part XVII	343–351	Official languages
Part XVIII	352–360	Emergency provisions
Part XIX	361–367	Miscellaneous provision—exemption of President and Governors from criminal proceedings
Part XX	368	Amendment of constitution
Part XXI	369–392	Temporary, transitional, and special provisions
Part XXII	393–395	Short title, commencement, and repeal of the constitution

Schedules in the Constitution of India

1. *First Schedule:* List of states and union territories
2. *Second Schedule:* Salaries of president, governors, chief judges, judges of high court and supreme court, comptroller, and auditor general
3. *Third Schedule:* Forms of oaths and affirmations
4. *Fourth Schedule:* Allocation of seats for each state of India in Rajya Sabha
5. *Fifth Schedule:* Administration and control of scheduled areas and tribes
6. *Sixth Schedule:* Provisions for administration of tribal areas in Assam, Meghalaya, Tripura, Mizoram, and Arunachal Pradesh
7. *Seventh Schedule:* Gives allocation of powers and functions between union and states. It contains three lists.

1	Union List	97 subjects
2	State List	66 subjects
3	Concurrent List	47 subjects

Both centre and states can legislate on the Concurrent List.

8. *Eighth Schedule:* List of 22 languages of India recognized by the Constitution are as follows:

1. Assamese	2. Bengali
3. Gujarati	4. Hindi
5. Kannada	6. Kashmiri
7. Manipuri	8. Malayalam
9. Konkani	10. Marathi
11. Nepali	12. Oriya
13. Punjabi	14. Sanskrit
15. Sindhi	16. Tamil
17. Telugu	18. Urdu
19. Santhali	20. Bodo
21. Maithili	22. Dogri

Is there any official language in India:

India has no official language. The official language of the union government of Republic of India is Hindi, while English is the secondary official language. The constitution of India states that "The official language of the Union shall be Hindi in Devanagari script", which was supported by a High Court ruling. However, languages listed in the Eighth Schedule of the Indian Constitution are sometimes referred to, without legal standing, as the National Languages of India.

Sindhi was added in 1967 by the 21st Amendment. Konkani, Manipuri, and Nepali were added in 1992 by the 71st Amendment. Santhali, Maithili, Bodo, and Dogri were added in 2003 by the 92nd Amendment.

9. *Ninth Schedule:* Added by the 1st Amendment in 1951; it contains acts and orders related to land tenure, land tax, railways, industries (right to property is not a fundamental right now).
10. *Tenth Schedule:* Added by the 52nd Amendment in 1985; it contains provisions for disqualification on grounds of defection.
11. *Eleventh Schedule:* Added by the 73rd Amendment in 1992; it contains provisions for Panchayati Raj.
12. *Twelfth Schedule:* Added by the 74th Amendment in 1992; it contains provisions for municipal corporation.

Fundamental Rights

The fundamental rights are in Part III of the Indian Constitution, 1949, from Article 12 to 35. The framer of the Indian constitution borrowed it from USA. Part III of the Constitution is rightly described as the 'Magna Carta of India'. The Fundamental Rights are guaranteed by the Constitution to all persons without any discrimination. The Fundamental Rights are named so because they are guaranteed and protected by the Constitution, which is the fundamental law of the land.

Originally, the right to property was also included in the Fundamental Rights. However, the 44th Amendment, passed in 1978, revised the status of property rights by stating that 'No person shall be deprived of his or her property save by authority of law'.

The Fundamental Rights are given below.

Right to Equality

Article 14: Equality before law and equal protection of law

Article 15: Prohibition of discrimination on grounds of religion, race, caste, sex or place of birth

Article 16: Equality of opportunity in matters of public employment

Article 17: End of untouchability

Article 18: Abolition of titles; military and academic distinctions are, however, exempted

Right to Freedom

Article 19: It guarantees the citizens of India the following six fundamentals freedoms:

1. Freedom of speech and expression
2. Freedom of assembly
3. Freedom to form associations
4. Freedom of movement
5. Freedom of residence and settlement
6. Freedom of profession, occupation, trade, and business

Article 20: Protection in respect of conviction for offences

Article 21: Protection of life and personal liberty

Article 22: Protection against arrest and detention in certain cases

Right against Exploitation

Article 23: Trafficking of human beings is prohibited
Article 24: No child below the age of 14 can be employed

Right to Freedom of Religion

Article 25: Freedom of conscience and free profession, practice, and propagation of religion
Article 26: Freedom to manage religious affairs
Article 27: Prohibits taxes on religious grounds
Article 28: Freedom as to attendance at religious ceremonies in certain educational institutions

Cultural and Educational Rights

Article 29: Protection of interests of minorities
Article 30: Right of minorities to establish and administer educational institutions
Article 31: Omitted by the 44th Amendment Act

Note: Minority Institutions – 'All minorities ... shall have the right to establish and administer education institutions of their own' _____ is the mandate, as per Article 30(1) of the Constitution. Government is committed to address the existing backwardness in education of minorities, especially the Muslims, constituting the major chunk of the minorities. Therefore, the Prime Minister's New 15 Point Programme, inter-alia, aims to enhance opportunities for education of minorities ensuring an equitable share in economic activities and employment.

In January 2016, Government stated that Aligarh Muslim University, Aligarh and Jamia Millia Islamia, New Delhi, were set up by acts of Parliament. Hence, they are not minority institutions.

Right to Constitutional Remedies

Article 32: The right to move the Supreme Court in case of violation of any right (called the heart and soul of the constitution by Dr B. R. Ambedkar)

Forms of Writ

As per the Right to Constitutional Remedies (Articles 32–35), a citizen has the right to move the court for securing his or her fundamental rights. Citizens can go to the Supreme Court or the High Court for getting their fundamental rights enforced. It empowers the courts to issue directions, orders or writs for this purpose.

The different forms of writs have been discussed below:

Habeas corpus means to have the body. It is in the nature of an order, calling upon a person who has unlawfully detained another person to produce the latter before the court.

Mandamus: It literally means command. It is thus an order of a superior court, commanding a person holding a public office or a public authority (including the government) to do or not to do something, in the nature of public duty.

Prohibition: A writ of prohibition is issued by a superior court to an inferior court or a tribunal to prevent it from exceeding its jurisdiction and to compel it to keep within the limits of its jurisdiction.

Certiorari: A writ of certiorari has much in common with a writ of prohibition. The only difference between the two is, whereas a writ of prohibition is issued to prevent an inferior court or tribunal to go ahead with the trial of a case in which it has assumed excess of jurisdiction, a writ of certiorari is issued to quash the order passed by an inferior court or a tribunal in excess of jurisdiction.

Quo Warranto: Quo warranto means what is your authority? A writ of quo warranto is issued against the holder of a public office in order to show the court under what authority he holds the office.

Writs can be initiated by the following institutions:

1. The Supreme and High Courts
2. The National Human Rights Commission
3. The State Human Rights Commissions and Human Rights Courts
4. Non-Governmental Organizations such as People's Union for Civil Liberties and Amnesty International

Fundamental Duties

Our constitution has explicitly laid down certain fundamental duties of its citizens in Article 51A, emphasizing that every Indian citizen would:

1. Promote harmony and spirit of common brotherhood, transcending religious, linguistic, and regional or sectoral diversities
2. Renounce practices derogatory to the dignity of women
3. Value and preserve the rich heritage of our composite culture
4. Protect and improve the natural environment
5. Develop scientific temper
6. Abjure violence and strive towards excellence in all spheres of individual and collective activity so that the nation constantly rises to higher levels of endeavour and achievement

President of India

1. *Qualification:* Must be a citizen of India
2. *Age:* Completed 35 years of age
3. *Eligibility:* Eligible to be a member of Lok Sabha. Must not hold any government post except the following posts:
   (a) President or Vice President
   (b) Governor of any state
   (c) Minister of the Union or of any State
4. *Election:* President is indirectly elected through the electoral college consisting of elected members of both the houses of the parliament and elected members of the Legislative Assemblies of the states (no nominated members). Supreme Court inquires all disputes regarding the President's election. The elected president takes oath in the presence of the Chief Justice of India, or in his absence, the senior-most judge of the Supreme Court.
5. *Terms and emoluments:* The terms and emoluments of the President are as follows:
   (a) Five-year term
   (b) Article 57 says that there is no upper limit on the number of times a person can become a President
   (c) Can give his or her resignation to the Vice President before full term
6. *Impeachment:* Quasi-judicial procedure. Can be impeached only on grounds of violation of the constitution. The impeachment procedure can be initiated in both the houses of the Parliament.
7. *Vacancy:* In case if the office of the President falls vacant due to death, resignation or removal, the Vice President act as President. If he is not available then the Chief Justice, if not, then the senior-most judge of the Supreme Court shall act as the President of India.

   The election is to be held within six months from the date of vacancy.
8. *Powers:* The powers of the President are given below.
   (i) Appoints the PM, ministers, Chief Justice and the judges of Supreme Court and High Court, chairman and members of UPSC, Comptroller and Auditor General, Attorney General, Chief Election Commissioner and other members of Election Commission of India, Governors, members of Finance Commission, Ambassadors, and so on.
   (ii) Summon and prorogue the sessions of the two houses and can dissolve the Lok Sabha.
   (iii) Appoints the Finance Commission (after every five years) that recommends the distribution of taxes between the union and the state governments.
   (iv) Supreme Commander of the Defence Forces of India
   (v) Appoints the Chief of Army, Navy, and Air Force.
   (vi) Declares wars and concludes peace to the approval of the Parliament
   (vii) No money bill or demand for grant can be introduced or moved in the Parliament unless it has been recommended by the President.

(viii) He has the power to grant pardon, reprieve, or remit punishment or commute death sentences.

9. *Emergency powers:* The President can promulgate three types of emergencies.

Type of emergency	Article
National emergency	352
State emergency (President's rule)	356
Financial emergency	360

Prime Minister of India

1. Prime Minister is the real executive authority.
2. He is the ex-officio Chairman of the National Institution for Transforming India (NITI Aayog, erstwhile Planning Commission), National Development Council, National Integration Council, and Interstate Council.
3. The President convenes and prorogues all sessions of Parliament in consultation with the Prime Minister.
4. He can recommend the dissolution of Lok Sabha before expiry.
5. He appoints the council of ministers.
6. He allocates portfolios, and he can ask a minister to resign and can get him dismissed by the President.
7. He has the power to recommend to the President to declare emergency on grounds of war, external aggression, or armed rebellion.
8. He advises the President about President's rule in the state or in case of emergency due to financial instability.
9. He is the leader of the house.

Vice President of India

1. *Election:* Elected by both the houses (Electoral College) in accordance with the system of proportional representation by means of a single transferable vote and the vote being secret. Nominated members also participate in his election.

   The Supreme Court has the final and exclusive jurisdiction for resolving disputes and doubts relating to the election of the Vice President of India
2. *Criteria:* Citizen of India
3. *Age:* More than 35 years of age
4. *Eligibility:* Possesses the qualification for membership of Rajya Sabha

   Does not hold any office of profit under union, state, or local authority. However, for this purpose, the President, Vice President, Governor of a state, and a minister of the union or a state are not held to be holding an office of profit.

Holds office for five years and can be re-elected for any number of terms.

Term can be cut short if he resigns or by a resolution of the Rajya Sabha, passed by a majority of all the members of the Rajya Sabha and agreed to by the Lok Sabha.

He is the ex-officio Chairman of the Rajya Sabha. As he is not a member of Rajya Sabha, he has no right to vote.

Being the Vice President of India, he is not entitled to any salary, but is entitled to the salary and allowances payable to the Chairman of Rajya Sabha.

All bills, resolution, and motion can be taken in Rajya Sabha after his consent.

Can discharge the functions of the President; the Vice President shall not perform the duties of the office of the Chairman of Rajya Sabha and shall not be entitled to receive to salary of the Chairman. During this period, he is entitled for the salary and privileges of the President of India.

Citizenship

Citizen of a nation is a person who enjoys full civil and political rights in that nation. Aliens are people who do not enjoy all these rights.

Rights Available to a Citizen

In India, the following rights are available to its citizens only:

1. The right to not be discriminated against on grounds of religion, race, caste, sex, or place of birth

2. The right to equality of opportunity in matters of public employment
3. The right to the six freedoms of Article 19, namely, right to speech, assembly, association, movement, residence, and occupation
4. Cultural and educational rights
5. The right to vote for elections to the Parliament and the Legislative Assemblies of the states
6. Certain offices, for example, the President, Prime Minister, Vice President, Judges of the Supreme or High Court, can be occupied only by Indian citizens.

The right to equality before law and equal protection of the law, right to the protection of life and personal liberty, and the right to freedom of religion, are available to aliens also.

Single and Dual Citizenship

India has single citizenship. It means a person can be only a citizen of India, not of any of the states of India. Also, the Indian constitution forbids dual citizenship, whereby a person may be a citizen of two countries at the same time, or of a country and of one of its units or state at the same time.

A person can only be a citizen of India, and claim the rights and privileges that go with citizenship.

Who are the Citizens of India?

Constitutional Provisions

The constitution describes the classes of people who would be considered citizens of India at the time of commencement of the constitution.

1. *Citizens by domicile:* Those who live in India and fulfil any one of the following conditions, namely (a) they were born in India, (b) their parents were born in India, or (c) they must have lived in India for at least five years before the commencement of the constitution are called citizens by domicile.
2. *Migrants from Pakistan to India:* Migrants from Pakistan to India are to be considered Indian citizens if they, or their parents, were born in undivided India.
3. *Migrants from India to Pakistan:* Any person who migrated to Pakistan after March 1, 1947, ceases to be a citizen of India.
4. *People of Indian origin residing outside India:* Those who reside outside India, but whose parents or grandparents were born in undivided India can claim citizenship by registering as citizen with the diplomatic representatives of India.

Citizenship Acts

The Parliament passed the Citizenship Act (1955) and Citizenship (Amendment) Act (2003) laying down ways in which a person may acquire or lose Indian citizenship. According to these acts, a person may become a citizen of India:

1. By birth
2. By descent
3. By registration
4. By naturalization
5. By incorporation of territory

A person who has lived in India, or has served the Government of India, for at least seven years, knows one of the official languages of India, has renounced the citizenship of his country of origin, and has taken the oath of allegiance of India, and is of good character, can apply for citizenship through naturalization.

Loss of Citizenship

According to these acts, a person can lose his citizenship by the following:

1. *Renunciation:* An Indian citizen can make a declaration of renouncing his citizenship, and have this declaration registered.
2. *Termination:* When a person becomes a citizen of another country voluntarily, he automatically loses his citizenship of India.
3. *Deprivation:* A person who becomes a citizen of India by naturalization or registration can be deprived of his citizenship if found that he gained it through false means, showed disrespect to the Indian constitution,

was disloyal to the country, or was convicted of an offence within five years of getting the citizenship.

Citizenship (Amendment) Act of 2003 also made it possible for people to be the overseas citizens of India, if they are of Indian origin and hold the citizenship of some selected countries (West European and North American countries). This allows them to easily travel to and from India, but otherwise does not give them the privileges of people who are complete citizens of India.

Parliament

The Parliament of India consists of the President and the two houses namely, the Lower House or Lok Sabha and the Upper House or Rajya Sabha.

Rajya Sabha

It is the upper house of parliament. It consists of representatives of states and represents the federal character of the constitution. The membership of a state is based on the population of that state.

The maximum strength of the Rajya Sabha is 250. Of these, 238 represent the states and union territories and the remaining 12 are nominated by the President from amongst persons who have distinguished themselves in the field of literature, art, science, social service, and so on.

Its members are elected by the members of state Legislative Assemblies on the basis of proportional representation through a single transferable vote.

Tenure

Rajya Sabha is a permanent body, and not subject to dissolution. One-third of its members retire every two years. The members are elected by the elected members of the state Legislative Assemblies for a six-year term. There are no seats reserved for scheduled castes and tribes in the Rajya Sabha.

Qualifications for Membership

To be qualified to become a member of the Rajya Sabha, a person must be

1. A citizen of India
2. Not less than 30 years of age
3. Registered as a voter in any parliamentary constituency

Chairman and Deputy Chairman of Rajya Sabha

The Vice President of India is the ex-officio Chairman of the Rajya Sabha. He presides over the proceedings of the Rajya Sabha. In his absence, the Deputy Chairman of the Rajya Sabha presides over. Deputy Chairman is elected by the members of the Rajya Sabha amongst themselves.

Lok Sabha

Lok Sabha is the lower house of the parliament. It consists of representatives elected by the people on the basis of universal adult franchise through a secret ballot. The constitution prescribes a membership of not more than 530 representatives of the states, not more than 20 representatives of the union territories and not more than two members of the Anglo-Indian Community nominated by the President, if in the opinion of the President the Anglo-Indian community is not adequately represented in the Lok Sabha.

The constitution empowers the Parliament to readjust the seats in the Lok Sabha on the basis of population after every census.

Tenure

The normal term of Lok Sabha is five years. However, it may be dissolved earlier by the President. The 42nd Amendment Act, 1976 extended the normal life of the Lok Sabha to six years. However, the 44th Amendment Act, 1978 has set it at five years as the original constitution envisaged.

The life of the Lok Sabha can be extended by the Parliament beyond the five-year term, when a proclamation of emergency under Article 352 is in force. The Parliament cannot extend the normal life of Lok Sabha for more than one year at a time, but in any case, such extensions cannot continue beyond a period of six months after the proclamation comes to an end.

Qualifications for Membership to Lok Sabha

In order to be a member of the Lok Sabha, a person must have the following qualifications:

1. A citizen of India
2. Not less than 25 years of age
3. Registered as a voter in any parliamentary constituency.

Speaker and Deputy Speaker of Lok Sabha

Speaker is the Chief Presiding Officer of the Lok Sabha. Speaker and the Deputy Speaker of Lok Sabha are elected by the members of Parliament amongst themselves. Deputy Speaker performs the duties of Speaker in case of vacancy or absence.

Speaker and Deputy Speaker remain in office as long as they are the members of the House. Speaker continues in office, even after dissolution of the House till the newly elected Lok Sabha is constituted.

Speaker and Deputy Speaker may be removed from their office by a resolution of the House after serving a 14-day notice to them. Speaker can exercise his casting vote in case of a tie, that is, in case of equality of votes on a bill.

Speaker possesses certain powers that do not belong to the Chairman of the Rajya Sabha. They are as follows:

1. To preside over a joint sitting of the Houses of the Parliament
2. Power of certification of a money bill when transmitted from the Lok Sabha to the Rajya Sabha
3. The decision of the Speaker as to whether the money bill is final.

Special Powers of the Lok Sabha

The Lok Sabha enjoys the following powers that are not available to the Rajya Sabha:

1. A confidence or no-confidence motion can be initiated and passed only in the Lok Sabha.
2. Money and financial bills can be introduced only in the Lok Sabha. It controls the purse of the government.

Rajya Sabha cannot reject or amend a money bill by virtue of its legislative powers. It can only recommend changes in the money bill and can delay it for a maximum period of 14 days only. Lok Sabha enjoys full legislative powers in this regard.

Under Article 352, Lok Sabha, in a special sitting, can disapprove the continuance in force of a national emergency proclaimed by the President. In such a case, the President shall revoke the national emergency.

The Parliament generally meets in three sessions in a year. These sessions are as follows:

1. Budget session – (January – March/April)
2. Monsoon session (Jul–Aug)
3. Winter session (Nov–Dec)

The President can call a joint sessions of the two houses if a bill passed by one house is rejected by the other house, if the amendments proposed to a bill by one house are not acceptable to the other house or a house does not take any action on a bill remitted to it for six months. Decision is taken by a majority of the total members present. The deadlock over a bill in a joint sitting is resolved by members present and voting.

Since the Lok Sabha has a larger membership in a joint sitting, generally the will of the Lok Sabha prevails. After the passage of the bill in a joint sitting, it is presented to the President for his assent. However, no joint sitting can be summoned to resolve a deadlock in case of a money bill or a Constitutional Amendment Bill. With effect from year 2017, the budget is to be presented in month of January. Railway Budget has now been merged with General Budget.

Important Terms in Parliamentary Proceedings

1. *Question hour:* Normally, the first hour of the business of a house is devoted to questions every day and is called the question hour.
2. *Adjournment motions:* An adjournment motion is an extraordinary procedure, which if admitted, leads to setting aside the normal business of the house for discussing a definite matter of urgent public importance.

3. *Call-attention motion:* A member of Parliament may, with prior permission of the Speaker call the attention of a minister to any matter of urgent public importance and the minister may make a brief statement or ask for time to make a statement at a later hour or date.
4. *No confidence motion:* A motion moved by a member to express lack of confidence in the government for any reason, is called no-confidence motion. The motion if allowed, is debated upon. At the conclusion of the debate, a vote of confidence is sought by the government and if it fails to get the required majority of votes, the government has to resign.

Parliamentary Committees

The work done by Parliament varies not only in nature, but considerably in volume too. A good deal of its business is transacted by Parliamentary Committees.

Ad hoc and Standing Committees

As the name suggests, Ad hoc Committees are appointed for a specific purpose. They cease to exist once the task is complete and they submit a report. The main Ad hoc Committees are the Select and the Joint Committees on bills.

Apart from the Ad hoc Committees, each House of Parliament has Standing Committees such as the Business Advisory Committee, the Committee on Petitions, Committee of Privileges, and the Rules Committee.

Other Committees

Some committees act as Parliament's watch dogs over the Executive. These are the Committees on Subordinate Legislation, Government Assurances, Estimates, Public Accounts and the Public Undertakings, and Departmentally Related Standing Committees (DRSCs).

Attorney General

Attorney General is the first law officer of the Government of India. He is the primary lawyer in the Supreme Court of India. He must be a person qualified to be appointed as the Judge of the Supreme Court.

AG is appointed by the President of India under Article 76(1) of the Constitution. He/she holds office during the pleasure of the President.

His duties are to advise the government on legal matters and to perform other legal duties, which are referred to or assigned to him by the President and to discharge the functions conferred to him by the constitution. Though he is not a member of the cabinet, he has the right to speak in both the Houses of the Parliament; or any committee thereof, but has no right to vote. In performance of his official duties, the Attorney General shall have the rights of an audience in all the courts in the territory of India.

Attorney General represents the government but is allowed to take up private practice, provided the other party is not the state. Due to this, he is not paid a salary but a retainer to be determined by the President. The Attorney General gets a retainer equivalent to the salary of a judge of the Supreme Court.

Comptroller and Auditor General of India

Comptroller and Auditor General of India is appointed by the President. He holds office until the age of 65 years or at the expiry of six-year term, whichever is earlier.

He is the guardian of the public purse. His duties are to keep the accounts of the union and the states. CAG also ensures that no money is spent out of the Consolidated Fund of India or of the states without the sanction of the Parliament or of the state legislatures.

Constitution contains provisions to ensure impartiality of the office and to make it independent of the Executive.

He can be removed from his office only on grounds of proved misbehaviour or incapacity in the same manner a judge of the Supreme Court is removed, that is each House of the Parliament passes a resolution supported by two-thirds of the members present who vote and by a majority of the House.

His salary and conditions of service cannot be changed to his disadvantage during his term of office, except under a financial emergency. His salary is charged on the consolidated Fund of India and is not subject to vote of the Parliament. He is paid a salary equivalent to that of a judge of the Supreme Court.

Union Public Service Commission (UPSC)

UPSC is India's central agency authorised to conduct the Civil Services and many other exams. The agency's charter is granted by the Constitution of India. Articles 315 to 323 of Part XIV of the constitution, titled as Services under the Union and the States, provide for a Public Service Commission for the Union and for each state. The Royal Commission on the Superior Civil Services in India under the Chairmanship of Lord Lee, which submitted its Report in 1924, recommended the setting up of the Public Service Commission. This led to the establishment of the first Public Service Commission on 1 October 1926 under the Chairmanship of Sir Ross Barker.

The limited advisory function accorded to the Public Service Commission and the continued stress on this aspect by the leaders of our freedom movement resulted in the setting up of a Federal Public Service Commission under the Government of India Act, 1935. The Federal Public Service Commission became the Union Public Service Commission after Independence, and it was given a Constitutional status with promulgation of Constitution of India on 26 January 1950.

The Commission consists of a chairman and ten members. The terms and conditions of service of chairman and members of the commission are governed by the Union Public Service Commission (Members) Regulations, 1969. The chairman and other members of the UPSC (Union Public Service Commission) are appointed by the President of India. Every member holds office for a term of six years or until he attains the age of sixty-five years, whichever is earlier.

Executives at the State Level

The executives at the state level have been modelled on the central pattern. It consists of the Governor, the Council of ministers, and the Chief Minister.

Governor

The executive power of the state is vested in the Governor and all the executive actions of the state have to be taken in the name of the Governor. Normally, there is a Governor for each state; however, it is possible to appoint the same person as a Governor for two or more states.

Appointment, Term of Office, and Qualifications

The Governor is appointed by the President. He can hold office during the pleasure of the President. The appointment is done for 5 years. He can relinquish his office earlier by tendering his resignation to the President. The President can also remove him from office before the expiry of his term. The Governor can be given charge for more than one state.

To be eligible for appointment as a Governor, a person:

1. Must be a citizen of India.
2. Must have completed 35 years of age.
3. Should not be a member of either House of Parliament or the state legislature.
4. Must possess the qualifications prescribed for membership of the state legislatures.
5. Must not hold any office of profit.

Powers and Functions

The constitution vests quite extensive powers in the Governor and he is expected to exercise on the advice of the council of ministers.

Executive Powers

The Governor is the executive head of the state and all executive actions of the state are taken in his name. He also appoints all important officials of the state including the chief minister, ministers, advocate general, chairman, and members of the state Public Service Commission.

Legislative Powers

Governor is a part of the state legislature. He has the power to

1. Summon and dissolve state Legislature.
2. Appoint one-sixth of the members of Legislative Council.
3. Appoint one member from the Anglo-Indian community to the state Legislative Assembly.
4. Give assent to the bills passed by the state legislature.
5. Reserve certain bills passed by the legislature for the assent of the President.
6. Make laws through ordinances during the recess of the state legislatures.

Financial Powers

1. To ensure that the budget of the state is laid before the state legislature every year.
2. All money bills can be introduced in the state legislature only on recommendation of the Governor.
3. Administers the contingency fund of the state and can advance money out of it to meet any unforeseen expenditure pending its authorization by the legislature.

Judicial Powers

1. Consulted by the President while appointing the Chief Justice and judges of the state High Court.
2. Appoints judges of courts below the High Court.
3. Power to grant pardons, reprieves, respites, or remissions of punishment to persons convicted of an offence against the state laws.

Emergency Powers

Governor has the power to make a report to the President whenever he is sure that a situation has arisen in which governance of the state cannot be carried on in accordance with the provisions of the constitution (Article 356), thereby inviting the President to assume to himself the functions of the government of the state or any of them. When the state is placed under President's rule, the Governor acts as the representative of the President in the state and assumes extensive powers.

Chief Minister

Governor is assisted in discharging his functions by a council of ministers headed by the Chief Minister. The Chief Minister, who is generally the leader of the majority party in the state assembly, is appointed by the Governor. He enjoys a term that runs parallel to that of the state legislature. CM recommends to the Governor, the names of council of ministers and allocates portfolios to them.

Council of Ministers

Any person can be appointed as a minister but he ceases to be one if he is not elected as a member of the state legislature within six months after his appointment as a minister. The council of ministers is collectively responsible to the Vidhan Sabha.

Advocate General

Advocate General is the first law officer of a state. The office corresponds to the office of the Attorney General of India and enjoys similar functions within the state. He is appointed by the Governor and holds office during the pleasure of the Governor. A person who is qualified to be appointed as a judge of a High Court can only be appointed as Advocate General. He has the right to participate in the proceedings of the houses of state legislatures without the right to vote and has the right of audience in any court in the state.

State Legislature

The constitution provides for a legislature for every state. The legislature of every state consists of the Governor and one or two houses. The legislatures in the state are either bicameral (consisting of two houses) or unicameral (consisting of one house). The lower house is always known as the Legislative Assembly (Vidhan Sabha) and the upper house, wherever it exists, as the Legislative

Council (Vidhan Parishad). At present only five states have a bicameral legislature, namely Bihar, Jammu and Kashmir, Karnataka, Maharashtra, and Uttar Pradesh. All other states have only one house. The Legislative Councils can be created or abolished in a state by the Parliament under Article 169 by a simple procedure. If the Legislative assembly of the state passes a resolution by a majority of the total membership of the assembly and by a majority of not less than two-third of the members present and voting, the Parliament may approve the resolution by a simple majority.

Composition of the Houses

The strength of the Legislative Assembly varies from 60 to 500 in different states according to the population. However, the Legislative Assembly of Sikkim has only 32 members. The members of the assembly are chosen directly by the people on the basis of adult franchise from territorial constituencies in the state. Seats are reserved for STs and SCs on the basis of population. If the Governor of a state is of the opinion that the Anglo-Indian community is not adequately represented in the Legislative Assembly, he may nominate one member of that community to the assembly as he considers appropriate.

Tenure

The normal tenure of the Legislative Assembly of every state is of five years; however, it may be dissolved earlier by the Governor. Similarly, its term can be extended by one year at a time by the Parliament during national emergency.

Qualifications

A person can become a member of the Legislative Assembly only if he:

1. Is a citizen of India.
2. Is more than 25 years of age.
3. Does not hold any office of profit under the state or central government.
4. Possesses such other qualifications as may be prescribed by law.

If any question arises as to whether a member of a house of the legislature of a state is subject to disqualification, the question shall be referred for the decision of the Governor and his decision shall be final.

Officers

A Legislative Assembly shall have its Speaker and Deputy Speaker elected from among its members.

Legislative Council

It is the upper house of the state legislature and contains various categories of members. It is popularly known as Vidhan Parishad. The membership of the council shall not be more than one-third of the membership of the legislature, but not less than 40. Broadly speaking, 5/6 of the total members of the council shall be indirectly elected and 1/6 shall be nominated by the Governor.

The Legislative Council is not subject to dissolution but after every two years, one-third of its members retire.

Qualifications

To be a member of the Legislative Council, a person:

1. Must be a citizen of India.
2. Must be more than 30 years of age.
3. Must not hold any office of profit under the state or union government.
4. Must possess other qualifications as may be prescribed by the Parliament.

Sessions of the Legislature

The state legislature must meet at least twice a year and the interval between any two sessions should not be more than six months.

Legislative Procedure

The legislative procedure in a state having a unicameral legislature is simple. All bills originate in the single chamber, that is, the Legislative Assembly and when duly passed, are presented to the Governor for his assent. However, in case of a bicameral legislature, the procedure is slightly different from that of the Parliament. If the Vidhan Sabha rejects a bill which originated in the Vidhan Parishad, then that is the end of the bill. In case of money bills, the procedure followed is exactly similar to that of the Parliament.

Finance Commission

The Finance Commission is set up under Article 280 of the constitution. It is constituted by the President, once in every five years. Its main function is to recommend about the (i) distribution of financial resources between the centre and the states and also among the states themselves, (ii) the principles which govern the grants-in-aid of the revenues amongst the states out of the consolidated fund of India.

Supreme Court

India opted for a unified and single judiciary and a single integrated system of courts for the union as well as the states, though it has opted for a federal system. Supreme Court stands at the apex of the judicial system of India. It consists of a chief justice and 25 other judges. The Supreme Court normally sits at New Delhi.

Appointment

Chief justice of the Supreme Court is appointed by the President in consultation with other judges of the Supreme Court and High Courts, as he may deem necessary for the purpose. The other judges of the Supreme Court are appointed by the President in consultation with the Chief Justice.

Qualification of a Judge

A person, in order to be qualified for appointment as a judge of the Supreme Court must:

1. Be a citizen of India.
2. Have been a judge of the High Court or two or more such courts in succession for at least five years or
3. Have been an advocate of a high court or two or more such courts in succession for at least 10 years or
4. A distinguished jurist in the opinion of the President.

Tenure

A judge of the Supreme Court vacates his office on attaining 65 years of age or by resignation addressed to the President or on removal by the President upon a resolution passed by both the Houses of the Parliament, supported by a majority of the total membership of that House and by a majority of not less than two-thirds of the members present and voting on grounds of proved misbehaviour or incapacity.

Independence of Supreme Court Judges

The constitution has made provisions to ensure independence of the judges. Some of these provisions are as follows:

1. The salaries and allowances of judges are charged on the consolidated fund of India; thus, they are not subject to a vote of Parliament. Moreover, the salaries and other service conditions of judges cannot be changed to their disadvantage during their tenure.
2. The Constitution's Articles 124 and 217 dealt with the appointment of judges of the higher judiciary. According to these articles, judges could be appointed by the President of India after consulting the chief justice of India (CJI) and other judges.

   The present system for appointment of judges that was adopted in 1993 is also called as Collegium system.

   Note: The Government sought to replace the system with National Judicial Appointments Commission (NJAC) that proposes a transparent and broad-based process of selection of judges of the Supreme Court and High Courts. They were to be selected by the commission whose members were drawn from the judiciary, legislature, and civil society for future appointment of judges.

The constitution was also amended for the purpose. In its October 17, 2015, judgement, Supreme Court struck down the new laws on NJAC on the ground of encroachment into judicial independence.

3. Once appointed, a judge of the Supreme Court can only be removed from office by the President, on the basis of a resolution passed by both the Houses of the Parliament with a majority of total membership and a majority of not less than two-thirds of the members present and voting in each house, on grounds of proved misbehaviour or incapacity of the judge in question.

Jurisdiction of the Supreme Court

The jurisdiction of the Supreme Court is five-fold, which is as follows:

1. *Original jurisdiction:* The original jurisdiction of the Supreme Court is purely federal in character, and it has exclusive authority to decide any dispute (a) between the centre and one or more states and (b) between two or more states
2. *Writ jurisdiction:* Article 32 confers jurisdiction on the Supreme Court to enforce the fundamental rights. The power to issue writs for enforcement of the fundamental rights is given by the constitution to the Supreme Court and High courts.
3. *Appellate jurisdiction:* Supreme Court is the highest court of appeal and its writs and decrees run throughout the country.
4. *Advisory jurisdiction:* Under Article 143 of the constitution, Supreme Court renders advice to the President on any matter of law or fact whenever he seeks such advice. However, the advice is not binding on the President.
5. *Revisory jurisdiction:* Supreme Court, under Article 137 is empowered to review any judgement or order made by it with a view to remove any mistake or error that might have crept in the judgement or order.

Supreme Court and Power of Judicial Review

Supreme Court has been vested with the power of judicial review. Judicial review can be defined as the competence of a court of law to declare the constitutionality or otherwise of a legislative enactment. It can ensure that the laws passed by the legislature and the orders issued by the Executive do not contravene any provision of the constitution. If they go against any provision of the constitution, it can declare them unconstitutional or null and void.

High Court

The judiciary in states consists of a High Court and subordinate courts. The Parliament can, however, establish by law, a common High Court for two or more such states, or for one or more state and one or more union territories.

Appointment of Judges

Every High Court shall consist of a Chief Justice and such other judges as the President may appoint from time to time. As in the case of Supreme Court, there is no fixed maximum number of judges of a High Court. The decision is left on to the President.

The President has the power to appoint: (i) additional judges for a temporary period, not exceeding two years to clear pending cases or (ii) an acting judge, when the permanent judge of a High Court is temporarily absent or unable to perform his duties.

Qualifications

To qualify for appointment as a judge of the High Court, a person:

1. Must be a citizen of India
2. Should have been an advocate of a High Court or two or more such courts in succession for at least 10 years or
3. Should have held a judicial office in Indian territory for a period of at least 10 years

Tenure

The judge of High Court holds office till he attains the age of 62 years. He can resign from his position. The removal procedure is same as is the case of a judge of the Supreme Court.

Independence of the Judges

As in the case of a judge of the Supreme Court, the constitution seeks to maintain the independence of the judges of the High Court by a number of provisions.

Election Commission

The constitution provides for an independent election commission to ensure free and fair elections. Election commission consists of a Chief Election Commissioner and such other commissioners as the President may decide from time to time. In October 1993, the Government promulgated an act which provided for the appointment of election commissioners. At present, there is a Chief Election Commissioner and two other Election Commissioners who are appointed by the President for a five-year term. The term can be cut short on account of resignation or removal by the President on grounds of proved misbehaviour or incapacity on the recommendations of the Parliament.

Functions of the Election Commission

1. To superintend, direct and control elections to the Parliament and the state legislature
2. To conduct elections to the post of the President and Vice President
3. To lay down general rules for elections
4. To determine constituencies and to control the preparation of electoral rolls, allot symbols to recognized political parties
5. To settle any disputes arising in connection with the elections
6. To conduct counting and declare results
7. To postpone or countermand elections for specific reasons

Panchayati Raj Institutions

Panchayati Raj is an important feature of the Indian political system, which ensures direct participation of people at the grass root level. After independence, the framers of the constitution decided to give them importance and under Article 40 of the Directive Principles, directed the states to organize village panchayats as units of self-government. A number of committees were appointed such as the Balwantrai Mehta Committee and Ashok Mehta Committee to suggest measures for improvement of working of Panchayati Raj institutions. The constitution passed the 73rd and 74th Amendment Acts, 1992, which were related to the working of panchayats and municipalities.

Apart from mandatory provisions for reservation of SCs/STs and women, there are voluntary provisions for reservation of members from backward classes also. The Ministry of Panchayati Raj was created in the year 2004 to look after ongoing process of decentralization and local governance in the states.

The constitution envisages a three-tier system of Panchayats:

1. The village level
2. The district panchayat at the district level
3. The intermediate panchayat, which stands between the village and district panchayats in those states where the population is above 20 lakhs

All the seats in a panchayat are filled by persons chosen by direct election from territorial constituencies in the panchayat area.

The electorate is named as the Gram Sabha, consisting of persons registered in the electoral rolls relating to a village comprised within the area of a panchayat. Seats are reserved for SCs and STs and also for women. A state may, by law, make provisions for similar reservation of the offices of chairpersons in panchayats at the village and other levels. Chairperson is elected according to the law passed by the state.

Duration of a Panchayat

Each panchayat shall continue for five years from the date of its first meeting. However, it can be dissolved earlier in accordance with the procedure prescribed by the state law.

Qualifications for Membership

All persons who are qualified to be chosen to the state legislature shall be qualified to be chosen as a member of the panchayat. The only difference is that a person who has attained the age of 21 years will be eligible to be a member of the panchayat.

Powers and Functions of Panchayats

State legislatures have the legislative power, to confer on the panchayat, such powers and authority as may be necessary to enable them to function as institutions of self-government. They are usually entrusted with the responsibility of the following:

1. Preparing plans for economic development and social justice
2. Implementation of schemes for economic development and social justice
3. Matters listed in the 11th Schedule. This schedule contains 29 items, for example, land improvement, minor irrigation, animal husbandry, fisheries, education, and women and child development. A state may, by law, authorize a panchayat to levy, collect and appropriate taxes, duties, tolls, and so on.

A State Election Commission consisting of a State Election Commissioner is appointed by the Governor, to conduct elections to the panchayats. Any question with respect to elections shall be referred to such authority as the state legislature may provide by law. Courts will have no jurisdiction in this matter.

Municipalities

Institutions of self-government in urban areas are called municipalities. They are of three types:

1. Nagar panchayat, for a transitional area (that is being transformed from a rural area to an urban area)
2. Municipal council for a smaller urban area
3. Municipal corporation for a larger urban area

Composition of Municipalities

The members of a municipality are generally elected by direct election. The legislature of a state may, by law, provide for representation in a municipality.

For one or more wards comprised within the territorial area of a municipality having a population of three lakhs or more, it would be obligatory to constitute ward committees.

Duration of Municipalities

Every municipality shall continue for five years from the date of its first meeting. However, it may be dissolved earlier according to law.

Qualifications for Membership

All persons who are qualified to be chosen to the state legislature shall be qualified for being a member of the municipality. There is an important difference. Persons who have attained the age of 21 years shall be eligible to be a member, while for election to the state legislature, a person should have attained the age of 25 years.

A state legislature may, by law, authorize a municipality to levy, collect, and appropriate taxes, duties, tolls, and so on.

The State Election Commission shall have the power to conduct elections to municipalities.

Apart from giving constitutional recognition to municipalities, the 74th Amendment lays down that in every state two committees shall be constituted, namely,

1. At the district level, a district planning committee
2. In every metropolitan area, a metropolitan planning committee

Union Budget (Article 112)

The budget is the annual financial statement of the government. It is a government bill and is classified as a Money Bill. It is presented to the Lok Sabha upon the recommendation of the President. The budget is a statement of the estimated receipts and expenditures of the government of India for the following financial year. All the expenditures approved through various demands for grants and expenses charged on the consolidated fund of India are then presented in the form of a single bill called the appropriation bill. The proposals for taxation to raise revenue are presented in the form of financial bill.

Consolidated Fund of India

It is a fund to which all the revenue, loans raised and income of the Government of India are deposited.

Charged expenditures are expenditures that do not require the approval of the Parliament to be spent out of the consolidated fund of India.

Contingency Fund of India

This fund was created in 1950 by an act of Parliament on the basis of powers provided under Article 267. It has a limit of 50 crores. It is placed at the disposal of the President to meet unforeseen expenditures where the Parliament's approval cannot be obtained owing to time factor.

Public Account of India

It accounts for flows for those transactions where the government is merely acting as a banker. This fund was constituted under Article 266 (2) of the Constitution. Examples of those are provident funds, small savings, and so on. These funds do not belong to the government. They have to be paid back at some time to their rightful owners. Because of this nature of the fund, expenditures from it are not required to be approved by the Parliament.

NITI Aayog

National Institution for Transforming India (NITI Aayog) is a policy think-tank of government that replaces Planning Commission and aims to involve the states in economic policy-making in India. It will be providing strategic and technical advice to the central and the state governments. Government had announced the formation of NITI Aayog on 1 January 2015.
It has the following levels:

1. Prime Minister of India will be the Chairperson.
2. Governing Council comprises the Chief Ministers of all the States and Lieutenant Governors of Union Territories.
3. Regional Councils will be formed to address specific issues and contingencies impacting more than one state or a region. These will be formed for a specified tenure.
4. Experts, specialists, and practitioners with relevant domain knowledge as special invitees will be nominated by the Prime Minister.

Higher Education System

1. The main governing body at the tertiary level of education in India is
(a) NCERT (b) CBSE
(c) AICTE (d) UGC

2. Government established the University Grants Commission by an act of Parliament in the year (*June 2007*)
(a) 1980 (b) 1948
(c) 1950 (d) 1956

3. The tertiary education includes
(a) Primary and secondary education
(b) Higher education
(c) Vocational education and training
(d) Both (b) and (c)

4. Which of the following is the regulator of higher education?
(a) NCERT (b) AICTE
(c) UGC (d) MHRD

5. The idea of Four Pillars of Education was suggested by
(a) UNICEF (b) UGC
(c) NCTE (d) UNESCO

6. The name of the plan to increase enrolment in the higher education institutions is
   (a) Rashtriya Uchchatar Shiksha Abhiyan (RUSA)
   (b) Sarva Shiksha Abhiyan
   (c) Both (a) and (b)
   (d) None of the above
7. Which of the following agency put forward the concept of proactive university?
   (a) UNDP (b) UNESCO
   (c) AICTE (d) UGC
8. 'Destiny of India is being shaped in her classroom'. This is stated in
   (a) National Policy on Education (1986)
   (b) National Knowledge Commission (2005)
   (c) Education Commission (1964–66)
   (d) University Education Commission (1948–49)
9. CHEER stands for
   (a) Children Enrichment Education through Radio
   (b) Child health education electronic recording
   (c) Children for Engineers and Energy Requirement
   (d) None of the above
10. Educational TV was first introduced in India in the year
    (a) 1961 (b) 1959
    (c) 1968 (d) 1965
11. Which of the following agencies or organizations was constitutionally assigned the task of coordination and determination of standards of institutions in higher education?
    (a) UGC
    (b) Concerned state governments
    (c) Union government
    (d) None of the above
12. Which of the following documents is termed as the Magna Carta of English education in India?
    (a) Charles Wood's dispatch
    (b) Macaulay minutes
    (c) Mountstuart Elphinstone's minutes
    (d) Wardha system
13. In which of the following years, Presidency Universities of Calcutta, Bombay, and Madras were set up following the recommendations of Woods' dispatch?
    (a) 1854 (b) 1857
    (c) 1858 (d) 1861
14. The University of Allahabad was founded in the year
    (a) 1887 (b) 1901
    (c) 1905 (d) 1911
15. Which of the following institution was set up in 1945 to look after the functioning of three Central Universities of Aligarh, Banaras, and Delhi?
    (a) University Grants Commission
    (b) University Grants Committee
    (c) Inter University Board
    (d) Association of Indian Universities
16. The report of central advisory board of education on post war educational development in India is also termed as
    (a) Sargent report (b) Nehru report
    (c) Wardha report (d) None of the above
17. Which section of the UGC Act provides for the promotion and coordination of university education and for the maintenance of standards of teaching, examination, and research?
    (a) Section 12 (b) Section 15
    (c) Section 25 (d) Section 28
18. It is said that the present higher education system has its origin in Mountstuart Elphinstone's minutes, which stressed upon the need for establishing schools for teaching English and European sciences. This reported was presented in the year
    (a) 1823 (b) 1835
    (c) 1858 (d) 1861
19. Inter University Board was set up in 1925 to promote university activities, by sharing information and cooperation in the field of education, culture, sports, and allied areas. Now, it is known as
    (a) Association of Indian Universities
    (b) Central Advisory Board of Education

(c) Central Board of Secondary Education
(d) None of the above

20. Which of the following is known as Calcutta University Commission?
(a) Saddler Commission
(b) Kothari Commission
(c) Hunter Commission
(d) Wood Dispatch

21. Which of the following is regarded as the first policy measure regarding higher education in India?
(a) Wood's dispatch
(b) Macaulay's minutes
(c) Elphinstone report
(d) None of the above

22. Which of the following is a precursor to 10 + 2 + 3?
(a) Saddler commission
(b) Wood dispatch
(c) Kothari commission
(d) None of the above

23. Which of the following commissions recommended setting up UGC and is also known as the University Education Commission?
(a) Radhakrishnan commission
(b) Mudaliar commission
(c) Wardha commission
(d) Kothari commission

24. Which of the following commission's report is titled as education and national development report?
(a) Radhakrishnan commission
(b) Kothari commission
(c) Mudaliar commission report
(d) None of the above

25. National committee on 10 + 2 + 3 education structure set up in 1972 was headed by
(a) Dr P. D. Shukla
(b) Dr D. S. Kothari
(c) Dr Radhakrishnan
(d) None of the above

26. The following commissions were set up by the government or its agencies after independence. Arrange the following in a chronological order (in terms of their occurrence)
I University Education Commission
II Secondary Education Commission
III Education Commission
Codes:
(a) III, II, and I (b) II, I, and III
(c) I, II, and III (d) I, III, and II

27. Which of the following committees recommended the spending of ₹500 crores to be spent on research in basic sciences every year by UGC every year?
(a) M. M. Sharma committee
(b) Kakodkar committee
(c) Prof. Yashpal committee
(d) None of the above

28. The committee set up by the Ministry of Human Resource Development which recommended autonomy of IITs was headed by
(a) Prof. Anil Kakodkar
(b) Prof. Yashpal
(c) Sam Pitroda
(d) None of the above

29. National knowledge commission (NKC) was headed by
(a) Prof. Anil Kakodkar
(b) Prof. Yashpal
(c) Sam Pitroda
(d) None of the above

30. A committee was set up in 1990 to review NPE (1986). Its report titled as 'Towards an Enlightened and Humane Society' stated that system of higher education encourages memorization of facts and regurgitation rather than creativity. The head of the committee was
(a) Acharya Ramamurti
(b) Prof. Yashpal
(c) Prof. M. M. Joshi
(d) None of the above

31. Which of the following committees recommended the setting up of National Commission for Higher Education and Research (NCHER) for prescribed standards of academic quality and defining policies for advancement of knowledge in higher educational institutions?
(a) Sam Pitroda committee
(b) Prof. Yashpal committee

(c) M. M. Sharma committee
(d) Gnanam committee

32. Chairman of UGC committee appointed in 1969 for the purpose of administrative legislation of the universities was
(a) Dr D. S. Kothari
(b) Dr P. B. Gajendragadkar
(c) Prof. Yashpal
(d) None of the above

33. Which of the following personalities headed the committee recommended setting up of 1500 universities so as to achieve the target gross enrolment of 30%?
(a) Dr D. S. Kothari (b) Sam Pitroda
(c) Prof. Yashpal (d) None of the above

34. Which of the following percentage figures was recommended by both Kothari Commission and National Policy that should be spent on education (1986)?
(a) 4% of GDP (b) 5% of GDP
(c) 6% of GDP (d) None of the above

35. Which of the following states has the maximum number of central universities?
(a) Uttar Pradesh (b) Delhi
(c) Both (a) and (b) (d) None of the above

36. Which of the following institution or organization publishes Universities Handbook?
(a) University Grants Commission
(b) Association of Indian Universities
(c) Inter University Centres
(d) Central Advisory Board of Education

37. In which year was the Association of Indian Universities (AIU) originally set up?
(a) 1925 (b) 1945
(c) 1953 (d) None of the above

38. Which of the following authorities is not empowered to bring a university into existence?
(a) State government
(b) Central government
(c) UGC
(d) None of the above

39. How many universities were set up under Central Universities Act, 2009?
(a) 12 (b) 16
(c) 40 (d) 43

40. Which among the following constitute the majority of institutions within the university system?
(a) Central universities
(b) State universities
(c) Deemed universities
(d) Private universities

41. Which among the following constitute the majority of enrolments within the university system?
(a) Central universities
(b) State universities
(c) Deemed universities
(d) Private universities

42. Universities having central campus for imparting education are called (*June 2007*)
(a) Central universities
(b) Deemed universities
(c) Residential universities
(d) Open universities

43. Which of the following agencies provide funding to Indira Gandhi National Open University?
(a) University Grants Commission
(b) Ministry of Human Resource Development
(c) Both (a) and (b)
(d) None of the above

44. The university that telecasts interactive educational programmes through its own channel is (*June 2007*)
(a) Dr B. R. Ambedkar Open University, Hyderabad
(b) IGNOU
(c) University of Pune
(d) Annamalai University

45. Which of the following pairs of authorities are at the top of hierarchy in the case of a Central University?
(a) Visitors and Chancellor
(b) Visitors and Vice Chancellor
(c) Chancellor and Vice Chancellor
(d) Vice President & Vice Chancellor

46. The state with most universities is
(a) Tamil Nadu (b) Andhra Pradesh
(c) Rajasthan (d) Uttar Pradesh

47. The state with most deemed universities is
(a) Tamil Nadu (b) Andhra Pradesh
(c) Maharashtra (d) Karnataka

48. According to Times Higher Education's research findings to rank the world's higher educational institutions, which of the following educational has top rank in India?
(a) Delhi University, Delhi
(b) IIT- Mumbai
(c) Panjab University, Chandigarh
(d) IIT- Delhi

49. Institute of National Importance is an institution in higher education which serves as a pivotal player in developing highly skilled personnel within the specified region of the country or state. This status can be conferred upon them by
(a) University Grants Commission
(b) An act of Parliament
(c) All Indian Council for Technical Education
(d) All of the above

50. Commonwealth of learning (CoL) is the only official Commonwealth agency located outside Britain. It is located in
(a) New Delhi, India
(b) Vancouver, Canada
(c) Sydney, Australia
(d) Islamabad, Pakistan

51. As envisaged in 12th Five Year Plan, under the concept of College Cluster Universities, a minimum number of colleges in the vicinity of a city or district can establish a university. What is the minimum number of such colleges?
(a) 25 (b) 50
(c) 60 (d) 100

52. EHEI stands for
(a) Equity in Higher Education Institutions
(b) Equity in Higher Education Index
(c) Equality in Higher Education Index
(d) Equity in Hidden Education Income

53. API stands for
(a) Academic Parameter Indicator
(b) Academic Performance Indicator
(c) Academic Paid Instalment
(d) None of the above

54. National literacy mission was established in
(a) 1996 (b) 1988
(c) 1999 (d) 2000

55. The main aim of National Council for Teacher Education is
(a) To open college of education
(b) To promote research in education
(c) To maintain standards in colleges of education
(d) To provide grant to colleges of education

56. National Council of Educational Research and Training was established in
(a) 1961 (b) 1962
(c) 1963 (d) 1964

57. Which of the following organizations set up the National Assessment and Accreditation Council?
(a) AICTE (b) UGC
(c) MHRD (d) None of the above

58. National Assessment and Accreditation Council (NAAC) is headquartered in
(a) New Delhi (b) Mumbai
(c) Hyderabad (d) Bengaluru

59. NUEPA is mainly concerned with
(a) Educational Supervision
(b) Educational Unity
(c) Educational Planning
(d) Educational Evaluation

60. The title of Yashpal Committee Report (1993) is
(a) lCT in Teacher education
(b) Learning without burden
(c) Learning through Broadcasting
(d) None of the above

61. The number of representatives of Central Government in UGC is
(a) 9 (b) 2 (c) 6 (d) 3

62. Which of the following agencies or institutions set up the Accreditation Board (AB)?
(a) Indian Council of Agricultural Research
(b) All India Council for Technical Education
(c) University Grants Commission
(d) Ministry of Human Resource Development

63. The National Board of Accreditation (NBA) was set up in the year 1987 by
(a) AICTE (b) UGC
(c) MHRD (d) IGNOU

64. In which of the following years 'The National Policy of Education' was revised and a 'Programme of Action' was also attached to it?
(a) 1968 (b) 1976
(c) 1986 (d) 1992

65. Which of the following days is celebrated as National Education Day?
(a) September 5 (b) October 2
(c) November 11 (d) November 14

66. The purpose of National Education Policy is
(a) Universalization of primary education
(b) Vocationalization of education
(c) To review the education
(d) To give equal opportunity of education to all

67. According to Vision Paper of 12th Five Year Plan, the targeted staff strength (in terms of teacher–student ratio) envisaged for science and technology in higher education is
(a) 1 : 10 (b) 1 : 15
(c) 1 : 20 (d) 1 : 30

68. According to Vision Paper of 12th Five Year Plan, the targeted staff strength (in terms of teacher–student ratio) envisaged for social sciences, humanities, management and arts subjects in higher education courses is
(a) 1 : 10 (b) 1 : 15
(c) 1 : 20 (d) 1 : 30

69. In order to achieve the 12th Five Year Plan's Inclusive and Qualitative Expansion of Higher Education, the number of proposed women universities is
(a) 10 (b) 15 (c) 20 (d) 30

70. Apart from few short-term programmes, academic staff colleges set up for teachers' training basically offer
(a) Subject-specific refresher courses
(b) General orientation programmes
(c) Both (a) and (b)
(d) None of the above

71. Which of the following institutes is/are funded by central government?
(a) National Institute of Foundry and Forge Technology, Ranchi
(b) North Eastern Regional Institute of Science and Technology, Itanagar
(c) Sant Longowal Institute of Engineering and Technology, Longowal, Punjab
(d) All of the above

72. The first Committee to be constituted after independence by the Government of India on Women's Education was
(a) Dr. Radhakrishnan Commission
(b) The Mudaliar Commission
(c) The Shri Sri Prakasa Committee
(d) Dr. Durgabai Deshmukh Committee

73. Which article of the constitution provides for the rights of minorities to establish and administer the institutions of their choice?
(a) Article 21 (1) (b) Article 30 (1)
(c) Article 32 (d) None of the above

74. In which of the following year National Commission for Minorities Educational Institutions (NCMI) was set up
(a) 2001 (b) 2003
(c) 2004 (d) 2005

75. Which of the following is a specialized agency of UN to deal with copyright and other intellectual property rights?
(a) WIPO (b) GATS
(c) GATT (d) None of the above

76. The name of pilot project to provide education through massive satellite connectivity up to grass-root level is
(a) Sarva Shiksha Abhiyan
(b) Women Empowerment Project
(c) Rajiv Gandhi Project
(d) None of the above

77. Which of the following universities has been assigned the status of central university in 2013?
(a) Panjab University
(b) Osmania University
(c) Nalanda University
(d) Indira Gandhi National Tribal University

78. The number of Central Universities in India is
(a) 40 (b) 41 (c) 42 (d) 46

79. Rashtriya Sanskrit Vidyapeetha is located in
(a) Tirupati (b) Chennai
(c) Hyderabad (d) Jaipur

80. Which of the following languages was assigned the status of classical language in 2013?
(a) Sanskrit (b) Tamil
(c) Hindi (d) Malayalam

81. Match List I with List II and select the correct answer from the codes given below:

List I		List II	
A	National Council of Rural Institutes	I	New Delhi
B	Indian Council of Historical Research	II	Hyderabad
C	Indian Council of Philosophical Research	III	Shimla
D	Indian Institute of Advanced Study	IV	Bangalore

Codes:
(a) A-II, B-IV, C-I, and D-III
(b) A-II, B-IV, C-III, and D-I
(c) A-II, B-III, C-IV, and D-I
(d) A-II, B-I, C-IV, and D-III

82. The first virtual university of India came up in
(a) Andhra Pradesh
(b) Maharashtra
(c) Uttar Pradesh
(d) Tamil Nadu *(December 2013)*

83. Which of the following project(s) is/are funded by external agencies?
(a) Technical Education Quality Improvement Programme
(b) Technician Education Project
(c) Colombo Plan Staff College, Manila
(d) All of the above

84. The South Asian University is located at
(a) New Delhi (b) Jaipur
(c) Kathmandu (d) Islamabad

85. The Vikram Sarabhai Space Research Centre is located at
(a) Thiruvananthapuram
(b) Sriharikota
(c) Pune
(d) Bengaluru

86. Which one of the following Councils has been disbanded in 2013?
(a) Distance Education Council (DEC)
(b) National Council for Teacher Education (NCTE)
(c) National Council of Educational Research and Training (NCERT)
(d) National Assessment and Accreditation Council (NAAC)

87. Centre for Cellular and Molecular Biology is located in
(a) Hyderabad (b) Chennai
(c) Bengaluru (d) Ahmedabad

88. Which of the following days is celebrated as National Education Day?
(a) September 5 (b) October 2
(c) November 11 (d) November 14

89. Which of the following regulatory bodies does not enjoy a statutory status as a professional body?
(a) Bar Council of India
(b) All India Council for Technical Education
(c) Medical Council of India
(d) None of the above

90. Under which of the following constitutional amendments, education was transferred to the concurrent list?
(a) 42nd (b) 73rd
(c) 74th (d) None of the above

91. UGC gets its funding from
    (a) Central government only
    (b) State governments
    (c) Both central and state governments
    (d) None of the above
92. Which of the following universities in India has Prime Minister as its chancellor?
    (a) Indira Gandhi National Open University
    (b) Visva – Bharti University
    (c) Indian Maritime University
    (d) Indian Defence University
93. Faculty Improvement Programme of UGC aims at
    (a) Appointment of additional faculty
    (b) Make faculty research oriented
    (c) Improving physical infrastructure
    (d) None of the above
94. Mahatma Gandhi Antarrashtriya Hindi Vishwavidyalaya is located at
    (a) New Delhi (b) Jaipur
    (c) Porbandar (d) Wardha
95. CABE was set up in the year
    (a) 1925 (b) 1857
    (c) 1956 (d) 1992
96. IGNOU was set up in the year
    (a) 1985 (b) 1988
    (c) 1991 (d) 1992
97. The apex body for open and distance learning (ODL) system in the country is
    (a) DEC (b) IGNOU
    (c) MHRD (d) None of the above
98. The ex-officio chairperson of Distance Education Council (DEC) is
    (a) Vice Chancellor, IGNOU
    (b) HRD Minister
    (c) Either (a) or (b)
    (d) None of the above
99. The Ministry of Human Resource Development was created in the year
    (a) 1972 (b) 1980
    (c) 1985 (d) 1991
100. Government has set a target to increase the gross enrolment ratio in higher education to 30% by the year
    (a) 2015 (b) 2020
    (c) 2025 (d) 2030
101. Which of the following personalities was the first chairman of UGC?
    (a) Dr Shanti Swaroop Bhatnagar
    (b) Dr Manmohan Singh
    (c) Shri Humayun Kabir
    (d) Shri C. D. Deshmukh
102. First open university in India was
    (a) Andhra Pradesh Open University
    (b) Indira Gandhi National Open University
    (c) Delhi University
    (d) None of the above
103. The first university in India to start correspondence course was
    (a) Andhra Pradesh Open University
    (b) IGNOU
    (c) Delhi University
    (d) None of the above
104. The rank of India in terms of enrolment in higher education institutions is
    (a) First (b) second
    (c) Third (d) Fourth
105. The National Knowledge Commission, a high level advisory body to Prime Minister of India, with the objective of transforming India into a knowledge society was set up in the year
    (a) 2005 (b) 2006
    (c) 2007 (d) 2008
106. The concept of a countrywide network for higher education that would allow students the flexibility to design their own curriculum and combine subjects of their choice is basically of
    (a) Innovation University
    (b) Meta University
    (c) Central University
    (d) Deemed university
107. The concept of Meta University was first propounded by
    (a) Massachusetts Institute of Technology
    (b) Jawaharlal Nehru University
    (c) Harvard Business School
    (d) Delhi University

108. The universities with NAAC 'A' Grade and 10 years of standing can get financial support from UGC for innovative teaching or educational programmes; these universities are known as
(a) Meta Universities
(b) Innovation Universities
(c) Central Universities
(d) None of the above

109. In which of the following countries, the Humboldtian Concept of University Education originated?
(a) USA (b) Poland
(c) France (d) Germany

110. The major concept underlying distance education is
(a) Continuing education
(b) Simplicity
(c) Cost effectiveness
(d) Objectivity

111. The course content of professional degree emphasizes on
(a) Acquiring skills and practical analysis
(b) Theory and research
(c) Building concepts
(d) None of the above

112. The number of universities at the time of independence was
(a) 15 (b) 20 (c) 28 (d) 35

113. Networking of libraries through electronic media is called (*June 2007*)
(a) Inflibnet (b) Libinfnet
(c) The Internet (d) HTML

114. Match List I with List II and select the correct answer from the codes given below:

List I (Institutions)		List II (Locations)	
A	Vikram Sarabhai Space Research Centre	I	Thiruvananthapuram
B	Centre for Cellular and Molecular Biology	II	Hyderabad
C	Indian Space Research Organization	III	Bengaluru
D	The Energy and Resources Institute	IV	New Delhi

Codes:
(a) A-I, B-II, C-III, and D-IV
(b) A-I, B-III, C-II, and D-IV
(c) A-III, B-II, C-I, and D-IV
(d) A-III, B-I, C-II, and D-IV

115. In which year was the NBA set up?
(a) 1991 (b) 1994
(c) 2001 (d) 2005

116. Aligarh Muslim University was set up in the year
(a) 1857 (b) 1875
(c) 1905 (d) 1916

117. Who among the following was the first Education Minister of independent India?
(a) Abul Kalam Azad
(b) S. Vallabhbhai Patel
(c) S. Radhakrishnan
(d) None of the above

118. There is a proposal to establish innovation universities aiming at world class standards. The proposed number of such institutions is
(a) 10 (b) 14
(c) 25 (d) None of the above

119. Which of the following satellite channel was launched on 26 January, 2003 for the spread of technical growth and development of distance education in India?
(a) Eklavya (b) Dronacharya
(c) Gyan Darshan (d) Gyan Vani

120. Which of the following institutions have been set up by the MHRD?
(a) National Bal Bhawan, New Delhi
(b) ISRO
(c) DRDO
(d) None of the above

121. SITE means
(a) Satellite Instructional Television Experiment
(b) Satellite Informational Television Experiment
(c) Satellite Instructional Telecom Experiment
(d) Satellite Informational Telecom Experiment

122. Name of the research station on Antarctic set up by India is
(a) Dakshin Gangotri
(b) Dakshin Ganga
(c) Dakshin Godawari
(d) None of the above

123. The foundation training of selected IAS officers is conducted at
(a) LBS National Academy of Public Administration, Mussoorie
(b) MG Institute of Public Administration, Chandigarh
(c) UPSC, New Delhi
(d) All state capitals

124. The main objective of 'National Mission on Teachers and Training' is to improve
(a) Students' enrolment
(b) Quality of teaching
(c) Women education
(d) All of the above

125. PACER is acronym for
(a) Professionals Action Committee for Educational Reforms
(b) Professionals Accreditation Committee for Educational Reforms
(c) Professionals Action Committee for Educational Research
(d) None of the above

126. Mahila Samakhya was born out of the New Education Policy of 1986 which stressed the need for an intervention to create gender equality through women's education. It was launched in the year
(a) 1989 (b) 1992
(c) 1996 (d) 1998

127. Who was the chairman of University Education Commission set up in 1948?
(a) Dr S. Radhakrishnan
(b) Dr D. S. Kothari
(c) Maulana Abul Kalam Azad
(d) C. D. Deshmukh

128. University Education Commission recommended the setting up of UGC on the lines of University Grants Commission of
(a) USA (b) Great Britain
(c) Germany (d) USSR

129. Which of the following agency or institution proposed introduction of India Education Index (IEI) for ranking institutes based on academic, research, performance, and other parameters?
(a) AICTE (b) NAAC
(c) UGC (d) IIT-Delhi

130. The largest university in the world in terms of student enrolment is
(a) Beijing University, Beijing, China
(b) Dr B. R. Ambedkar University Open University, Hyderabad
(c) Indira Gandhi National Open University, New Delhi
(d) None of the above

131. The first inter university centre which was established by UGC in 1984 is
(a) Inter University Accelerator Centre (Nuclear Science Centre)
(b) Inter University Centre for Astronomy and Astro-Physics (IUCAA)
(c) Inter University Accelerator Centre (formerly Nuclear Science Centre)
(d) None of the above

132. Distance Education Council set up the Arjun Singh Centre for Distance and Open Learning in the year 2002 in
(a) Jamia Millia Islamia University
(b) Delhi University
(c) Jawaharlal Nehru University
(d) IGNOU

133. Which of the following was the first private institution to be granted the status of a deemed university in 1976?
(a) Manipal Academy of Higher Education
(b) Symbiosis Institute, Pune
(c) Thapar University, Patiala
(d) Amity University, Noida

134. Match List I with List II and select the correct answer from the codes given below:

List I		List II	
A	Chinmaya International Foundation	I	Delhi
B	The Oriental Institute	II	Baroda
C	Academy of Sanskrit Research	III	Melkote (Karnataka)
D	Rashtriya Veda Vidya Pratishthan	IV	Ernakulum

Codes:

(a) A-IV, B-II, C-III, and D-I
(b) A-II, B-IV, C-III, and D-I
(c) A-II, B-III, C-IV, and D-I
(d) A-II, B-I, C-IV, and D-III

135. Through which of the following constitutional amendments Article 21A was inserted in the constitution to provide for free and compulsory education to all children of age group between 6 and 14 years as a fundamental right
(a) 73rd (b) 74th
(c) 86th (d) None of the above

136. Match List I with List II and select the correct answer from the codes given below:

List I (Institutions)		List II (Locations)	
A	National Law Institute	I	Shimla
B	Indian Institute of Advanced Studies	II	Bhopal
C	National Judicial Academy	III	Hyderabad
D	National Savings Institute	IV	Nagpur

Codes:

(a) A-III, B-II, C-IV, and D-I
(b) A-I, B-II, C-III, and D-IV
(c) A-IV, B-III, C-I, and D-II
(d) A-III, B-I, C-II, and D-IV

137. Indian Institute of Mass Communication is located in
(a) Ahmedabad
(b) New Delhi
(c) Hyderabad
(d) Jaipur

138. Indian National Defence University (INDU), India's first defence university, was inaugurated on May 2013 is proposed to be located at
(a) Rohtak (b) Pune
(c) Hyderabad (d) Gurgaon

Governance, Polity, Administration, and Institutions

Our Constitution: Basic Features

139. The modern state is described as
(a) A police state
(b) A welfare state
(c) A laissez faire state
(d) Autocratic state

140. The chief source of political power in India is
(a) The people
(b) The constitution
(c) The Parliament
(d) The Parliament and the state legislatures

141. Which of the following is not an essential element of the state?
(a) Population (b) Territory
(c) Sovereignty (d) Democracy

142. Which of the following factors is/are responsible for increase of the role of government in developing countries? (*December 2004*)

I Economic planning
II Rising expectation of people
III Privatization
IV Emergence of concept of welfare state

Select the most appropriate answer from the code given below.

Codes:

(a) I and IV (b) I, II, and IV
(c) Only III (d) Only IV

143. The Preamble to the constitution states 'We, the people of India, having solemnly resolved to constitute India into a sovereign, socialist, secular, democratic republic...'

By which of the following amendments were the words socialist and secular were added to it?

(a) 42nd Amendment
(b) 72nd Amendment
(c) 73rd Amendment
(d) 83rd Amendment

144. In a federal state

(a) States are more powerful than the centre
(b) Centre is more powerful than the states
(c) A presidential form of government functions
(d) None of the above

145. A federal system

(a) Must have a written constitution
(b) Must have an unwritten constitution
(c) May have either written or unwritten constitution
(d) May not have any constitution

146. The Constituent Assembly (which framed our constitution) was set up in the year

(a) 1942 (b) 1945
(c) 1946 (d) 1947

147. When was the Indian constitution passed by the Constituent Assembly?

(a) 26 November 1949
(b) 26 January 1949
(c) 26 January 1950
(d) None of the above

148. Which of the following personalities was the chairperson of the Drafting Committee of Indian constitution?

(a) Rajendra Prasad
(b) Tej Bahadur Sapru
(c) Rajagopalachari
(d) Dr B. R. Ambedkar

149. The time taken by the constituent assembly to frame the constitution for the country was

(a) 3 years 2 months and 10 days
(b) 2 years 11 months and 18 days
(c) 2 years 10 months and 11 days
(d) None of the above

150. India, that is Bharat, shall be a union of states. The states and the territories, thereof, shall be as specified in the

(a) First Schedule
(b) Second Schedule
(c) Third Schedule
(d) None of the above

151. In India, with several characteristics of a federal government, the supremacy lies in the

(a) Constitution (b) Parliament
(c) Supreme Court (d) Bureaucracy

152. An interpretation of Indian Constitution is based on the spirit of

(a) Preamble
(b) Directive principles
(c) Fundamental rights
(d) None of the above

153. The Constitution of India is divided into

(a) 20 parts (b) 22 parts
(c) 24 parts (d) 42 parts

154. Which of the following has the most profound impact on our constitution?

(a) Government of India Act, 1935
(b) Constitution of USA
(c) Constitution of UK
(d) Constitution of Ireland

155. The Indian Constitution closely follows the constitutional system of

(a) USA (b) UK
(c) Switzerland (d) Russia

156. The secular character of the Constitution of India denotes that

(a) State has no official religion.
(b) Equal opportunity to everybody to profess, practice, and propagate of religion of their choice
(c) Single citizenship to assured to all people irrespective of their religion
(d) All of the above

157. Directive Principles of State Policy included in the Constitution of India have been inspired by the constitution of
(a) USA (b) Ireland
(c) Canada (d) Australia

158. Which of the following depicts the true nature of Indian Constitution?
(a) Unitary
(b) Federal
(c) Parliamentary
(d) Federal in form and unitary in spirit

159. Fundamental duties were incorporated in the Indian Constitution by the
(a) 32nd Amendment
(b) 42nd Amendment
(c) 44th Amendment
(d) 76th Amendment

160. What does the phrase equality before the law used in Article 14 mean?
(a) All individuals are equal.
(b) All laws are the same for everybody.
(c) All individuals are equally subjected to the ordinary law of the land.
(d) Law in equal circumstances should treat everybody equally.

161. Who headed the committee appointed the constitution assembly to finalize the fundamental rights of Indian citizens
(a) Dr B. R. Ambedkar
(b) Jawaharlal Nehru
(c) Sardar Patel
(d) All of the above

162. What is the number of fundamentals rights as enshrined in our constitution?
(a) Six (b) Eight
(c) Ten (d) Twelve

163. Which of the following articles provides for the Fundamental Rights in our constitution?
(a) Articles 13–36 (b) Articles 12–35
(c) Articles 15–39 (d) None of the above

164. Which of the following articles guarantees Right to freedom of religion?
(a) 12–19 (b) 12–14
(c) 25–28 (d) 21–28

165. Which among the following is not guaranteed by the Constitution of India?
(a) Freedom to own, acquire, and dispose of property anywhere in the country
(b) Freedom to move freely throughout the country
(c) Freedom to assemble peacefully without arms
(d) Freedom to practise any trade or profession

166. According to Supreme Court verdict, Right to Property is a
(a) Constitutional right
(b) Legal right
(c) Fundamental right
(d) Directive Principles

167. Which of the following is not a Fundamental Right? (*December 2005*)
(a) Right to equality
(b) Right against exploitation
(c) Right to freedom of speech and expression
(d) Right of free compulsory education of all children up to the age of 14

168. Which of the following Fundamental Rights have been deleted from our constitution through an amendment?
(a) Right against exploitation
(b) Right to freedom of religion
(c) Right to property
(d) Freedom of speech and expression

169. The authority to issue writs for the enforcement of fundamental rights rests with
(a) All the courts in India
(b) The Parliament
(c) The Supreme Court
(d) The President of India

170. How can Fundamental Rights be protected by a citizen?

(a) By approaching the Supreme Court, who will issue writs against the authority.
(b) Parliament will take note of such violations and tell the courts.
(c) The Executive will inform the courts.
(d) It is automatically protected.

171. Which Fundamental Right is concerned with the abolition of social distinctions?
(a) Right to equality
(b) Right against exploitation
(c) Right to life and liberty
(d) Cultural and educational rights

172. Fundamental rights can be suspended during
(a) President's rule
(b) National emergency
(c) Financial emergency
(d) Can never be suspended

173. To uphold and protect the sovereignty, unity, and integrity of India, a provision has been made in the
(a) Directive Principles
(b) Preamble to the constitution
(c) Fundamental Duties
(d) Fundamental Rights

174. How do Directive Principles of State Policy differ from Fundamental Rights?
(a) The former are meant for UTs, whereas the latter are for states.
(b) The former are not enforceable, whereas the latter are enforceable.
(c) The former are not a part of the constitution, whereas the latter are the part of the constitution.
(d) None of the above

175. Which of the following instruments may be used by the Supreme Court for the enforcement of fundamental rights?
(a) A decree (b) An ordinance
(c) A notification (d) A writ

176. Which of the following writs may be issued to enforce a fundamental right?
(a) Habeas corpus (b) Mandamus
(c) Prohibition (d) Certiorari

177. Right to free education within certain limits is
(a) Guaranteed as a fundamental right
(b) Enshrined in the Directive Principles of State policy
(c) Outlined in the Preamble of the constitution
(d) Ignored by constitution

178. Which of the following article deals with the amendment to our constitution?
(a) 356 (b) 368 (c) 370 (d) 372

179. Distributive justice is the common aim of
(a) Articles 44 and 45
(b) Articles 38 and 39
(c) Articles 29 and 30
(d) Articles 45 and 46

180. Which of the following legislative measure introduced the concept of collective responsibility of the cabinet in India?
(a) Minto–Morley Reforms
(b) Independence Act, 1947
(c) Constitution of India
(d) Government of India Act, 1935

181. In the case of a conflict between the centre and a state in respect of a subject included in Concurrent List
(a) Union law prevails
(b) State law prevails
(c) Both may prevail
(d) Decided by the President

182. The idea of democratic decentralization in India was popularized by *(December 2004)*
(a) A. D. Gorwala Committee, 1951
(b) Paul H. Appleby Committee, 1953
(c) B. R. Mehta Committee, 1957
(d) Ashok Mehta Committee, 1978

183. Match List I with List II and select the correct answer from the codes given below:

List I (Schedules)		List II (Matters)	
A	First	I	Territory States and Union Territories
B	Eighth	II	Languages

C	Ninth	III	Acts passed by Legislature
D	Tenth	IV	Disqualification of MPs/MLAs on defection

Codes:

(a) A-II, B-I, C-III, and D-IV
(b) A-II, B-I, C-IV, and D-III
(c) A-I, B-II, C-IV, and D-III
(d) A-I, B-II, C-III, and D-IV

184. Legislative Council in a state can be created by the
(a) State Legislative Assembly alone
(b) President on recommendation of the Governor
(c) Parliament alone
(d) Parliament on recommendation of the State Legislature

185. Match List I with List II and select the correct answer from the codes given below: *(June 2010)*

List I (Articles)		List II (Institutions)	
A	Article 280	I	Administrative Tribunals
B	Article 324	II	Election Commission
C	Article 323	III	Finance Commission
D	Article 315	IV	UPSC

Codes:

(a) A-I, B-II, C-III, and D-IV
(b) A-III, B-II, C-I, and D-IV
(c) A-II, B-III, C-IV, and D-I
(d) A-II, B-IV, C-III, and D-I

Parliament

186. The most essential feature of the Parliamentary form of government is the
(a) Sovereignty of Parliament
(b) Written constitution
(c) Accountability of the Executive to the Legislature
(d) Independence of the judiciary

187. The Parliament of India consists of
(a) Lok Sabha only
(b) Rajya Sabha only
(c) Lok Sabha and Rajya Sabha
(d) Lok Sabha, Rajya Sabha, and President

188. In a parliamentary form of government, the real powers of the state are vested in the
(a) Council of ministers
(b) President
(c) Government
(d) Parliament

189. The maximum strength of Lok Sabha and Rajya Sabha, respectively, is
(a) 552 and 250 (b) 537 and 275
(c) 525 and 238 (d) 545 and 250

190. An ordinance promulgated by the President
(a) Will lapse automatically after two months
(b) Will continue to be in force till is superseded by an Act of the Parliament
(c) Will automatically become a law after six months
(d) Will lapse on the expiration of six weeks from the meeting of the Parliament

191. An ordinance can be promulgated in case
(a) Of conflict between two Houses on a bill
(b) Both Houses of Parliament are not in session
(c) The Lok Sabha has been dissolved
(d) Of elections

192. For removal of which of the following dignitaries Parliament's resolution is not needed?
(a) Judge of Supreme Court
(b) Comptroller and Auditor General
(c) Chief Election Commissioner
(d) Governor of a state

193. To which of the following bills the President must accord his sanction without sending it back for fresh consideration?
(a) Finance Bills
(b) Bill seeking amendment to the constitution
(c) Ordinary bills
(d) Bills passed by both the Houses of the Parliament

194. Vice President of India presides over
(a) House of People
(b) Rajya Sabha
(c) Both (a) and (b)
(d) Union Cabinet

195. Which of the following is the ex-officio Chairman of Rajya Sabha?
(a) President (b) Vice President
(c) Prime Minister (d) None of the above

196. During zero hour
(a) Money Bill is introduced in the Lok Sabha
(b) Matters of utmost importance are raised
(c) Opposition members raise their questions
(d) MPs take a break

197. Bills are normally introduced in the Parliament
(a) During question hour
(b) During zero hour
(c) Soon after lunch break
(d) Shortly before the House adjourns for the day

198. A bill referred to a joint sitting of the two Houses of the Parliament can be passed by
(a) Absolute majority
(b) A simple majority
(c) Two-third majority
(d) None of the above

199. A bill for alteration of boundaries of states shall not be introduced in the Parliament without the recommendation of
(a) The presiding officers of both Houses of Parliament
(b) The legislatures of the states concerned
(c) The Supreme Court
(d) The President

200. Match List I with List II and select the correct answer from the codes given below:

List I (Institutions)		List II (Functions)	
A	Parliament	I	Formulation of budget
B	C and AG	II	Enactment of budget
C	Ministry of Finance	III	Implementation of budget
D	Executing Departments	IV	Legality of expenditure
		V	Justification of income

Codes:
(a) A-III, B-IV, C-II, and D-I
(b) A-II, B-IV, C-I, and D-III
(c) A-V, B-III, C-IV, and D-II
(d) A-IV, B-II, C-III, and D-V

201. The first elected Lok Sabha under the new constitution came into being in
(a) 1950 (b) 1951
(c) 1952 (d) 1953

202. Money can be spent out of the Consolidated Fund of India with the approval of the
(a) President
(b) Parliament
(c) Comptroller and Auditor General
(d) Finance Minister

203. Which of the following states has the maximum representation in the Lok Sabha?
(a) Uttar Pradesh (b) Bihar
(c) Maharashtra (d) West Bengal

204. Who has the authority to decide whether a particular bill is a Money Bill or not?
(a) The Prime Minister
(b) The Lok Sabha Speaker
(c) The President
(d) The Chief Justice of India

205. Which of the following bills cannot be introduced first in the Rajya Sabha?

(a) Money Bills
(b) Non-finance Bill
(c) Both (a) and (b)
(d) None of the above

206. Parliament can legislate on matters listed in the state list (*June 2006*)
(a) With prior permission of the President
(b) Only after the constitution is amended suitably
(c) In case of inconsistency among state legislatures
(d) At the request of two or more states

207. How many members of the Rajya Sabha are nominated by the President of India?
(a) 10 (b) 12 (c) 15 (d) 18

208. The joint sitting of both houses of Parliament is presided over by the
(a) President
(b) Lok Sabha Speaker
(c) Vice President
(d) Chief Justice of India

209. The time gap between two sessions of the Parliament should not exceed
(a) Three months (b) One year
(c) Nine months (d) Six months

210. According to Article 120 of the Constitution of India, the business in Parliament shall be transacted in
(a) English only
(b) Hindi only
(c) English and Hindi both
(d) All the languages included in Eight Schedule of the constitution

211. One-third of the members of the Rajya Sabha retire after every
(a) Second year (b) Fifth year
(c) One year (d) Third year

212. A Money Bill passed by the Lok Sabha has to be passed by Rajya Sabha within
(a) Three months
(b) Fourteen days
(c) Twenty-one days
(d) One month

213. Which of the following is not a standing committee of the Parliament?
(a) Estimates Committee
(b) Committee on Public Undertakings
(c) Committee on Welfare of SCs and STs
(d) Committee on Public Accounts

214. When the Lok Sabha is dissolved, the Speaker continues in office till a new
(a) Presiding officer is appointed
(b) Speaker is elected when the new House meets
(c) Lok Sabha is formed
(d) Deputy Speaker is appointed

215. Which of the following Houses of Parliament is also called the House of Elders?
(a) Lok Sabha (b) Vidhan Sabha
(c) Rajya Sabha (d) Gram Sabha

216. Which of the following authorities appoint the Chairman of the Public Accounts Committee of the Parliament?
(a) The Speaker of Lok Sabha
(b) The Finance Minister
(c) The Prime Minister
(d) The President

217. The tenure of Rajya Sabha is
(a) Two years (b) Five years
(c) Six years (d) Permanent

218. Lok Sabha can be dissolved before the expiry of its normal five-year term by (*December 2005*)
(a) The Prime Minister
(b) The Speaker of Lok Sabha
(c) The President on the recommendation of Prime Minister
(d) None of the above

219. The minimum age requirement of a candidate to become a member of the Rajya Sabha is
(a) Twenty-five years
(b) Thirty-five years
(c) Thirty years
(d) Twenty-one years

220. Members of the Rajya Sabha are elected according to
(a) Cumulative vote system
(b) Single non-transferable vote system
(c) Single transferable vote system
(d) None of the above

221. Under whose advice does the President of India declare emergency under Article 352?
(a) Council of ministers
(b) Cabinet
(c). Chief Ministers of all states
(d) Prime Minister

222. Which subject was transferred from state list to Concurrent List by the 42nd amendment of the constitution?
(a) Agriculture
(b) Education
(c) Irrigation
(d) Local self-government

223. According to our constitution, the maximum number of members representing the union territories in the Lok Sabha cannot exceed
(a) 20 (b) 25
(c) 10 (d) 15

224. The central GST bill, the Integrated GST bill, the Union Territory GST bill and a bill to compensate states for revenue losses arising from the transition to GST were introduced in March 2017 as
(a) Money Bills
(b) Ordinary Bills
(c) Finance Bills
(d) Constitutional Amendment Bills

225. What is the minimum age for being the member of the Parliament?
(a) Twenty-one years
(b) Twenty-five years
(c) Thirty-five years
(d) None of the above

President and Prime Minister

226. The Prime Minister is the
(a) Head of the State
(b) Head of the Government
(c) Head of the State and the Head of the Government
(d) None of the above

227. Appointment of the members of the Council of Ministers is made by the President
(a) On the advice of the Chief Justice of India
(b) On the advice of the Vice President
(c) On the advice of the Prime Minister
(d) None of the above

228. President of India is
(a) The head of the government
(b) The head of the state
(c) The head of the parliament
(d) The head of the judiciary

229. The minimum age for being eligible to become the Prime Minister of India is
(a) Twenty-one years
(b) Twenty-five years
(c) Thirty years
(d) Thirty-five years

230. Who among the following is the ex officio Chairman of the NITI Aayog?
(a) President (b) Vice President
(c) Speaker (d) Prime Minister

231. The President of India is elected indirectly by an Electoral College consisting of elected members of
(a) Only Lok Sabha
(b) Only Rajya Sabha
(c) State assemblies and state Legislative Councils
(d) All of the above

232. Which of the following authorities can proclaim emergency in the states?
(a) The Governor
(b) The Chief Minister
(c) The President
(d) The Prime Minister

233. The oath of office to the President is administered by the
(a) Chief Justice of India
(b) Speaker
(c) Prime Minister
(d) Vice President

234. Which of the following authorities can impose reasonable restrictions on fundamental rights?
(a) The President
(b) The Chief Justice of India
(c) The Parliament
(d) The Lok Sabha

235. Who decides the disputes regarding the election of the President?
(a) The Speaker
(b) The Supreme Court
(c) The Election Commission
(d) The Parliament

236. Article 356 of the Constitution of India deals with
(a) Autonomy of States
(b) The proclamation of President's Rule in a State
(c) The removal of a Chief Minister
(d) The appointment of a Governor

237. In which of the following situations does the President act in his own discretion?
(a) In appointing the Prime Minister
(b) In returning a proposal to the council of ministers for reconsideration
(c) Both of these
(d) None of the above

238. Prime Minister resigns when he does not command majority in the Lower House of Parliament. This is
(a) In accordance with a stipulation in the constitution
(b) Not explicitly stated in the constitution but followed as a convention
(c) Peculiar to Indian democracy
(d) A legacy of the Government of India Act, 1919

239. Which of the following articles empowers the President to appoint Prime Minister of India?
(a) Article 74
(b) Article 75
(c) Article 76
(d) None of the above

240. The Governor of a state is appointed by the
(a) Chief Minister (b) Chief Justice
(c) President (d) Prime Minister

Other Important Public Institutions

241. Which of the following authorities recommends the principles governing the grants-in-aid of revenues of states out of Consolidated Fund of India?
(a) Public Accounts Committee
(b) Inter State Council
(c) Union Ministry of Finance
(d) Finance Commission

242. Consider the following statements regarding the Attorney General of India:
I There is no age limit to his appointment.
II He can be a member of a Parliamentary Committee.
III He shall have the right of audience in all the courts.
IV The term of his office is fixed by the Constitution of India.
Select the correct answer from the codes given below.
Codes:
(a) I and II are correct.
(b) I, II, and III are correct.
(c) II, III, and IV are correct.
(d) III and IV are correct.

243. Which of the following has the constitutional authority to decide tax share of states?
(a) Finance minister
(b) Finance commission
(c) NITI Aayog
(d) Union cabinet

244. In India, a political party is recognized as a National or Regional party by the (*December 2004*)
(a) The President of India
(b) The Election Commission of India
(c) The law ministry in consultation with the Law Commission of India
(d) The union Parliament in consultation with state Legislature

245. Which of the following non-members of Parliament has the right to address it?
(a) The Chief Election Commissioner
(b) The Comptroller and Auditor General
(c) The Attorney General of India
(d) The Solicitor General of India

246. Which part of the constitution directs the state to establish Panchayati Raj Institution in the country?

(a) Preamble
(b) Directive Principles of State Policy
(c) fundamental rights
(d) None of the above

247. By which of the following measures NITI Aayog was established?
(a) Cabinet resolution
(b) Parliament resolution
(c) President
(d) Prime Minister

248. Which of the following authority appoints the Chief Election Commissioner of India?
(a) President
(b) Prime Minister
(c) Parliament
(d) Chief Justice of India

249. Who is the highest Law Officer of a state?
(a) Attorney General
(b) Advocate General
(c) Solicitor General
(d) Secretary General

250. Members of the Union Public Service Commission function for
(a) 60 years (b) 58 years
(c) 62 years (d) 65 years

251. The Panchayati Raj System was adopted to
(a) Make people aware of politics
(b) Decentralize the power of democracy
(c) Educate the peasants
(d) None of the above

252. Panchayati Raj was first introduced in
(a) Rajasthan (b) Gujarat
(c) Uttar Pradesh (d) Bihar

253. Under which of the following amendments, the historic Panchayati Raj Bill was passed by the Parliament in 1992
(a) 70th Amendment
(b) 72nd Amendment
(c) 74th Amendment
(d) 68th Amendment

254. Which of the following statements are correct about the Central Information Commission?
I The Central Information Commission is a statutory body.
II The Chief Information Commissioner and other Information Commissioners are appointed by the President of India.
III The Commission can impose a penalty up to a maximum of 25,000/-
IV It can punish an errant officer.
Select the correct answer from the codes given below.
Codes:
(a) I and II only (b) I, II, and IV
(c) I, II, and III (d) II, III, and IV

255. Which is at the apex of the three-tier system of Panchayati Raj ?
(a) Gram Sabha (b) Gram Panchayat
(c) Zila Parishad (d) Panchayat Samiti

256. Which article of the constitution directs the government to organize village panchayats?
(a) Article 32 (b) Article 40
(c) Article 48 (d) Article 51

257. NITI Aayog is a
(a) Statutory body
(b) Executive body
(c) Autonomous body
(d) Advisory and non-statutory body

258. Consider the following statements:
Assertion (A): Rights and duties are the two sides of the same **coin.**
Reason (R): It is not the duty of the state to maintain the rights of the citizens.
(a) Both (A) and (R) are true, and (R) is correct explanation of (A)
(b) Both (A) and (R) are true, but (R) is not the correct explanation of (A)
(c) (A) is true, but (R) is false
(d) (A) is false, but (R) is true

259. Who holds the power of judicial review in India?
(a) President (b) Prime Minister
(c) Supreme Court (d) Parliament

260. Supreme Court of India consists of a Chief Justice and
   (a) Seven judges
   (b) Nine judges
   (c) Twenty-Five judges
   (d) Thirty judges

261. What is the minimum duration of a stay, before a person can apply for Indian citizenship?
   (a) Five years (b) Three years
   (c) Seven years (d) Ten years

262. CAG is the Chief Accountant and Auditor for
   (a) Union Government
   (b) State Governments
   (c) Union and State Governments
   (d) Neither Union nor State Government

Miscellaneous

263. Ministry of Human Resource Development includes (*June 2006*)
   (a) Department of Elementary Education and Literacy
   (b) Department of Secondary Education and Higher Education
   (c) Department of Women and Child Development
   (d) All of the above

264. A uniform civil code has been recommended in the Directive Principles to ensure
   (a) To control the population growth
   (b) National security
   (c) National integration
   (d) Support for weaker sections of society

265. The language which enjoys special status in Article 351 of the Constitution of India as the primary source language for the development of the official standard of Hindi is
   (a) Sanskrit (b) Tamil
   (c) Bhojpuri (d) Maithili

266. Which of the following is the official language(s) as per Indian constitution?
   (a) Hindi
   (b) English
   (c) Hindi with English as an additional language
   (d) No official language

267. The National Language of India is
   (a) Hindi
   (b) English
   (c) Both English and Hindi
   (d) No national language

268. Which of the following High Courts gave ruling that India has no national language?
   (a) Mumbai (b) Gujarat
   (c) Lucknow (d) Patna

269. The Right of Children to Free and Compulsory Education Act, also popular as Right to Education Act (RTE Act) was enacted in the year
   (a) 2008 (b) 2009
   (c) 2010 (d) 2011

270. Right to Education Act (RTE) makes it mandatory to provide free and compulsory education for children age group between
   (a) 6 and 14 years (b) 6 and 12 years
   (c) 8 and 14 years (d) None of the above

271. The Right to Education Act came into force in the year
   (a) 2008 (b) 2009
   (c) 2010 (d) None of the above

272. Which of the following articles of constitution states that the official language of the union shall be Hindi in Devanagari script?
   (a) 343 (1) (b) 356
   (c) 75 (d) 351

273. The first language to have been assigned the status of classical language in 2004 is
   (a) Tamil (b) Sanskrit
   (c) Kannada (d) Malayalam

274. Odia has been assigned the status of classical language in February 2014. With this, the number of classical languages in India is
   (a) Three (b) Four
   (c) Five (d) Six

275. Ninety-third Constitution Amendment Bill seeks
   (a) To grant statehood to Uttaranchal
   (b) To make elementary education compulsory
   (c) To make army service mandatory
   (d) None of the above

276. Which of the following parts of the Indian Constitution enjoins upon the state to provide free and compulsory education for children up to 14 years of age?
   (a) Directive Principles of State Policy
   (b) fundamental rights
   (c) Fundamental Duties
   (d) Special Provisions related to certain classes

277. Select the correct sequence in ascending order.
   (a) Deputy Ministers, Ministers of State, and Cabinet Ministers
   (b) Ministers of State, Deputy Ministers, and Cabinet Ministers
   (c) Ministers of State, Cabinet Ministers, and Deputy Ministers
   (d) Cabinet Ministers, Ministers of State, and Deputy Ministers

278. Which of the following pairs of articles of the Constitution of India and the subjects dealt with by them are correctly matched?
   I Article 352: Proclamation of emergency
   II Article 370: Special status in respect of Jammu and Kashmir
   III Article 14: Equality of opportunity in matters of public employment
   IV Article 40: Organization of village panchayats
   Select the correct answer using the codes given below:
   Codes:
   (a) I and II (b) II, III, and IV
   (c) I, II, and IV (d) I, III, and IV

279. Which of the following is an example of extra-constitutional power of the Governor of a state in India?
   (a) His role as Chancellor of the universities in the state
   (b) His power to dismiss the ministry
   (c) His power to dissolve the state Legislative Assembly
   (d) His power to return a bill to the state Legislative Assembly for reconsideration

280. If Prime Minister of India belongs to the upper house of Parliament,
   (a) He will not be able to vote in his favour in the event of a no-confidence motion
   (b) He will not be able to speak on the budget in the lower house
   (c) He can make statements only in the upper house
   (d) He becomes a member of the lower house within six months after being sworn-in as the Prime Minister

281 Two statements, one labelled as Assertion (A) and the other labelled as Reason (R), are given:
   Assertion (A): The reservation of 33% of seats for women in Parliament and State Legislatures does not require constitutional amendment.
   Reason (R): Political parties contesting elections can allocate 33% seats they contest to women candidates without any constitutional amendment.
   In the context of these two statements, which of the following is correct?
   (a) Both (A) and (R) are true, and (R) is the correct explanation of (A)
   (b) Both (A) and (R) are true, but (R) is not the correct explanation of (A)
   (c) (A) is true, but (R) is false
   (d) (A) is false, but (R) is true

282 Which of the following is/are stated in the Constitution of India?
   I The President shall not be member of either house of Parliament
   II The Parliament shall consist of the President and two houses
   Choose the correct answer from the codes given below:

Codes:

(a) Neither I nor II (b) Both I and II
(c) I alone (d) II alone

283 Match List I with List II:

List I (Article of constitution)		List II (Subject)	
A	Art 54	I	President's Election
B	Art 75	II	Prime Minister Appointment
C	Art 155	III	Appointment of Governor
D	Art 164	IV	Appointment of Chief Minster

Codes:

(a) A-IV, B-II, C-III and D-I
(b) A-I, B-III, C-II and D-IV
(c) A-I, B-II, C-III and D-IV
(d) A-IV, B-III, C-II and D-I

284 Which of the following amendments relates to the local government institutions?
(a) 52nd Amendment
(b) 73rd Amendment
(c) 66th Amendment
(d) 70th Amendment

285 The real executive authority of the state is
(a) The Governor
(b) The Speaker
(c) The Council of Ministers
(d) The Chief Justice of High Court

286 Which of the following is the lengthiest amendment to the Constitution of India so far?
(a) 24th Amendment
(b) 30th Amendment
(c) 42nd Amendment
(d) 44th Amendment

287 The only President of India who was elected unopposed is
(a) S. Radhakrishnan
(b) Dr Zakir Hussain
(c) Neelam Sanjeeva Reddy
(d) Fakhruddin Ali Ahmed

288 Which of the following state Governors enjoys special powers with regard to the administration of tribal areas?
(a) Odisha (b) Madhya Pradesh
(c) Bihar (d) Assam

289 The normal tenure of the Governor of a state is
(a) Five years
(b) Till he/she enjoys the confidence of the President
(c) Till he/she enjoys the confidence of the Chief Minister
(d) None of the above

290 The Legislative Council in a state may be created or abolished by the
(a) President, on the recommendation of the Governor
(b) Parliament
(c) Parliament after the state Legislative Assembly passes a resolution to that effect
(d) Governor on a recommendation by the state cabinet

291 Which of the following introduced Indian Penal Code?
(a) Lord Macaulay (b) Lord Dalhousie
(c) Lord Curzon (d) Lord Ripon

292 Constitution of India does not mention the post of
(a) Deputy Prime Minister
(b) Deputy Chairman of the Rajya Sabha
(c) Deputy Speaker of the state Legislative Assembly
(d) None of the above

293 Which of the following age groups is taken into consideration for constituting Gender Parity Index for higher education?
(a) 15–22 years (b) 18–23 years
(c) 16–22 years (d) 18–25 years

294 There was a major announcement in Budget 2016-17 in the form of Higher Education Funding Agency.
Which of the following statements are correct in this context?

I. An initial capital base of Rs 1,000 cr
II. Joint participation of Government and philanthropic donors
III. Quality infrastructure in IITs, NITs, IIITs, etc.

Codes:

(a) I and II (b) II and III
(c) I and III (d) All of the above

295 According to 2011 Census Report, the difference between literacy rates of men and women in India is about
(a) 10% (b) 17% (c) 21% (d) 27%

296 For equality of educational opportunities among women, the Constitution has provision under
(i) Article 45
(ii) Article 15(3)
(iii) Article 16(1) and (2)
(iv) All the above
Which of the above is correct?
(a) Only (i) is correct.
(b) (i) and (ii) are correct.
(c) (i) and (iii) are correct.
(d) (iv) is correct.

297 Equality of educational opportunities is possible by
(a) Extending portals of educational institutions to all without any discrimination
(b) Opening more educational institutions
(c) Privatizing the education system in the country
(d) Public funding of Education

298 Who have signed MOU for recognition of Teacher Education in Special Education Programme in India?
(a) NCTE and NAAC
(b) RCI and NCERT
(c) NCDS and RCI
(d) RCI and NCTE

299 National youth day, observed across India on 12 January commemorates the birth anniversary of which famous Indian personality?
(a) Swami Dayanand Saraswati
(b) Swami Vivekanand
(c) Aurobindo Ghosh
(d) Rabindranath Tagore

Answer Keys

1. (d) 2. (d) 3. (d) 4. (c) 5. (d)
6. (a) 7. (b) 8. (c) 9. (a) 10. (c)
11. (a) 12. (a) 13. (b) 14. (a) 15. (b)
16. (a) 17. (a) 18. (a) 19. (b) 20. (a)
21. (a) 22. (a) 23. (a) 24. (b) 25. (a)
26. (c) 27. (a) 28. (a) 29. (c) 30. (a)
31. (b) 32. (b) 33. (b) 34. (c) 35. (b)
36. (b) 37. (a) 38. (c) 39. (b) 40. (b)
41. (b) 42. (b) 43. (b) 44. (b) 45. (a)
46. (a) 47. (a) 48. (c) 49. (b) 50. (b)
51. (a) 52. (b) 53. (b) 54. (b) 55. (c)
56. (a) 57. (b) 58. (d) 59. (c) 60. (b)
61. (b) 62. (a) 63. (a) 64. (d) 65. (c)
66. (c) 67. (b) 68. (b) 69. (c) 70. (c)
71. (d) 72. (d) 73. (b) 74. (c) 75. (a)
76. (c) 77. (c) 78. (d) 79. (a) 80. (d)
81. (a) 82. (b) 83. (b) 84. (a) 85. (a)
86. (a) 87. (a) 88. (c) 89. (d) 90. (a)
91. (a) 92. (b) 93. (b) 94. (d) 95. (a)
96. (a) 97. (a) 98. (a) 99. (c) 100. (b)
101. (d) 102. (a) 103. (c) 104. (b) 105. (a)
106. (a) 107. (a) 108. (b) 109. (d) 110. (a)
111. (a) 112. (b) 113. (a) 114. (a) 115. (b)
116. (b) 117. (a) 118. (b) 119. (a) 120. (a)
121. (a) 122. (a) 123. (a) 124. (b) 125. (a)
126. (a) 127. (a) 128. (b) 129. (b) 130. (c)
131. (c) 132. (a) 133. (a) 134. (a) 135. (c)
136. (d) 137. (b) 138. (d)

Our Constitution: Basic Features

139. (b) 140. (a) 141. (d) 142. (b) 143. (a)
144. (a) 145. (a) 146. (c) 147. (a) 148. (d)
149. (b) 150. (a) 151. (a) 152. (a) 153. (b)
154. (a) 155. (b) 156. (d) 157. (a) 158. (d)

159. (b) 160. (c) 161. (b) 162. (a) 163. (b)
164. (c) 165. (a) 166. (b) 167. (d) 168. (c)
169. (c) 170. (a) 171. (a) 172. (b) 173. (c)
174. (b) 175. (d) 176. (a) 177. (b) 178. (b)
179. (b) 180. (d) 181. (a) 182. (c) 183. (d)
184. (a) 185. (b)

Parliament

186. (a) 187. (d) 188. (a) 189. (d) 190. (d)
191. (b) 192. (a) 193. (a) 194. (b) 195. (b)
196. (b) 197. (b) 198. (b) 199. (b) 200. (b)
201. (c) 202. (b) 203. (a) 204. (b) 205. (a)
206. (d) 207. (b) 208. (a) 209. (d) 210. (c)
211. (a) 212. (b) 213. (d) 214. (b) 215. (c)
216. (a) 217. (c) 218. (c) 219. (c) 220. (c)
221. (b) 222. (b) 223. (a) 224. (a) 225. (b)

President and Prime Minister

226. (b) 227. (c) 228. (b) 229. (b) 230. (d)
231. (d) 232. (c) 233. (a) 234. (a) 235. (b)
236. (b) 237. (b) 238. (a) 239. (b) 240. (c)

Other Important Public Institutions

241. (d) 242. (b) 243. (b) 244. (b) 245. (c)
246. (b) 247. (a) 248. (a) 249. (b) 250. (d)
251. (b) 252. (a) 253. (b) 254. (c) 255. (c)
256. (b) 257. (d) 258. (c) 259. (c) 260. (d)
261. (a) 262. (c)

Miscellaneous

263. (d) 264. (c) 265. (a) 266. (c) 267. (d)
268. (b) 269. (b) 270. (a) 271. (c) 272. (d)
273. (a) 274. (d) 275. (b) 276. (a) 277. (a)
278. (c) 279. (a) 280. (a) 281. (d) 282. (b)
283. (c) 284. (b) 285. (a) 286. (c) 287. (c)
288. (d) 289. (a) 290. (c) 291. (a) 292. (a)
293. (b) 294. (b) 295. (b) 296. (d) 297. (a)
298. (d) 299. (b)

MAIN HIGHER EDUCATION INSTITUTIONS

Delhi

- Central Council for Research in Homoeopathy
- Council of Scientific and Industrial Research
- CSIR Human Resources Development Group
- Defence Research and Development Organisation
- Indian Council of Agricultural Research
- Directorate of Wheat Research
- Indian Council of Medical Research (ICMR)
- Indian Council for Research on International Economic Relations
- National Brain Research Centre
- National Bureau of Plant Genetic Resources
- National Centre for Agricultural Economics and Policy Research
- Nuclear Science Centre
- Science and Engineering Research Council
- The Energy and Resources Institute (TERI)
- Petroleum Conservation Research Association

Bangalore

- Central Power Research Institute
- Centre for Artificial Intelligence and Robotics
- Centre for Mathematical Modelling and Computer Simulation (CSIR)
- Indian Academy of Science
- Indian Institute of Science
- Indian Space Research Organisation (ISRO)
- Jawaharlal Nehru Centre for Astronomy and Astrophysics
- Jawaharlal Nehru Centre for Advanced Scientific Research
- National Aerospace Laboratories
- National Centre for Biological Sciences
- Raman Research Institute

Chennai

- Central Electrochemical Research Institute
- Central Institute of Brackishwater Aquaculture
- Indian Institute of Technology
- The Institute of Mathematical Sciences
- National Institute of Ocean Technology
- Structural Engineering Research Centre

Kolkata

- Indian Statistical Institute
- Inter University Consortium on DAE Facilities

- Saha Institute of Nuclear Physics
- S.N.Bose National Centre for Basic Sciences
- Variable Energy Cyclotron Centre

Mumbai

- Bhabha Atomic Research Centre
- Centre for Monitoring the Indian Economy
- Indian Institute of Geomagnetism
- Indira Gandhi Institute of Development Research
- National Centre for Software Technology
- Society for Applied Microwave Electronic Engineering and Research
- Tata Institute of Fundamental Research

Hyderabad

- Centre for Cellular and Molecular Biology
- Environment Protection Training and Research Institute
- International Crops Research Institute for the Semi-Arid Tropics (ICRISAT), Patancheru
- National Geophysical Research Institute
- Indian Institute of Chemical Technology

Thiruvananthapuram

- Centre for Development Studies
- Centre for Earth Science Studies
- Electronic Research and Development Centre
- Rajiv Gandhi Centre for Biotechnology

Lucknow

- Central Drug Research Institute
- Indian Council of Philosophy Research
- Industrial Toxicology Research Centre
- National Botanical Research Institute
- National Research Laboratory for Conservation of Cultural Property

Ahmedabad

- Institute for Plasma Research
- Physical Research Laboratory

Dehradun

- Forest Research Institute
- Indian Institute of Petroleum
- Wildlife Institute of India

Barrackpore (West Bengal)

- Central Inland Capture Fisheries Research Institute

Bhopal

- Central Institute of Agricultural Engineering

Bhubaneswar

- Institute of Physics
- Regional Research Laboratory

Chandigarh

- Post Graduate Institute of Medical Education and Research

Dirang (Arunachal Pradesh)

- National Research Centre on Yak

Durgapur

- Central Mechanical Engineering Research Institute

Eluru (Andhra Pradesh)

- National Research Centre for Oil Palm
- National Atmospheric Research Laboratory, Gadanki

Gandhi Nagar

- Institute for Plasma Research

Goa

- National Institute of Oceanography

Indore

- Centre for Advanced Technology

Jammu

- Regional Research Laboratory

Jhansi (Uttar Pradesh)

- National Research Centre for Agroforestry

Jodhpur (Rajasthan)

- Central Arid Zone Research Institute

Kanpur

- Indian Institute of Pulses Research

Kasaragod

- Central Plantation Crops Research Institute

Kharagpur

- Indian Institute of Technology

Kochi

- Central Marine Fisheries Research Institute

Mathura

- Central Institute for Research on Goats

Palampur (Himachal Pradesh)

- Institute of Himalayan Bioresource Technology

Pilani

- Central Electronics Research Institute
- Birla Institute of Technology and Science

Pune (Maharashtra)

- Centre for Development of Advanced Computing
- Inter-University Centre for Astronomy and Astrophysics
- National Chemical Laboratory

Roorkee (Uttar Pradesh)

- Central Building Research Institute

UGC NET PAPER 1 DECEMBER 2012

1. The English word *communication* is derived from the words
   (a) Communis and communicare
   (b) Communist and commune
   (c) Communism and communalism
   (d) Communion and common sense
2. Chinese Cultural Revolution leader Mao Zedong used a type of communication to talk to the masses known as
   (a) Mass line communication
   (b) Group communication
   (c) Participatory communication
   (d) Dialogue communication
3. Conversing with the spirits and ancestors is termed as
   (a) Transpersonal communication
   (b) Intrapersonal communication
   (c) Interpersonal communication
   (d) Face-to-face communication
4. The largest circulated daily newspaper among the following is
   (a) The Times of India
   (b) The Indian Express
   (c) The Hindu
   (d) The Deccan Herald
5. The pioneer of silent feature film in India was
   (a) K. A. Abbas (b) Satyajit Ray
   (c) B. R. Chopra (d) Dadasaheb Phalke
6. Classroom communication of a teacher rests on the principle of
   (a) Infotainment (b) Edutainment
   (c) Entertainment (d) Power equation
7. The missing number in the series
   0, 6, 24, 60, 120, ?, 336, is
   (a) 240 (b) 220 (c) 280 (d) 210
8. A group of 7 members having a majority of boys is to be formed out of 6 boys and 4 girls. The number of ways the group can be formed is
   (a) 80 (b) 100 (c) 90 (d) 110
9. The number of observations in a group is 40. The average of the first 10 members is 4.5, and the average of the remaining 30 members is 3.5. The average of the whole group is
   (a) 4 (b) 15/2 (c) 15/4 (d) 6
10. If 'MOHAN' is represented by the code 'KMFYL', then 'COUNT' will be represented by
    (a) AMSLR (b) MSLAR
    (c) MASRL (d) SAMLR
11. The sum of the ages of two persons A and B is 50. Five years ago, the ratio of their ages was 5:3. The present age of A and B are

(a) 30 and 20 (b) 35 and 15
(c) 38 and 12 (d) 40 and10

12. Let A mean minus (–), B mean multiplied by (×), C mean divided by (÷), and D mean plus (+). The value of 90 D 9 A 29 C 10 B 2 is
(a) 8 (b) 10 (c) 12 (d) 14

13. Consider the **Assertion I** and **Assertion II** and select the right code given below.
Assertion I: Even bank lockers are not safe. Thieves can break them and take away your wealth. However, thieves cannot go to heaven. So, you should keep your wealth in heaven.
Assertion II: The difference in skin colour of living beings is because of the distance from the sun and not because of some permanent traits. Skin colour is the result of body's reaction to the sun and its rays.
Codes:
(a) Both the assertions are forms of argument.
(b) Assertion I is an argument, but Assertion II is not.
(c) Assertion II is an argument, but Assertion I is not.
(d) Both the assertions are explanations of facts.

14. By which of the following proposition, the proposition, some men are not honest, is contradicted?
(a) All men are honest.
(b) Some men are honest.
(c) No men are honest.
(d) All of the above

15. A stipulative definition is
(a) Always true
(b) Always false
(c) Sometimes true sometimes false
(d) Neither true nor false

16. Choose the appropriate alternative given in the codes to replace the question mark.
Examiner – examinee, Pleader – client, Preceptor – ?
(a) Customer (b) Pathfinder
(c) Perceiver (d) Disciple

17. If the statement, most of the students are obedient, is taken to be true, which one of the following pair of statements can be claimed to be true?
I. All obedient persons are students.
II. All students are obedient.
III. Some students are obedient.
IV. Some students are not disobedient.
Codes:
(a) I and II (b) II and III
(c) III and IV (d) II and IV

18. Choose the right code:
A deductive argument claims that:
I. The conclusion does not claim something more than that is contained in the premises.
II. The conclusion is supported by the premise or premises conclusively.
III. If the conclusion is false, then premise or premises may be either true or false.
IV. If premise or combination of premises is or are true, then conclusion must be true.
Codes:
(a) I and II (b) I and III
(c) II and III (d) All of the above

On the basis of the data given in the following table, give answers to questions from 19 to 24:

Government Expenditures on Social Services (as per cent of total expenditure)

Sl. No.	Items	2007–08	2008–09	2009–10	2010–11
	Social services	11.06	12.94	13.06	14.02
(a)	Education, sports, and youth affairs	4.02	4.04	3.96	4.46
(b)	Health and family welfare	2.05	1.91	1.90	2.03

Sl. No.	Items	2007–08	2008–09	2009–10	2010–11
(c)	Water supply, housing, etc.	2.02	2.31	2.20	2.27
(d)	Information and broadcasting	0.22	0.22	0.20	0.22
(e)	Welfare of SC/ST and OBC	0.36	0.35	0.41	0.63
(f)	Labour and employment	0.27	0.27	0.22	0.25
(g)	Social welfare and nutrition	0.82	0.72	0.79	1.06
(h)	North-eastern areas	0.00	1.56	1.50	1.75
(i)	Other social services	1.29	1.55	1.87	1.34
	Total government expenditure	100.00	100.00	100.00	100.00

19. How many activities of social services have shown the expenditure to be less than 5% of the total expenditures incurred on social services in 2008–2009?
(a) One (b) Three
(c) Five (d) All of the above

20. In which year, the expenditures on social services increased with the highest rate?
(a) 2007–2008 (b) 2008–2009
(c) 2009–2010 (d) 2010–2011

21. Which of the following activities remain almost stagnant in terms of shares of expenditure?
(a) North-eastern areas
(b) Welfare of SC/ST and OBC
(c) Information and broadcasting
(d) Social welfare and nutrition

22. Which of the following item's expenditure share is almost equal to the remaining three items in the given years?
(a) Information and broadcasting
(b) Welfare of SC/ST and OBC
(c) Labour and employment
(d) Social welfare and nutrition

23. Which of the following items of social services have registered the highest rate of increase in expenditure during 2007–2008 to 2010–2011?
(a) Education, sports, and youth affairs
(b) Welfare of SC/ST and OBC
(c) Social welfare and nutrition
(d) Overall social services

24. Which of the following items have registered the highest rate of decline in terms of expenditure during 2007–2008 to 2009–2010?
(a) Labour and employment
(b) Health and family welfare
(c) Social welfare and nutrition
(d) Education, sports, and youth affairs

25. ALU stands for
(a) American Logic Unit
(b) Alternate Local Unit
(c) Alternating Logic Unit
(d) Arithmetic Logic Unit

26. A personal computer uses a number of chips mounted on a circuit board called
(a) Microprocessor (b) System board
(c) Daughter board (d) Mother board

27. Computer virus is a
(a) Hardware (b) Bacteria
(c) Software (d) None of the above

28. Which one of the following is correct?
(a) $(17)_{10} = (17)_{16}$ (b) $(17)_{10} = (17)_8$
(c) $(17)_{10} = (10111)_2$ (d) $(17)_{10} = (10001)_2$

29. The file extension of MS-Word document in Office 2007 is ________
(a) .pdf (b) .doc (c) .docx (d) .txt

30. ________ is a protocol used by e-mail clients to download e-mails to your computer
(a) TCP (b) FTP
(c) SMTP (d) POP

31. Which of the following is a source of methane?
(a) Wetlands
(b) Foam industry

(c) Thermal power plants
(d) Cement industry

32. Minamata disease in Japan was caused by pollution due to
(a) Lead (b) Mercury
(c) Cadmium (d) Zinc

33. Biomagnification means increase in the
(a) Concentration of pollutants in living organisms
(b) Number of species
(c) Size of living organisms
(d) Biomass

34. Nagoya Protocol is related to
(a) Climate change (b) Ozone depletion
(c) Hazardous waste (d) Biodiversity

35. The second most important source after fossil fuels contributing to India's energy needs is
(a) Solar energy (b) Nuclear energy
(c) Hydropower (d) Wind energy

36. In case of earthquakes, an increase in magnitude 1 on Richter scale implies
(a) A ten-fold increase in the amplitude of seismic waves
(b) A ten-fold increase in the energy of the seismic waves
(c) A two-fold increase in the amplitude of seismic waves
(d) A two-fold increase in the energy of seismic waves

37. Which of the following is not a measure of human development index?
(a) Literacy rate (b) Gross enrolment
(c) Sex ratio (d) Life expectancy

38. India has the highest number of students in colleges after
(a) UK (b) USA
(c) Australia (d) Canada

39. Which of the following statement(s) is/are not correct about the Attorney General of India?
I. The President appoints a person, who is qualified to be a judge of a High Court, to be the Attorney General of India.
II. He has the right of audience in all the courts of the country.
III. He has the right to take part in the proceedings of the Lok Sabha and the Rajya Sabha.
IV. He has a fixed tenure.

Select the correct answer from the codes given below:

Codes:
(a) I and IV (b) II, III, and IV
(c) III and IV (d) III only

40. Which of the following prefixes President Pranab Mukherjee desires to discontinue while interacting with Indian dignitaries as well as in official notings?
I. His Excellency
II. Mahamahim
III. Hon'ble
IV. Shri/Smt

Select the correct answer from the codes given below:

Codes:
(a) I and III (b) II and III
(c) I and II (d) I, II, and III

41. Which of the following can be done under conditions of financial emergency?
I. State Legislative Assemblies can be abolished.
II. Central government can acquire control over the budget and expenditure of states.
III. Salaries of the judges of High Courts and the Supreme Court can be reduced.
IV. Right to constitutional remedies can be suspended.

Select the correct answer from the codes given below:

Codes:
(a) I, II, and III (b) II, III, and IV
(c) I and II (d) II and III

42. Match List I with List II and select the correct answer from the codes given below:

	List I		List II
A	Poverty Reduction Programme	I	Mid-day Meals

List I		List II	
B	Human Development Scheme	II	Indira Awaas Yojana (IAY)
C	Social Assistance Scheme	III	National Old Age Pension (NOAP)
D	Minimum Need Scheme	IV	MNREGA

Codes:
(a) A-IV, B-I, C-III, and D-II
(b) A-II, B-III, C-IV, and D-I
(c) A-III, B-IV, C-I, and D-II
(d) A-IV, B-III, C-II, and D-I

43. For an efficient and durable learning, learner should have
(a) Ability to learn only
(b) Requisite level of motivation only
(c) Opportunities to learn only
(d) Desired level of ability and motivation

44. Classroom communication must be
(a) Teacher-centric (b) Student-centric
(c) General-centric (d) Textbook-centric

45. The best method of teaching is to
(a) Impart information
(b) Ask students to read books
(c) Suggest good reference material
(d) Initiate a discussion and participate in it

46. Interaction inside the classroom should generate
(a) Argument (b) Information
(c) Ideas (d) Controversy

47. 'Spare the rod and spoil the child' gives the message that
(a) Punishment in the class should be banned
(b) Corporal punishment is not acceptable
(c) Undesirable behaviour must be punished
(d) Children should be beaten with rods

48. The type of communication that a teacher has in the classroom is termed as
(a) Interpersonal
(b) Mass communication
(c) Group communication
(d) Face-to-face communication

49. Which of the following is an indication of the quality of a research journal?
(a) Impact factor (b) *h*-index
(c) *g*-index (d) *i10*-index

50. Good research ethics means
(a) Not disclosing the holdings of shares or stocks in a company that sponsors your research
(b) Assigning a particular research problem to one PhD or research student only
(c) Discussing with your colleagues confidential data from a research paper that you are reviewing for an academic journal
(d) Submitting the same research manuscript for publishing in more than one journal

51. Which of the following sampling methods is based on probability?
(a) Convenience sampling
(b) Quota sampling
(c) Judgement sampling
(d) Stratified sampling

52. Which one of the following references is written according to American Psychological Association (APA) format?
(a) Sharma, V. (2010). Fundamentals of Computer Science. New Delhi: Tata McGraw Hill
(b) Sharma, V. 2010. Fundamentals of Computer Science. New Delhi: Tata McGraw Hill
(c) Sharma, V. 2010. Fundamentals of Computer Science, New Delhi: Tata McGraw Hill
(d) Sharma, V. (2010), Fundamentals of Computer Science, New Delhi: Tata McGraw Hill

53. Arrange the following steps of research in correct sequence:
I. Identification of research problem
II. Listing of research objectives
III. Collection of data
IV. Methodology
V. Data analysis
VI. Results and discussion

Codes:

(a) I, II, III, IV, V, and VI
(b) I, II, III, IV, V, and VI
(c) II, I, III, IV, V, and VI
(d) II, I, IV, III, V, and VI

54. Identify the incorrect statement.
(a) A hypothesis is made on the basis of limited evidence as a starting point for further investigations.
(b) A hypothesis is a basis for reasoning without any assumption of its truth.
(c) A hypothesis is a proposed explanation for a phenomenon.
(d) A scientific hypothesis is a scientific theory.

Read the following passage carefully and answer the questions from 55 to 60.

The popular view of towns and cities in developing countries and of urbanization process is that despite the benefits and comforts it brings, the emergence of such cities connotes environmental degradation, generation of slums and squatters, urban poverty, unemployment, crimes, lawlessness, traffic chaos, and so on. But what is the reality? Given the unprecedented increase in urban population over the past 50 years from 300 million in 1950 to 2 billion in 2000 in developing countries, the wonder is how well the world has coped and not how badly.

In general, the urban quality of life has improved in terms of availability of water and sanitation, power, health and education, communication, and transport. By way of illustration, a large number of urban residents have been provided with improved water in urban areas in Asia's largest countries such as China, India, Indonesia, and Philippines. Despite that, the access to improved water in terms of percentage of total urban population seems to have declined during the past decade of 20th century, although in absolute numbers, millions of additional urbanites have been provided improved services. These countries have made significant progress in the provision of sanitation services too, together, providing for an additional population of more than 293 million citizens within a decade (1990–2000). These improvements must be viewed against the backdrop of rapidly increasing urban population, fiscal crunch, and strained human resources and efficient and quality-oriented public management.

55. The popular view about the process of urbanization in developing countries is
(a) Positive (b) Negative
(c) Neutral (d) Unspecified

56. The average annual increase in the number of urbanites in developing countries, from 1950 to 2000 AD, was close to
(a) 30 million (b) 40 million
(c) 50 million (d) 60 million

57. The reality of urbanization is reflected in
(a) How well the situation has been managed
(b) How badly the situation has gone out of control
(c) How fast has been the tempo of urbanization
(d) How fast the environment has degraded

58. Which one of the following is not considered as an indicator of urban quality of life?
(a) Tempo of urbanization
(b) Provision of basic services
(c) Access to social amenities
(d) All of the above

59. The author in this passage has tried to focus on
(a) Extension of knowledge
(b) Generation of environmental consciousness
(c) Analytical reasoning
(d) Descriptive statement

60. In the above passage, the author intends to state
(a) The hazards of the urban life
(b) The sufferings of the urban life
(c) The awareness of human progress
(d) The limits of growth

ANSWER KEYS

1. (a)	7. (d)	13. (b)	19. (b)	25. (d)	31. (a)	37. (c)	43. (d)	49. (a)	55. (b)
2. (a)	8. (b)	14. (a)	20. (b)	26. (d)	32. (b)	38. (b)	44. (b)	50. (b)	56. (a)
3. (a)	9. (c)	15. (c)	21. (c)	27. (c)	33. (a)	39. (a)	45. (d)	51. (d)	57. (a)
4. (a)	10. (a)	16. (d)	22. (d)	28. (d)	34. (d)	40. (c)	46. (c)	52. (a)	58. (a)
5. (d)	11. (a)	17. (c)	23. (b)	29. (c)	35. (c)	41. (d)	47. (c)	53. (b)	59. (c)
6. (b)	12. (d)	18. (a)	24. (a)	30. (d)	36. (a)	42. (a)	48. (c)	54. (d)	60. (d)

HINTS AND SOLUTIONS

1. (a): The word 'Communication' is derived from the Latin word *Communicare* meaning to impart, share, or make common, which later entered English language in the 14th and 15th centuries. In the word *communication*, the key root is *mun-* (not *uni*), which is related to words such as 'community'.

2. (a): The mass line is the political, organizational, and leadership methods developed by Mao Zedong during the Chinese Revolution, and the communication used in the process is termed as mass line communication.

3. (a): Transpersonal communication: trans means beyond; hence, transpersonal means beyond persons or human beings. Interpersonal means between two persons, and intrapersonal means talking to himself or herself.

4. (a): The Times of India started as Bombay Times was setup in 1838 and is the most widely read English language newspaper. The answer choices are among English Newspapers only. Otherwise, Dainik Jagran and Dainik Bhaskar are the largest read newspapers in India, both published in Hindi.

5. (d): Dadasaheb Phalke was the pioneer of the silent feature film in India; 'Shree Pundalik' (Marathi), which was made by him and released in 1912, was the first silent film in India. He also made the next silent feature film 'Raja Harishchander' in 1913.

6. (b): Edutainment in classroom is combination of education and entertainment; it means that effective education has to take place in a humorous environment.

7. (d): Here, the pattern is $0 \times 1 \times 2$, $1 \times 2 \times 3$, $2 \times 3 \times 4$, $3 \times 4 \times 5$, $4 \times 5 \times 6$, $5 \times 6 \times 7$, $6 \times 7 \times 8$, and so on.

8. (b): It is a question of combination and we have to make use of concept of probability. Here, to make a group of 7 people consisting majority of boys can have following combinations: = (6 boys and 1 girl) or (5 boys and 2 girls) or (4 boys and 3 girls).
$= ({}^6C_6 \times {}^4C_1) + ({}^6C_5 \times {}^4C_2) + ({}^6C_4 \times {}^4C_3)$
$= (1 \times 4) + (6 \times 6) + 60$
$= 100$
Here, it should be noted that as the keyword is OR; we have to make use of addition theorem and also the number of combinations $= {}^nC_r$ where n is total number of elements and r means making r selections out of n.
${}^nC_r = n!/r!\,(n - r)!$

9. (c): It is a question of combined average. Combined average $= (N_1 \cdot X_1 + N_2 \cdot X_2)/(N_1 + N_2)$, where N_1 and N_2 are the respective number of elements in two groups, and X_1 and X_2 are their respective averages.
$(10 \times 4.5 + 30 \times 3.5)/40 = (45 + 105)/40 = 150/40 = 15/4$

10. (a)

M	O	H	A	N
–2	–2	–2	–2	–2
K	M	F	Y	L

Similarly,

C	O	U	N	T
–2	–2	–2	–2	–2
A	M	S	L	R

11. (a): The sum of the ages of two persons A and B is 50. Five years ago, the ratio of their ages was 5:3.

Ten years ago, the sum of ages must be 10 years less (5 years less for each of A and B), it means that the sum of ages must be 40 years.
Total of ratios = 5 + 3 = 8
So, 5 years ago A's age = 5/8 × 40 = 25 years
Present age of A = 25 + 5 = 30 years
So, 5 years ago B's age = 3/8 × 40 = 15 years
Present age of B = 15 + 5 = 20 years

12. (d): 90 + 9 − 29 × by 10 × by 2 = 14. The solution does not follow BODMAS.

13. (b): Assertion I is an argument to 'keep your wealth in heaven', whereas Assertion II is an explanation to a query a probable query about skin colour.

15. (c): Stipulative definition: A definition that is stipulated by someone and that is not a standard usage, so this can be right or wrong.

16. (d): Here, the second term is being supervised or facilitated by the first term, so the answer is disciple.

17. (c): Looking at the Venn diagram, I and II cannot be true. In this type of statement, the subjects 'most' and 'some' carry the same sense, so III is true. When we rest the language of statement IV, it should be read as 'Some students are obedient'.

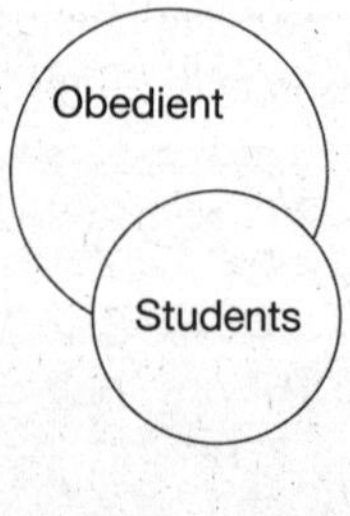

18. (a): According to the definition of deductive argument, I, II, and IV follow. Since III is wrong, answer choices (b) and (c) are omitted.

19. (b): Here, we have to calculate the expenditure incurred on different activities individually as a percentage of expenditure on social services:

- Education, sports, and youth affairs = (4.04/12.94) × 100 × 100 = 31.22%
- Health and family welfare = (1.91/12.94) × 100 = 14.76%
- Water supply and housing = (2.31/12.94) × 100 = 17.85%
- Information and broadcasting = (0.22/12.94) × 100 = 1.70%
- Welfare to SC/ST and OBC = (0.35/12.94) × 100 = 2.70%
- Labour and employment = (0.27/12.94) × 100 = 2.08%
- Social welfare and nutrition = (0.72/12.94) × 100 = 5.56%
- Northeast states = (1.56/12.94) × 100 = 12.05%
- Other social services = (1.55/12.94) × 100 = 11.97%

Thus, there are three service activities where the expenditure has been less than 5% of total expenditure incurred on social services. So, (b) is the answer. In this question, approximate calculations of percentage figures can also help in solving the problem.

20. (b): In this question, since all figures are in the form of common size statement, wherein all figures have been reduced to percentage figures, we need to convert these figures to absolute figures to get correct answer as it cannot be ruled out that the absolute government expenditure might have reduced.

As per answer choices, if we assume that total government expenditure is kept at the same level in absolute figures (in terms of rupees), then 2008–2009 is the answer.

$$\frac{12.94 - 11.06}{11.06} \times 100 = 16.99\%$$

For 2009–2010,

$$\frac{13.06 - 12.94}{12.94} \times 100 = 0.12/12.94 \sim 1\%$$

For 2010–2011,

$$\frac{14.02-13.06}{13.06}\times 100$$
$$=(0.06/13.06)\times 100 \sim 0.5\%$$

So, clearly (b) is the answer when the increase in the expenditure is maximum at 16.99%.

21. (c): Information and broadcasting
Just by observing and assuming that total government expenditure stands at the same level, (c) is the answer.

22. (d): Here, the approach should be to pick the largest figure among the answer choices and just see that total of remaining three is approximately equal to them or not for verification. Here, among the choices, the largest figure is social welfare and nutrition for different years. For 2008–2009, the total of information and broadcasting, welfare to SC/ST and OBC, and labour and employment is 0.85, which is comparable to that of social welfare and nutrition at 0.82. Same is case for other years as well.

23. (b): The percentage increases between the years 2007–2008 and 2010–2011 for different items have been calculated as given below:
 (a) Education, sports, and youth affairs = (4.46 – 4.02)/4.02 × 100 = 10.94%
 (b) Welfare to SC/ST and OBC = (0.63 – 0.36)/0.36 × 100 = 0.27/0.36 × 100 = 75%
 (c) Social welfare and nutrition = (1.06 – 0.82)/0.82 × 100 = 0.24/0.82 × 100 = 29.26%
 (d) Overall social services = (14.02 – 11.06)/11.06 × 100 = 2.96/11.06 × 100 = 26.76%

24. (a): Decline in percentage terms for different items during 2007–2008 to 2009–2010:
 (a) Labour and employment = (0.27 – 0.22)/0.27 × 100 = 18.51%
 (b) Health and family welfare = (2.05 – 1.90)/2.05 × 100 = 0.15/2.05 × 100 = 7.31%
 (c) Social welfare and nutrition = 0.82 – 0.79/0.82 × 100 = 0.03/0.82 × 100 = 3.65%
 (d) Education, sports, and youth affairs = 4.02 – 3.96/4.02 × 100 = 1.49%

So, (a) is the answer as the decline is maximum in percentage terms.

28. (d): There is no need to explore answer choices (a) and (b) as there is same number, that is, on both sides of the equation with different bases.
Solving (c), we get
$(10111)_2 = 1\times 2^4 + 0\times 2^3 + 1\times 2^2 + 1\times 2^1 + 1\times 2^0 = 16 + 4 + 2 + 1 = 23$
Solving (d), we get
$(10001)_2 = 1\times 2^4 + 0\times 2^3 + 0\times 2^2 + 0\times 2^1 + 1\times 2^0 = 16 + 1 = 17$
So, $(17)_{10} = (10001)_2$

34. (d): Nagoya Protocol on Access to Genetic Resources and the Fair and Equitable Sharing of Benefits Arising from their Utilization (ABS) to the Convention on Biological Diversity is a supplementary agreement to the Convention on Biological Diversity (CBD). It was adopted on 29 October 2010 in Nagoya, Japan.

35. (c): Hydropower contributes around 17% in meeting energy needs of India. Nuclear energy contributes around 3–4%, and wind energy and solar energy just 1–2%.

UGC NET PAPER 1 JUNE 2013

1. 'www' stands for
   (a) work with web (b) word wide web
   (c) world wide web (d) worth while web
2. A hard disk is divided into tracks which is further subdivided into
   (a) Clusters (b) Sectors
   (c) Vectors (d) Head
3. A computer program that translates a program statement by statement into machine language is called a/an
   (a) Compiler (b) Simulator
   (c) Translator (d) Interpreter
4. A gigabyte is equal to
   (a) 1024 Megabytes (b) 1024 Kilobytes
   (c) 1024 Terabytes (d) 1024 Bytes
5. A compiler is software that converts
   (a) Characters to bits
   (b) High-level language to machine language
   (c) Machine language to high-level language
   (d) Words to bits
6. Virtual memory is
   (a) an extremely large main memory
   (b) an extremely large secondary memory
   (c) an illusion of extremely large main memory
   (d) a type of memory used in super computers
7. The phrase 'tragedy of commons' is in the context of
   (a) tragic event related to damage caused by release' of poisonous gases
   (b) tragic conditions of poor people
   (c) degradation of renewable free access resources
   (d) climate change
8. 'Kyoto Protocol' is related to
   (a) Ozone depletion (b) Hazardous waste
   (c) Climate change (d) Nuclear energy
9. Which of the following is a source of emission leading to the eventual formation of surface ozone as a pollutant?
   (a) Transport sector
   (b) Refrigeration and Air conditioning
   (c) Wetlands
   (d) Fertilizers
10. The smog in cities in India mainly consists of
    (a) Oxides of sulphur
    (b) Oxides of nitrogen and unburnt hydrocarbons
    (c) Carbon monoxide and SPM
    (d) Oxides of sulphur and ozone
11. Which of the following types of natural hazards have the highest potential to cause damage to humans?

(a) Earth quakes
(b) Forest fires
(c) Volcanic eruptions
(d) Droughts and floods

12. The percentage share of renewable energy sources in the power production in India is around
(a) 2–3 % (b) 22–25%
(c) 10–12% (d) < 1%

13. In which of the following categories the enrolment of students in higher education in 2010–2011 was beyond the percentage of seats reserved?
(a) OBC students (b) SC students
(c) ST students (d) Woman students

14. Which one of the following statements is not correct about the University Grants Commission (UGC)?
(a) It was established in 1956 by an Act of Parliament.
(b) It is tasked with promoting and coordinating higher education.
(c) It receives Plan and Non-Plan funds from the Central Government.
(d) It receives funds from State Governments in respect of State Universities.

15. Consider the statement which is followed by two arguments (I) and (II)

Statement: Should India switch over to a two-party system?

Arguments:
(I) Yes, it will lead to stability of Government.
(II) No, it will limit the choice of voters.
(a) Only argument (I) is strong.
(b) Only argument (II) is strong.
(c) Both the arguments are strong.
(d) Neither of the arguments is strong.

16. Consider the statement which is followed by two arguments (I) and (II):

Statement: Should persons with criminal background be banned from contesting elections?

Arguments:
(I) Yes, it will decriminalize politics.
(II) No, it will encourage the ruling party to file frivolous cases against their political opponents.
(a) Only argument (I) is strong.
(b) Only argument (II) is strong.
(c) Both the arguments are strong.
(d) Neither of the arguments is strong.

17. Which of the following statement(s) is/are correct about a Judge of the Supreme Court of India?
1. A Judge of the Supreme Court is appointed by the President of India.
2. He holds office during the pleasure of the President.
3. He can be suspended, pending an inquiry.
4. He can be removed for proven misbehaviour or incapacity.

Select the correct answer from the codes given below:

Codes:
(a) 1, 2 and 3 (b) 1, 3 and 4
(c) 1 and 3 (d) 1 and 4

18. In the warrant of precedence, the Speaker of the Lok Sabha comes next only to
(a) The President
(b) The Vice-President
(c) The Prime Minister
(d) The Cabinet Ministers

19. The blackboard can be utilized best by a teacher for
(a) Putting the matter of teaching in black and white
(b) Making the students attentive
(c) Writing the important and notable points
(d) Highlighting the teacher himself

20. Nowadays, the most effective mode of learning is
(a) Self study
(b) Face-to-face learning
(c) e-Learning
(d) Blended learning

21. At the primary school stage, most of the teachers should be women because they
(a) can teach children better than men
(b) know basic content better than men

(c) are available on lower salaries
(d) can deal with children with love and affection

22. Which one is the highest order of learning?
(a) Chain learning
(b) Problem-solving learning
(c) Stimulus-response learning
(d) Conditioned-reflex learning

23. A person can enjoy teaching as a profession when he
(a) has control over students
(b) commands respect from students
(c) is more qualified than his colleagues
(d) is very close to higher authorities

24. 'A diagram speaks more than 1,000 words'. The statement means that the teacher should
(a) use diagrams in teaching
(b) speak more and more in the class
(c) use teaching aids in the class
(d) not speak too, much in the class

25. A research paper
(a) is a compilation of information on a topic
(b) contains original research as deemed by the author
(c) contains peer-reviewed original research or the evaluation of research conducted by others.
(d) can be published in more than one journal.

26. Which one of the following belongs to the category of good 'research ethics'?
(a) Publishing the same paper in two research journals without telling the editors.
(b) Conducting a review of the literature that acknowledges the contributions of other people in the relevant field or relevant prior work.
(c) Trimming outliers from a data set without discussing your reasons in a research paper.
(d) Including a colleague as an author on a research paper in return for a favour even though the colleague did not make a serious contribution to the paper.

27. Which of the following sampling methods is not based on probability?
(a) Simple random sampling
(b) Stratified sampling
(c) Quota sampling
(d) Cluster sampling

28. Which one of the following references is written as per Modem Language Association (MLA) format?
(a) Hall, Donald. Fundamentals of Electronics, New Delhi : Prentice Hall of India, 2005
(b) Hall, Donald, Fundamentals of Electronics, New Delhi : Prentice Hall of India, 2005
(c) Hall, Donald, Fundamentals of Electronics, New Delhi : Prentice Hall of India, 2005
(d) Hall, Donald. Fundamentals of Electronics. New Delhi : Prentice Hall of India, 2005

29. A workshop is
(a) a conference for discussion on a topic
(b) a meeting for discussion on a topic
(c) a class at a college or a university in which a teacher and the students discuss a topic
(d) a brief intensive course for a small group, emphasizing the development of a skill or technique for solving a specific problem.

30. A working hypothesis is
(a) a proven hypothesis for an argument
(b) not required to be tested
(c) a provisionally accepted hypothesis for further research
(d) a scientific theory

Read the following passage carefully and answer the questions (31 to 36):

The Taj Mahal has become one of the world's best known monuments. This domed white marble structure is situated on a high plinth at the southern end of a four-quartered garden, evoking the gardens of paradise, enclosed within walls measuring 305 by 549 metres. Outside the walls, in an area known as Mumtazabad, were living quarters for attendants, markets, serais and other structures built by local merchants and nobles. The tomb complex and the other imperial structures of Mumtazabad were maintained by the income from thirty villages given specifically for the tomb's support. The name Taj Mahal is unknown in Mughal chronicles, but it is used by contemporary Europeans in India, suggesting that this was the tomb's popular name. In contemporary texts, it is simply called the illuminated tomb (Rauza-i-Munavvara).

Mumtaz Mahal died shortly after delivering her fourteenth child in 1631. The Mughal court was then residing in Burhanpur. Her remains were temporarily buried by the grief-stricken emperor in a spacious garden known as Zainabad on the bank of River Tapti. Six months later, her body was transported to Agra, where it was interred in land chosen for the mausoleum. This land, situated south of the Mughal city on the bank of River Jamuna, had belonged to the Kachwaha rajas since the time of Raja Man Singh and was purchased from the then current raja, Jai Singh. Although contemporary chronicles indicate Jai Singh's willing cooperation in this exchange, extant farmans (imperial commands) indicate that the final price was not settled until almost two years after the mausoleum's commencement. Jai Singh's further cooperation was insured by imperial orders issued between 1632 and 1637 demanding that he provide stone masons and carts to transport marble from the mines at Makrana, within his 'ancestral domain', to Agra where both the Taj Mahal and Shah Jahan's additions to the Agra fort were constructed concurrently.

Work on the mausoleum was commenced early in 1632. Inscriptional evidence indicates much of the tomb was completed by 1636. By 1643, when Shah Jahan most lavishly celebrated the 'Urs ceremony for Mumtaz Mahal', the entire complex was virtually complete.

31. Marble stone used for the construction of Taj Mahal was brought from the ancestral domain of Raja Jai Singh. The name of the place where mines of marble is
    (a) Burhanpur (b) Makrana
    (c) Amber (d) Jaipur

32. The popular name Taj Mahal was given by
    (a) Shah Jahan
    (b) Tourists
    (c) Public
    (d) European travellers

33. Point out the true statement from the following:
    (a) Marble was not used for the construction of Taj Mahal.
    (b) Red sandstone is non-visible in Taj Mahal complex.
    (c) Taj Mahal is surrounded by a four-quartered garden known as Chahar Bagh.
    (d) Taj Mahal was constructed to celebrate the 'Urs ceremony for Mumtaz Mahal'.

34. In the contemporary texts, Taj Mahal is known
    (a) Mumtazabad
    (b) Mumtaz Mahal
    (c) Zainabad
    (d) Rauza-i-Munavvara

35. The construction of Taj Mahal was completed between the period
    (a) 1632–1636 A.D. (b) 1630–1643 A.D.
    (c) 1632–1643 A.D. (d) 1636–1643 A.D.

36. The documents indicating the ownership of land, where Taj Mahal was built, known as
    (a) Farman
    (b) Sale deed
    (c) Sale-purchase deed
    (d) None of the above

37. In the process of communication, which one of the following is in the chronological order?
    (a) Communication, medium, receiver, effect, message
    (b) Medium, communicator, message, receiver, effect
    (c) Communicator, message, medium, receiver, effect
    (d) Message, communicator, medium, receiver, effect

38. Bengal Gazette, the first Newspaper in India, was started in 1780 by
(a) Dr Annie Besant
(b) James Augustus Hicky
(c) Lord Cripson
(d) A. O. Hume

39. Press censorship in India was imposed during the tenure of the Prime Minister
(a) Rajeev Gandhi (b) Narasimha Rao
(c) Indira Gandhi (d) Deve Gowda

40. Communication via New media such as computers, teleshopping, the Internet and mobile telephony is termed as
(a) Entertainment
(b) Interactive communication
(c) Development communication
(d) Communitarian

41. Classroom communication of a teacher rest on the principle of
(a) Infotainment (b) Edutainment
(c) Entertainment (d) Enlightenment

42. __________ is important when a teacher communicates with his/her student
(a) Sympathy (b) Empathy
(c) Apathy (d) Antipathy

43. In a certain code, GALIB is represented by HBMJC. TIGER will be represented by
(a) UJHFS (b) UHJSF
(c) JHUSF (d) HUJSF

44. In a certain cricket tournament, 45 matches were played. Each team played once against each of the other teams. The number of teams participated in the tournament is
(a) 8 (b) 10 (c) 12 (d) 14

45. The missing number in the series 40, 120, 60, 180, 90, ?, 135 is
(a) 110 (b) 270 (c) 105 (d) 210

46. The odd numbers from 1 to 45 which are exactly divisible by 3 are arranged in ascending order. The number at 6th position is
(a) 18 (b) 24 (c) 33 (d) 36

47. The mean of four numbers a, b, c, d is 100. If c = 70, then the mean of the remaining numbers is
(a) 30 (b) 85/2 (c) 170/3 (d) 110

48. If the radius of a circle is increased by 50%, the perimeter of the circle will increase by
(a) 20% (b) 30% (c) 40% (d) 50%

49. If the statement 'some men are honest' is false, which among the following statements will be true?
Choose the correct code given below.
(i) All men are honest.
(ii) No men are honest.
(iii) Some men are not honest.
(iv) All men are dishonest.

Codes:
(a) (i), (ii) and (iii) (b) (ii), (iii) and (iv)
(c) (i), (iii) and (iv) (d) (ii), (i) and (iv)

50. Choose the proper alternative given in the codes to replace the question Bee - Honey, Cow - Milk, Teacher - ?
(a) Intelligence (b) Marks
(c) Lessons (d) Wisdom

51. P is the father of R and S is the son of Q and T is the brother of P, If R is the sister of S, how is Q related to T?
(a) Wife (b) Sister-in-law
(c) Brother-in-law (d) Daughter-in-law

52. A definition put forward to resolve a dispute by influencing attitudes or stirring emotions is called
(a) Lexical (b) Persuasive
(c) Stipulative (d) Precisions

53. Which of the codes given below contains only the correct statements?

Statements:
(i) Venn diagram is a clear method of notation.
(ii) Venn diagram is the most direct method of testing the validity of categorical syllogisms.
(iii) In Venn diagram method, the premises and the conclusion of a categorical syllogism is diagrammed.
(iv) In Venn diagram method, the three overlapping circles are drawn for testing a categorical syllogism.

Codes:

(a) (i), (ii), and (iii) (b) (i), (ii), and (iv)
(c) (ii), (iii), and (iv) (d) (i), (iii), and (iv)

54. Inductive reasoning presupposes
(a) Unity in human nature
(b) Integrity in human nature
(c) Uniformity in human nature
(d) Harmony in human nature

Read the table below, and based on this table, answer questions from 55 to 60.

Area under major horticulture crop (in lakh hectares)

Year	Fruits	Vegetables	Flowers	Total horticulture area
2005–06	53	72	1	187
2006–07	56	75	1	194
2007–08	58	78	2	202
2008–09	61	79	2	207
2009–10	63	79	2	209

55. Which of the following two year have recorded the highest rate increase in area under the total horticulture?
(a) 2005–06 and 2006–07
(b) 2006–07 and 2008–09
(c) 2007–08 and 2008–09
(d) 2006–07 and 2007–08

56. Shares of the area under flowers, vegetables, and fruits in the area under total horticulture are, respectively,
(a) 1, 38, and 30 per cent
(b) 30, 38, and 1 per cent
(c) 38, 30, and 1 per cent
(d) 35, 36, and 2 per cent

57. Which of the following has recorded the highest rate of increase in area during 2005–06 to 2009–10?
(a) Fruits (b) Vegetables
(c) Flowers (d) Total horticulture

58. Find out the horticultural crop that has recorded an increase of area by around 10 per cent from 2005–06 to 2009–10.
(a) Fruits (b) Vegetables
(c) Flowers (d) Total horticulture

59. What has been the share of area under fruits, vegetables, and flowers in the area under total horticulture in 2007–08?
(a) 53 per cent
(b) 68 per cent
(c) 79 per cent
(d) 100 per cent

60. In which year, area under fruits has recorded the highest rate of increase?
(a) 2006–07 (b) 2007–08
(c) 2008–09 (d) 2009–10

Answer Keys

1. (b)	7. (c)	13. (a)	19. (c)	25. (c)	31. (b)	37. (c)	43. (a)	49. (a)	55. (d)
2. (b)	8. (c)	14. (d)	20. (d)	26. (b)	32. (d)	38. (b)	44. (b)	50. (d)	56. (a)
3. (d)	9. (a)	15. (c)	21. (d)	27. (c)	33. (d)	39. (c)	45. (b)	51. (b)	57. (c)
4. (a)	10. (d)	16. (a)	22. (b)	28. (d)	34. (d)	40. (b)	46. (c)	52. (b)	58. (b)
5. (b)	11. (a)	17. (d)	23. (b)	29. (d)	35. (c)	41. (b)	47. (d)	53. (a)	59. (b)
6. (b)	12. (c)	18. (c)	24. (a)	30. (c)	36. (a)	42. (b)	48. (d)	54. (c)	60. (a)

Hints and Solutions

7. (c): First used by Garrett Hardin in 1968; this term is used in context of economy and ecology. This is related to over exploitation of common natural resources to benefit few people.

9. (a): It is also called 'Tropospheric Ozone' and also known as 'bad ozone' as it can damage living tissues. This ground-level ozone is considered as a pollutant. Tropospheric ozone is formed by the interaction of sunlight, particularly ultraviolet light, with hydrocarbons and nitrogen oxides, which are emitted by automobiles, gasoline vapours, fossil fuel power plants, refineries, and certain other industries.

14. (d): Statements under choices (a) and (b) are known facts. UGC receives funds from Central Government. There are two kinds of grants for universities, institutions deemed to be universities, and colleges; they are Development (Plan) Grants and Maintenance (Non-plan) Grants. Central universities and colleges affiliated to them and institutions deemed to be university receive both the plan and non-plan grants. However, the state universities and their affiliated colleges receive only plan grants.

15. (c): Two-party system governments are more stable, for example, USA is a testimony to it. So argument I follows.

India is a very diverse society, with regional parties assuming increasingly larger role in parliamentary democratic set up. So two-party system may not work in present situation. So argument II also follows.

16. (a): Argument I is explicit, that is the obvious purpose of statement. As far as Argument II is concerned, filing frivolous cases against opponents is one thing and proving them in court of law is another.

20. (d): A blended learning approach combines face-to-face classroom methods with computer-mediated activities to form an integrated instructional approach. The goal of a blended approach is to join the best aspects of both, face-to-face and online instruction.

27. (c): Convenience sampling, quota sampling, and judgmental sampling are other types of non-probability sampling types.

39. (c): The emergency was imposed for a period of 21 months during 1975–77 when President Fakhruddin Ali Ahmed, upon request by PM Indira Gandhi, declared a state of emergency under Article 352 of the Constitution of India, effectively bestowing on her the power to rule by decree, suspending elections and civil liberties.

41. (b): Edutainment = Education + Entertainment. Here, entertainment means using sense of humour in class.

43. (a)

G	A	L	I	B
+1	+1	+1	+1	+1
H	B	M	J	C

Similarly,

T	I	G	E	R
+1	+1	+1	+1	+1
U	J	H	F	S

44. (b): In these types of questions, first of all, we identify whether it is a question of permutation or combination. Whether one team playing with another, or vice versa, it will be considered as one match. So it is a question of combination.

According to the formula of combination, $^nC_r = n!/\, r!\, (n-r)!$

Here, n is the total number of teams playing.

As two teams at a time are selected for playing with each other, $r = 2$.

By solving, we get $n = 10$.

45. (b): Multiply by three, then divide by 2, again multiply by 3, then again divide by 2, and so on. It can be solved as a question of mixed series also.

46. (c): <u>3</u>, 6. <u>9</u>, 12, <u>15</u>, 18, <u>21</u>, 24, <u>27</u>, 30, <u>33</u>, 36, <u>39</u>, and so on. The underlined numbers are both odd as well as divisible by 3. So 33 is the answer.

47. (d): $a + b + c + d = 400$

$c = 70$

$a + b + d = 400 - 70 = 330$

Average of a, b, and c = 330/3 = 110

48. (d): Perimeter = $2\pi r$

After increase in 50%, r is $3/2r$.

New perimeter = $2\pi \times 3/2r$

$= 3\pi r$

Increase in perimeter = $3\pi r - 2\pi r$

$= 1\pi r$

Percentage increase in perimeter = $1\pi r/2\pi r \times 100 = 50\%$

50. (d): Teacher delivers wisdom that enables us to take right decisions in life. Opting for 'lessons' and 'marks' are narrow choices. Intelligence is a gift of nature.

51. (b)

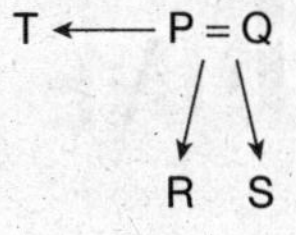

53. (a): The circles may not be necessarily overlapping. So (iv) can be safely omitted.

UGC NET PAPER 1 RECONDUCT JUNE 2013 (IN SEPTEMBER, 2013)

Note:

- This paper contains sixty (60) multiple choice questions, each question carrying two (2) marks.
- Candidate is expected to answer any fifty (50) questions.
- In case more than fifty (50) questions are attempted, only the fifty (50) questions will be evaluated.

1. The world population growth rate at a certain reference year was 3.5%. Assuming exponential growth of population, after how many years, the population of the world would have increased by a factor 16?
   (a) ~80 years (b) ~40 years
   (c) ~160 years (d) ~320 years
2. Telephone is an example of
   (a) Linear communication
   (b) Non–linear communication
   (c) Circular
   (d) Mechanized
3. Means of grapevine communication are
   (a) Formal (b) Informal
   (c) Critical (d) Corporate
4. Communication issues at the international level are addressed by
   (a) ILO (b) ITU
   (c) UNDP (d) UNESCO
5. Referential framing used by TV audience connects media with
   (a) Reality (b) Falsity
   (c) Negativity (d) Passivity
6. The communicated knowledge in a classroom is considered as
   (a) Non-pervasive treasure
   (b) Limited judgment
   (c) Autonomous virtue
   (d) Cultural capital
7. Classroom communication is normally considered as
   (a) Effective (b) Affective
   (c) Cognitive (d) Non-selective
8. A person writes all the numbers from 0 to 99. The number of times digit 3 will be written as
   (a) 18 (b) 19 (c) 20 (d) 21
9. Starting from point A, Ajit walks 14 metres towards west, he then turns to his right and walks 14 metres and then turns to his left and walks 10 metres. He again turns to his left and walks 14 metres and reaches to the point E. The shortest distance between A and E is
   (a) 38 (b) 42 (c) 52 (d) 24
10. A, B, C, D, E, and F are sitting around a round table. A is between E and F. E is opposite to

D and C is not in either of the neighbouring seats of E. The person opposite to B is
(a) C (b) D (c) A (d) F

11. The missing number in the series 2, 7, 24, 77, ?, 723 is
(a) 238 (b) 432 (c) 542 (d) 320

12. In a certain city, the taxi charges comprise of a fixed charge and the charge of the distance travelled. A person paid ₹156 for a journey of 16 km and another person paid ₹204 for the journey of 24 km. The amount paid by a passenger who has travelled 30 km is
(a) 236 (b) 240 (c) 248 (d) 256

13. In certain code, HEALTH is written as KHDOWK. The code of NORTH will be
(a) QRUWK (b) RQWUK
(c) RWQUK (d) RWUKQ

14. Yedav, Arjun, Rajesh, and Kamal play cricket. Rajesh and Kamal play tennis but do not play football. Yadav does not play badminton but play golf. Arjun does not play tennis. Kamal sometimes plays badminton. Who does play only cricket?
(a) Yadav (b) Arjun
(c) Rajesh (d) Kamal

15. A deductive argument cannot be valid:
(a) If its premise/premises is/are true, then its conclusion is true.
(b) If its premise/premises is/are true, then its conclusion is false.
(c) If its premise/premises is/are false, then its conclusion is false.
(d) If its premise/premises is/are false, then its conclusion is true.

16. An analogical argument is strengthened by
(a) making the claim bolder while its premises remain unchanged
(b) reducing the claim made on the basis of the premises affirmed
(c) remaining the claim unchanged while the evidence in its support is found to exhibit greater frailty
(d) None of the above

17. If two propositions cannot be false but may be true, then what is the relation between the two propositions?
(a) Contrary (b) Subcontrary
(c) Subalternation (d) Contradictory

18. Given below are some codes of arrangements of three items in order of wider scope. Select the correct code.
(a) Garments, cloth, and shirts
(b) Cloth, garments, and shirts
(c) Shirts, garments, and cloth
(d) Garments, shirts, and cloth

19. What is equivalent of the statement 'All atheists are pessimists'?
(a) All non-pessimists are non-atheists.
(b) All non-atheists are non-pessimists.
(c) All pessimists are atheists.
(d) None of the above

In the following table, trends in the production of energy in India by primary sources are given. Study the table and answer Question 20 to 23: (production in petajoules)

Year	Coal & lignite	Crude petroleum	Natural gas	Electricity (Hydro & nuclear)	Total
2006–07	7,459	1,423	1,223	4,763	14,868
2007–08	7,926	1,429	1,248	4,944	15,547
2008–09	8,476	1,403	1,265	5,133	16,277
2009–10	9,137	1,411	1,830	4,511	16,889
2010–11	9,207	1,579	2,012	5,059	17,857

20. In which year, primary sources recorded the lowest growth in total production of energy?
(a) 2007–08 (b) 2008–09
(c) 2009–10 (d) 2010–11

21. Which source of energy has shown the highest growth rate in production during 2006–07 to 2010–11?
(a) Coal and lignite
(b) Crude petroleum
(c) Hydro and nuclear electricity
(d) Total production of energy

22. Which one of the following primary sources of energy has recorded the highest growth in production in 2008–09?
(a) Coal and lignite
(b) Crude petroleum
(c) Natural gas
(d) Hydro and nuclear electricity

23. In which year, the production of hydro and nuclear electricity was almost double the production of crude petroleum and natural gas taken together?
    (a) 2006–07 (b) 2007–08
    (c) 2008–09 (d) 2009–10
24. The Internet ethical protocol is called
    (a) Net protocol (b) Netiquette
    (c) Net ethics (d) Net morality
25. Commercial messages on the net are identified as
    (a) Net ads
    (b) The Internet commercials
    (c) Webmercials
    (d) Viral advertisements
26. Manuel Castells was the first to use the term
    (a) The Internet society
    (b) Electronic society
    (c) Network society
    (d) Telematic society
27. GIF stands for
    (a) Global Information Format
    (b) Graphics Information Format
    (c) Graphics Interchange File
    (d) Graphics Interchange Format
28. Which one of the following is <u>not</u> an Operating System?
    (a) IBM AIX (b) Linux
    (c) Sun Solaris (d) Firefox
29. Which of the following is/are a minority institution(s)?
    I Punjabi University, Patiala
    II Osmania University, Hyderabad
    III Kashmir University, Srinagar
    IV St. Stephens College, Delhi

    Select the correct answer from the code given below.

    Codes:
    (a) I and II (b) II and IV
    (c) II only (d) IV only
30. Which of the following statements are correct about the National Advisory Council (NAC)?
    I The National Advisory Council is a statutory body.
    II It is headed by the Prime Minister of India.
    III It facilitates constant interaction with the leaders of civil society.
    IV It provides policy and legislative inputs to the Government of India.

    Select the correct answer from the code given below.

    Codes:
    (a) I, II, and III (b) II, III, and IV
    (c) I, III, and IV (d) III and IV
31. Which of the following are voluntary provisions in the 73rd Constitutional Amendment Act (1992)?
    I Minimum age of 21 for contesting elections to Panchayats
    II Indirect elections to the post of Chairperson Panchayats at the intermediate and district levels.
    III Representation of Members of Parliament and State Legislature on Panchayati Raj institutions
    IV Reservation of seats for backward classes.

    Select the correct answer from the code given below.

    Codes:
    (a) I, II, and IV (b) II, III, and IV
    (c) I, II, and III (d) III and IV
32. In which of the following states the segment of population, which is in majority, enjoys the benefit of reservation of seats in the state assembly?
    (a) Meghalaya and Mizoram
    (b) Assam and Nagaland
    (c) Madhya Pradesh and Assam
    (d) Rajasthan and Arunachal Pradesh
33. Which of the following are the ways of acquiring Indian citizenship?
    I Birth
    II Descent
    III Naturalization
    IV Incorporation of territory

    Select the correct answer from the code given below.

Codes:

(a) I and II (b) I and IV
(c) I, II, and III (d) I, II, III, and IV

34. Which of the following statements about the Union Public Service Commission are correct?

I UPSC is a constitutional body.
II It serves as an advisory body.
III It is called upon to advise the government in regard to representation of the Scheduled Castes and Scheduled Tribes in the Civil Service.
IV It is consulted on appointments of Chairman and members of Tribunals and Commissions.

Select the correct answer from the code given below.

Codes:

(a) I, II, and III (b) I, II, and IV
(c) I, III, and IV (d) I and II

Read the following passage carefully and answer Questions from 35 to 40:

I had occasion to work with her closely during the Women's International Year in 1975 when she was chairing a Steering Committee and made me the member in charge of publicity. Representatives from different political parties and women's organizations were on the committee and though the leftists claimed a sort of proprietary right over her, Aruna encouraged and treated all members alike. It was not her political affiliations or her involvement in a particular cause, which won her respect and recognition, but her utter honesty in public life, her integrity, and her compassion for the oppressed, which made her an adorable person. She had the courage to differ with and defy the mightiest in the land; yet her human spirit prompted her to work in the worst of slums to offer succour to the poor and the exploited.

In later years—around late eighties and early nineties—Aruna Asaf Ali's health began to deteriorate. Although her mind remained alert, she could not actively take up her pet causes such as action for women's advancement, planning for economic justice, role of media, reaffirmation of values in public affairs, etc. Slowly, her movements were restricted, and Aruna who had drawn sustenance from common people, from her involvement in public life, became a lonely person. She passed away in July 1996.

35. Which committee was chaired by Aruna ?
(a) Women's International Year's Committee
(b) Steering Committee of Women's International Year
(c) A Committee of Publicity
(d) Women's Organizations

36. Who were made the members of the Committee of Publicity?

Choose the answer from codes given below:

I Representatives from different political parties
II Representatives from the leftist parties
III Representatives from the women's organizations
IV None of the above

Codes:

(a) I and III (b) I and II
(c) I, II, and III (d) IV only

37. Aruna earned respect because of
(a) She identified with the leftists
(b) She did not associate with any political party
(c) Chairing a Steering Committee
(d) She identified with women's organizations

38. Who tried to monopolize Aruna as their proprietary right?
(a) Women Organizations
(b) Leftists
(c) Steering Committee
(d) Some Political Parties

39. Aruna's health began to deteriorate from
(a) 1985–2002 (b) 1998–2000
(c) 1981–2000 (d) 1989–2001

40. Aruna's pet cause(s) in her life was/were
(a) Role of media
(b) Economic justice
(c) Reaffirmation of values in public affairs
(d) All of the above

41. A good teacher must be
    (a) Resourceful and autocratic
    (b) Resourceful and participative
    (c) Resourceful and authoritative
    (d) Resourceful and dominant
42. Which one of the following is the best method of teaching?
    (a) Lecture method
    (b) Discussion method
    (c) Demonstration method
    (d) Question-answer method
43. Successful communication in classroom teaching is
    (a) Circular (b) Reciprocal
    (c) Directional (d) Influential
44. Which one of the following types of evaluation assesses the learning progress to provide continuous feedback to both teachers and students during instruction?
    (a) Placement evaluation
    (b) Formative evaluation
    (c) Diagnostic evaluation
    (d) Summative evaluation
45. Which one of the following is a scaled down teaching situation?
    (a) Macroteaching
    (b) Team teaching
    (c) Cooperative teaching
    (d) Micro teaching
46. CLASS stands for
    (a) Complete Literacy and Studies in Schools
    (b) Computer Literates and Students in Schools
    (c) Computer Literacy and Studies in Schools
    (d) Centre for Literacy and Studies in Schools
47. Which one of the following is not a type of experimental method?
    (a) Single group experiment
    (b) Residual group experiment
    (c) Parallel group experiment
    (d) Rational group experiment
48. Which one of the following is not a non-parametric test?
    (a) *t*-test (b) Sign test
    (c) Chi-square test (d) Run test
49. Read the following statements—one labelled as Assertion (*A*) and the other as Reason (*R*):

    Assertion (A): Qualitative research in India has a long way to go to reach international standards.

    Reason (R): Because the funding agencies do not support qualitative research in academic institutions.

    Find the correct answer from the codes given below:
    (a) Both (*A*) and (*R*) are true and (*R*) is the correct explanation of (*A*).
    (b) Both (*A*) and (*R*) are true, but (*R*) is not the correct explanation of (*A*).
    (c) (*A*) is true, but (*R*) is false.
    (d) Both (*A*) and (*R*) are false.
50. Identify the correct sequence of research steps:
    (a) Selection of topic, review of literature, data collection, and interpretation of findings
    (b) Review of literature, selection of topic, data collection, and interpretation of findings
    (c) Selection of topic, data collection, review of literature, and interpretation of findings
    (d) Selection of topic, review of literature, interpretation of findings, and data collection
51. Deconstruction is a popular method of research in
    (a) Basic science (b) Applied science
    (c) Social science (d) Literature
52. With that one of the following techniques communality is associated?
    (a) Univariate analysis
    (b) Factor analysis
    (c) Case studies
    (d) SWOT analysis
53. The variable that impacts the relationship between an independent variable and a dependent variable is known as

(a) Antecedent variable
(b) Precedent variable
(c) Predictor variable
(d) Control variable

54. Which one of the following is a non-probability sampling method?
(a) Simple random sampling
(b) Stratified sampling
(c) Cluster sampling
(d) Quota sampling

55. By the year 2022, the Climate Change Action Plan of Government of India aims at installing
(a) 20,000 MW of wind power
(b) 25,000 MW of wind power
(c) 20,000 MW of solar power
(d) 10,000 MW of solar power

56. Which one of the following biosphere reserves has UNESCO recognition?
(a) Manas
(b) Kanchenjunga
(c) Seshachalam Hills
(d) Greater Nicobar

57. Which activity contributes to water pollution more than any other throughout world?
(a) Agriculture
(b) Hydroelectric power generation
(c) Industry
(d) Urbanization

58. Match List – I with List – II and find the correct answer from the codes given below:

List I		List I	
A	Nilgiri	I	Deccan Peninsula
B	Manas	II	Chhattisgarh
C	Simlipal	III	Eastern Himalaya
D	Achankmar-Amarkantak	IV	Western Ghat

Codes:

	A	B	C	D
(a)	I	II	III	IV
(b)	II	III	IV	I
(c)	III	IV	II	I
(d)	IV	III	I	II

59. G5 are the five most important emerging economies of world. Which one of the following does not form part of G5?
(a) Mexico (b) Brazil
(c) China (d) Korea

60. Which of the following nations has the maximum per capita emissions of carbon di-oxide?
(a) China (b) Japan
(c) USA (d) India

ANSWER KEYS

1. (a)	7. (c)	13. (a)	19. (a)	25. (c)	31. (d)	37. (b)	43. (b)	49. (c)	55. (c)
2. (a)	8. (c)	14. (b)	20. (c)	26. (c)	32. (a)	38. (b)	44. (b)	50. (a)	56. (d)
3. (b)	9. (d)	15. (b)	21. (a)	27. (d)	33. (d)	39. (c)	45. (d)	51. (d)	57. (a)
4. (b)	10. (d)	16. (b)	22. (a)	28. (d)	34. (d)	40. (d)	46. (c)	52. (b)	58. (d)
5. (a)	11. (a)	17. (b)	23. (c)	29. (d)	35. (b)	41. (b)	47. (b)	53. (d)	59. (d)
6. (d)	12. (b)	18. (b)	24. (b)	30. (d)	36. (a)	42. (c)	48. (a)	54. (d)	60. (c)

HINTS AND SOLUTIONS

1. (a): The geometric growth means 2, 4, 6, 8……
The exponential growth means 2, 4, 8, 16 ……
Exponential means compounded growth in population.
Consider population as 1, since as factor it will cancel from both side anyway,
Let number of years = 1 $(1 + 3.5/100)^x$ = 1 +16
So, $(1.035)^x = 17$
So, $x = \log 17/\log 1.035 = 1.23044/0.0149403 = 82.35743$
So, approximate number of years = 80

2. (a): Other examples of linear communication are face-to-face communication, email, chats, etc.

3. (b): Communication in informal groups is basically grapevine communication where hierarchy may not be followed.

7. (c): Cognitive means development of intellectual capability and is considered as the core learning domain. The candidates can refer to page 1.6 for better clarification.

9. (d):

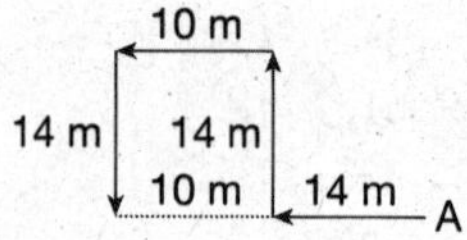

10. (d):

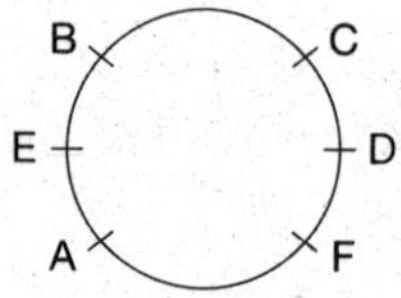

11. (a): $2 \times 3 + 1 = 7$; $7 \times 3 + 3 = 24$; $24 \times 3 + 5 = 77$; $77 \times 3 + 7 = 238$; $238 \times 3 + 9 = 723$

12. (b): We need not to calculate to fixed charges.

Variable charges for 8 km (that is, 24 km −16 km) = 204 −156 = ₹48

Variable for 1 km = 48/8 = ₹6

Extra variable charges for 6 km = 6 × 6 = ₹36

These can be added for total charges for 24 km to get total charges for 30 kms = 204 + 36 = ₹240

13. (a):

H	E	A	L	T	H
+3	+3	+3	+3	+3	+3
K	H	D	O	W	K

N	O	R	T	H
+3	+3	+3	+3	+3
Q	R	U	W	K

14. (b):

	Cricket	Tennis	Football	Badminton	Golf
Yadav	✓			X	✓
Arjun	✓	X			
Rajesh	✓	✓	X		
Kamal	✓	✓	X	✓	

20. (c): The growth rate for different years: 4.56% for 2007–08; 4.69% for 2008–09; 3.75% for 2009–10; 5.73% for 2010–11. So (c) is the answer.

21. (a): The growth figures for different primary sources of energy in India: For coal and lignite −23.43%; crude petroleum −10.96%; Hydro and Nuclear electricity −6.21%; Total production of energy −20.10 %.

28. (d): Mozilla Firefox 3.5 is one of the most popular browsers.

29. (d): Additional Information: National Commission for Minority Educational Institutions (NCMEI) was established in 2004.

31. (d): Need to focus on key word - voluntary provisions. voluntary provisions. Otherwise, reservation for SCs/STs and women is compulsory.

44. (b): Please refer to page 1.19.

48. (a): In question, not a non-parametric test means the it is asking about parametric test. t-test, z-test, F-test for analysis of variance are the main examples of parametric tests.

52. (b): The communality is a measure of variance in a given variable that is explained by all the factors combined together. It also reflects upon the reliability of the indicator.

56. (d): There are 18 biosphere in Government of India's Man and Biosphere (MAB) List. Out of these eighteen, ten are recognized in UNESCO's Man and Biosphere List. These nine biosphere reserves are Achanakmar-Amarkantak (Chhattisgarh, Madhya Pradesh), Gulf of Mannar (Tamil Nadu), Nanda Devi (Uttarakhand), Great Nicobar Islands, Nilgiri (TamilNadu, Kerala, Karnataka), Nokrek (Meghalaya), Pachmarhi (Madhya Pradesh), Simlipal (Odisha), Sundarbans (West Bengal) and Agasthyamala Biosphere Reserve (Kerala and Tamilnadu).

UGC NET Paper 1 December 2013

1. Which is the main objective of research?
   (a) To review the literature
   (b) To summarize what is already known
   (c) To get an academic degree
   (d) To discover new facts or to make fresh interpretation of known facts
2. Sampling error decreases with the
   (a) Decrease in sample size
   (b) Increase in sample size
   (c) Process of randomization
   (d) Process of analysis
3. The principles of fundamental research are used in
   (a) Action research
   (b) Applied research
   (c) Philosophical research
   (d) Historical research
4. Users who use media for their own ends are identified as
   (a) Passive audience (b) Active audience
   (c) Positive audience (d) Negative audience
5. Classroom communication can be described as
   (a) Exploration
   (b) Institutionalization
   (c) Unsignified narration
   (d) Discourse
6. Ideological codes shape our collective
   (a) Productions (b) Perceptions
   (c) Consumptions (d) Creations
7. In communication, myths have power, but are
   (a) Uncultural (b) Insignificant
   (c) Imprecise (d) Unpreferred
8. The first multi-lingual news agency of India was
   (a) Samachar
   (b) API
   (c) Hindustan Samachar
   (d) Samachar Bharati
9. Organizational communication can also be equated with
   (a) Intra-personal communication
   (b) Inter-personal communication
   (c) Group communication
   (d) Mass communication
10. If two propositions having the same subject and predicate terms are such that one is the denial of the other, then the relationship between them is called
    (a) Contradictory (b) Contrary
    (c) Sub-contrary (d) Sub-alternation
11. Ananya and Krishna can speak and follow English. Bulbul can write and speak Hindi as Archana does. Archana talks with Ananya also in Bengali. Krishna can not follow Bengali. Bulbul talks with Ananya in Hindi. Who can speak and follow English, Hindi, and Bengali?
    (a) Archana (b) Bulbul
    (c) Ananya (d) Krishna

12. A stipulative definition may be said to be
    (a) Always true
    (b) Always false
    (c) Sometimes true, sometimes false
    (d) Neither true nor false
13. When the conclusion of an argument follows from its premise(s) conclusively, then the argument is called
    (a) Circular argument
    (b) Inductive argument
    (c) Deductive argument
    (d) Analogical argument
14. Saturn and Mars are planets like the Earth. They borrow light from the Sun and moves around the Sun as the Earth does. So those planets are inhabited by various orders of creatures as the Earth.
    What type of argument is contained in the above passage?
    (a) Deductive (b) Astrological
    (c) Analogical (d) Mathematical
15. Given below are two premises. Four conclusions are drawn from those two premises in four codes. Select the code that states the conclusion validly drawn.
    Premises:
    (i) All saints are religious. (major)
    (ii) Some honest persons are saints. (minor)
    Codes:
    (a) All saints are honest.
    (b) Some saints are honest.
    (c) Some honest persons are religious.
    (d) All religious persons are honest.

Following table provides details about the Foreign Tourist Arrivals (FTAs) in India from different regions of the world in different years. Study the table carefully and answer the Questions from **16** to **19** based on this table.

Region	**Number of foreign tourist arrivals**		
	2007	**2008**	**2009**
Western Europe	1686083	1799525	1610086
North America	1007276	1027297	1024469
South Asia	982428	1051846	982633
South East Asia	303475	332925	348495
East Asia	352037	355230	318292
West Asia	171661	215542	201110
Total FTAs in India	5081504	5282603	5108579

16. Find out the region that contributed around 20 percent of the total foreign tourist arrivals in India in 2009.
    (a) Western Europe (b) North America
    (c) South Asia (d) South East Asia
17. Which of the following regions has recorded the highest negative growth rate of foreign tourist arrivals in India in 2009?
    (a) Western Europe (b) North America
    (c) South Asia (d) West Asia
18. Find out the region that has been showing declining trend in terms of share of foreign tourist arrivals in India in 2008 and 2009.
    (a) Western Europe (b) South East Asia
    (c) East Asia (d) West Asia
19. Identify the region that has shown hyper growth rate of foreign tourist arrivals than the growth rate of the total FTAs in India in 2008.
    (a) Western Europe (b) North America
    (c) South Asia (d) East Asia
20. The post-industrial society is designated as
    (a) Information society
    (b) Technology society
    (c) Mediated society
    (d) Non-agricultural society
21. The initial efforts for internet based communication was for
    (a) Commercial communication
    (b) Military purposes
    (c) Personal interaction
    (d) Political campaigns
22. Internal communication within institutions is done through

(a) LAN (b) WAN
(c) EBB (d) MMS

23. Virtual reality provides
(a) Sharp pictures
(b) Individual audio
(c) Participatory experience
(d) Preview of new films

24. The first virtual university of India came up in
(a) Andhra Pradesh
(b) Maharashtra
(c) Uttar Pradesh
(d) Tamil Nadu

25. Arrange the following books in chronological order in which they appeared. Use the code given below:

(i) *Limits to Growth*

(ii) *Silent Spring*

(iii) *Our Common Future*

(iv) *Resourceful Earth*

Codes:
(a) (i), (iii), (iv), (ii)
(b) (ii), (iii), (i), (iv)
(c) (ii), (i), (iii), (iv)
(d) (i), (ii), (iii), (iv)

26. Which one of the following continents is at a greater risk of desertification?
(a) Africa (b) Asia
(c) South America (d) North America

27. 'Women are closer to nature than men'. What kind of perspective is this?
(a) Realist (b) Essentialist
(c) Feminist (d) Deep ecology

28. Which one of the following is not a matter of a global concern in the removal of tropical forests?
(a) Their ability to absorb the chemicals that contribute to depletion of ozone layer.
(b) Their role in maintaining the oxygen and carbon balance of the earth.
(c) Their ability to regulate surface and air temperatures, moisture content, and reflectivity.
(d) Their contribution to the biological diversity of the planet.

29. The most comprehensive approach to address the problems of man–environment interaction is one of the following:
(a) Natural Resource Conservation Approach
(b) Urban-industrial Growth-oriented Approach
(c) Rural-agricultural Growth-oriented Approach
(d) Watershed Development Approach

30. The major source of the pollutant gas, carbon mono-oxide (CO), in urban areas is
(a) Thermal power sector
(b) Transport sector
(c) Industrial sector
(d) Domestic sector

31. In a fuel cell-driven vehicle, the energy is obtained from the combustion of
(a) Methane (b) Hydrogen
(c) LPG (d) CNG

32. Which one of the following Councils has been disbanded in 2013?
(a) Distance Education Council (DEC)
(b) National Council for Teacher Education (NCTE)
(c) National Council of Educational Research and Training (NCERT)
(d) National Assessment and Accreditation Council (NAAC)

33. Which of the following statements are correct about the National Assessment and Accreditation Council?

(i) It is an autonomous institution.

(ii) It is tasked with the responsibility of assessing and accrediting institutions of higher education.

(iii) It is located in Delhi.

(iv) It has regional offices.

Select the correct answer from the codes given below:

Codes:
(a) (i) and (iii) (b) (i) and (ii)
(c) (i), (ii), and (iv) (d) (ii), (iii), and (iv)

34. The power of the Supreme Court of India to decide disputes between two or more States falls under its
(a) Advisory Jurisdiction
(b) Appellate Jurisdiction
(c) Original Jurisdiction
(d) Writ Jurisdiction

35. Which of the following statements are correct?
(i) There are seven Union Territories in India.
(ii) Two Union Territories have Legislative Assemblies
(iii) One Union Territory has a High Court.
(iv) One Union Territory is the capital of two States.

Codes:
(a) (i) and (iii) only
(b) (ii) and (iv) only
(c) (ii), (iii), and (iv) only
(d) (i), (ii), (iii), and (iv)

36. Which of the following statements are correct about the Central Information Commission?
(i) The Central Information Commission is a statutory body.
(ii) The Chief Information Commissioner and other Information Commissioners are appointed by the President of India.
(iii) The Commission can impose a penalty upto a maximum of ₹25,000/-
(iv) It can punish an errant officer.

Select the correct answer from the codes given below:

Codes:
(a) (i) and (ii) only
(b) (i), (ii), and (iv)
(c) (i), (ii), and (iii)
(d) (ii), (iii), and (iv)

37. Who among the following conducted the CNN-IBN–The Hindu 2013 Election Tracker Survey across 267 constituencies in 18 States?
(a) The Centre for the Study of Developing Societies (CSDS)
(b) The Association for Democratic Reforms (ADR)
(c) CNN and IBN
(d) CNN, IBN and The Hindu

38. In a certain code, 'TEACHER' is written as 'VGCEJGT'. Then, the code of 'CHILDREN' will be
(a) EKNJFTGP (b) EJKNFTGP
(c) KNJFGTP (d) None of these

39. A person has to buy both apples and mangoes. The cost of one apple is ₹7, whereas that of a mango is ₹5. If the person has ₹38, the number of apples he can buy is
(a) 1 (b) 2 (c) 3 (d) 4

40. A man pointing to a lady said, "The son of her only brother is the brother of my wife". The lady is related to the man as
(a) Mother's sister
(b) Grand mother
(c) Mother-in-law
(d) Sister of Father-in-law

41. In this series 6, 4, 1, 2, 2, 8, 7, 4, 2, 1, 5, 3, 8, 6, 2, 2, 7, 1, 4, 1, 3, 5, 8, 6, how many pairs of successive numbers have a difference of 2 each?
(a) 4 (b) 5 (c) 6 (d) 8

42. The mean marks obtained by a class of 40 students is 65. The mean marks of half of the students is found to be 45. The mean marks of the remaining students is
(a) 85 (b) 60
(c) 70 (d) 65

43. Anil is twice as old as Sunita. Three years ago, he was three times as old as Sunita. The present age of Anil is
(a) 6 years (b) 8 years
(c) 12 years (d) 16 years

44. Which of the following is a social network?
(a) amazon.com (b) eBay
(c) gmail.com (d) Twitter

45. The population information is called parameter, whereas the corresponding sample information is known as
(a) Universe (b) Inference
(c) Sampling design (d) Statistics

Read the following passage carefully and answer the Questions from 46 to 51:

Heritage conservation practices improved worldwide after the International Centre for the Study of the Preservation and Restoration of Cultural Property (ICCROM) was established with UNESCO's assistance in 1959. The intergovernmental organization with 126 member states has done a commendable job by training more than 4000 professionals, providing practice standards, and sharing technical expertise. In this golden jubilee year, as we acknowledge its key role in global conservation, an assessment of international practices would be meaningful to the Indian conservation movement. Consistent investment, rigorous attention, and dedicated research and dissemination are some of the positive lessons to imbibe. Countries like Italy have demonstrated that prioritizing heritage with significant budget provision pays. On the other hand, India, which is no less endowed in terms of cultural capital, has a long way to go. Surveys indicate that in addition to the 6600 protected monuments, there are over 60,000 equally valuable heritage structures that await attention. Besides the small group in the service of Archaeological Survey of India, there are only about 150 trained conservation professionals. In order to overcome this severe shortage, the emphasis has been on setting up dedicated labs and training institutions. It would make much better sense for conservation to be made part of mainstream research and engineering institutes, as has been done in Europe.

Increasing funding and building institutions are the relatively easy part. The real challenge is to redefine international approaches to address local contexts. Conservation cannot limit itself to enhancing the art-historical value of the heritage structures, which international charters perhaps overemphasize. The effort has to be broad-based: It must also serve as a means of improving the quality of life in the area where the heritage structures are located. The first task, therefore, is to integrate conservation efforts with sound development plans that take care of people living in the heritage vicinity. Unlike in western countries, many traditional building crafts survive in India, and conservation practices offer an avenue to support them. This has been acknowledged by the Indian National Trust for Art and Cultural Heritage charter for conservation but is yet to receive substantial state support. More strength for heritage conservation can be mobilized by aligning it with the green building movement. Heritage structures are essentially eco-friendly and conservation could become a vital part of the sustainable building practices campaign in future.

46. The outlook for conservation heritage changed
(a) After the establishment of the International Centre for the Study of the Preservation and Restoration of Cultural Property
(b) After training the specialists in the field
(c) After extending UNESCO's assistance to the educational institutions
(d) After ASI's measures to protect the monuments

47. The inter-government organization was appreciated because of
(a) Increasing number of members to 126
(b) Imparting training to professionals and sharing technical expertise
(c) Consistent investment in conservation
(d) Its proactive role in renovation and restoration

48. Indian conservation movement will be successful if there would be
(a) Financial support from the Government of India
(b) Non-governmental organizations, role and participation in the conservation movement
(c) consistent investment, rigorous attention, and dedicated research and dissemination of awareness for conservation
(d) Archaeological Survey of India's meaningful assistance

49. As per the surveys of historical monuments in India, there is very small number of protected monuments. As per the given total number of monuments and enlisted number of protected monuments, percentage comes to
(a) 10 per cent (b) 11 per cent
(c) 12 per cent (d) 13 per cent

50. What should India learn from Europe to conserve our cultural heritage?
(i) There should be significant budget provision to conserve our cultural heritage.
(ii) Establish dedicated labs and training institutions.
(iii) Force the government to provide sufficient funds.
(iv) Conservation should be made part of mainstream research and engineering institutes.
Choose correct answer from the codes given below:
(a) (i), (ii), (iii), and (iv) (b) (i), (ii), and (iv)
(c) (i) and (ii) (d) (i), (iii), and (iv)

51. INTACH is known for its contribution for conservation of our cultural heritage. The full form of INTACH is
(a) International Trust for Art and Cultural Heritage
(b) Intra-national Trust for Art and Cultural Heritage
(c) Integrated Trust for Art and Cultural Heritage
(d) Indian National Trust for Art and Cultural Heritage

52. While delivering lecture if there is some disturbance in the class, a teacher should
(a) Keep quiet for a while and then continue.
(b) Punish those causing disturbance.
(c) Motivate to teach those causing disturbance.
(d) Not bother of what is happening in the class.

53. Effective teaching is a function of
(a) Teacher's satisfaction
(b) Teacher's honesty and commitment
(c) Teacher's making students learn and understand
(d) Teacher's liking for professional excellence

54. The most appropriate meaning of learning is
(a) Acquisition of skills
(b) Modification of behaviour
(c) Personal adjustment
(d) Inculcation of knowledge

55. Arrange the following teaching process in order:
(i) Relate the present knowledge with previous one
(ii) Evaluation
(iii) Reteaching
(iv) Formulating instructional objectives
(v) Presentation of instructional materials
Codes:
(a) (i), (ii), (iii), (iv), (v)
(b) (ii), (i), (iii), (iv), (v)
(c) (v), (iv), (iii), (i), (ii)
(d) (iv), (i), (v), (ii), (iii)

56. CIET stands for
(a) Centre for Integrated Education and Technology
(b) Central Institute for Engineering and Technology
(c) Central Institute for Education Technology
(d) Centre for Integrated Evaluation Techniques

57. Teacher's role at higher education level is to
(a) Provide information to students
(b) Promote self learning in students
(c) Encourage healthy competition among students
(d) Help students to solve their problems

58. The Verstehen School of Understanding was popularized by
(a) German Social Scientists
(b) American Philosophers
(c) British Academicians
(d) Italian Political Analysts

59. The sequential operations in scientific research are
(a) Co-variation, Elimination of Spurious Relations, Generalization, and Theorization
(b) Generalization, Co-variation, Theorization, and Elimination of Spurious Relations

(c) Theorization, Generalization, and Elimination of Spurious Relations, Covariation
(d) Elimination of Spurious Relations, Theorization, and Generalization, Covariation

60. In sampling, the lottery method is used for
(a) Interpretation (b) Theorization
(c) Conceptualization (d) Randomization

Answer Keys

1. (d)	7. (c)	13. (c)	19. (c)	25. *	31. (b)	37. (a)	43. (c)	49. (a)	55. (d)
2. (b)	8. (c)	14. (c)	20. (a)	26. (a)	32. (a)	38. (b)	44. (d)	50. (b)	56. (c)
3. (b)	9. (c)	15. (c)	21. (b)	27. (b)	33. (b)	39. (d)	45. (d)	51. (d)	57. (b)
4. (b)	10. (a)	16. (b)	22. (a)	28. (a)	34. (c)	40. (d)	46. (a)	52. (c)	58. (a)
5. (d)	11. (c)	17. (a)	23. (c)	29. (d)	35. (d)	41. (c)	47. (b)	53. (c)	59. (a)
6. (b)	12. (d)	18. (c)	24. (d)	30. (b)	36. (c)	42. (a)	48. (c)	54. (b)	60. (d)

'*' denotes marks given to all candidates.

Hints and Solutions

1. (d): Refer pages 2.1 and 2.2
2. (b): Refer 'Step 4: Selecting samples' on pages 2.22 and 2.23.
3. (b): Refer 'Classification of Research on the Basis of Application' on page 2.7.
10. (a): Refer 'Squares of Opposition' on pages 6.12 and 6.13.
11. (c): One need to go step-by-step to solve this question and update this table in every step. In the solution given below, S stands for speak, F for follow, and W for write.

	English	Hindi	Bengali
Ananya	S & F	S & F	S & F
Krishna	S & F		
Bulbul		W & S	
Archana		W & S	S & F

So, Ananya is the answer.

12. (d): Refer 'Types of Definitions' on page 6.15.
13. (c): Refer pages 6.1 and 6.2
14. (c): Refer page 6.4
15. (c): This question can be solved with the help of Venn diagram as well.

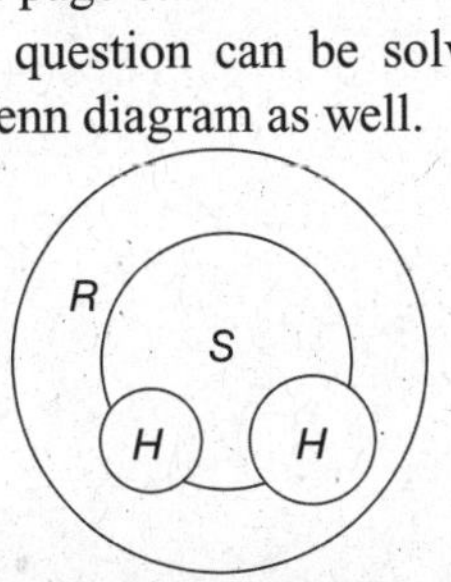

Here, *R*, *S*, and *H* stand for Religious, Saints, and Honest, respectively. There are two ways through which *H* can be shown. Note that 'Some honest persons are saints' does not mean that some saints are honest. Hence, (b) is not true.

16. (b): Some approximation can be applied by ignoring last four digits in all the figures-

30. (b): Refer Table 9.1 on page 9.10.

32. (a): Refer 'Open and Distance Education' on page 10.16

33. (a): Refer page number 10.16

34. (c): Refer page number 10.41

38. (b)

T	E	A	C	H	E	R
+1	+1	+1	+1	+1	+1	+1
V	G	C	E	J	G	T

Similarly,

C	H	I	L	D	R	E	N
+1	+1	+1	+1	+1	+1	+1	+1
E	J	K	N	F	T	G	P

40. (d): We can make use of standard symbols to draw family diagram.

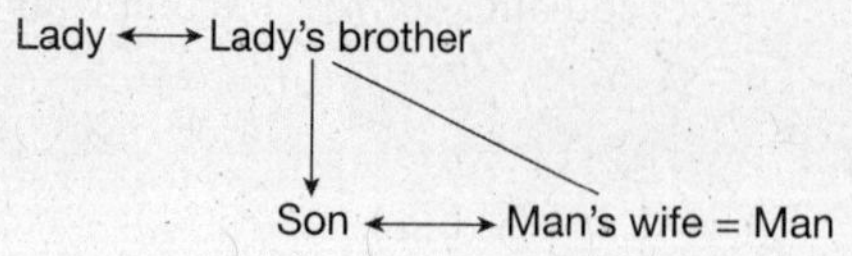

The diagram shows that lady's brother is father-in-law of man, so the lady in question is 'sister of father-in-law'. So, (d) is the answer.

42. (a): It's a question of Combined Arithmetic Mean.

43. (c): Let's assume that present age of Anil = x years;
Then, Sunita's age = $x/2$ years
$x - 3 = 3\,(x/2 - 3)$
By solving the equation, the present age of Anil = 12 years

45. (d): Refer 'Step 4: Selecting Samples' on page 2.22

52. (c): Refer page 1.30. In answering these types of questions, lot of subjectivity is there. Motivating students is always the best approach. In case of misbehaviour, teacher should stop teaching for a while.

53. (c): Effective means to ensure that end objective is achieved. End objective in teaching is 'making students learn and understand'.

54. (b): Learning is basically a psychological concept. Refer page 1.15

58. Refer page 2.2. Verstehen is linked with teaching as well.

59. (a) In research, first of all, we look for similarities (covariation) across a range of situations to help us narrow down specific attributions. Thus elimination of spurious relationships logically becomes the second step. Factor analysis mentioned on page 2.15 is the statistical technique that can be used for this purpose. Generalisation and Theory are the ultimate desirable aims of almost every research.

60. One of the most desirable feature of research is objectivity. For that data collection and sampling should be unbiased to the extent possible. Random sample means every member of population has equal chance of being selected. Candidates need to refer 'Randomisation' on page 2.18 and 'Types of sampling techniques' on page 2.22.

UGC NET PAPER 1 JUNE 2014

1. Break-down in verbal communication is described as
   (a) Short circuit
   (b) Contradiction
   (c) Unevenness
   (d) Entropy

2. The Telephone Model of Communication was first developed in the area of
   (a) Technological theory
   (b) Dispersion theory
   (c) Minimal effects theory
   (d) Information theory

3. The Dadasaheb Phalke Award for 2013 has been conferred on
   (a) Karan Johar (b) Amir Khan
   (c) Asha Bhonsle (d) Gulzar

4. Photographs are not easy to
   (a) Publish (b) Secure
   (c) Decode (d) Change

5. The grains that appear on a television set when operated are also referred to as
   (a) Sparks (b) Green dots
   (c) Snow (d) Rain drops

6. In circular communication, the encoder becomes a decoder when there is
   (a) Noise (b) Audience
   (c) Criticality (d) Feedback

7. In a post- office, stamps of three different denominations of ₹7, ₹8, and ₹10 are available. The exact amount for which one cannot buy stamps is
   (a) 19 (b) 20 (c) 23 (d) 29

8. In certain coding method, the word QUESTION is encoded as DOMESTIC. In this coding, what is the code word for the word RESPONSE?
   (a) OMESUCEM (b) OMESICSM
   (c) OMESICEM (d) OMESISCM

9. If the series 4, 5, 8, 13, 14, 17, 22, ... is continued in the same pattern, then which one of the following is not a term of this series?
   (a) 31 (b) 32 (c) 33 (d) 35

10. Complete the series BB, FE, II, ML, PP, ______ by choosing one of the following option given:
    (a) TS (b) ST (c) RS (d) SR

11. A man started walking from his house towards south. After walking 6 km, he turned to his left and walked 5 km. Then he walked further 3 km after turning left. He then turned to his left and continued his walk for 9 km. How far is he away from his house?
    (a) 3 km (b) 4 km
    (c) 5 km (d) 6 km

12. One writes all numbers from 50 to 99 without the digits 2 and 7. How many numbers have been written?
(a) 32 (b) 36 (c) 40 (d) 38

13. 'If a large diamond is cut up into little bits, it will lose its value just as an army is divided up into small units of soldiers, it loses its strength'.

The argument put above may be called as
(a) Analogical (b) Deductive
(c) Statistical (d) Causal

14. Given below are some characteristics of logical argument. Select the code which expresses a characteristic which is not of inductive in character.
(a) The conclusion is claimed to follow from its premises.
(b) The conclusion is based on causal relation.
(c) The conclusion conclusively follows from its premises.
(d) The conclusion is based on observation and experiment.

15. If two propositions having the same subject and predicate terms can both be true but both cannot be false, then the relation between those two propositions is called
(a) Contradictory
(b) Contrary
(c) Subcontrary
(d) Subaltern

16. Given below are two premises and four conclusions drawn from those premises. Select the code that expresses conclusion drawn validly from the premises (separately or jointly).

Premises:

(a) All dogs are mammals.
(b) No cats are dogs.

Conclusions:

(i) No cats are mammals.
(ii) Some cats are mammals.
(iii) No dogs are cats.
(iv) No dogs are non-mammals.

Codes:

(a) (i) only (b) (i) and (ii)
(c) (iii) and (iv) (d) (ii) and (iii)

17. Given below is a diagram of three circles A, B, and C inter-related with each other. The Circle A represents the class of Indians, the Circle B represents the class of scientists, and Circle C represents the class of politicians. p, q, r, s represent different regions. Select the code containing the region that indicates the class of Indian scientists who are not politicians.

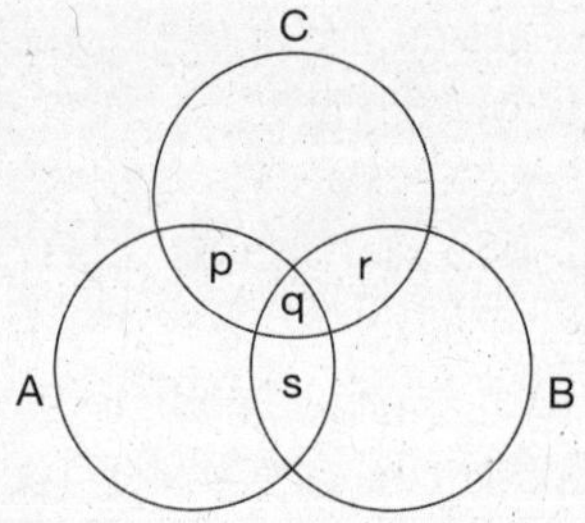

Codes:

(a) q and s only
(b) s only
(c) s and r only
(d) p, q, and s only

Read the following table carefully. Based upon this table answer the Questions from 18 to 22:

Net area under irrigation by sources in a country (thousand hectares)

Year	Government canals	Private canals	Tanks	Tube wells & other wells	Other sources	Total
1997–98	17,117	211	2593	32,090	3102	55,173
1998–99	17,093	212	2792	33,988	3326	57,411
1999–00	16,842	194	2535	34,623	2915	57,109
2000–01	15,748	203	2449	33,796	2880	55,076
2001–02	15,031	209	2179	34,906	4347	56,672
2002–03	13,863	206	1802	34,250	3657	53,778
2003–04	14,444	206	1908	35,779	4281	56,618
2004–05	14,696	206	1727	34,785	7453	58,867
2005–06	15,268	207	2034	35,372	7314	60,196

18. Which of the following sources of irrigation has registered the largest percentage of decline in net area under irrigation during 1997–98 and 2005–06?
(a) Government canals
(b) Private canals
(c) Tanks
(d) Other sources

19. Find out the source of irrigation that has registered the maximum improvement in terms of percentage of net irrigated area during 2002–03 and 2003–04.
(a) Government canals
(b) Tanks
(c) Tube wells and other wells
(d) Other sources

20. In which of the following years, net irrigation by tanks increased at the highest rate?
(a) 1998–99 (b) 2000–01
(c) 2003–04 (d) 2005–06

21. Identify the source of irrigation that has recorded the maximum incidence of negative growth in terms of net irrigated area during the years given in the table.
(a) Government canals
(b) Private canals
(c) Tube wells and other wells
(d) Other sources

22. In which of the following years, shares of the tube wells and other wells in the total net irrigated area was the highest?
(a) 1998–99 (b) 2000–01
(c) 2002–03 (d) 2004–05

23. The acronym FTP stands for
(a) File Transfer Protocol
(b) Fast Transfer Protocol
(c) File Tracking Protocol
(d) File Transfer Procedure

24. Which one of the following is not a/an image/graphic file format?
(a) PNG (b) GIF (c) BMP (d) GUI

25. The first web browser is
(a) Internet Explorer
(b) Netscape
(c) World Wide Web
(d) Firefox

26. When a computer is booting, BIOS is loaded to the memory by
(a) RAM (b) ROM
(c) CD-ROM (d) TCP

27. Which one of the following is not the same as the other three?
(a) MAC address
(b) Hardware address
(c) Physical address
(d) IP address

28. Identify the IP address from the following:
(a) 300 · 215 · 317 · 3
(b) 302 · 215@ 417 · 5
(c) 202 · 50 · 20 · 148
(d) 202 – 50 – 20 – 148

29. The population of India is about 1.2 billion. Take the average consumption of energy per person per year in India as 30 megajoule. If this consumption is met by carbon-based fuels and the rate of carbon emissions per kilojoule is 15×10^6 kg, then the total carbon emissions per year from India will be
(a) 54 million metric tonnes
(b) 540 million metric tonnes
(c) 5400 million metric tonnes
(d) 2400 million metric tonnes

30. Which of the following cities has been worst affected by urban smog in recent times?
(a) Paris (b) London
(c) Los Angeles (d) Beijing

31. The primary source of organic pollution in fresh water bodies is
(a) Run-off urban areas
(b) Run-off from agricultural forms
(c) Sewage effluents
(d) Industrial effluents

32. 'Lahar' is a natural disaster involving
(a) Eruption of large amount of material
(b) Strong winds
(c) Strong water waves
(d) Strong winds and water waves

33. In order to avoid catastrophic consequences of climate change, there is general agreement among the countries of the world to limit the rise in average surface temperature of earth compared to that of pre-industrial times by
(a) 1.5°C to 2°C (b) 2.0°C to 3.5°C
(c) 0.5°C to 1.0°C (d) 0.25°C to 0.5°C

34. The National Disaster Management Authority functions under the Union Ministry of
(a) Environment (b) Water Resources
(c) Home Affairs (d) Defence

35. Match List–I and List–II and select the correct answer from the codes given below:

List – I		List – II	
A	Flood	I	Lack of rainfall of sufficient duration
B	Drought	Ii	Tremors produced by the passage of vibratory waves through the rocks of the earth
C	Earthquake	III	A vent through which molten substances come out
D	Volcano	IV	Excess rain and uneven distribution of water

Codes:
(a) A-IV, B-I, C-II, D-III
(b) A-II, B-III, C-IV, D-I
(c) A-III, B-IV, C-II, D-I
(d) A-IV, B-III, C-I, D-II

36. Which one of the following green house gases has the shortest residence time in the atmosphere?
(a) Chlorofluorocarbon
(b) Carbon dioxide
(c) Methane
(d) Nitrous oxide

37. Consider the following statements and select the correct answer from the code given below:
(i) Rajasthan receives the highest solar radiation in the country.
(ii) India has the fifth largest installed wind power in the world.
(iii) The maximum amount of wind power is contributed by Tamil Nadu.
(iv) The primary source of uranium in India is Jaduguda.

Codes:
(a) (i) and (ii) (b) (i), (ii), and (iii)
(c) (ii) and (iii) (d) (i) and (iv)

38. Who among the following is the de facto executive head of the Planning Commission?
(a) Chairman
(b) Deputy Chairman
(c) Minister of State for Planning
(d) Member Secretary

39. Education as a subject of legislation figures in the
(a) Union List
(b) State List
(c) Concurrent List
(d) Residuary Powers

40. Which of the following are Central Universities?
(i) Pondicherry University
(ii) Vishwa Bharati
(iii) H.N.B. Garhwal University
(iv) Kurukshetra University

Select the correct answer from the codes given below:

Codes:
(a) (i), (ii), and (iii) (b) (i), (iii), and (iv)
(c) (ii), (iii), and (iv) (d) (i), (ii), and (iv)

41. Consider the statement which is followed by two arguments (i) and (ii).

Statement: India should have a very strong and powerful Lokpal.

Arguments:
(i) Yes, it will go a long in eliminating corruption in bureaucracy.
(ii) No, it will discourage honest officers from making quick decisions.

Codes:
(a) Only argument (i) is strong.
(b) Only argument (ii) is strong.

(c) Both the arguments are strong.
(d) Neither of the arguments is strong.

42. Which of the following universities has adopted the meta university concept?
(a) Assam University
(b) Delhi University
(c) Hyderabad University
(d) Pondicherry University

43. Which of the following statements are correct about a Central University?
(i) Central University is established under an Act of Parliament.
(ii) The President of India acts as the visitor of the University.
(iii) The President has the power to nominate some members to the Executive Committee or the Board of Management of the University.
(iv) The President occasionally presides over the meetings of the Executive Committee or Court.

Select the correct answer from the code given below:

Codes:

(a) (i), (ii), and (iv) (b) (i), (iii), and (iv)
(c) (i), (ii), and (iii) (d) (i), (ii), (iii), and (iv)

44. Which one of the following is considered a sign of motivated teaching?
(a) Students asking questions
(b) Maximum attendance of the students
(c) Pin drop silence in the classroom
(d) Students taking notes

45. Which one of the following is the best method of teaching?
(a) Lecture (b) Discussion
(c) Demonstration (d) Narration

46. Dyslexia is associated with
(a) Mental disorder
(b) Behavioural disorder
(c) Reading disorder
(d) Writing disorder

47. The e-content generation for under-graduate courses has been assigned by the Ministry of Human Resource Development to
(a) INFLIBNET
(b) Consortium for Educational Communication
(c) National Knowledge Commission
(d) Indira Gandhi National Open University

48. Classroom communication is normally considered as
(a) Effective (b) Cognitive
(c) Affective (d) Selective

49. Who among the following, propounded the concept of paradigm?
(a) Peter Haggett (b) Von Thunen
(c) Thomas Kuhn (d) John K. Wright

50. In a thesis, figures and tables are included in
(a) The appendix
(b) A separate chapter
(c) The concluding chapter
(d) The text itself

51. A thesis statement is
(a) An observation
(b) A fact
(c) An assertion
(d) A discussion

52. The research approach of Max Weber to understand how people create meanings in natural settings is identified as
(a) Positive paradigm
(b) Critical paradigm
(c) Natural paradigm
(d) Interpretative paradigm

53. Which one of the following is a non-probability sampling?
(a) Simple random
(b) Purposive
(c) Systematic
(d) Stratified

54. Identify the category of evaluation that assesses the learning progress to provide continuous feedback to the students during instruction.
(a) Placement (b) Diagnostic
(c) Formative (d) Summative

55. The research stream of immediate application is
    (a) Conceptual research
    (b) Action research
    (c) Fundamental research
    (d) Empirical research

Read the following passage carefully and answer the Questions from 56 to 60:

Traditional Indian values must be viewed both from the angle of the individual and from that of the geographically delimited agglomeration of people or groups enjoying a common system of leadership which we call the 'State'. The Indian 'State's' special feature is the peaceful, or perhaps mostly peaceful, co-existence of social groups of various historical provenances that mutually adhere in a geographical, economic, and political sense, without ever assimilating to each other in social terms, in ways of thinking, or even in language. Modern Indian law will determine certain rules, especially in relation to the regime of the family, upon the basis of how the loincloth is tied, or how the turban is worn, for this may identify the litigants as members of a regional group, and therefore as participants in its traditional law, though their ancestors left the region three or four centuries earlier. The use of the word 'State' above must not mislead us. There was no such thing as a conflict between the individual and the State, atleast before foreign governments became established, just as there was no concept of state 'sovereignty' or of any church-and-state dichotomy.

Modern Indian 'secularism' has an admittedly peculiar feature: it requires the state to make a fair distribution of attention and support amongst all religions. These blessed aspects of India's famed tolerance (Indian kings so rarely persecuted religious groups that the exceptions prove the rule) at once struck Portuguese and other European visitors to the West Coast of India in the sixteenth century, and the impression made upon them in this and other ways gave rise, at one remove, to the basic constitution of Thomas More's Utopia. There is little about modern India that strikes one at once as Utopian: but, the insistence upon the inculcation of norms and the absence of bigotry and institutionalized exploitation of human or natural resources are two very different features that link the realities of India and her tradition with the essence of all Utopians.

56. Which of the following is a special feature of the Indian State?
    (a) Peaceful co-existence of people under a common system of leadership
    (b) Peaceful co-existence of social groups of different historical provenances attached to each other in a geographical, economic, and political sense
    (c) Social integration of all groups
    (d) Cultural assimilation of all social groups

57. The author uses the word 'State' to highlight
    (a) Antagonistic relationship between the state and the individual throughout the period of history
    (b) Absence of conflict between the state and the individuals upto a point in time
    (c) The concept of state sovereignty
    (d) Dependence on religion

58. Which one is the peculiar feature of modern Indian 'secularism'?
    (a) No discrimination on religious considerations
    (b) Total indifference to religion
    (c) No space for social identity
    (d) Disregard for social law

59. The basic construction of Thomas More's Utopia was inspired by
    (a) Indian tradition of religious tolerance
    (b) Persecution of religious groups by Indian rulers
    (c) Social inequality in India
    (d) European perception of Indian State

60. What is the striking feature of modern India?
    (a) A replica of Utopian State
    (b) Uniform laws
    (c) Adherence to traditional values
    (d) Absence of Bigotry

Answer Keys

1. (d)	7. (a)	13. (a)	19. (d)	25. (c)	31. (c)	37. (*)	43. (c)	49. (c)	55. (b)
2. (d)	8. (c)	14. (c)	20. (d)	26. (b)	32. (a)	38. (b)	44. (a)	50. (d)	56. (b)
3. (d)	9. (c)	15. (c)	21. (a)	27. (d)	33. (a)	39. (c)	45. (c)	51. (c)	57. (b)
4. (c)	10. (a)	16. (c)	22. (c)	28. (c)	34. (c)	40. (a)	46. (c)	52. (d)	58. (a)
5. (c)	11. (c)	17. (b)	23. (a)	29. (*)	35. (a)	41. (a)	47. (b)	53. (b)	59. (a)
6. (d)	12. (a)	18. (c)	24. (d)	30. (d)	36. (c)	42. (b)	48. (b)	54. (c)	60. (d)

"*" denotes that marks are given to those candidates who have attempted this question within their first fifty attempted questions.

Hints and Solutions

7. (a): Elimination of choices is required to solve this question. Look at (a). For exact amount of 19, no combination fits, for (b) $10 \times 2 = 20$; (c) $(8 \times 2) + (7 \times 1) = 23$; (d) $(7 \times 3) + (8 \times 1) = 29$. Thus, (a) is the answer.

8. (c)

Q	U	E	S	T	I	O	N
↓	↓	↓	↓	↓	↓	↓	↓
D	O	M	E	S	T	I	C

Similarly,

R	E	S	P	O	N	S	E
↓	↓	↓	↓	↓	↓	↓	↓
?	M	E	?	I	C	E	M

Only one choice is possible that is matching of last four letters ICEM. Hence, (c) is the answer.

9. (c): Difference of 1, 3, 5 is the pattern. The terms after 22 will be 23, 26, 31, 32, 35…… Hence, 33 is not the term, and (c) is the answer.

10. (a)

B	+3	F	+2	I	+3	M	+2	P	+3	T
B	+2	E	+3	I	+2	L	+3	P	+2	S

Hence, TS is the answer.

11. (c)

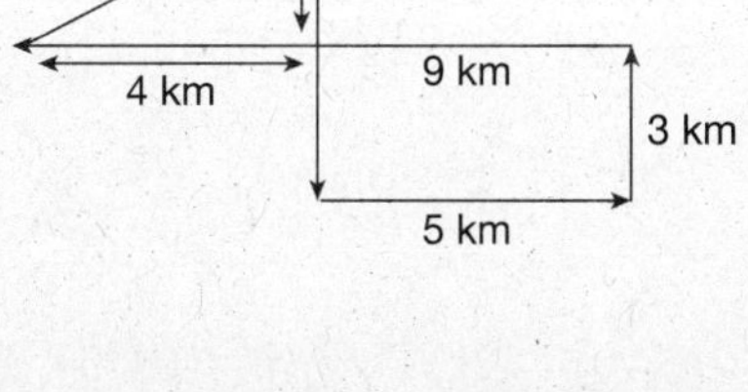

Using Pythagoras, theorem (adding squares of 3 and 4, and then taking their square root), the answer is 5 km.

12. (a) Hint – total numbers is 50. Eighteen numbers are to be deducted from it.

13. (a): Refer page 6.4

14. (c): Refer pages 6.1–6.2

15. (c): Refer 'Squares of Opposition' on pages 6.12-6.13.

16. (c): Let us assume that M stands for mammals, D for dogs and C for Cats.

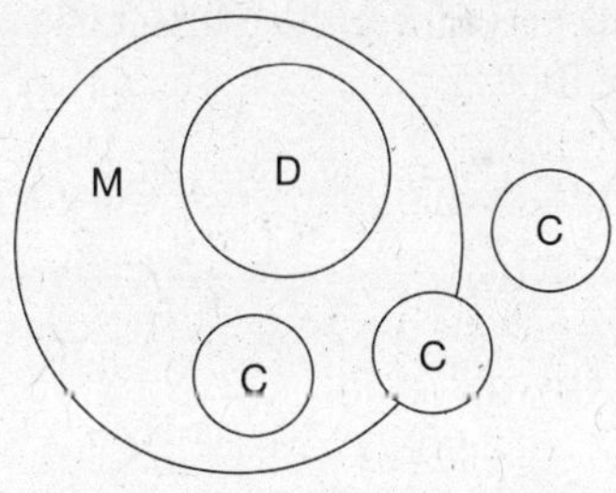

There can be three scenarios for C as shown in the above diagram.

29. * - None of the choices are correct. Marks were given to candidates who attempted this question. Solution is still provided here for the understanding of candidates.

Population of India = 1.2 billion = 1.2×10^9

Total energy consumption in India $= 1.2 \times 10^9 \times 30 \times 10^6 = 36 \times 10^{15}$ Joules

Carbon emission per kilojoule = 15×10^6 kg

Carbon emission per Joule = $15 \times 10^6/10^3 = 15 \times 10^3$ kg

Total carbon emissions from India = $36 \times 10^{15} \times 15 \times 10^3$ kgs = 540×10^{18} kg

None of choices match the answer.

30. (d)

Note: Beijing Red Alert was issued in Beijing in December 2015 as well for alarming levels of pollution. There are four levels of pollution alert in Beijing, red alert being the most severe and PM2.5 being alarmingly high.

33. (a): The temperature increase limits is called as tipping point, beyond which the climate change will be catastrophic and irreversible. Some research scientists mention 4°C as the tipping point.

35. (a): Refer 'Natural Hazards and their mitigation' on page 9.17

36. (c): CH_4 emitted today lasts about a decade on average, which is much less time than CO_2. However, CH_4 also absorbs much more energy than CO_2. The net effect of the shorter lifetime and higher energy absorption is reflected in the Global Warming Potential (GWP). GWP of methane is much higher than that of CO_2. The methane GWP also accounts for some indirect effects, such as the fact that methane is a precursor to ozone, and ozone is itself a greenhouse gas. For further details, the candidates may visit www3.epa.gov/climatechange/ghgemissions/gwps.html.

38. (b): On January 1, 2015, Planning Commission was replaced with NITI Ayog—National Institution for Transforming India (details in Unit 10).

39. (c): Refer 'Education Subject in Concurrent List (1976)' on page 10.4

42. (b): Refer page 10.10

43. (c): Refer page 10.7

46. (c): Dyslexia is the most common learning disability in children; it is characterized by trouble with reading despite normal intelligence and persists throughout the life.

Steve Jobs, the founder of Apple also suffered from this disorder.

51. (c): Refer page 2.29.

53. (b): Refer 'selecting samples' on page 2.22

54. (c): Refer page 1.19

55. (b): Refer page 2.7

CBSE-UGC NET Paper 1 December 2014

1. The term 'Yellow Journalism' refers to
   (a) sensational news about terrorism and violence
   (b) sensationalism and exaggeration to attract readers/viewers.
   (c) sensational news about arts and culture
   (d) sensational news prints in yellow paper.

2. In the classroom, the teacher sends the message either as words or images. The students are really
   (a) Encoders (b) Decoders
   (c) Agitators (d) Propagators

3. Media is known as
   (a) First Estate (b) Second Estate
   (c) Third Estate (d) Fourth Estate

4. The mode of communication that involves a single source transmitting information to a large number of receivers simultaneously, is called
   (a) Group Communication
   (b) Mass Communication
   (c) Intrapersonal Communication
   (d) Interpersonal Communication

5. A smart classroom is a teaching space which has
   (i) Smart portion with a touch panel control system.
   (ii) PC/Laptop connection and DVD/VCR player.
   (iii) Document camera and specialized software
   (iv) Projector and screen

   Select the correct answer from the codes given below:
   (a) (i) and (ii) only
   (b) (ii) and (iv) only
   (c) (i), (ii) and (iii) only
   (d) (i), (ii), (iii) and (iv)

6. Digital Empowerment means
   (i) Universal digit literacy
   (ii) Universal access to all digital resources.
   (iii) Collaborative digital platform for participative governance.
   (iv) Probability of all entitlements for individuals through cloud.

   Choose the correct answer from the codes given below:
   (a) (i) and (ii) only
   (b) (ii) and (iii) only
   (c) (i), (ii) and (iii) only
   (d) (i), (ii), (iii) and (iv)

7. The next term in the series:
   2, 7, 28, 63, 126, _______ is
   (a) 215 (b) 245 (c) 276 (d) 296

8. The next term in the series:
   AB, ED, IH, NM, ________ is
   (a) TS (b) ST (c) TU (d) SU

9. If STREAMERS is coded as UVTGALDQR, then KNOWLEDGE will be coded as
(a) MQPYLCDFD (b) MPQYLDCFD
(c) PMYQLDFCD (d) YMQPLDDFC

10. A is brother of B. B is the brother of C. C is the husband of D. E is the father of A. D is related to E as
(a) Daughter (b) Daughter-in-law
(c) Sister-in-law (d) Sister

11. Two numbers are in the ratio 3:5. If 9 is subtracted from the numbers, the ratio becomes 12:23. The numbers are
(a) 30, 50 (b) 36, 60
(c) 33, 55 (d) 42, 70

12. The mean of the ages of father and his son is 27 years. After 18 years, father will be twice as old as his son. Their present ages are
(a) 42, 12 (b) 40, 14
(c) 30, 24 (d) 36, 18

Read the following passage carefully and answer questions 13 to 17:

The literary distaste for politics, however, seems to be focused not so much on the largely murky practice of politics in itself as a subject of literary representation but rather more on how it is often depicted in literature, i.e., on the very politics of such representation. A political novel often turns out to be not merely a novel about politics but a novel with a politics of its own, for it seeks not merely to show us how things are but has fairly definite ideas about how things should be, and precisely what one should think and do in order to make things move in that desired direction. In short, it seeks to convert and enlist the reader to a particular cause or ideology; it often is (in an only too familiar phrase) not literature but propaganda. This is said to violate the very spirit of literature which is to broaden our understanding of the world and the range of our sympathies rather than to narrow them down through partisan commitment. As John Keats said, 'We hate poetry that has a palpable design upon us'.

Another reason why politics does not seem amenable to the highest kind of literary representation seems to arise from the fact that politics by its very nature is constituted of ideas and ideologies. If political situations do not lend themselves to happy literary treatment, political ideas present perhaps an even greater problem in this regard. Literature, it is argued, is about human experiences rather than about intellectual abstractions; it deals in what is called the 'felt reality' of human flesh and blood, and in sap and savour *(rasa)* rather than in arid and lifeless ideas. In an extensive discussion of the matter in her book *Ideas and the Novel,* the American novelist Mary McCarthy observed that 'ideas are still today felt to be unsightly in the novel' though that was not so in 'former days', i.e., in the 18th and 19th centuries. Her formulation of the precise nature of the incompatibility between ideas on the one hand and the novel on the other betrays perhaps a divided conscience in the matter and a sense of dilemma shared by many writers and readers: 'An idea cannot have loose ends, but a novel, I almost think, needs them. Nevertheless, there is enough in common for the novelists to feel... the attraction of ideas while taking up arms against them – most often with weapons of mockery.'

13. According to the passage, a political novel often turns out to be a
(a) Literary distaste for politics
(b) Literary representation of politics
(c) Novel with its own politics
(d) Depiction of murky practice of politics

14. A political novel reveals
(a) Reality of the things
(b) Writer's perception
(c) Particular ideology of the readers
(d) The spirit of literature

15. The constructs of politics by its nature is
(a) Prevalent political situation
(b) Ideas and Ideologies
(c) Political propaganda
(d) Understanding of human nature

16. Literature deals with
    (a) Human experiences in politics
    (b) Intellectual abstractions
    (c) Dry and empty ideas
    (d) Felt reality of human life

17. The observation of the novelist, Mary McCarthy reveals
    (a) unseen felt ideas of today in the novel
    (b) dichotomy of conscience on political ideas and novels
    (c) compatibility between idea and novel
    (d) endless ideas and novels

18. When in a group of propositions, one proposition is claimed to follow from the others, that group of propositions is called
    (a) An argument
    (b) A valid argument
    (c) An explanation
    (d) An invalid argument

19. Namita and Samita are brilliant and studious. Anita and Karabi are obedient and irregular. Babita and Namita are irregular but brilliant. Samita and Kabita are regular and obedient. Who among them is/are brilliant, obedient, regular and studious?
    (a) Samita alone
    (b) Namita and Samita
    (c) Kabita alone
    (d) Anita alone

20. Warrior is related to sword, carpenter is related to saw, farmer is related to plough. In the same way, the author is related to
    (a) Book (b) Fame
    (c) Reader (d) Pen

21. Given below is a diagram of three circles A, B and C over-lapping each other. The circle A represents the class of honest people, the circle B represents the class of sincere people and circle C represents the class of politicians. p, q, r, s, U, X, Y represent different regions. Select the code that represents the region indicating the class of honest politicians who are not sincere.

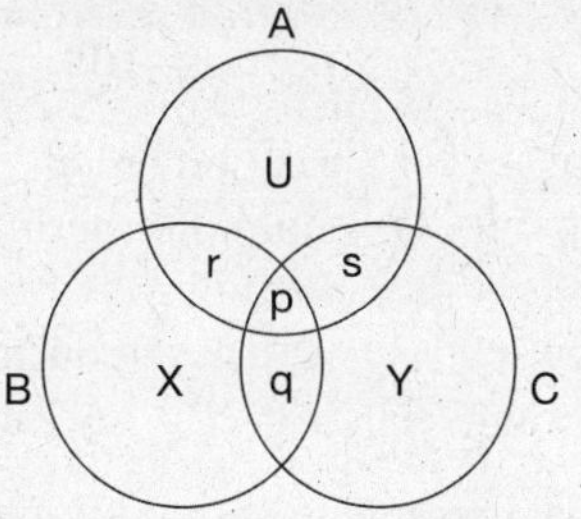

Codes:
(a) X (b) q (c) p (d) s

22. "A man ought no more to value himself for being wiser than a woman if he owes his advantage to a better education, than he ought to boast of his courage for beating a man when his hands were tied."
    The above passage is an instance of
    (a) Deductive argument
    (b) Hypothetical argument
    (c) Analogical argument
    (d) Factual argument

23. By which of the following proposition, the proposition 'wise men are hardly afraid of death' is contradicted?
    (a) Some wise men are afraid of death.
    (b) All wise men are afraid of death.
    (c) No wise men is afraid of death.
    (d) Some wise men are not afraid of death.

For a country CO_2 emissions (million metric tons) from various sectors are given in the following table. Answer the questions (**24** to **29**) based on the data given:

CO_2 emissions (million metric tons)

Sector / Year	Power	Industry	Commercial	Agriculture	Domestic
2005	500	200	150	80	100
2006	600	300	200	90	110
2007	650	320	250	100	120

(Continued)

CO_2 emissions (million metric tons)

Year \ Sector	Power	Industry	Commercial	Agriculture	Domestic
2008	700	400	300	150	150
2009	800	450	320	200	180

24. What is the percentage (%) growth of CO_2 emissions from power sector during 2005 to 2009?
(a) 60 (b) 50 (c) 40 (d) 80

25. Which sector has recorded maximum growth in CO_2 emissions during 2005 to 2009?
(a) Power (b) Industry
(c) Commercial (d) Agriculture

26. By what percentage (%), the total emissions of CO_2 have increased from 2005 to 2009?
(a) ~89.32% (b) ~57.62%
(c) ~40.32% (d) ~113.12%

27. What is the average annual growth rate of CO_2 emissions in power sector?
(a) ~12.57% (b) ~16.87%
(c) ~30.81% (d) ~50.25%

28. What is the percentage contribution of power sector to total CO_2 emissions in the year 2008?
(a) ~30.82% (b) ~41.18%
(c) ~51.38% (d) ~60.25%

29. In which year, the contribution (%) of industry to total sectoral CO_2 emissions was minimum?
(a) 2005 (b) 2006
(c) 2007 (d) 2009

30. Symbols A-F are used in which one of the following?
(a) Binary number system
(b) Decimal number system
(c) Hexadecimal number system
(d) Octal number system

31. Which one of the following is not a search engine?
(a) Google (b) Chrome
(c) Yahoo (d) Bing

32. CSS stands for
(a) Cascading Style Sheets
(b) Collecting Style Sheets
(c) Comparative Style Sheets
(d) Comprehensive Style Sheets

33. MOOC stands for
(a) Media Online Open Course
(b) Massachusetts Open Online Course
(c) Massive Open Online Course
(d) Myrind Open Online Course

34. Binary equivalent of decimal number 35 is
(a) 100011 (b) 110001
(c) 110101 (d) 101011

35. gif, jpg, bmp, png are used as extensions for files which store
(a) audio data (b) image data
(c) video data (d) text data

36. Which of the anthropogenic activity accounts for more than $\frac{2}{3}$rd of global water consumption?
(a) Agriculture
(b) Hydropower generation
(c) Industry
(d) Domestic and Municipal usage

37. One of the anthropogenic sources of gaseous pollutants chlorofluorocarbons (CFCs) in air is
(a) Cement industry
(b) Fertiliser industry
(c) Foam industry
(d) Pesticide industry

38. In terms of total CO_2 emissions from a country, identify the correct sequence:
(a) U.S.A. > China > India > Russia
(b) China > U.S.A. > India > Russia
(c) China > U.S.A. > Russia > India
(d) U.S.A. > China > Russia > India

39. Match List – I and List – II and identify the correct code:

List – I		List – II	
A	World Health Day	I	16th September
B	World Population Day	II	1st December
C	World Ozone Day	III	11th July
D	World AIDS Day	IV	7th April

Codes:
(a) A-I, B-II, C-III, D-IV
(b) A-IV, B-III, C-I, D-II
(c) A-II, B-III, C-IV, D-I
(d) A-III, B-IV, C-II, D-I

40. The cyclone 'Hudhud' hit the coast of which State?
(a) Andhra Pradesh (b) Karnataka
(c) Kerala (d) Gujarat

41. Which of the following is not a renewable natural resource?
(a) Clean air (b) Fresh water
(c) Fertile soil (d) Salt

42. The maximum number of fake institutions/ universities as identified by the UGC in the year 2014 are in the State/Union territory of
(a) Bihar (b) Uttar Pradesh
(c) Tamil Nadu (d) Delhi

43. Which of the following institutions are empowered to confer or grant degrees under the UGC Act, 1956?
1. A university established by an Act of Parliament.
2. A university established by an Act of Legislature.
3. A university/institution established by a linguistic minority.
4. An institution which is a deemed to be university.

Select the correct answer from the codes given below:
(a) 1 and 2 (b) 1, 2 and 3
(c) 1, 2 and 4 (d) 1, 2, 3 and 4

44. Which of the following are the tools of good governance?
1. Social Audit
2. Separation of Powers
3. Citizen's Charter
4. Right to Information

Select the correct answer from the codes given below:
(a) 1, 3 and 4 (b) 2, 3 and 4
(c) 1 and 4 (d) 1, 2, 3 and 4

45. Which of the following powers, the President has in relation to Lok Sabha?
1. Summoning
2. Adjournment – sine die
3. Prorogation
4. Dissolution

Select the correct answer from the codes given below:
(a) 1 and 4 (b) 1, 2 and 3
(c) 1, 3 and 4 (d) 1, 2, 3 and 4

46. The interval between two sessions of parliament must not exceed
(a) 3 months (b) 6 months
(c) 4 months (d) 100 days

47. Right to Privacy as a Fundamental Right is implied in
(a) Right to Freedom
(b) Right to Life and Personal Liberty
(c) Right to Equality
(d) Right against Exploitation

48. Which of the following organizations deals with 'capacity building program' on Educational Planning?
(a) NCERT (b) UGC
(c) NAAC (d) NUEPA

49. "Education is the manifestation of perfection already in man" was stated by
(a) M.K. Gandhi
(b) R.N. Tagore
(c) Swami Vivekanand
(d) Sri Aurobindo

50. Which of the following is not a prescribed level of teaching?
(a) Memory
(b) Understanding
(c) Reflective
(d) Differentiation

51. Maximum participation of students during teaching is possible through

(a) Lecture method
(b) Demonstration method
(c) Inductive method
(d) Textbook method

52. Diagnostic evaluation ascertains
(a) Students performance at the beginning of instructions.
(b) Learning progress and failures during instructions.
(c) Degree of achievement of instructions at the end.
(d) Causes and remedies of persistent learning problems during instructions.

53. Instructional aids are used by the teacher to
(a) glorify the class
(b) attract the students
(c) clarify the concepts
(d) ensure discipline

54. Attitude of the teacher that affects teaching pertains to
(a) Affective domain
(b) Cognitive domain
(c) Connative domain
(d) Psychomotor domain

55. When planning to do as social research, it is better to
(a) approach the topic with an open mind
(b) do a pilot study before getting stuck into it
(c) be familiar with literature on the topic
(d) forget about theory because this is a very practical

56. When academicians are called to deliver lecture or presentation to an audience on certain topics or a set of topics of educational nature, it is called
(a) Training Program (b) Seminar
(c) Workshop (d) Symposium

57. The core elements of a dissertation are
(a) Introduction; Data Collection; Data Analysis; Conclusions and Recommendations
(b) Executive Summary; Literature review; Data gathered; Conclusions; Bibliography
(c) Research Plan; Research Data; Analysis; References
(d) Introduction; Literature Review; Research Methodology; Results; Discussion and Conclusion

58. What is a Research Design?
(a) A way of conducting research that is not grounded in theory.
(b) The choice between using qualitative or quantitative methods.
(c) The style in which you present your research findings e.g. a graph.
(d) A framework for every stage of the collection and analysis of data.

59. 'Sampling Cases' means
(a) Sampling using a sampling frame
(b) Identifying people who are suitable for research
(c) Literally the researcher's brief case
(d) Sampling of people, newspapers, television programmes etc.

60. The frequency distribution of a research data which is symmetrical in shape similar to a normal distribution but center peak is much higher, is
(a) Skewed (b) Mesokurtic
(c) Leptokurtic (d) Platykurtic

Answer Keys

1. (b)	7. (a)	13. (c)	19. (a)	25. (d)	31. (b)	37. (c)	43. (c)	49. (c)	55. (c)
2. (b)	8. (a)	14. (b)	20. (d)	26. (a)	32. (a)	38. (b)	44. (b)	50. (d)	56. (b)
3. (d)	9. (b)	15. (b)	21. (d)	27. (a)	33. (c)	39. (b)	45. (c)	51. (b)	57. (d)
4. (b)	10. (b)	16. (d)	22. (c)	28. (b)	34. (a)	40. (a)	46. (b)	52. (d)	58. (d)
5. (d)	11. (c)	17. (a)	23. (b)	29. (a)	35. (b)	41. (d)	47. (b)	53. (c)	59. (d)
6. (d)	12. (a)	18. (a)	24. (a)	30. (c)	36. (a)	42. (b)	48. (d)	54. (a)	60. (c)

Hints and Solutions

1. (b): **Yellow journalism** is a sensational style of newspaper reporting that emerged at the end of the nineteenth century when rival newspaper publishers William Randolph Hearst and Joseph Pulitzer competed for sales in the coverage of events leading up to and during the Spanish-American War, and it's a type of reporting that continues today.

3. Fourth Estate refers to the news media. The origin of the term is attributed to Edmund Burke, who used it in a parliamentary debate in 1787 in the House of Commons of Great Britain.

7. (a): $1^3 + 1, 2^3 - 1, 3^3 + 1, 4^3 - 1, 5^3 + 1$ and so on. Hence, answer is 126.

8. (a): B + 2 gives D, D + 1 (and reversing order) gives ED, again D + 4 gives H and so on, hence (a) is the answer.

9. (b)

S	T	R	E	A	M	E	R	S
+2	+2	+2	+2		−1	−1	−1	−1
U	V	T	G	A	L	D	Q	R

K	N	O	W	L	E	D	G	E
+2	+2	+2	+2		−1	−1	−1	−1
M	P	Q	Y	L	D	C	F	D

Hence, (b) is the correct option.

11. (c): Let's assume that numbers are $3x$ and $5x$. According to statement, $(3x - 9)/(5x - 9) = 12/23$ solving it we get $x = 11$, hence numbers are 33 and 55.

18. An argument is a form of communication that tries to persuade its audience to adopt a particular position about a topic. Arguments have three main parts: a claim that states the position to be argued; reasons that logically explain why the claim should be accepted; and evidence that supports the reasons with facts, anecdotes, statistics, expert testimony, and examples. The statements a writer makes to offer a claim, reasons, and evidence can weaken or strengthen an argument. (*Source:* study.com)

19. (a)

	Brillent	Obedient	Regular	Studious
Namita	✓			✓
Samita	✓	✓	✓	✓
Anitha		✓		
Karabi		✓		
Babita	✓			
Kabita		✓	✓	

23. Refer 'Squares of Opposition' on pages 6.12 and 6.13.

36. (a): Refer Water Pollution and its types on page 9.12. Different sources have different percentage figures.

38. (b): refer to Carbon Emissions Table on page 9.40.

40. (a): The practice of naming storms (tropical cyclones) began in order to help in the quick identification of storms in warning messages because names are presumed to be far easier to remember than numbers and technical terms. This is mainly taken care of by World Metereological Organisation. For details, visit the link https://www.wmo.int/pages/prog/www/tcp/Storm-naming.html.

52. Refer 'Types of Evaluation Systems on the Basis of Phase of Instruction' on page 1.21.

54. Refer 'Bloom's Classification of Teaching and Instructional Objectives' on page 1.7.

55. Refer 'Social Research Is Basically Qualitative Research' on page 2.9.

56. Refer page 2.35

60.

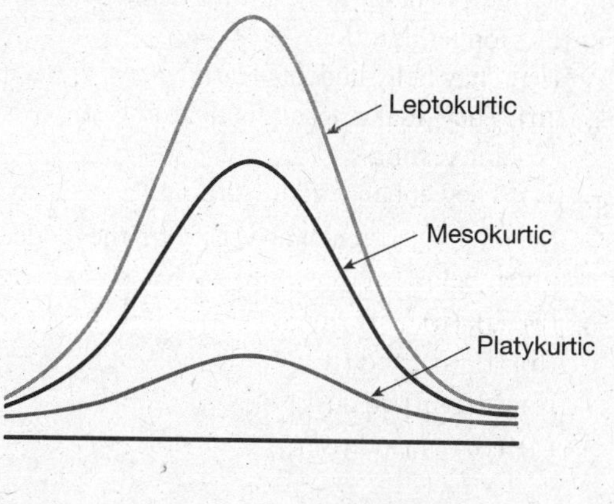

CBSE-UGC NET PAPER 1
JUNE 2015

1. Which of the following is the highest level of cognitive ability?
   (a) Knowing (b) Understanding
   (c) Analysing (d) Evaluating

2. Which of the following factors does **not** impact teaching?
   (a) Teacher's knowledge
   (b) Class room activities that encourage learning
   (c) Socio-economic background of teachers and students
   (d) Learning through experience

3. Which of the following statements about teaching aids are correct?
   (i) They help in retaining concepts for longer duration.
   (ii) They help students learn better.
   (iii) They make teaching learning process interesting.
   (iv) They enhance rote learning.

   Select the correct answer from the codes given below:
   (a) (i), (ii), (iii), and (iv)
   (b) (i), (ii), and (iii)
   (c) (ii), (iii), and (iv)
   (d) (i), (ii), and (iv)

4. Techniques used by a teacher to teach include:
   (i) Lecture
   (ii) Interactive lecture
   (iii) Group work
   (iv) Self study

   Select the correct answer from the codes given below:
   (a) (i), (ii), and (iii)
   (b) (i), (ii), (iii), and (iv)
   (c) (ii), (iii), and (iv)
   (d) (i), (ii), and (iv)

5. Achievement tests are commonly used for the purpose of:
   (a) Making selections for a specific job
   (b) Selecting candidates for a course
   (c) Identifying strengths and weaknesses of learners
   (d) Assessing the amount of learning after teaching

6. A good teacher is one who
   (a) Gives useful information
   (b) Explains concepts and principles
   (c) Gives printed notes to students
   (d) Inspires students to learn

7. Which of the following statements regarding the meaning of research are correct?
   (i) Research refers to a series of systematic activity or activities undertaken to find out the solution of a problem.
   (ii) It is a systematic, logical, and an unbiased process wherein verification of hypothesis, data analysis, interpretation, and formation of principles can be done.
   (iii) It is an intellectual enquiry or quest towards truth.
   (iv) It leads to enhancement of knowledge.

   Select the correct answer from the codes given below:
   (a) (i), (ii), and (iii) (b) (ii), (iii), and (iv)
   (c) (i), (iii), and (iv) (d) (i), (ii), (iii), and (iv)

8. A good thesis writing should involve :
   (i) reduction of punctuation and grammatical errors to a minimum.
   (ii) careful checking of references.
   (iii) consistency in the way the thesis is written.
   (iv) a clear and well-written abstract.

   Select the correct answer from the codes given below:
   (a) (i), (ii), (iii), and (iv)
   (b) (i), (ii), and (iii)
   (c) (i), (ii), and (iv)
   (d) (ii), (iii), and (iv)

9. Jean Piaget gave a theory of cognitive development of humans on the basis of his:
   (a) Fundamental research
   (b) Applied research
   (c) Action research
   (d) Evaluation research

10. 'Male and female students perform equally well in a numerical aptitude test'. This statement indicates a
    (a) Research hypothesis
    (b) Null hypothesis
    (c) Directional hypothesis
    (d) Statistical hypothesis

11. The conclusions/findings of which type of research cannot be generalized to other situations?
    (a) Historical research
    (b) Descriptive research
    (c) Experimental research
    (d) Causal comparative research

12. Which of the following steps are required to design a questionnaire?
    (i) Writing primary and secondary aims of the study
    (ii) Review of the current literature
    (iii) Prepare a draft of questionnaire
    (iv) Revision of the draft

    Select the correct answer from the codes given below:
    (a) (i), (ii), and (iii)
    (b) (i), (iii), and (iv)
    (c) (ii), (iii), and (iv)
    (d) (i), (ii), (iii), and (iv)

Read the following passage carefully and answer Questions from 13 to 18.

Storytelling is not in our genes. Neither it is an evolutionary history. It is the essence of what makes us Human.

Human beings progress by telling stories. One event can result in a great variety of stories being told about it. Sometimes those stories differ greatly. Which stories are picked up and repeated and which ones are dropped and forgotten often determine how we progress. Our history, knowledge, and understanding are all the collections of the few stories that survive. This includes the stories that we tell each other about the future, and how the future will turn out depends partly, possibly largely, on which stories we collectively choose to believe.

Some stories are designed to spread fear and concern. This is because some storytellers feel that there is a need to raise some tensions. Some stories are frightening: they are like totemic warnings: 'Fail to act now and we are all doomed'. Then, there are stories that indicate that all will be fine so long as we leave everything upto a few especially able adults. Currently, this trend is being led by those who call themselves 'rational optimists'. They tend to claim that it is human nature to compete and to succeed and also to profit at the expense of others. The rational optimists, however, do not realize how humanity has progressed overtime through amiable social networks and how large groups work in less selfishness and in the process accommodate rich and poor, high and low alike. This aspect in storytelling is considered by the 'Practical Possibles', who sit between those who say all is fine and cheerful and be individualistic in your approach to a successful future, and those who ordain pessimism and fear that we are doomed.

What the future holds for us is which stories we hold on to and how we act on them.

Answer the following questions:

13. Our knowledge is a collection of
    (a) All stories that we have heard during our life-time
    (b) Some stories that we remember
    (c) A few stories that survive
    (d) Some important stories

14. Story telling is
    (a) An art
    (b) A science
    (c) In our genes
    (d) The essence of what makes us human

15. How the future will turn out to be, depends upon the stories
    (a) We collectively choose to believe in
    (b) Which are repeatedly narrated
    (c) Designed to spread fear and tension
    (d) Designed to make prophecy

16. Rational optimists
    (i) Look for opportunities
    (ii) Are sensible and cheerful
    (iii) Are selfishly driven
    Identify the correct answer from the codes given below:
    (a) (i), (ii), and (iii) (b) (i) only
    (c) (i) and (ii) only (d) (ii) and (iii) only

17. Humans become less selfish when
    (a) They work in large groups
    (b) They listen to frightening stories
    (c) They listen to cheerful stories
    (d) They work in solitude

18. 'Practical Possibles' are the ones who
    (a) Follow midway path
    (b) Are doom-mongers
    (c) Are self-centre
    (d) Are cheerful and carefree

19. Effectiveness of communication can be traced from which of the following?
    (i) Attitude surveys
    (ii) Performance records
    (iii) Students attendance
    (iv) Selection of communication channel
    Select the correct answer from the codes given below:
    (a) (i), (ii), (iii), and (iv)
    (b) (i), (ii), and (iii)
    (c) (ii), (iii), and (iv)
    (d) (i), (ii), and (iv)

20. ***Assertion (A):*** Formal communication tends to be fast and flexible.
    Reason (R): Formal communication is a systematic and orderly flow of information.
    (a) Both (*A*) and (*R*) are correct, and (*R*) is correct explanation of (*A*).
    (b) Both (*A*) and (*R*) are correct, but (*R*) is not correct explanation of (*A*).
    (c) (*A*) is correct, but (*R*) is false.
    (d) (*A*) is false, but (*R*) is correct.

21. Which of the following are the characteristic features of communication?
    (i) Communication involves exchange of ideas, facts, and opinions.
    (ii) Communication involves both information and understanding.
    (iii) Communication is a continuous process.
    (iv) Communication is a circular process.
    Select the correct answer from the codes given below:
    (a) (i), (ii), and (iii) (b) (i), (ii), and (iv)
    (c) (ii), (iii), and (iv) (d) (i), (ii), (iii), and (iv)

22. The term 'grapevine' is also known as
    (a) Downward communication
    (b) Informal communication
    (c) Upward communication
    (d) Horizontal communication

23. Which of the following is not a principle of effective communication?
    (a) Persuasive and convincing dialogue
    (b) Participation of the audience
    (c) One-way transfer of information
    (d) Strategic use of grapevine

24. In communication, the language is
   (a) The verbal code
   (b) Intrapersonal
   (c) The symbolic code
   (d) The non-verbal code

25. The next term in the series is
   2, 5, 9, 19, 37, ?
   (a) 73 (b)75 (c) 78 (d) 8 0

26. In certain code, MATHURA is coded as JXQEROX. The code of HOTELS will be
   (a) LEQIBP (b) ELQBIP
   (c) LEBIQP (d) ELIPQB

27. One day Prakash left home and walked 10 km towards south, turned right and walked 5 km, turned right and walked 10 km and turned left and walked 10 km. How many km will he have to walk to reach his home straight?
   (a) 10 (b) 20 (c) 15 (d) 30

28. A girl introduced a boy as the son of the daughter of the father of her uncle. The boy is related to the girl as
   (a) Brother (b) Uncle
   (c) Nephew (d) Son

29. In an examination, 10,000 students appeared. The result revealed the number of students who have

Passed in all five subjects	=	5583
Passed in three subjects only	=	1400
Passed in two subjects only	=	1200
Passed in one subject only	=	735
Failed in English only	=	75
Failed in Physics only	=	145
Failed in Chemistry only	=	140
Failed in Mathematics only	=	200
Failed in Bio-science only	=	157

   The number of students passed in at least four subjects is
   (a) 6300 (b) 6900 (c) 7300 (d) 7900

30. At present, a person is 4 times older than his son and is 3 years older than his wife. After 3 years, the age of the son will be 15 years. The age of the person's wife after 5 years will be
   (a) 42 (b) 48 (c) 45 (d) 50

31. If we want to seek new knowledge of facts about the world, we must rely on reason of the type
   (a) Inductive (b) Deductive
   (c) Demonstrative (d) Physiological

32. A deductive argument is invalid if
   (a) Its premises and conclusions are all false.
   (b) Its premises are true but its conclusion is false.
   (c) Its premises are false but its conclusion is true.
   (d) Its premises and conclusions are all true.

33. Inductive reasoning is grounded on
   (a) Integrity of nature
   (b) Unity of nature
   (c) Uniformity of nature
   (d) Harmony of nature

34. Among the following statements **two** are contradictory to each other. Select the correct code that represents them.

   Statements:
   (i) All poets are philosophers.
   (ii) Some poets are philosophers.
   (iii) Some poets are not philosophers.
   (iv) No philosopher is a poet.

   Codes:
   (a) (i) and (ii) (b) (i) and (iv)
   (c) (i) and (iii) (d) (ii) and (iii)

35. Which of the codes given below contains only the **correct** statements? Select the code :

   Statements:
   (i) Venn diagram represents the arguments graphically.
   (ii) Venn diagram can enhance our understanding.
   (iii) Venn diagram may be called valid or invalid.
   (iv) Venn diagram is clear method of notation.

   Codes:
   (a) (i), (ii), and (iii) (b) (i), (ii), and (iv)
   (c) (ii), (iii), and (iv) (d) (i), (iii), and (iv)

36. When the purpose of a definition is to explain the use or to eliminate ambiguity, then the definition is called
(a) Stipulative (b) Theoretical
(c) Lexical (d) Persuasive

Question numbers 37 to 42 are based on the tabulated data given below:

A company has 20 employees with their age (in years) and salary (in thousand rupees per month) mentioned against each of them:

S.No.	Age (in years)	Salary (in thousand rupees per month)
1.	44	35
2.	32	20
3.	54	45
4.	42	35
5.	31	20
6.	53	60
7.	42	50
8.	51	55
9.	34	25
10.	41	30
11.	33	30
12.	31	35
13.	30	35
14.	37	40
15.	44	45
16.	36	35
17.	34	35
18.	49	50
19.	43	45
20.	45	50

37. Classify the data of age of each employee in class interval of 5 years. Which class interval of 5 years has the maximum average salary?
(a) 35–40 years (b) 40–45 years
(c) 45–50 years (d) 50–55 years

38. What is the frequency (%) in the class interval of 30–35 years?
(a) 20% (b) 25% (c) 30% (d) 35%

39. What is the average age of the employees?
(a) 40.3 years (b) 38.6 years
(c) 47.2 years (d) 45.3 years

40. What is the fraction (%) of employees getting salary ≥ 40,000 per month?
(a) 45% (b) 50% (c) 35% (d) 32%

41. What is the average salary (in thousand per month) in the age group 40–50 years?
(a) 35 (b) 42.5 (c) 40.5 (d) 36.5

42. What is the fraction of employees getting salary less than the average salary of all the employees?
(a) 45% (b) 50% (c) 55% (d) 47%

43. Encoding or scrambling data for transmission across a network is known as:
(a) Protection (b) Detection
(c) Encryption (d) Decryption

44. Which of the following is **not** an output device?
(a) Printer (b) Speaker
(c) Monitor (d) Keyboard

45. Which of the following represents one billion characters?
(a) Kilobyte (b) Megabyte
(c) Gigabyte (d) Terabyte

46. Which of the following is not open source software?
(a) Internet explorer
(b) Fedora Linux
(c) Open office
(d) Apache HTTP server

47. Which one of the following represents the binary equivalent of the decimal number 25?
(a) 10101 (b) 01101
(c) 11001 (d) 11011

48. Which is an instant messenger that is used for chatting?
(a) AltaVista (b) MAC
(c) Microsoft Office (d) Google Talk

49. In which of the countries per capita use of water is maximum?
(a) USA (b) European Union
(c) China (d) India

50. India's contribution to total global carbon dioxide emissions is about
(a) ~3% (b) ~6%
(c) ~10% (d) ~15%

51. Two earthquakes A and B happen to be of magnitude 5 and 6, respectively, on Richter scale. The ratio of the energies released E_B/E_A will be approximately
(a) ~ 8 (b) ~ 16 (c) ~ 32 (d) ~ 64

52. Which of the following combinations represent renewable natural resources?
(a) Fertile soil, fresh water, and natural gas
(b) Clean air, phosphates, and biological diversity
(c) Fishes, fertile soil, and fresh water
(d) Oil, forests, and tides

53. In the recently launched Air Quality Index in India, which of the following pollutants is not Included?
(a) Carbon monoxide
(b) Fine particulate matter
(c) Ozone
(d) Chlorofluorocarbons

54. The factors that are most important in determining the impact of anthropogenic activities on environment are
(a) Population, affluence per person, and land available per person
(b) Population, affluence per person, and the technology used for exploiting resources
(c) Atmospheric conditions, population, and forest cover
(d) Population, forest cover, and land available per person

55. The session of the parliament is summoned by
(a) The President
(b) The Prime Minister
(c) The Speaker of the Lok Sabha
(d) The Speaker of the Lok Sabha and the Chairman of the Rajya Sabha

56. Civil Service Day is celebrated in India on
(a) 21st April (b) 24th April
(c) 21st June (d) 7th July

57. The South Asia University is situated in the city of:
(a) Colombo (b) Dhaka
(c) New Delhi (d) Kathmandu

58. The University Grants Commission was established with which of the following aims?
(i) Promotion of research and development in higher education
(ii) Identifying and sustaining institutions of potential learning
(iii) Capacity building of teachers
(iv) Providing autonomy to each and every higher educational institution in India
Select the correct answer from the codes given below:
(a) (i), (ii), (iii), and (iv)
(b) (i), (ii), and (iii)
(c) (ii), (iii), and (iv)
(d) (i), (ii), and (iv)

59. The Gross Enrolment Ratio (GER) in institutions of higher education in India at present (2015) is about
(a) 8 per cent (b) 12 per cent
(c) 19 per cent (d) 23 per cent

60. The total number of central universities in India in April 2015 was:
(a) 08 (b) 14 (c) 27 (d) 43

Answer Keys

1. (d)	7. (d)	13. (c)	19. (b)	25. (b)	31. (a)	37. (d)	43. (c)	49. (b)	55. (a)
2. (c)	8. (a)	14. (d)	20. (d)	26. (b)	32. (b)	38. (d)	44. (d)	50. (b)	56. (a)
3. (b)	9. (a)	15. (a)	21. (d)	27. (c)	33. (c)	39. (a)	45. (c)	51. (c)	57. (c)
4. (a)	10. (b)	16. (a)	22. (b)	28. (a)	34. (c)	40. (a)	46. (a)	52. (c)	58. (b)
5. (d)	11. (a)	17. (a)	23. (c)	29. (a)	35. (b)	41. (b)	47. (c)	53. (d)	59. (c)
6. (d)	12. (d)	18. (a)	24. (a)	30. (d)	36. (c)	42. (c)	48. (d)	54. (b)	60. (d)

HINTS AND SOLUTIONS

1. (d): Refer page 1.7.

   Under Bloom's classification of teaching and instructional objectives, there are six levels under cognitive domain: (i) knowledge, (ii) comprehension, (iii) application, (iv) analysis, (v) synthesis, and (vi) evaluation.
2. (c): Refer 'Effective Teaching Practices' on page 1.5.
3. (b): Refer 'Benefits of Teaching Aids' on page 1.21.
4. (a): Refer 'Teaching Methods' on page 1.8.
5. (d): Refer 'Evaluation Systems' on page 1.19.
6. (d): Refer 'Effective Teaching Practices' on page 1.5.
7. (d): Refer 'Research Concept and Definitions' on page 2.1.
8. (a): Refer page 2.29
10. (b): Here, null means no difference. Thus, null hypothesis means no difference between two sets of students here—one male and other female. Then, we collect data to test the hypothesis. refer page 2.15 for more details
12. (d): Refer page 2.21 and 2.22
19. (b): Effectiveness of communication (specifically classroom communication) is gauzed through enhancement in learning that further aims at permanent change in behaviour. Thus, (i), (ii), and (iii) are applicable.
20. (d): Refer 'Classification of Communication Based on Purpose and Style' on page 4.9.
21. (d): Refer pages 4.1–4.3
22. (b): Refer 'Informal Communication' on page 4.9.
23. (c): Effective communication is a two-way process. Also, refer point 3 under 'Nature and Characteristics of Communication' on page 4.2.
24. (a): Refer page 4.3
25. (b): x 2 + 1, x 2 – 1, x 2 + 1 and so on.
   2 x 2 + 1, 5 x 2 – 1, 9 x 2 + 1, 19 x 2 –1 and so on.
26. (b):

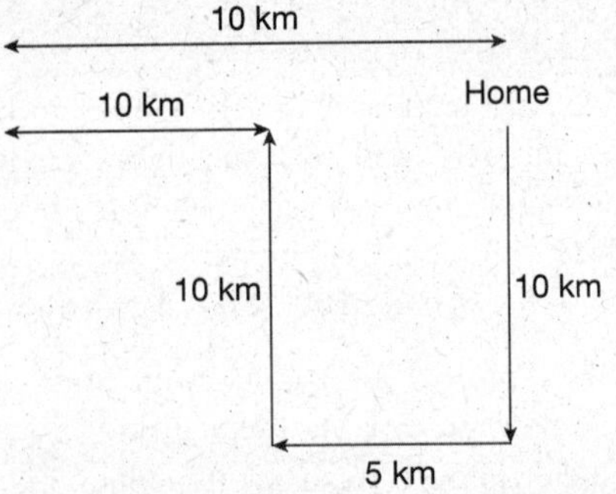

29. (a): Venn diagram for 5 variables is a difficult approach.

   Let's solve it by method that is usually described under probability topic. Number of students passed in at least four subjects = Number of students passed exactly in four subjects + Number of students exactly passed in five subjects (i)

   But, number of students passed in four subjects = Number of students failed in one subject only = Failed in English only + … Failed in Bioscience only = 75 + 145 + 140 + 200 + 157 = 717

   Substituting it in (i), number of students passed in at least four subjects = 5583 + 717 = 6300
30. (d): Let us assume that present age of person = x years

   Hence, son's age = $x/4$ years

   According to the statement $x/4 = 15 - 3 = 12$ years $\Longrightarrow x = 48$ years

   Hence, wife's age = 48 – 3 = 45 years

   Wife's age after 5 years = 45 + 5 = 50 years
31. (a): Refer page 6.1. Here, some examples are also mentioned.
32. (b): Refer pages 6.2 and 6.3
33. (c): Refer page 6.1
36. (c): Refer 'Types of definitions' on page 6.15.

37. (d):

Classes (age groups)	Class frequencies	Sum of salaries for different classes (in thousands)	Average group salaries (in Rs) = Sum of salaries /class frequencies
30–35	~~IIII~~II = 7	30 + 30 + … = 2,00,000	28,571
35–40	II = 2	40 + 35 = 75,000	37,500
40–45	~~IIII~~I = 6	2,40,000	40,000
45–50	II = 2	= 1,00,000	50,000
50–55	III = 3	= 1,60,000	53,333

Hence, class 50–55 has the maximum average salary.

38. (d): Required percentage = $7/20 \times 100 = 35\%$

39. (a): Total of ages (from the question table) = 44 + 32 + 54…43 + 45 = 806 years

Average age = 806/20 = 40.3 years

40. (a): Required percentage = $9/20 \times 100 = 45\%$

41. (b): Required average salary in the age group (45–50) = 340/8 = 42.5 years

42. (c): Average salary of all ages = 7,75,000 /20 = Rs 38,750

45. (c): A gigabyte (GB) is a measure of computer data storage capacity that is roughly equivalent to 1 billion bytes.

46. (a): Open-source software (OSS) is computer software with its source code made available with a license in which the copyright holder provides the rights to study, change, and distribute the software to anyone and for any purpose.

47. (c): This question is quite simple. We have to solve all choices one by one.

16 8 4 2 1

1 0 1 0 1 = $16 \times 1 + 8 \times 0 + 4 \times 1 + 2 \times 0 + 1 \times 1 = 21$

Similarly, solve for other options also. Option (c) is the right answer.

1 1 0 0 1 = $1 \times 16 + 1 \times 8 + 0 \times 4 + 0 \times 2 + 1 \times 1 = 25$

Students can visit http://www.cimt.plymouth.ac.uk for more examples.

49. (b): Visit www.unwater.org for facts relating to water.

51. (c): Magnitudes are based on a logarithmic scale (base 10). It means that for each whole number you go up on the magnitude scale, the amplitude of the ground motion recorded by a seismograph goes up 10 times. Using this scale, a magnitude 6 earthquake would result in 10 times the level of ground shaking as a magnitude 5 earthquake (and 32 times as much energy would be released).

53. (d): Refer page 9.9

54. (b): Refer pages 9.36

55. (a): Article 87(1) of the Constitution provides: 'At the commencement of the first session after each general election to the House of the People and at the commencement of the first session of each year, the President shall address both Houses of Parliament assembled together and inform Parliament of the causes of its summons'.

57. (c): Refer 'Note' in the list of Central universities on page 10.9

58. (b): Refer page 10.6 and 10.7 (University Education System, aims of Higher Education and UGC)

59. (c): Refer page 10.23. Here, some basic information is given about GER is given under 'Key Issues Facing Spread of Higher Education in India'.

60. (d): The updated list is given on page 10.7 onwards according to UGC/MHRD sources.

CBSE-UGC NET PAPER 1 DECEMBER 2015

1. Greater the handicap of the students coming to the educational institutions, greater the demand on the
(a) Family (b) Society
(c) Teacher (d) State

2. What are the characteristics of Continuous and Comprehensive Evaluation?
(i) It increases the workload on students by taking multiple tests.
(ii) It replaces marks with grades.
(iii) It evaluates every aspect of the student.
(iv) It helps in reducing examination phobia.
Select the correct answer from the codes given below:
(a) (i), (ii), (iii), and (iv)
(b) (ii) and (iv)
(c) (i), (ii), and (iii)
(d) (ii), (iii), and (iv)

3. Which of the following attributes denote great strengths of a teacher?
(i) Full-time active involvement in the institutional management
(ii) Setting examples
(iii) Willingness to put assumptions to the test
(iv) Acknowledging mistakes
Select the correct answer from the codes given below:
(a) (i), (ii), and (iv) (b) (ii), (iii), and (iv)
(c) (i), (iii), and (iv) (d) (i), (ii), (iii), and (iv)

4. Which one of the following statements is correct in the context of multiple-choice type questions?
(a) They are more objective than true–false type questions.
(b) They are less objective than essay type questions.
(c) They are more subjective than short answer type questions.
(d) They are more subjective than true–false type questions.

5. As Chairman of an independent commission on education, Jacques Delors' report to UNESCO was titled
(a) International Commission on Education Report
(b) Millennium Development Report
(c) Learning : The Treasure Within
(d) World Declaration on Education for All

6. What are required for good teaching?
(i) Diagnosis (ii) Remedy
(iii) Direction (iv) Feedback
Select the correct answer from the codes given below:
(a) (i), (ii), (iii), and (iv) (b) (i) and (ii)
(c) (ii), (iii), and (iv) (d) (iii) and (iv)

7. Which of the following statements is not true in the context of participatory research ?
   (a) It recognizes knowledge as power.
   (b) It emphasises on people as experts.
   (c) It is a collective process of enquiry.
   (d) Its sole purpose is production of knowledge.

8. Which of the following statements is true in the context of the testing of a hypothesis?
   (a) It is only the alternative hypothesis that can be tested.
   (b) It is only the null hypothesis that can be tested.
   (c) Both the alternative and the null hypotheses can be tested.
   (d) Both the alternative and the null hypotheses cannot be tested.

9. Which of the following are the basic rules of APA style of referencing format?
   (i) Italicize titles of shorter works such as journal articles or essays
   (ii) Invert authors' names (last name first)
   (iii) Italicize titles of longer works such as books and journals
   (iv) Alphabetically index reference list

   Select the correct answer from the codes given below:
   (a) (i) and (ii) (b) (ii), (iii), and (iv)
   (c) (iii) and (iv) (d) (i), (ii), (iii), and (iv)

10. Which of the following are the characteristics of a seminar?
    (i) It is a form of academic instruction.
    (ii) It involves questioning, discussion, and debates.
    (iii) It involves large groups of individuals.
    (iv) It needs involvement of skilled persons.

    Select the correct answer from the codes given below:
    (a) (ii) and (iii) (b) (ii) and (iv)
    (c) (ii), (iii), and (iv) (d) (i), (ii), and (iv)

11. A researcher is interested in studying the prospects of a particular political party in an urban area. What tool should he prefer for the study?
    (a) Rating scale (b) Interview
    (c) Questionnaire (d) Schedule

12. Ethical norms in research do not involve guidelines for
    (a) Thesis format
    (b) Copyright
    (c) Patenting policy
    (d) Data sharing policies

Read the following passage carefully and answer the questions from 13 to 17.

I did that thing recently where you have to sign a big card—which is a horror unto itself, especially as the keeper of the Big Card was leaning over me at the time. Suddenly I was on the spot, a rabbit in the headlights, torn between doing a fun message or some sort of in-joke or a drawing. Instead overwhelmed by the myriad options available to me, I decided to just write: 'Good luck, best, Joel'.

It was then that I realised, to my horror, that I had forgotten how to write. My entire existence is 'tap letters into computer'. My shopping lists are hidden in the notes function of my phone. If I need to remember something I send an e-mail to myself. A pen is something I chew when I am struggling to think. Paper is something I pile beneath my laptop to make it a more comfortable height for me to type on.

A poll of 1000 teens by the stationers, Bic found that one in 10 do not own a pen, a third have never written a letter, and half of 13 to 19 years old have never been forced to sit down and write a thank you letter. More than 80% have never written a love letter, 56% do not have letter paper at home, and a quarter have never known the unique torture of writing a birthday card. The most a teen ever has to use a pen is on an exam paper.

Bic, have you heard of mobile phones? Have you heard of e-mail, Facebook, and snap chatting? This is the future. Pens are dead. Paper is dead. Handwriting is a relic.

'Handwriting is one of the most creative outlets we have and should be given the same importance as other art forms such as sketching, painting, or photography'.

Answer the following questions:

13. When confronted with signing a big card, the author felt like 'a rabbit in the headlight'. What does this phrase mean?

(a) A state of confusion
(b) A state of pleasure
(c) A state of anxiety
(d) A state of pain

14. According to the author, which one is not the most creative outlet of pursuit?
(a) Handwriting (b) Photography
(c) Sketching (d) Reading

15. The entire existence of the author revolves round
(i) Computer
(ii) Mobile phone
(iii) Typewriter
Identify the correct answer from the codes given below:
(a) (ii) only (b) (i) and (ii) only
(c) (i), (ii), and (iii) (d) (ii) and (iii) only

16. How many teens, as per the Bic survey, do not own a pen?
(a) 800 (b) 560 (c) 500 (d) 100

17. What is the main concern of the author?
(a) The teens use social networks for communication.
(b) The teens use mobile phones.
(c) The teens use computer.
(d) The teens have forgotten the art of handwriting.

18. The main objectives of student evaluation of teachers are:
(i) To gather information about student weaknesses.
(ii) To make teachers take teaching seriously.
(iii) To help teachers adopt innovative methods of teaching.
(iv) To identify the areas of further improvement in teacher traits.
Identify the correct answer from the codes given below:
(a) (i) and (ii) only
(b) (ii), (iii), and (iv) only
(c) (i), (ii), and (iii) only
(d) (i) only

19. Using the central point of the classroom communication as the beginning of a dynamic pattern of ideas is referred to as
(a) Systemisation
(b) Problem-orientation
(c) Idea protocol
(d) Mind mapping

20. Aspects of the voice, other than the speech are known as
(a) Physical language
(b) Personal language
(c) Para language
(d) Delivery language

21. Every type of communication is affected by its
(a) Reception (b) Transmission
(c) Non-regulation (d) Context

22. Attitudes, actions, and appearances in the context of classroom communication are considered as
(a) Verbal (b) Non-verbal
(c) Impersonal (d) Irrational

23. Most often, the teacher–student communication is
(a) Spurious (b) Critical
(c) Utilitarian (d) Confrontational

24. In a classroom, a communicator's trust level is determined by
(a) The use of hyperbole
(b) The change of voice level
(c) The use of abstract concepts
(d) Eye contact

25. Find the next term in the series
2, 5, 10, 17, 26, 37, ___?___.
(a) 50 (b) 57 (c) 62 (d) 72

26. A group of 210 students appeared in some test. The mean of $\frac{1}{3}$ rd of students is found to be 60. The mean of the remaining students is found to be 78. The mean of the whole group will be
(a) 80 (b) 76 (c) 74 (d) 72

27. Anil after travelling 6 km towards East from his house realized that he has travelled in a wrong direction. He turned and travelled 12 km towards West, turned right, and travelled 8 km to reach his office. The straight distance of the office from his house is
(a) 20 km (b) 14 km
(c) 12 km (d) 10 km

28. Find the next term in the series
B2E, D5H, F12K, H27N, ?.
(a) J56I (b) I62Q (c) Q62J (d) J58Q

29. A party was held in which a grandmother, father, mother, four sons, their wives and one son and two daughters to each of the sons were present. The number of females present in the party is
(a) 12 (b) 14 (c) 18 (d) 24

30. P and Q are brothers. R and S are sisters. The son of P is brother of S. Q is related to R as
(a) Son (b) Brother
(c) Uncle (d) Father

31. Consider the argument given below:
'Pre-employment testing of teachers is quite fair because doctors, architects, and engineers who are now employed had to face such a testing'.
What type of argument it is?
(a) Deductive (b) Analogical
(c) Psychological (d) Biological

32. Among the following propositions, two are related in such a way that they can both be true although they cannot both be false. Which are those propositions? Select the correct code.
Propositions:
(i) Some priests are cunning.
(ii) No priest is cunning.
(iii) All priests are cunning.
(iv) Some priests are not cunning.
Codes:
(a) (i) and (ii) (b) (iii) and (iv)
(c) (i) and (iii) (d) (i) and (iv)

33. A cluster of propositions with a structure that exhibits some inference is called
(a) An inference (b) An argument
(c) An explanation (d) A valid argument

34. Consider the following assertion (*A*) and reason (*R*) and select the correct code given below:
(*A*): No man is perfect.
(*R*): Some men are not perfect.
(a) Both (*A*) and (*R*) are true, but (*R*) does not provide sufficient reason for (*A*).
(b) Both (*A*) and (*R*) are true, and (*R*) provides sufficient reason for (*A*).
(c) (*A*) is true, but (*R*) is false.
(d) (*A*) is false, but (*R*) is true.

35. A definition that has a meaning that is deliberately assigned to some symbol is called
(a) Lexical (b) Precising
(c) Stipulative (d) Persuasive

36. If the proposition 'No men are honest' is taken to be false, then which of the following proposition/propositions can be claimed certainly to be true?
Propositions:
(a) All men are honest.
(b) Some men are honest.
(c) Some men are not honest.
(d) No honest person is man.

Given below in the table is the decadal data of population and electrical power production of a country.

Year	Population (million)	Electrical power production (GW)*
1951	20	10
1961	21	20
1971	24	25
1981	27	40
1991	30	50
2001	32	80
2011	35	100

* 1 GW = 1000 million watt

Based on the above table, answer the questions from 37 to 42.

37. Which decade registered the maximum growth rate (%) of population?
(a) 1961–71 (b) 1971–81
(c) 1991–2001 (d) 2001–2011

38. Average decadal growth rate (%) of population is
(a) ~ 12.21% (b) ~ 9.82%
(c) ~ 6.73% (d) ~ 5%

39. Based on the average decadal growth rate, what will be the population in the year 2021?
(a) 40.34 million (b) 38.49 million
(c) 37.28 million (d) 36.62 million

40. In the year 1951, what was the power availability per person?
(a) 100 W (b) 200 W
(c) 400 W (d) 500 W

41. In which decade, the average power availability per person was maximum?
(a) 1981–1991 (b) 1991–2001
(c) 2001–2011 (d) 1971–1981

42. By what percentage (%) the power production increased from 1951 to 2011?
(a) 100% (b) 300%
(c) 600% (d) 900%

43. NMEICT stands for
(a) National Mission on Education through ICT
(b) National Mission on E-governance through ICT
(c) National Mission on E-commerce through ICT
(d) National Mission on E-learning through ICT

44. Which of the following is an instant messaging application?
(i) WhatsApp
(ii) Google Talk
(iii) Viber

Select the correct answer from the codes given below:
(a) (i) and (ii) only (b) (ii) and (iii) only
(c) (i) only (d) (i), (ii), and (iii)

45. In a Computer, a byte generally consists of
(a) 4 bits (b) 8 bits
(c) 16 bits (d) 10 bits

46. Which of the following is not an input device?
(a) Microphone (b) Keyboard
(c) Joystick (d) Monitor

47. Which of the following is an open source software?
(a) MS Word (b) Windows
(c) Mozilla Firefox (d) Acrobat Reader

48. Which of the following enables us to send the same letter to different persons in MS Word?
(a) Mail join (b) Mail copy
(c) Mail insert (d) Mail merge

49. Inside rural homes, the source(s) of Nitrogen Oxide Pollution may be
(i) Unvented gas stoves
(ii) Wood stoves
(iii) Kerosene heaters
Choose the correct code:
(a) (i) and (ii) only (b) (ii) and (iii) only
(c) (ii) only (d) (i), (ii), and (iii)

50. Which of the following pollutants can cause cancer in humans?
(a) Pesticides (b) Mercury
(c) Lead (d) Ozone

51. ***Assertion (A):*** People population control measures do not necessarily help in checking environmental degradation.
Reason (R): The relationship between population growth and environmental degradation is rather complex.
Choose the correct answer from the following:
(a) Both (A) and (R) are true, and (R) is the correct explanation of (A).
(b) Both (A) and (R) are true, but (R) is not the correct explanation of (A).
(c) (A) is true, but (R) is false.
(d) (A) is false, but (R) is true.

52. Which of the following phenomena is not a natural hazard?
(a) Wildfire
(b) Lightning
(c) Landslide
(d) Chemical contamination

53. As a part of National Climate Change Policy, Indian government is planning to raise the installed capacity of renewable energy by the year 2030 to
(a) 175 GW (b) 200 GW
(c) 250 GW (d) 350 GW

54. At present, in terms of per capita energy consumption (kWh/year), identify the correct sequence.
(a) Brazil > Russia > China > India
(b) Russia > China > India > Brazil
(c) Russia > China > Brazil > India
(d) China > Russia > Brazil > India

55. Which of the following are the objectives of Rashtriya Uchchatar Shiksha Abhiyan (RUSA)?
   (i) To improve the overall quality of state institutions.
   (ii) To ensure adequate availability of quality faculty.
   (iii) To create new institutions through upgradation of existing autonomous colleges.
   (iv) To downgrade universities with poor infrastructure into autonomous colleges.

   Select the correct answer from the codes given below:
   (a) (i), (ii), (iii), and (iv)
   (b) (i), (ii), and (iii)
   (c) (i), (iii), and (iv)
   (d) (i), (ii), and (iv)

56. The grounds on which discrimination in admission to educational institutions is constitutionally prohibited are
   (i) Religion (ii) Sex
   (iii) Place of birth (iv) Nationality

   Select the correct answer from the codes given below:
   (a) (ii), (iii), and (iv)
   (b) (i), (ii), and (iii)
   (c) (i), (ii), and (iv)
   (d) (i), (ii), (iii), and (iv)

57. Which of the following statements are correct about Lok Sabha?
   (i) The Constitution puts a limit on the size of the Lok Sabha.
   (ii) The size and shape of the Parliamentary Constituencies are determined by the Election Commission.
   (iii) First - past - the Post electoral system is followed.
   (iv) The Speaker of Lok Sabha does not have a casting vote in case of an equality of votes.

   Select the correct answer from the codes given below:
   (a) (i), and (iii) (b) (i), (ii), and (iii)
   (c) (i), (iii), and (iv) (d) (i), (ii), (iii), and (iv)

58. Public order as an item in the Constitution figures in
   (a) the Union List
   (b) the State List
   (c) the Concurrent List
   (d) the Residuary Powers

59. The term of office of the Advocate General of a state is
   (a) 4 years
   (b) 5 years
   (c) 6 years or 65 years of age whichever is earlier
   (d) Not fixed

60. Which among the following States has the highest number of seats in the Lok Sabha?
   (a) Maharashtra (b) Rajasthan
   (c) Tamil Nadu (d) West Bengal

Answer Keys

1. (c)	7. (d)	13. (a)	19. (d)	25. (a)	31. (b)	37. (a)	43. (a)	49. (d)	55. (b)
2. (d)	8. (b)	14. (d)	20. (c)	26. (d)	32. (d)	38. (b)	44. (d)	50. (a)	56. (b)
3. (b)	9. (b)	15. (b)	21. (d)	27. (d)	33. (b)	39. (b)	45. (b)	51. (a)	57. (a)
4. (a)	10. (d)	16. (d)	22. (b)	28. (d)	34. (a)	40. (d)	46. (d)	52. (d)	58. (b)
5. (c)	11. (c)	17. (d)	23. (c)	29. (b)	35. (c)	41. (c)	47. (c)	53. (d)	59. (d)
6. (a)	12. (a)	18. (b)	24. (d)	30. (c)	36. (b)	42. (d)	48. (d)	54. (c)	60. (a)

Hints and Solutions

1. This is happening due to formalisation of education also.
2. Refer 'Desirable Characteristics of Evaluation' on page 1.20.
5. For full text www.unesco.org/education/pdf/15_62.pdf can be visited.
6. Refer 'Maxims and Principles of Teaching under Best Teaching Practices' on page 1.5.

7. Refer 'Research Objectives' on page 2.1. The production of knowledge is not the sole objective of any kind of research.
8. Refer to the concept of null and alternative hypothesis on page 2.16. Rejection of null hypothesis means acceptance of alternative hypothesis. Only null hypothesis is tested.
9. Refer page 2.30
10. Refer page 2.36
18. Refer 'Functions of Evaluation' on page 1.20.
19. Refer pages 1.23 – 24
20. Among the forms of paralanguage, we find physical elements like facial expressions or gestures. There are also many vocal features that contribute to our interpretation of spoken language, such as voiced pauses or intonation.
21. Refer point number 11 under 'Nature and Characteristics of Communication' on page 4.3.
22. Refer 'Non-verbal Communication' on page 4.8.
23. Classroom communication takes place with certain clear objectives, so it is utilitarian.
25. +3, +5, +7, +9, …
26. It is the question of Combined Arithmetic Mean. $X_{12} = (X_1 N_1 + X_2 N_2)/N$, where X_1 and X_2 are arithmetic means of two groups and N_1 and N_2 are their respective frequencies. N is the total number of frequencies.

    Here, $N_1 = 70$, $N_2 = 210 - 70 = 140$

    Combined Arithmetic Mean $= (60 \times 70 + 78 \times 140)/210 = 72$
27.

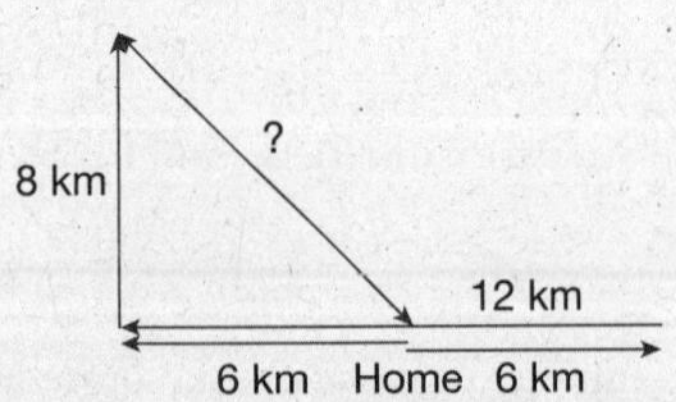

Making use of Pythagoras Theorem $= \sqrt{6^2 + 8^2} = 10\text{km}$

30.

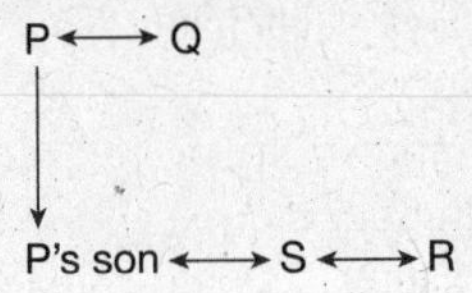

So, P's son, S and R are siblings. Hence, Q is the uncle of R.

33. Refer page 6.2
35. Refer 'Types of Definition' on page 6.15.
36. Refer page 6.8, here the solution to a similar kind of question is provided.
37. Here, we need to calculate the decadal growth: 1951–61,.61–71, …, 2001–2011.

    For example, decadal growth of 1951–61 = $(21 - 20)/20 \times 100 = 5\%$

    For 1961–71 = $(24 - 21)/21 \times 100 = 14.28\%$

    For 1971–81, it is 12.5%

    For 1981–91, it is 11.11%

    For 1991–2001 = 6.66%, and for 2001–2011, it is 9.375%

    Hence, (a) is the answer.
38. Making use of calculation done in solution for Q.No. 37, average growth rate = (5% + 14.28% + 12.5% … 9.375%)/6 = 9.82 %

    It is as per available choices, the compound annual growth calculation is most likely to be different.
39. Here, we have to make use of calculation done in Q.No. 38. The required answer = $[(100 + 9.82)/100] \times 35 = 38.49$ million
40. The required answer (per capita availability of power) = 10 GW/20 million = 10×1000 million watts/20 million = 500 watt
41. The calculation is to be done in the same manner as done is Q.No. 40.
42. The required answer (increase over 1951–2011) = $(100 - 10)/10 \times 100 = 900\%$
49. Refer 'Indoor Air Pollution' on page 9.12.
50. Refer Table 9.1 on page 9.10
52. Refer page 9.17
55. Refer page 10.11
56. Refer 'Right to Equality' on page 10.31.

57. The size and shape of Parliamentary constituencies are determined by Delimitation Commission of India, ideally on the basis of recent census. The representation from each state is not changed during this exercise. The constitution (under Article 81, Section 2) stipulates about the allocation of seats.

The Ninety-First Amendment to the Constitution has put off reallocation of seats between states up to 2026.

The Lok Sabha Speaker has the casting vote in case the vote of the house is evenly split.

60. Maharashtra - 48, Rajasthan - 25, Tamil Nadu - 39, and West Bengal - 42

Uttar Pradesh at 85 has the largest number of seats in Lok Sabha.

CBSE-UGC NET PAPER 1
JULY 2016

The following table shows the percentage profit (%) earned by two companies A and B during the years 2011–15. Answer Questions 1–3 based on the data contained in the table:

Profit earned by two companies

Year	Percentage profit (%)	
	A	B
2011	20	30
2012	35	40
2013	45	35
2014	40	50
2015	25	35

Where percent (%) Profit =

$$\frac{\text{Income} - \text{Expenditure}}{\text{Expenditure}} \times 100$$

1. In which year, the percentage profit earned by the company B is less than that of company A?
(a) 2012
(b) 2013
(c) 2014
(d) 2015

2. If the total expenditure of the two companies was ₹9 lakh in the year 2012 and the expenditure of A and B were in the ratio 2:1, then what was the income of the company A in that year?
(a) ₹9.2 lakh
(b) ₹8.1 lakh
(c) ₹7.2 lakh
(d) ₹6.0 lakh

3. What is the average percentage profit earned by the company B?
(a) 35%
(b) 42%
(c) 38%
(d) 40%

The following table shows the number of people in different age groups who responded to a survey about their favourite style of music. Use this information to answer the questions that follow: (Question 4–6) to the nearest whole percentage:

Number of people

Style of music \ Age	(Years) 15–20	(Years) 21–30	(Years) 31+
Classical	6	4	17
Pop	7	5	5
Rock	6	12	14
Jazz	1	4	11
Blues	2	3	15
Hip-Hop	9	3	4
Ambient	2	2	2

4. What percentage of respondents aged 31+ indicated a favourite style other than classical music?
(a) 64% (b) 60%
(c) 75% (d) 50%

5. Approximately what percentage of the total sample were aged 21–30?
(a) 31% (b) 23%
(c) 25% (d) 14%

6. Approximately what percentage of the total sample indicates that Hip-Hop is their favourite style of music?
(a) 6% (b) 8%
(c) 14% (d) 12%

7. The process of copying files to a CD-ROM is known as
(a) Burning (b) Zipping
(c) Digitising (d) Ripping

8. An unsolicited e-mail message sent to many recipients at once is a
(a) Worm (b) Virus
(c) Threat (d) Spam

9. The statement "the study, design, development, implementation, support or management of computer-based information systems, particularly software applications and computer Hardware" refers to
(a) Information Technology (IT)
(b) Information and Collaborative Technology (ICT)
(c) Information and Data Technology (IDT)
(d) Artificial Intelligence (AI)

10. If the binary equivalent of the decimal number 48 is 110000, then the binary equivalent of the decimal number 51 is given by
(a) 110011 (b) 110010
(c) 110001 (d) 110100

11. Identify the air pollutant in urban areas which irritates eyes and also respiratory tract of human beings.
(a) Particulate matter
(b) Oxides of nitrogen
(c) Surface ozone
(d) Carbon monoxide

12. Which of the following is the largest source of water pollution in major rivers of India?
(a) Untreated sewage
(b) Agriculture run-off
(c) Unregulated small scale industries
(d) Religious practices

13. Sustainable development goals have specific targets to be achieved by
(a) 2022 (b) 2030
(c) 2040 (d) 2050

14. Indian government's target of producing power from biomass by the year 2022, is
(a) 50 GW (b) 25 GW
(c) 15 GW (d) 10 GW

15. ***Assertion (A):*** Conserving our soil resources is critical to human survival.

Reason (R): Soil is home to many micro-organisms and contains minerals.

Choose the correct code:
(a) Both (A) and (R) are correct and (R) is the correct explanation of (A).
(b) Both (A) and (R) are correct but (R) is not the correct explanation of (A).
(c) (A) is true and (R) is false.
(d) (A) is false and (R) is true.

16. World Meteorological Organisation's (WMO) objective is to reduce the number of deaths due to hydro-meteorological disasters over the decade 2010–2019 by (with reference to the decade 1994–2003)
(a) 25% (b) 50%
(c) 75% (d) 80%

17. ________ is a type of memory circuitry that holds the computer's start-up routine.
(a) RIM (Read Initial Memory)
(b) RAM (Random Access Memory)
(c) ROM (Read Only Memory)
(d) Cache Memory

18. An ASCII is a character-encoding scheme that is employed by personal computers in order to represent various characters, numbers and control keys that the computer user selects on the keyboard. ASCII is an acronym for
(a) American Standard Code for Information Interchange
(b) American Standard Code for Intelligent Information

(c) American Standard Code for Information Integrity
(d) American Standard Code for Isolated Information

19. The National Judicial Appointments Commission (NJAC) has been declared unconstitutional by
(a) The Supreme Court of India
(b) The High Court
(c) The High Court and the Supreme Court both
(d) The President of India

20. Which of the following statement(s) about the Indian political system is/are correct?
(A) The President is both Head of the State and Head of the Government.
(B) Parliament is supreme.
(C) The Supreme Court is the guardian of the Constitution.
(D) The Directive Principles of State Policy are justiciable.

Select the correct answer from the codes given below:
(a) (A), (B), (C) and (D)
(b) (B), (C) and (D)
(c) (B) and (C)
(d) (C) only

21. Which of the following are the fundamental duties?
(A) To respect the National Flag
(B) To protect and improve the natural environment
(C) For a parent to provide opportunities for education to his/her child
(D) To protect monuments and places of national importance

Select the correct answer from the codes given:

Codes:
(a) (A), (B) and (C)
(b) (A), (B) and (D)
(c) (A), (C) and (D)
(d) (A), (B), (C) and (D)

22. Which of the following statements are correct in respect of NITI Aayog?
(A) It is a constitutional body.
(B) It is a statutory body.
(C) It is neither a constitutional body nor a statutory body.
(D) It is a think-tank.

Select the correct answer from the codes given below:
(a) (A) and (D)
(b) (B) and (D)
(c) (C) and (D)
(d) (B), (C) and (D)

23. Which of the following core values among the institutions of higher education are promoted by the NAAC (National Assessment and Accreditation Council)?
(A) Contributing to national development.
(B) Fostering global competencies among the students.
(C) Inculcating a value system among students and teachers.
(D) Promoting the optimum utilisation of the infrastructure.

Select the correct answer from the codes given below:

Codes:
(a) (B), (C) and (D)
(b) (A), (B) and (C)
(c) (A), (C) and (D)
(d) (A), (B), (C) and (D)

24. The best way for providing value education is through
(a) Discussions on scriptural texts
(b) Lectures/discourses on values
(c) Seminars/symposia on values
(d) Mentoring/reflective sessions on values

25. A college-level assistant professor has planned his/her lectures with an intent to develop cognitive dimensions of students centred on skills of analysis and synthesis. Below, given are two sets of items, Set - I consisting of levels of cognitive interchange and Set - II comprising basic requirements for promoting them. Match the two sets and indicate your answer by choosing the correct alternative from the codes given:

	Set - I (Levels of cognitive interchange)		Set - II (Basic requirements for promoting cognitive interchange)
A	Memory level	I.	Giving opportunity for discriminating examples and non-examples of a point.
B	Understanding level	II.	Recording the important points made during the presentations.
C	Reflective level	III.	Asking the students to discuss various items of information.
		IV.	Critically analysing the points to be made and discussed.

Codes:

	A	B	C
(a)	II	IV	I
(b)	III	IV	II
(c)	II	I	IV
(d)	I	II	III

26. Which set of learner characteristics may be considered helpful in designing effective teaching–learning systems? Select the correct alternative from the codes given below:
    (A) Prior experience of learners in respect of the subject.
    (B) Interpersonal relationships of learner's family friends.
    (C) Ability of the learners in respect of the subject.
    (D) Student's language background.
    (E) Interest of students in following the prescribed dress code.
    (F) Motivational-orientation of the students.

    Codes:
    (a) (A), (B), (C) and (D)
    (b) (A), (C), (D) and (F)
    (c) (B), (C), (D) and (E)
    (d) (C), (D), (E) and (F)

27. ***Assertion (A):*** The purpose of higher education is to promote critical and creative thinking abilities among students.

    Reason (R): These abilities ensure job placements.

    Choose the correct answer from the following code:
    (a) Both (A) and (R) are true and (R) is the correct explanation of (A).
    (b) Both (A) and (R) are true but (R) is not the correct explanation of (A).
    (c) (A) is true but (R) is false.
    (d) (A) is false but (R) is true.

28. Match the items of the first set with that of the second set in respect of evaluation system.

    Choose the correct code:

	Set - I		Set - II
A	Formative evaluation	I	Evaluating cognitive and co-cognitive aspects with regularity
B	Summative evaluation	II	Tests and their interpretations based on a group and certain yardsticks
C	Continuous and comprehensive evaluation	III	Grading the final learning outcomes
D	Norm and criterion referenced tests	IV	Quizzes and discussions

Codes:

	A	B	C	D
(a)	IV	III	I	II
(b)	I	II	III	IV
(c)	III	IV	II	I
(d)	I	III	IV	II

29. Select the alternative which consists of positive factors contributing to effectiveness of teaching:

List of factors:

(A) Teacher's knowledge of the subject.
(B) Teacher's socio-economic background.
(C) Communication skill of the teacher.
(D) Teacher's ability to please the students.
(E) Teacher's personal contact with students.
(F) Teacher's competence in managing and monitoring the classroom transactions.

Codes:

(a) (B), (C) and (D)
(b) (C), (D) and (F)
(c) (B), (D) and (E)
(d) (A), (C) and (F)

30. The use of teaching aids is justified on the grounds of
(a) Attracting students' attention in the class room
(b) Minimising indiscipline problems in the classroom
(c) Optimising learning outcomes of students
(d) Effective engagement of students in learning tasks

31. The format of thesis writing is the same as in
(a) Preparation of a research paper/article
(b) Writing of seminar presentation
(c) A research dissertation
(d) Presenting a workshop/conference paper

32. In qualitative research paradigm, which of the following features may be considered critical?
(a) Data collection with standardised research tools.
(b) Sampling design with probability sample techniques.
(c) Data collection with bottom-up empirical evidences.
(d) Data gathering to take place with top-down systematic evidences.

33. From the following list of statements, identify the set which has negative implications for 'research ethics':
(A) A researcher critically looks at the findings of another research.
(B) Related studies are cited without proper references.
(C) Research findings are made the basis for policy making.
(D) Conduct of practitioner is screened in terms of reported research evidences.
(E) A research study is replicated with a view to verify the evidences from other researches.
(F) Both policy making and policy implementing processes are regulated in terms of preliminary studies.

Codes:

(a) (A), (B) and (C)
(b) (B), (C) and (D)
(c) (B), (D) and (F)
(d) (A), (C) and (E)

34. In a research on the effect of child-rearing practices on stress-proneness of children in completing school projects, the hypothesis formulated is that 'child rearing practices do influence stress-proneness'. At the data-analysis stage a null hypothesis is advanced to find out the tenability of research hypothesis. On the basis of the evidence available, the null hypothesis is rejected at 0.01 level of significance. What decision may be warranted in respect of the research hypothesis?
(a) The research hypothesis will also be rejected.
(b) The research hypothesis will be accepted.
(c) Both the research hypothesis and the null hypothesis will be rejected.
(d) No decision can be taken in respect of the research hypothesis.

35. A researcher intends to explore the effect of possible factors for the organisation of effective mid-day meal interventions. Which research method will be most appropriate for this study?

(a) Historical method
(b) Descriptive survey method
(c) Experimental method
(d) Ex-post-facto method

36. Which of the following is an initial mandatory requirement for pursuing research?
(a) Developing a research design
(b) Formulating a research question
(c) Deciding about the data analysis procedure
(d) Formulating a research hypothesis

Read the following passage carefully and answer question numbers from 37 to 42:

In terms of labour, for decades, the relatively low cost and high quality of Japanese workers conferred considerable competitive advantage across numerous durable goods and consumer electronics industries (e.g., Machinery, automobiles, televisions, radios). Then labour-based advantages shifted to South Korea, then to Malaysia, Mexico and other nations. Today, China appears to be capitalising best on the basis of labour. Japanese firms still remain competitive in markets for such durable goods, electronics and other products, but the labour force is no longer sufficient for competitive advantage over manufacturers in other industrialising nations. Such shifting of labour-based advantage is clearly not limited to manufacturing industries. Today, a huge number of IT and service jobs are moving from Europe and North America to India, Singapore, and other countries with relatively well-educated, low-cost workforces possessing technical skills. However, as educational levels and technical skills continue to rise in other countries, India, Singapore, and other nations enjoying labour-based competitive advantage today are likely to find such advantage cannot be sustained through emergence of new competitors. In terms of capital, for centuries the days of gold coins and later even paper money restricted financial flows. Subsequently regional concentrations were formed where large banks, industries and markets coalesced. But today capital flows internationally at rapid speed. Global commerce no longer requires regional interactions among business players. Regional capital concentrations in places such as New York, London and Tokyo still persist, of course, but the capital concentrated there is no longer sufficient for competitive advantage over other capitalists distributed worldwide. Only if an organisation is able to combine, integrate and apply its resources (e.g., Land, labour, capital, IT) in an effective manner that is not readily imitable by competitors can such an organisation enjoy competitive advantage sustainable overtime. In a knowledge-based theory of the firm, this idea is extended to view organisational knowledge as a resource with at least the same level of power and importance as the traditional economic inputs. An organisation with superior knowledge can achieve competitive advantage in markets that appreciate the application of such knowledge. Semiconductors, genetic engineering, pharmaceuticals, software, military warfare, and like knowledge-intensive competitive arenas provide both time-proven and current examples. Consider semiconductors (e.g. computer chips), which are made principally of sand and common metals. These ubiquitous and powerful electronic devices are designed within common office buildings, using commercially available tools, and fabricated within factories in many industrialised nations. Hence, land is not the key competitive resource in the semiconductor industry.

Based on the passage answer the following questions:

37. How can an organisation enjoy competitive advantage sustainable overtime?
(a) Through regional capital flows.
(b) Through regional interactions among business players.
(c) By making large banks, industries and markets coalesced.
(d) By effective use of various instrumentalities.

38. What is required to ensure competitive advantages in specific markets?
(a) Access to capital
(b) Common office buildings
(c) Superior knowledge
(d) Common metals

39. The passage also mentions about the trend of
    (a) Global financial flow
    (b) Absence of competition in manufacturing industry
    (c) Regionalisation of capitalists
    (d) Organisational incompatibility
40. What does the author lay stress on in the passage?
    (a) International commerce
    (b) Labour-intensive industries
    (c) Capital resource management
    (d) Knowledge-driven competitive advantage
41. Which country enjoyed competitive advantages in automobile industry for decades?
    (a) South Korea (b) Japan
    (c) Mexico (d) Malaysia
42. Why labour-based competitive advantages of India and Singapore cannot be sustained in IT and service sectors?
    (a) Due to diminishing levels of skill.
    (b) Due to capital-intensive technology making inroads.
    (c) Because of new competitors.
    (d) Because of shifting of labour-based advantage in manufacturing industries.
43. What are the barriers to effective communication?
    (a) Moralising, being judgemental and comments of consolation.
    (b) Dialogue, summary and self-review.
    (c) Use of simple words, cool reaction and defensive attitude.
    (d) Personal statements, eye contact and simple narration.
44. The choice of communication partners is influenced by factors of
    (a) Proximity, utility and loneliness
    (b) Utility, secrecy and dissonance
    (c) Secrecy, dissonance and deception
    (d) Dissimilarity, dissonance and deviance
45. As a teacher, select the best option to ensure your effective presence in the classroom.
    (a) Use of peer command
    (b) Making aggressive statements
    (c) Adoption of well-established posture
    (d) Being authoritarian
46. Every communicator has to experience
    (a) Manipulated emotions
    (b) Anticipatory excitement
    (c) The issue of homophiles
    (d) Status dislocation
47. Imagine you are working in an educational institution where people are of equal status. Which method of communication is best suited and normally employed in such a context?
    (a) Horizontal communication
    (b) Vertical communication
    (c) Corporate communication
    (d) Cross communication
48. Identify the important element a teacher has to take cognizance of while addressing students in a classroom.
    (a) Avoidance of proximity
    (b) Voice modulation
    (c) Repetitive pause
    (d) Fixed posture
49. Two railway tickets from city A to B and three tickets from city A to C cost ₹177. Three tickets from city A to B and two tickets from city A to C cost ₹173. The fare for city B from city A will be
    (a) ₹25 (b) ₹27
    (c) ₹30 (d) ₹33
50. A person walks 10 m in front and 10 m to the right. Then every time turning to his left, he walks 5, 15 and 15 m, respectively. How far is he now from his starting point?
    (a) 20 m (b) 15 m
    (c) 10 m (d) 5 m
51. A is sister of B. F is daughter of G. C is mother of B. D is father of C. E is mother of D. A is related to D as
    (a) Granddaughter
    (b) Daughter
    (c) Daughter-in-law
    (d) Sister
52. In the series

    AB, EDC, FGHI, ...?...., OPQRST, the missing term is

(a) JKLMN (b) JMKNL
(c) NMLKJ (d) NMKLJ

53. Among the following propositions two are related in such a way that one is the denial of the other. Which are those propositions? Select the correct code:

Propositions:
(A) All women are equal to men.
(B) Some women are equal to men.
(C) Some women are not equal to men.
(D) No women are equal to men.

Codes:
(a) (A) and (B)
(b) (A) and (D)
(c) (C) and (D)
(d) (A) and (C)

54. In certain code, SELECTION is coded as QCJCARGML. The code of AMERICANS will be
(a) YKCPGAYLQ
(b) BNFSJDBMR
(c) QLYAGPCKY
(d) YQKLCYPAG

55. In the series

3, 11, 23, 39, 59, ...

The next term will be
(a) 63 (b) 73
(c) 83 (d) 93

56. Select the option which is not correct about Venn diagram:
(a) Venn diagram represents propositions as well as classes.
(b) It can provide clear method of notation.
(c) It can be either valid or invalid.
(d) It can provide the direct method of testing the validity.

57. Select the code which is not correct in the context of deductive argument with two premises:
(a) An argument with one true premise, one false premise and a false conclusion may be valid.
(b) An argument with two true premises and a false conclusion may be valid.
(c) An argument with one true premise, one false premise and a true conclusion may be valid.
(d) An argument with two false premises and a false conclusion may be valid.

58. Given below are two premises and four conclusions are drawn from them (taking singly or together). Select the code that states the conclusions validly drawn.

Premises: (I) All religious persons are emotional.

(II) Ram is a religious person.

Conclusions: (A) Ram is emotional.

(B) All emotional persons are religious.

(C) Ram is not a non-religious person.

(D) Some religious persons are not emotional.

Codes:
(a) (A), (B), (C) and (D)
(b) (A) only
(c) (A) and (C) only
(d) (B) and (C) only

59. If the proposition 'All thieves are poor' is false, which of the following propositions can be claimed certainly to be true?

Propositions:
(a) Some thieves are poor.
(b) Some thieves are not poor.
(c) No thief is poor.
(d) No poor person is a thief.

60. Consider the following statement and select the correct code stating the nature of the argument involved in it:

To suppose that the earth is the only populated world in the infinite space is as absurd as to assert that in an entire field of millet only one grain will grow.
(a) Astronomical
(b) Anthropological
(c) Deductive
(d) Analogical

ANSWER KEYS

1. (b)	7. (a)	13. (b)	19. (a)	25. (c)	31. (c)	37. (d)	43. (a)	49. (d)	55. (c)
2. (b)	8. (d)	14. (d)	20. (d)	26. (b)	32. (c)	38. (c)	44. (a)	50. (d)	56. (c)
3. (c)	9. (a)	15. (b)	21. (a)	27. (b)	33. (c)	39. (a)	45. (c)	51. (a)	57. (b)
4. (c)	10. (a)	16. (b)	22. (c)	28. (a)	34. (b)	40. (d)	46. (b)	52. (c)	58. (c)
5. (c)	11. (c)	17. (c)	23. (b)	29. (d)	35. (d)	41. (b)	47. (a)	53. (d)	59. (b)
6. (d)	12. (a)	18. (a)	24. (d)	30. (c)	36. (b)	42. (c)	48. (b)	54. (a)	60. (d)

HINTS AND SOLUTIONS

1. It is a question of simple observation
2. Total of radios = 2 + 1 = 3.

   Expenditure of company A in 2012

   $= \frac{2}{3} \times 9 = ₹6$ lakhs

   Given that Profit of company A in 2012 = 35%

   Thus, 35 = [(Income of Company A − 6) / 6] × 100

   Solving, it we get that Income of company A = ₹18.10 lakhs
3. Required percentage

   $= \frac{30+40+35+50+35}{5} = \frac{190}{5} = 38\%$

   Here, we calculate this percentage on the basis of assumption that expenditure figure is same for all years. Otherwise, none of choices is correct.
4. Required percentage

   $= \frac{5+14+11+15+4+2}{17+5+14+11+15+4+2} \times 100 = \frac{51}{68} \times 100$

   $= \frac{51}{68} = 75\%$
5. Total sample size = 134

   Total of people between ages 21 – 30 years = 33

   Required percentage $= \frac{33}{134} \times 100 = 25\%$
6. Required percentage $= \frac{\text{Hip} - \text{Hop Total}}{\text{Grand total}} \times 10$

   $= \frac{16}{134} \times 100 = 12\%$ (approx.)

10. As we need binary code for 51, we can find binary code for 3 and add it to that for 48.

    Binary for 48 = 110000 (Given)

2	3	1
2	2	1
	0	

    So binary for 3 = 011

    Binary for 51 = 110000 + 011
    = 110011
11. Refer Table 9.1 on page 9.10
12. The largest source of water pollution is major rivers in India is untreated sewage.
13. The SDGs came into effect in January 2016, and they will continue guide UNDP policy and funding for the next 15 years. Also known as Global Goals, they are a universal call to action to end poverty, protect the planet and ensure that all people enjoy peace and prosperity. Seventeen SDGs build on the successes of the Millennium Development Goals, while including new areas such as climate change, economic inequality, innovation, sustainable consumption, peace, and justice, among other priorities.
14. India has renewable energy generation target of 175 GW by 2022. Of the target capacity, 100 GW would be from solar power, 60 GW from wind, 10 GW from biomass and 5 GW from small hydro power.
19. Refer page 10.42
20. President is the head of State, and PM is the head of Government. In Indian context, people of the country are sovereign, whereas the Constitution of India is supreme. Parliament is the supreme law making body. The Directive Principles of State Policy are not justiciable.

21. Refer page 10.33
22. Refer page 10.46
23. Refer page 1.2–3
30. Refer page 1.22
31. Refer page 2.27
32. Refer page 2.2 and 2.9
33. Refer page 2.32
35. Refer 2.5–6
43. Refer page 4.10
47. Refer page 4.9
49. Let Railway fare from City A to City B = ₹x
And from City A to City C = ₹ y
According to question

$$2x + 3y = 177 \quad \text{(i)}$$
$$3x + 2y = 173 \quad \text{(ii)}$$

Solving equations (i) and (ii), we get x = ₹ 33, that is the required answer.

50.

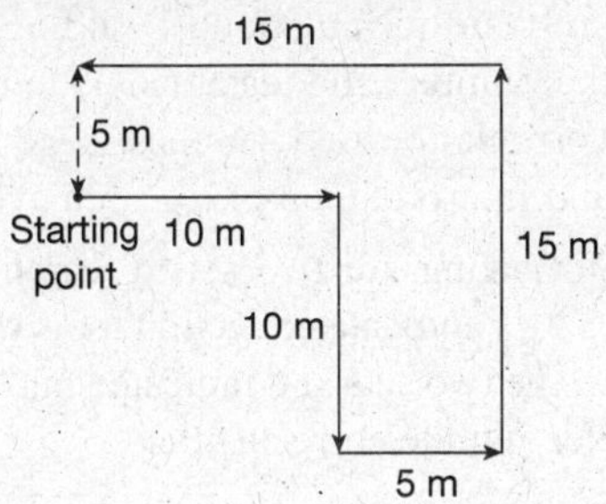

51.

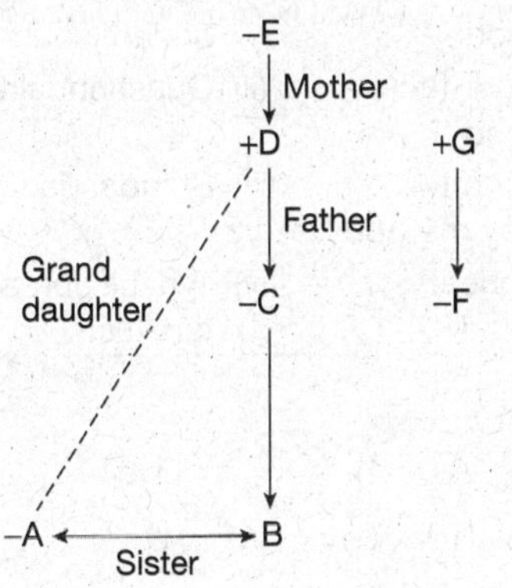

52. The number of alphabets is increasing by 1 and are alternatively being written in reverse order

AB, EDC, FGHI, NMLKJ, OPQRST

53. First proposition: 'All women are equal to men' is given among the answer choice. We can start with that.

All women are equal to men also mean that "some women are equal to men". It is based on rules of syllogism, which means that what applies to all also applies to part of it. Now, the denial of it is 'some women are not equal to men'. That is the third proposition.

54.

S	E	L	E	C	T	I	O	N
–2	–2	–2	–2	–2	–2	–2	–2	–2
Q	C	J	C	A	R	G	M	L

Similarly

A	M	E	R	I	C	A	N	S
–2	–2	–2	–2	–2	–2	–2	–2	–2
Y	K	C	P	G	A	Y	L	Q

55. +8, +12, +16, +20, +24 and so on.

58.

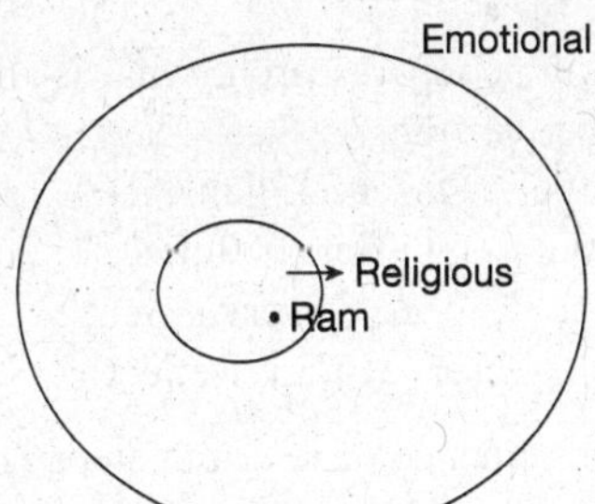

CBSE-UGC NET PAPER 1 JANUARY 2017

1. The principal of a school conducts an interview session of teachers and students with a view to explore the possibility of their enhanced participation in school programmers. Which type of research does this endeavourbe related to?
   (a) Evaluation research
   (b) Fundamental research
   (c) Action research
   (d) Applied research

2. In doing action research, what is the usual sequence of steps?
   (a) Reflect, Observe, Plan, Act
   (b) Plan, Act, Observe, Reflect
   (c) Plan, Reflect, Observe, Act
   (d) Act, Observe, Plan, Reflect

3. Which sequence of research steps is logical in the following list?
   (a) Problem formulation, Analysis, Development of Research design, Hypothesis Making, Collection of data, Arriving at generalizations, and conclusions
   (b) Development of Research Design, Hypothesis making, Problem Formulation, Data analysis, Arriving at conclusions, and Data collection
   (c) Problem Formulation, Hypothesis making, Development of a Research design, Collection of a Data, Data analysis and formulation of generalizations, and Conclusions
   (d) Problem formulation, Deciding about the sample and data collection tools, Formulation of Hypothesis, Collection and Interpretation of research evidence

4. The following are two sets:research methods (Set-I) and data collection tools (Set-II). Match the two sets and indicate your answer by selecting the correct code:

Set-I	Set-II
A Experimental method	(i) Using primary secondary sources
B Ex post-facto method	(ii) Questionnaire
C Descriptive survey method	(iii) Standardised tests
D Historical method	(iv) Typical characteristics tests

Codes:

	A	B	C	D
(a)	(ii)	(i)	(iii)	(iv)
(b)	(iii)	(iv)	(ii)	(i)
(c)	(ii)	(iii)	(i)	(iv)
(d)	(ii)	(iv)	(iii)	(i)

5. The issue of 'research ethics' may be considered pertinent at which stage of research?
   (a) At the stage of problem formulation and its definition
   (b) At the stage of defining the population of research
   (c) At the stage of data collection and interpretation
   (d) At the stage of reporting the findings
6. In which of the following, reporting format is formally prescribed?
   (a) Doctoral-level thesis
   (b) Conference of researchers
   (c) Workshops and seminars
   (d) Symposia

Read the following passage carefully and answer Questions from 7 to 12:

The last Great War, which nearly shook the foundations of the modern world, had little impact on Indian literature beyond aggravating the popular revulsions against violence and adding to growing disillusionment with the 'humane pretensions' of the Western World. This was eloquently voiced in Tagore's poems and his last testament, 'Crisis in Civilization'. The Indian intelligentsia was in a state of moral dilemma. On the one hand, it could not help sympathising with the England's dogged courage in the hour of peril, with the Russians fighting with their backs on the wall against ruthless Nazi hordes, and with the China groaning under the heel of Japanese militarism; on the other hand, their own country was practically under the military occupation of their own soil and the Indian army under Subhas Bose was trying from the opposite camp to liberate their country. No creative impulse could issue from such confusion of loyalties. One would imagine that the achievement of Indian independence in 1947, which came in the wake of the Allies victory and was followed by collapse of colonialism in the neighbouring countries of South East Asia, would have released an upsurge of the creative energy. No doubt it did, but it was soon submerged in the great agony of partition with the inhuman slaughter of innocents and the uprooting of the millions of the people from their homeland followed by the martyrdom of Mahatma Gandhi. These tragedies along with Pakistan's invasion of Kashmir and its later atrocities in Bangladesh, did indeed provoke a pregnant writing, particularly in the languages of the regions most affected, Bengali, Hindi, Kashmiri, Punjabi, Sindhi, and Urdu. Both poignant or passionate writing does not by itself make great literature. What reserves of enthusiasm and confidence served these disasters have been mainly absorbed in the task of national reconstruction and economic development. Great literature has always emerged out of chains of convulsions. Indian literature is richer today in terms of volume, range, and variety than it ever was in the past.

7. What was the impact of the last great war on Indian literature?
   (a) It had no impact.
   (b) It aggravated popular revulsion against violence.
   (c) It shook the foundations of literature.
   (d) It offered eloquent support to the Western World.
8. What did Tagore articulate in his last testament?
   (a) Offered support to Subhas Bose
   (b) Exposed the humane pretensions of the Western World
   (c) Expressed loyalty to England
   (d) Encouraged the liberation of countries
9. What was the stance of Indian intelligentsia during the period of great war?
   (a) Indifference to Russia's plight
   (b) They favoured Japanese militarism
   (c) They prompted creativity out of confused loyalties
   (d) They expressed sympathy for England's dogged courage
10. Identify the factor responsible for the submergence creative energy in Indian literature.
   (a) Military occupation of one's own soil
   (b) Resistance to colonial occupation
   (c) Great agony of partition
   (d) Victory of Allies

11. What was the aftermath that survived tragedies in Kashmir and Bangladesh?
(a) Suspicion of other countries
(b) Continuance of rivalry
(c) Menace of war
(d) National reconstruction

12. The passage has the message that
(a) Disasters are inevitable
(b) Great literature emerges out of chains of convulsions
(c) Indian literature does not have a marked landscape
(d) Literature has no relation with war and independence

13. Effective communication pre-supposes
(a) Non-alignment
(b) Domination
(c) Passivity
(d) Understanding

14. When verbal and non-verbal messages are contradictory, it is said that most people believe in
(a) Indeterminate messages
(b) Verbal messages
(c) Non-verbal messages
(d) Aggressive messages

15. The typical feature of information-rich classroom lecture is in the nature of being
(a) Sedentary
(b) Staggered
(c) Factual
(d) Sectoral

16. Expressive communication is driven by
(a) Passive aggression
(b) Encoder's personality characteristics
(c) External clues
(d) Encoder–decoder contract

17. Positive classroom communication leads to
(a) Coercion
(b) Submission
(c) Confrontation
(d) Persuasion

18. Classroom communication is the basis of
(a) Social identity
(b) External inanities
(c) Biased passivity
(d) Group aggression

19. The missing term in the series 1, 4, 27, 16, ?, 36, 243,... is
(a) 30
(b) 49
(c) 125
(d) 81

20. The next term in the series
YEB, WFD, UHG, SKI, _?_ will be
(a) TLO
(b) QOL
(c) QLO
(d) GQP

21. If A is coded as C, M as I, N as P, S as O, I as A, P as N, E as M, O as E, and C as S, then the code of COMPANIES will be
(a) SPEINMOAC
(b) NCPSEIOMA
(c) SMOPIEACN
(d) SEINCPAMO

22. Among the following, identify the continuous type of data
(a) Number of languages a person speaks
(b) Number of children in a household
(c) Population in cities
(d) Weight of students in a class

23. Ali buys a glass, a pencil box and a cup and pays ₹21 to the shopkeeper. Rakesh buys a cup, two pencil boxes, and a glass, and he pays ₹28 to the shopkeeper. Preeti buys two glasses, a cup, and two pencil boxes, and she pays ₹35 to the shopkeeper. Then, the cost of 10 cups will be
(a) ₹40
(b) ₹60
(c) ₹80
(d) ₹70

24. Out of the following four cities, three are alike in some manner while the fourth one is different. Identify the odd one.
(a) Lucknow
(b) Rishikesh
(c) Allahabad
(d) Patna

25. The following are some characteristics of reasoning. Select the code that states a characteristic that is not a deductive reasoning
    (a) The conclusion must be based on observation and experiment.
    (b) The conclusion should be supported by the premise/premises.
    (c) The conclusion must follow from the premise/premises necessarily.
    (d) The argument may be valid or invalid.
26. If two standard-form categorical propositions with the same subject and predicate are related in such a manner that is: when one is undermined and the other must be undetermined, what is their relation?
    (a) Contrary
    (b) Sub-contrary
    (c) Contradictory
    (d) Subaltern
27. Men and women may have different reproductive strategies but neither can be considered inferior or superior to the other, any more than a bird's wings can be considered superior or inferior to a fish's fins. Select the code that states those two propositions
    (a) Biological
    (b) Physiological
    (c) Analogical
    (d) Hypothetical
28. Among the following propositions, two are related in such a way that they cannot both be true but can be false. Select the code states those two propositions

    Propositions:
    (i) Every student is attentive
    (ii) Some students are attentive
    (iii) Students are never attentive
    (iv) Some students are not attentive

    Codes:
    (a) (i) and (ii)
    (b) (i) and (iii)
    (c) (ii) and (iii)
    (d) (iii) and (iv)
29. The following are two premised (A) and (B). From those two premises, four conclusions i, ii, iii, iv are drawn. Select the code that states the conclusions validly drawn from the premises (taking singly or jointly)

    Premises: (A) Untouchability is a curse
    (B) All hot pans are untouchable

    Conclusions:
    (i) All hot pans are curse
    (ii) Some untouchable things are hot pans
    (iii) All curses are untouchable
    (iv) Some curses are untouchable

    Codes:
    (a) (i) and (ii)
    (b) (ii) and (iii)
    (c) (iii) and (iv)
    (d) (ii) and (iv)
30. If the statement 'None but the brave wins the race' is false, which of the following statements can be claimed to be true?
    (a) All brave persons win the race
    (b) Some persons who win the race are not brave
    (c) Some persons who win the race are brave
    (d) No person who wins the race is brave

The following table embodies data on the sales revenue (₹in lakhs) generated by a publishing house during the years 2012–2015 while selling books, magazines, and journals as three categories of items. Answer questions 31–33 based on the data given in the table

Sales revenue (₹In lakh)

Year → / Item ↓	2012	2013	2014	2015
Journals	46	47	45	44
Magazines	31	39	46	51
Books	73	77	78	78
Total				

31. In 2015, approximately what percent of total revenue come from books?

(a) 45%
(b) 55%
(c) 35%
(d) 25%

32. The number of years in which there was an increase in revenue from at least two categories of items is
(a) 0
(b) 1
(c) 2
(d) 3

33. If the year 2016 were to show the same growth in terms of total sales revenue as the year 2015 over the year 2014, then the revenue in the year 2016 must be approximately:
(a) ₹194 lakh
(b) ₹187 lakh
(c) ₹172 lakh
(d) ₹177 lakh

A university professor maintains data on MCA students tabulated by performance and gender of the students. The data is kept on a computer hard disk, but accidentally some of its data are lost because of a computer virus. Only the following could be recovered:

Gender	Average	Good	Excellent	Total
Male			10	
Female				32
Total		30		

Panic buttons were pressed but to no avail. An expert committee was formed, which decided that the following facts were self-evident:

(i) Half the students were either excellent or good.
(ii) 40% of the students were females
(iii) One-third of the male students were average

Answer questions 34–36 based on the data given above:

34. How many female students are excellent?
(a) 0
(b) 8
(c) 16
(d) 32

35. What proportion of female students are good?
(a) 0
(b) 0.25
(c) 0.50
(d) 0.75

36. Approximately, what proportion of good students are male?
(a) 0
(b) 0.73
(c) 0.43
(d) 0.27

37. Which of the following statement(s) is/are TRUE?

S1: The decimal number 11 is larger than the hexadecimal number 11

S2: In the binary number 1110.101, the fractional part has the decimal value as 0.625

(a) S1 Only
(b) S2 Only
(c) Both S1 and S2
(d) Neither S1 nor S2

38. Read the following two statements:

I: Information and Communication Technology (ICT) is considered as a subset of Information Technology (IT)

II: The 'right to use' a piece of software is termed as copyright

Which of the above mentioned statement(s) is/are CORRECT?
(a) Both I and II
(b) Neither I nor II
(c) II Only
(d) I Only

39. Which of the following correctly lists the types of the computer memory from highest to lowest speed?

(i) Secondary Storage
(ii) Main Memory (RAM)
(iii) Cache Memory
(iv) CPU Registers

Codes:
(a) (i), (ii), (iii), (iv)
(b) (iv), (iii), (i), (ii)
(c) (iv), (iii), (ii), (i)
(d) (iii), (iv), (ii), (i)

40. Which of the following is a characteristic of Web 2.0 applications?
(a) Multiple users schedule their time to use Web 2.0 applications one by one.
(b) Web2.0 applications are focused on the ability for people to collaborate and share information online.
(c) Web2.0 applications provide users with content rather than facilitating users to create it.
(d) Web2.0 applications use only static pages.

41. With regard to a word processing software, the process of combining static information in a publication together with variable information in a data source to create one merged publication is called
(a) Electronic mail
(b) Data sourcing
(c) Mail merge
(d) Spam mail

42. DVD technology uses an optical media to store the digital data. DVD is an acronym for
(a) Digital Vector Disc
(b) Digital Volume Disc
(c) Digital Versatile Disc
(d) Digital Visualization Disc

43. ***Assertion (A):*** Sustainable development critical to well-being of human society.

Reason (R): Environmentally sound policies do not harm the environment or deplete the natural resources.

Choose the correct code:
(a) Both (A) and (R) are correct and (R) is the correct explanation of (A).
(b) Both (A) and (R) are correct, but (R) is not the correct explanation of (A).
(c) (A) is true and (R) is true
(d) (A) is false and (R) is true

44. The dominant source of pollution due to oxides of nitrogen (NOx) in urban areas is
(a) Road transport
(b) Commercial Sector
(c) Energy use in industry
(d) Power plants

45. Which of the following is not a water-borne disease?
(a) Typhoid
(b) Hepatitis
(c) Cholera
(d) Dengue

46. The Government of India has set targets for power production from small hydro-projects by the year 2022 is
(a) 1 Giga-Watt
(b) 5 Giga-Watt
(c) 10 Giga-Watt
(d) 15 Giga-Watt

47. In which country, the recent international agreement on phasing out HydroFluoroCarbons (HFCs) was signed?
(a) Rwanda
(b) Morocco
(c) South Africa
(d) Algeria

48. Which of the following natural hazards is not hydro-meteorological?
(a) Snow avalanche
(b) Sea erosion
(c) Tropical cyclone
(d) Tsunami

49. Which of the following are the demerits of globalization of higher education?
(i) Exposure to global curriculum
(ii) Promotion of elitism in education
(iii) Commodification of higher education
(iv) Increase in the cost of education

Select the correct answer from the following codes:

Codes:
(a) (i) and (iv)
(b) (i), (iii), and (iv)
(c) (ii), (iii), and (iv)
(d) (i), (ii), (iii), and (iv)

50. Which of the following statements are correct about deemed universities?

(i) The Governor of the State is the chancellor of deemed universities.

(ii) They can design their own syllabus and course work.

(iii) They can frame their own guidelines regarding admission and fees.

(iv) They can grant degrees.

Select the correct answer from the following codes:

Codes:
(a) (i), (ii), and (iii)
(b) (ii), (iii), and (iv)
(c) (i), (iii), and (iv)
(d) (i), (ii), (iii), and (iv)

51. The purpose of value education is best served by focusing on
(a) Cultural practices prevailing in the society.
(b) Norms of conduct laid down by a social group
(c) Concern for human values
(d) Religious and moral practices and instructions.

52. Which of the following statements are correct?

(i) Rajya Sabha is a permanent house that can be dissolved only during national emergency.
(ii) Rajya Sabha does not represent the local interests of the States.
(iii) Members of the Rajya Sabha are not bound to vote at the dictates of the states they represent.
(iv) No Union territory has a representative in the Rajya Sabha.

Select the correct answer from the following codes:

Codes:
(a) (i) and (iv)
(b) (ii) and (iii)
(c) (ii), (iii), and (iv)
(d) (i), (ii), (iii), and (iv)

53. Which of the following are not necessarily the immediate consequences of the proclamation of the President's Rule in a State?

(i) Dissolution of the State of Ministers in the State

(ii) Removal of the Council of Ministers in the State

(iii) Takeover of the State administration by the Union Government

(iv) Appointment of a new Chief Secretary

Select the correct answer from the following codes:

Codes:
(a) (i) and (iv)
(b) (i), (ii), and (iii)
(c) (i), (ii), (iii), and (iv)
(d) (ii) and (iii)

54. Instead of holding the office during the pleasure of the President who among the following hold (s) office during good behaviour?

(i) Governor of a state

(ii) Attorney General of India

(iii) Judges of the High Court

(iv) Administrator of a Union Territory

Select the correct answer from the following codes:

Codes:
(a) (i) Only
(b) (iii) Only
(c) (i) and (iii)
(d) (i), (ii), (iii), and (iv)

55. Which of the following set of statements represents acceptable propositions with respect to teaching–learning relationships? Choose the correct code to indicate your answer.

(i) When students fail in a test, it is the teacher who fails

(ii) Every teaching must aim at ensuring learning

(iii) There can be teaching without learning taking place

(iv) There can be no learning without teaching

(v) A teacher teaches but learns also

(vi) Real learning implies rote learning

Codes:

(a) (ii), (iii), (iv), and (v)
(b) (i), (ii), (iii), and (v)
(c) (iii), (iv), (v), and (vi)
(d) (i), (ii), (v), and (vi)

56. ***Assertion (A):*** Learning is a life-long process.

Reason (R): Learning to be useful must be linked with life processes.

Choose the correct answer from the following code:

(a) Both (A) and (R) are true and (R) is the correct explanation of (A).
(b) Both (A) and (R) are true, but (R) is not the correct explanation of (A).
(c) (A) is true, but (R) is false
(d) (A) is false, but (R) is true.

57. Effectiveness of teaching has to be judged in terms of

(a) Course coverage
(b) Students' interest
(c) Learning outcomes of students
(d) Use of teaching aids in the classroom

58. In which teaching method, learner's participation is made optimal and proactive?

(a) Discussion method
(b) Buzz session method
(c) Brainstorming session method
(d) Project method

59. One of the most powerful factors affecting teaching effectiveness is related to the

(a) Social system of the country
(b) Economic status of the society
(c) Prevailing political system
(d) Educational system

60. ***Assertion (A):*** Formative evaluation tends to accelerate the pace of learning.

Reason (R): As against summative evaluation, formative evaluation is highly reliable.

Choose the correct answer from the following code:

(a) Both (A) and (R) are true and (R) is the correct explanation of (A).
(b) Both (A) and (R) are true, but (R) is not the correct explanation of (A).
(c) (A) is true, but (R) is false.
(d) (A) is false, but (R) is true

Answer Keys

1. (c)	7. (b)	13. (d)	19. (c)	25. (a)	31. (a)	37. (b)	43. (b)	49. (c)	55. (b)
2. (b)	8. (b)	14. (c)	20. (b)	26. (c)	32. (c)	38. (b)	44. (a)	50. (b)	56. (b)
3. (c)	9. (d)	15. (c)	21. (d)	27. (c)	33. (d)	39. (c)	45. (d)	51. (c)	57. (c)
4. (b)	10. (c)	16. (b)	22. (d)	28. (b)	34. (a)	40. (b)	46. (b)	52. (b)	58. (d)
5. (c)	11. (d)	17. (d)	23. (d)	29. (d)	35. (b)	41. (c)	47. (a)	53. (a)	59. (d)
6. (a)	12. (b)	18. (a)	24. (a)	30. (b)	36. (b)	42. (c)	48. (d)	54. (b)	60. (c)

Hints and Solutions

1. Refer page 2.7; action research has many applications in solving the local problems, specifically in education sector.
2. Refer page 2.7
3. Refer Table 2.3 on page 2.11
4. Refer types of research on page 2.5
6. Refer page 2.27 under 'Research Process' gives detailed description about research report/thesis.
14. Refer page 4.9 under concept of kinesics it has been mentioned that words account for 71%. Tone of voice is 38% and body language accounts for 55% of communication.
15. Information rich means more facts are being delivered in lecture.
16. Implied in the question statement itself.

17. Positive classroom communication means it should motivate or persuade students to learn.

18. A social identity is the portion of an individual's self-concept derived from perceived membership in a relevant social group. Social identity has been explained in a way that makes it easy to explain intergroup behaviour.

19. It's a question of mixed series.
First series: $1^3, 3^3, 5^3, 7^3, \ldots.$
Second Series: $2^2, 4^2, 6^2, \ldots.$
Thus, 5^3, i.e., 125 is the right answer.

20. Refer "EJOTY" on page 5.3.

E F G H I J K L M N O P

1+ 2+ 3+ 4+

Thus (b) is the answer.

21.

A	N	M	S	I	P	E	O	C
C	I	P	O	A	N	M	E	S
5	3	6	9	7	4	8	2	1

So, code for companies will be SEINCPAMO

22. Refer page 2.14. There are two types of variables:
   (i) **Discrete:** Definite values such as 1, 2... 4, 5 and so on. For example, number of chairs can only be 1, 2, 3 ..... and not value 1.2357 etc
   (ii) **Continuous Variables:** Take possible value with in a range. For example weight, weight of a boy can be anything such as 5.23125.....kg.

23. Let's g students for glass, p for pencil box & c for cup.
Ali: $1g + 1p + 1c = ₹21$ (i)
Rakesh: $1g + 2p + 1c = ₹28$ (ii)
Preeti: $2g + 2p + 1c = ₹35$ (iii)
Comparing (i) & (iii) $1p = ₹7$
Comparing (ii) & (iii) we can say that cost of $1g = ₹7$
substituting them in equation (i), we get $1c = ₹7$
So cost of 10 cups $= 7 \times 10 = ₹70$

24. Lucknow is on the bank of River Gomti, whereas all others are on banks of Holy Ganga.

25. Refer page 2.8 under Inductive Research, the first point denotes 'observe the different phenomena'. It means first choice in the question is about inductive reasoning & not deductive reasoning.

26. Refer page 6.12 - Square of Opposition

27. Refer page 6.4 - Analogous arguments

28. On page 6.5, there are rules for converting common language statements into their logical forms. Thus proposition (a) will become 'All the students are attentive'. Similarly, Proposition (c) will become 'No student is attentive'.
Propositions (a) and (c) comply with the conditions mentioned in question statement. So (b) is the answer.

29. Draw the Venn diagram

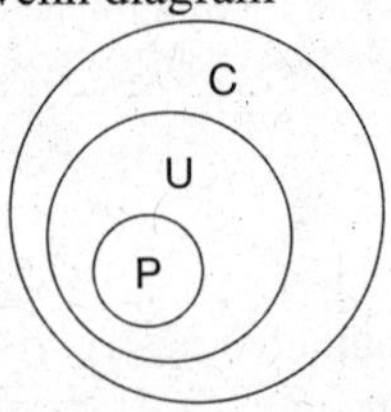

C – Curses

U – Untouchable

P – Pans

Conclusions (i), (ii) & (iv) seems to be valid, but according to official answer key (d) is the right answer.

31. First of all, total of each column should be done.
2012 – 150, 2013 – 163, 2014 – 169, 2015 – 173
Required % age = $(78/173) \times 100 = 45\%$ (approx).

32. By simple observation, we can find the answer. In 2013, there was increase in sales in all categories. In 2014, there was increase in sales in magazines and books in comparison to previous years.

33. Percentage increase in 2015
$$= (173 - 169)/169 \times 100 = 2.36\%$$

Now desired sales revenue in 2016 = 173 + 2.36% of 173 = ₹176.97 lakh or ₹177 lakh approx.

34.

	Average	Good	Excellent	Total
M	16[3]	22[4]	10	48[2]
F	24	8	0[6]	32
T	40	30	10[5]	80[1]

(Good + Excellent = 40)

From statement (b), 40% of Total students = 32

Thus Total students = 32 × 100/40 = 80[1]

From this we can say, Total of Male Students = 80 – 32 = 48[2]

From statement (c), number of Male students who are average = 1/3 × 48 = 16[3]

Number of Male students who are good = 48 – (16 + 10) = 22[4]

Half the students were either excellent or good = 1/2 × 80 = 40

Thus total of Excellent students = 40 – 30 = 10[5]

Thus Number of female student who are Excellent = 10 –10 = 0[6]

35. Proportion of Female students who are good = 8/32 = 0.25

36. Proportion of good students who are male = 22/30 = 0.73

39. Refer page 8.14–15

40. Refer social media on page 8.26

44. Refer page 9.11

57. Refer page 1.1. This fact is mentioned in the definition of teaching itself.

58. Refer page 1.9

59. All factors mentioned here affect the teaching effectiveness but 'Educational system' is the most direct.

CBSE-UGC NET PAPER 1 NOVEMBER 2017

1. Which of the following set of statements best represents the nature and objective of teaching and learning?
   (A) Teaching is like selling and learning is like buying.
   (B) Teaching is a social act while learning is a personal act.
   (C) Teaching implies learning whereas learning does not imply teaching.
   (D) Teaching is a kind of delivery of knowledge while learning is like receiving it.
   (E) Teaching is an interaction and is triadic in nature whereas learning is an active engagement in a subject domain.

   Codes:
   (a) (A), (D) and (E) (b) (B), (C) and (E)
   (c) (A), (B) and (C) (d) (A), (B) and (D)

2. From the list given below identify the learner characteristics which would facilitate teaching-learning system to become effective. Choose the correct code to indicate your answer.
   (A) Prior experience of learner
   (B) Learner's family lineage
   (C) Aptitude of the learner
   (D) Learner's stage of development
   (E) Learner's food habits and hobbies
   (F) Learner's religious affiliation

   Codes:
   (a) (A), (C) and (D) (b) (D), (E) and (F)
   (c) (A), (D) and (E) (d) (B), (C) and (F)

3. ***Assertion (A):*** All teaching implies learning.
   Reason (R): Learning to be useful must be derived from teaching.
   Choose the correct answer from the following:
   (a) Both (A) and (R) are true, and (R) is the correct explanation of (A).
   (b) Both (A) and (R) are true, but (R) is not the correct explanation of (A).
   (c) (A) is true, but (R) is false.
   (d) (A) is false, but (R) is true.

4. On the basis of summative tests, a teacher is interpreting his/her students, performance in terms of their wellness life style evident in behaviour. This will be called:
   (a) Formative testing
   (b) Continuous and comprehensive evaluation
   (c) Norm-referenced testing
   (d) Criterion-referenced testing

5. Which one of the following is a key behaviour in effective teaching?
   (a) Using student ideas and contribution
   (b) Structuring
   (c) Instructional variety
   (d) Questioning

6. Which of the following research types focuses on ameliorating the prevailing situations?
   (a) Fundamental Research
   (b) Applied Research
   (c) Action Research
   (d) Experimental Research
7. A researcher attempts to evaluate the effect of method of feeding on anxiety-proneness of children. Which method of research would be appropriate for this?
   (a) Case study method
   (b) Experimental method
   (c) Ex-post-facto method
   (d) Survey method
8. In which of the following arrangements a wider spectrum of ideas and issues may be made possible?
   (a) Research Article
   (b) Workshop mode
   (c) Conference
   (d) Symposium
9. In finalizing a thesis writing format which of the following would form part of supplementary pages?
   (a) List of tables and figures
   (b) Table of contents
   (c) Conclusions of the study
   (d) Bibliography and Appendices
10. Which of the following is susceptible to the issue of research ethics?
    (a) Inaccurate application of statistical techniques
    (b) Faulty research design
    (c) Choice of sampling techniques
    (d) Reporting of research findings

Read the following passage carefully and answer Questions from 11 to 15:

Climate change is considered to be one of the most serious threats to sustainable development, with adverse impacts on the environment, human health, food security, economic activity, natural resources and physical infrastructure. Global climate varies naturally. According to the Intergovernmental Panel on Climate Change (IPCC), the effects of climate change have already been observed, and scientific findings indicate that precautionary and prompt action is necessary. Vulnerability to climate change is not just a function of geography or dependence on natural resources; it also has social, economic and political dimensions which influence how climate change affects different groups. Poor people rarely have insurance to cover loss of property due to natural calamities, i.e., drought, floods, super cyclones etc. The poor communities are already struggling to cope with the existing challenges of poverty and climate variability and climate change could push many beyond their ability to cope or even survive. It is vital that these communities are helped to adapt to the changing dynamics of nature. Adaptation is a process through which societies make themselves better able to cope with an uncertain future. Adapting to climate change entails taking the right measures to reduce the negative effects of climate change (or exploit the positive ones) by making the appropriate adjustments and changes. These range from technological options such as increased sea defences or flood-proof houses on stilts to behavioural change at the individual level, such as reducing water use in times of drought. Other strategies include early warning systems for extreme events, better water management, improved risk management, various insurance options and biodiversity conservation. Because of the speed at which climate change is happening due to global temperature rise, it is urgent that the vulnerability of developing countries to climate change is reduced and their capacity to adapt is increased and national adaptation plans are implemented. Adapting to climate change will entail adjustments and changes at every level from community to national and international. Communities must build their resilience, including adopting appropriate technologies while making the most of traditional knowledge, and diversifying their livelihoods to cope with current and future climate stress. Local coping strategies and knowledge need to be used in synergy with government and local interventions. The need of adaptation interventions depends on national circumstances.

There is a large body of knowledge and experience within local communities on coping with climatic variability and extreme weather events. Local communities have always aimed to adapt to variations in their climate. To do so, they have made preparations based on their resources and their knowledge accumulated through experience of past weather patterns. This includes times when they have also been forced to react to and recover from extreme events, such as floods, drought and hurricanes. Local coping strategies are an important element of planning for adaptation. Climate change is leading communities to experience climatic extremes more frequently, as well as new climate conditions and extremes. Traditional knowledge can help to provide efficient, appropriate and time - tested ways of advising and enabling adaptation to climate change in communities who are feeling the effects of climate changes due to global warming.

11. Given below are the factors of vulnerability of poor people to climate change. Select the code that contains the correct answer.
    (A) Their dependence on natural resources
    (B) Geographical attributes
    (C) Lack of financial resources
    (D) Lack of traditional knowledge

    Codes:

    (a) (A), (B) and (C)
    (b) (B), (C) and (D)
    (c) (A), (B), (C) and (D)
    (d) (C) only

12. Adaptation as a process enables societies to cope with:
    (A) An uncertain future
    (B) Adjustments and changes
    (C) Negative impact of climate change
    (D) Positive impact of climate change

    Select the most appropriate answer from the following code:
    (a) (A), (B), (C) and (D)
    (b) (A) and (C)
    (c) (B), (C) and (D)
    (d) (C) only

13. To address the challenge of climate change, developing countries urgently require:
    (a) Imposition of climate change tax
    (b) Implementation of national adaptation policy at their level
    (c) Adoption of short-term plans
    (d) Adoption of technological solutions

14. The traditional knowledge should be used through:
    (a) Its dissemination
    (b) Improvement in national circumstances
    (c) Synergy between government and local interventions
    (d) Modern technology

15. The main focus of the passage is on:
    (a) Combining traditional knowledge with appropriate technology
    (b) Co-ordination between regional and national efforts
    (c) Adaptation to climate change
    (d) Social dimensions of climate change

16. The interaction between a teacher and students creates a zone of proximal:
    (a) Difference
    (b) Confusion
    (c) Development
    (d) Distortion

17. The spatial audio reproduction in a classroom can reduce the students':
    (a) Cognitive load in understanding
    (b) Respect for the teacher
    (c) Motivation for excellence
    (d) Interest in technology-orientation

18. The classroom communication should essentially be:
    (a) Contrived
    (b) Empathetic
    (c) Abstract
    (d) Non-descriptive

19. A good communicator begins his/her presentation with a:
    (a) Complex question
    (b) Non-sequitur
    (c) Repetitive phrase
    (d) Ice-breaker

20. In a classroom, the probability of message reception can be enhanced by:
(a) Establishing a viewpoint
(b) Exposing the ignorance of students
(c) Increasing the information load
(d) Using high decibel audio tools

21. In the series 1, 6, 15, 28, 45, ... the next term will be:
(a) 66 (b) 76
(c) 56 (d) 84

22. The next term in the series ABD, DGK, HMS, MTB, ... is:
(a) NSA (b) SBL (c) PSK (d) RUH

23. In certain code, "COVALENT" is coded as BWPDUOFM. The code of "ELEPHANT" will be:
(a) MFUIQRTW (b) QMUBIADH
(c) QFMFUOBI (d) EPHNTEAS

24. Ajay is a friend of Rakesh. Pointing to an old man Ajay asked Rakesh who is he? Rakesh said "His son is my son's uncle". The old man is related to Rakesh as:
(a) Grandfather (b) Father-in-law
(c) Father (d) Uncle

25. A postman walked 20 m straight from his office, turned right and walked 10 m. After-turning left he walked 10 m and after turning right walked 20 m. He again turned right and walked 70 m. How far he is from his office?
(a) 50 m (b) 40 m (c) 60 m (d) 20 m

26. It is Truism to say that no one was there when life first appeared on earth. Any assertion about life's origin, thus, should be treated as a theory.

The above two statements constitute:
(a) A historical explanation
(b) A narrative
(c) An argument
(d) A conjecture

27. Given below are four statements. Among them two are related in such a way that they can both be true but they cannot both be false. Select the code that indicates those two statements:

Statements:
(A) Honest people never suffer.
(B) Almost all honest people do suffer.
(C) Honest people hardly suffer.
(D) Each and every honest person suffers.

Codes:
(a) (A) and (B) (b) (A) and (C)
(c) (A) and (D) (d) (B) and (C)

28. A deductive argument is invalid if:
(a) Its premises and conclusion are all true.
(b) Its premises and conclusion are all false.
(c) Its premises are all false but its conclusion is true.
(d) Its premises are all true but its conclusion is false.

29. Given below are two premises (a and b). From those two premises four conclusions (i), (ii), (iii), and (iv) are drawn. Select the code that states the conclusion/conclusions drawn validly

(taking the premises singularly or jointly).

Premises: (A) All bats are mammals.
(B) No birds are bats.

Conclusions: (i) No birds are mammals.
(ii) Some birds are not mammals.
(iii) No bats are birds.
(iv) All mammals are bats.

Codes:
(a) (i) only (b) (i) and (ii) only
(c) (iii) only (d) (iii) and (iv) only

30. Just as melting ice - cubes do not cause a glass of water to overflow, melting sea - ice does not increase oceanic volume.

What type of argument is it?
(a) Analogical (b) Hypothetical
(c) Psychological (d) Statistical

Answer the questions 31 to 35 based on the data given in the table below.
Table: Number of registered vehicles in India and India's population.

Year	Total vehicles (Lakhs)	Two wheelers (Lakhs)	Cars, Jeeps, Taxis (Lakhs)	Buses (Lakhs)	Goods vehicles (Lakhs)	Others (Lakhs)	Population (India) (Millions)
1961	6.65	0.88	3.1	0.57	1.68	0.42	439.23
1971	18.65	5.76	6.82	0.94	3.43	1.70	548.15
1981	53.91	26.18	11.60	1.62	5.54	8.97	683.32
1991	213.74	142.00	29.54	3.31	13.56	25.33	846.42
2001	549.91	385.56	70.58	6.34	29.48	57.95	1028.73
2011	1417.58	1018.65	191.23	16.04	70.64	121.02	1210.19

31. The maximum decadal growth in population of India is registered in the period:
(a) 1961–1971 (b) 1991–2001
(c) 2001–2011 (d) 1981–1991

32. In which year the decadal growth (%) in number of cars surpassed that of the two wheelers?
(a) 1991 (b) 2001 (c) 1981 (d) 2011

33. What was the average decadal growth in the number of cars during 1961–2011?
(a) ~ 131% (b) ~ 68%
(c) ~ 217% (d) ~ 157%

34. In the year 2001, out of total number of vehicles, the number of passenger vehicles (4 wheelers) accounted for:
(a) ~ 14% (b) ~ 24%
(c) ~ 31% (d) ~ 43%

35. What was the per capita ownership of two wheelers in India in the year 2011?
(a) ~ 0.084% (b) ~ 0.0084%
(c) ~ 0.84% (d) ~ 0.068%

36. What is the name for a webpage address?
(a) Domain (b) Directory
(c) Protocol (d) URL

37. The data storage hierarchy consists of:
(a) Bytes, bits, fields, records, files, and databases
(b) Bits, bytes, fields, records, files, and databases
(c) Bits, bytes, records, fields, files, and databases
(d) Bits, bytes, fields, files, records, and databases

38. Which of the following domains is used for - profit businesses?
(a) .org (b) .net (c) .edu (d) .com

39. What is the full form of USB as used in computer related activities?
(a) Ultra Security Block
(b) Universal Security Block
(c) Universal Serial Bus
(d) United Serial Bus

40. Which of the following represents billion characters?
(a) Terabytes (b) Megabytes
(c) Kilobytes (d) Gigabytes

41. Which of the following pollutants is the major cause of respiratory diseases?
(a) Suspended fine particles
(b) Nitrogen oxides
(c) Carbon monoxide
(d) Volatile organic compounds

42. ***Assertion (A):*** In urban areas, smog episodes occur frequently in winters.

Reason (R): In winters, a lot of biomass is burnt by people for heating purposes or to keep themselves warm.

Choose the correct answer from the code given below:
(a) Both (A) and (R) are true, and (R) is the correct explanation of (A)
(b) Both (A) and (R) are true, but (R) is not the correct explanation of (A)
(c) (A) is true and (R) is false
(d) Both (A) and (R) are false

43. Occurrence of natural hazards is affected by:
    (A) Land use changes
    (B) Drainage and construction
    (C) Ozone depletion
    (D) Climate change

    Choose the correct answer from the code given below:
    (a) (A), (C) and (D) (b) (A), (B) and (C)
    (c) (A), (B) and (D) (d) (B), (C) and (D)

44. Which of the following pollutant gases is not produced both naturally and as a result of industrial activity?
    (a) Chlorofluoro carbons
    (b) Nitrous oxide
    (c) Methane
    (d) Carbon dioxide

45. Among the following fuels of energy, which is the most environment friendly?
    (a) Ethanol (b) Biogas
    (c) CNG (d) Hydrogen

46. Which of the following are the goals of higher education in India?
    (A) Access
    (B) Equity
    (C) Quality and Excellence
    (D) Relevance
    (E) Value based education
    (F) Compulsory and free education

    Select the correct answer from the code given below:
    (a) (A), (B) and (E) only
    (b) (A), (B), (E) and (F)
    (c) (A), (B), (C), (D) and (E)
    (d) (A), (B), (C), (D), (E) and (F)

47. Which of the following has been ranked the best college in the country (2017) as per the National Institutional Ranking Framework (NIRF)?
    (a) Miranda House, Delhi
    (b) St. Stephen's College, Delhi
    (c) Fergusson College, Pune
    (d) Maharaja's College, Mysore

48. Which of the following universities has received the Visitor's Award for the best Central University in India in Feb. 2017?
    (a) Jawaharlal Nehru University
    (b) Banaras Hindu University
    (c) Tezpur University
    (d) University of Hyderabad

49. Who among the following can be removed by the President without Parliament's resolution?
    (a) Judge of a High Court
    (b) Governor of a State
    (c) Chief Election Commissioner
    (d) Comptroller and Auditor-General

50. Which of the following come(s) within the ambit of the term 'corruption'?
    (A) Misuse of official position
    (B) Deviation from rules, laws and norms
    (C) Non-action when action is required
    (D) Harm to public good

    Select the correct answer from the code given below:
    (a) (A) only
    (b) (A) and (B) only
    (c) (A), (B) and (D)
    (d) (A), (B), (C) and (D)

Answer Keys

1. (b)	6. (c)	11. (a)	16. (c)	21. (a)	26. (c)	31. (a)	36. (d)	41. (a)	46. (c)
2. (a)	7. (c)	12. (a)	17. (a)	22. (b)	27. (d)	32. (d)	37. (b)	42. (b)	47. (a)
3. (c)	8. (c)	13. (b)	18. (b)	23. (c)	28. (d)	33. (a)	38. (d)	43. (c)	48. (a)
4. (d)	9. (d)	14. (c)	19. (d)	24. (c)	29. (c)	34. (a)	39. (c)	44. (a)	49. (b)
5. (c)	10. (d)	15. (c)	20. (a)	25. (a)	30. (a)	35. (*)	40. (d)	45. (d)	50. (d)

"*" Answers should not be in percentages. So marks allotted to all candidates.

Hints and Solutions

1. (b): Learning is basically a psychological concept, so depends upon individual to a great extent. It is active engagement in a subject domain.

   In (a) and (d), teaching is being described as a kind of commodity, so they are to be eliminated. Teaching is triadic in nature as shown in the diagram below.

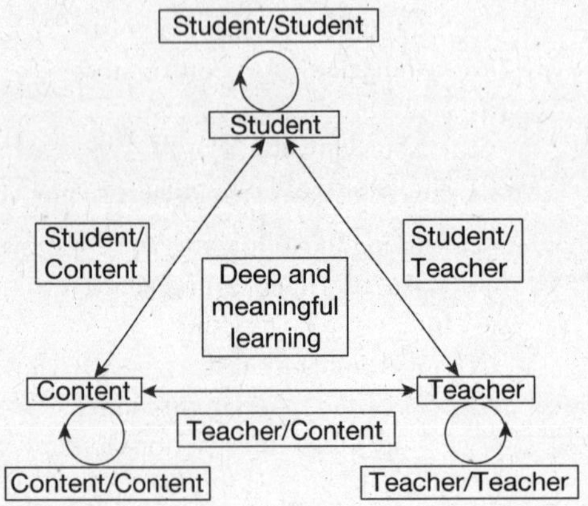

3. (c): Assertion (A) is right, as ultimate objective of teaching is to make students learn. Reason (R) is false, as learning is a lifelong process and not all of it is takes place in classroom. In a broader perspective, a great deal of learning takes place in actual life situations as well.
4. (d): Summative tests are usually conducted by external agencies with well-defined criteria. These are tests that measure a particular student's performance against a standard or **criterion**. They should not be confused with the **norm-referenced** assessments that measure a student's performance against that of other students. The content and skills in a **criterion-referenced** assessment are more specific.
5. (c): The main objective of using instructional variety is to ensure optimum involvement of all senses so that understanding and retention is better, for example, multi-modal teaching.
6. (c): Action research mainly focuses on providing solutions/insights into immediate problems/issues.
7. (c): Ex-post-facto method: Here, the effects of feeding on anxiety may be ascertained after a long time gap.
8. (c): Refer Page 2.36 for detailed explanation.
9. (d): **Appendices are always supplementary to the research paper.** As such, your study must be able to stand alone without the appendices, and the paper must contain all information including tables, diagrams, and results necessary to understand the research problem. The key point to remember when including an appendix is that the information is non-essential; if it were removed, the reader would still be able to comprehend the significance, validity, and implications of your research.
10. (d): Research findings, specifically, in social sciences are prone to subjective interpretation.

16. (c): Vygotsky developed a Theory of Cognitive Development that focused on the role of culture in the development of higher mental functions. Zone of Proximal Development (ZPD) is defined as the range of tasks that a child can perform with the help and guidance of others but cannot yet perform independently. Within ZPD, there are two levels—**actual development level** and **potential development level**.

    For future exams, NET aspirants must remember that closely related to ZPD is the concept of 'scaffolding' where a teacher should provide clues about how to proceed through the problem.
17. (a): Developed by Sweller in late 1980s, **Cognitive Load** Theory focuses on amount of mental effort being used in working memory and how instructional design can be used to reduce **cognitive load** in learners.
19. (d): The main objective of ice-breaking questions/interactions is to create congenial, humorous, and motivating environment for discussion.

20. (a): This is specifically true when students move to higher classes.

21. (a): 1 6 15 28 45 66

Difference 5 9 13 17 21

+4 +4 +4 +4

22. (b):

A	+3	D	+4	H	+5	M	+6	S
B	+5	G	+6	M	+7	T	+8	B
D	+7	K	+8	S	+9	B	+10	L

23. (c):

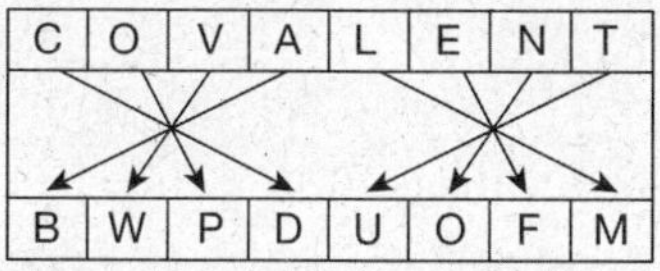

Similarly,

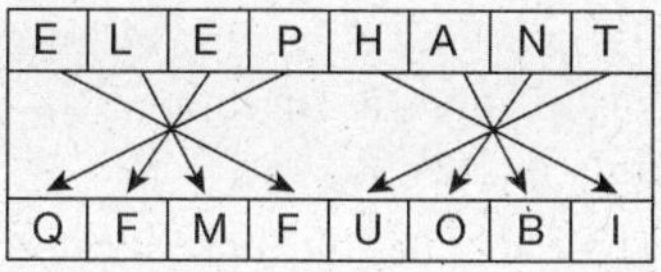

24. (c):

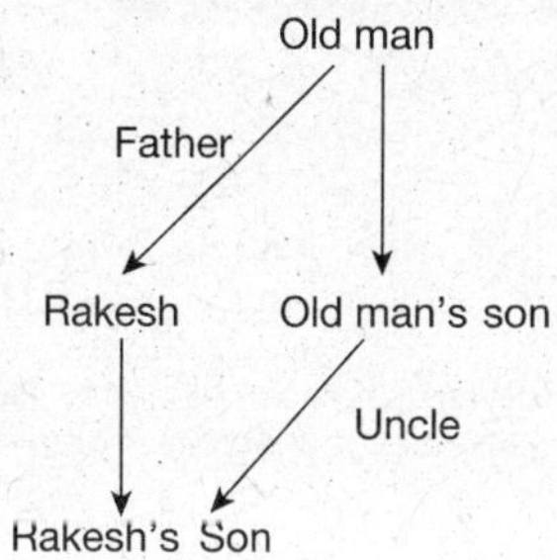

25. (a):

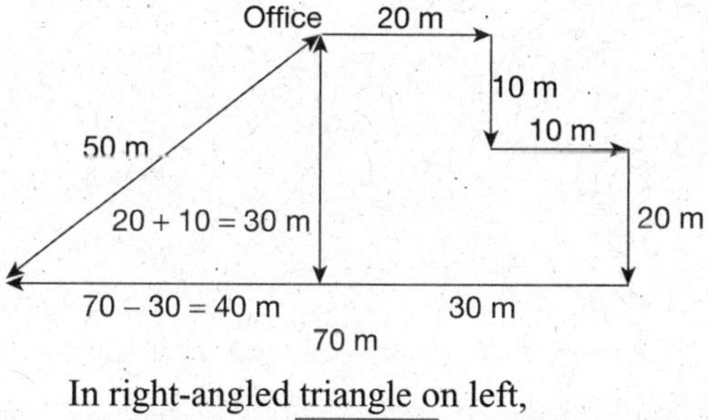

In right-angled triangle on left,

Hypotenuse $= \sqrt{40^2 + 30^2} = \sqrt{2500} = 50\,\text{m}$

Thus, distance from office to destination is 50 m.

27. (d): Refer rules mentioned on pages 6.5–6.7 to convert these statements into their logical forms. Once that is done, refer to pages 6.12–6.14 (Square of Opposition).

	Given statement	Logical form	Type of proposition
(a)	Honest people never suffer.	No honest person suffers.	E Type
(b)	Almost all honest people do suffer.	Some honest people suffer.	I Type
(c)	Honest people hardly suffer.	Some honest people don't suffer.	O Type
(d)	Each and every honest person suffers.	All honest persons suffer.	A Type

Now, as per question, they can both be true, but they cannot both be false; the propositions are to be sub-contrary. I-Type and O-Type makes sub-contrary. Thus, (B) and (C) are to be answers. Accordingly, (d) is the right answer.

28. (d): Refer pages 6.2–6.3.

29. (c): Based upon premises, there can be three Venn diagrams:

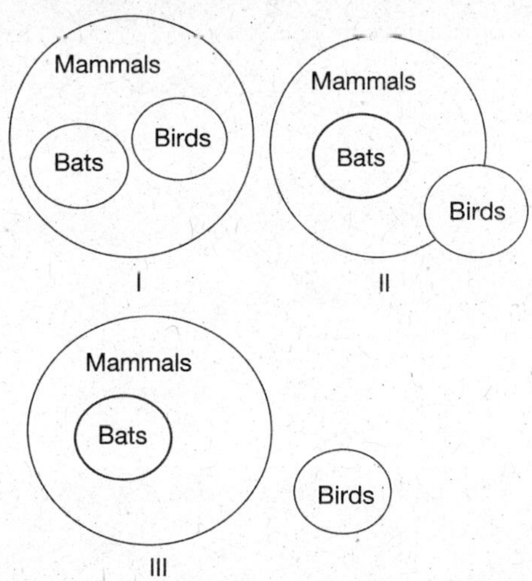

Now looking at all conclusions:

(i) No birds are mammals: May or may not be, so its invalid.

(ii) Some birds are not mammals: May or may not be, so its invalid.

(iii) No bats are birds: Valid

(iv) All mammals are bats: May or may not be, so its invalid.

Thus, only (c) is valid, it is the right answer.

31. (a): Growth for 1961–1971 = [(548.15 – 439.23)/439.23] × 100 = 24.79%

Similarly, it growth rate can be calculated for decades given in answer choices.

Here, (a) is the right answer.

32. (d): In question 33, we have to calculate decadal growth for cars. The same is to be done in case of two wheelers. Students can eliminate choices by doing some approximation.

For year 2011, decadal growth rate of two wheelers = [(1018.65 – 385.56)/385.56] × 100

= (633.09/385.56) × 100 = 164.40%

For year 2011, decadal growth rate of cars = [(70.58 – 29.54)/29.54] × 100

= (41.04/29.54) × 100 = 138.93%

Hence, (d) is the right answer.

33. (a): In this question, calculations are to be done for all the five decades. Then averaging is done for all of these growth figures.

34. (a):

$$\text{Passenger vehicles} = \frac{(70.58 + 6.34)}{549.91} = 13.9\%$$

35. Here, all figures should be converted into lakhs or millions. Let's convert them into smaller units, that is, lakhs.

Population = 1210.19 million = 1210.19×10^6

Two wheelers = 1018.65 lakhs = 1018.65×10^5

Per Capita availability of two wheelers = Number of two wheelers/Total Population = $1018.65 \times 10^5 / 1210.19 \times 10^6 = 0.084$

Answer should not be in percentage as mentioned in question paper.

42. (b): Both A and R are true. However, biomass is mainly used in rural areas. So, (b) is the right answer.

45. (d): Hydrogen has the highest calorific value and there is no residue on its burning.

47. (a): Refer page 10.17.

CBSE-UGC NET PAPER 1 JULY 2018

1. Which of the following set of statements best describes the nature and objectives of teaching?
   (A) Teaching and learning are integrally related.
   (B) There is no difference between teaching and training.
   (C) Concern of all teaching is to ensure some kind of transformation in students.
   (D) All good teaching is formal in nature.
   (E) A teacher is a senior person.
   (F) Teaching is a social act whereas learning is a personal act.

   Select the correct answer from the codes given below:
   (a) (A), (B) and (D)
   (b) (B), (C) and (E)
   (c) (A), (C) and (F)
   (d) (D), (E) and (F)

2. Which of the following learner characteristics is highly related to effectiveness of teaching?
   (a) Prior experience of the learner
   (b) Educational status of the parents of the learner
   (c) Peer groups of the learner
   (d) Family size from which the learner comes.

3. In the two sets given below Set –I indicates methods of teaching while Set –II provides the basic requirements for success/effectiveness. Match the two sets and indicate your answer by choosing from the code:

   Set – I (Method of teaching)
   (A) Lecturing
   (B) Discussion in groups
   (C) Brainstorming
   (D) Programmed Instructional procedure

   Set – II (Basic requirements for success/effectiveness)
   (i) Small step presentation with feedback provided
   (ii) Production of large number of ideas
   (iii) Content delivery in a lucid language
   (iv) Use of teaching-aids
   (v) Theme based interaction among participants

	(A)	(B)	(C)	(D)
(a)	(i)	(ii)	(iii)	(iv)
(b)	(ii)	(iii)	(iv)	(v)
(c)	(iii)	(v)	(ii)	(i)
(d)	(iv)	(ii)	(i)	(iii)

4. From the list of evaluation procedures given below identify those which will be called 'formative evaluation'.

Indicate your answer by choosing from the code:

(A) A teacher awards grades to students after having transacted the course work.
(B) During interaction with students in the classroom, the teacher provides corrective feedback.
(C) The teacher gives marks to students on a unit test.
(D) The teacher clarifies to doubts of students in the class itself.
(E) The overall performance of a student's us reported to parents at every three months interval.
(F) The learner's motivation is raised by the teacher through a question-answer session.

Select the correct answer from the codes given below:

(a) (A), (B) and (C)
(b) (B), (C) and (D)
(c) (A), (C) and (E)
(d) (B), (D) and (F)

5. ***Assertion (A)***: All teaching should aim at ensuring learning.

Reason (R): All learning results from teaching.

Choose the correct answer from the following code:

(a) Both (A) and (R) are true, and (R) is the correct explanation of (A).
(b) Both (A) and (R) are true, but (R) is not the correct explanation of (A).
(c) (A) is true, but (R) is false.
(d) (A) is false, but (R) is true.

6. There are two sets given below.

Set – I specifies the types of research, while Set –II indicates their characteristics. Match the two and given your answer by selecting the appropriate code.

Set – I (Research types)

(A) Fundamental research
(B) Applied research
(C) Action research
(D) Evaluative research

Set – II (Characteristics)

(i) Finding out the extent of perceived impact of an intervention
(ii) Developing an effective explanation through theory building
(iii) Improving an existing situation through use of interventions
(iv) Exploring the possibility of a theory for use in various situations
(v) Enriching technological resources

	(A)	**(B)**	**(C)**	**(D)**
(a)	(ii)	(iv)	(iii)	(i)
(b)	(v)	(iv)	(iii)	(ii)
(c)	(iii)	(ii)	(iii)	(iv)
(d)	(ii)	(iii)	(iv)	(v)

7. Which of the sets of activities best indicate the cyclic nature of action research strategy?

(a) Reflect, Observe, Plan, Act
(b) Observe, Act, Reflect, Plan
(c) Act, Plan, Observe, Reflect
(d) Plan, Act, Observe, Reflect

8. Which of the following sequence of research steps is nearer to scientific method?

(a) Suggested solution of the problem, deducing the consequences of the solution, perceiving the problem situation, location of the difficulty and testing the solutions.
(b) Perceiving the problem situation, locating the actual problem and its definition, hypothesizing, deducing the consequences of the suggested solution and testing the hypothesis in action.
(c) Defining a problem, identifying the causes of the problem, defining a population, drawing a sample, collecting data and analysing results.
(d) Identifying the causal factors, defining the problem, developing a hypothesis, selecting a sample, collecting data and arriving at generalization and conclusions.

9. The problem of 'research ethics' is concerned with which aspect of research activities?

(a) Following the prescribed format of a thesis
(b) Data analysis through qualitative or quantitative technique
(c) Defining the population of research
(d) Evidence based research reporting

10. In which of the following activities, potential for nurturing creative and critical thinking is relatively greater?
(a) Preparing research summary
(b) Presenting a seminar paper
(c) Participation in research conference
(d) Participation in a workshop

Reading Comprehension: Read the following passage carefully and answer questions from 11 to 15:

If India has to develop her internal strengths, the nation has to focus on the technological imperatives, keeping in mind three dynamic dimensions: the people, the overall economy and the strategic interests. These technological imperatives also take into account a 'fourth' dimensions, time, and offshoot of modern day dynamism in business, trade, and technology that leads to continually shifting targets. We believe that technological strengths are especially crucial in dealing with this fourth dimension underlying continuous change in the aspirations of the people, the economy in the global context, and the strategic interests. The progress of technology lies at the heart of human history. Technological strengths are the key to creating more productive employment in an increasingly competitive market place and to continually upgrade human skills. Without a pervasive use of technologies, we cannot achieve overall development of our people in the years to come. The direct linkages of technology to the nation's strategic strengths are becoming more and more clear, especially since 1990s. India's own strength in a number of core areas still puts it in a position of reasonable strength in geo-political context. Any nation aspiring to become a developed one needs to have strengths in various strategic technologies and also the ability to continually upgrade them through its own creative strengths. For people-oriented actions as well, whether for the creation of large scale productive employment or for ensuring nutritional and health security for people, or for better living conditions, technology is the only vital input. The absence of greater technological impetus could lead to lower productivity and wastage of precious natural resources. Activities with low productivity or low value addition, in the final analysis hurt the poorest most important. India, aspiring to become a major economic power in terms of trade and increase in GDP, cannot succeed on the strength of turnkey projects designed and built abroad or only through large-scale imports of plant machinery, equipment and know how. Even while being alive to the short-term realities, medium and long-term strategies to develop core technological strengths within our industry are vital for envisioning a developed India.

11. According to the above passage, which of the following are indicative of the fourth dimension?
(A) Aspirations of people
(B) Modern day dynamism
(C) Economy in the global context
(D) Strategic interests
Select the correct answer from the codes given below:
(a) (A), (B) and (C) only
(b) (B), (C) and (D) only
(c) (A), (C) and (D) only
(d) (A), (B) and (D) only

12. More productive employment demands:
(a) Pervasive use of technology
(b) Limiting competitive market place
(c) Geo-political considerations
(d) Large industries

13. Absence of technology would lead to:
(A) Less pollution
(B) Wastage of precious natural resources
(C) Low value addition
(D) Hurting the poorest most
Select the correct answer from the codes given below:

(a) (A), (B) and (C) only
(b) (B), (C) and (D) only
(c) (A), (B) and (D) only
(d) (A), (C) and (D) only

14. The advantage of technological inputs would result in:
(a) Unbridled technological growth
(b) Importing plant machinery
(c) Sideling environmental issues
(d) Lifting our people to a life of dignity

15. Envisioning a developed India requires:
(a) Aspiration to become a major economic player
(b) Dependence upon projects designed abroad
(c) Focus on short-term projects
(d) Development of core technological strengths

16. Differentiation between acceptance and non-acceptance of certain stimuli in classroom communication is the basis of:
(a) Selective expectation of performance
(b) Selective affiliation to peer groups
(c) Selective attention
(d) Selective morality

17. **Assertion (A):** The initial messages to students in the classroom by a teacher need not be critical to establish interactions later.

Reason (R): More control over the communication process means more control over what the students are learning.
(a) Both (A) and (R) are true, and (R) is the correct explanation of (A).
(b) Both (A) and (R) are true, but (R) is not the correct explanation of (A).
(c) (A) is true, but (R) is false.
(d) (A) is false, but (R) is true.

18. **Assertion (A):** To communicate well in the classroom is a natural ability.

Reason (R): Effective teaching in the classroom demands knowledge of the communication process.
(a) Both (A) and (R) are true, and (R) is the correct explanation of (A).
(b) Both (A) and (R) are true, but (R) is not the correct explanation of (A).
(c) (A) is true, but (R) is false.
(d) (A) is false, but (R) is true.

19. **Assertion (A):** Classroom communication is a transactional process.

Reason (R): A teacher does not operate under the assumption that students' responses are purposive.
(a) Both (A) and (R) are true, and (R) is the correct explanation of (A).
(b) Both (A) and (R) are true, but (R) is not the correct explanation of (A).
(c) (A) is true, but (R) is false.
(d) (A) is false, but (R) is true.

20. Which of the following set of statements is correct for describing the human communication process?
(A) Non-verbal communication can stimulate ideas.
(B) Communication is a learnt ability.
(C) Communication is not a universal panacea.
(D) Communication cannot break-down.
(E) More communication means more effective learning by students.
(F) Value of what is learnt through classroom communication is not an issue for students.

Select the correct answer from the codes given below:
(a) (A), (C), (E) and (F)
(b) (B), (D), (E) and (F)
(c) (A), (B), (C) and (D)
(d) (A), (D), (E) and (F)

21. The next term in the series -1, 5, 15, 29, ________, ... is
(a) 36 (2) 47
(3) 59 (4) 63

22. The next term in the series: ABD, DGK, HMS, MTB, SBL, ________, ... is:
(a) ZKU (b) ZCA
(c) ZKW (d) ZKU

23. If VARANASI is coded as WCUESGZQ, then the code of KOLKATA will be:
(a) LOQOZEH (b) HLZEOOQ
(c) ZELHOQO (d) LQOOFZH

24. Introducing, Rakesh to her husband a women said, 'His brother's father is the only son of my grandfather'.
The woman is related to Rakesh as:
(a) Aunt (b) Mother
(c) Sister (d) Daughter

25. Two numbers are in the ratio 2: 5. If 16 is added to both the numbers, their ratio becomes 1: 2.
The numbers are:
(a) 6, 40 (b) 20, 50
(c) 28, 70 (d) 32, 80

26. Superiority of intellect depends upon its power of concentration on one theme in the same way as a concave mirror collects all the rays that strike upon it into one point.
(a) Mathematical (b) Psychological
(c) Analogical (d) Deductive

27. Given below are two premises (A and B). Four conclusions are drawn from them. Select the code that states validity drawn conclusion (s) (taking the premises individually or jointly).

Premises:

(A) Most of the dancers are physically fit.

(B) Most of the singers are dancers.

Conclusions:
(A) Most of the singers are physically fit.
(B) Most of the dancers are singers.
(C) Most of the physically fit persons are dancers.
(D) Most of the physically fit persons are singers.
Select the correct answer from the codes given below:
(a) (A) and (B) (b) (B) and (C)
(c) (C) and (D) (d) (D) and (A)

28. Which one among the following is a presupposition in inductive reasoning?
(a) Law of identity
(b) Unchangeability in nature
(c) Harmony in nature
(d) Uniformity of nature

29. If the proposition 'domestic animals are hardly ferocious' is taken to be false, which of the following proposition/propositions can be claimed to be certainly true? Select the correct code:
Propositions:
(A) All domestic animals are ferocious.
(B) Most of the domestic animals are ferocious.
(C) No domestic animal is ferocious.
(D) Some domestic animals are non-ferocious.
Select the correct answer from the codes given below:
(a) (A) and (B) (b) (A) only
(c) (C) and (D) (d) (B) only

30. Which one of the following statements is not correct in the context of Venn diagram method?
(a) It is a method of testing the validity of arguments.
(b) It represents both the premises of a syllogism in one diagram.
(c) It requires two overlapping circles for the two premises of a standard-form categorical syllogism.
(d) It can be used to represent classes as well as propositions.

Data interpretation: The table below embodies data on the production, exports and per capita consumption of rice in country P for the five years from 2012 to 2016. Answer Questions 31–35 based on the data contained in the table.

Year-wise Production, Exports and Per Capita Consumption of Rice

Year	Production (in million kg)	Experts (in million kg)	Per Capita Consumption (in kg)
2012	186.5	114	36.25
2013	202	114	35.2
2014	238	130	38.7
2015	221	116	40.5
2016	215	88	42

Where, per capita consumption = (consumption in million kg) / (population in million) and consumption (in million kg) = production – exports.

31. The percentage increase in the consumption of rice over the previous year was the highest in which year?
(a) 2013 (b) 2014
(c) 2015 (d) 2016

32. What is the population of the country in the year 2014 (in million)?
(a) 2.64 (b) 2.72
(c) 2.79 (d) 2.85

33. The ratio of exports to consumption in the given period was the highest in the year:
(a) 2012 (b) 2013
(c) 2014 (4) 2015

34. In which year, the population of country was the highest?
(a) 2013 (b) 2014
(c) 2015 (d) 2016

35. What is the average consumption of rice (in million kg) over the years 2012–2016?
(a) 104 (b) 102.1
(c) 108 (d) 100.1

36. Which of the following statements, regarding the term ICT is/are TRUE?
P: ICT is an acronym that stands for Indian Classical Technology.
Q: Converging technologies that exemplify ICT include the merging of audio-visual, telephone and computer networks through a common cabling system.
(a) P Only (b) Q Only
(c) P and Q (d) Neither P nor Q

37. A new Laptop has been produced that weighs less, is smaller and uses less power previous Laptop models.
Which of the following technologies has been used to accomplish this?
(a) Universal Serial Bus Mouse
(b) Faster Random Access Memory
(c) Blu Ray Drive
(d) Solid State Hard Drive

38. Given the following email fields, which of the email addresses will '*swami*' be able to see when he receives the message?

To ...	ram@test.com
Cc ...	raj@test.com; ravi@test.com
Bcc ...	swami@test.com; rama@test.com

(a) ram@test.com
(b) ram@test.com; raj@test.com; ravi@test.com
(c) ram@test.com; rama@test.com
(d) ram@test.com; rama@test.com; raj@test.com; ravi@test.com

39. Put the following units of storage into the correct order, starting with the smallest unit first and going down to the largest unit:
(A) Kilobyte (B) byte
(C) Megabyte (D) Terabyte
(E) Gigabyte (F) Bit
Select the correct answer from the codes given below:
(a) (F), (B), (A), (C), (D), (E)
(b) (F), (B), (A), (D), (E), (C)
(c) (F), (B), (A), (C), (E), (D)
(d) (F), (B), (A), (D), (C), (E)

40. With regard to computer memory, which of the following statement (s) is/are TRUE?
P: Read Only Memory (ROM) is 'volatile' memory.
Q: Random Access Memory (RAM) is 'volatile' memory.
R: Secondary Memory is 'volatile' memory.
(a) P only (b) Q only
(c) P and Q only (d) P and R only

41. 'Fly ash' produced in thermal power plants is an ecofriendly resource for use in:
(A) agriculture as micro-nutrient
(B) wasteland development
(C) dam and water holding structures
(D) brick industry
Choose the correct answer from the code given below:
(a) (A), (B) and (D) only
(b) (B), (C) and (D) Only
(c) (A), (C) and (D) Only
(d) (A), (B), (C) and (D)

42. Which of the following types of natural disasters has no definite beginning and end?
(a) Earthquakes (b) Landsides
(c) Hurricanes (d) Droughts

43. **Assertion (A):** Indoor air pollution is serious hazard.

Reason (R): The dispersal of air pollutants is rather limited in indoor environment.

Choose the correct answer from the code given below:

(a) Both (A) and (R) are true and (R) is the correct explanation of (A)
(b) Both (A) and (R) are true and (R) is not the correct explanation of (A)
(c) (A) is true and (R) is false.
(d) Both (A) and (R) are false.

44. In terms of their contribution to the total power generation in India, Identify the correct sequence of energy sources – Thermal Power Plants (TPP), Large Hydropower Projects (LHP), Nuclear Energy (NE) and Renewable Energy (RE) which includes solar energy, wind energy, biomass and small hydropower projects.

(a) TPP > RE > LHP > NE
(b) TPP > LHP > RE > NE
(c) LHP > TPP > RE > NE
(d) LHP > TPP > NE > RE

45. Which of the following is considered as major source of pollution in rivers of India?

(a) Unregulated small scale industry
(b) Untreated sewage
(c) Agricultural run-off
(d) Thermal power plants

46. India has the largest higher education system in the world after:

(A) United States of America
(B) Australia
(C) China
(D) United Kingdom (UK)

Select the correct answer from the codes given below:

(a) (A), (B), (C) and (D)
(b) (A), (B) and (C) only
(c) (A), (C) and (D) only
(d) (A) and (C) only

47. Prime Minister Research Fellowship is for students pursuing Ph. D programme in:

(a) State and Central Universities
(b) Central Universities, IISc, IITs, NITs, IISERs and IIITs
(c) IISc, IITs, NITs, IISERs, IIITs, State and Central Universities
(d) IITs and IISc

48. Leader of the opposition is a member of committees which select:

(A) Central Information Commissioner
(B) Central Vigilance Commissioner
(C) Chairperson of National Human Rights Commission
(D) Chairperson of National Commission for women

Select the correct answer from the codes given below:

(a) (A), (B), (C) and (D)
(b) (A), (B) and (C) only
(c) (A), (C) and (D) only
(d) (A), (B) and (D) only

49. Which of the following statements are correct about gender budgeting?

(A) It is separates budget addressing the specific needs of women.
(B) It assesses the impact of government budget on women.
(C) It is an accounting exercise.
(D) It is another budgeting innovation.

Select the correct answer from the codes given below:

(a) (B) and (D) only
(b) (A) and (D) only
(c) (A), (C) and (D) only
(d) (A) and (B) only

50. Which of the following are the barriers to citizen-centric administration in India?

(A) Wooden and inflexible attitude of the civil servants
(B) Ineffective implementation of laws and rules
(C) Awareness of rights and duties of citizens
(D) Lack of job opportunities for the youth

Select the correct answer from the codes given below:

(a) (A), (B), (C) and (D)
(b) (A), (B) and (C) only
(c) (A), (B) and (D) only
(d) (A) and (B) only

Answer Keys

1. (c)	7. (d)	13. (b)	19. (c)	25. (d)	31. (b)	37. (d)	43. (a)	49. (a)
2. (a)	8. (b)	14. (d)	20. (c)	26. (c)	32. (c)	38. (b)	44. (a)	50. (d)
3. (c)	9. (d)	15. (d)	21. (b)	27. (b)	33. (a)	39. (c)	45. (b)	
4. (d)	10. (c)	16. (c)	22. (c)	28. (d)	34. (d)	40. (b)	46. (d)	
5. (c)	11. (c)	17. (d)	23. (d)	29. (a)	35. (d)	41. (d)	47. (d)	
6. (a)	12. (a)	18. (d)	24. (c)	30. (c)	36. (b)	42. (d)	48. (b)	

Hints and Solutions

1. We need to look at the statements one by one:
   (A) Refer Pages 1.6 and 1.7. Under objectives of teaching, the last line clearly mentions that the objectives of teaching and learning must integrate.
   (B) Page 1.4, LHS Column – Teaching is a wider concept than training.
   (C) Page 1.15: LHS, under definition of learning, 1st, 2nd, 3rd points talk about transformation.
   (D) Page 1.1, LHS, 1st Paragraph under 'Concept of Teaching' – first three lines.
   (E) Page 1.5: 'Maxims of Teaching' do not indicate that a teacher is to be a senior person. Questions 39 – 94 deal with requisite qualities of a teacher.
   (F) Page 1.15, LHS, Heading – Learner's Characteristics are mainly about individual differences reflect that learning is a personal act. Types of learners also reflect upon this point.
2. On Page 1.5, under Effective Teaching Practices / Maxims of Teaching, point 2 clearly mentions, "Known to Unknown" that retention is always better if new knowledge can be linked with the known one that is basically prior experience of learner.
3. All of these methods have been mentioned – Lecture Method (Page 1.8), Discussion (Page 1.9), Brainstorming (Page 1.10), Programmed Instruction (Page 1.13).
4. Formative means judging while the program activities are *forming* (in progress. formative evaluation is mentioned under 'types of evaluation on the basis of phase of instruction' on Page 1.21.

   For future exams, NET aspirants should refer to ADDIE Process also –
   1. Analysis
   2. Design
   3. Development
   4. Implement
   5. Evaluate

   It is considered part of part of the ISD (Instructional System Design).
5. On Page 1.1, Teaching definitions refer to learning as main objective.

   On Page 1.7, 'Objectives of Teaching' mentions 'intended learning outcomes'. On Page 1.8, under Gagne and Griggs Classification of Teaching Objectives, there is mention of learning outcomes.

   Thus, Assertion (A) is right.

   Learning is modification of behaviour, not necessarily through teaching. On Page 1.1, under concept of teaching, it is mentioned that there are informal agencies such as family that teach in an informal manner, so Reason (R) is wrong.
6. Pages 2.5–2.10 – 'Types of Research'.
7. Refer Page 2.7.
8. Refer Page 2.11–2.26 deal with Research Process in a comprehensive manner.
9. Refer Page 2.32, there is a list of 'desirable elements to ensure ethics in research'. On Page 2.34, there is mention of 'avoiding

bias' and other points under Ethical issues relating to the researcher that emphasise 'objectivity' or 'evidence based research reporting'.

10. A research paper is an essay in which one explains what has been learnt after exploring some topic in depth. The information can be included from sources such as books, articles, interviews, and Internet sites. One can also use one's own ideas, knowledge, and opinions. It should be in one's own words.

    A workshop is a period of discussion or practical work on a particular subject in which a group of people share their knowledge or experience.

16. Selective attention is a cognitive process in which a person attends to one or a few sensory inputs/stimuli while ignoring the other ones.

    'Selective Expectation of Performance' is also seemingly right but it is not a standardised term. Students are aware of differential classroom treatment - high achievers receive more frequent and challenging opportunities to participate in class, more appreciation, more trust and greater autonomy.

    NET aspirants can refer to terms 'sensory buffer', 'filtering of messages', 'selective perception' etc for future exams.

    On Page 4.11, there is mention of 'competing stimuli' on LHS Column.

17. Refer to Page 4.13 – Principles of Effective Classroom Communication. A teacher sometimes mentions 'expected learning outcomes' at the beginning of lecture.

18. Refer to Page 4.13 – Principles of Effective Classroom Communication. To communicate well in the classroom is more a learnt ability than a natural ability. So (A) is false.

    Effective teaching is helped by knowledge of communication process.

19. Refer Page 4.3 – Classroom Communication Process – Classroom communication is basically a transactional model wherein a sender represents the individual who has important information that needs to reach someone else, and a feedback mechanism is very crucial to ensure its effectiveness.

    Reason (R) is incorrect as teaching is effective only if there is some feedback mechanism and students' responses are to be taken seriously.

    'Cole and Chan Model' is considered as two way 'interactive' communication process.

20. **Refer Page 4.2,** Nature and importance of communication.

21. Difference is increasing by 4, so next difference is 18, and next term should be 47.

    $5-(-1) = 6; 15 - 5 = 10, 29 - 15 = 14$

22.

A	+3	D	+4	H	+5	M	+6	S	+7	Z
B	+5	G	+6	M	+7	T	+8	B	+9	K
D	+7	K	+8	S	+9	B	+10	L	+11	W

23.

V	A	R	A	N	A	S	I
+1	+2	+3	+4	+5	+6	+7	+8
W	C	U	E	S	G	Z	Q

Similarly

K	O	L	K	A	T	A
+1	+2	+3	+4	+5	+6	+7
L	Q	O	O	F	Z	H

24.

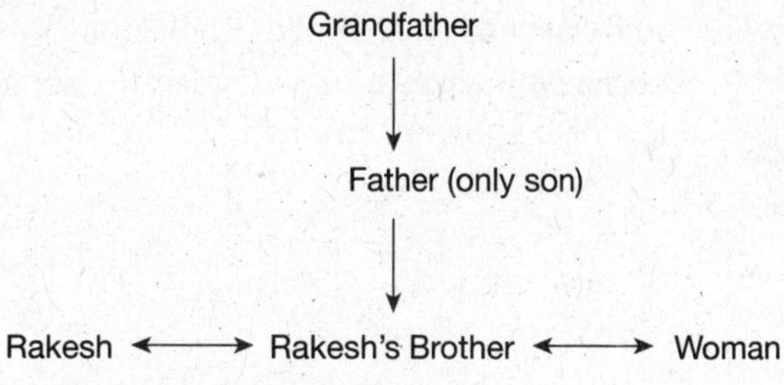

25. Let the numbers be $2x : 5x$

    $(2x + 16) / (5x + 16) = 1/2$

    Solving this $x = 16$

    Hence, the numbers are

    $2 \times 16 = 32$ and $5 \times 16 = 80$

26. Refer Page: 6.16, its analogus definition. The statement draws analogy between 'power of concentration' and 'concave mirror collects all the rays'.

27. Refer "Converting Common Language Statements into their Logical forms" on page 6.5 (RHS), replace 'Most of the' with "some" in premises and conclusions. As there are exactly three terms in premises, we can go for their alignment if required.

Some of the dancers are physically fit.

Some of the singers are dancers.

After alignment

Some of physically fit are dancers - (I-Type)
Some of dancers are singers – (I-Type)
I-Type + I-Type – No conclusion.
NET aspirants should note that alignment of sentences is not of any use in this case as I + I in any case doesn't give any conclusion.
Thus, (A) some of singers are physically fit and (B) some of physically fit are singers both statements don't apply.
Now we can go for immediate inference by refer table 6.2 on Page 6.7 to check for statements (B) and (C).

Some of physically fit are dancers – (I-Type)
After conversion: Some dancers are physically fit
Some of dancers are singers – (I-Type)
After conversion: Some singers are dancers.
Thus, (B) and (C) are valid conclusions.
Alternatively, we can try to solve the same question by Venn diagrams also.

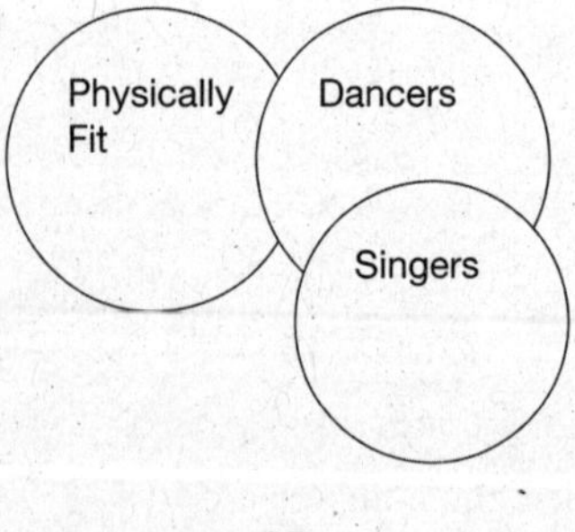

OR

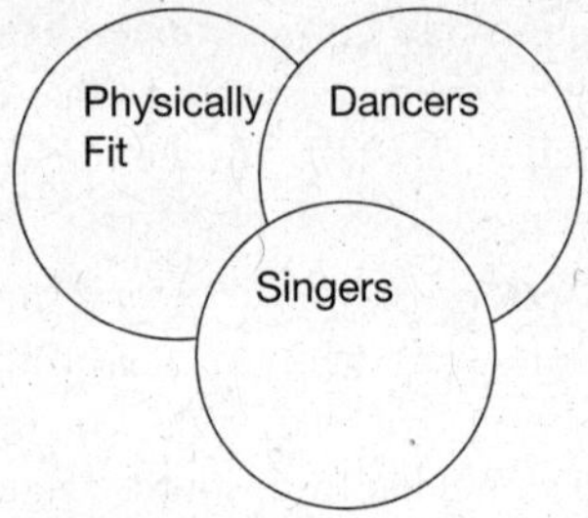

Conclusion (A) - Some of singers are physically fit. Keeping in view with two possibilities in Venn diagrams may be true or may not be true. In case of doubt, it is not a valid conclusion. Similarly, conclusion (D) is also not a valid conclusion.
Thus, both (B) and (C) apply, thus (B) is the right answer.

28. According to immediate inference, b and c are valid conclusions. This is directly mentioned on Page 6.2, RHS Column.

29. These types of questions require conceptual clarity, thorough practice and patience. Refer to 'Converting common language statements into their Logical Forms' on Pages 6.5 to 6.7.

First look at the main proposition. Sentences containing words as few, seldom, hardly, scarcely, are to be reduced to O if there is no sign of negation (use of word in this case). Thus 'domestic animals are hardly ferocious' is converted into O-type proposition 'some domestic animals are not ferocious'.

Now refer to square of opposition on Pages 6.12 – 6.14.

Here it is mentioned that is statement is taken to be false. If **O Type** is false, then **E** Type is false. Here E-type false means 'No domestic animals are ferocious'. It means that (C) is false.

(A) Since "O" and "A" are contradictories, if "O" is false, then "A" must be true. All domestic animals are ferocious. If an **O**-proposition is *false*, then you can conclude that the **A**-proposition would be True.

(B) We need to convert Most of the domestic animals are ferocious into its logical form some domestic animals are ferocious, that is I-type. Since 'I' and 'O' type are subcontraries, if one is false, then the other must be true. If 'O' is false, then 'I' must be true, thus (B) is valid.

All domestic animals are ferocious is valid conclusion.

(C) Again, if an **O**-proposition is *false*, then you can conclude that the **E**-proposition would be false. Since these fall under *subalternation*, if the particular is false, then the corresponding universal must be false. It means 'No domestic animal is ferocious' is not valid.

Keeping in view choices, we can say that (1) is the right answer.

We can try to solve this question in a very simple manner. If proposition 'domestic animals are hardly ferocious' is taken to be false, then 'all domestic animals are ferocious' is true. Accordingly (A) is correct. Again as per mediate inference rules 'some' is part of 'all'. So, (B) is also true. Thus, (1) is the correct answer.

30. A syllogism is a two premises argument having three terms, each of which is used twice in the argument. Since we have three classes, we expect to have three overlapping circles.

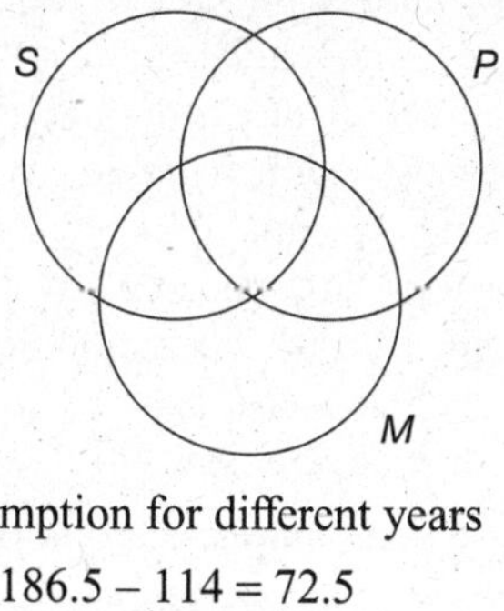

31. Consumption for different years

2012: 186.5 – 114 = 72.5

2013: 202 – 114 = 88

2014: 238 – 130 = 108

2015: 221 – 116 = 105

2016: 215 – 88 = 127

For year 2013, percentage increase

= (88 – 72.5)/72.5 × 100 = 21.37%

For year 2014, percentage increase

= (108 – 88)/88 × 100 = 22.72%

For year 2015, there is decrease in consumption.

For year 2016, percentage increase

= (127 × 105)/105 × 100 = 20.95%

32. Per Capita Consumption = (Consumption in million kg) / (Population in million)

Or population in million = consumption in million kg / per capita consumption

= 108 million kg / 38.7 kg = 2.79 million

Note: As population is to be calculated in million, there is no need for conversion of units as consumption is also given in millions. Kg in both numerator and numerators will cancel out each other.

33. We have already calculated consumption in question

For 2012, desired ratio = 114 : 72.5 = 1.57

For 2013, desired ratio = 114 : 88 = 1.29

For 2014, desired ratio = 130 : 108 = 1.20

For 2015, desired ratio = 116 : 105 = 1.10

For 2016, desired ratio = 88 : 127 = 0.69

34. Population = consumption (in million kg) / per capita consumption (in kgs)

Population for 2013 = 88 / 35.2 = 2.5 million

Population for 2014 = 2.79 (already calculated)

Population for 2015 = 105 / 40.5

= 2.59 million

Population for 2016 = 127 / 42

= 3.02 million

35. Average consumption

= (72.5 + 88 + 108 + 105 + 127) / 5

= 500.5/5 = 100.1 million kg

36. Refer Page 8.1, under Meaning of ICT, 2nd paragraph, there is mention that different tools are now able to work together and combined to form our networked world – a massive infrastructure of interconnected telephone services, standardised computerised hardware, internet, radio, TV etc.

37. Solid State Drive (SSD) is another type of Hard Disk drive (HDD). SSD has no moving mechanical components. A conventional hard disk drive has magnetic discs on which data is stored. SSD has an integrated circuit that stores data. The Advantages over conventional HDD includes higher speed, shock resistant, security of data, lighter in weight, smaller size, drastic decrease in boot times, much less power consumption.

39. Refer Page 8.17- RHS. A bit is a digit within binary number system.

40. Refer Page 8.14.

41. The most common use of fly ash is as a partial replacement for portland cement used in producing concrete.

42. Refer Page 9.22, RHS Column, 1st point - drought has been described as "slow onset of disaster and is difficult to demarcate the time of its onset and the end".

43. Refer Page: 9.12, RHS, last paragraphs.

44.

Fuel	MW	% of Total
Total Thermal	2,22,693	64.8%
Coal	1,96,958	57.3%
Gas	24,897	7.2%
Oil	838	0.2%
Hydro (Renewable)	45,403	13.2%
Nuclear	6,780	2.0%
RES* (MNRE)	69,022	20.1%
Total	343,899	

* Installed capacity in respect of RES (MNRE) as on 31.03.2018.

45. Refer question 98 on Page 9.55.

46. Refer Page 10.1, LHS, under Introduction to Higher Education, 2nd paragraph.

48. Some important points about leader of opposition:
   (a) The Leaders of Opposition (LoPs) in Lok Sabha and Rajya Sabha were given statutory recognition in the year 1977.
   (b) To become LoP, a political party needs atleast 10% strength of the house. The Speaker of Lok Sabha is the final judge to decide about leader of opposition. There is no LoP in 16th Lok Sabha (2014–2019) as no party could fulfil this condition
   (c) LoP gets the same salaries and allowances that are equivalent to a Cabinet minister.
   (d) LoP is necessary to ensure public confidence in candidate selection in the high posts. He/She is member of committees to select CIC, CVC, NHRC, Lokpal and NJAC. It is necessary to ensure public confidence in candidate selection in the high posts.
   (e) Law Commission in its March 2015 report recommended that the appointment of all election commissioners, including the CEC, be made by President in consultation with a three-member collegium, consisting of the PM, leader of the opposition in the Lok Sabha (or the leader of the largest opposition party in the lower house) and CJI.

49. The concept of 'Gender Budgeting' , also called as 'Budget for Gender Equity', was introduced in India in 2005–06. It is a powerful tool for achieving gender mainstreaming so as to ensure that benefits of development reach women as much as men. It started with two types of schemes—Women Specific Schemes (100% allocation for women) and Pro Women Schemes (at least 30% of the allocation for women).

50. On the contrary, awareness of rights and duties of citizens is facilitator of citizen-centric administration in India.